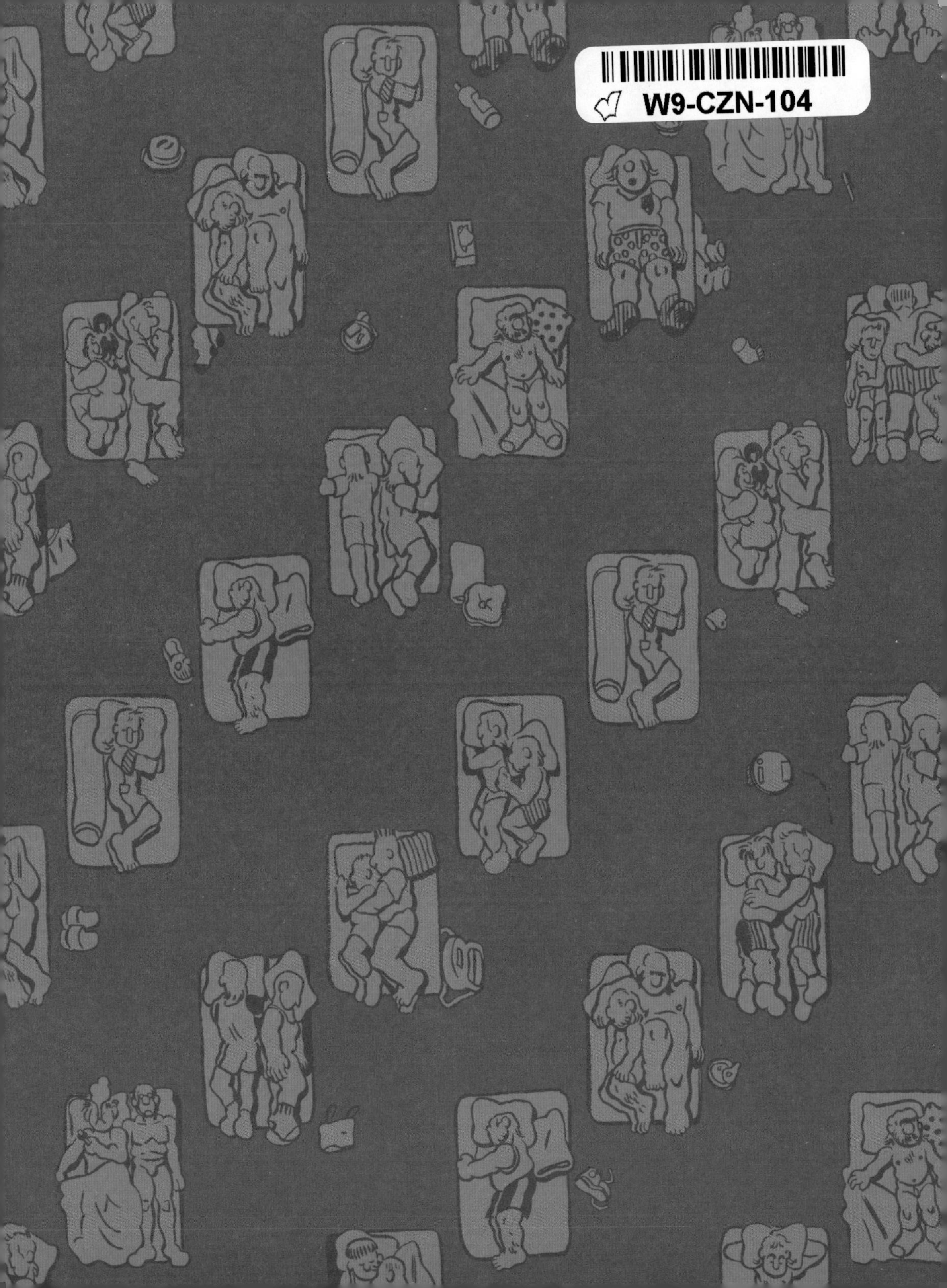

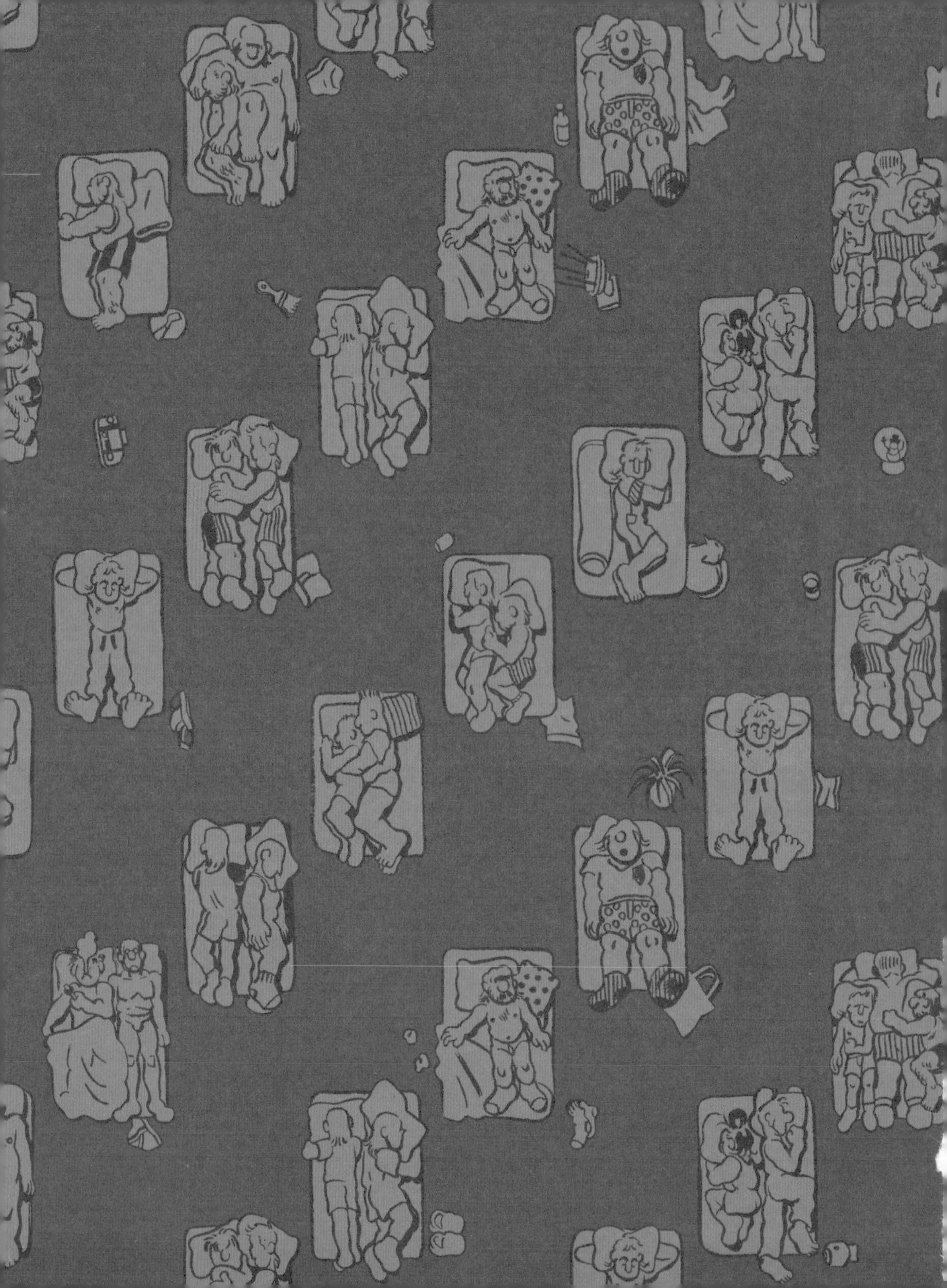

the short while ™

JEREMY SORESE

Published by
ARCHAIA ™

Design by
Jeremy Sorese and *Marie Krupina*

Assistant Editor
Allyson Gronowitz

Editor
Sierra Hahn

A very special thanks to ***Mitchell Kuga, Anthony Cudahy, Melissa Ling, Carta Monir, Molly Ellis and Kyle Turner for their early reading, encouragement and insight. For Scott Reed, who first brought me to the desert. For Adam J. Kurtz, for our work dates. For Jen Linnan, a champion of champions. And for Holden Brown, who looks more and more like home to me, each and every day.***

ARCHAIA™

BOOM! Studios, 5670 Wilshire Boulevard, Suite 400, Los Angeles, CA 90036-5679.
Printed in China. First Printing.

ISBN: 978-1-68415-746-4, eISBN: 978-1-64668-324-6

For Patrick Costello and Kevin Czap,
who believed in this book before I did.

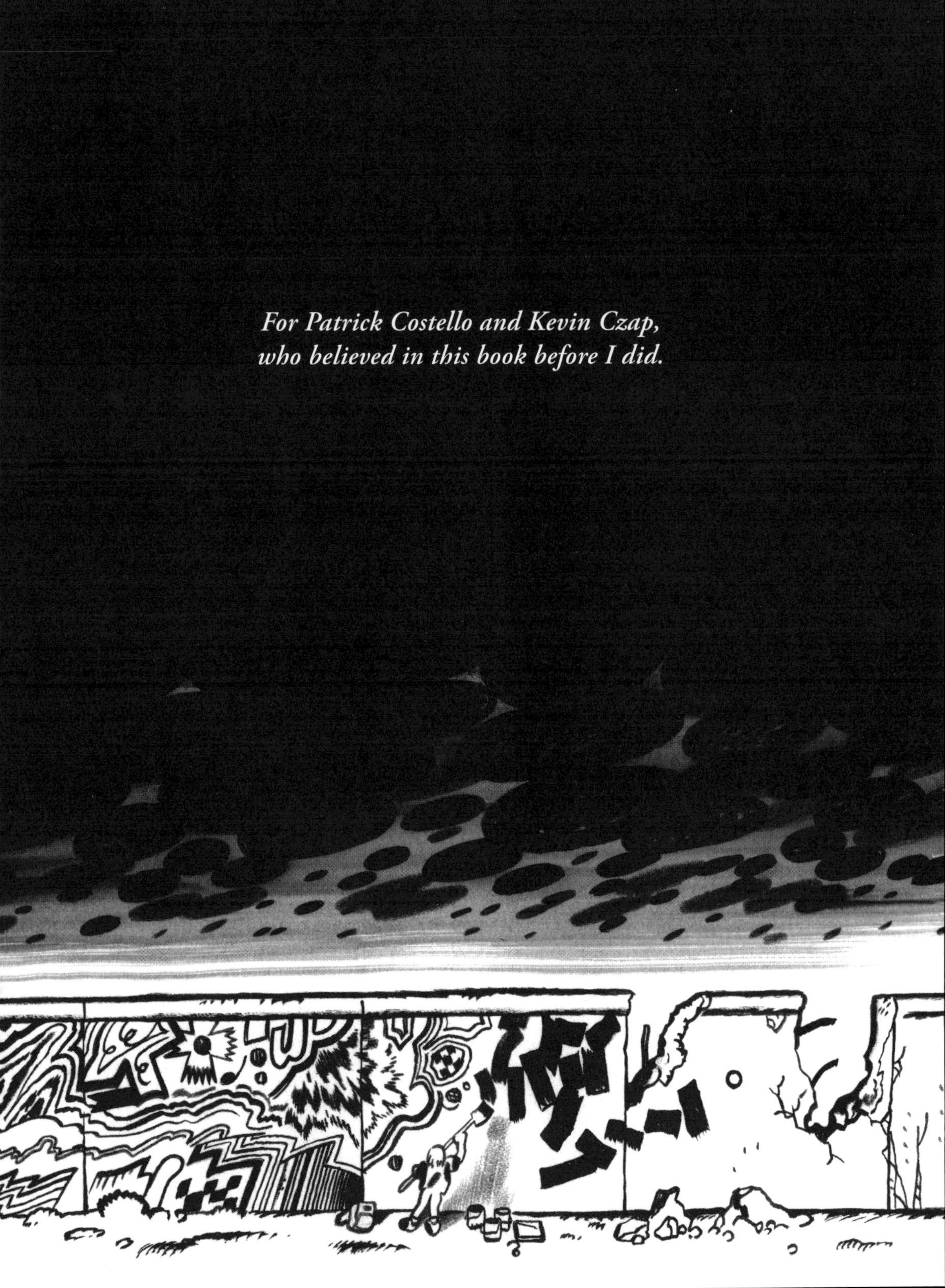

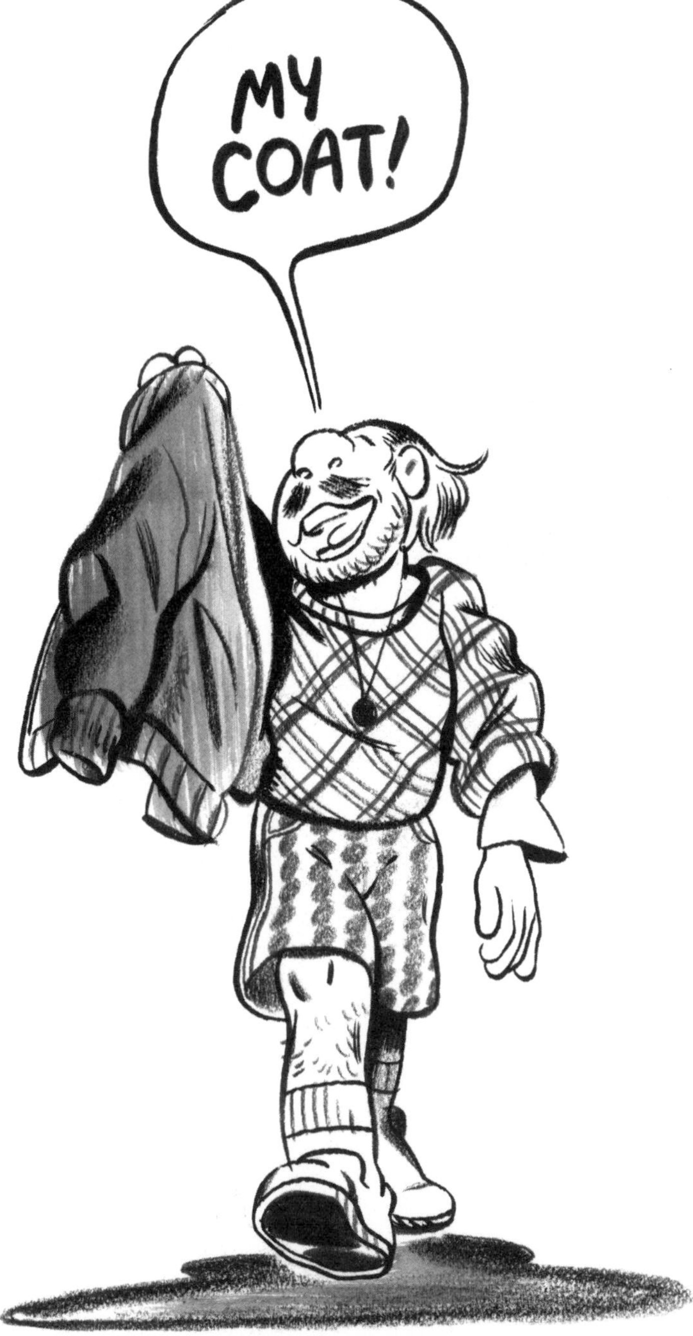
MY COAT!

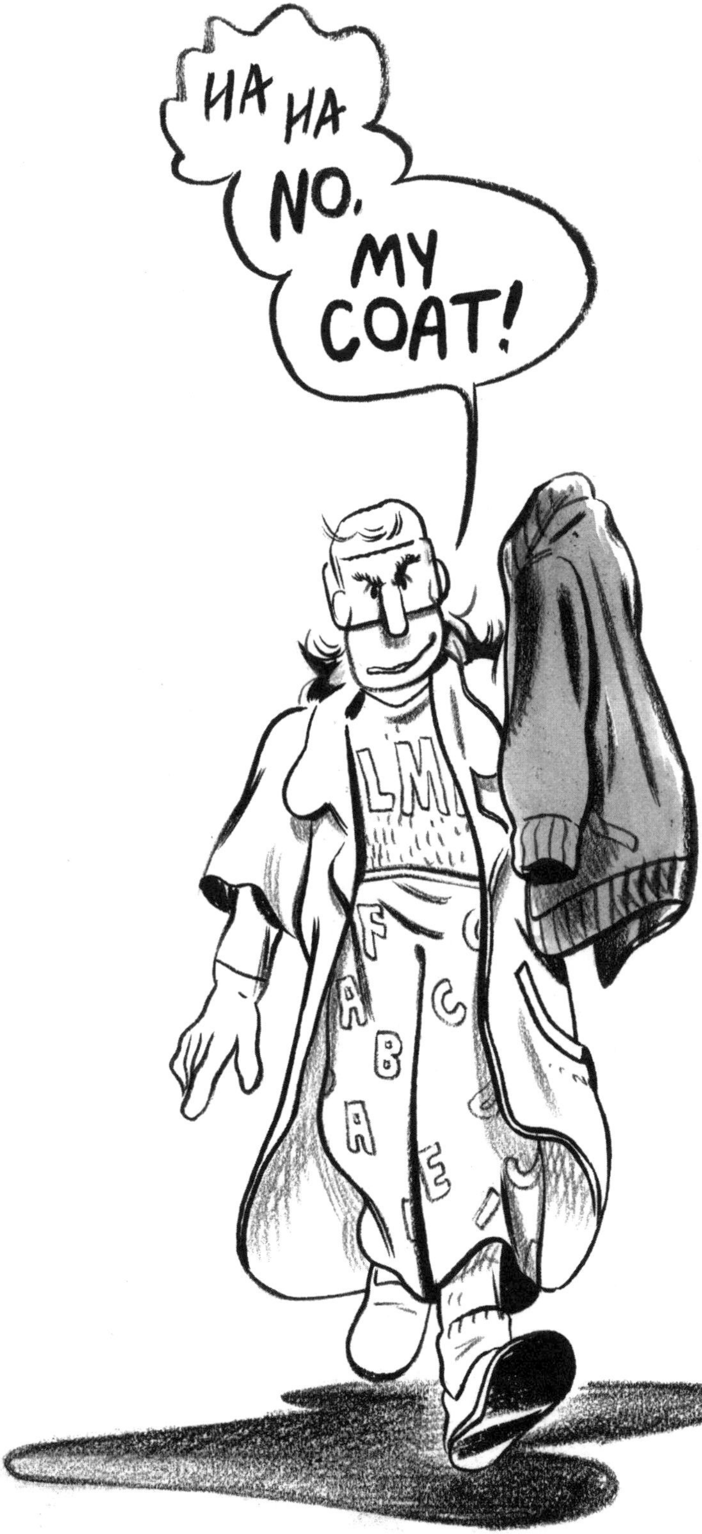
HA HA
NO, MY COAT!
LM
F
A C
B
A
E

[redacted]

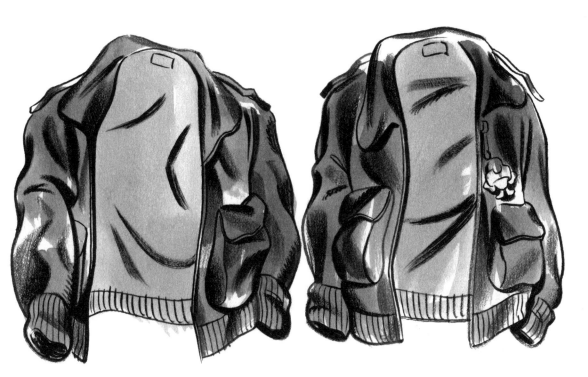

Colin and Paolo met after leaving a party while accidentally wearing each other's nearly identical leather jackets. Their jackets were heaped together on a bed in a darkened room, along with every other partygoer's discarded outer layers. The only noticeable difference between the two jackets was a small plastic toy hooked to the zipper of Paolo's.

The party had been thrown by a friend of Colin's named Avery, who remembered that both men arrived separately but dressed alike. Avery exchanged information on their behalf, suddenly obsessed with making sure the jackets were returned. Only after Colin and Paolo started talking did it occur to Colin that their lost jackets, and subsequent meeting, may have been orchestrated entirely by Avery, who wouldn't be above feigning innocence in an effort to spark some romance in Colin's life. Colin did appreciate their effort though—his jacket had originally belonged to his mom Minnie, purchased when she was his age.

Their first date lasted just long enough to swap jackets and promise a longer one to come.

Colin suggested they see a movie together, and they settled on a documentary titled *A View From All Sides*. Unexpectedly, Paolo started sobbing half way through, and they left before it was over.

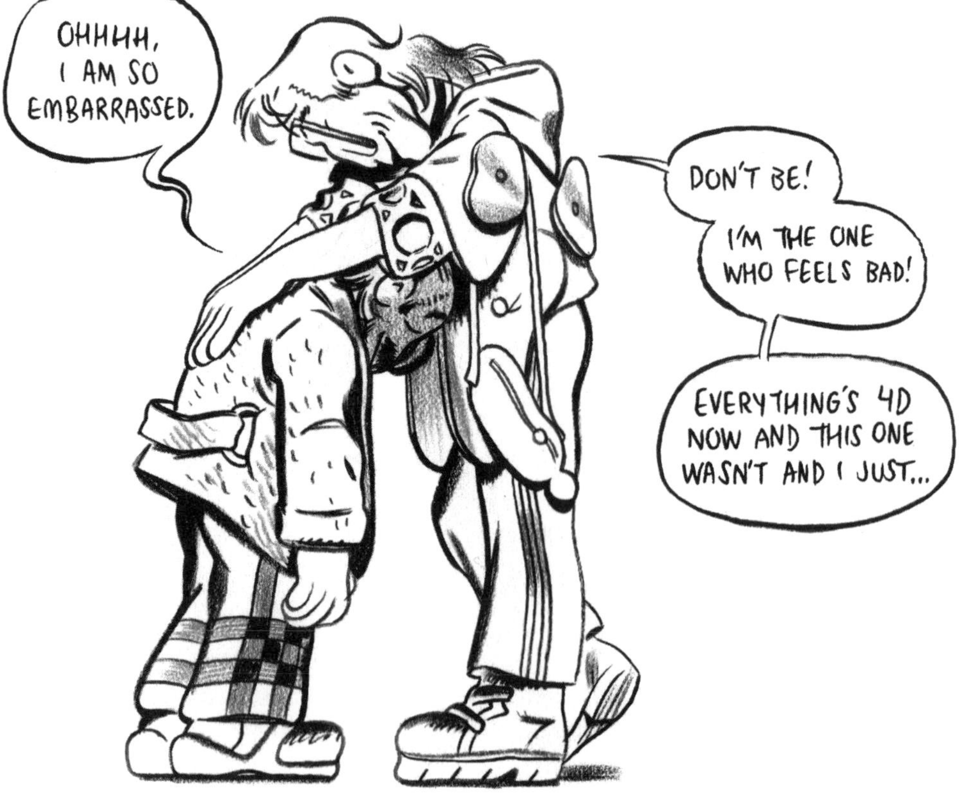
OHHHH, I AM SO EMBARRASSED.
DON'T BE!
I'M THE ONE WHO FEELS BAD!
EVERYTHING'S 4D NOW AND THIS ONE WASN'T AND I JUST...

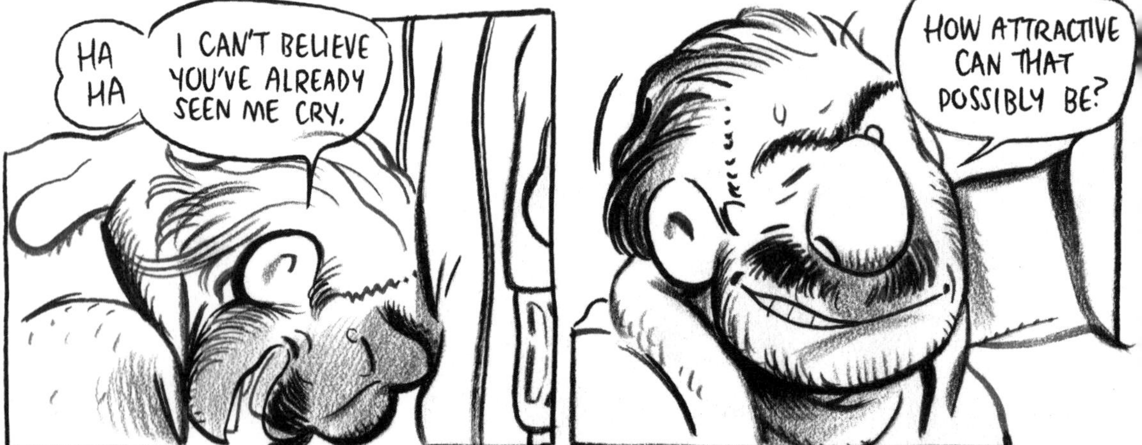
HA HA
I CAN'T BELIEVE YOU'VE ALREADY SEEN ME CRY.
HOW ATTRACTIVE CAN THAT POSSIBLY BE?

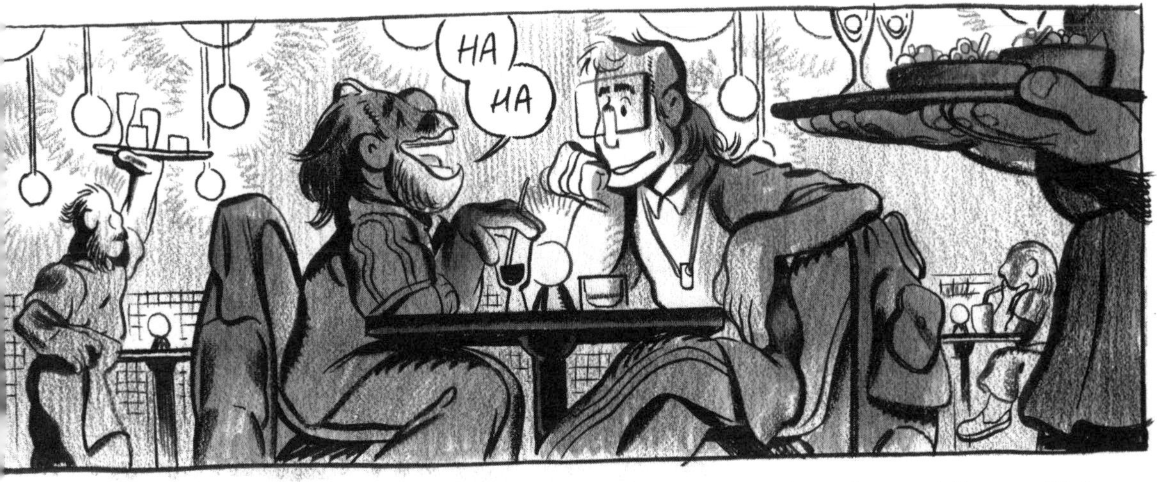
HA
HA

Truth was, Colin did find it attractive. He felt a soft spot for emotional people, especially men. Their uncontrolled feelings gave him a purpose—to be comforting, a little overbearing. Parental, but tender.

Paolo struggled with feeling like a burden. Admittedly, he was rarely difficult, often choosing to accept the decisions of others as if they were his own. Passive, but content.

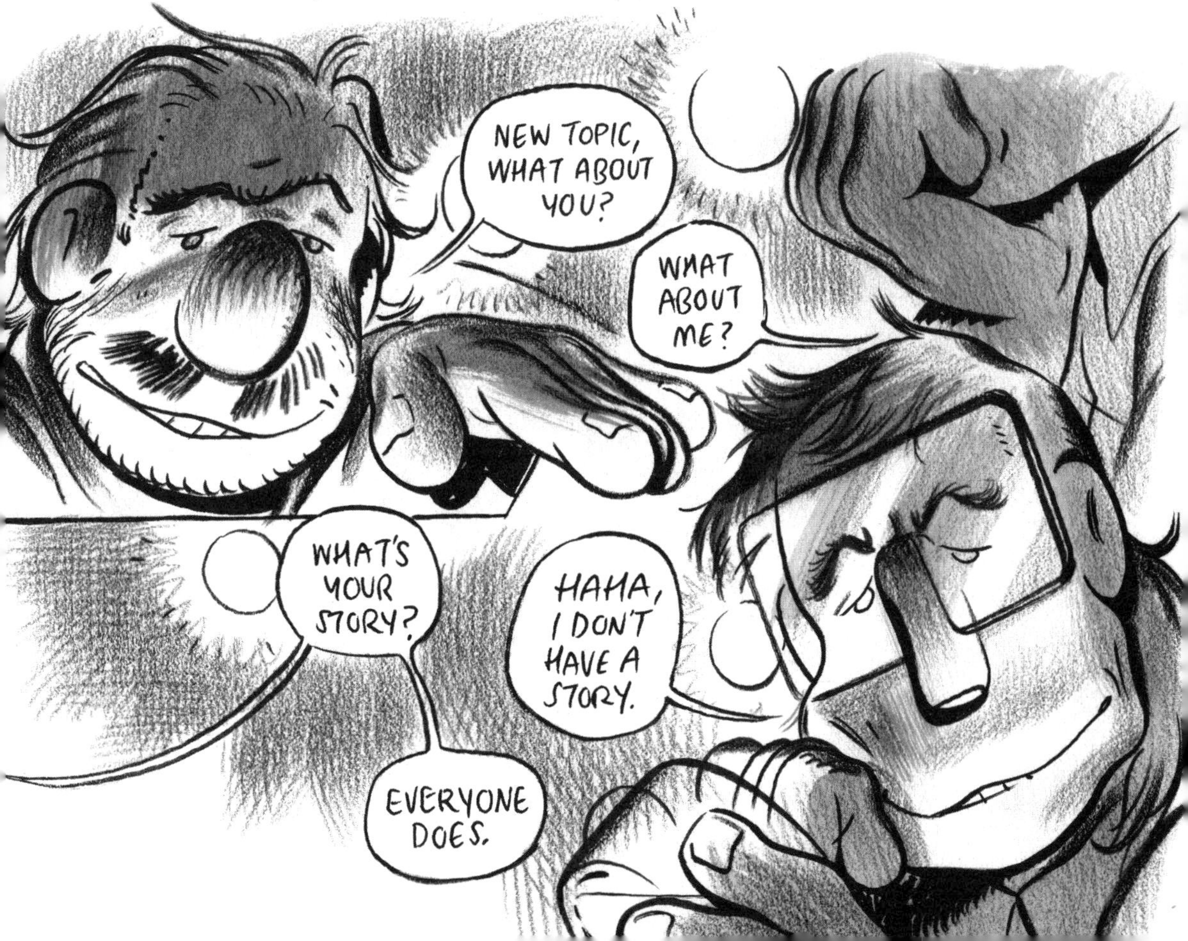
NEW TOPIC, WHAT ABOUT YOU?
WHAT ABOUT ME?
WHAT'S YOUR STORY?
HAHA, I DON'T HAVE A STORY.
EVERYONE DOES.

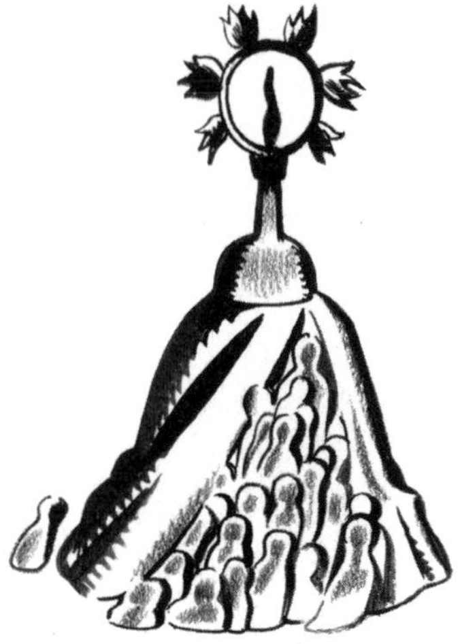
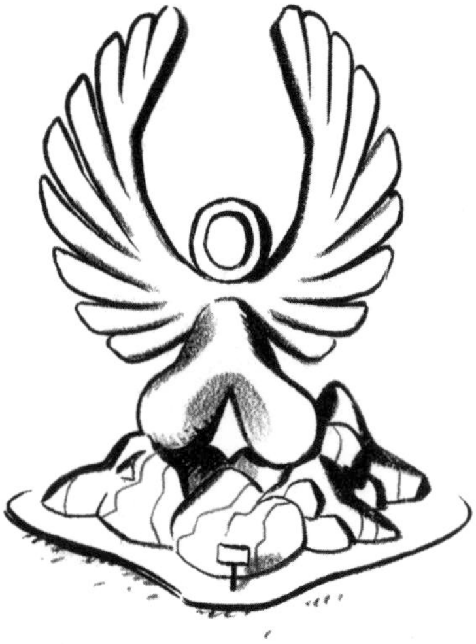
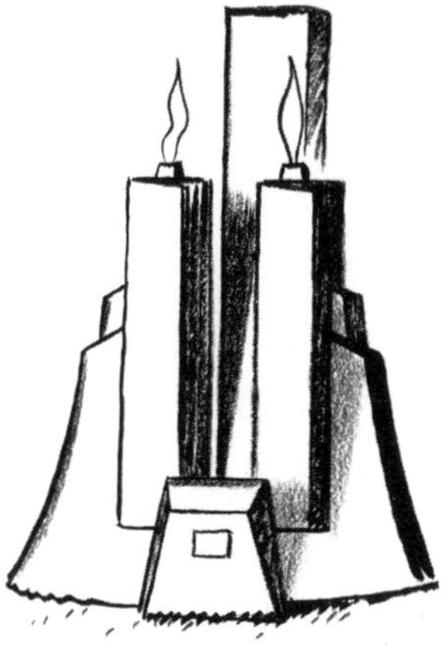

Colin worked for a Mayoral Advisory Committee regarding public monuments, acting as a project manager in their recent efforts to beautify the city. After the fall of the Administration, all evidence of that period in their country's history was eliminated. Monuments built in reverence to a more totalitarian vision of the world were destroyed and replaced with gentler, less specific, contemporary works. Some of the pieces deemed noteworthy were relocated to museums that could speak of the atrocities committed in a more nuanced way but most were recycled, the vast quantities of steel and stone set aside for something new.

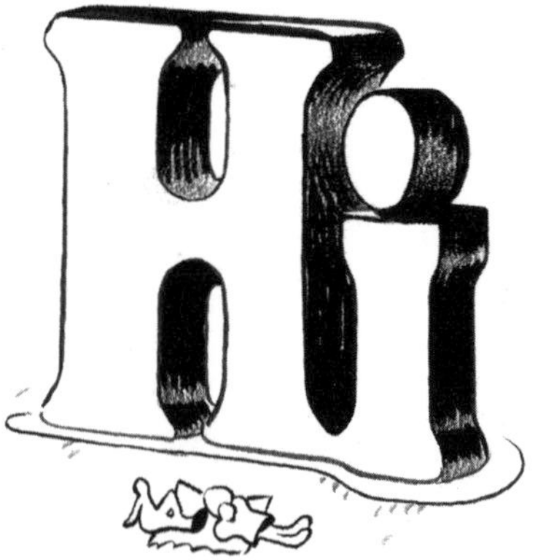
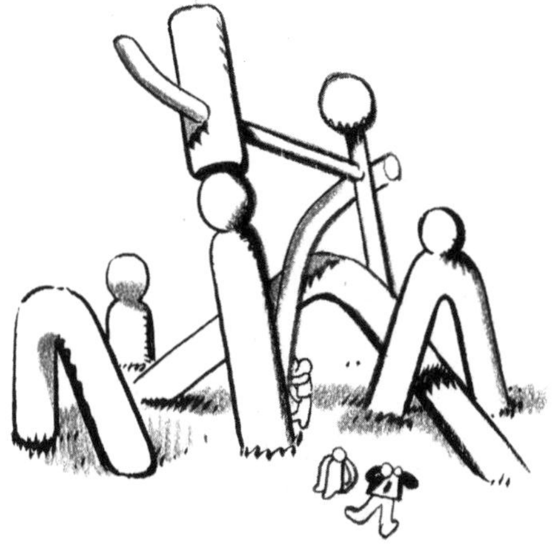
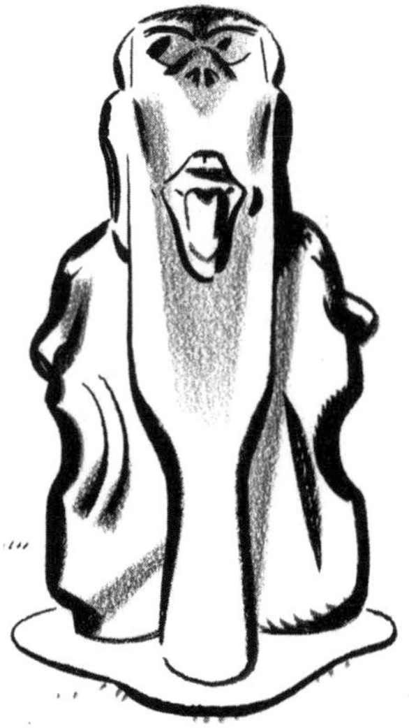

The Committee's intention was to help the general public forget what happened, or at least mis-remember, allowing their new memories of a revitalized urban center to replace the old. Colin's job was rewarding, but it also passed the burden of carrying this history onto him and his team.

Colin's mother Minnie had raised him as a member of *The Dance*, a spiritual guidance community focused on finding one's purpose in the Universe.

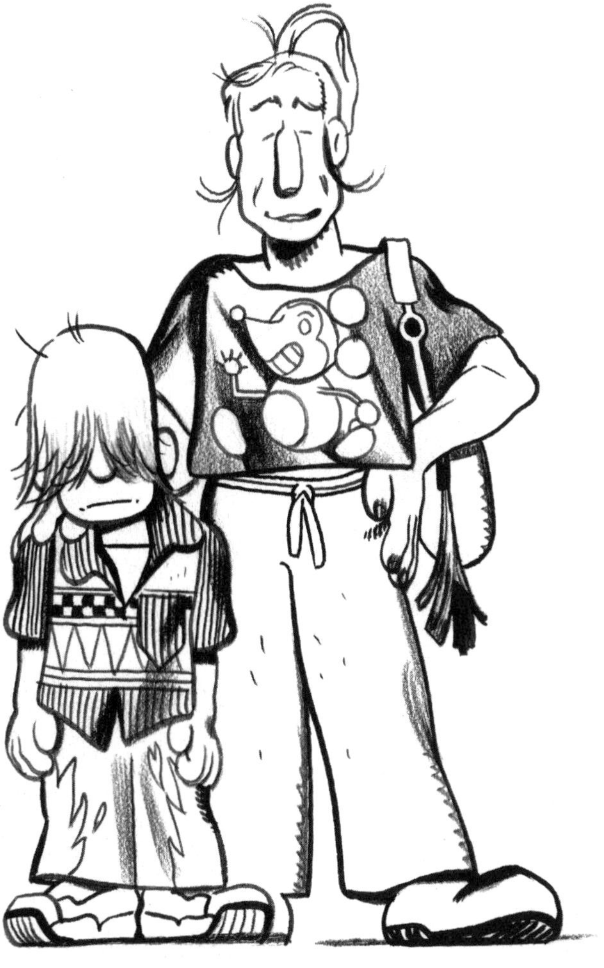

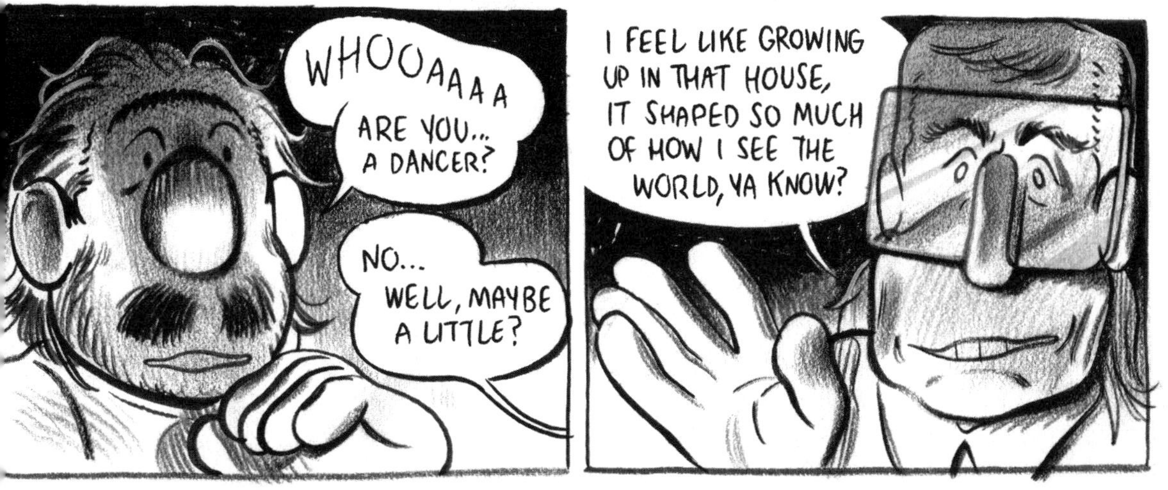
WHOOAAAA
ARE YOU... A DANCER?
NO... WELL, MAYBE A LITTLE?
I FEEL LIKE GROWING UP IN THAT HOUSE, IT SHAPED SO MUCH OF HOW I SEE THE WORLD, YA KNOW?

The organization known as *The Dance* was first started by a group of six friends.

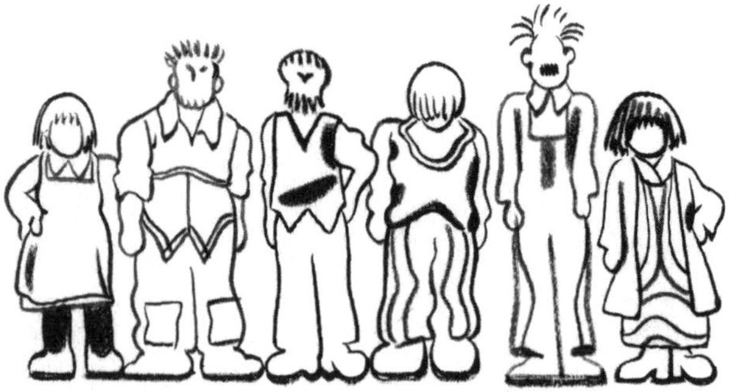

In the early days, "dancing" was an attempt to soothe their anxieties during a time when the country was pulling itself out of decades of brutality. Keeping the organization small also helped to quell any embarrassment anyone may have felt at being compared to a certain kind of free-spirited lifestyle. They didn't wear caftans or sell home-brewed organic concoctions. They spun around in open fields together and made out after work on evenings when their schedules permitted.

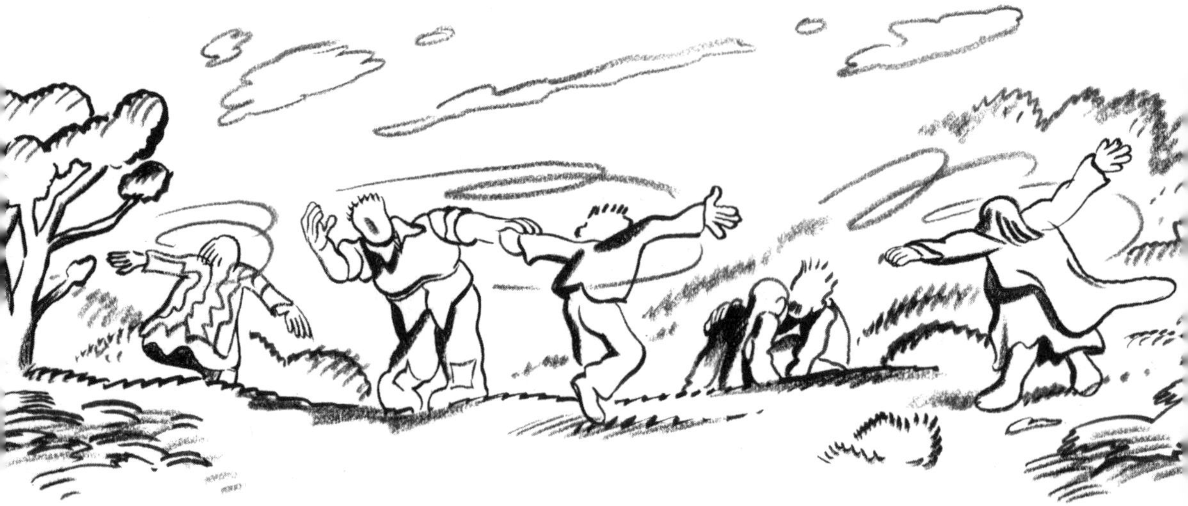

Their numbers inevitably grew, swelling from six to nearly fifty. An original member invited their new partner who, in turn, invited a close friend who, in turn, invited someone they didn't know very well. Larger numbers brought new problems. More members made explaining what they were doing harder. New members stopped spinning and just made out. Hallucinogens were introduced to help facilitate an easier emotional connection. Neighbors complained.

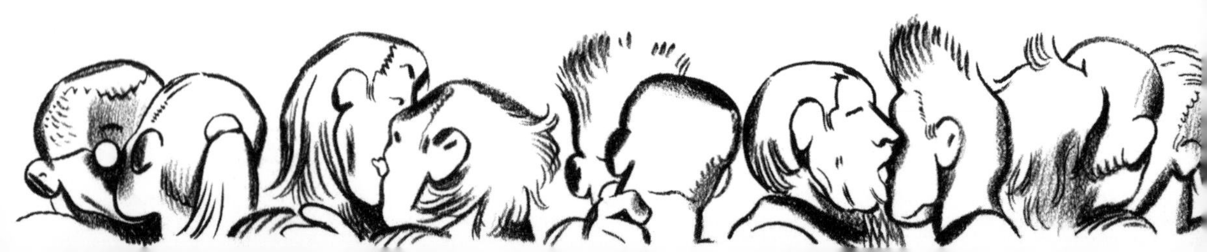

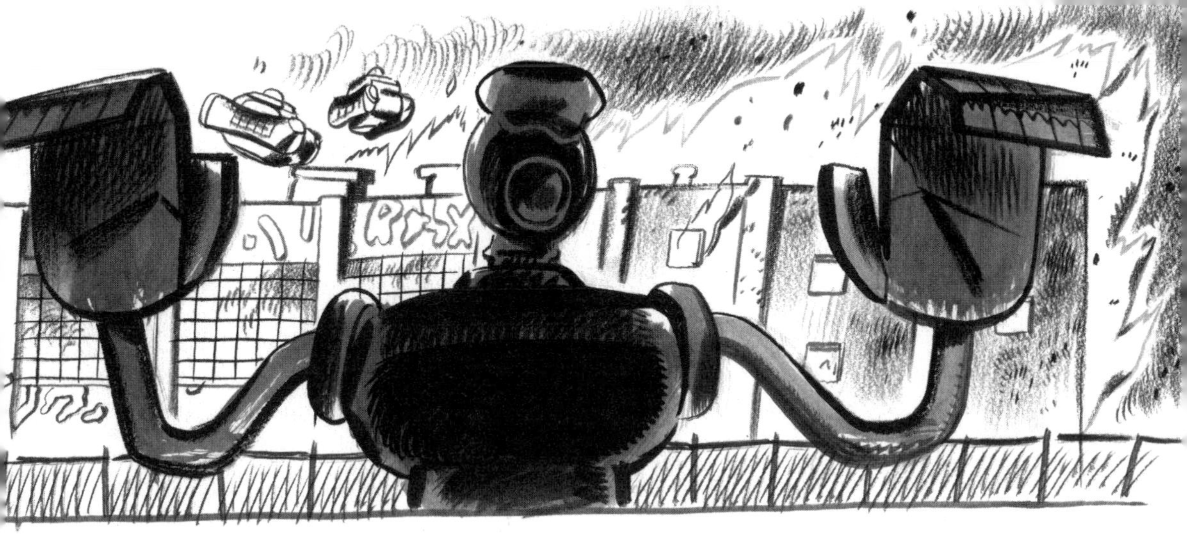

The original members abruptly broke away. The more recent members sought to monetize their newly discovered spiritual practice, buying an abandoned shoe-lace factory to establish as their headquarters. They were repeatedly busted by the local authorities on charges ranging from health code violations to tax evasion. After an intoxicated member fell from the roof of the building and died, the police sought to evict the residents. Shortly after, the factory burned down under mysterious circumstances.

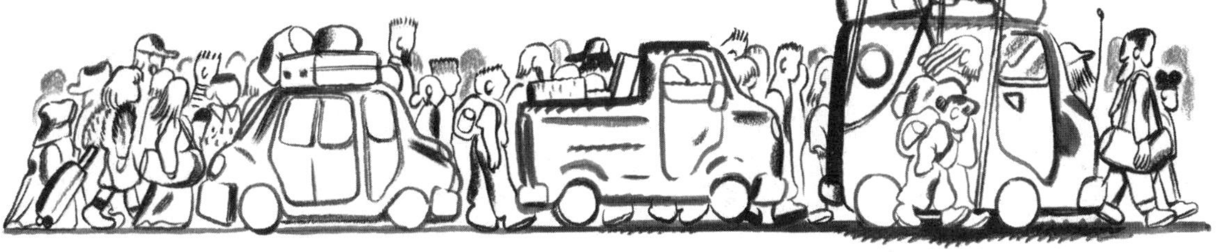

This only increased interest in *The Dance*. The surviving members of this second branch began proselytizing across the country, splintering into smaller, more mobile groups of devotees. They built a second center that was plagued by similar harassment from the police. Soon celebrities took an interest in *The Dance*, adopting the basic tenets to appear fashionable. Rumors circulated that Dancers secretly controlled both the global trade market and the film industry. But as *The Dance* rapidly expanded in scale, the organization collapsed in on itself. Interest waned once people found it harder to connect with their fellow Dancers.

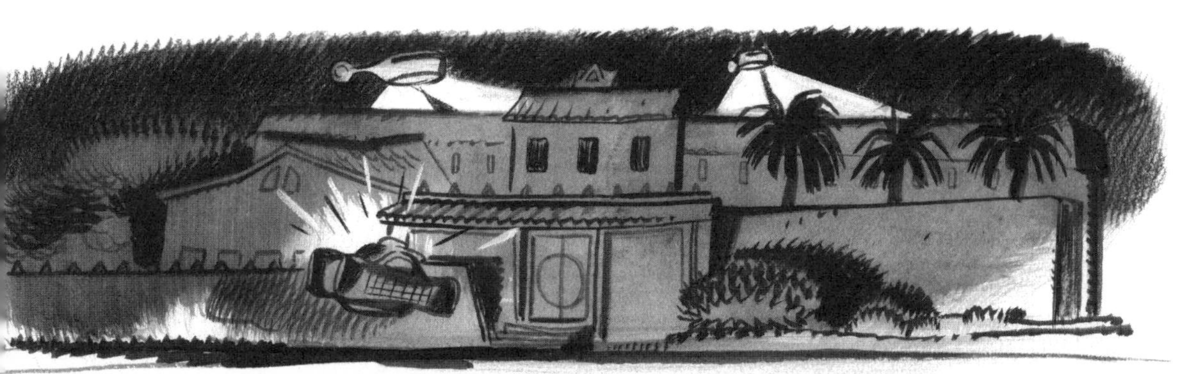

Even after their beloved organization morphed into something beyond their recognition, the six original Dancers stayed bound together by their shared history. The paths each of them had taken through life varied, but they still found time to meet up as a group. As their bodies aged, spinning in circles and making out made less sense. They began forming huddles, leaning on one another for support, which inevitably became a more widespread practice within the various splintered organizations.

The troupe gathers around the individual in the middle of the huddle. Troupes will often provide a cushion for the individual to lay down on during their session

The troupe forms a kind of web by linking arms with both the person next to them and across from them in the circle.

They found that the intimacy they continued to share opened up their beings to one another on a deeply spiritual level. Dancers believe that everyone they have ever met was meant to be, not as part of some grand cosmic plan—one of Heavens and Hells—but as part of a much smaller, more human one. To the more devoted Dancers, the idea of randomness discredits everyone's intrinsic value as an individual. Everyone has merit, regardless of their perceived worth, which they feel is a selfish way of judging another human being. Everyone from spouses to grocery store clerks, newborn babies to strangers on the bus, are all a part of this vast interconnected web.

This connection they feel allows their bodies to travel, or at least to feel as if they do, along the timeline of someone else's life, reliving major and minor events together, as though sharing one mind. This process of forming a huddle and connecting with a history larger than their singular individual one has become the cornerstone of *The Dance*.

The troupe members bring their left arms up, forming a kind of steeple with the person across from them in the circle.

To help facilitate the weaving of bodies, the troupe members begin to lean on one another, balancing their bodies against those of their fellow members.

A huddle can last less than an hour but have been known to last much longer. The longest recorded huddle was for almost two days.

Colin had never seen the inside of a huddle, but Minnie had, and claimed that it was the most beautiful experience of her life, second only to being a mom.

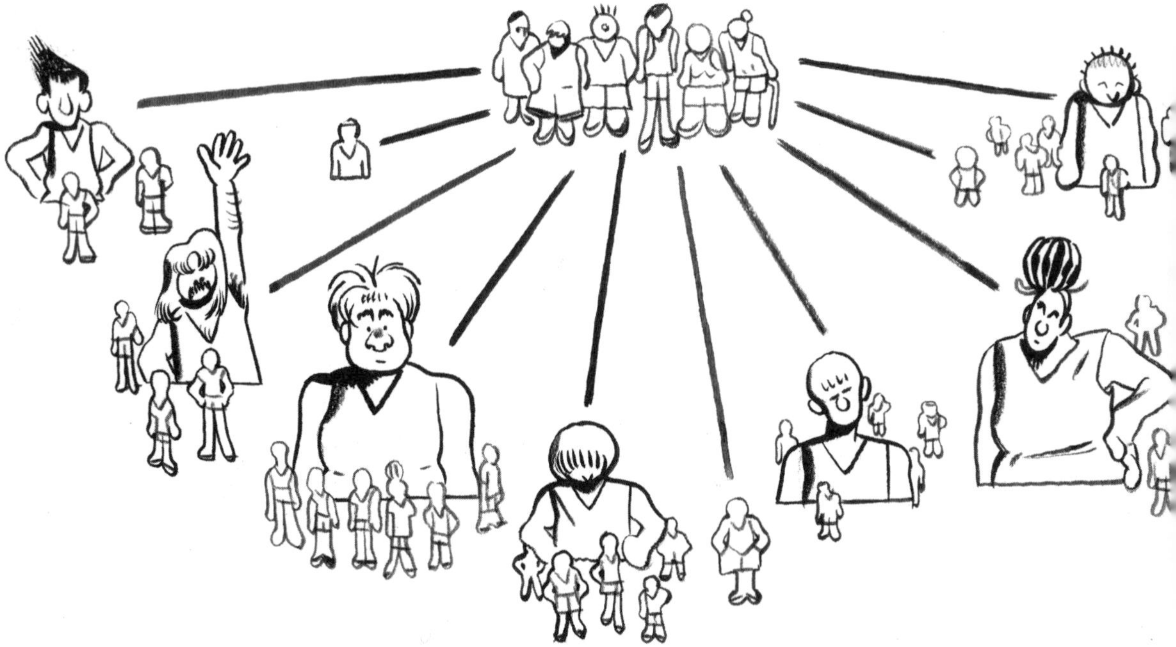

Though it never again reached the hysteria of its early years, the number of followers within the movement continued to grow. To maintain some sense of community, Dancers have assembled smaller troupes, limiting themselves to no more than twenty people. Smaller troupes allow for greater ease in forming emotional connections, which helps facilitate forming a successful huddle. Minnie has been a member of her troupe for nearly as long as Colin has been alive. They've been meeting in the same gymnasium of a local middle school for nearly that long as well.

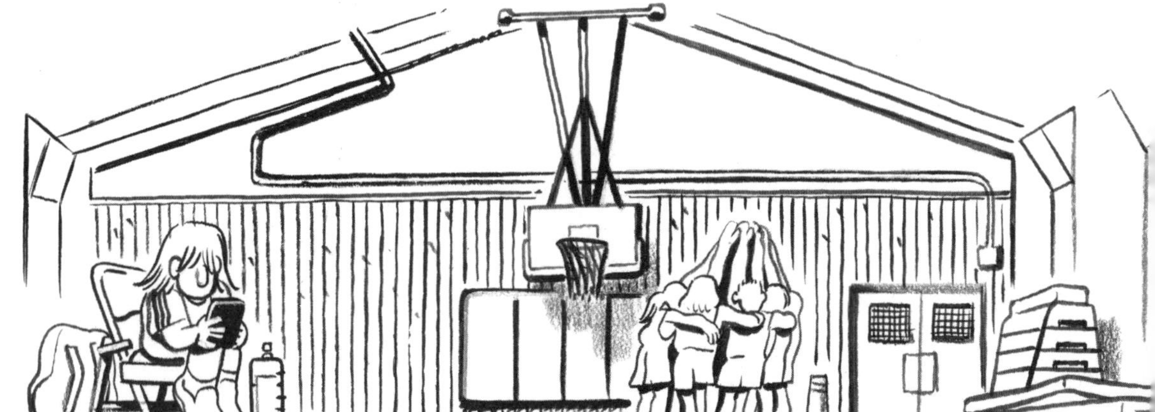

Minnie once saw a member of the original six Dancers speak. He had just cleared his sixty-fifth birthday, and the microphone amplified the sounds of his labored breathing throughout the convention center.

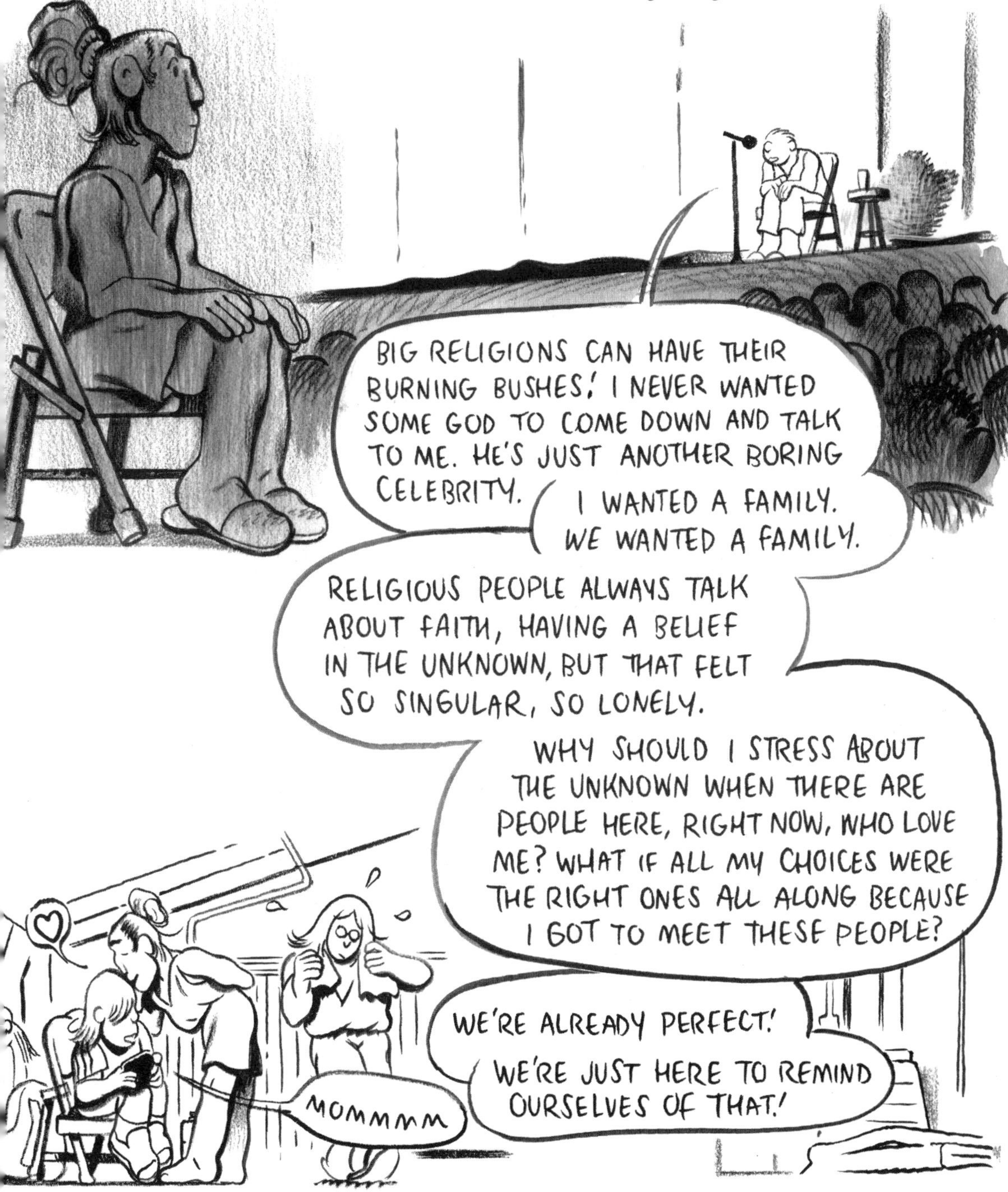

BIG RELIGIONS CAN HAVE THEIR BURNING BUSHES! I NEVER WANTED SOME GOD TO COME DOWN AND TALK TO ME. HE'S JUST ANOTHER BORING CELEBRITY.
I WANTED A FAMILY. WE WANTED A FAMILY.
RELIGIOUS PEOPLE ALWAYS TALK ABOUT FAITH, HAVING A BELIEF IN THE UNKNOWN, BUT THAT FELT SO SINGULAR, SO LONELY.
WHY SHOULD I STRESS ABOUT THE UNKNOWN WHEN THERE ARE PEOPLE HERE, RIGHT NOW, WHO LOVE ME? WHAT IF ALL MY CHOICES WERE THE RIGHT ONES ALL ALONG BECAUSE I GOT TO MEET THESE PEOPLE?
WE'RE ALREADY PERFECT!
WE'RE JUST HERE TO REMIND OURSELVES OF THAT!
MOMMMM

For Minnie, being a Dancer gave her life a simple answer to a complex world. In many ways, having Colin as a son did as well.

Colin had been a serious child, made even more so by Minnie's easy effervescence. Growing up as her only kid, his solemn demeanor became her life's solid foundation. The taut string of a wayward kite.

Once she conceived by way of a donor, Minnie found a clear purpose for her time on this planet. Deep down, she knew she would've loved whatever child the Universe had sent her way, but Colin, with his quiet, studious ways, was an easy child to obsess over.

As they both grew, she praised him for his sensitivity and warmth. He was the real partner she had created, one who, in theory at least, didn't present the same problems a spousal relationship did.

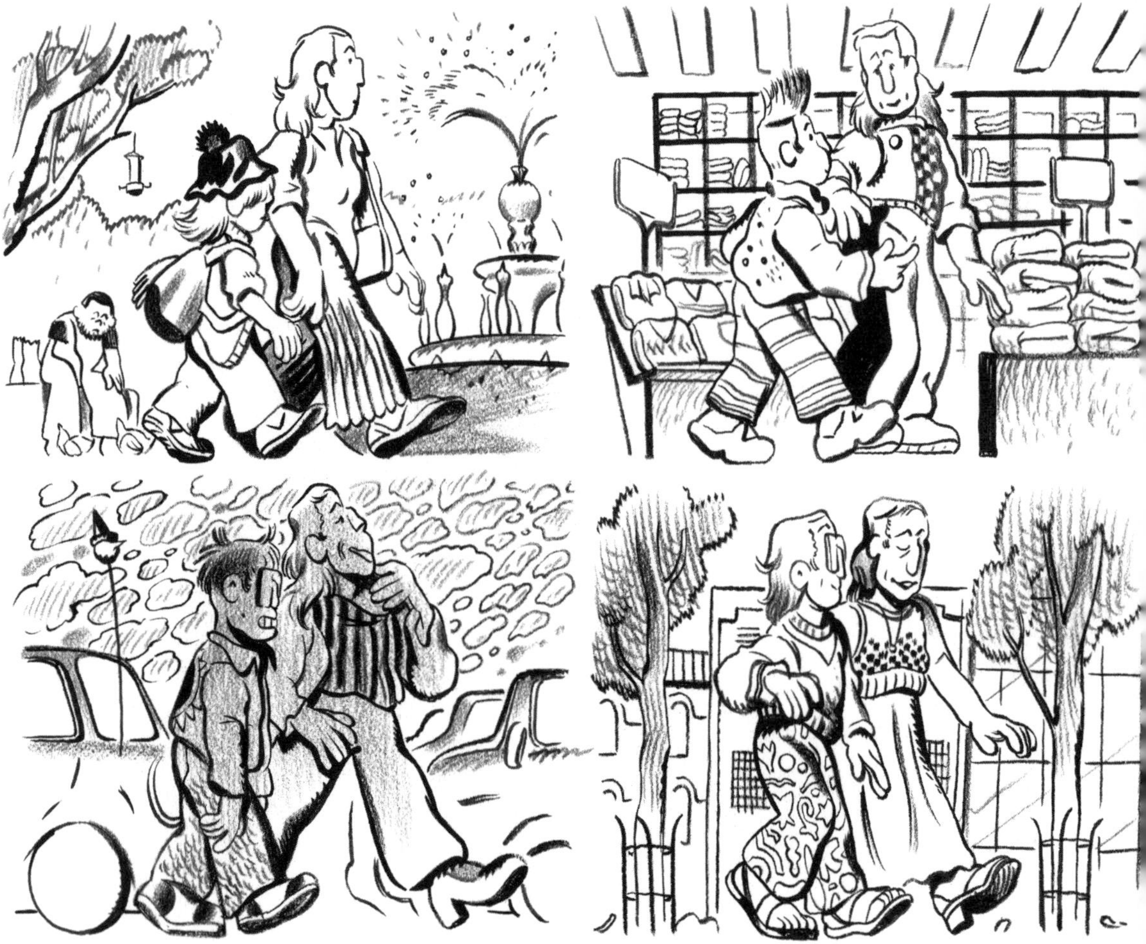

Minnie had been married five times.

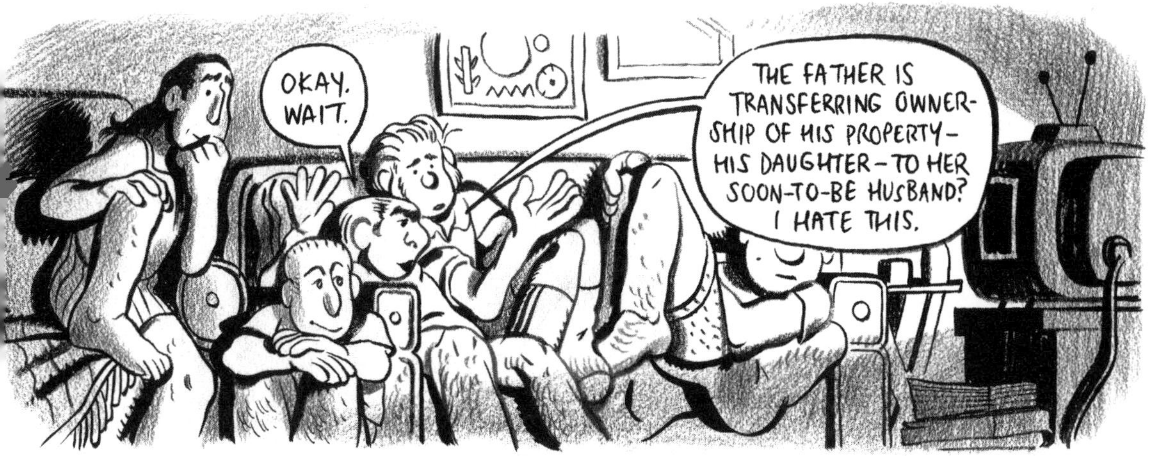
OKAY. WAIT.
THE FATHER IS TRANSFERRING OWNERSHIP OF HIS PROPERTY—HIS DAUGHTER—TO HER SOON-TO-BE HUSBAND? I HATE THIS.

Marriage fell out of fashion when Minnie was growing up. The right was denied to so many for so long that, when everyone finally could, why would they? Centuries of cultural artifacts were deemed confusing and irrelevant to the youth of Minnie's generation.

Her first marriage started off as a joke. Colin had seen the photos taken on that day, when Minnie married her first girlfriend Donna, someone Colin couldn't remember having ever known. Minnie and Donna were bored during a long break from school and raided a foreclosed bridal depot superstore that sat vacant in the crumbling town surrounding their university.

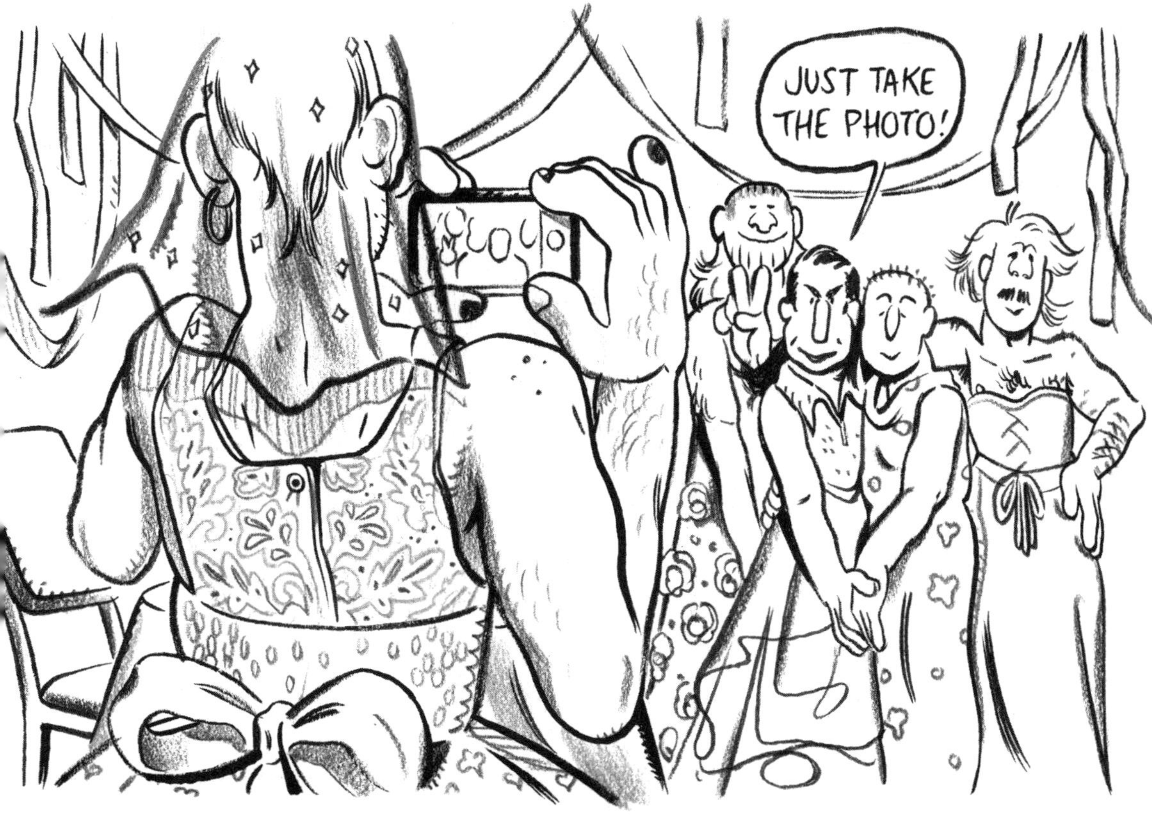
JUST TAKE THE PHOTO!

In an effort to stabilize their relationship, Minnie married Donna for a second time shortly before Colin was born. Their official marriage didn't last for long.

Colin was present for each of Minnie's subsequent weddings; he walked her down aisles and played mock officiant at intimate backyard gatherings in bare feet. He recognized them as nothing more than elaborate costume parties. At one point she was engaged to two people at once. Each of Minnie's marriages functioned outside of the clause "'til death do us part." These marriages were not a promise to maintain their romantic investment but a celebration of what they were feeling in that moment. After Donna, each of Minnie's partners understood this. And unlike Donna, each of Minnie's marriages ended happily.

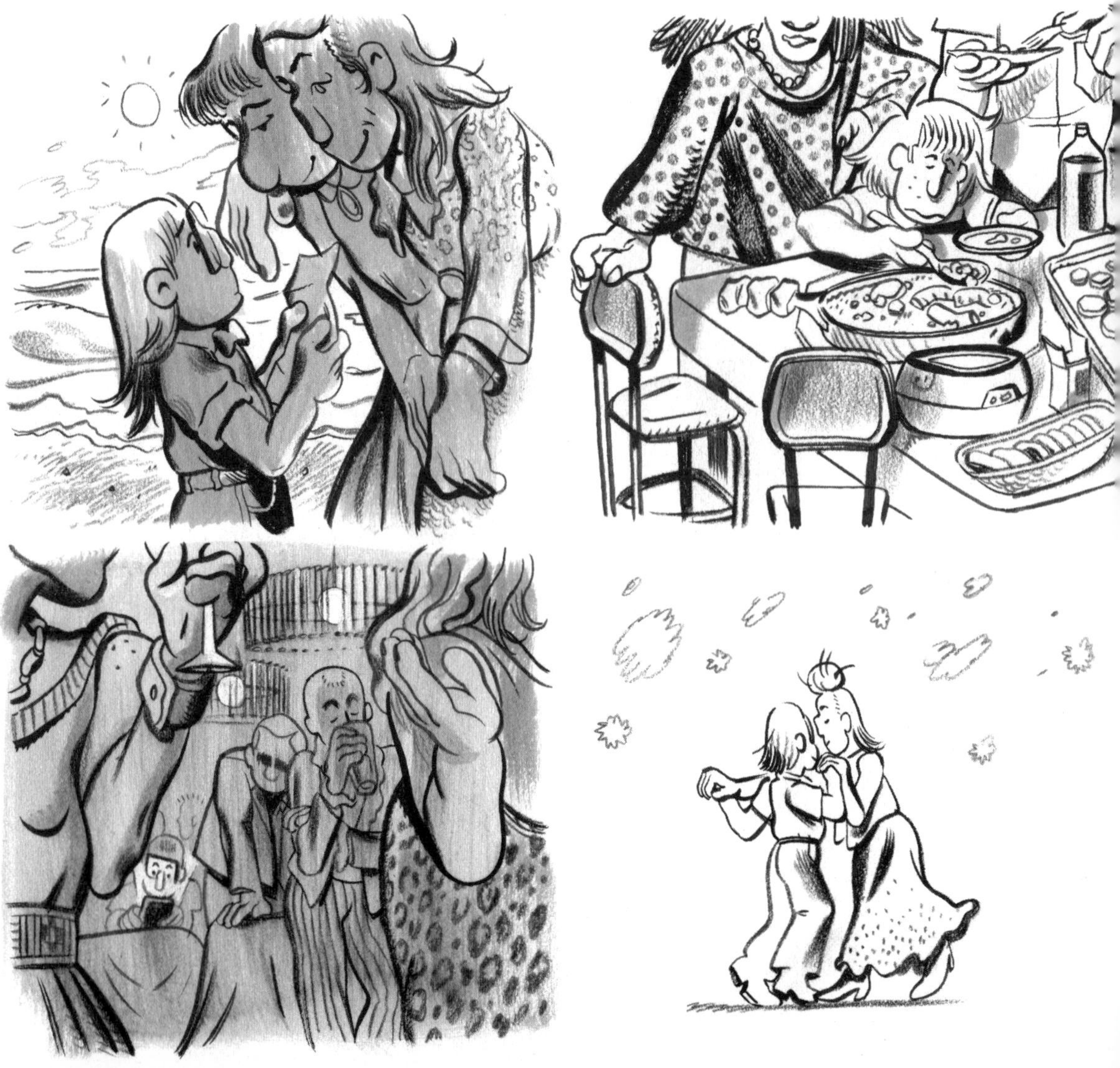

Minnie felt a deep curiosity for the lives of those around her. She was easily delighted by people and loved learning all that she could about them, slowly picking them like a lock.

Life was meant to be lived in a big way, and Colin, no matter how cautious and rational he became, agreed.

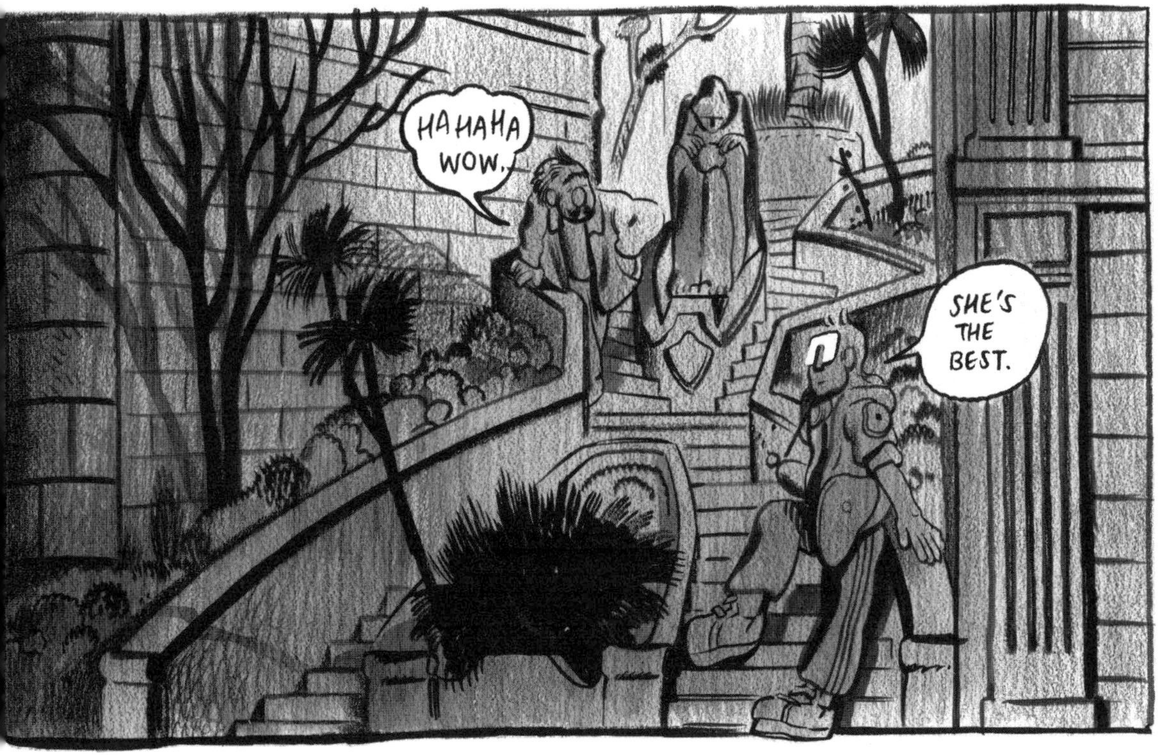
HAHAHA WOW.
SHE'S THE BEST.

As Colin grew up, Minnie was always the center of the stories he would tell at parties, the way he'd charm men on dates. If Colin was an immaculately cut glass vase, Minnie was the air bubble trapped within, full of something unknowable.

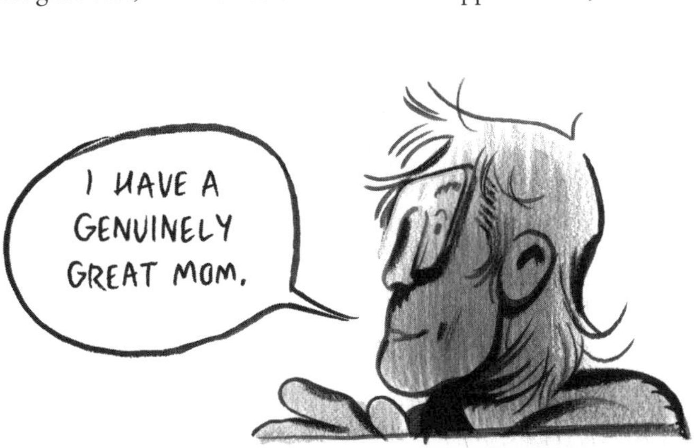
I HAVE A GENUINELY GREAT MOM.

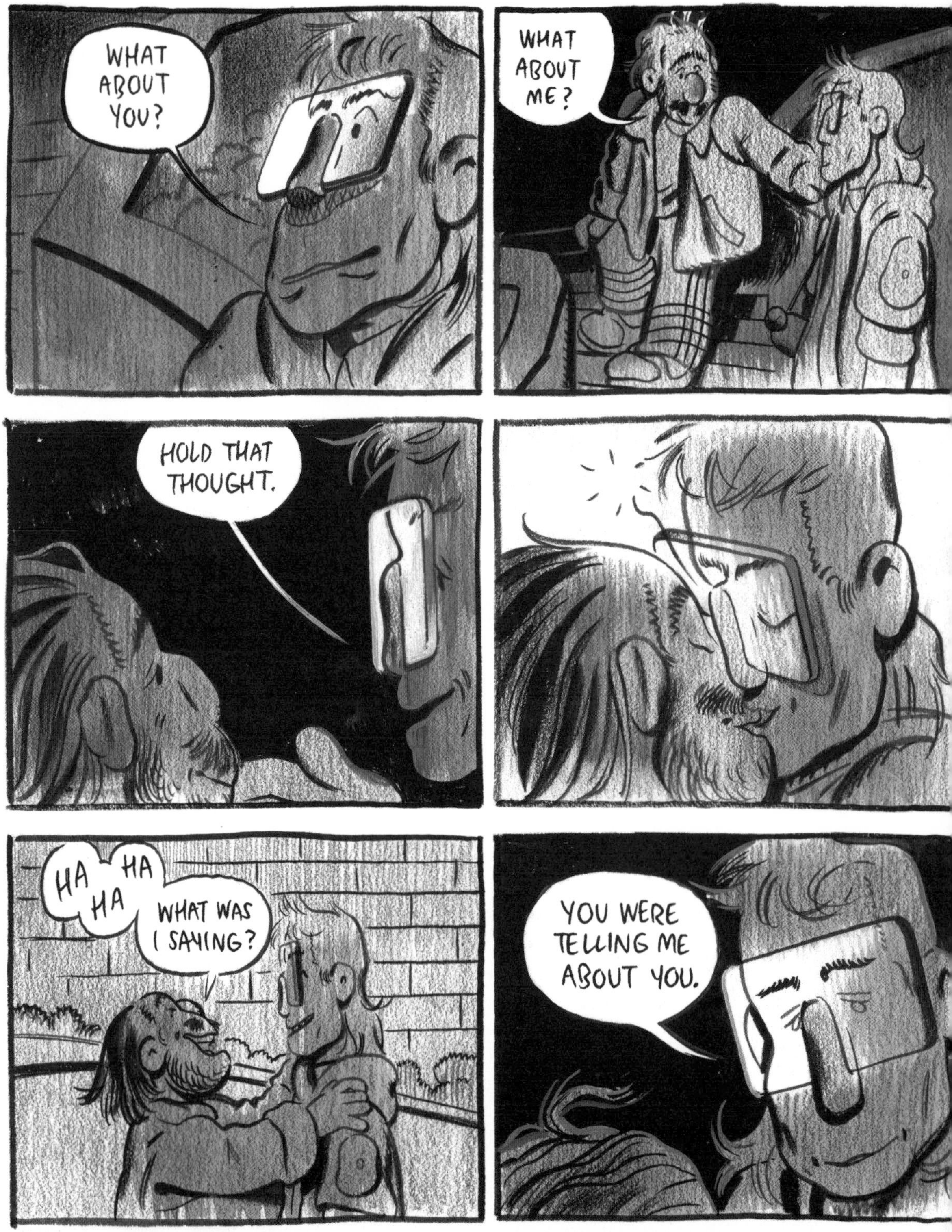
WHAT ABOUT YOU?
WHAT ABOUT ME?
HOLD THAT THOUGHT.
HA HA HA
WHAT WAS I SAYING?
YOU WERE TELLING ME ABOUT YOU.

Paolo wasn't working at the moment. He worked a series of odd jobs—landscaper, plot-line writer for erotic virtual reality experiences, barista at an organic beetle bar—but was taking time off to find a new direction, surviving on the guaranteed income provided by the city. He slept in. He took long walks. He pet cats at the local shelter. He had time to spare, which Colin never seemed to have enough of.

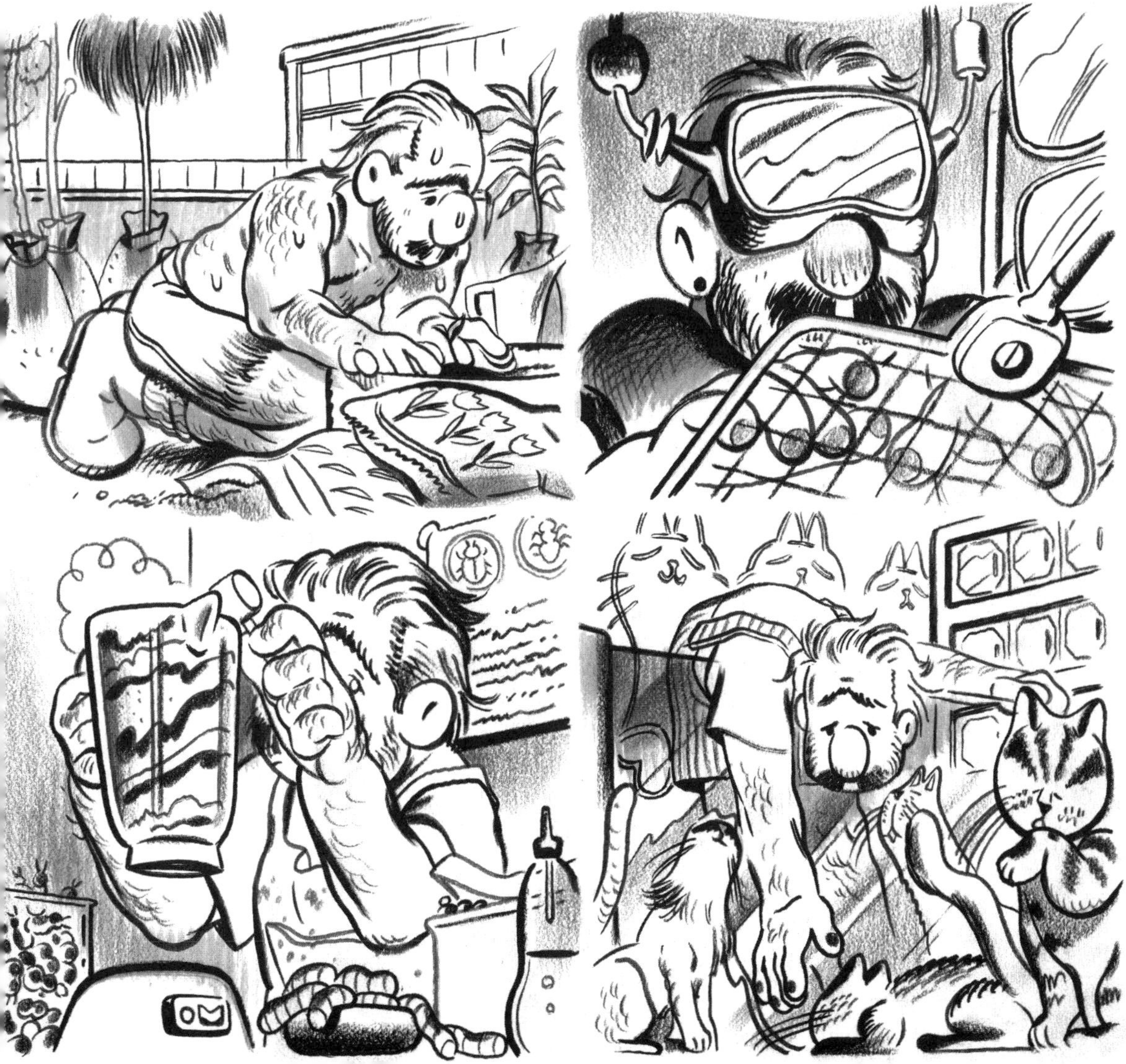

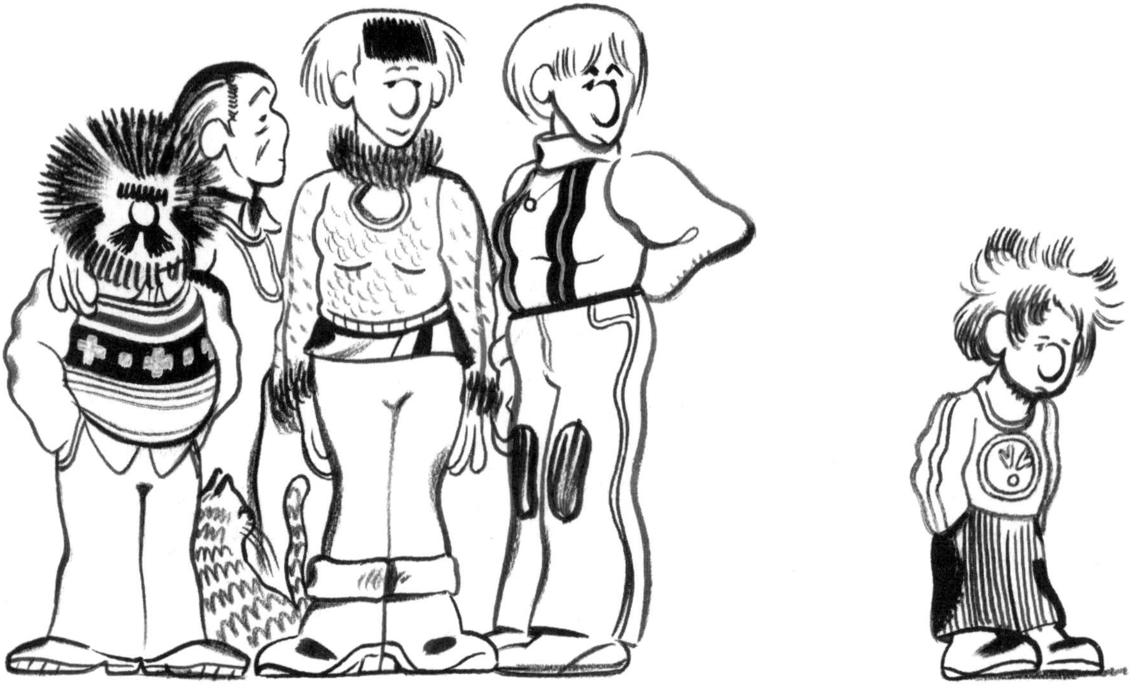

Paolo was the accidental third child of two immigrants from the crumbling European Union. After working for years to support their first two children—Paolo's twin sisters Karoline and Karolina—Donnino and Pina were reluctantly gifted a baby boy much later in life.

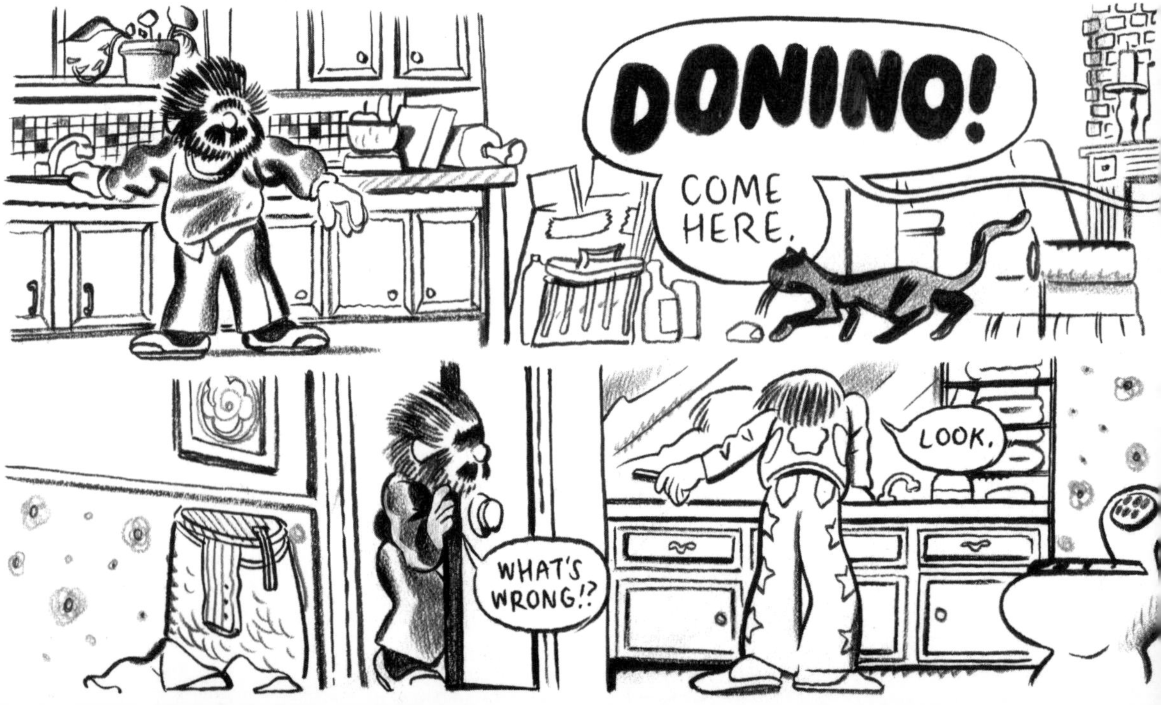
DONINO!
COME HERE.
WHAT'S WRONG!?
LOOK.

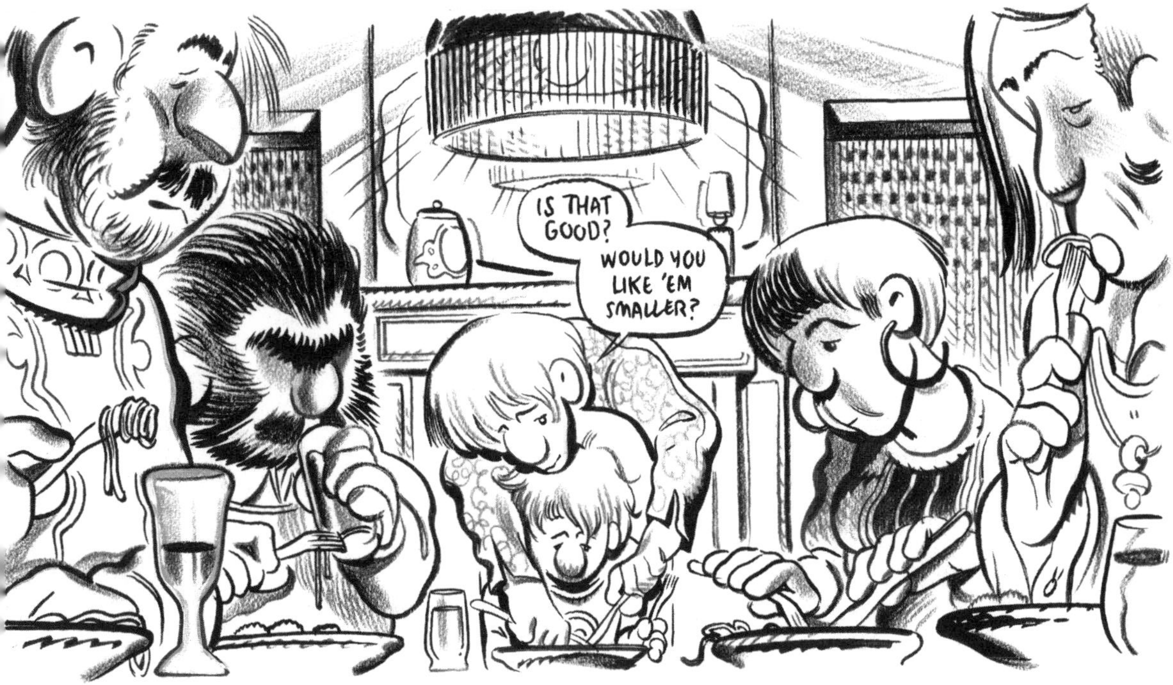
IS THAT GOOD?
WOULD YOU LIKE 'EM SMALLER?

While Colin felt comfortable being alone as a kid, Paolo had no other option. The fifteen-year age gap between Paolo and his older siblings meant his parents had little left to give him by the time he arrived and Karoline and Karolina were already moved out of the family's split-level solar home by the time he uttered his first word.

He spent his childhood wandering their neighborhood alone, unable to make friends easily and without the ability to occupy his time constructively. Outside of their extended family, the only company his parents ever entertained were the endless rotation of his sisters' boyfriends. Men who had nothing to say to a sullen preteen boy.

Later, Colin would come to understand that this was where Paolo's independent nature came from. His inability to ask for help. The stubbornness that closed him off from outside support. On their worst days, Colin reminded Paolo of the kind of older brother he had always wanted but had learned to do without.

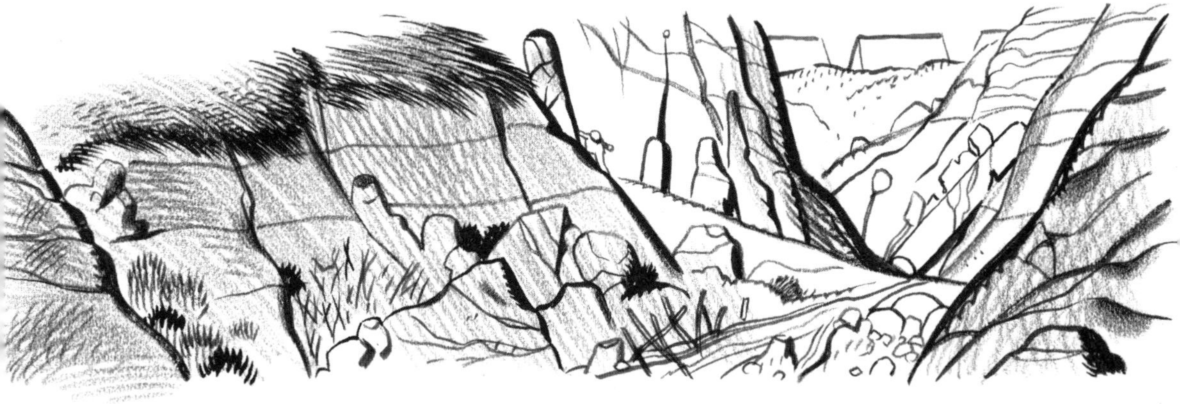

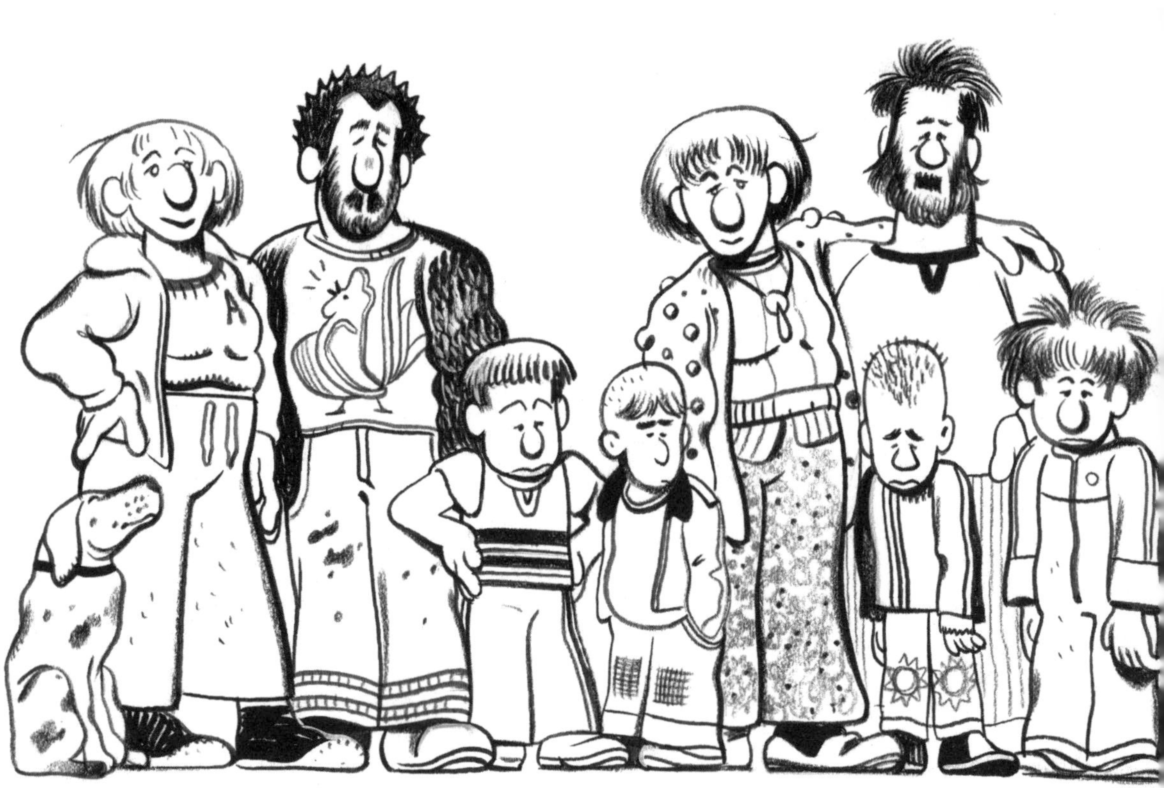

Karoline and Karolina worked as data analysts specializing in dismantling the large surveillance network created by the Administration. Shortly after being hired, the sisters were promoted, and in their new positions, they were ordered to reinstate this network for the current government. The network that not even a year before they had been taking apart.

They gave birth to two boys each: Kory and Korrie and Koren and Karl. Each boy was growing up to be bigger than Paolo—despite the ten-year age difference—which everyone commented on frequently. The lives of Paolo's older siblings made their parents proud. Having arrived in this country with so little, seeing their children prosper with large families and lucrative careers was all they could've hoped for.

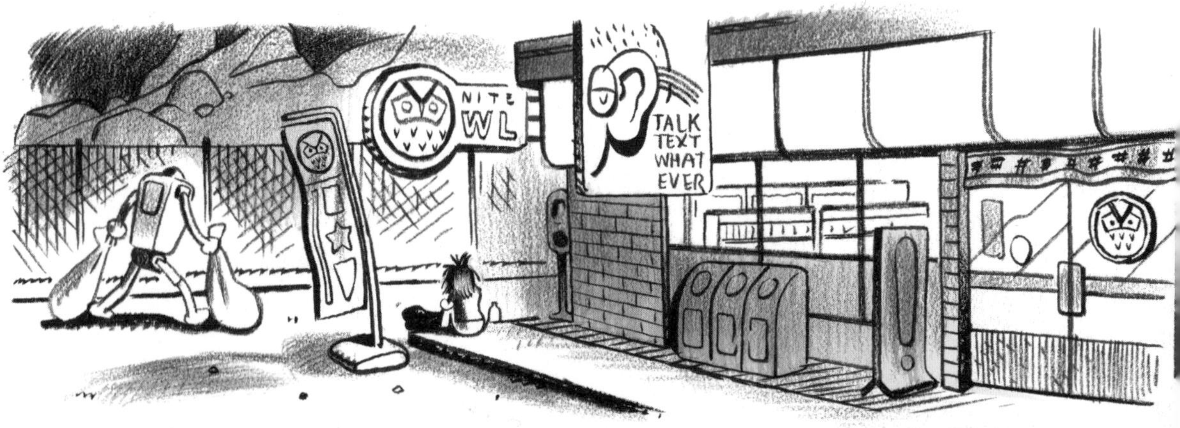
NITE OWL
TALK TEXT WHAT EVER

Family gatherings were intense—rooms overflowing with relatives whose names Paolo could never quite remember, loudly recalling anecdotes from a time he hadn't been alive to see, in a country that no longer existed. Paolo grew into a silent, difficult teenager, patiently waiting for the chance to strike out on his own.

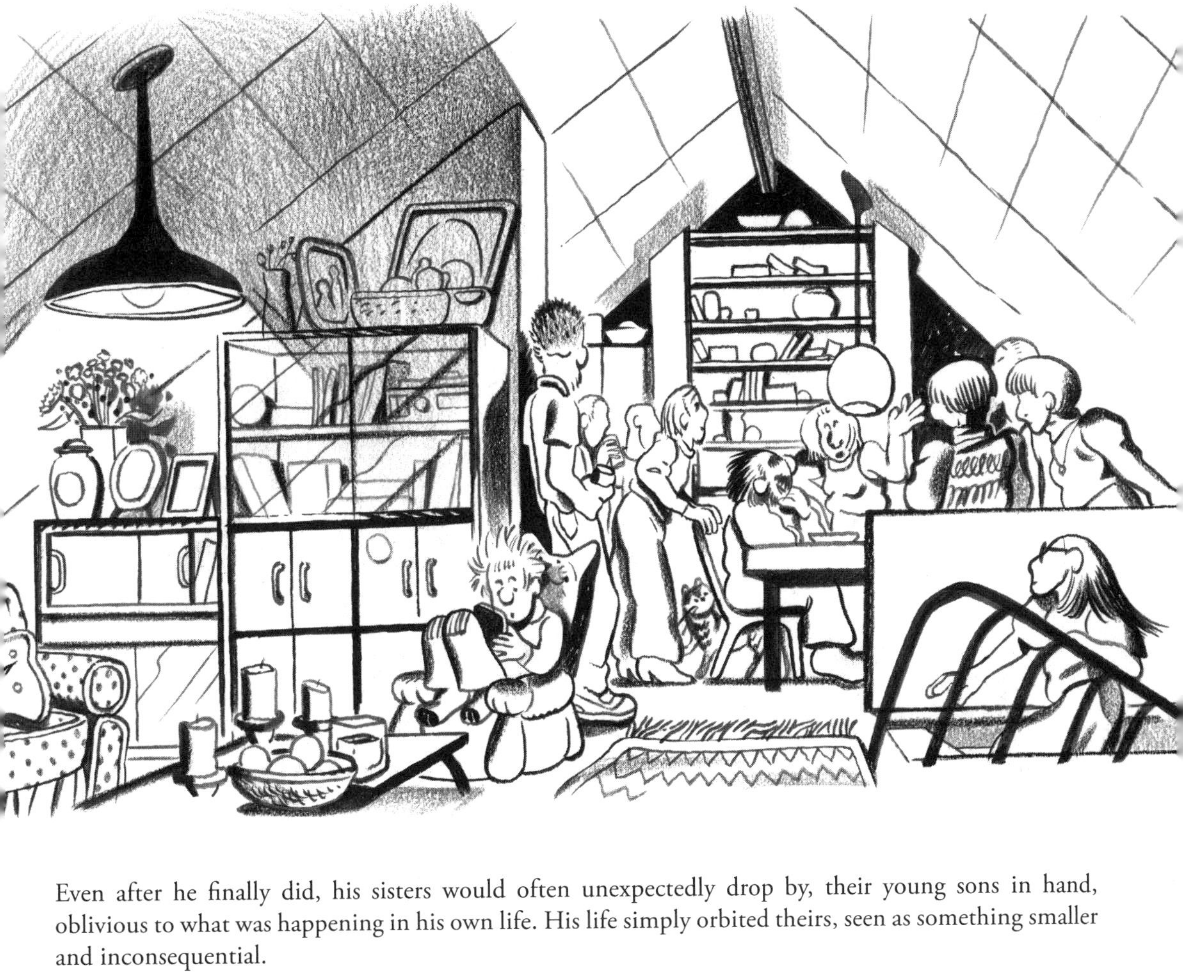

Even after he finally did, his sisters would often unexpectedly drop by, their young sons in hand, oblivious to what was happening in his own life. His life simply orbited theirs, seen as something smaller and inconsequential.

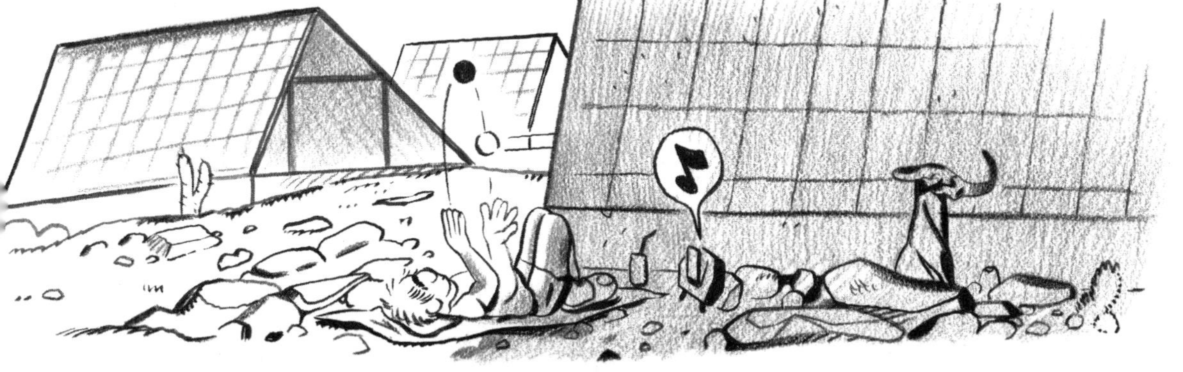

The language and cultural barrier Paolo felt living with two much older parents caused him to shrink in his ambition. He flitted between jobs, easily distracted from obtainable goals by loftier, more abstract ones. Because he knew he could never measure up to the expectations of his parents, he felt free to do whatever he wanted—but didn't know what that would be. He made his own way often by accident. Without anyone cheering for him from the sidelines, he lost motivation easily.

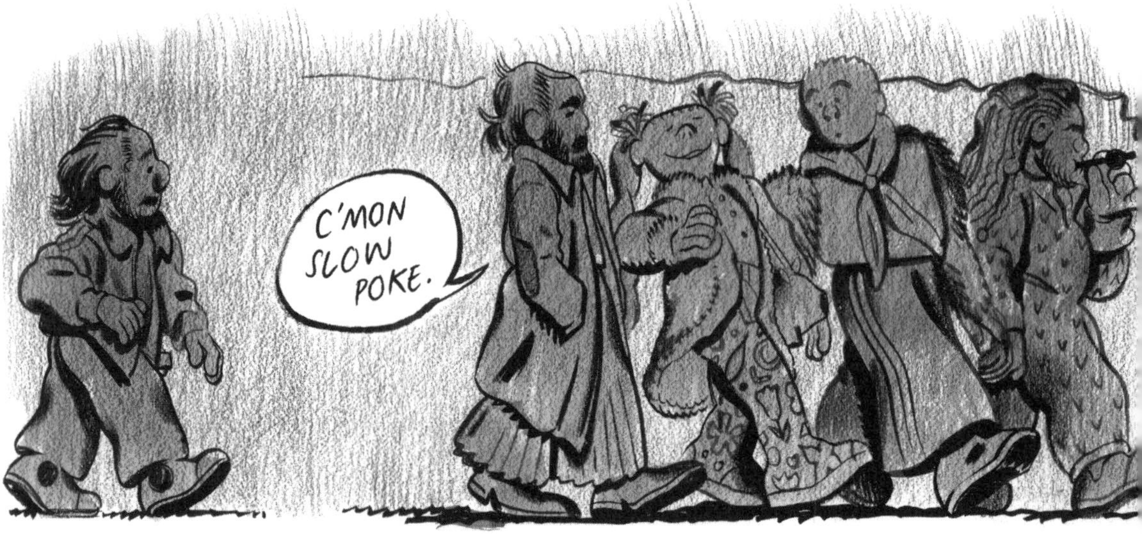
C'MON SLOW POKE.

He couldn't remember how he made any of his friends in the city. When those friends invited him to a party thrown by someone one of them had once worked with on a dinner cruise, he agreed to attend without much thought. He wore a leather jacket even though it was still a little too warm to wear comfortably in early December. He liked the jacket, picked out of a box of free clothes left behind in the lobby of someone he had once hooked up with.

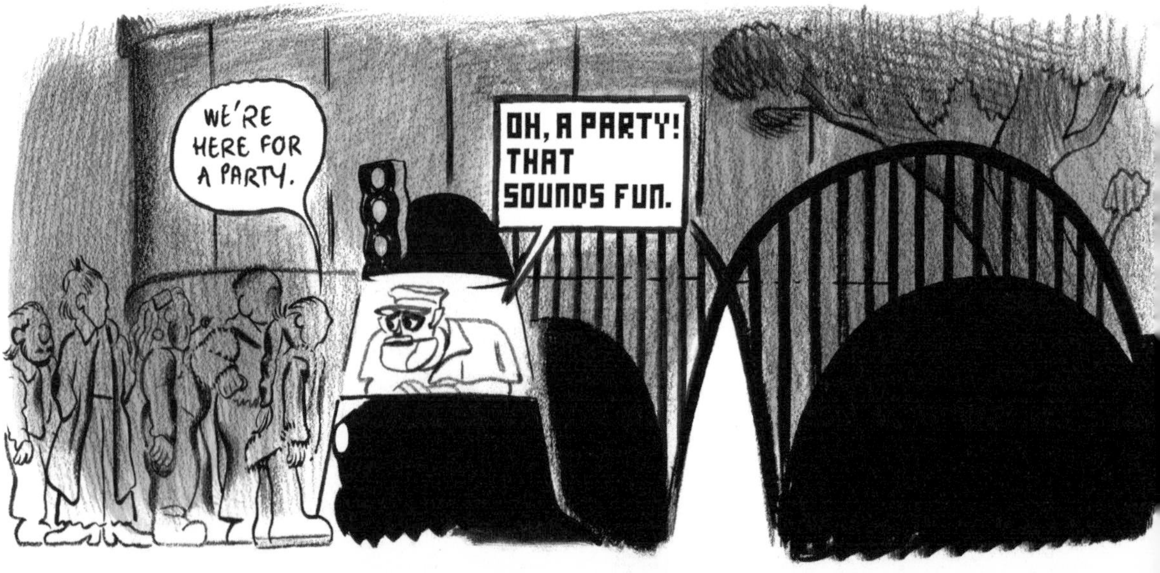
WE'RE HERE FOR A PARTY.
OH, A PARTY! THAT SOUNDS FUN.

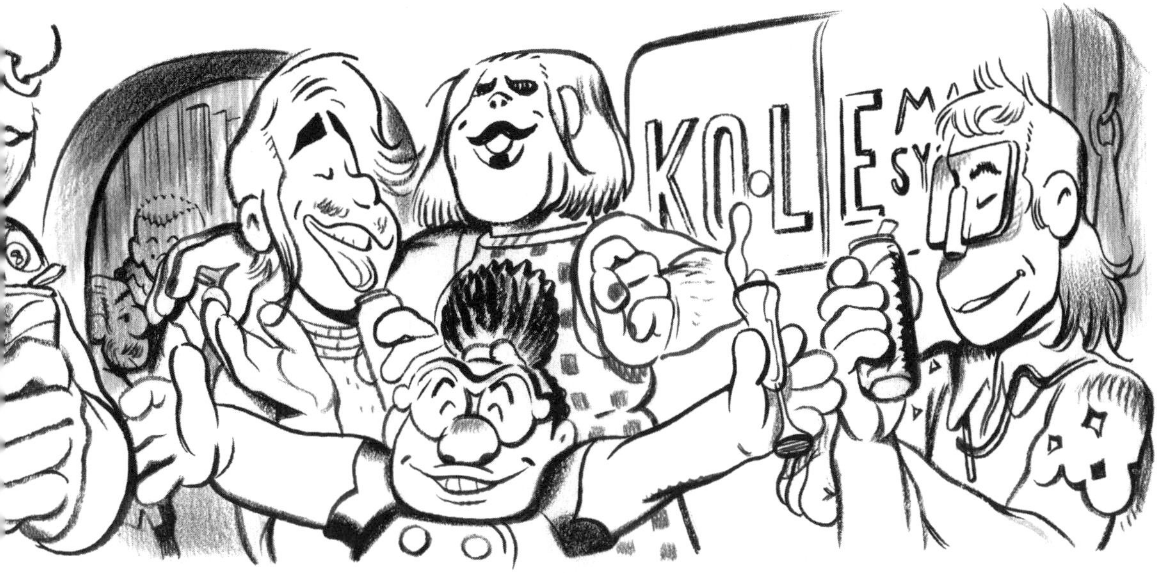

Paolo was disappointed in himself for not saying anything to Colin while they were both at the party. They even waited in the same line for the bathroom. Having felt invisible most of his life, Paolo thought of himself as impervious to embarrassment. Shyness was simply not him. And yet, despite his easygoing nature, something in Colin made him feel like he needed reassurance before stepping outside the safety of himself.

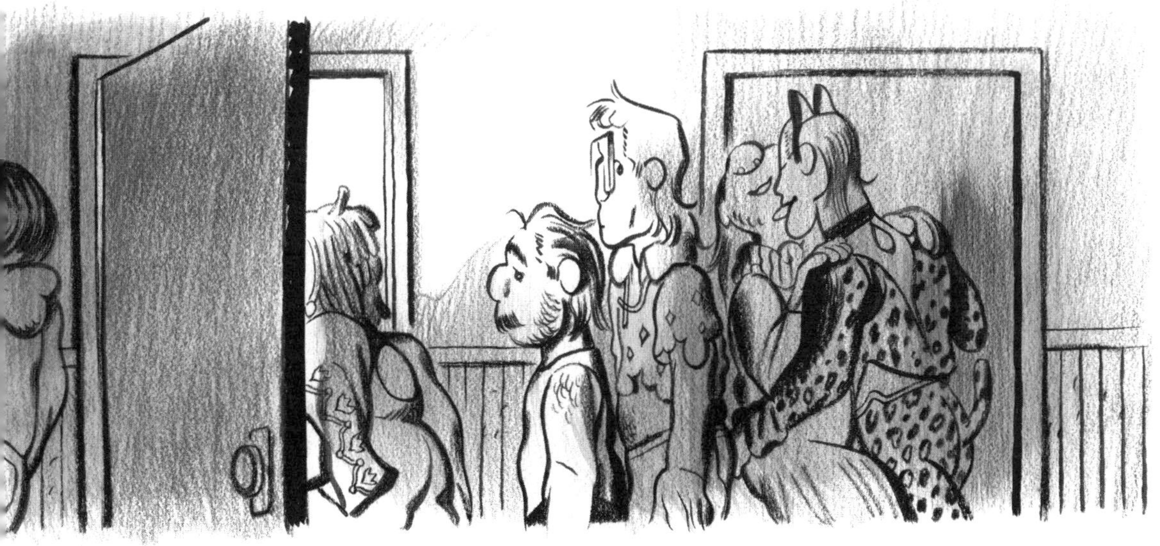

Colin didn't think of himself as inaccessible, but he knew he could be reserved. Not like the moon, in its cold distance, but the sun, the bright spot that keeps everyone tethered to it at a distance. Long after their relationship had come and gone, Paolo would always recall how this boyfriend had made him a little nervous at first. After years of feeling neglected, Colin seemed to Paolo like an impossible grand prize. A tall, handsome, trophy of a man who shone too brightly and couldn't possibly have been for Paolo to keep.

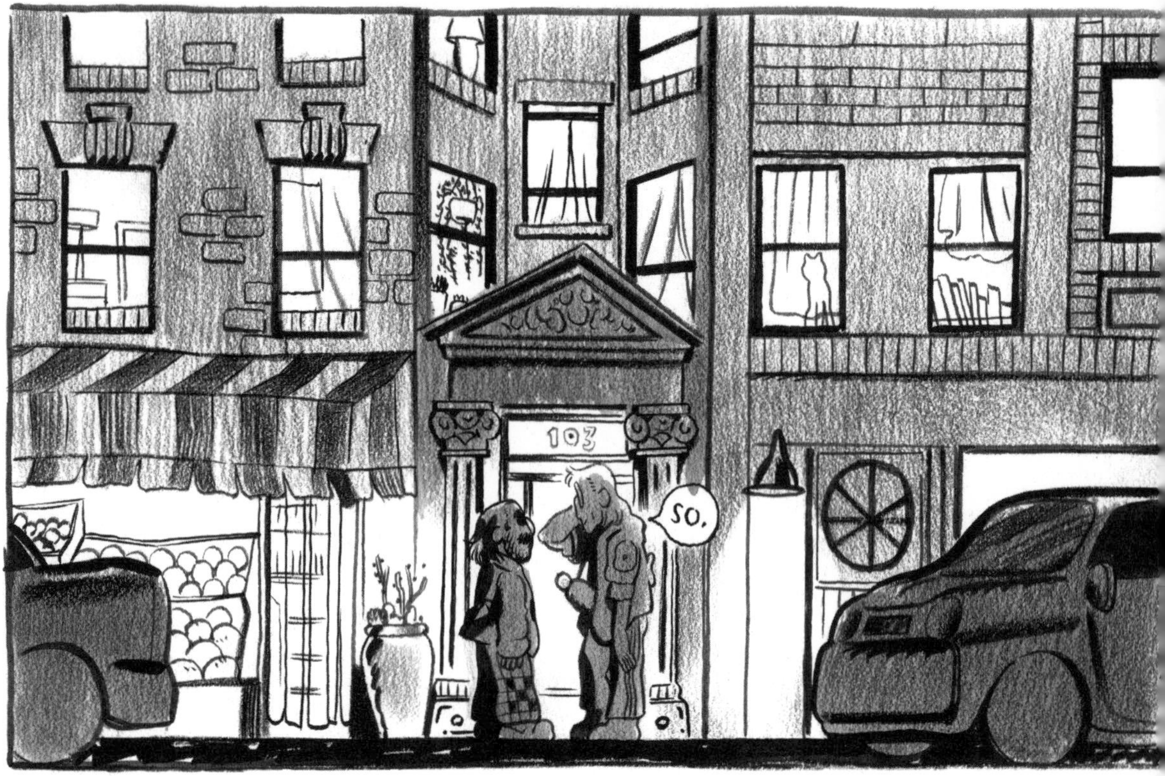
103
SO,

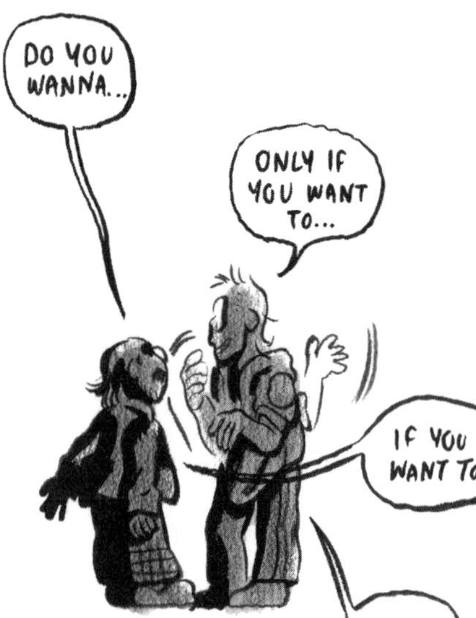
DO YOU WANNA...
ONLY IF YOU WANT TO...
IF YOU WANT TO!
THEN YEAH!

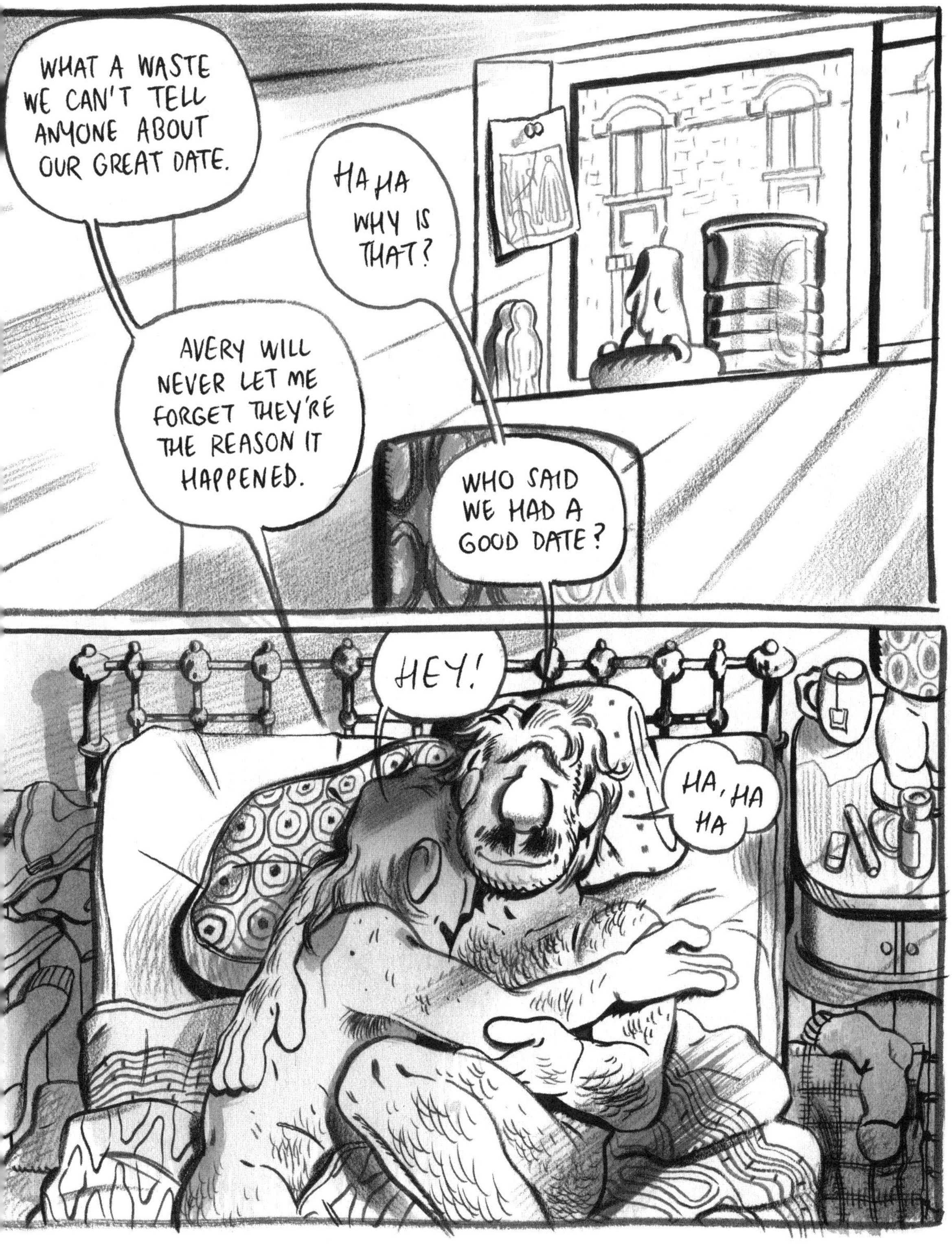
WHAT A WASTE WE CAN'T TELL ANYONE ABOUT OUR GREAT DATE.
HA HA WHY IS THAT?
AVERY WILL NEVER LET ME FORGET THEY'RE THE REASON IT HAPPENED.
WHO SAID WE HAD A GOOD DATE?
HEY!
HA, HA HA

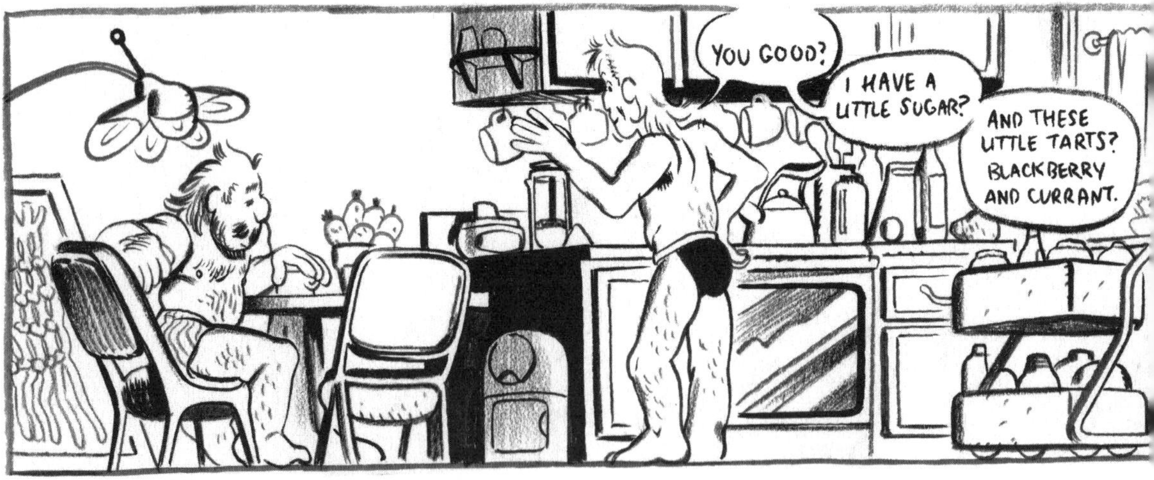
YOU GOOD?
I HAVE A LITTLE SUGAR?
AND THESE LITTLE TARTS? BLACKBERRY AND CURRANT.

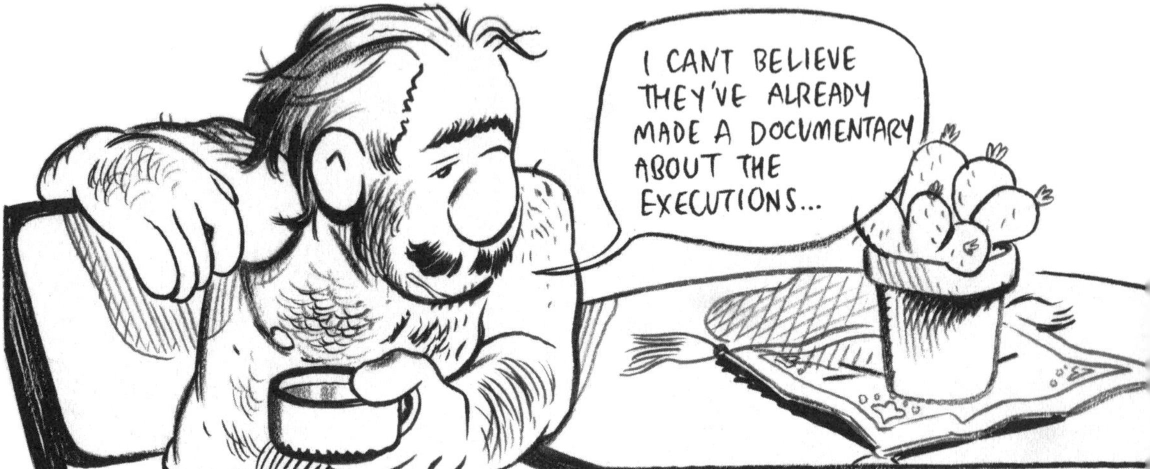
I CAN'T BELIEVE THEY'VE ALREADY MADE A DOCUMENTARY ABOUT THE EXECUTIONS...

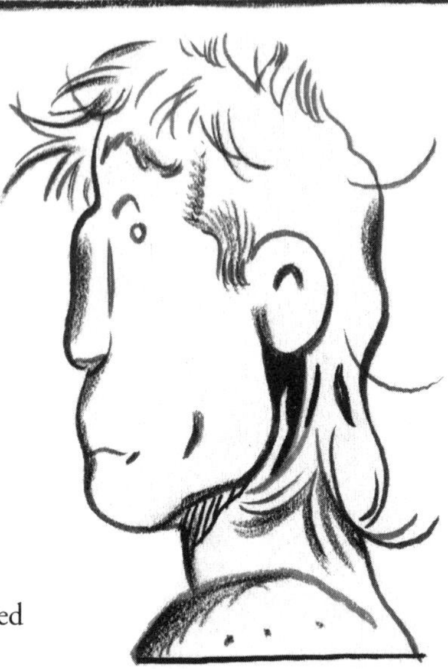

Colin realized Paolo wanted to talk about the documentary they had tried watching the night before. The one Paolo had wept through.

The documentary *A View From All Sides* follows the history of A.R.G_Os—also known as Aeronautic Relay Gyroscopes—and the various ways in which they've been implemented in the past sixty years.

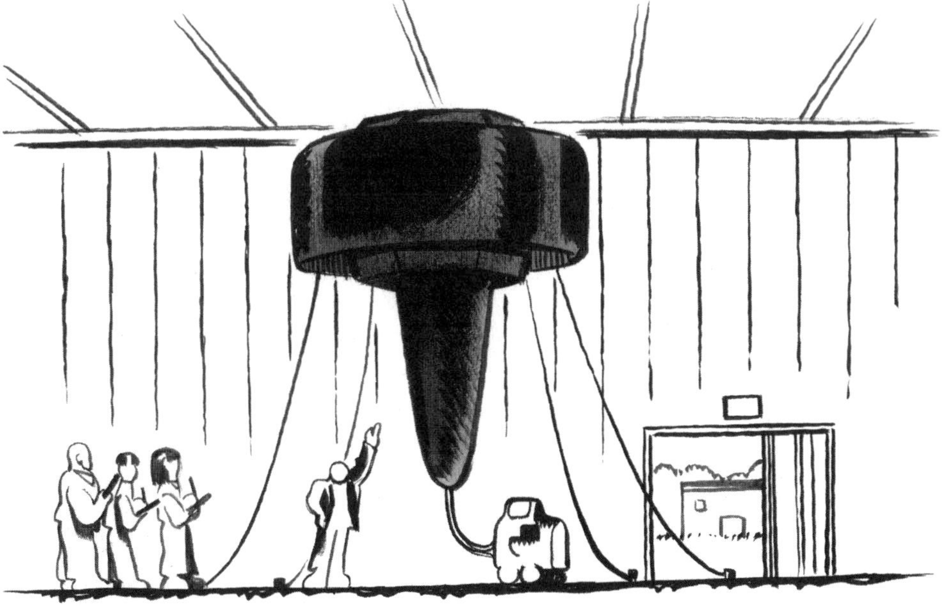

Designed by a man named Orville Obersteiner, the A.R.G_Os were first used to relay information to the farthest reaches of rapidly expanding city centers. Outdated infrastructure made most telecommunications an expensive and rare commodity, leaving large urban and suburban communities isolated. Local broadcasting stations without the budget to upkeep their own equipment could rent an A.R.G_O instead. Some were rented by neighborhoods to watch sporting events together which helped defray the cost. Occasionally they were used by local councils to remind their constituents of important information, such as when to vote in upcoming elections or where to get vaccinated.

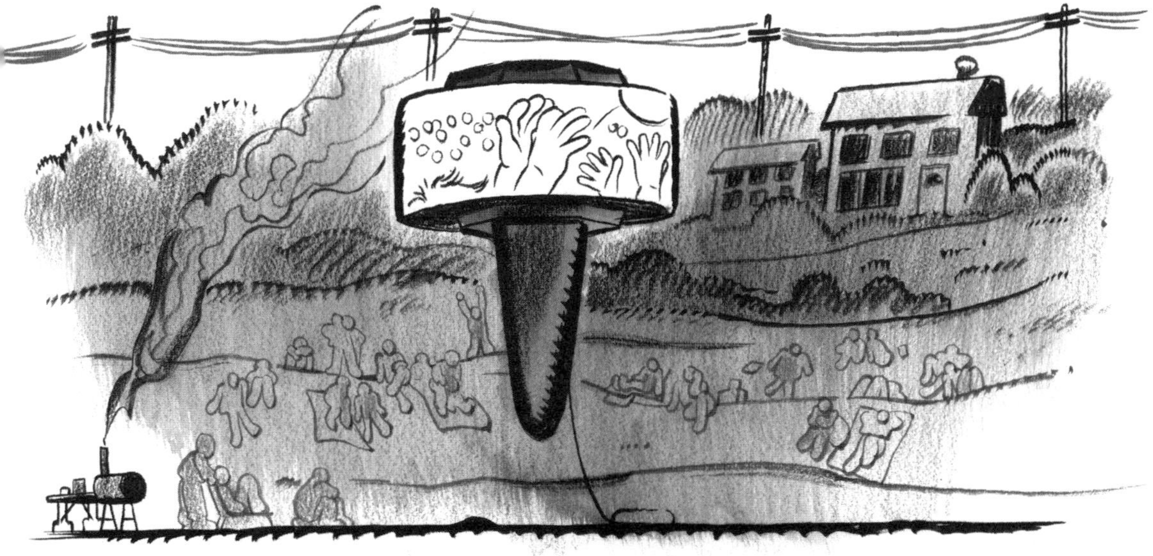

When the Administration rose to power, A.R.G_Os were quickly co-opted for their own purposes. Yet despite their connotations with a dark time in the nation's history, the A.R.G_Os are a key example of the importance of community and the lengths to which people will go to be heard.

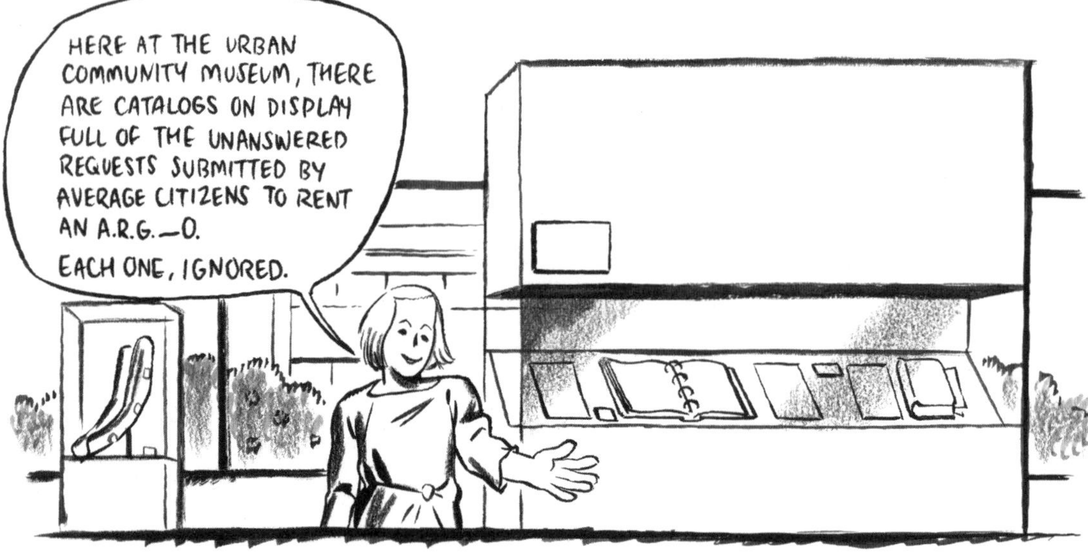
HERE AT THE URBAN COMMUNITY MUSEUM, THERE ARE CATALOGS ON DISPLAY FULL OF THE UNANSWERED REQUESTS SUBMITTED BY AVERAGE CITIZENS TO RENT AN A.R.G._O.
EACH ONE, IGNORED.

When the A.R.G_Os did return to circulation, the government privatized the entire fleet, making them unaffordable to the average citizen. At the time, no one knew what the Administration planned to do with them. For months, the A.R.G_Os drifted aimlessly, their dark screens looming ominously.

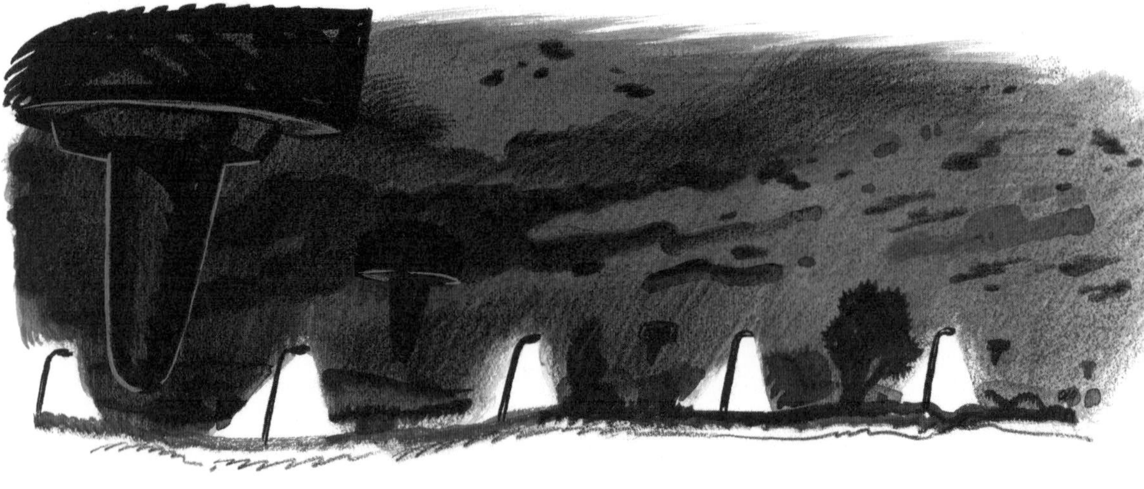

Soon the Administration began to use the A.R.G_Os to televise executions in an effort to intimidate. Initially, the executions on display were recordings from long before the Administration came into power, in an attempt to show they were more civilized than their predecessors. Inevitably new executions began, projected for everyone to see as a warning. Often these executions were of persons the Administration deemed dangerous or uncooperative with their new vision of the world. Very little documentation of these individuals exists beyond the televised executions themselves.

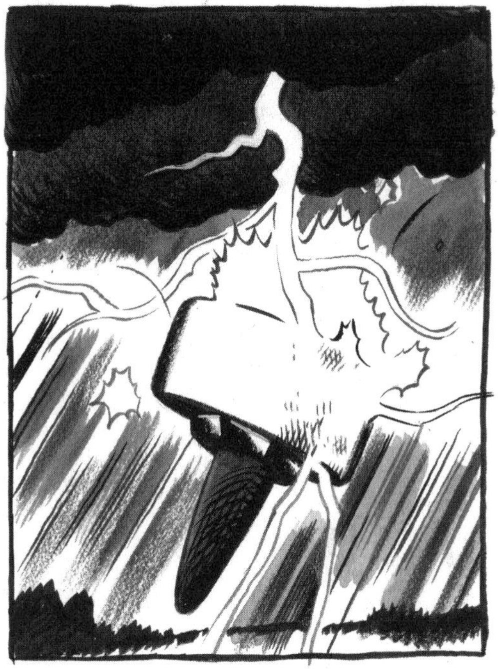

It didn't take long for the A.R.G_Os to become a symbol of the evil wrought by the Administration. As a form of quiet resistance, a photo began circulating of an A.R.G_O struck by lightning during an unexpected thunderstorm. Although the A.R.G_O didn't crash, this image became synonymous with anyone hoping to overthrow their oppressors. It graced album covers, advertisements, clothing brands, anything that would show support for radical change.

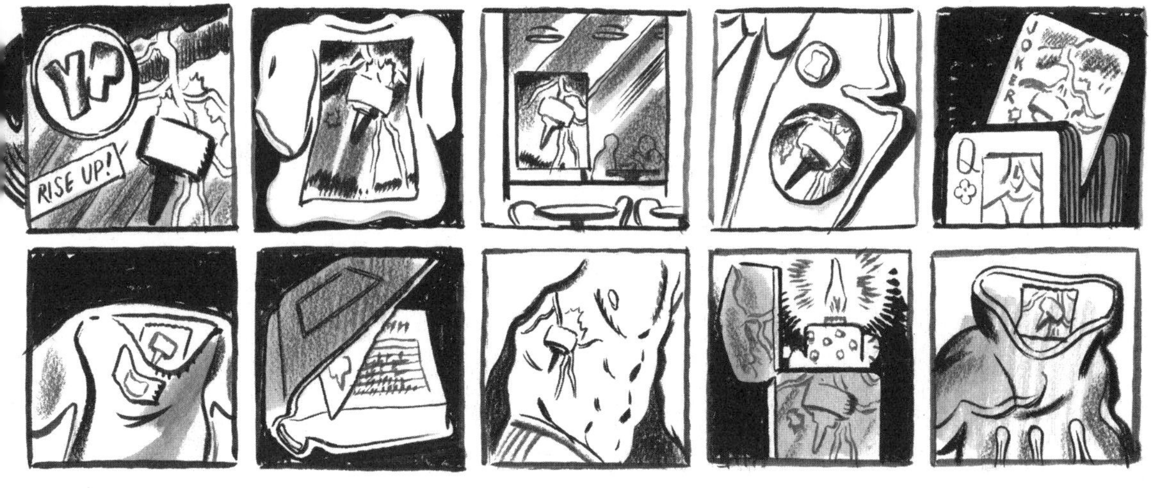
RISE UP!
JOKER

The Administration moved quickly to crack down on use of the image, and it wasn't long before those seen openly flaunting their support began to disappear. Even after that, there were still numerous examples of this image hidden away in the linings of jackets, printed on the inside of books. Even as a tattoo.

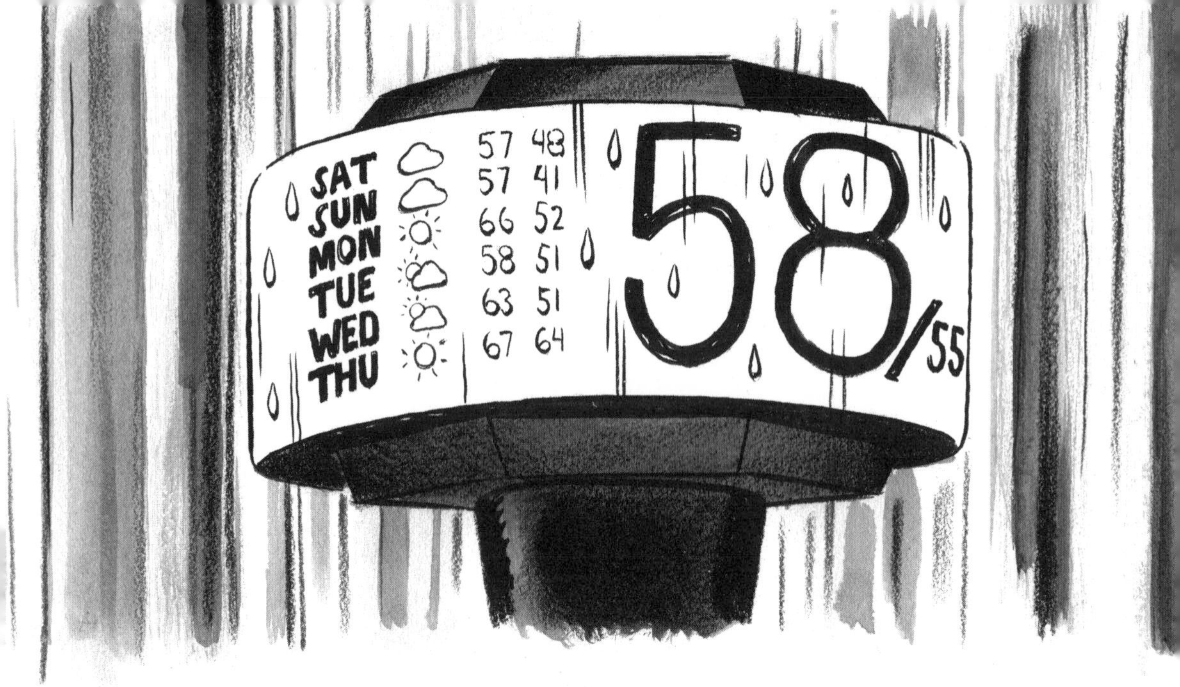
SAT
SUN
MON
TUE
WED
THU
57 48
57 41
66 52
58 51
63 51
67 64
58/55

After the fall of the Administration, the A.R.G_Os disappeared for a second time. Information was slow to circulate without well-supported news outlets, leaving many communities unaware of the shift in their government.

The government that came to replace the Administration was inundated with problems and lacked the resources to handle them properly. Despite their oppressive connotations, the A.R.G_Os were once again seen as an opportunity to reunite the shattered communities they were now trying to serve. Many older people who lived through the Administration were quick to speak out against their use, but, despite these initial protests, the A.R.G_Os were utilized to display simple information, like the seven-day weather forecast. Over time, they were expanded to include local events. Some communities allowed families to use them personally, having their local A.R.G_O display a birthday greeting for a child or a slideshow of photos taken on their recent vacation.

Unsurprisingly, their return to being used solely for public good was short-lived. Faced with the inability to broadcast news about the upcoming trials of key figures within the Administration's cabinet, the new government decided to once again use the A.R.G_Os to make examples of citizens seen as a threat to public safety.

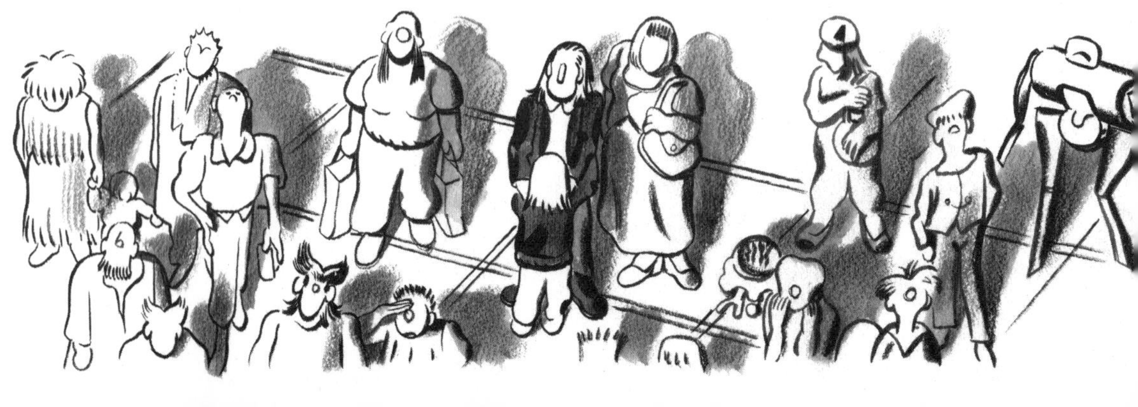

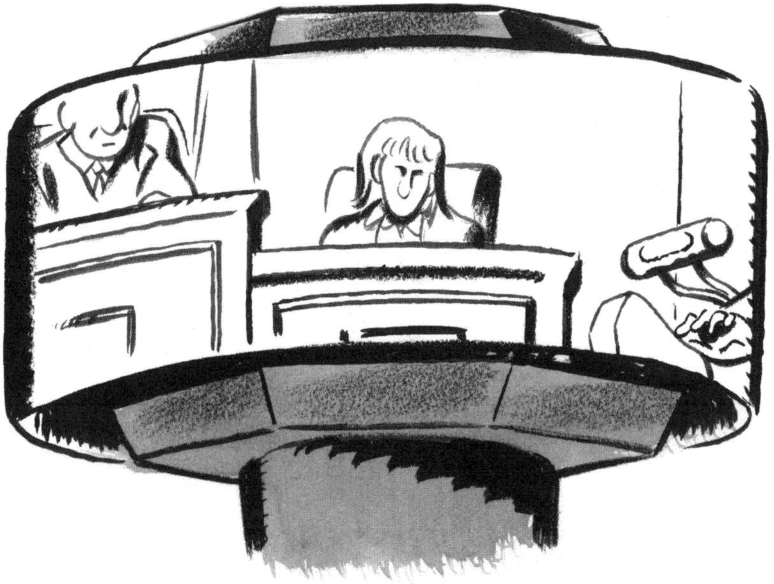

The backlash was swift and immediate but the A.R.G_Os stayed visible through each trial and subsequent sentencing. Some people were quick to recognize the poetic justice in condemning the Administration's Chief Media Strategist, Meaghan Johnson, on the very device she championed. Others lamented the A.R.G_Os as a cruel manipulative tool regardless of who was using them. The current government hoped for greater transparency than their predecessors but found themselves inevitably following in their footsteps.

When the crimes committed were deemed to warrant an execution, the A.R.G_Os once again served their purpose. Community organizers struggled to find a positive use for them that challenged this vicious history, continuing to run birth announcements and fun science facts for local children between passionate courtroom proceedings, but after nearly a year of preceding trials, their use in this way once again began to feel normal.

The executions took place over one week. Each day, a different cabinet member. Everyone could agree that what was happening was horrific, but the crimes committed by the Administration had already begun to fade, worn smooth and inconsequential by newer, more sensational horrors. This is what Colin and Paolo both remembered about that week; not the specifics of who had died but rather that people had died, hovering high up above their heads.

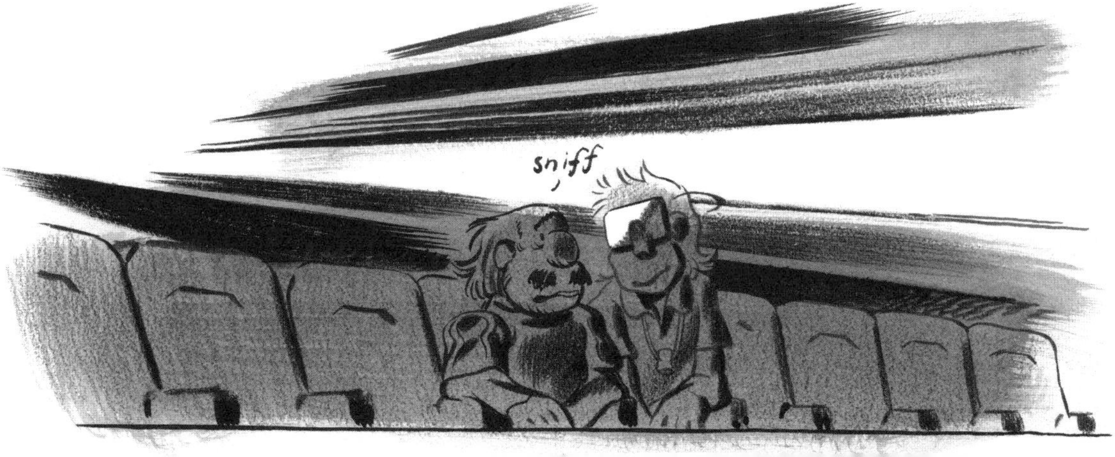
sniff

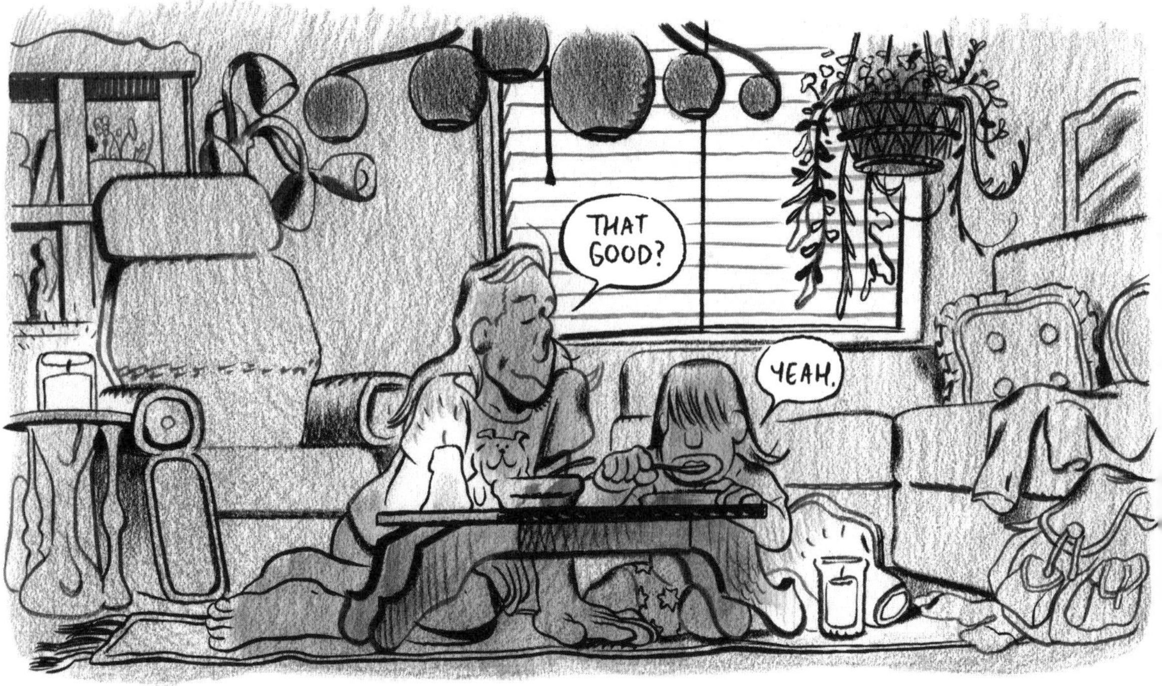
THAT GOOD?
YEAH.

Minnie kept Colin indoors that week, shut off from the final words of people she herself barely knew anything about. The Administration was of her parents' generation, and besides, Colin's well-being was more important than bearing witness to history her parents hadn't survived long enough to see. Each day at 6 p.m., when that day's convict was led into the execution chamber, Minnie would snip the energy converter in their apartment, which cut off not only electricity, but all broadcasted images from flowing into their home. She made the week into a kind of game, eating dinner together by candlelight as if they were weathering some ferocious storm.

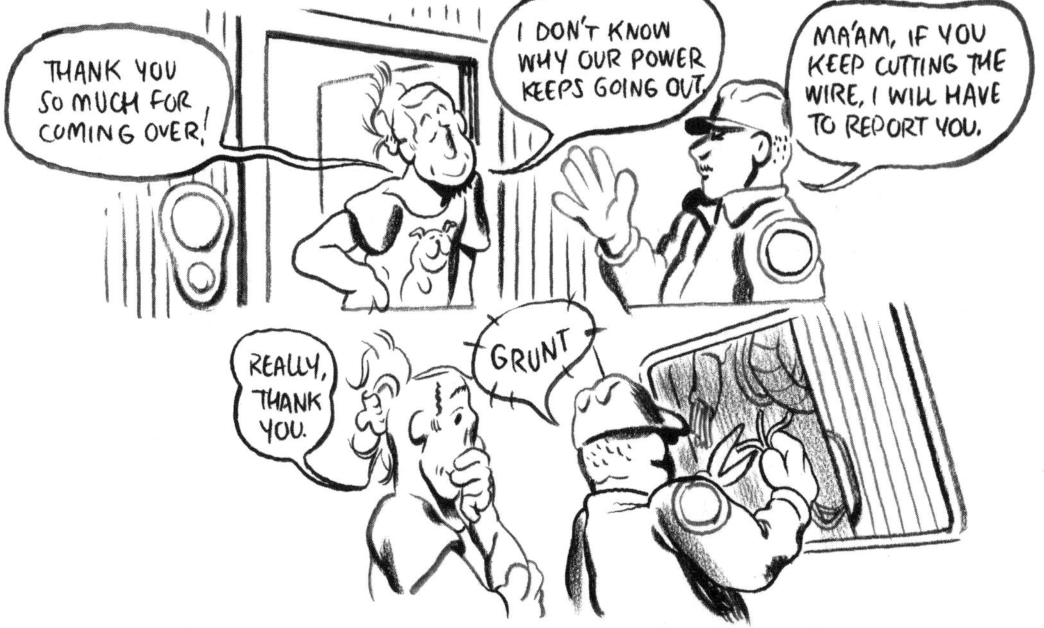
THANK YOU SO MUCH FOR COMING OVER!
I DON'T KNOW WHY OUR POWER KEEPS GOING OUT.
MA'AM, IF YOU KEEP CUTTING THE WIRE, I WILL HAVE TO REPORT YOU.
REALLY, THANK YOU.
GRUNT

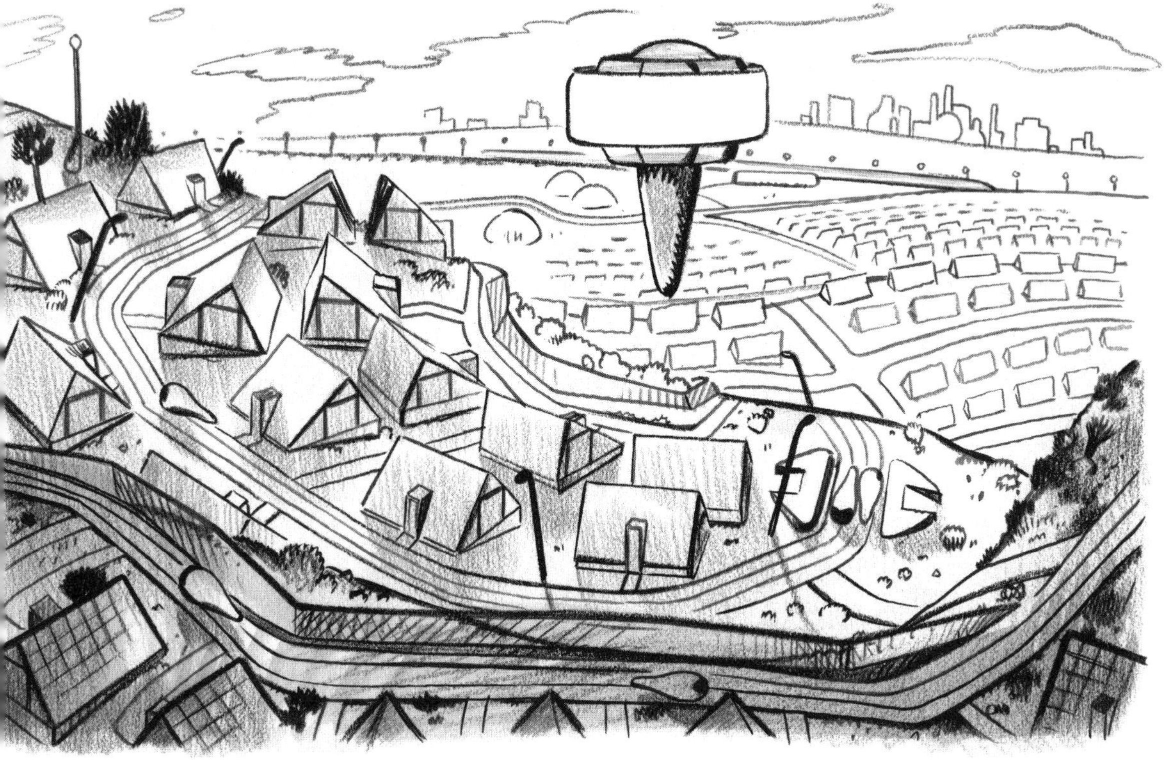

Paolo, on the other hand, remembered those days as particularly awful ones. When stressed, his mother would scream without warning—sometimes ear-piercingly loud, other times barely a yelp—and the daily executions, slowed by all-day televised commentary, meant she started well before noon.

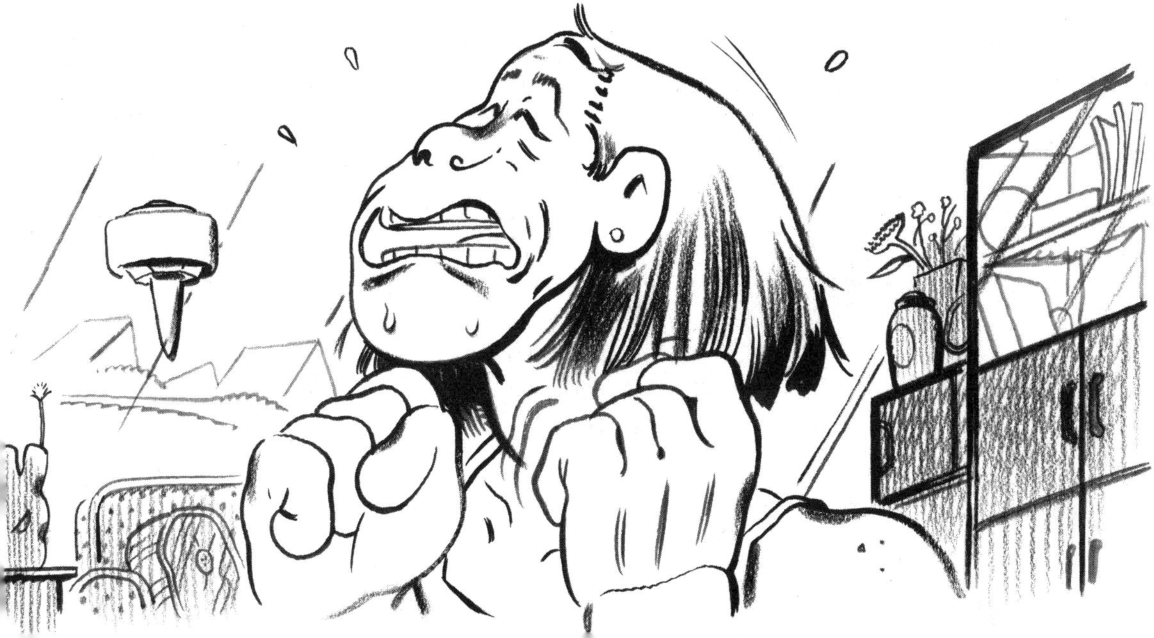

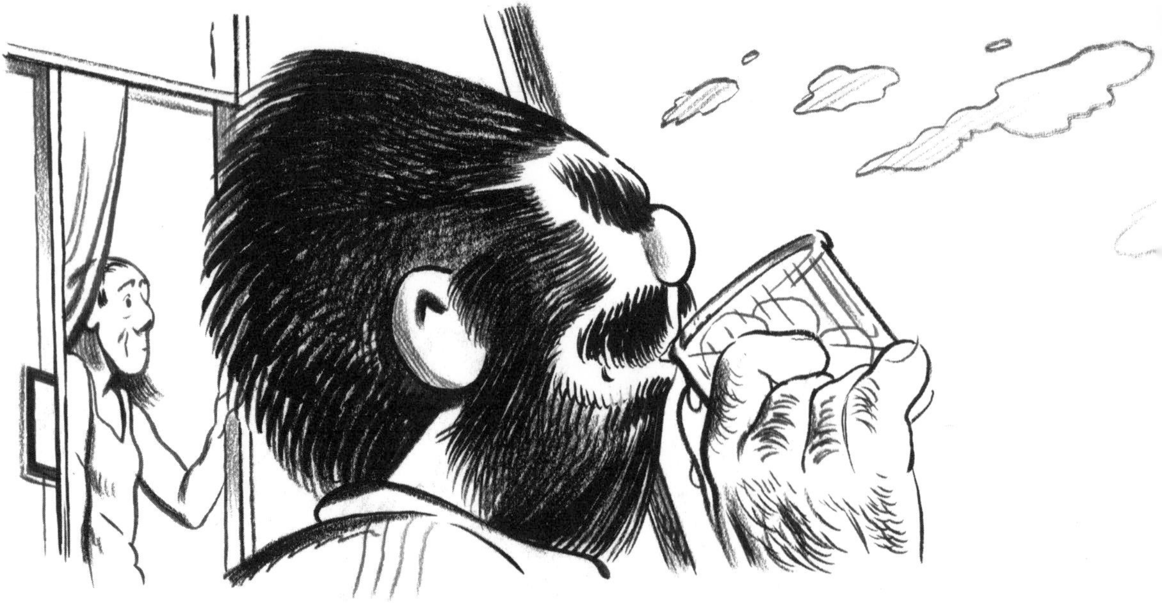

His father would drink to offset his wife's outbursts, watching each person die as his wife tearfully begged for him to come inside. Avoiding his parents, Paolo was stuck waiting in his room until each execution was over, unable to escape by just leaving as he normally would.

He would hide his telecommunicator in the closet, unable to shut off the live feed without cutting energy to the whole house. Even muffled under the dirty clothes in his closet, he could still hear each ragged, protracted breath.

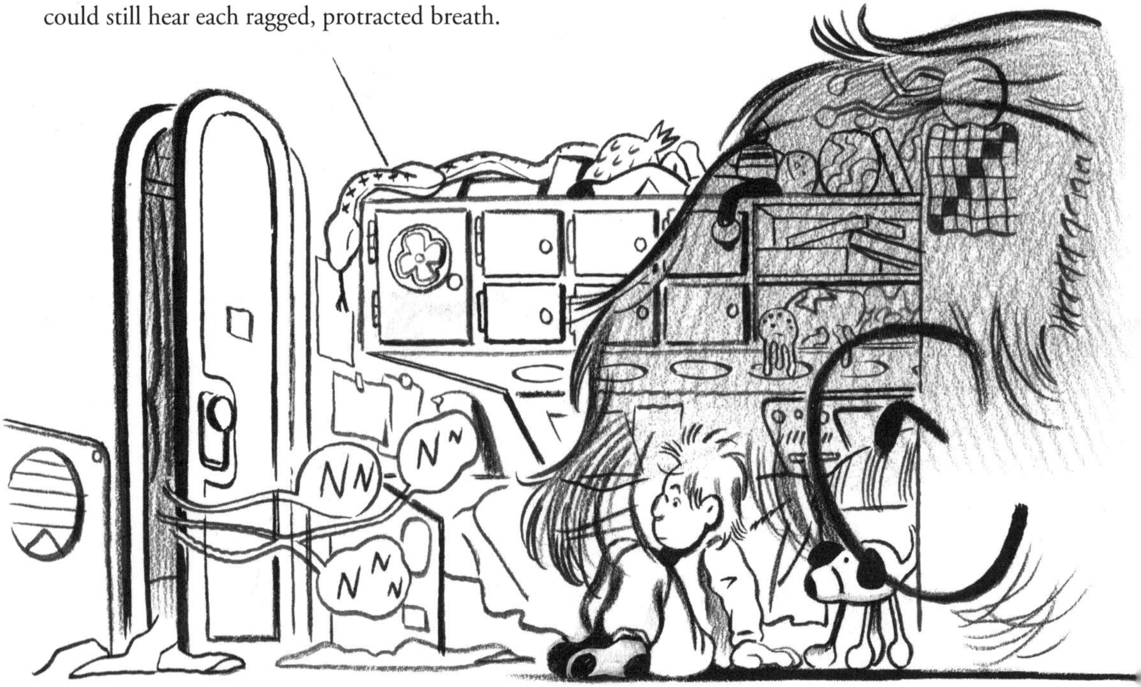
NN
NN
NNN

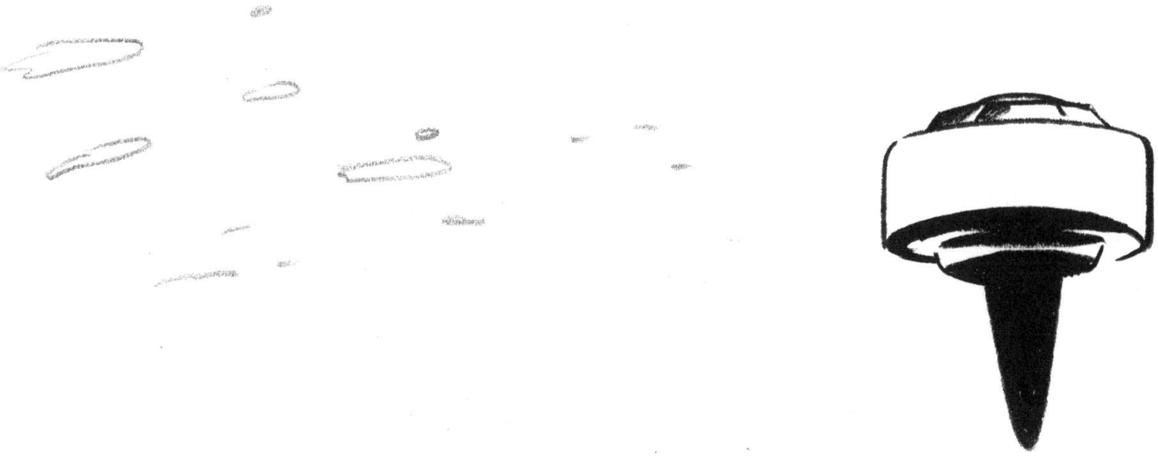

Even if he didn't know it at the time, it was in that moment of hearing Paolo describe that week of executions, of realizing Paolo had agreed to see that movie despite knowing it would be hard for him, that Colin decided he would do everything he could possibly do for Paolo.

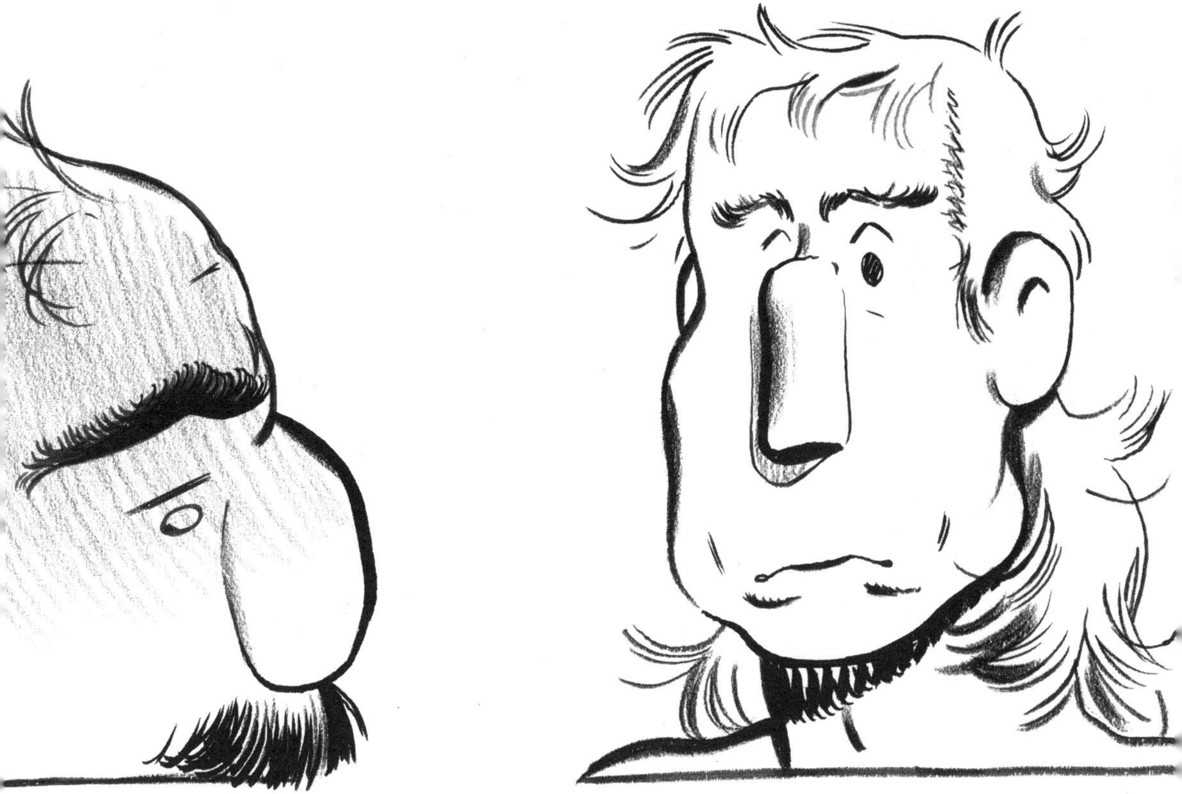

Which is what he did until he couldn't any more.

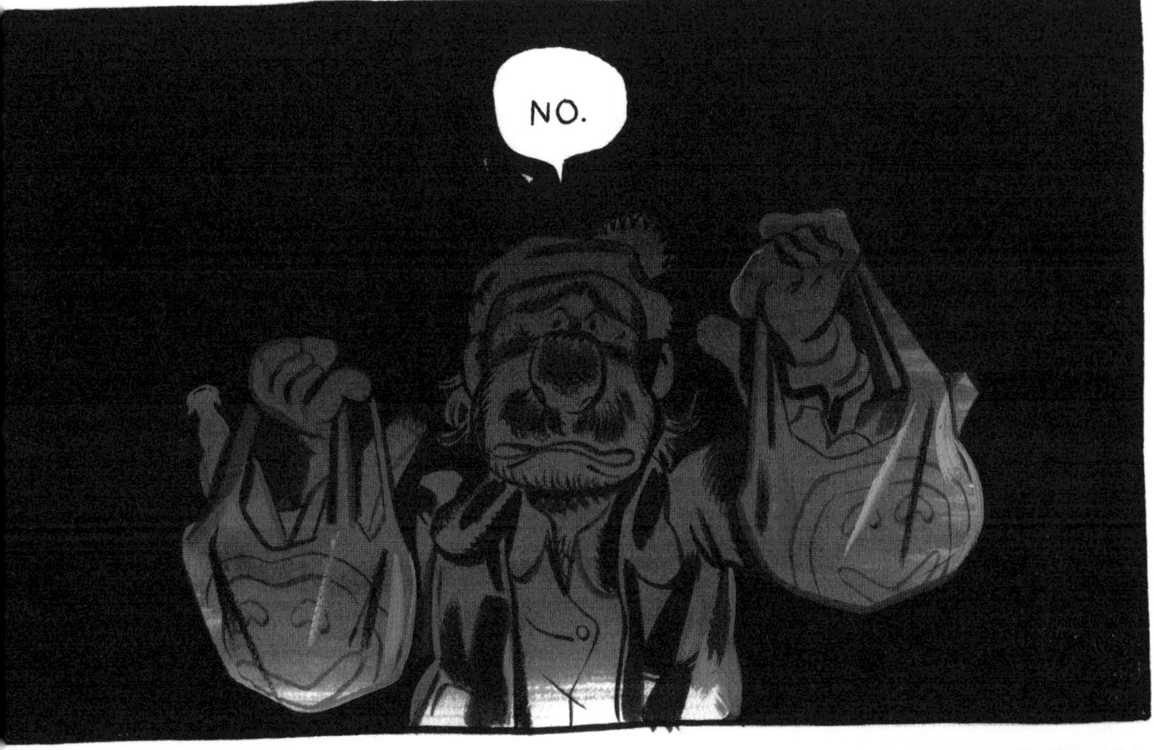
NO.

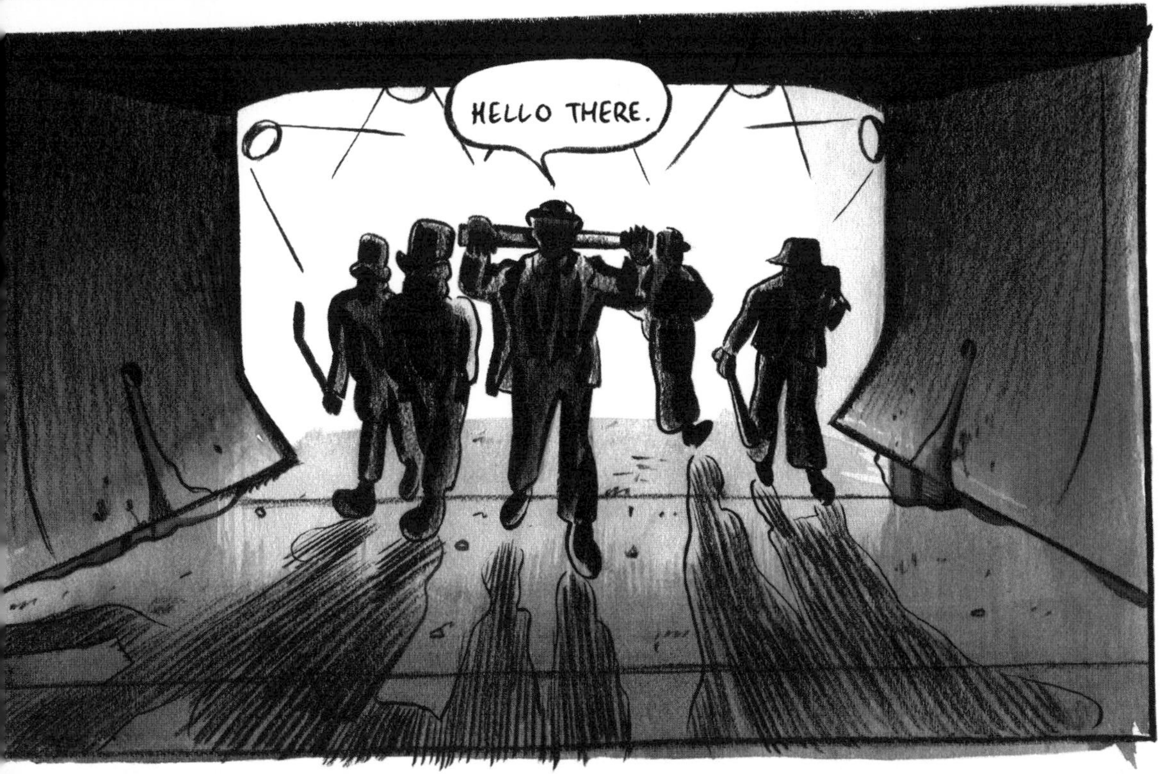
HELLO THERE.

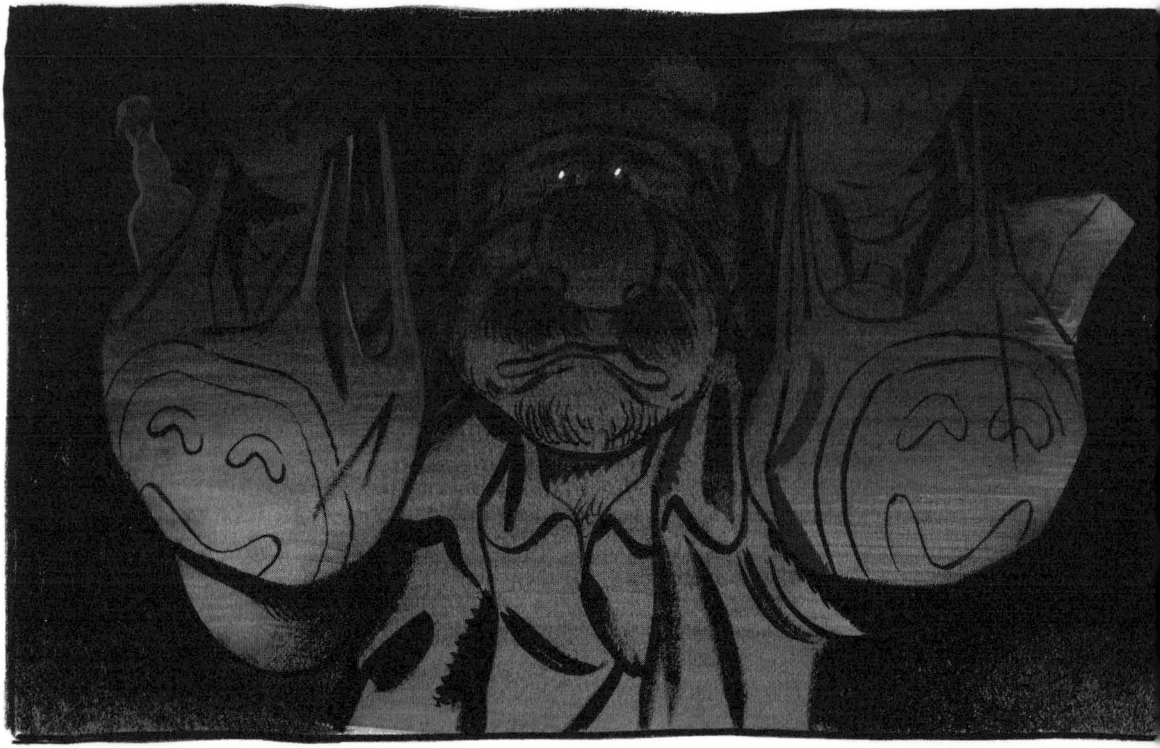

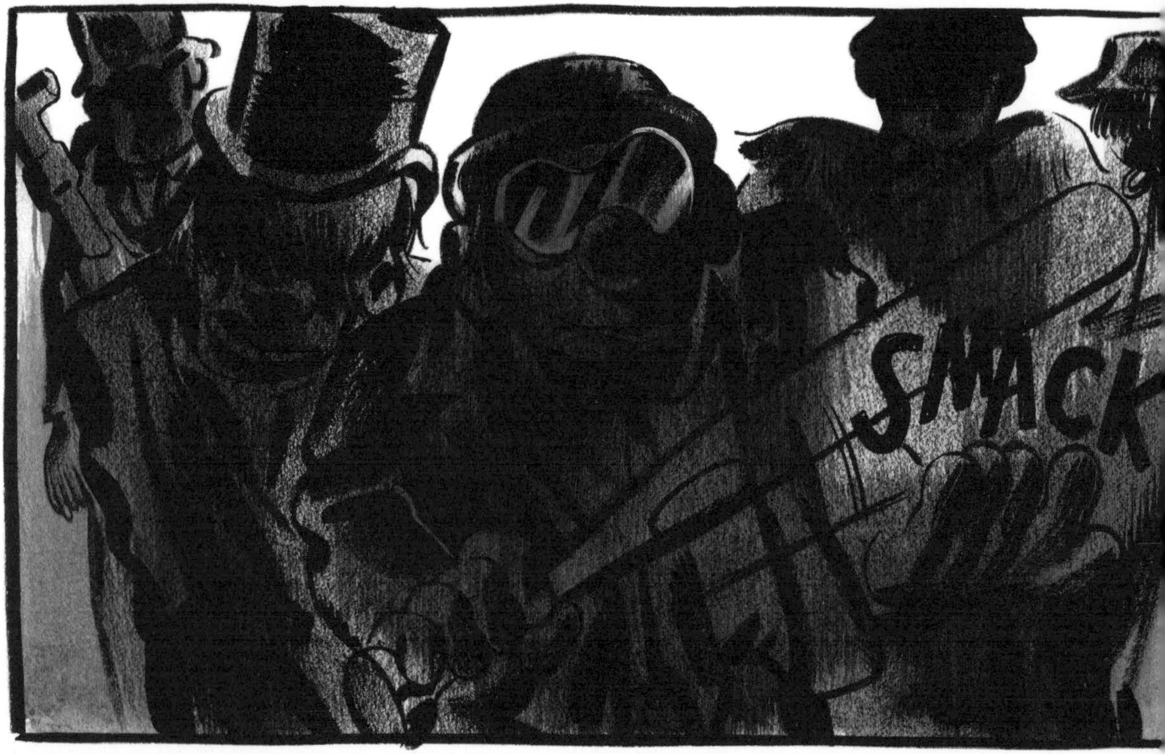
SMACK

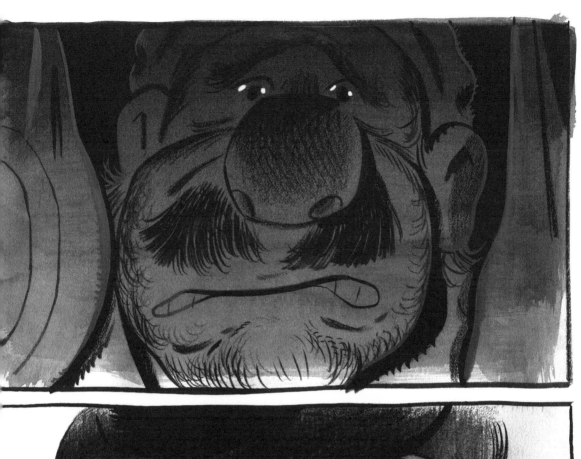

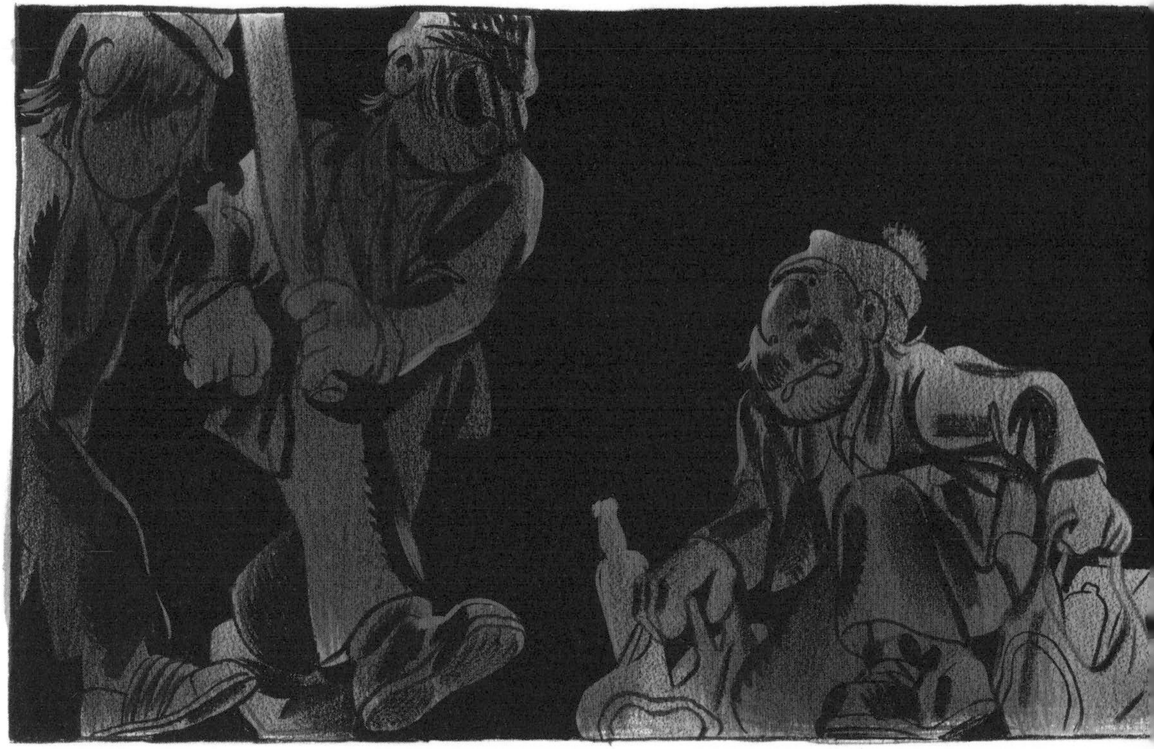
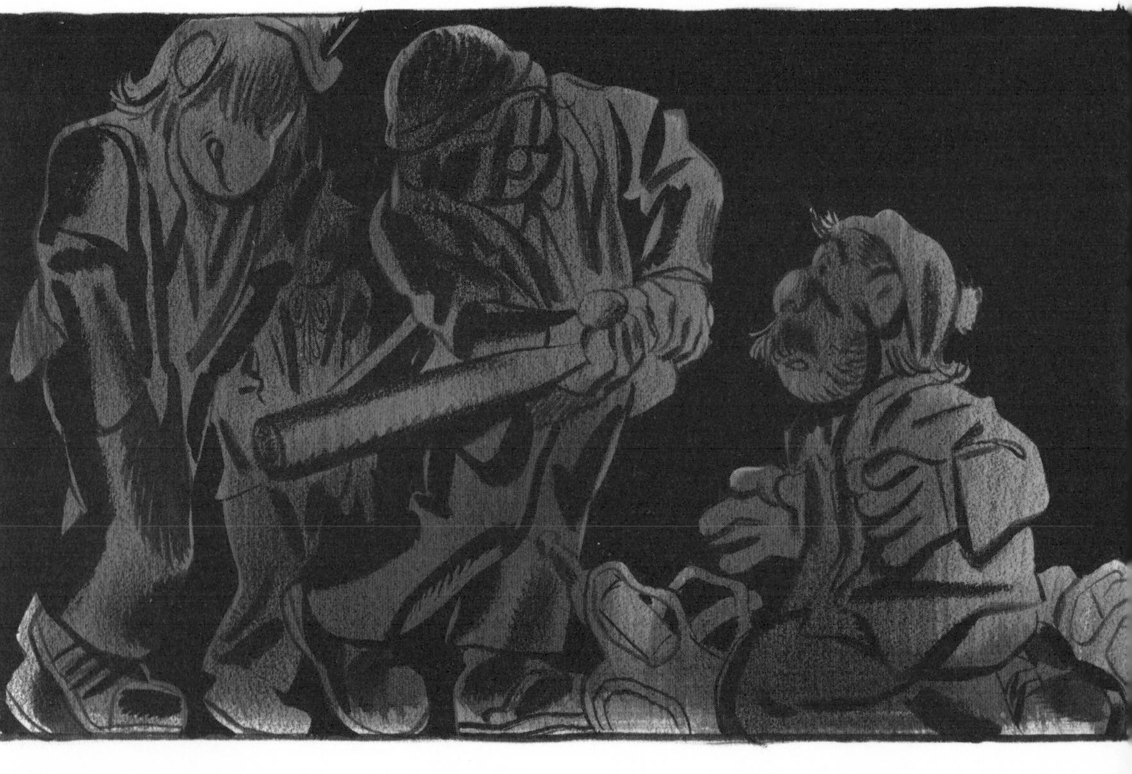

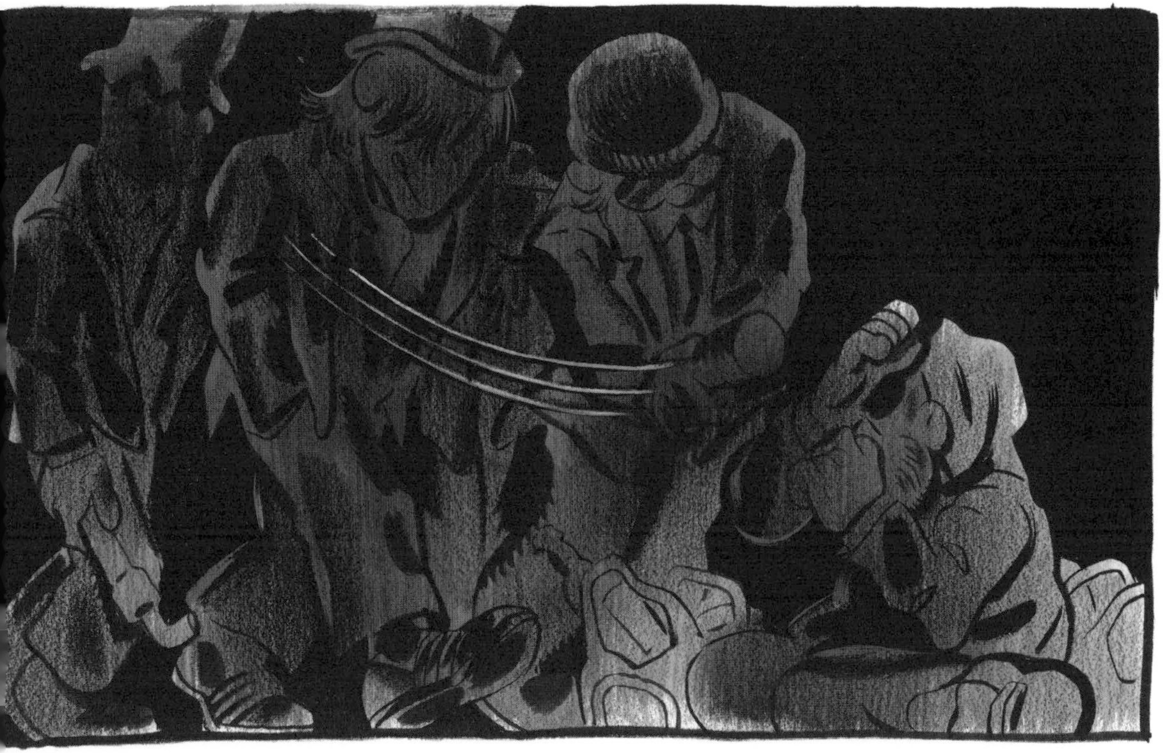

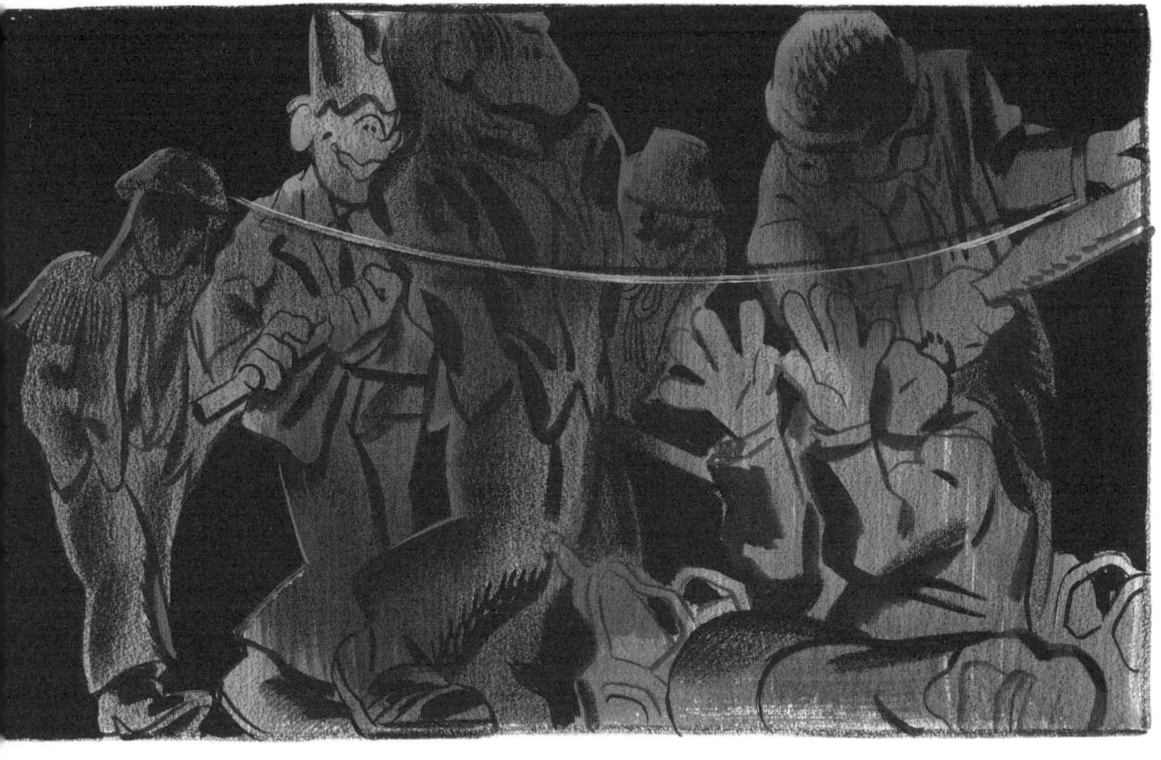

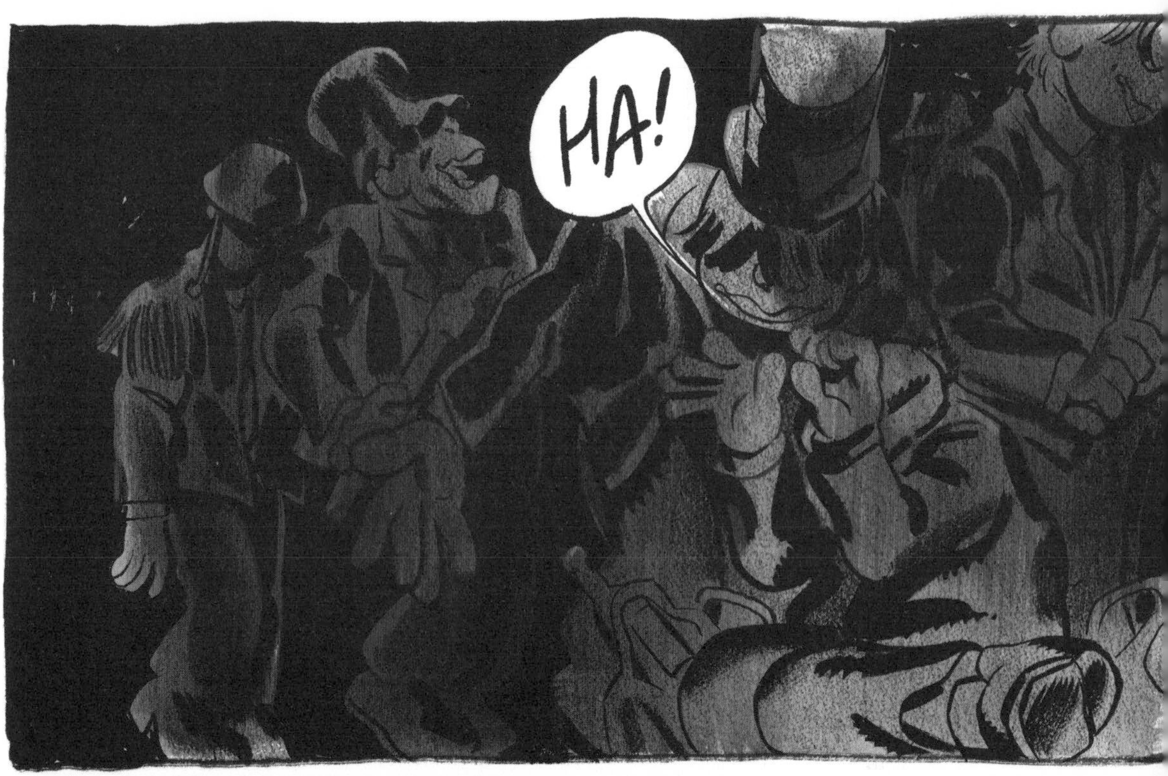
HA!

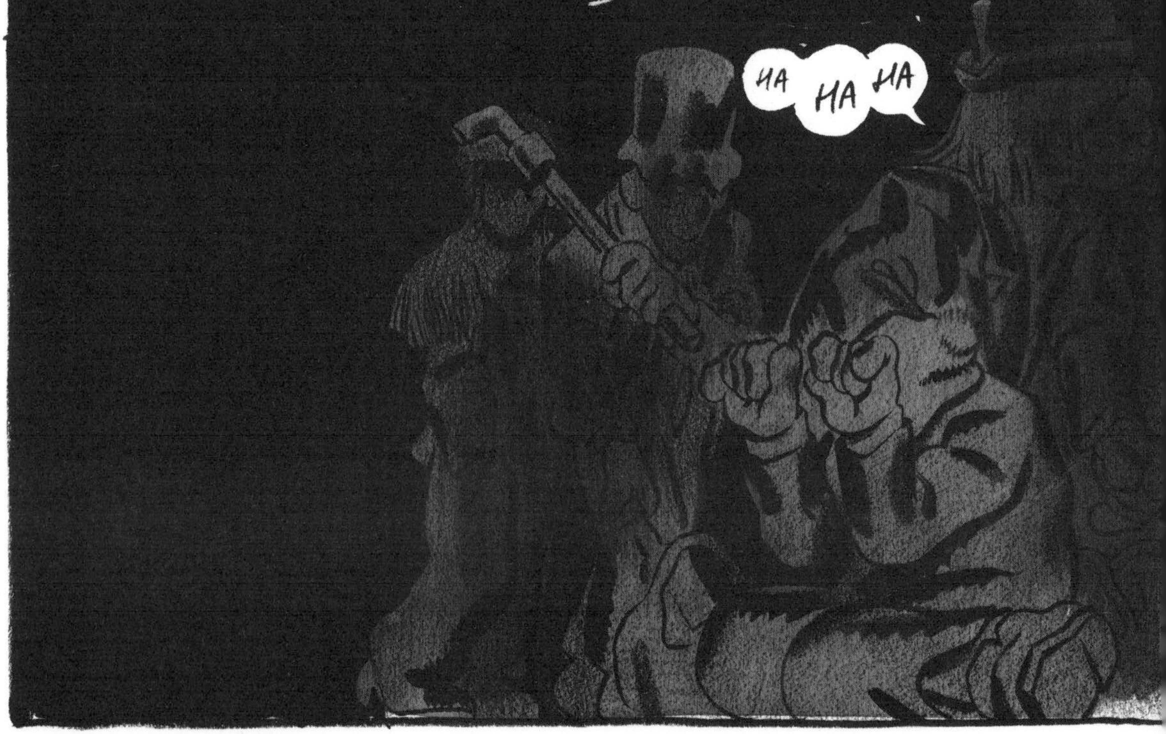
HA HA HA

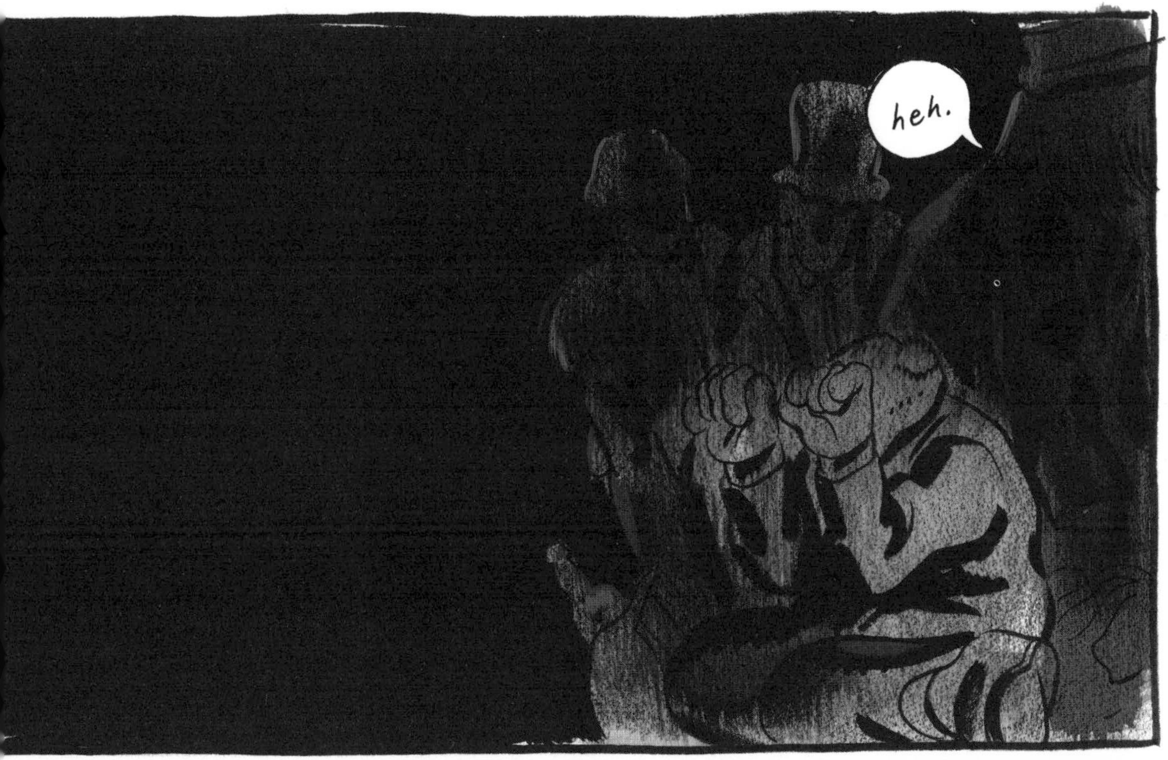
heh.
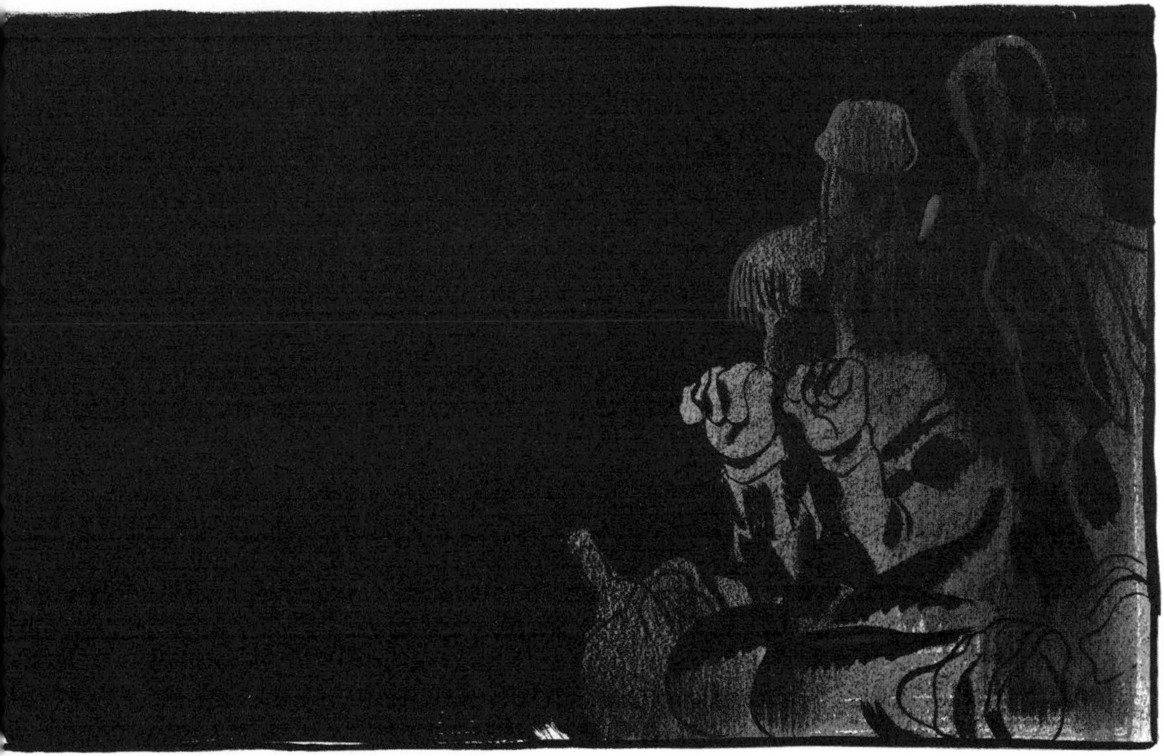

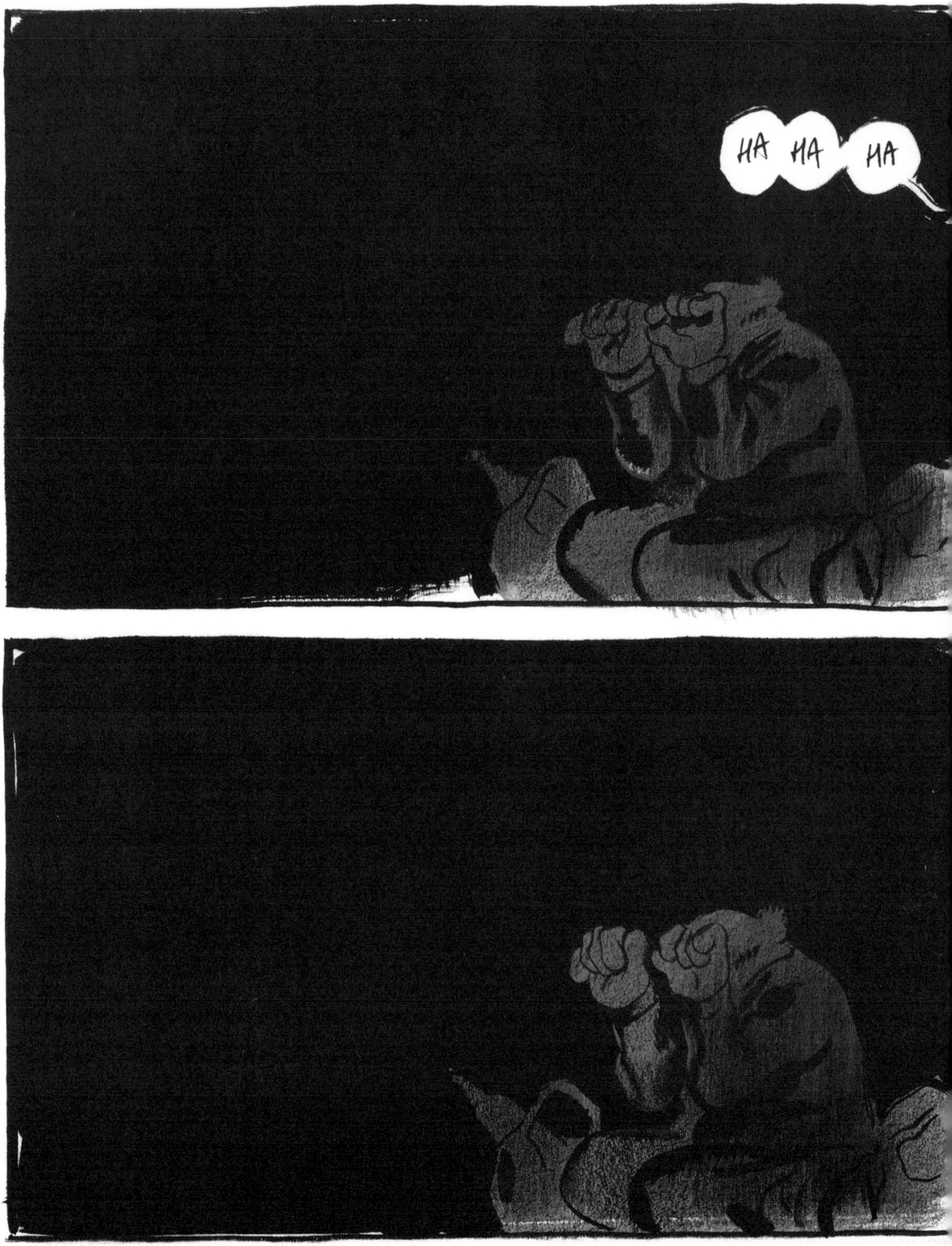
HA HA HA

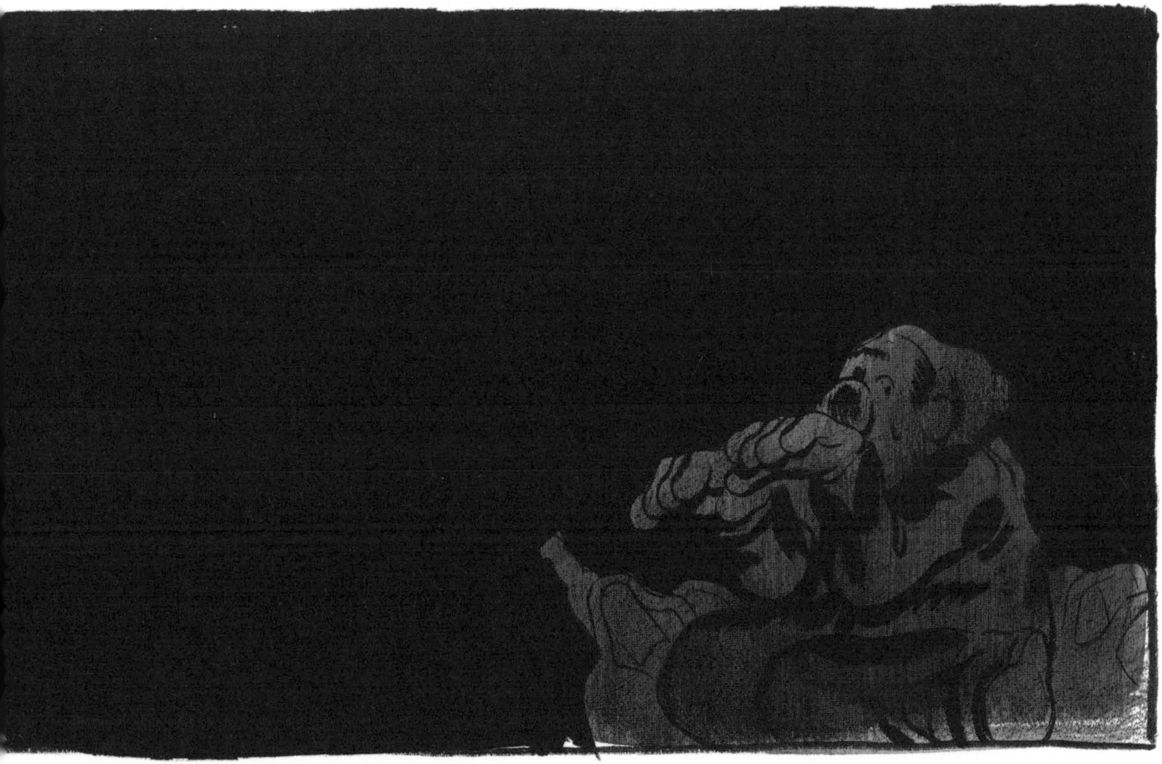

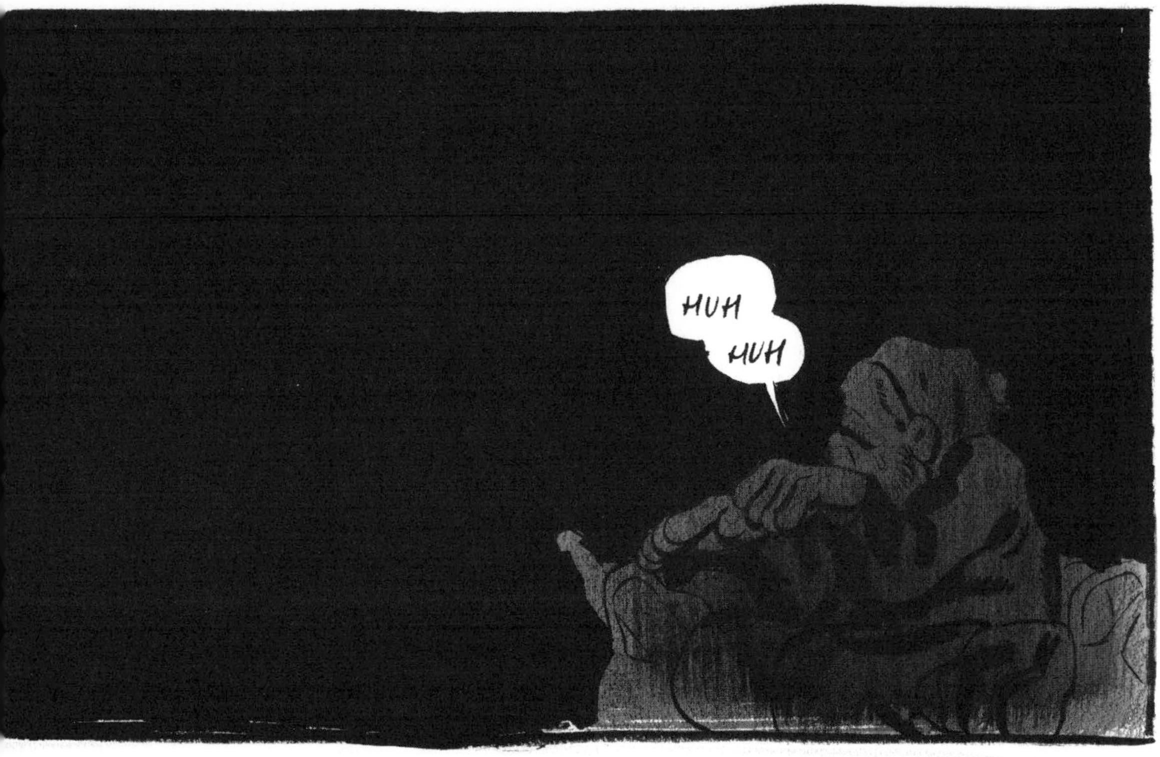
HUH
HUH

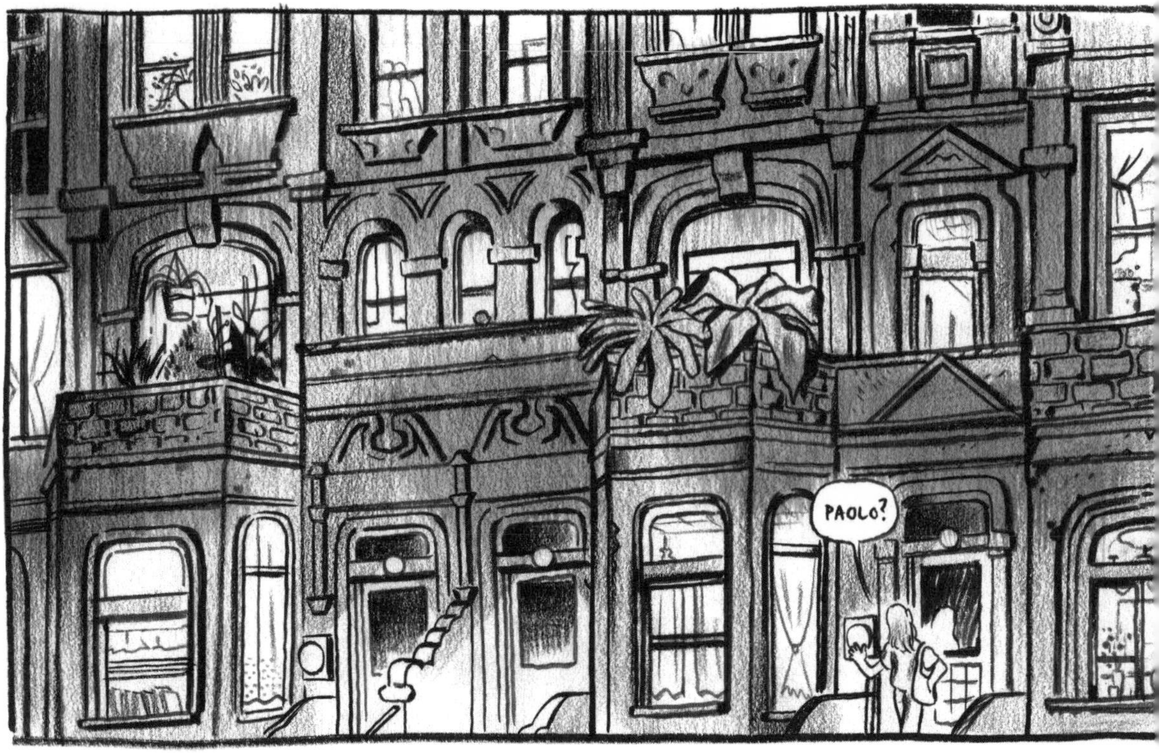
PAOLO?

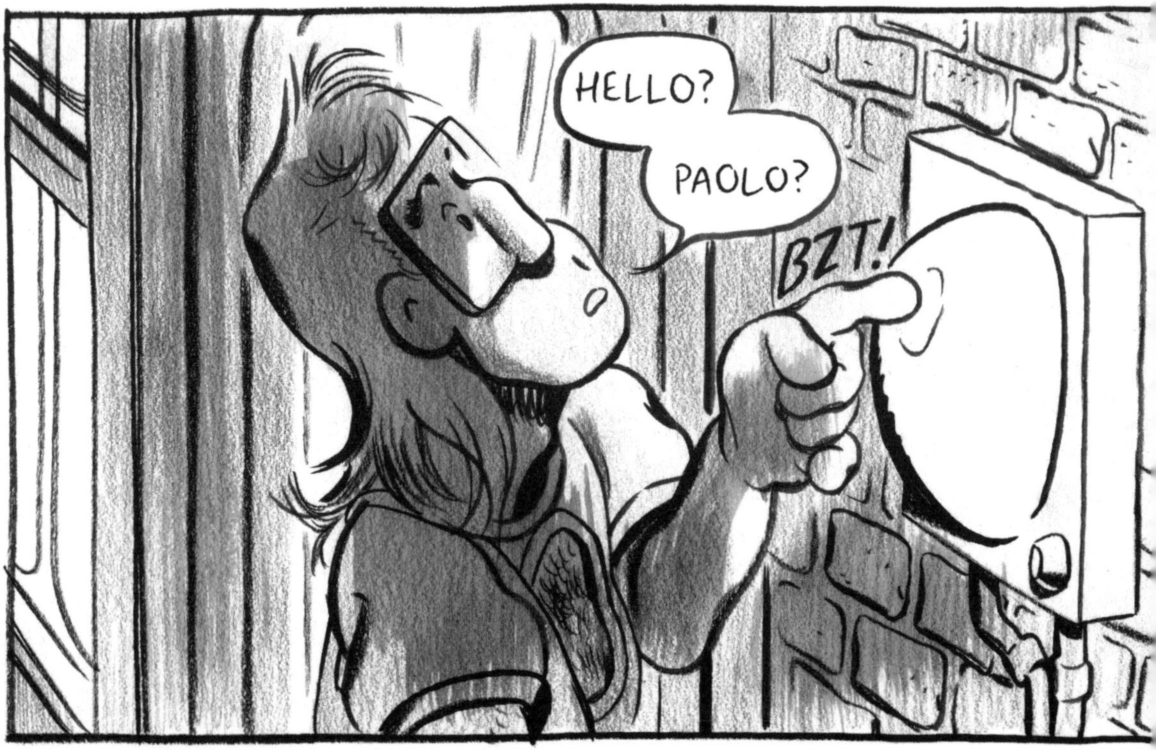
HELLO?
PAOLO?
BZT!

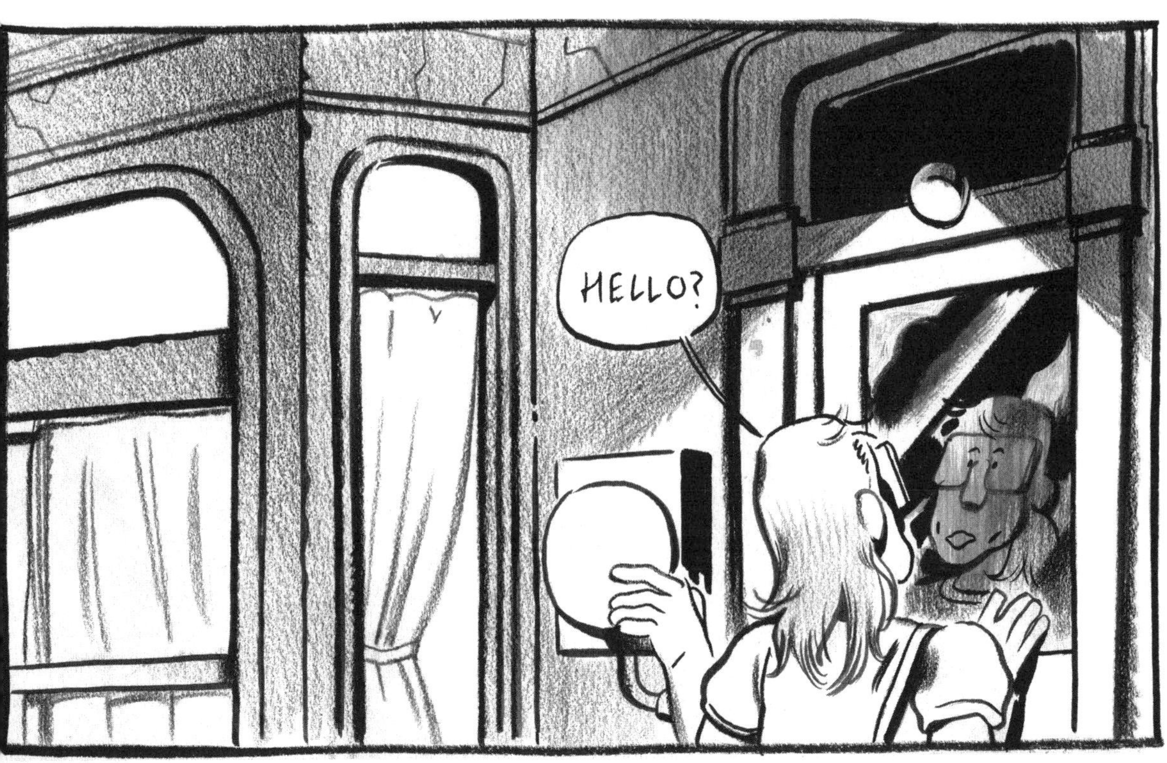
HELLO?

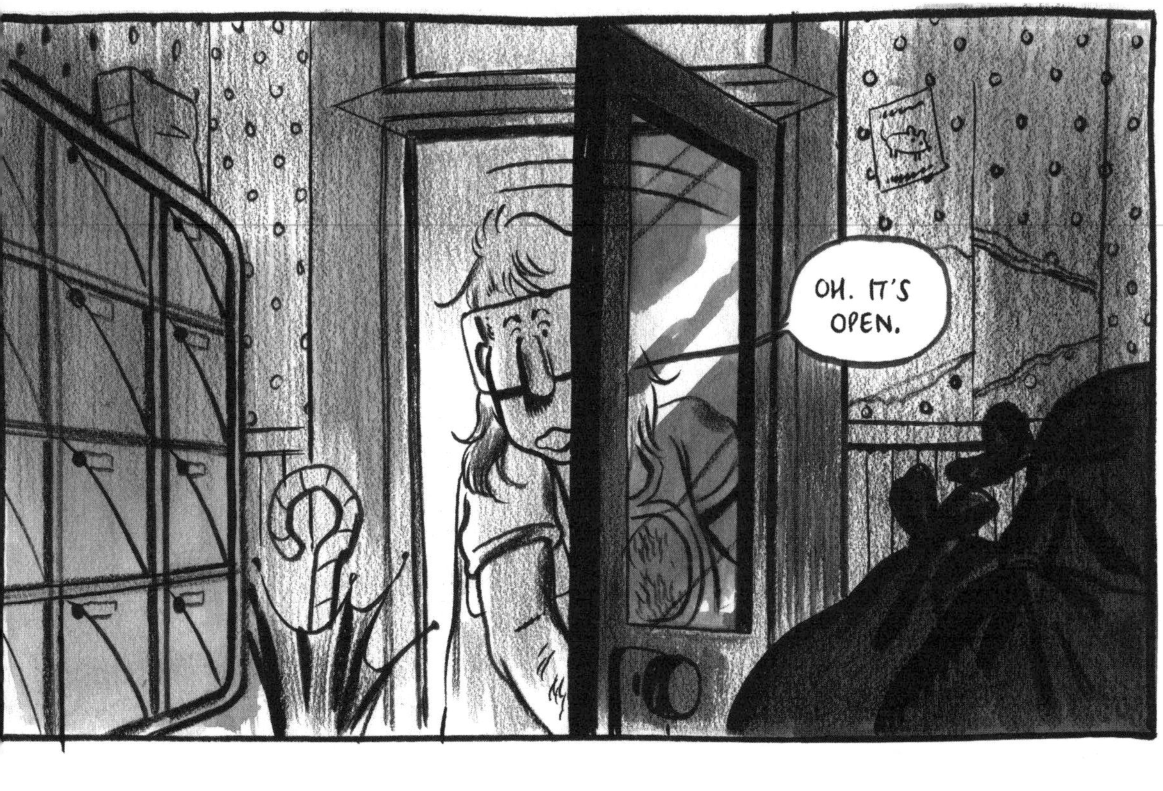
OH. IT'S OPEN.

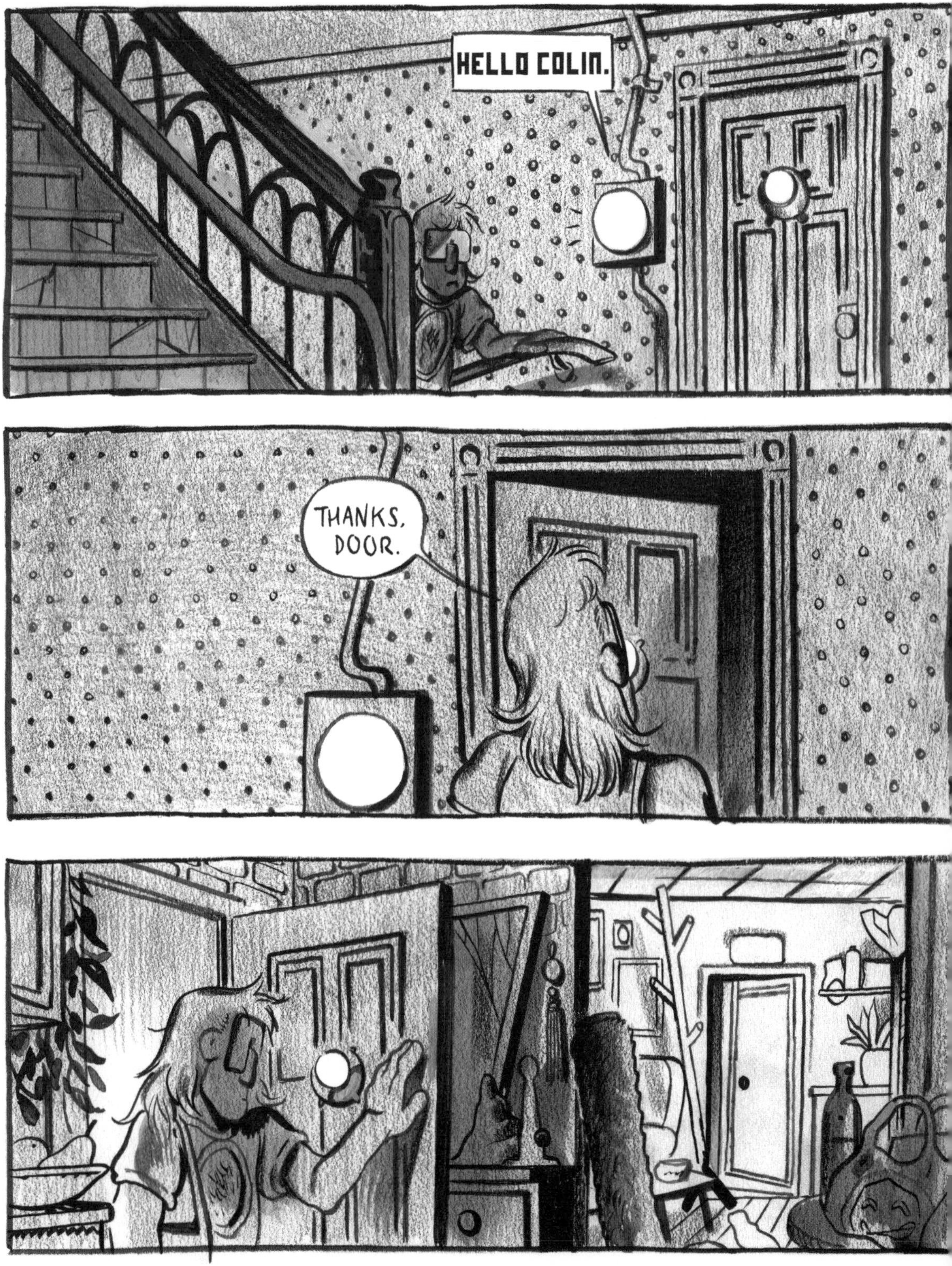
HELLO COLIN.
THANKS, DOOR.

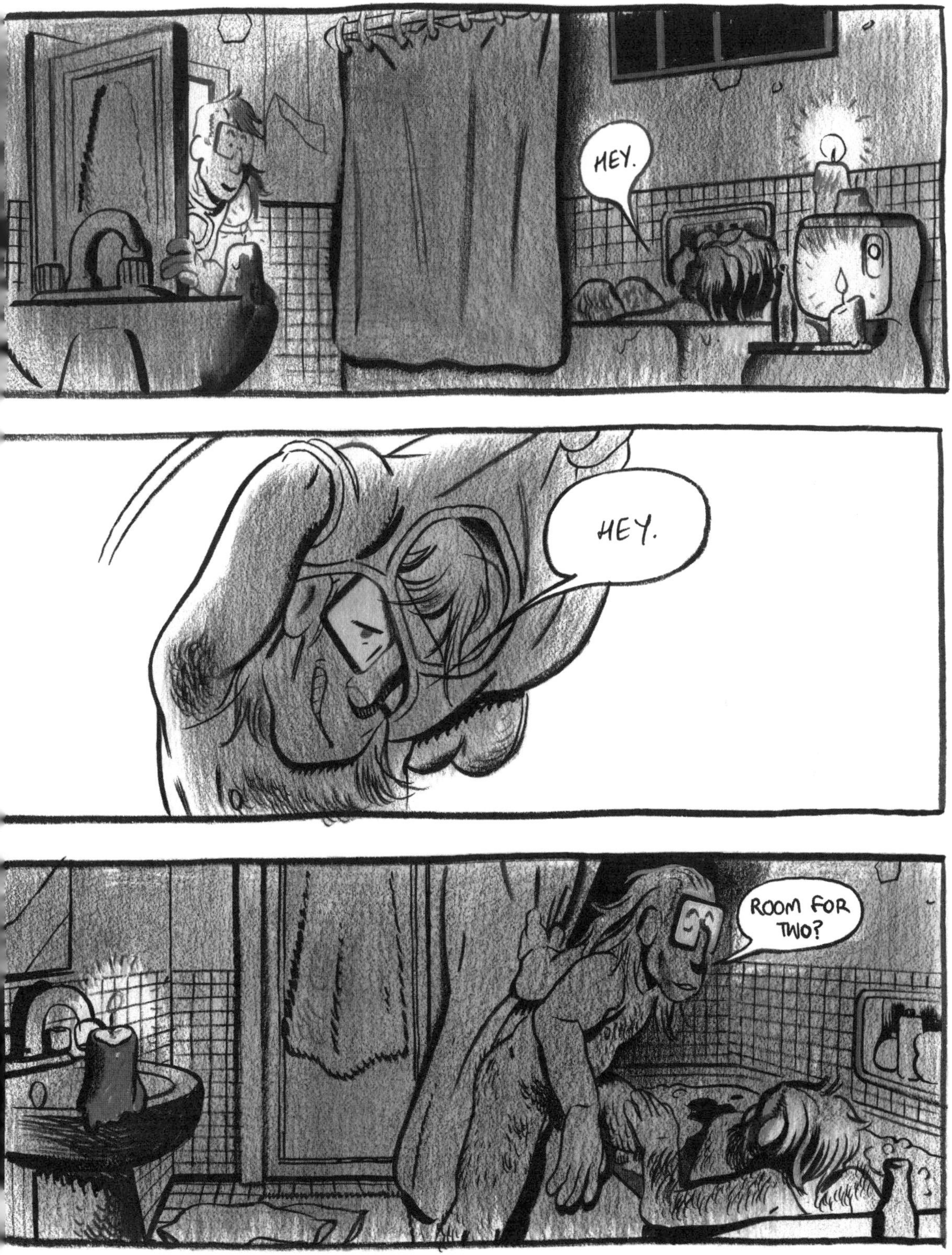
HEY.
HEY.
ROOM FOR TWO?

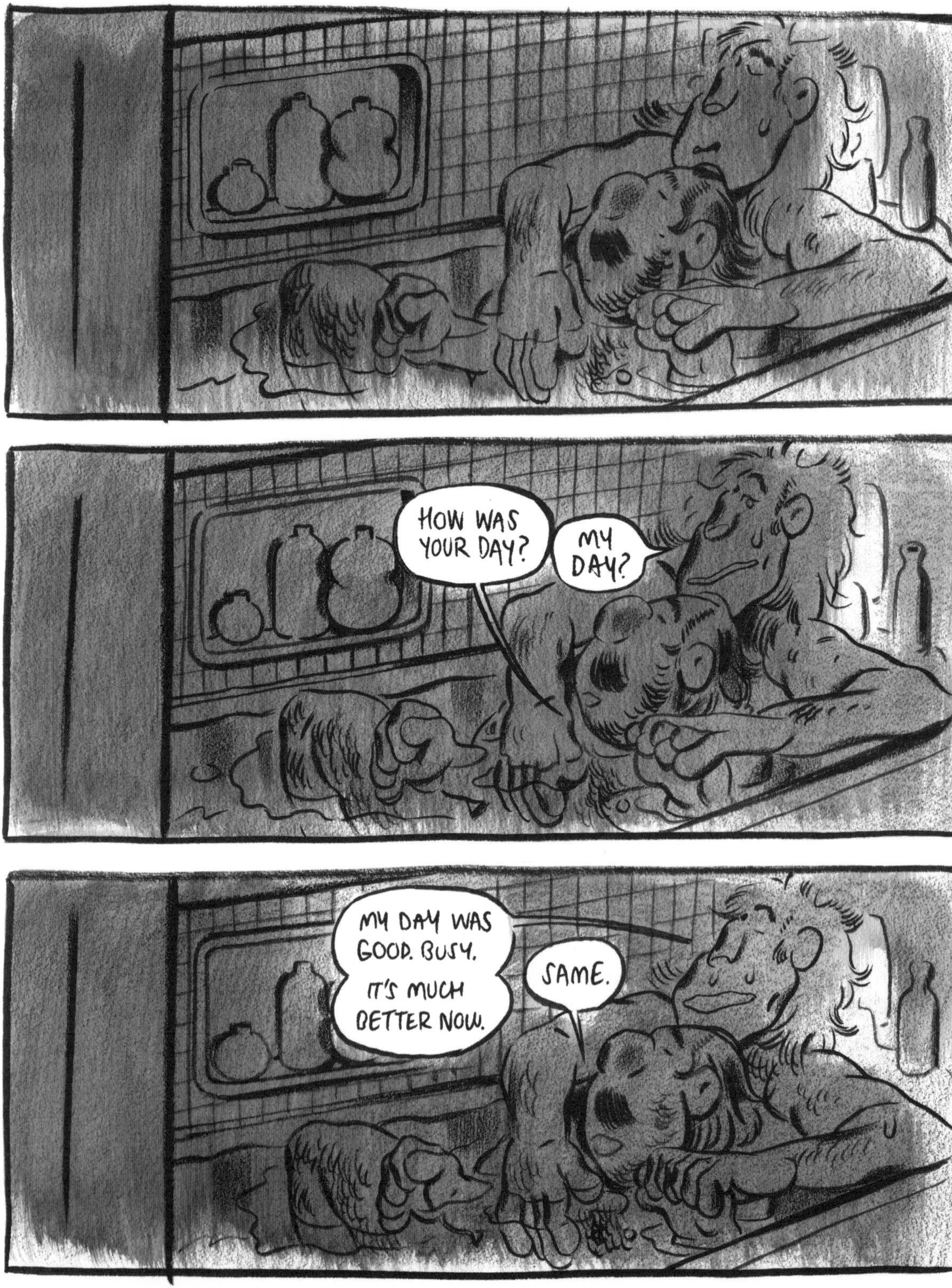
HOW WAS YOUR DAY?
MY DAY?
MY DAY WAS GOOD. BUSY.
IT'S MUCH BETTER NOW.
SAME.

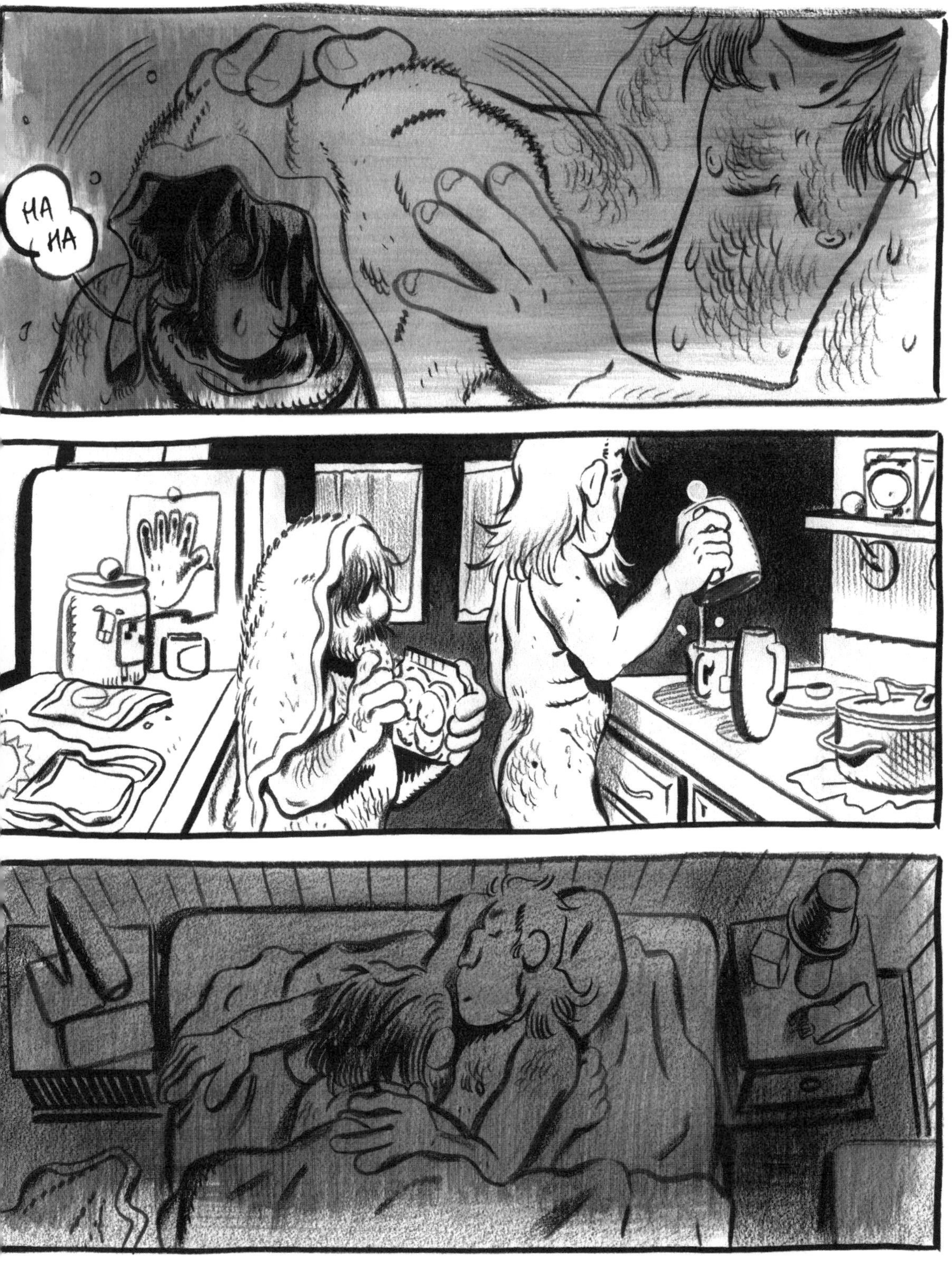
HA HA

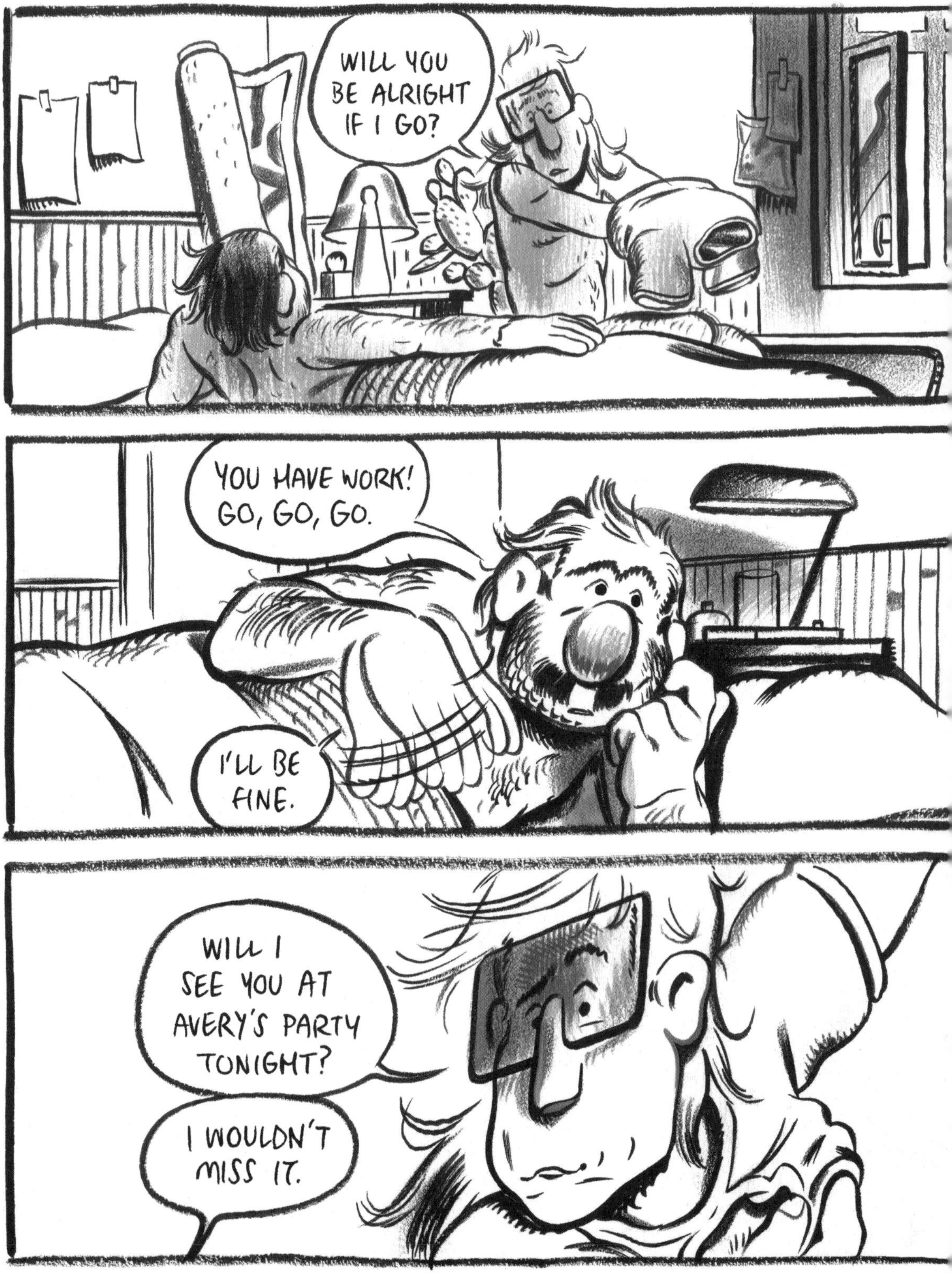
WILL YOU BE ALRIGHT IF I GO?
YOU HAVE WORK! GO, GO, GO.
I'LL BE FINE.
WILL I SEE YOU AT AVERY'S PARTY TONIGHT?
I WOULDN'T MISS IT.

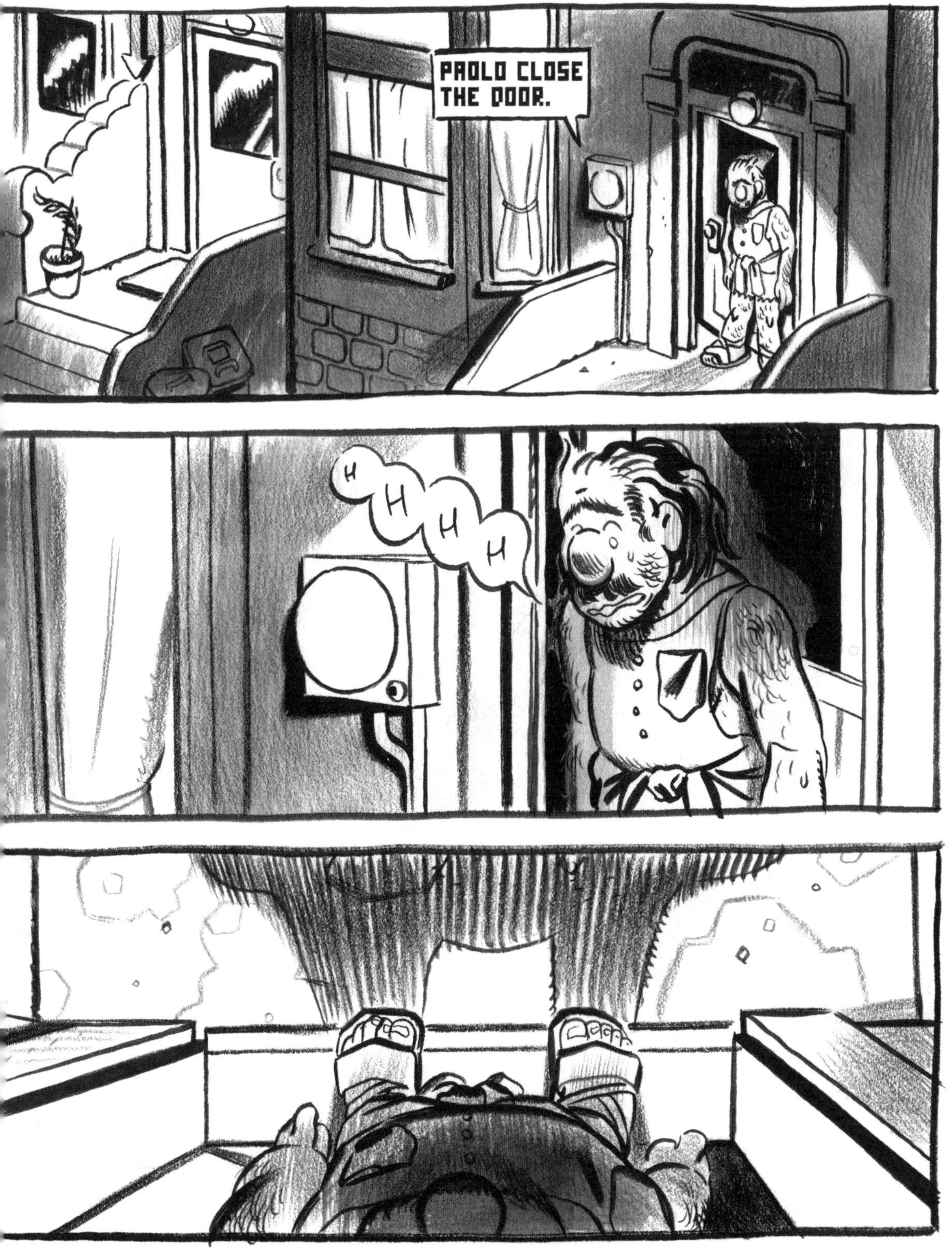

PAOLO CLOSE THE DOOR.
H H H H

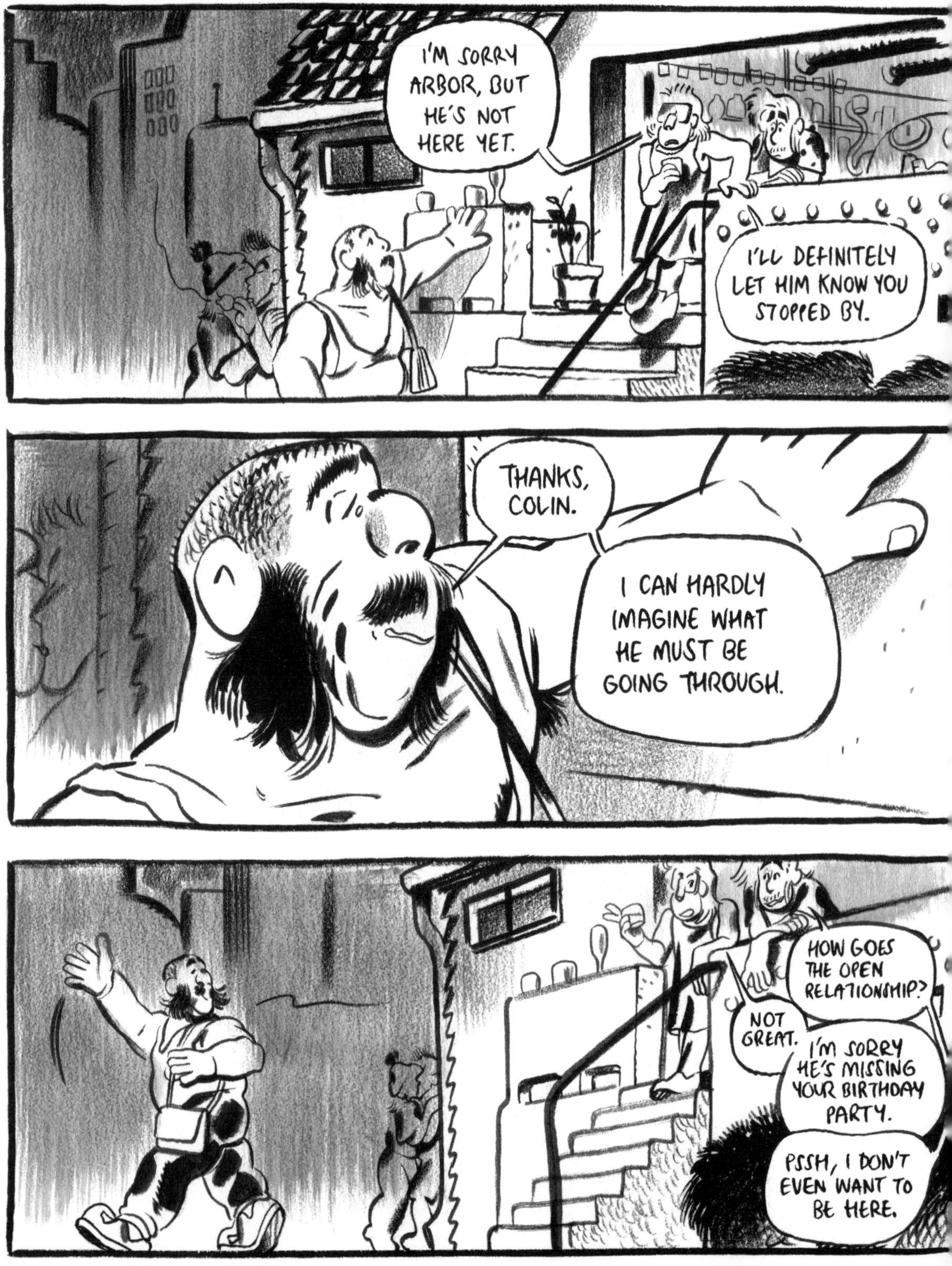
I'M SORRY ARBOR, BUT HE'S NOT HERE YET.
I'LL DEFINITELY LET HIM KNOW YOU STOPPED BY.
THANKS, COLIN.
I CAN HARDLY IMAGINE WHAT HE MUST BE GOING THROUGH.
HOW GOES THE OPEN RELATIONSHIP?
NOT GREAT.
I'M SORRY HE'S MISSING YOUR BIRTHDAY PARTY.
PSSH, I DON'T EVEN WANT TO BE HERE.

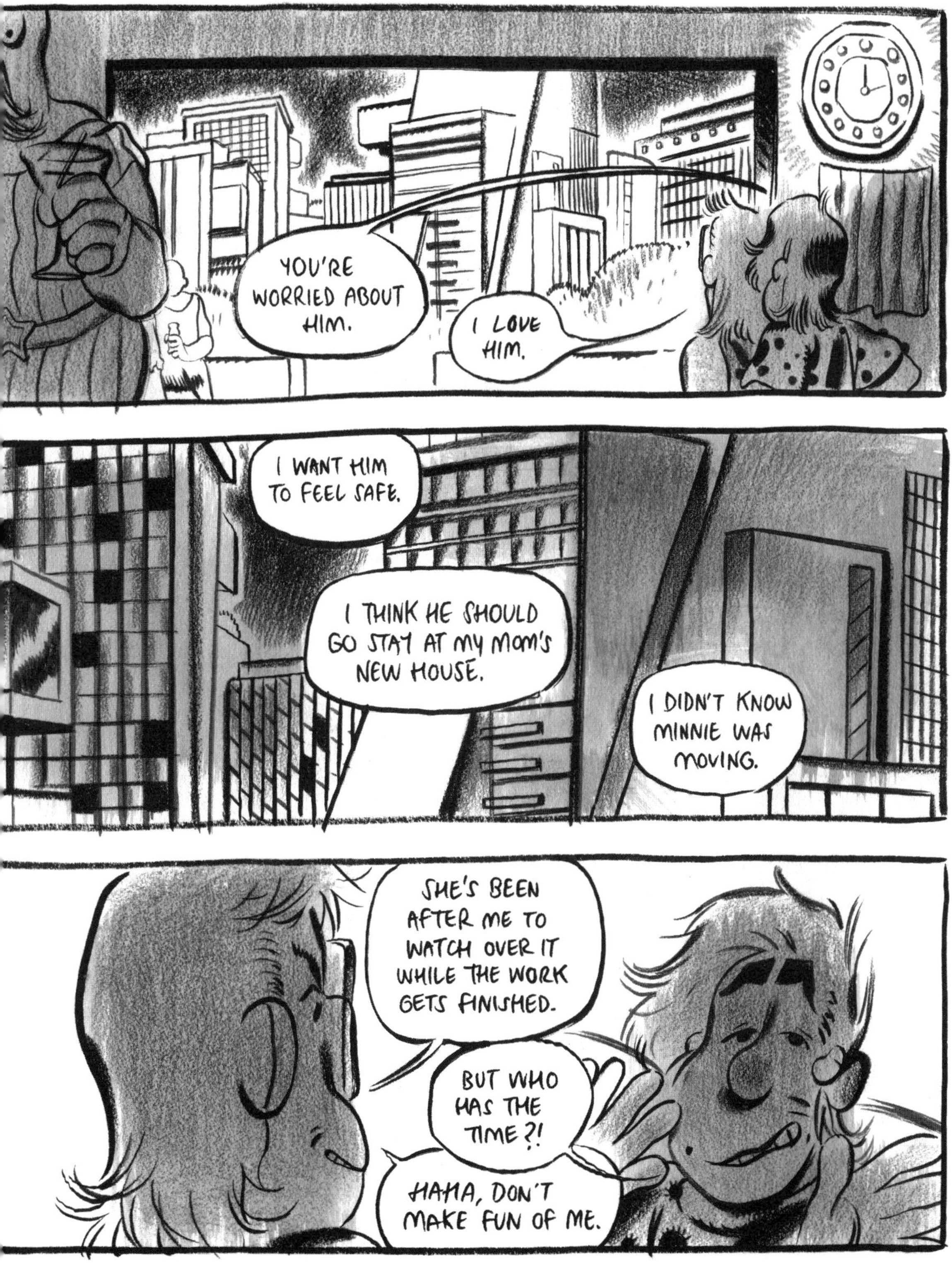
YOU'RE WORRIED ABOUT HIM.
I LOVE HIM.
I WANT HIM TO FEEL SAFE.
I THINK HE SHOULD GO STAY AT MY MOM'S NEW HOUSE.
I DIDN'T KNOW MINNIE WAS MOVING.
SHE'S BEEN AFTER ME TO WATCH OVER IT WHILE THE WORK GETS FINISHED.
BUT WHO HAS THE TIME?!
HAHA, DON'T MAKE FUN OF ME.

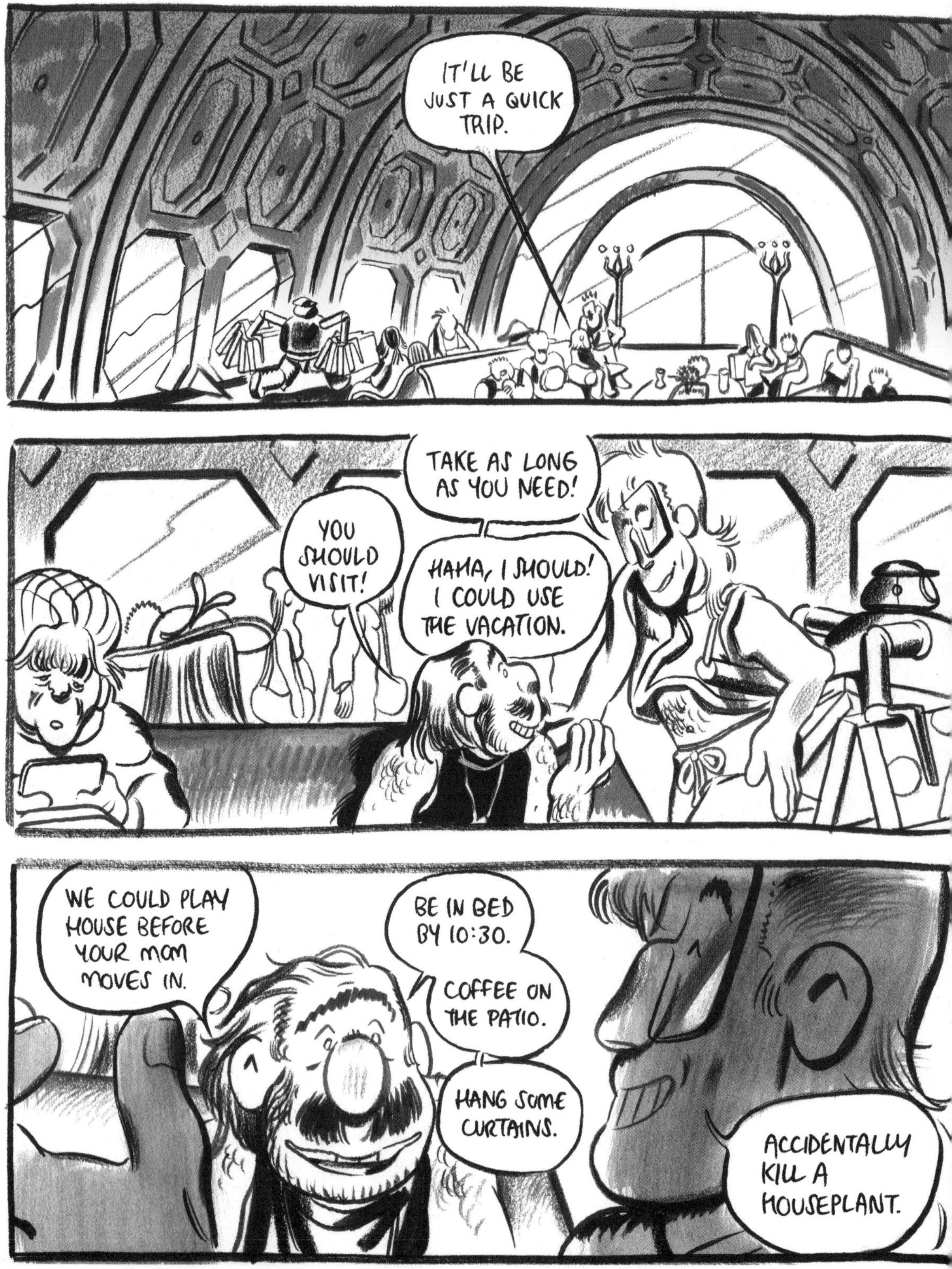
IT'LL BE JUST A QUICK TRIP.
YOU SHOULD VISIT!
TAKE AS LONG AS YOU NEED!
HAHA, I SHOULD! I COULD USE THE VACATION.
WE COULD PLAY HOUSE BEFORE YOUR MOM MOVES IN.
BE IN BED BY 10:30.
COFFEE ON THE PATIO.
HANG SOME CURTAINS.
ACCIDENTALLY KILL A HOUSEPLANT.

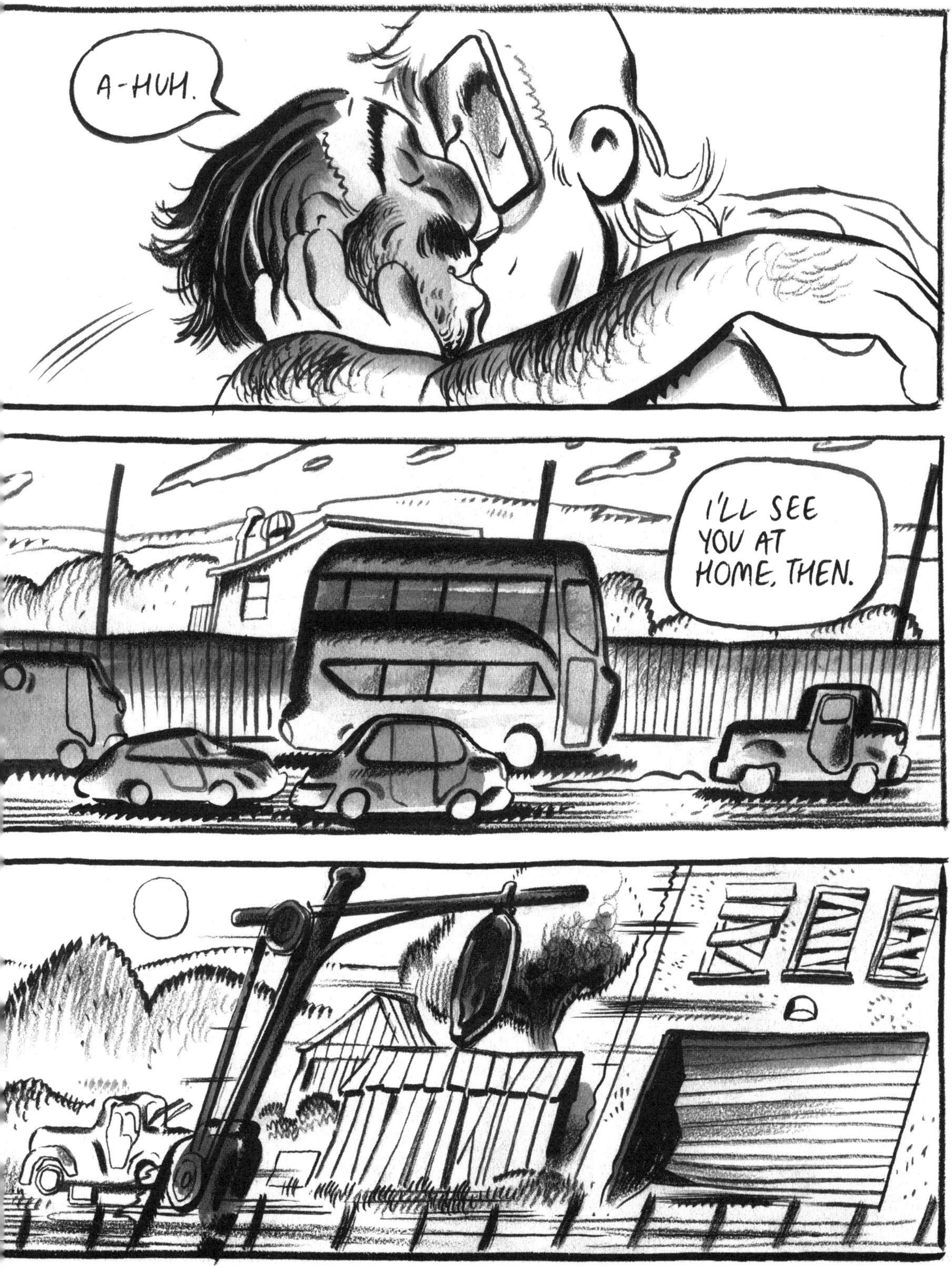
A-HUH.
I'LL SEE YOU AT HOME, THEN.

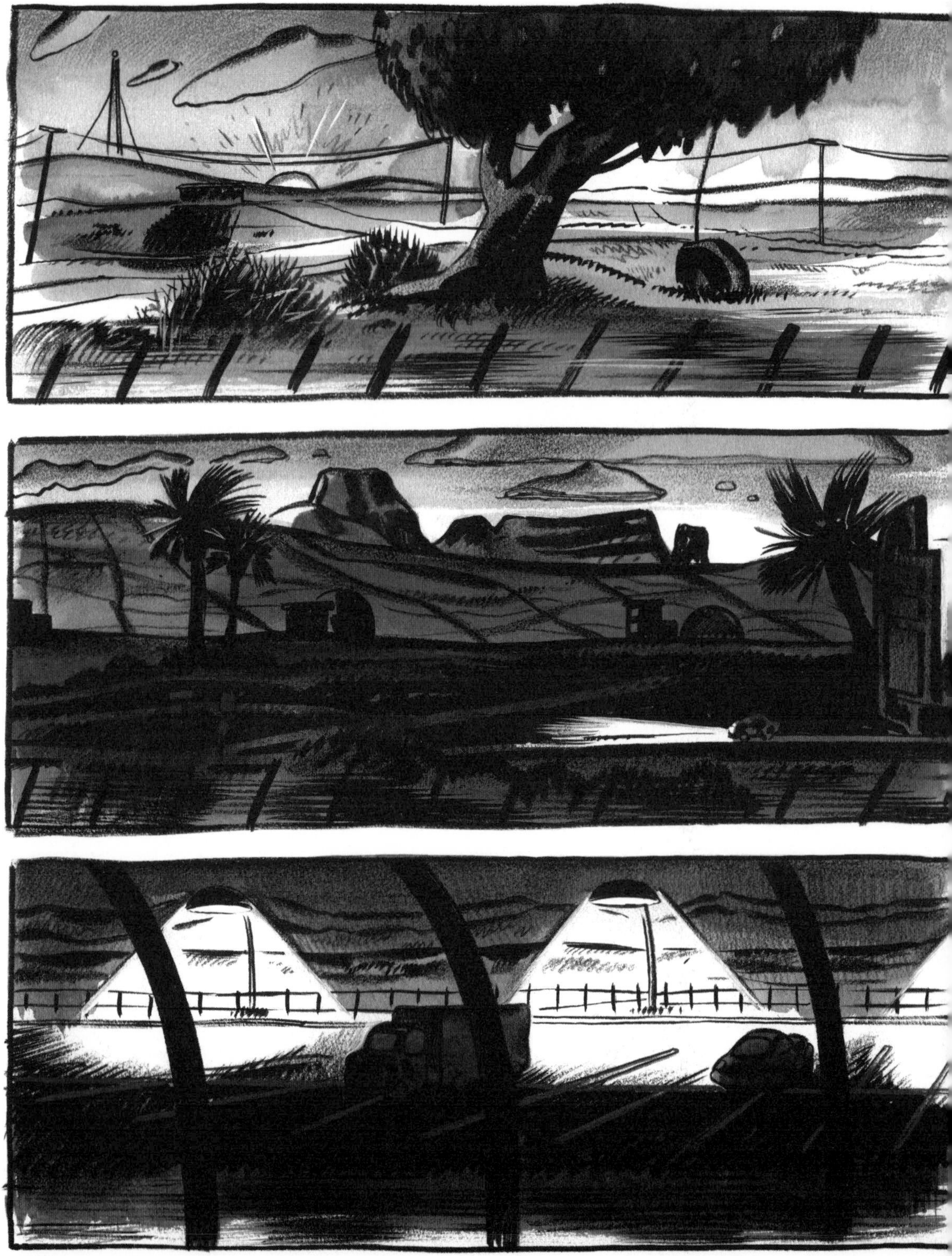

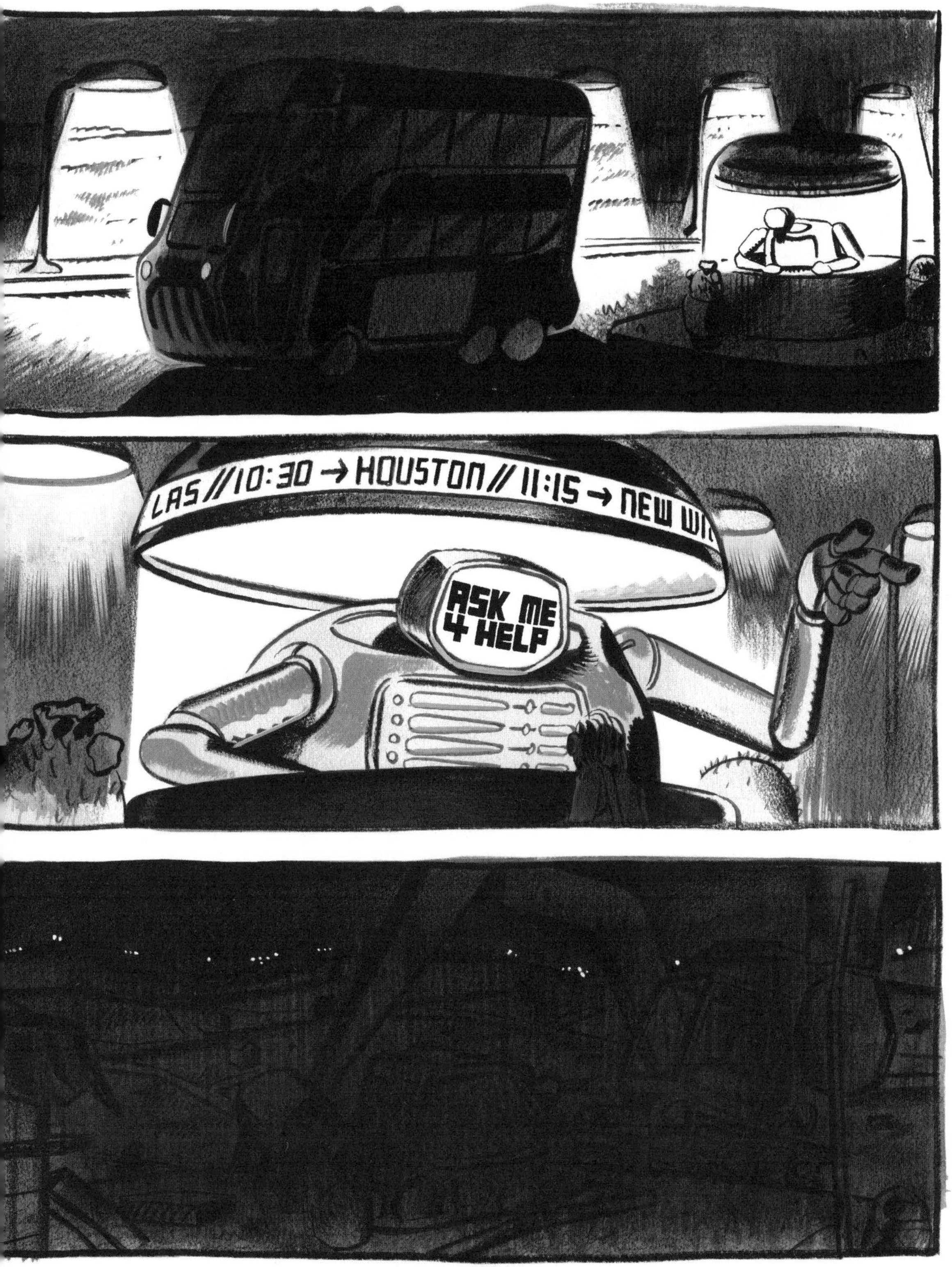
LAS // 10:30 → HOUSTON // 11:15 → NEW
ASK ME 4 HELP

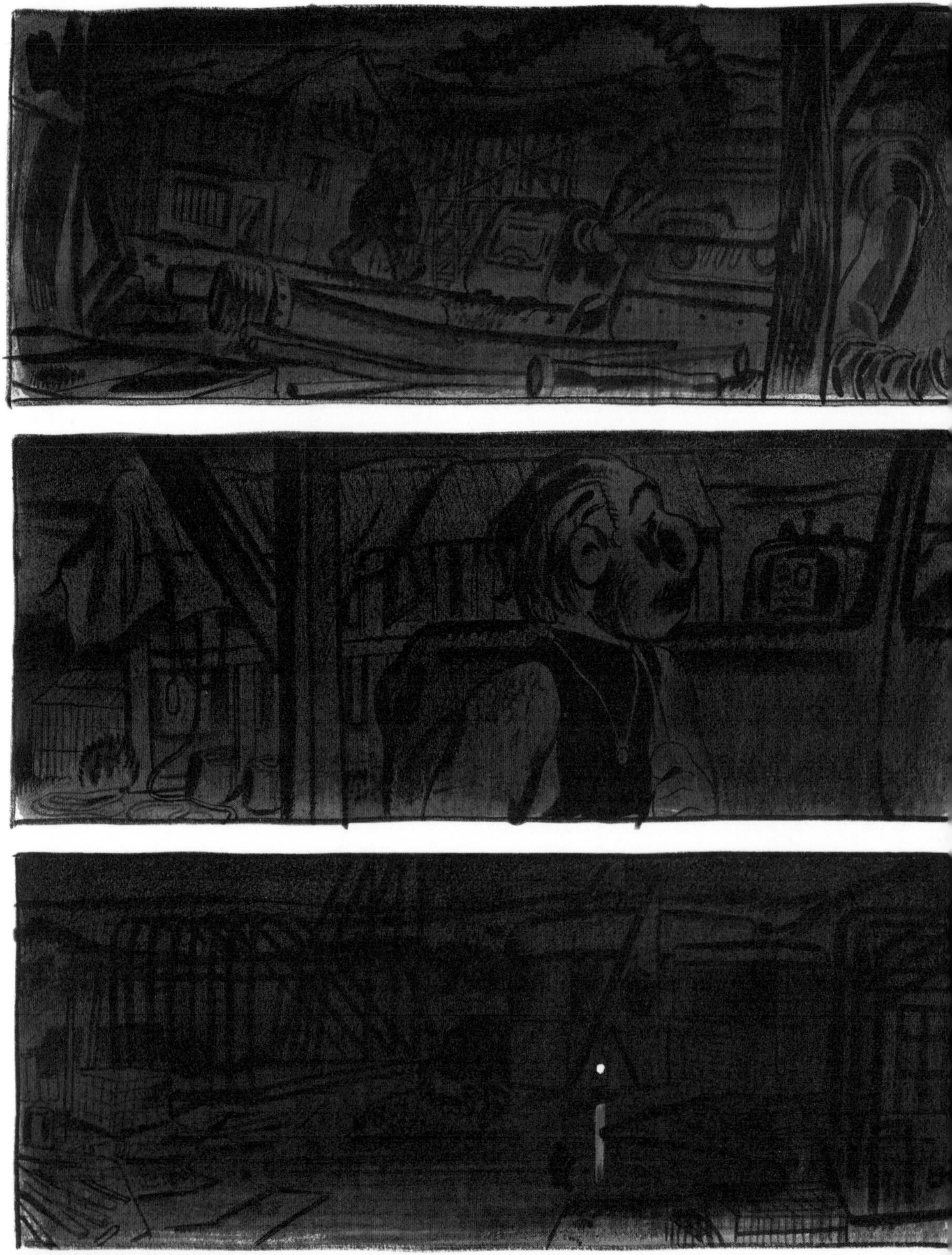

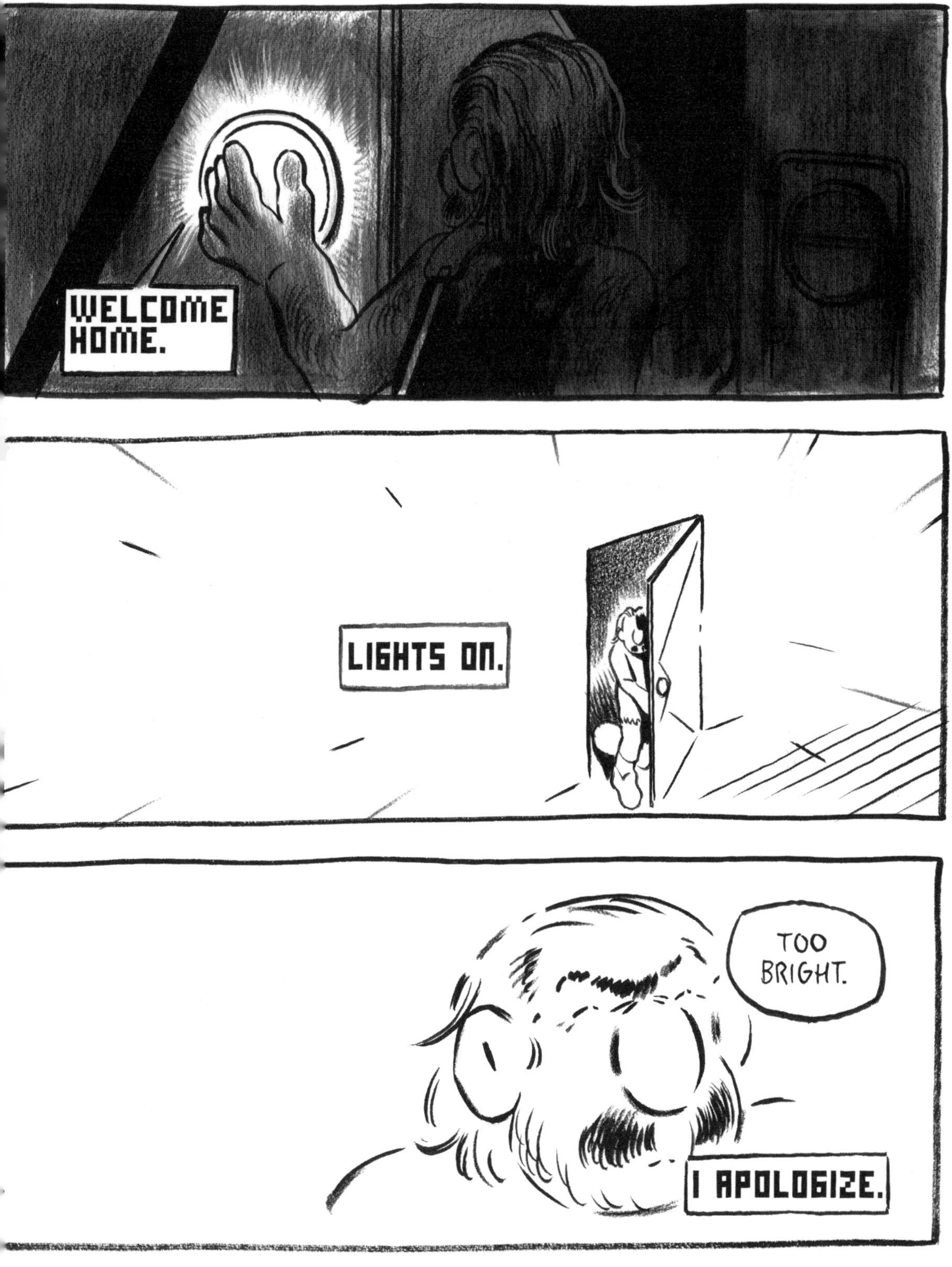
WELCOME HOME.
LIGHTS ON.
TOO BRIGHT.
I APOLOGIZE.

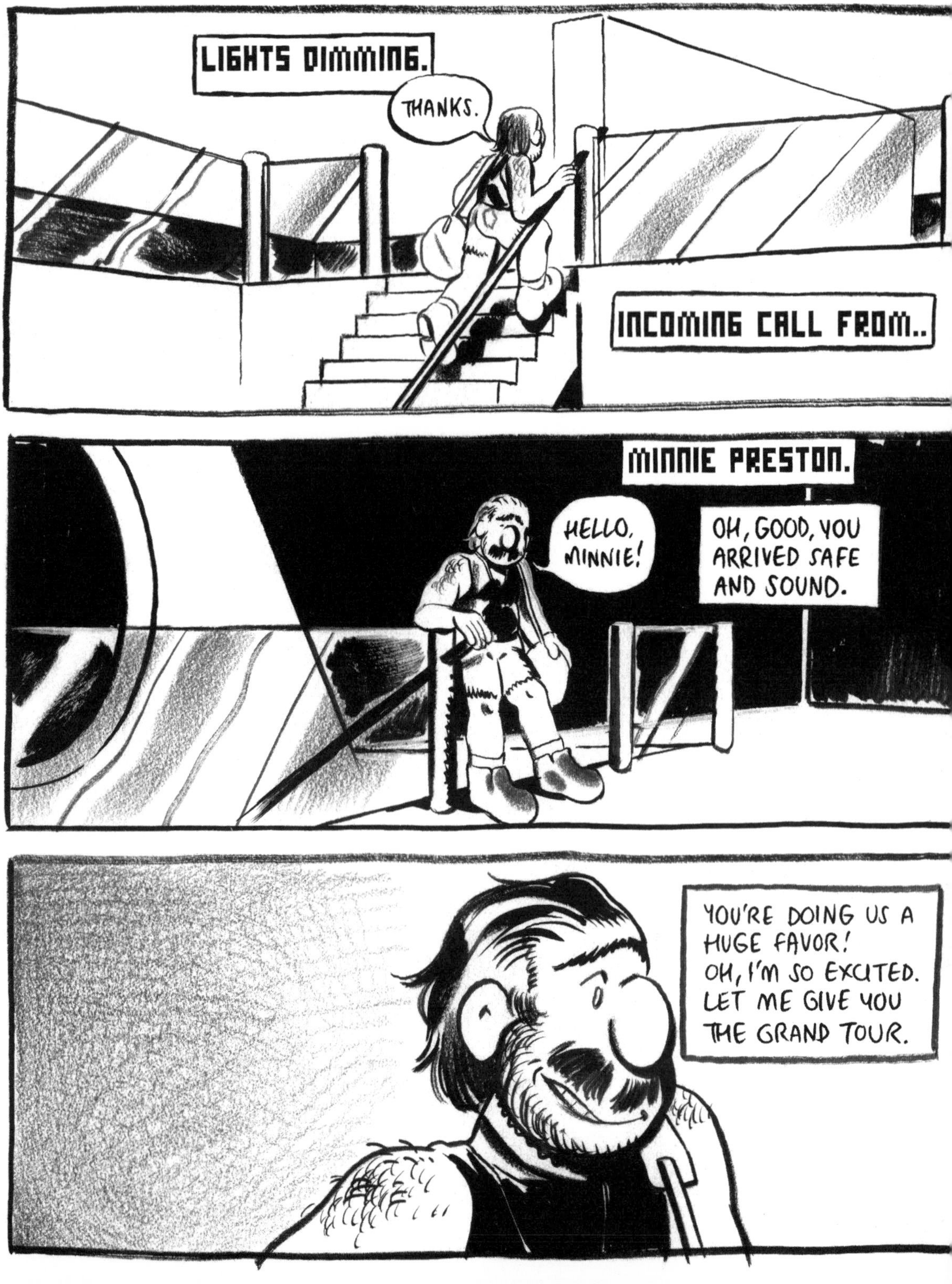

LIGHTS DIMMING.
THANKS.
INCOMING CALL FROM..
MINNIE PRESTON.
HELLO, MINNIE!
OH, GOOD, YOU ARRIVED SAFE AND SOUND.
YOU'RE DOING US A HUGE FAVOR! OH, I'M SO EXCITED. LET ME GIVE YOU THE GRAND TOUR.

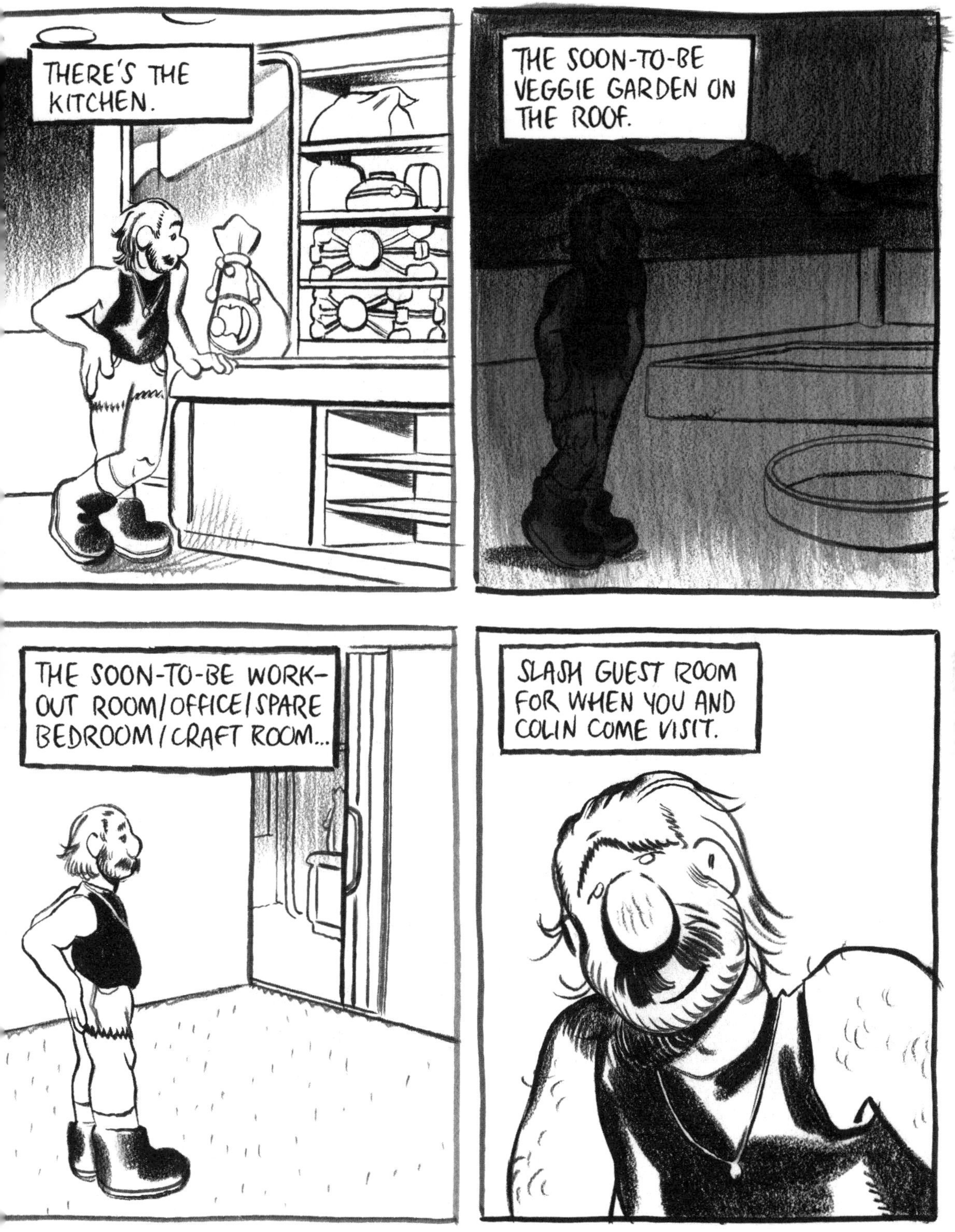
THERE'S THE KITCHEN.
THE SOON-TO-BE VEGGIE GARDEN ON THE ROOF.
THE SOON-TO-BE WORK-OUT ROOM/OFFICE/SPARE BEDROOM/CRAFT ROOM...
SLASH GUEST ROOM FOR WHEN YOU AND COLIN COME VISIT.

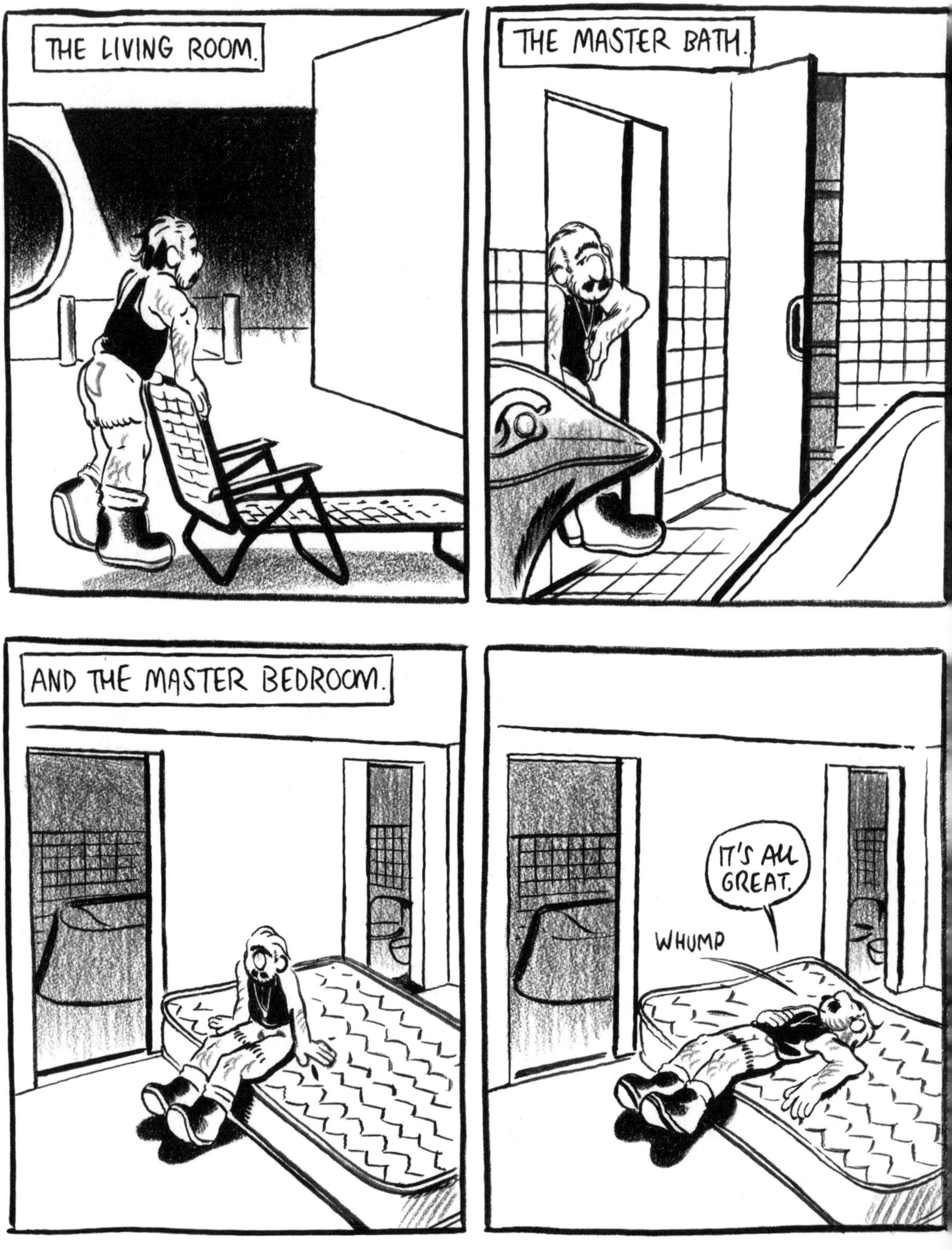
THE LIVING ROOM.
THE MASTER BATH.
AND THE MASTER BEDROOM.
WHUMP
IT'S ALL GREAT.

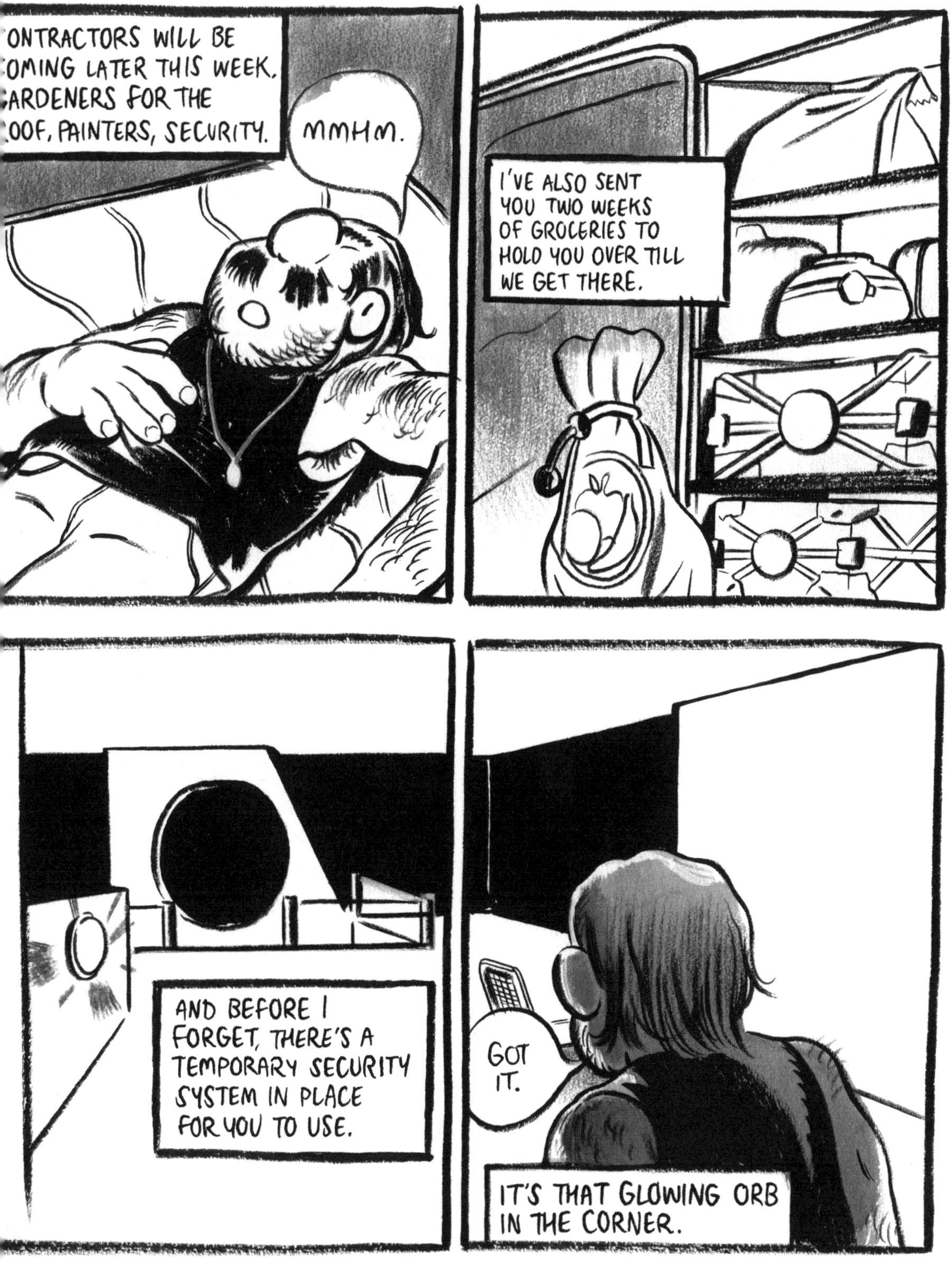
ONTRACTORS WILL BE
OMING LATER THIS WEEK.
ARDENERS FOR THE
OOF, PAINTERS, SECURITY.
MMHM.
I'VE ALSO SENT
YOU TWO WEEKS
OF GROCERIES TO
HOLD YOU OVER TILL
WE GET THERE.
AND BEFORE I
FORGET, THERE'S A
TEMPORARY SECURITY
SYSTEM IN PLACE
FOR YOU TO USE.
GOT
IT.
IT'S THAT GLOWING ORB
IN THE CORNER.

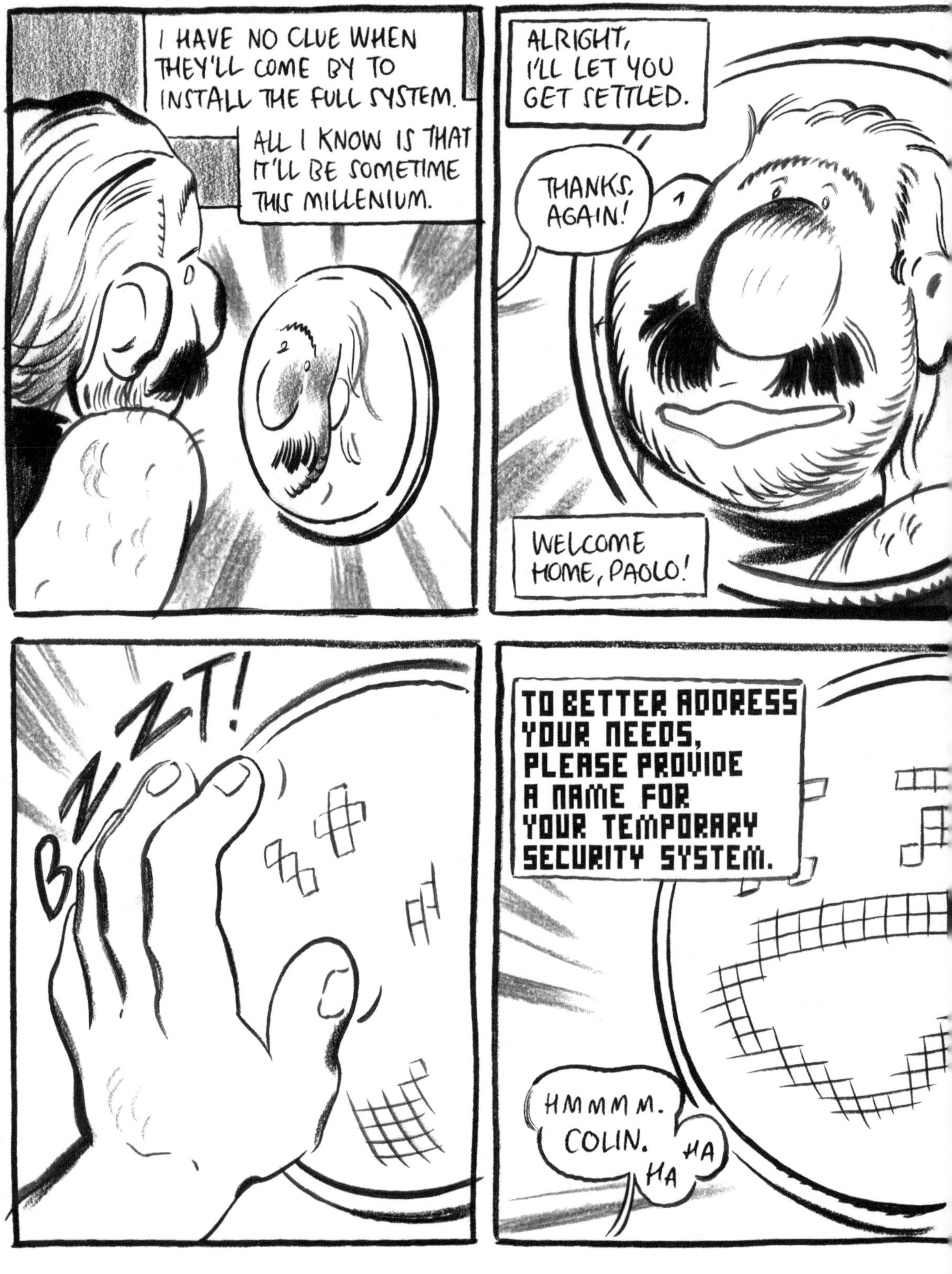
I HAVE NO CLUE WHEN THEY'LL COME BY TO INSTALL THE FULL SYSTEM.
ALL I KNOW IS THAT IT'LL BE SOMETIME THIS MILLENIUM.
ALRIGHT, I'LL LET YOU GET SETTLED.
THANKS, AGAIN!
WELCOME HOME, PAOLO!
BZZT!
TO BETTER ADDRESS YOUR NEEDS, PLEASE PROVIDE A NAME FOR YOUR TEMPORARY SECURITY SYSTEM.
HMMMM. COLIN.
HA HA

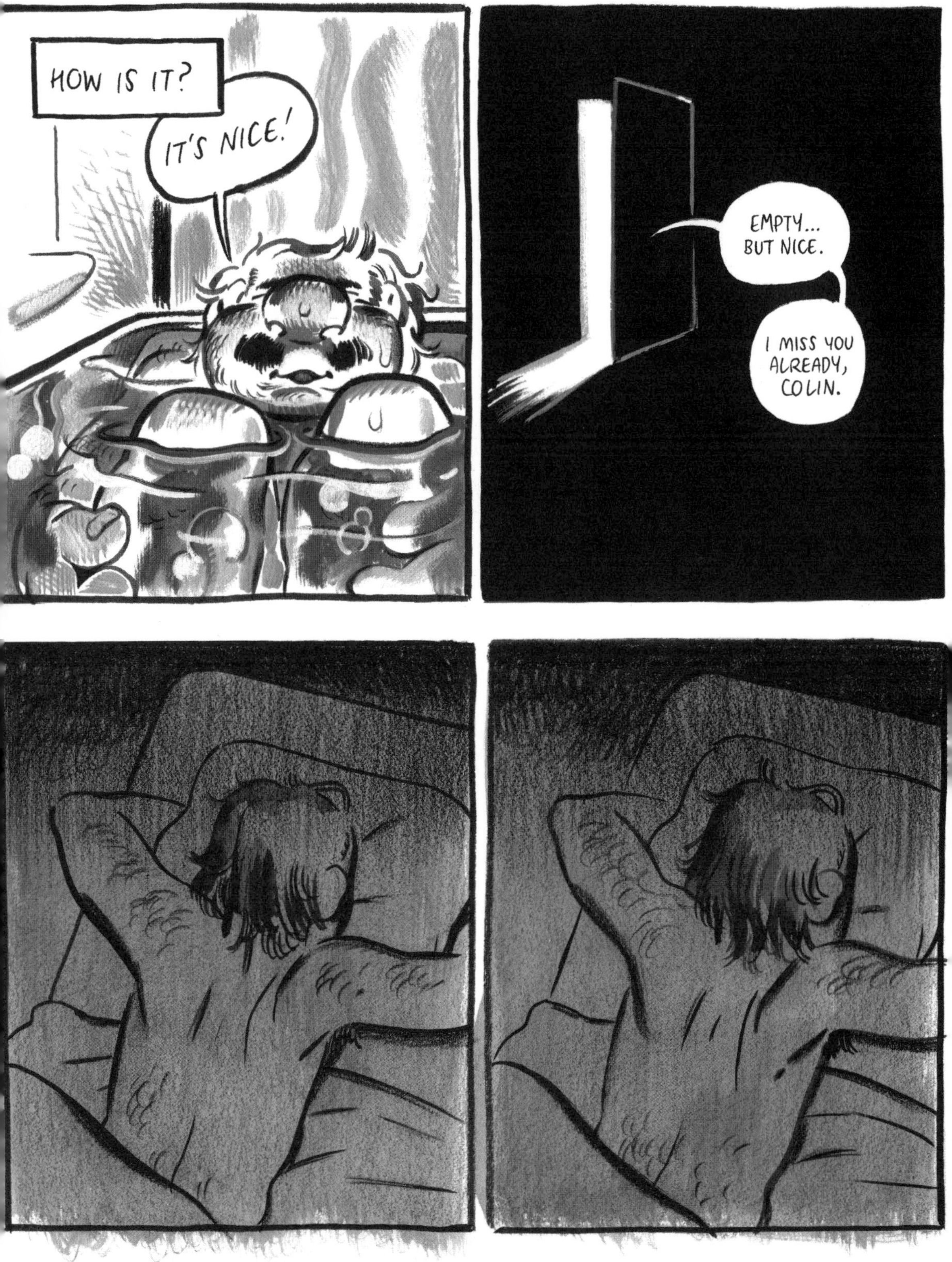
HOW IS IT?
IT'S NICE!
EMPTY... BUT NICE.
I MISS YOU ALREADY, COLIN.

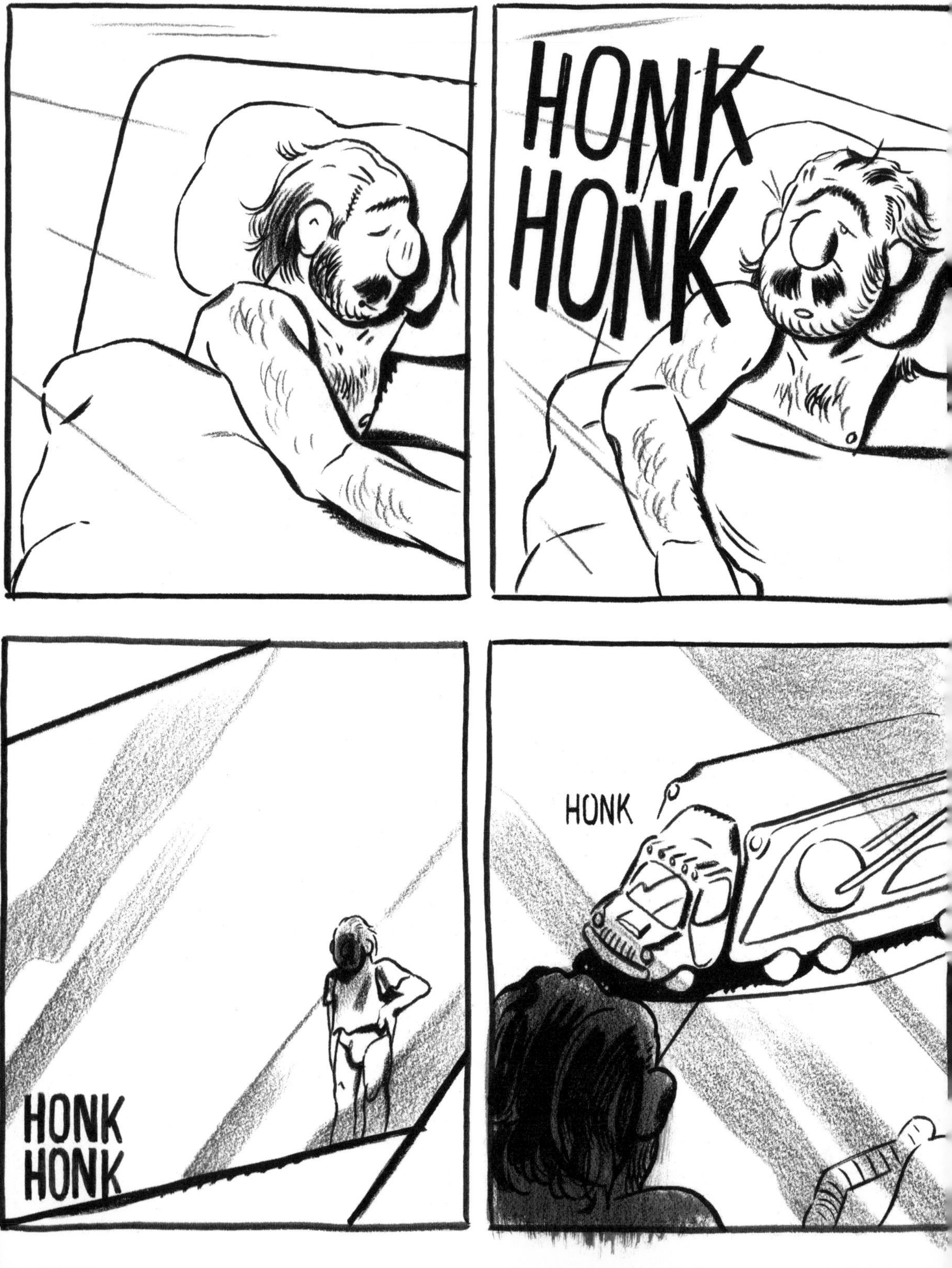
HONK
HONK
HONK
HONK
HONK

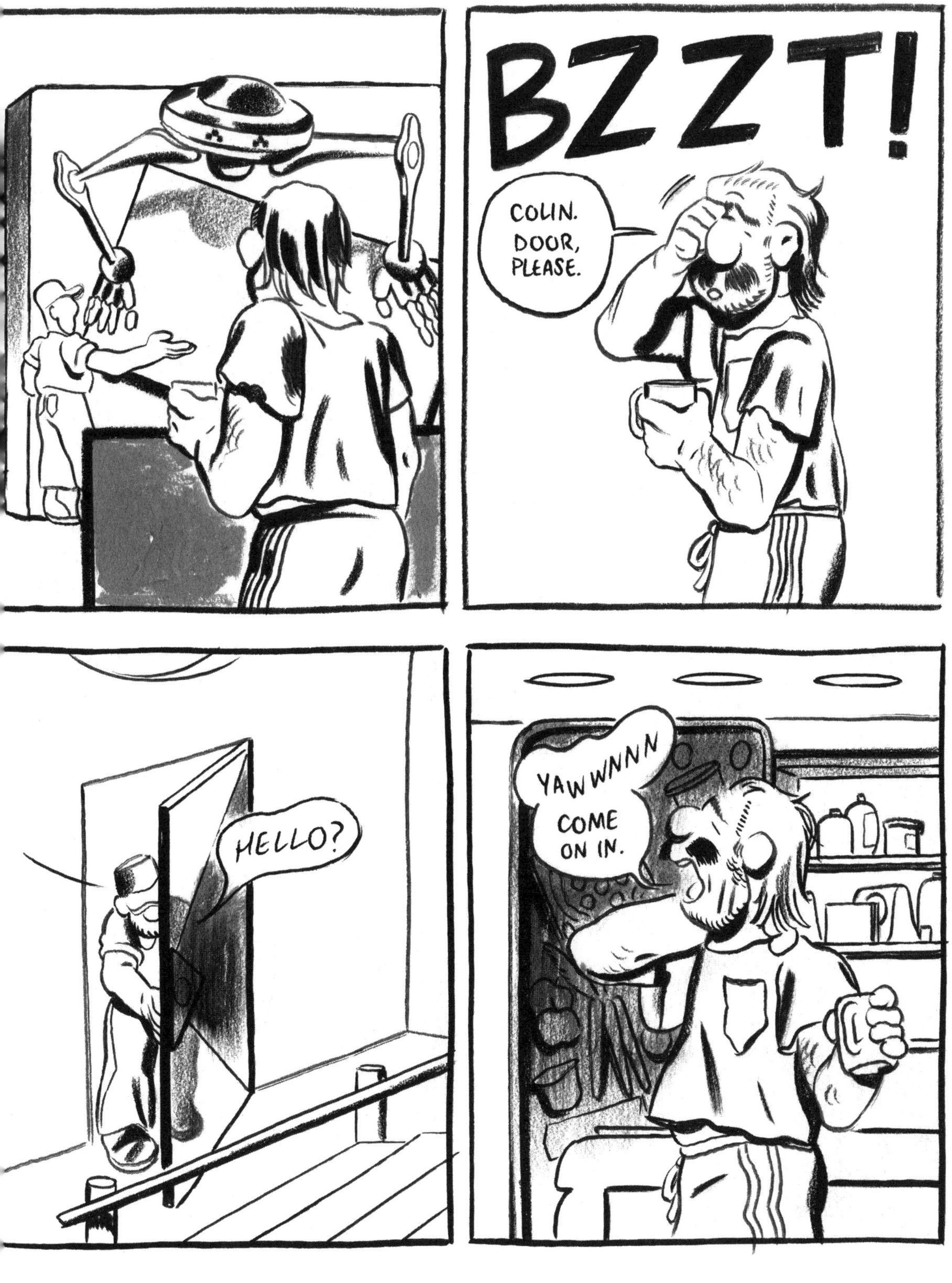
BZZZT!
COLIN. DOOR, PLEASE.
HELLO?
YAWWNNN
COME ON IN.

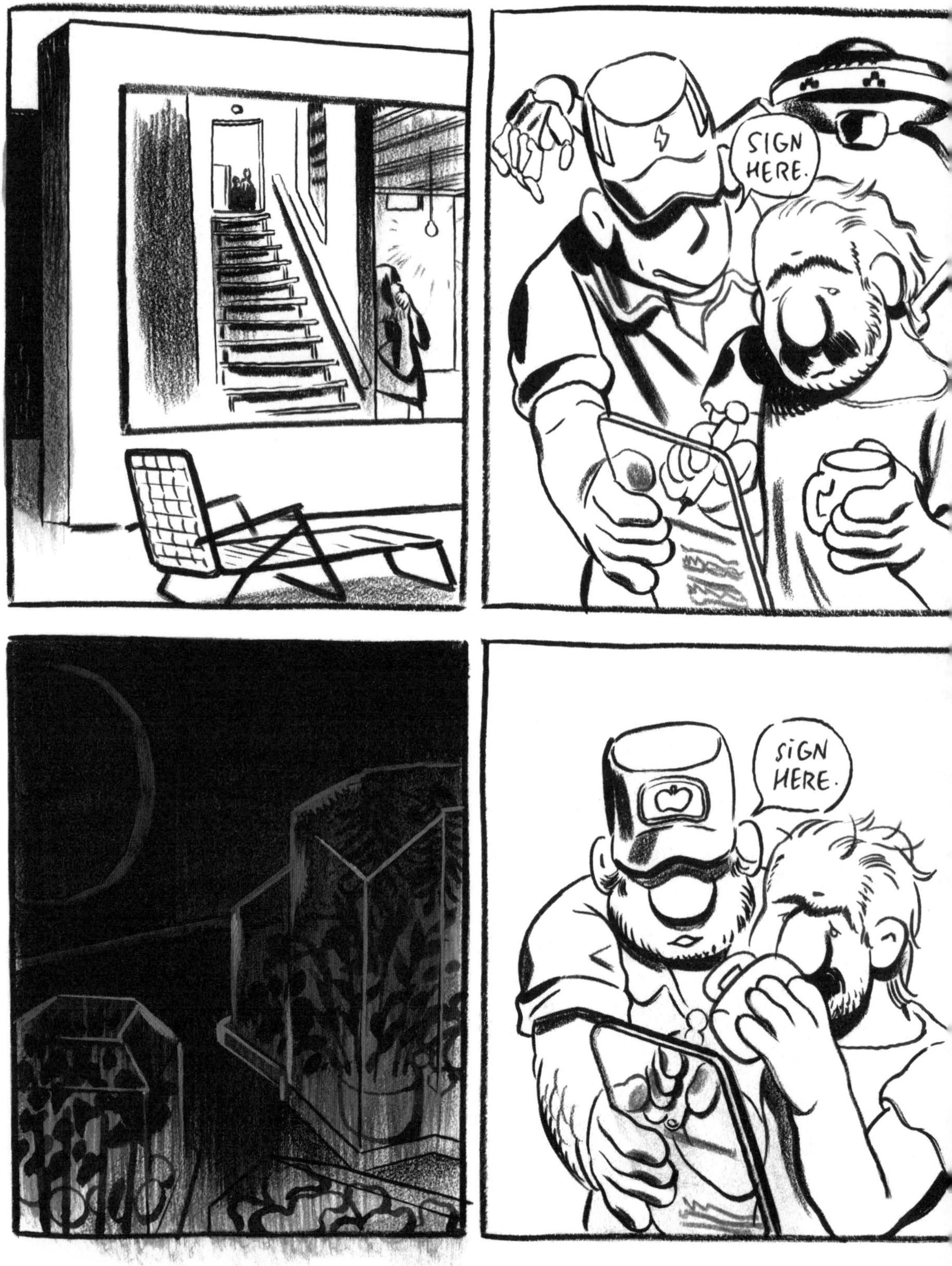
SIGN HERE.
SIGN HERE.

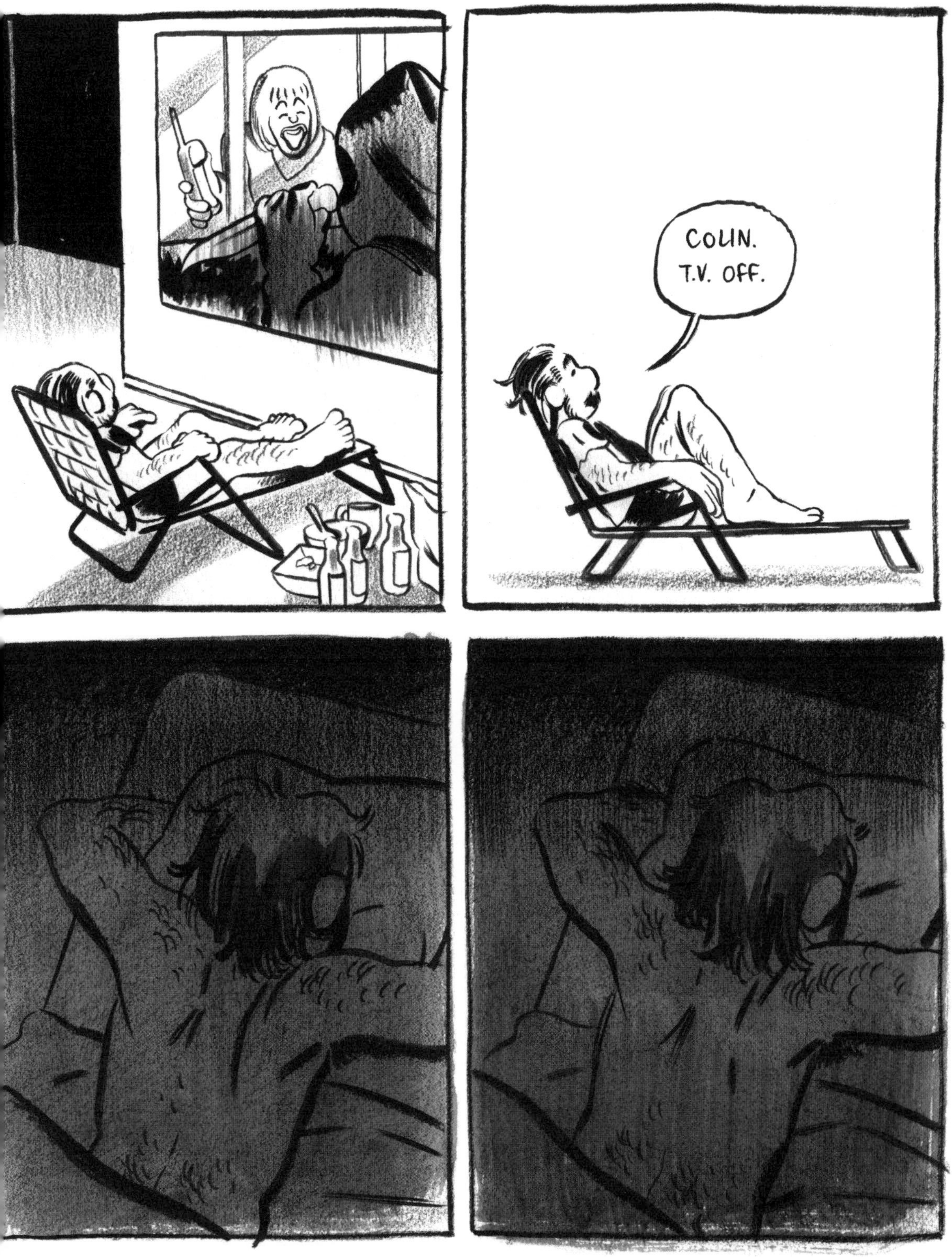
COLIN.
T.V. OFF.

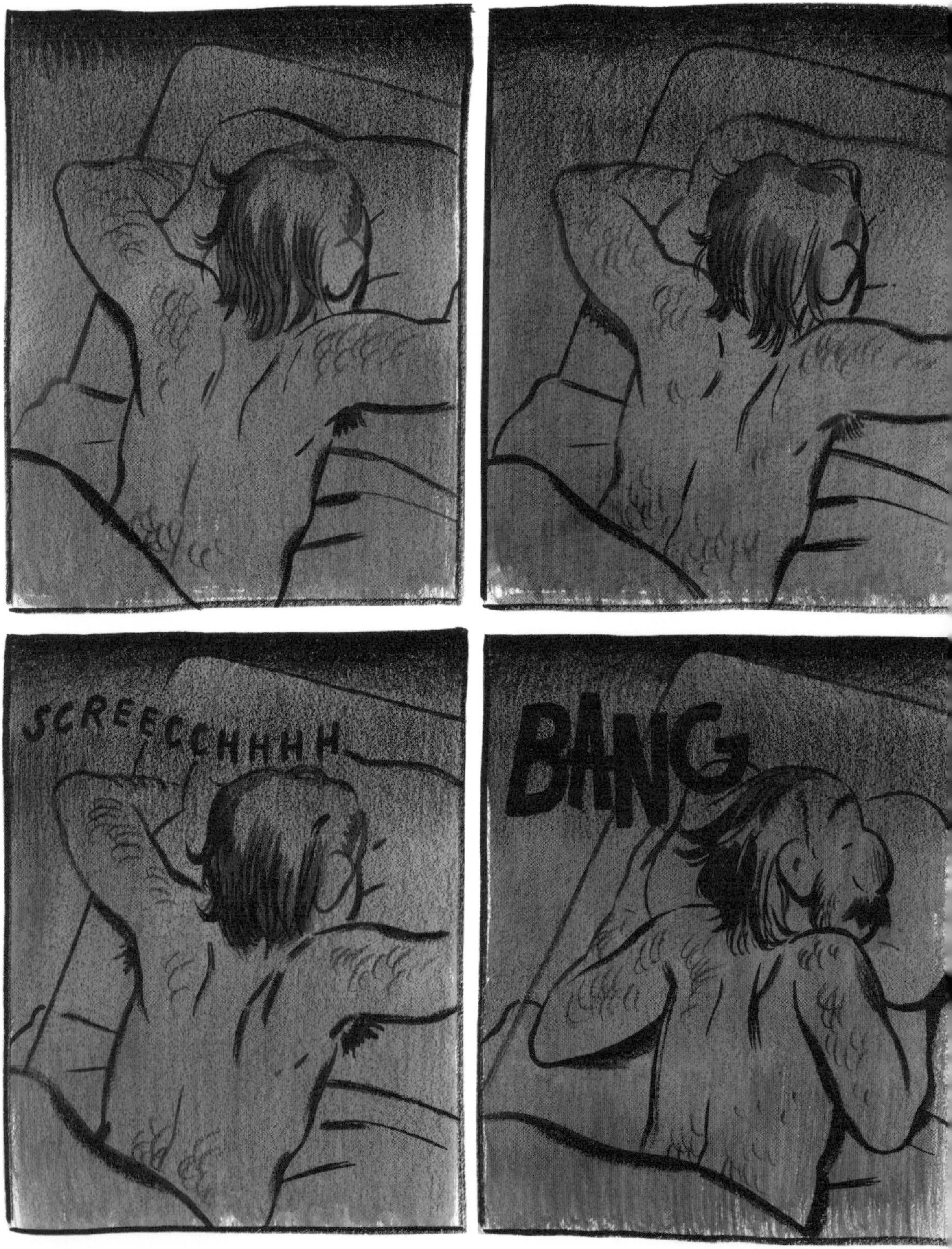
SCREECCHHHH
BANG

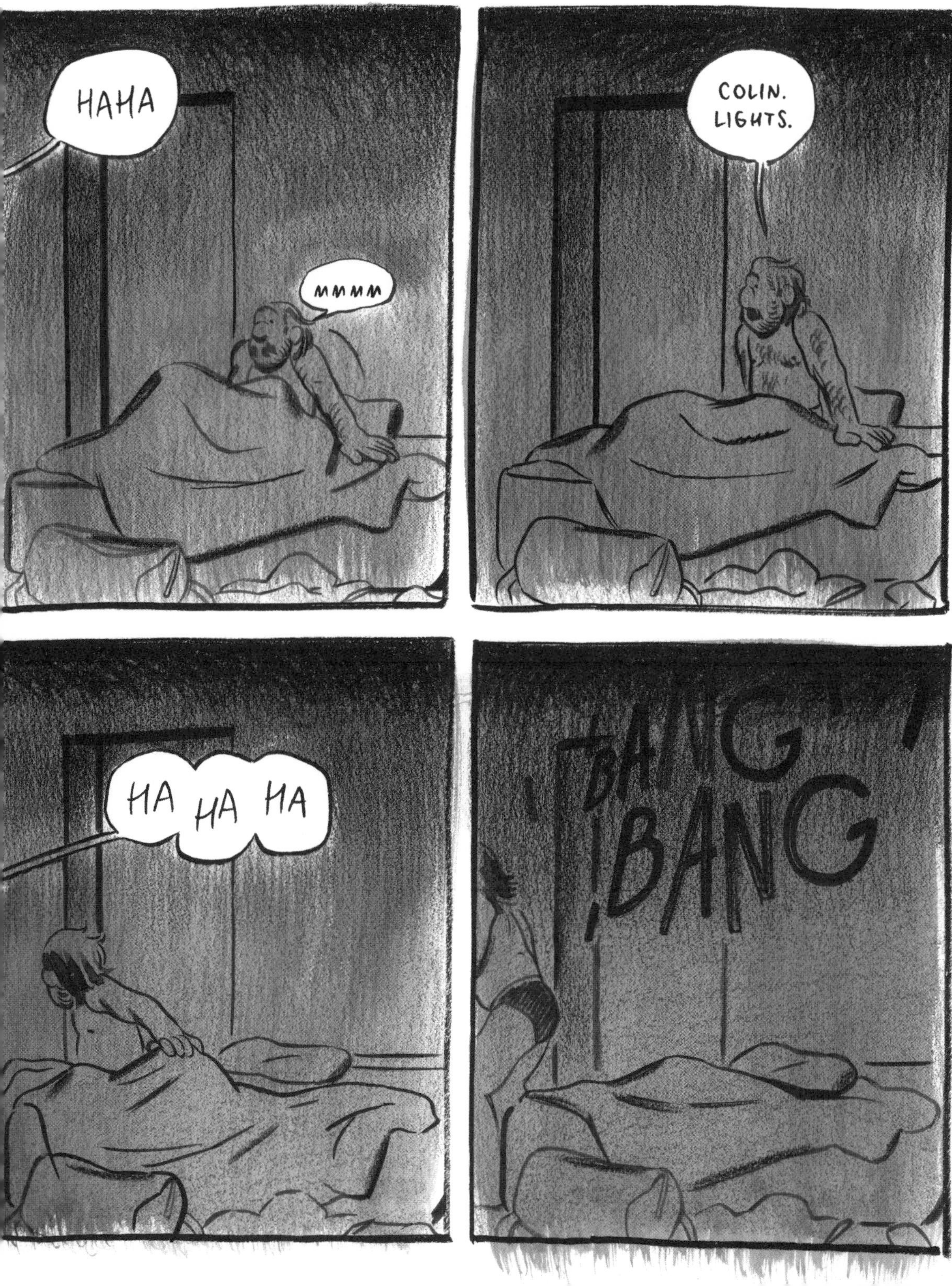
HAHA
MMMM
COLIN. LIGHTS.
HA HA HA
BANG
BANG

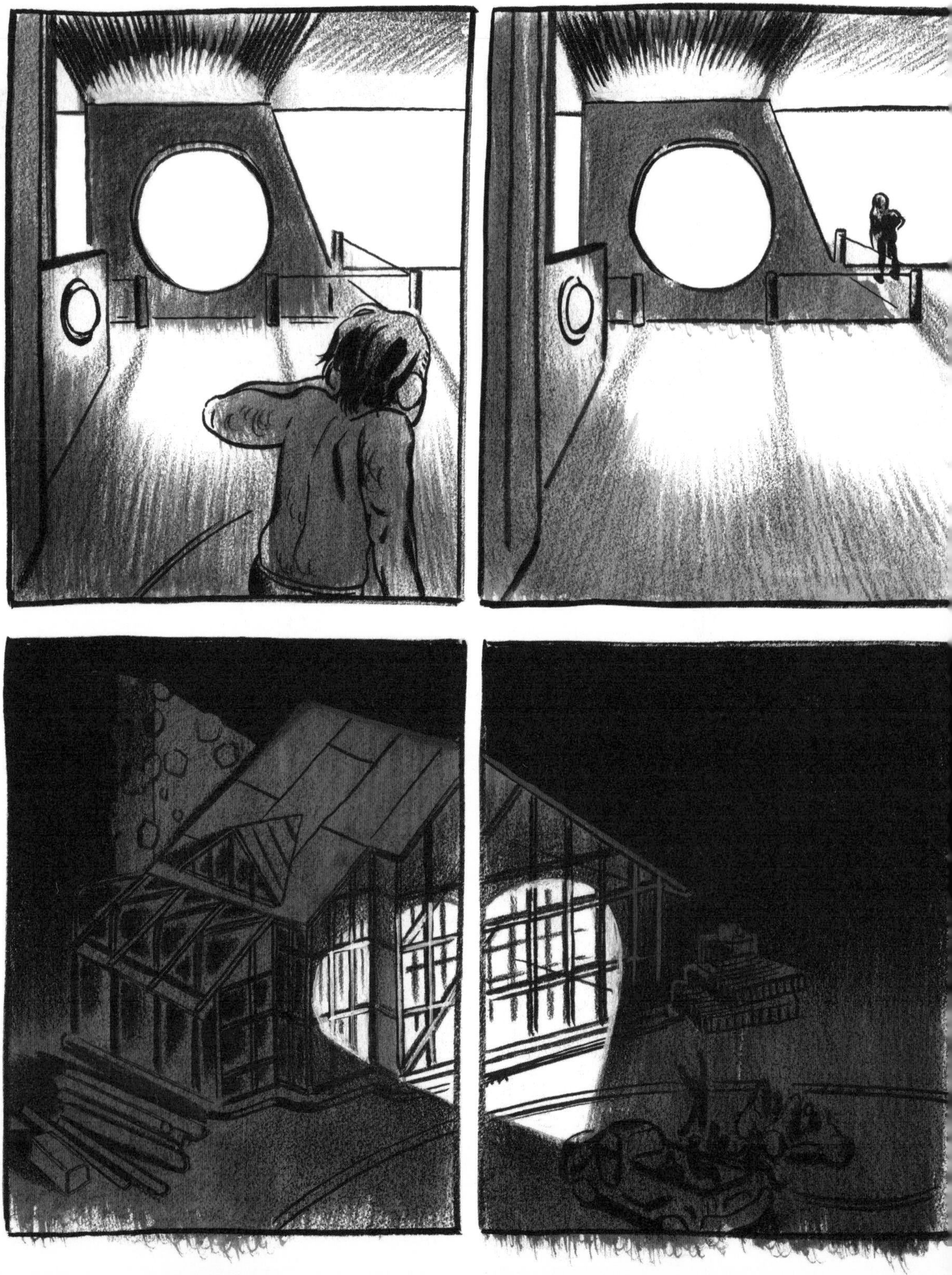

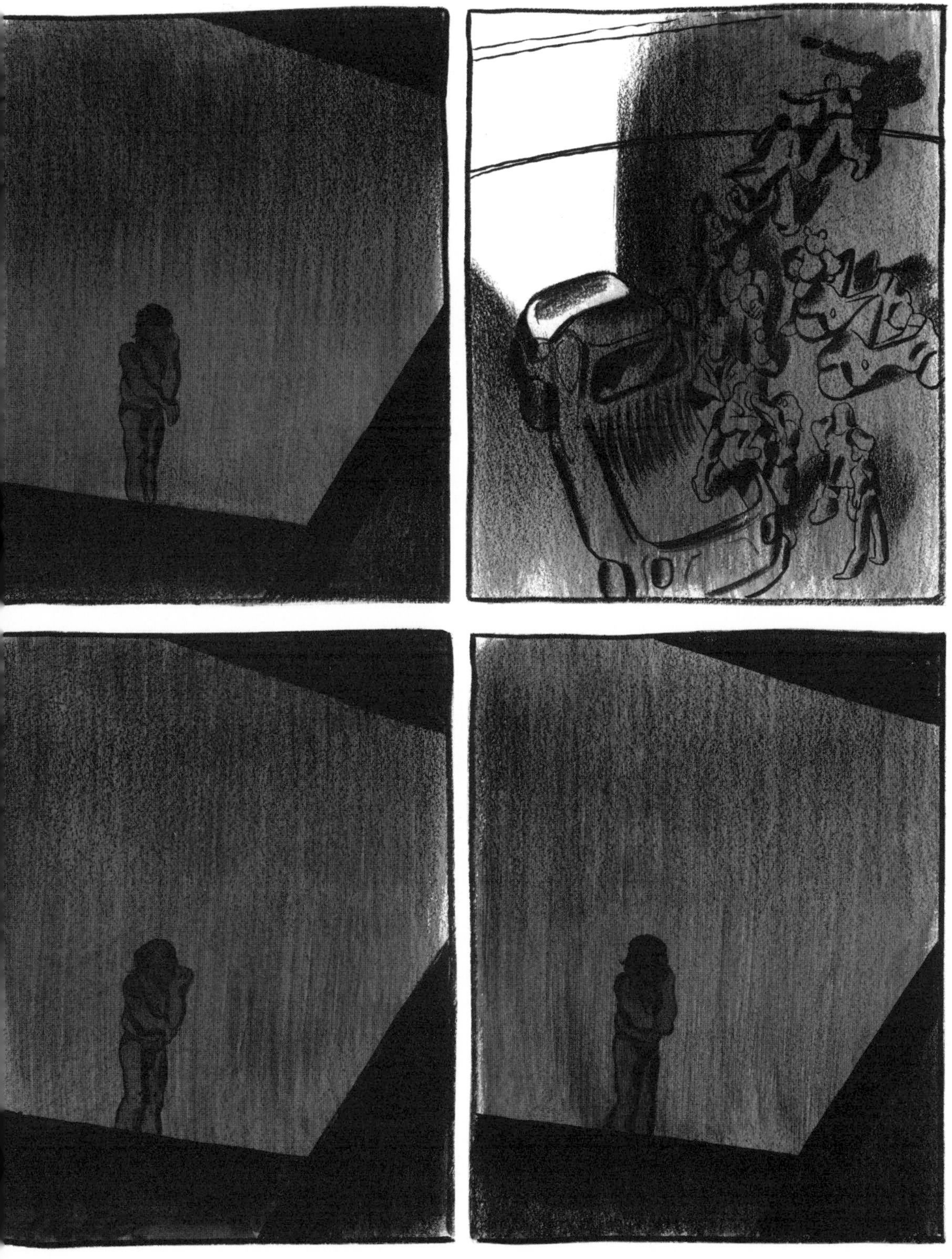

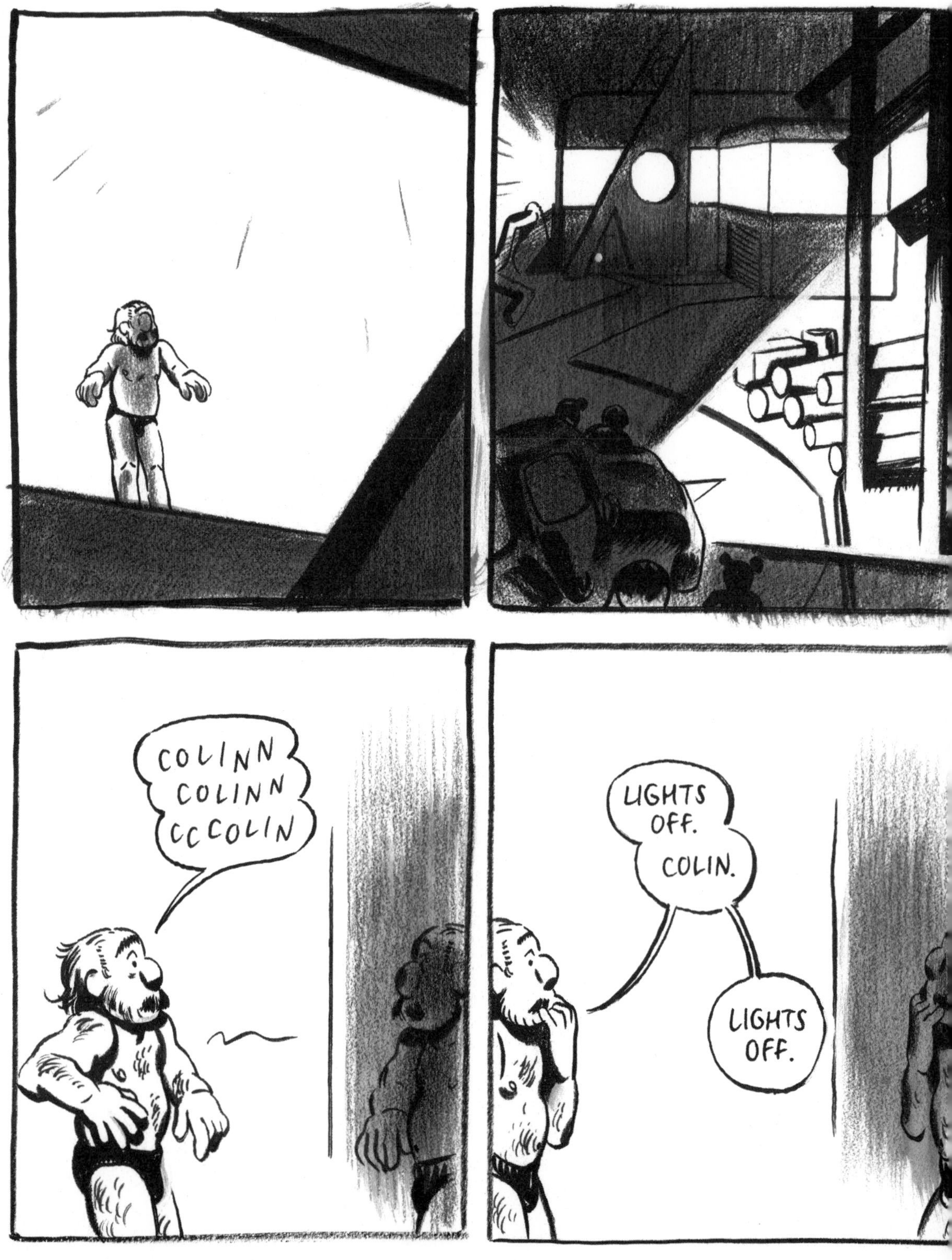
COLINN
COLINN
CCCOLIN
LIGHTS OFF.
COLIN.
LIGHTS OFF.

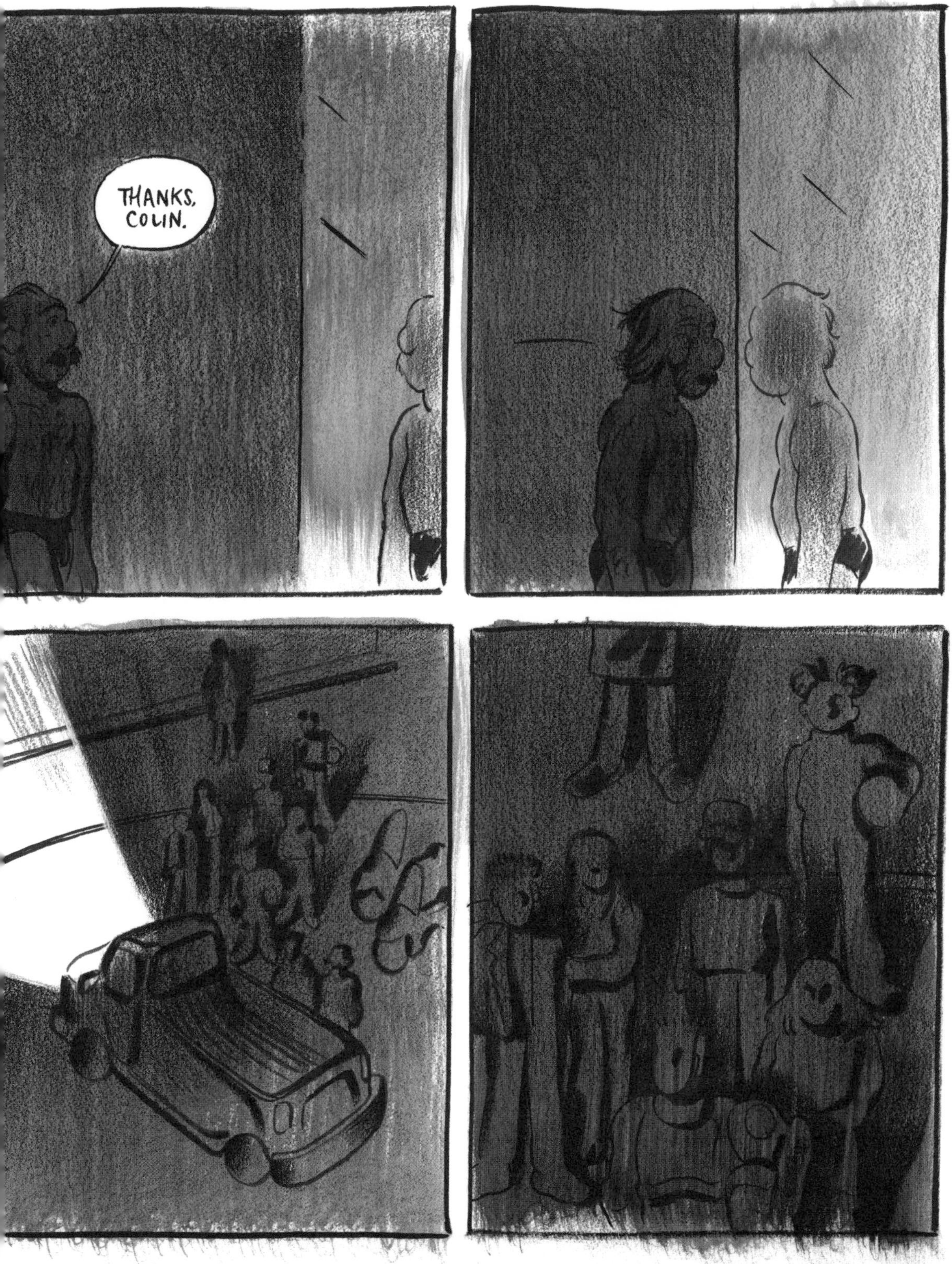
THANKS, COLIN.

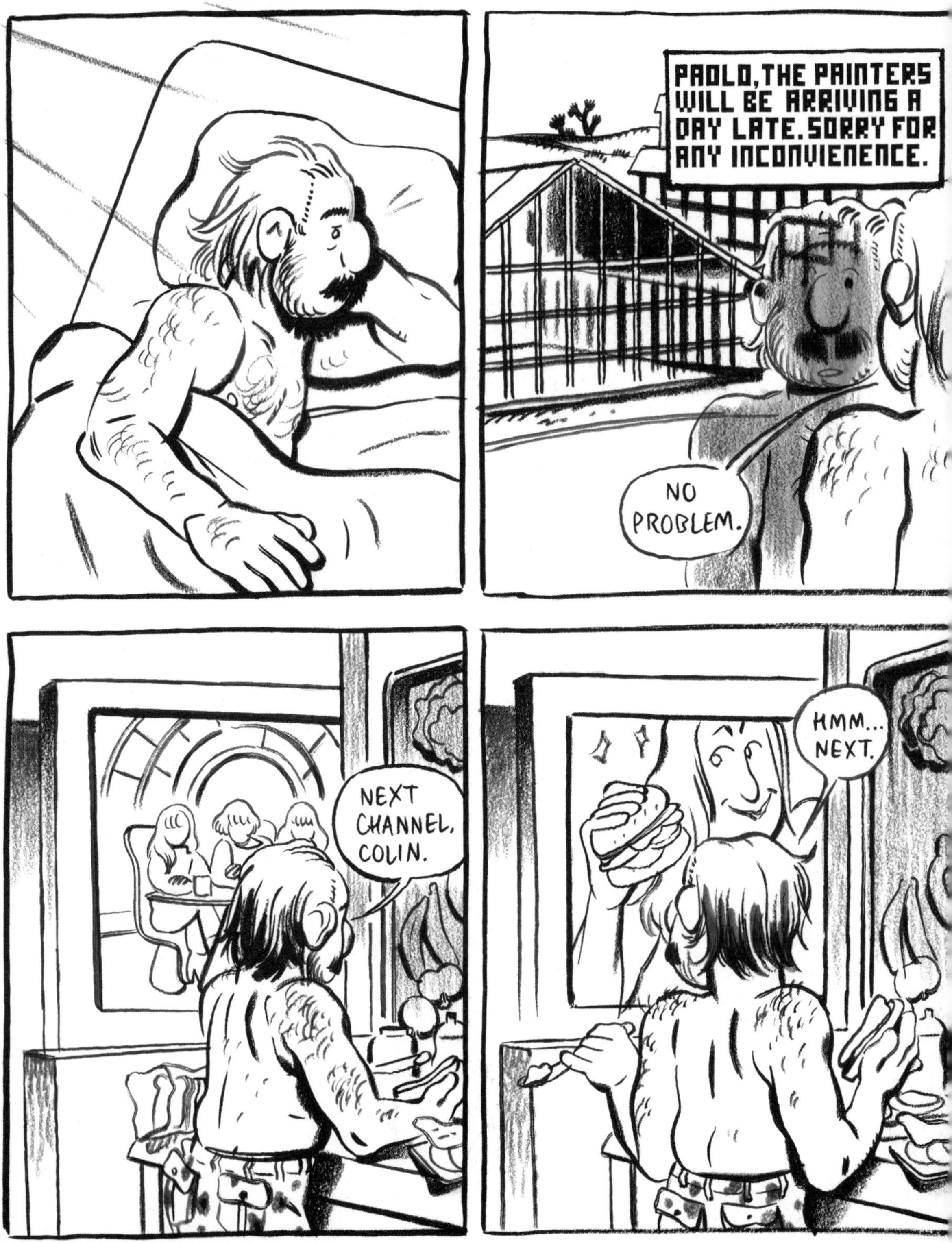
PAOLO, THE PAINTERS WILL BE ARRIVING A DAY LATE. SORRY FOR ANY INCONVIENENCE.
NO PROBLEM.
NEXT CHANNEL, COLIN.
HMM... NEXT.

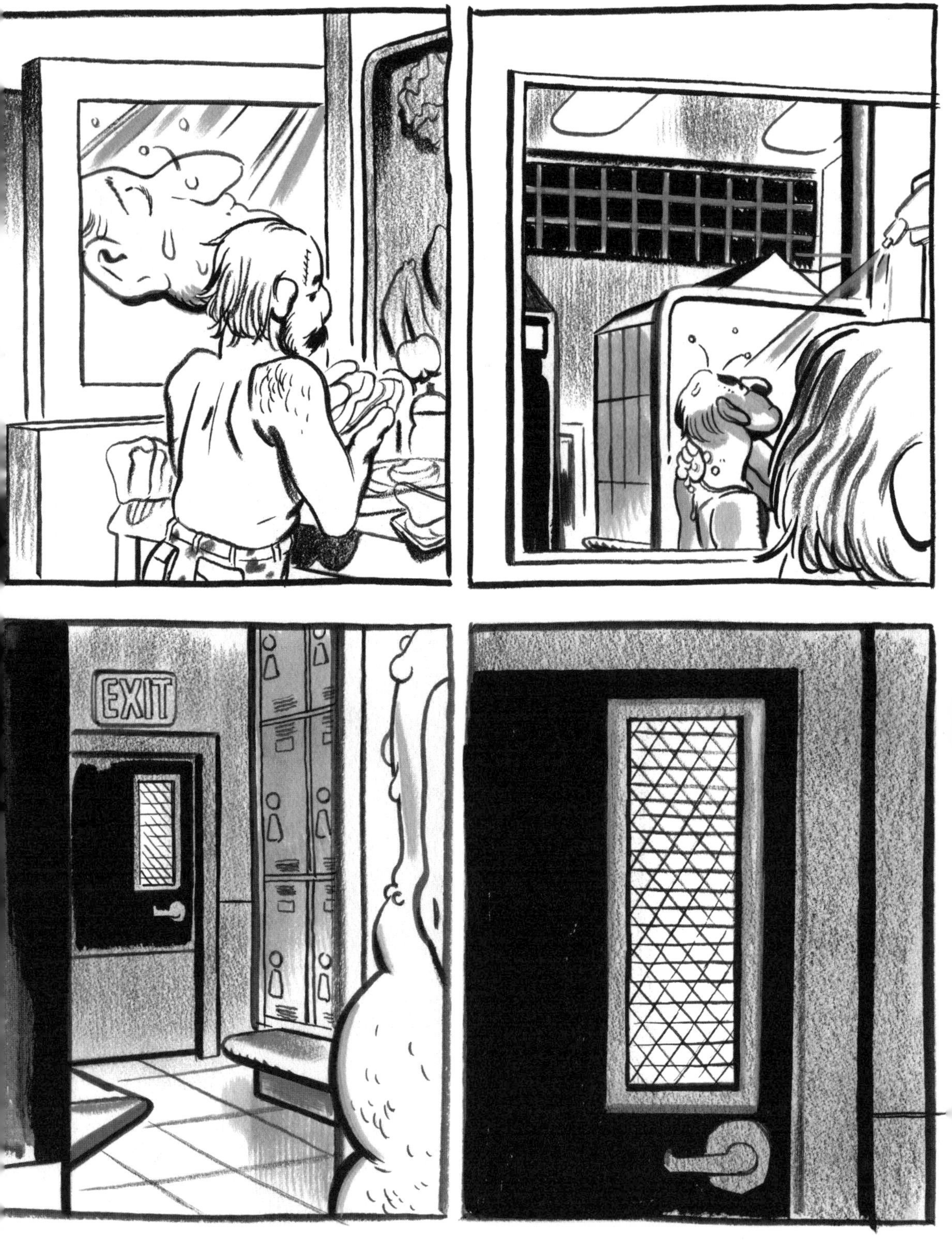
EXIT

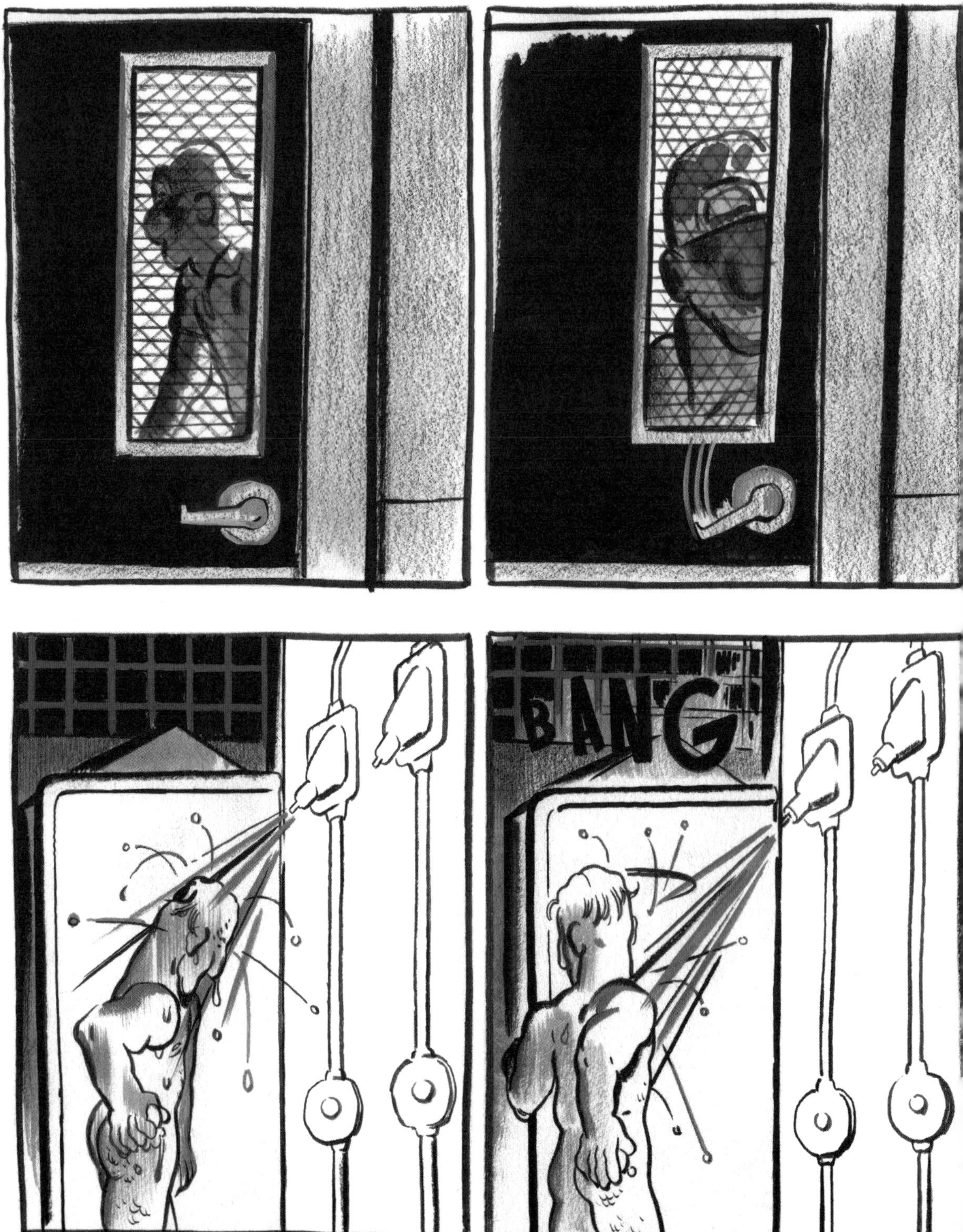
BANG

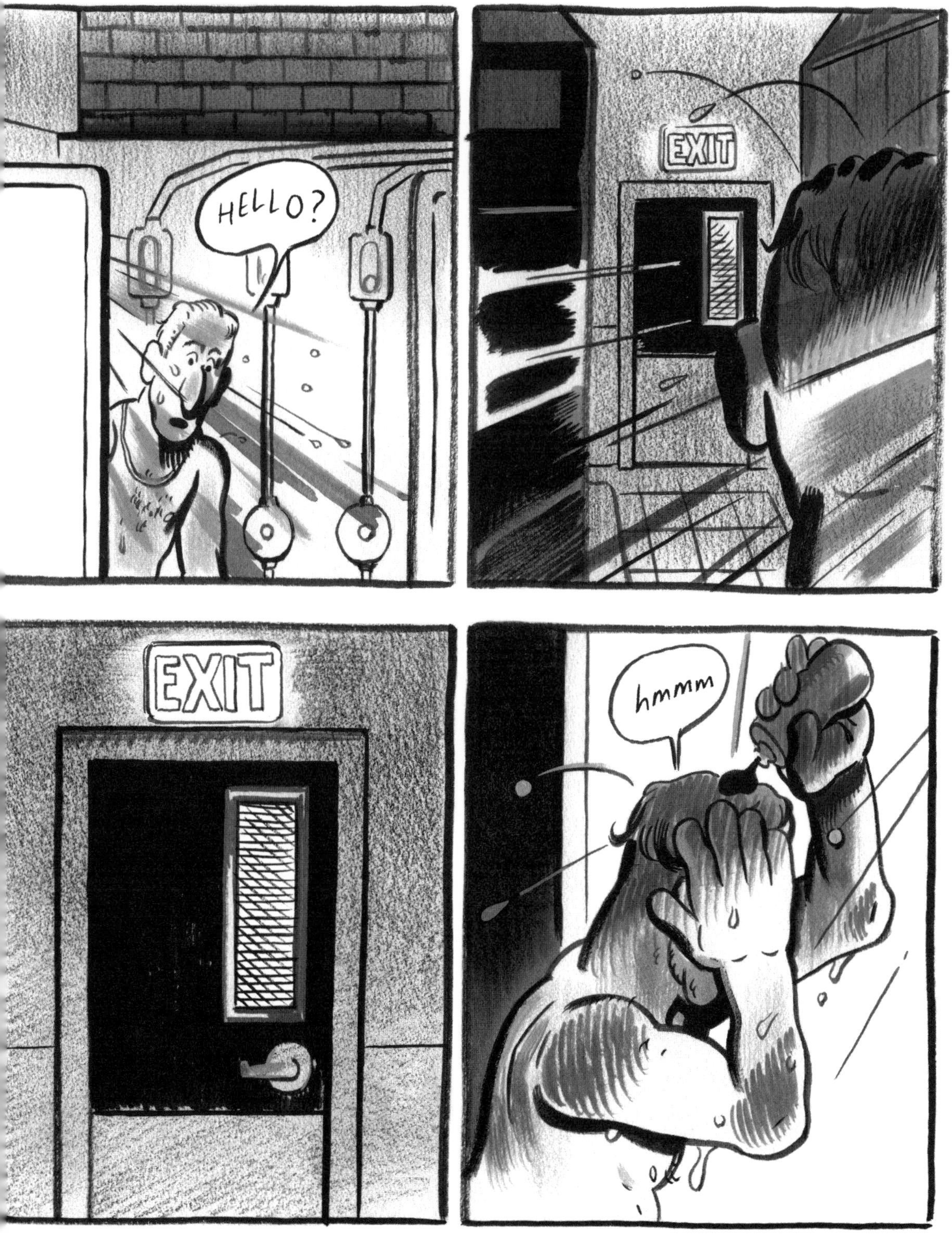
HELLO?
EXIT
EXIT
hmmm

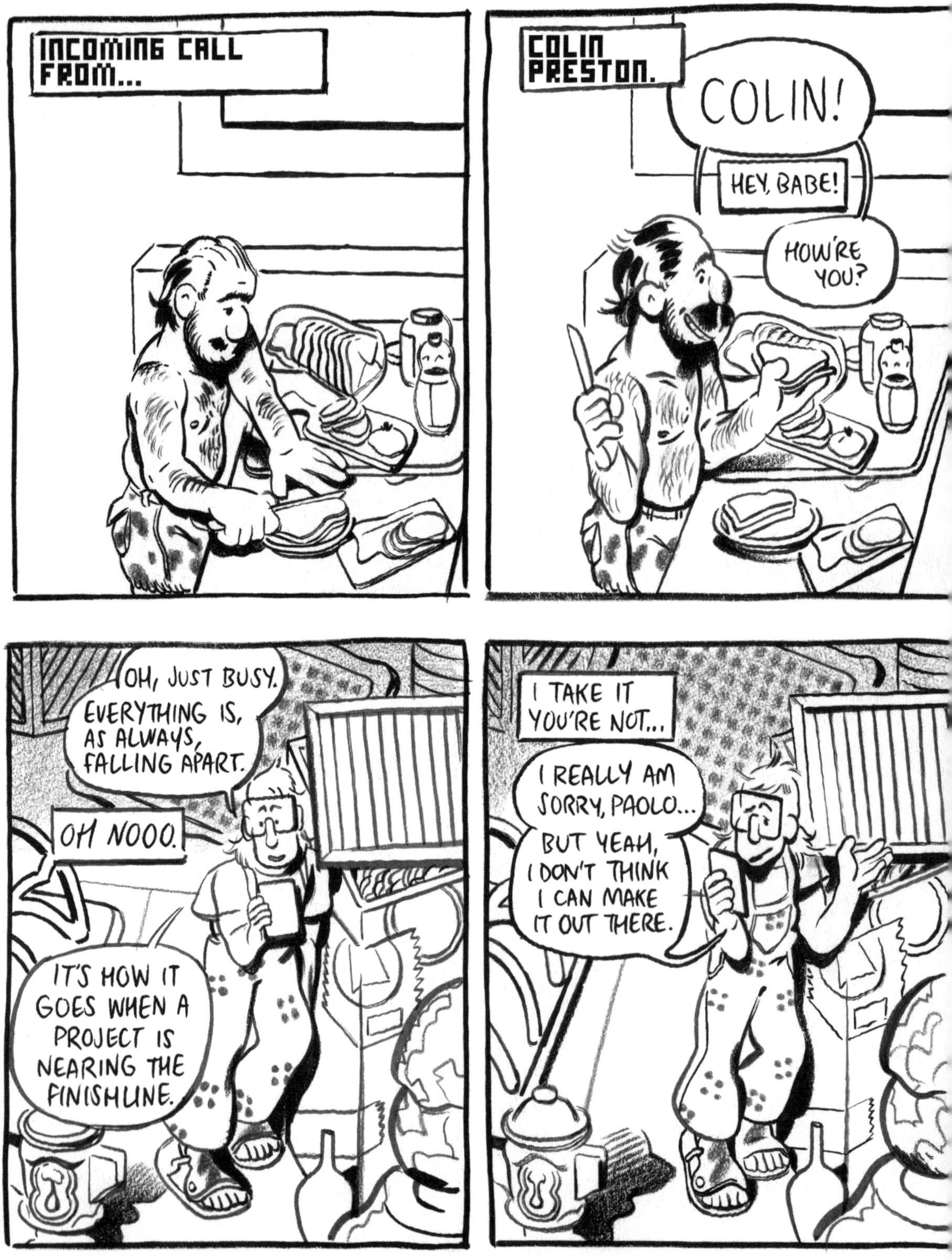
INCOMING CALL FROM...
COLIN PRESTON.
COLIN!
HEY, BABE!
HOW'RE YOU?
OH, JUST BUSY. EVERYTHING IS, AS ALWAYS, FALLING APART.
OH NOOO.
IT'S HOW IT GOES WHEN A PROJECT IS NEARING THE FINISHLINE.
I TAKE IT YOU'RE NOT...
I REALLY AM SORRY, PAOLO...
BUT YEAH, I DON'T THINK I CAN MAKE IT OUT THERE.

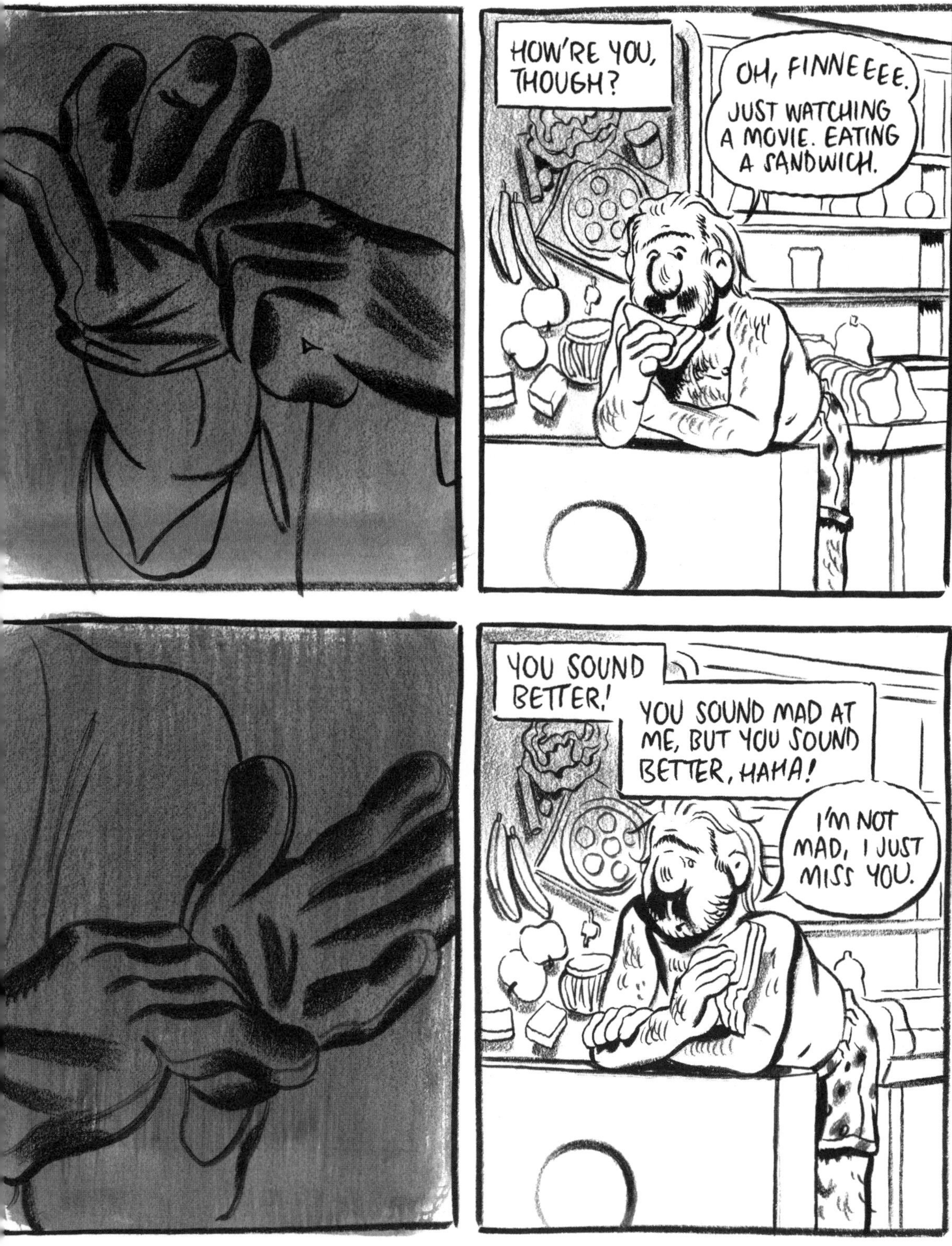
HOW'RE YOU, THOUGH?
OH, FINNEEEEE. JUST WATCHING A MOVIE. EATING A SANDWICH.
YOU SOUND BETTER!
YOU SOUND MAD AT ME, BUT YOU SOUND BETTER, HAHA!
I'M NOT MAD, I JUST MISS YOU.

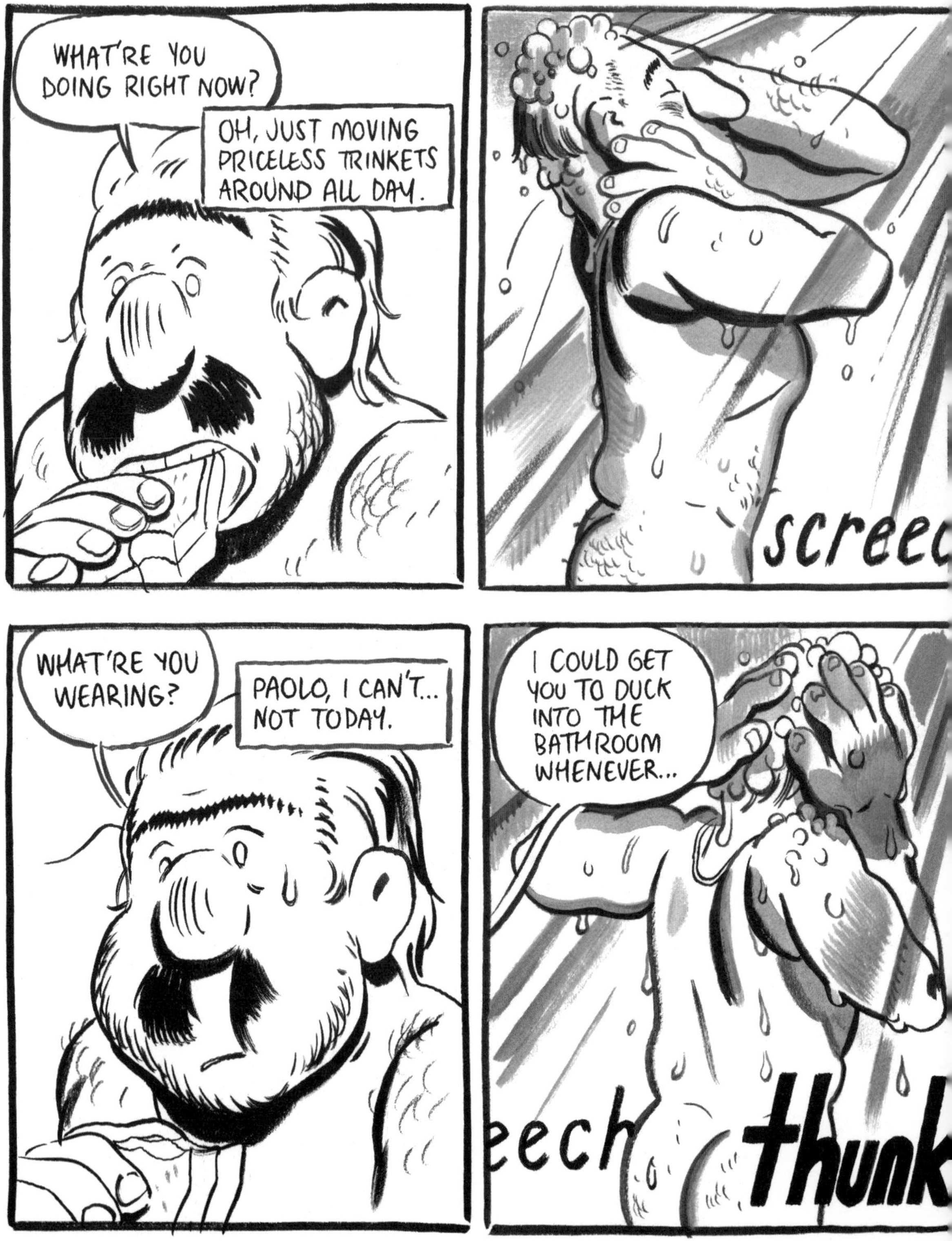
WHAT'RE YOU DOING RIGHT NOW?
OH, JUST MOVING PRICELESS TRINKETS AROUND ALL DAY.
screec
WHAT'RE YOU WEARING?
PAOLO, I CAN'T... NOT TODAY.
I COULD GET YOU TO DUCK INTO THE BATHROOM WHENEVER...
eech
thunk

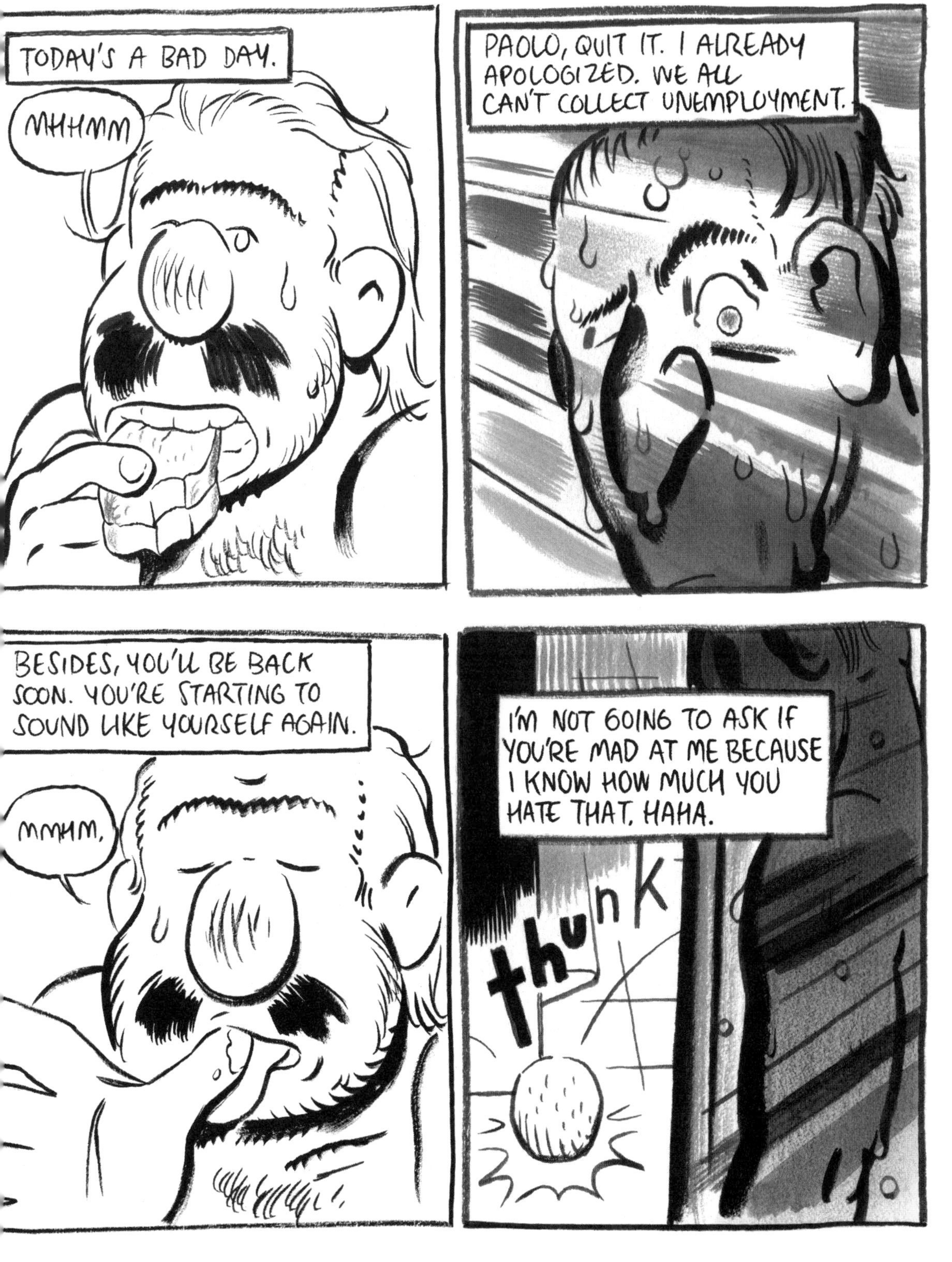
TODAY'S A BAD DAY.
MHHMM
PAOLO, QUIT IT. I ALREADY APOLOGIZED. WE ALL CAN'T COLLECT UNEMPLOYMENT.
BESIDES, YOU'LL BE BACK SOON. YOU'RE STARTING TO SOUND LIKE YOURSELF AGAIN.
MMHM.
I'M NOT GOING TO ASK IF YOU'RE MAD AT ME BECAUSE I KNOW HOW MUCH YOU HATE THAT. HAHA.
thunK

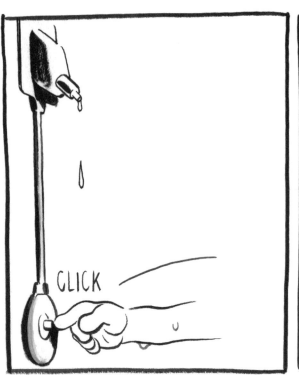

CLICK

I HAVE TO GO BUT WE'LL TALK SOON.

DRIP
DRIP

GASP!

CLACKITA

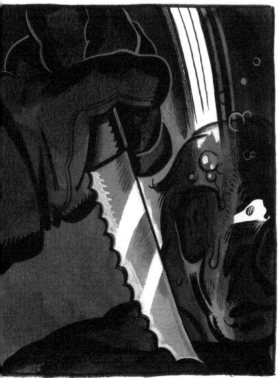

PAOLO?

YEAH YEAH.

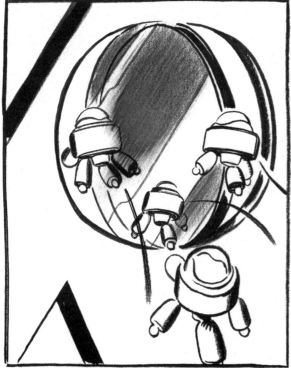

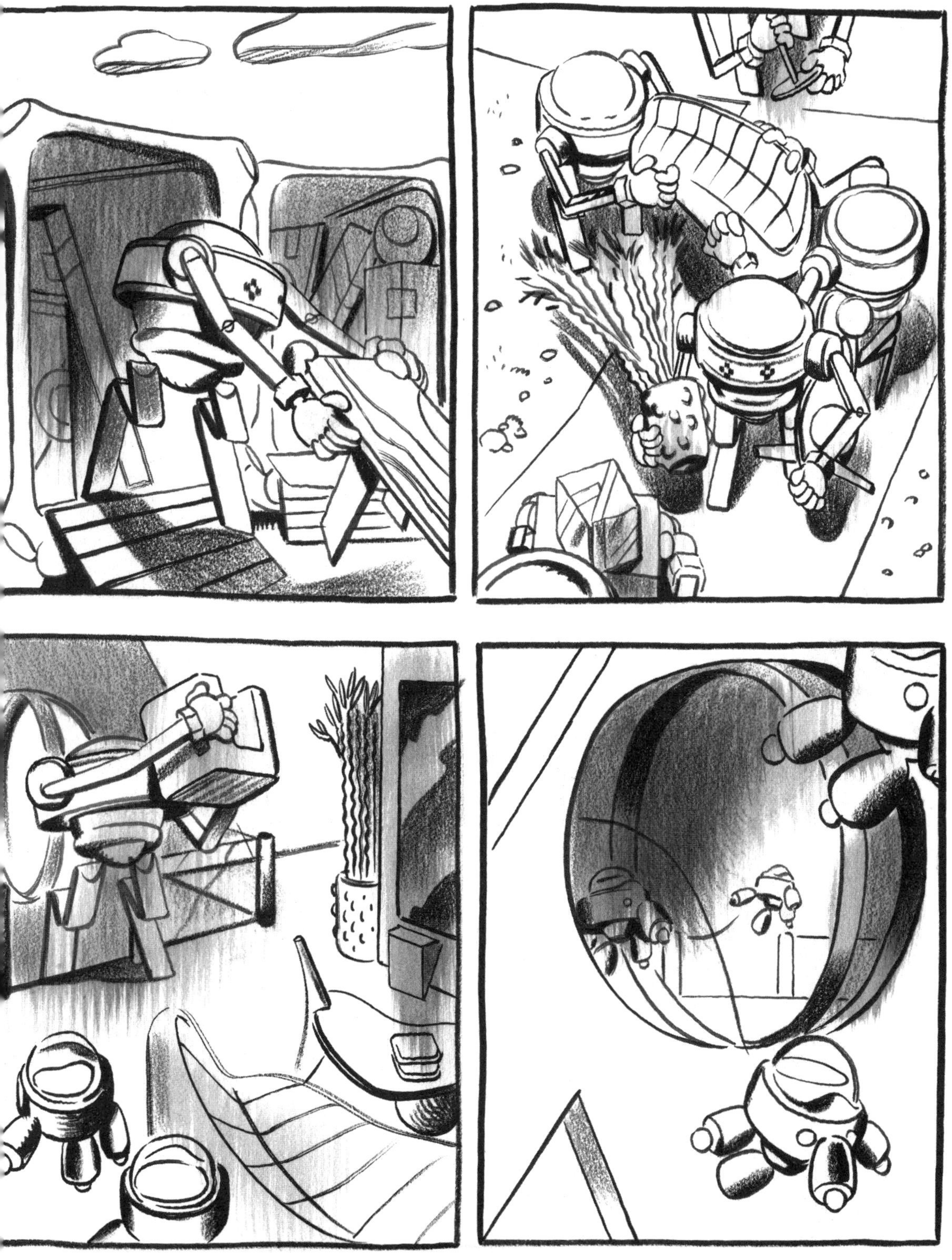

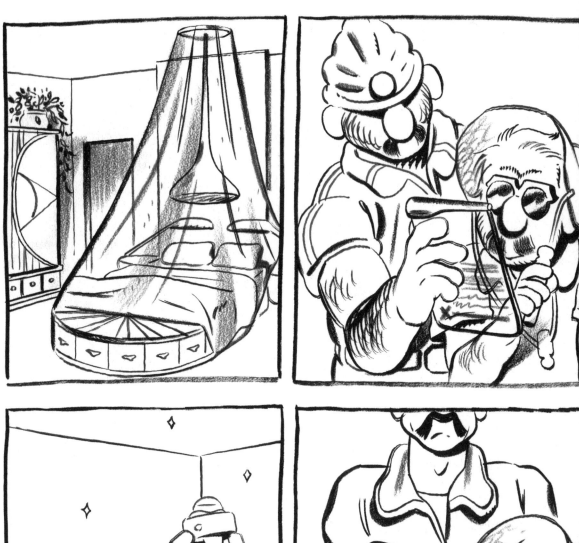

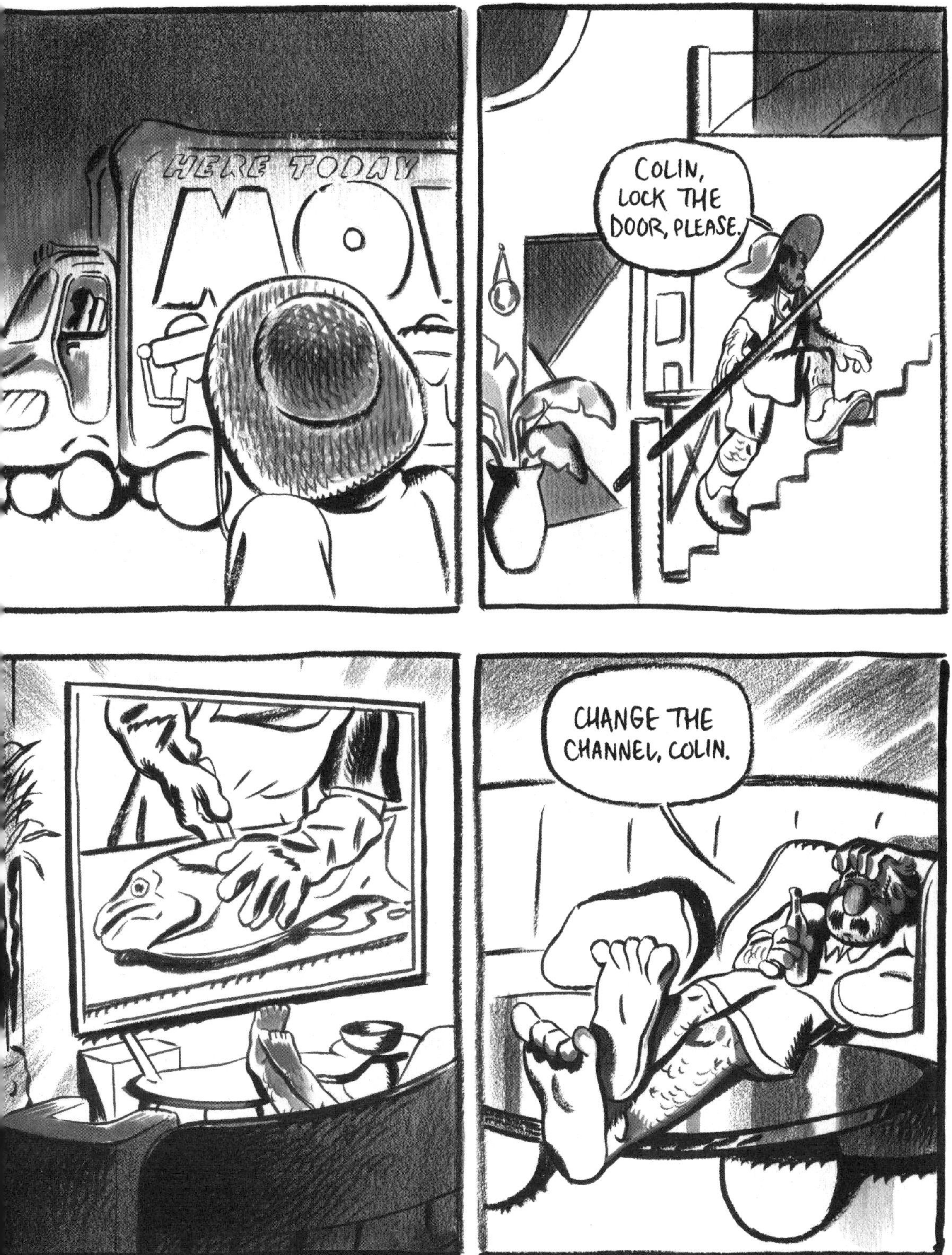
HERE TODAY
COLIN, LOCK THE DOOR, PLEASE.
CHANGE THE CHANNEL, COLIN.

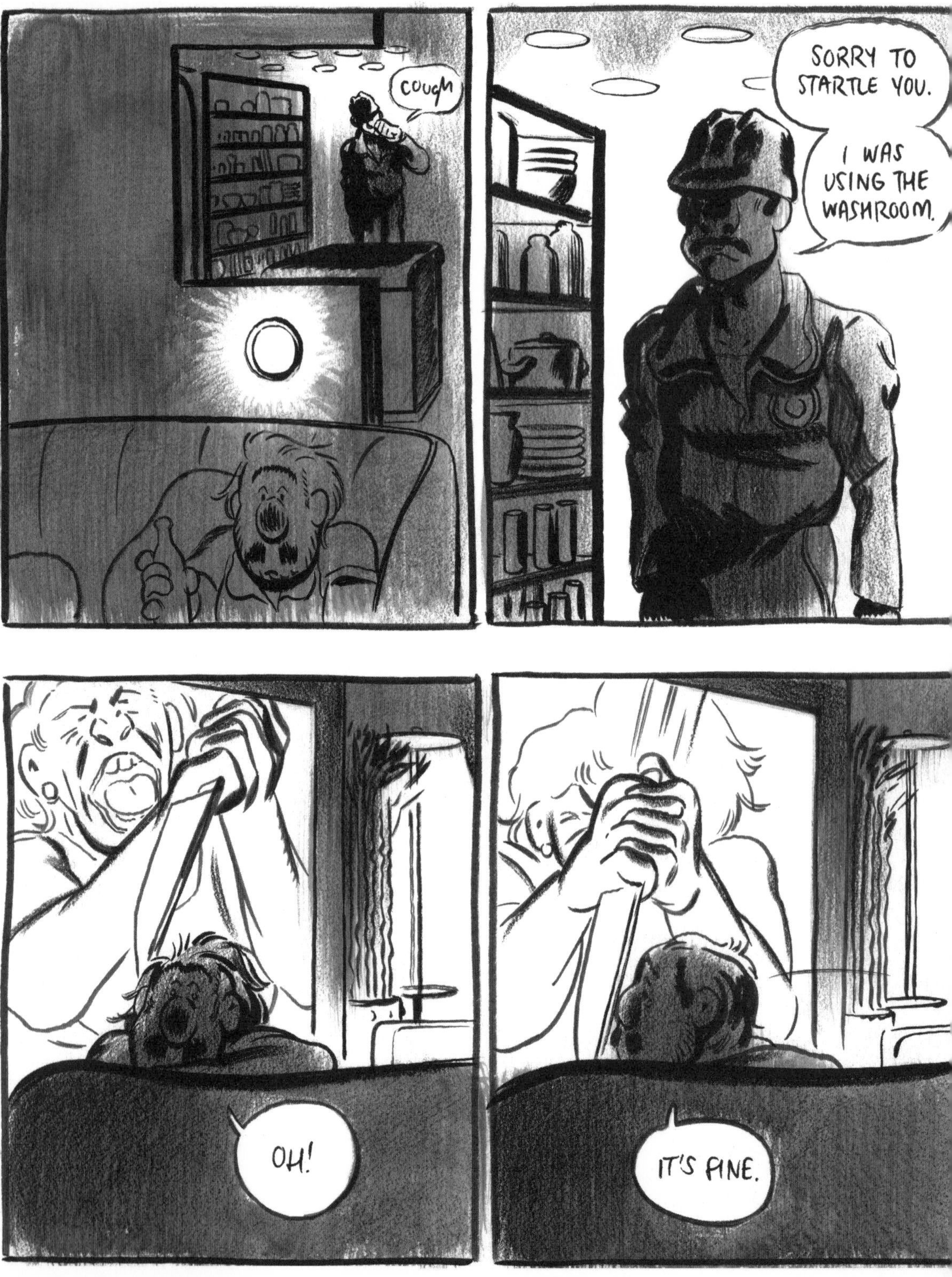
cough
SORRY TO STARTLE YOU.
I WAS USING THE WASHROOM.
OH!
IT'S FINE.

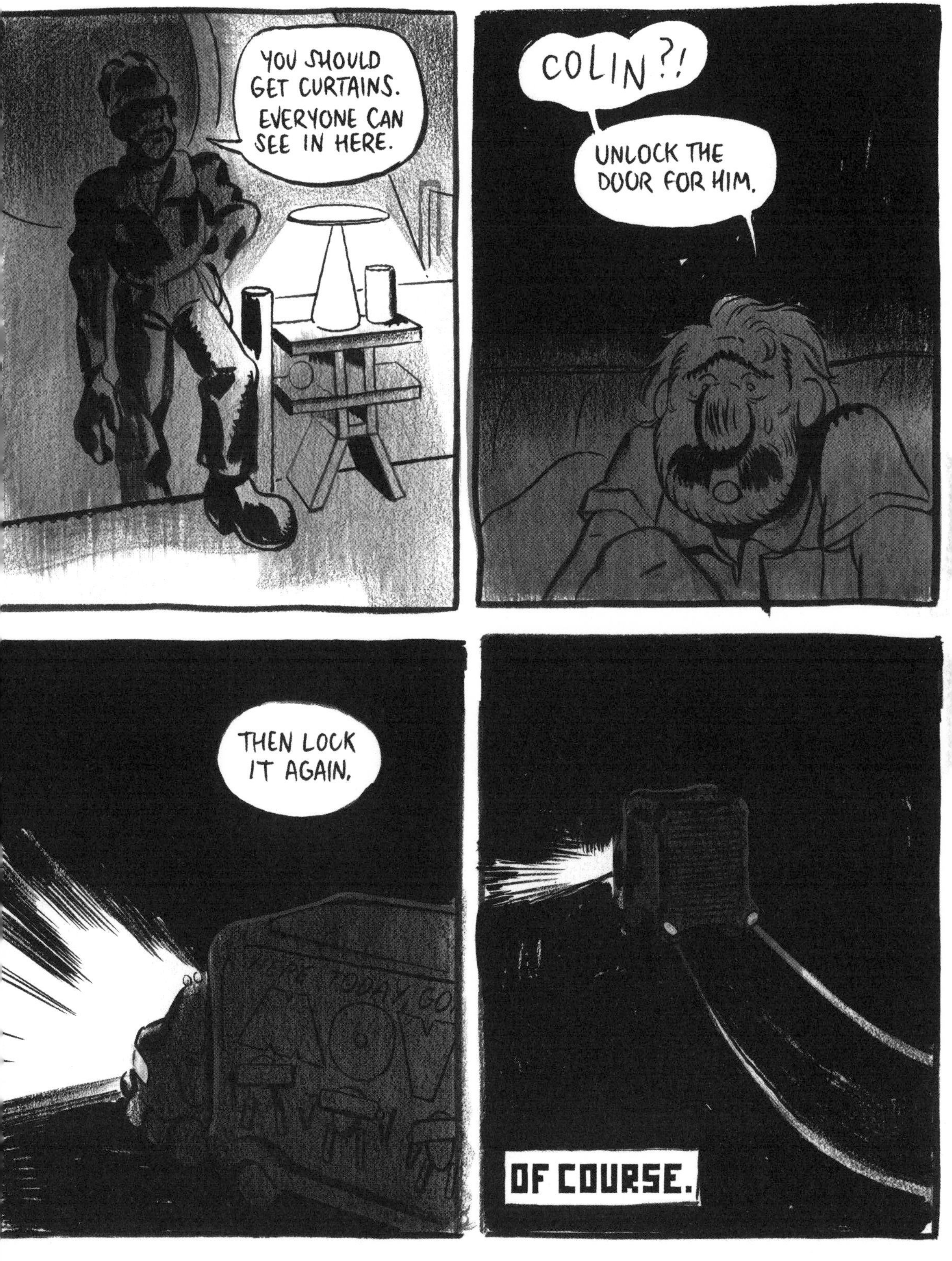
YOU SHOULD GET CURTAINS. EVERYONE CAN SEE IN HERE.
COLIN?!
UNLOCK THE DOOR FOR HIM.
THEN LOCK IT AGAIN.
OF COURSE.

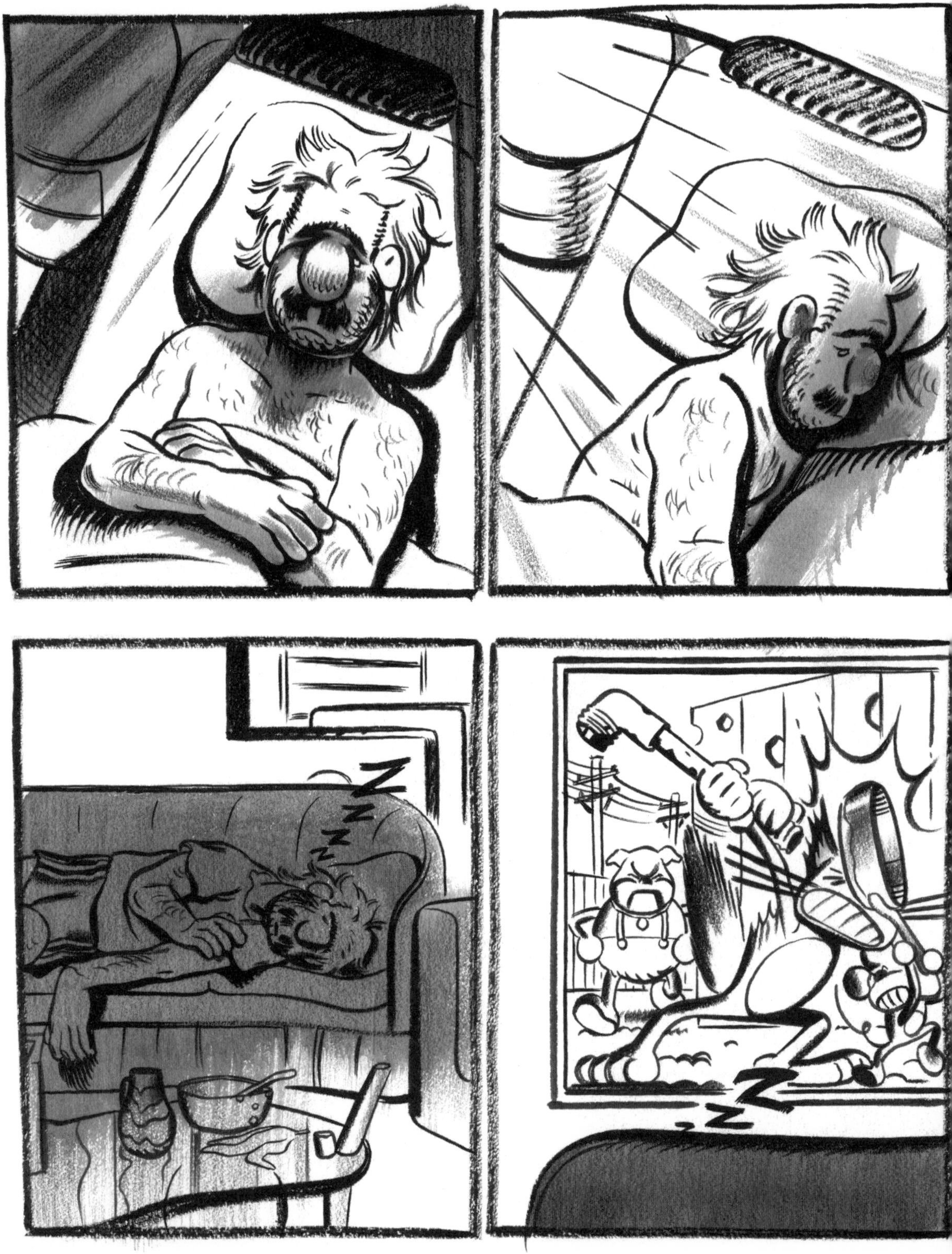

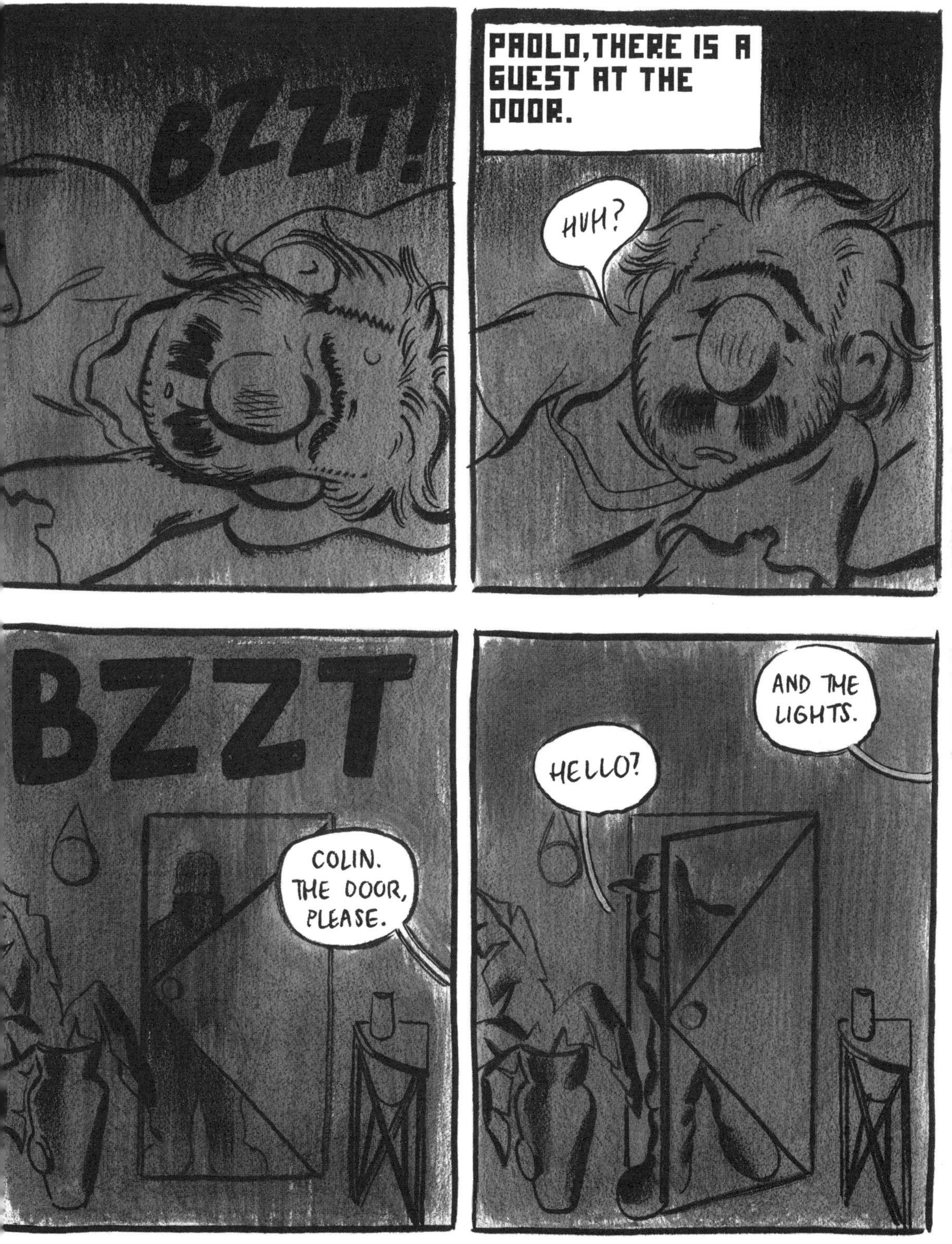
BZZT!
PAOLO, THERE IS A GUEST AT THE DOOR.
HUH?
BZZT
COLIN. THE DOOR, PLEASE.
HELLO?
AND THE LIGHTS.

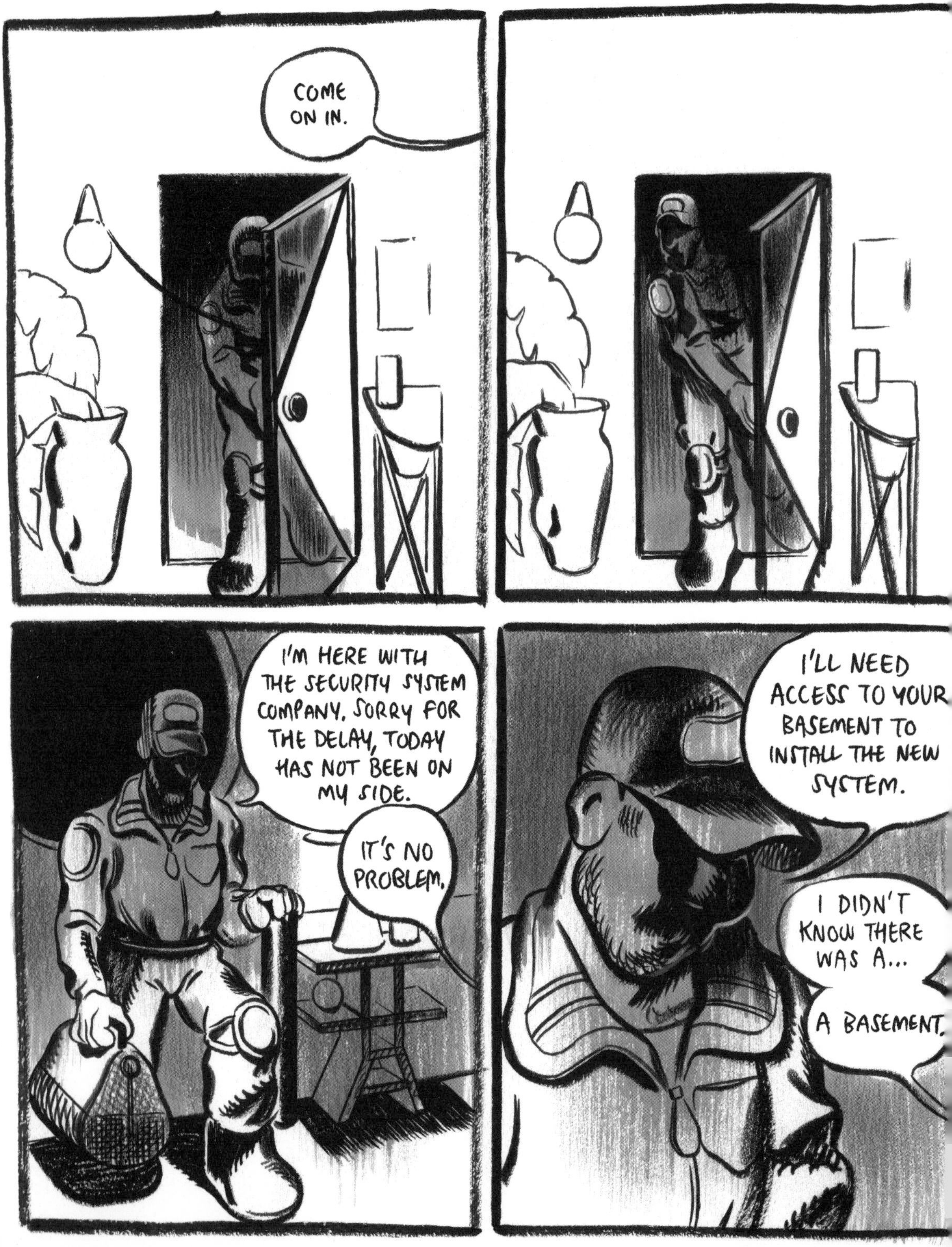
COME ON IN.
I'M HERE WITH THE SECURITY SYSTEM COMPANY. SORRY FOR THE DELAY, TODAY HAS NOT BEEN ON MY SIDE.
IT'S NO PROBLEM.
I'LL NEED ACCESS TO YOUR BASEMENT TO INSTALL THE NEW SYSTEM.
I DIDN'T KNOW THERE WAS A...
A BASEMENT.

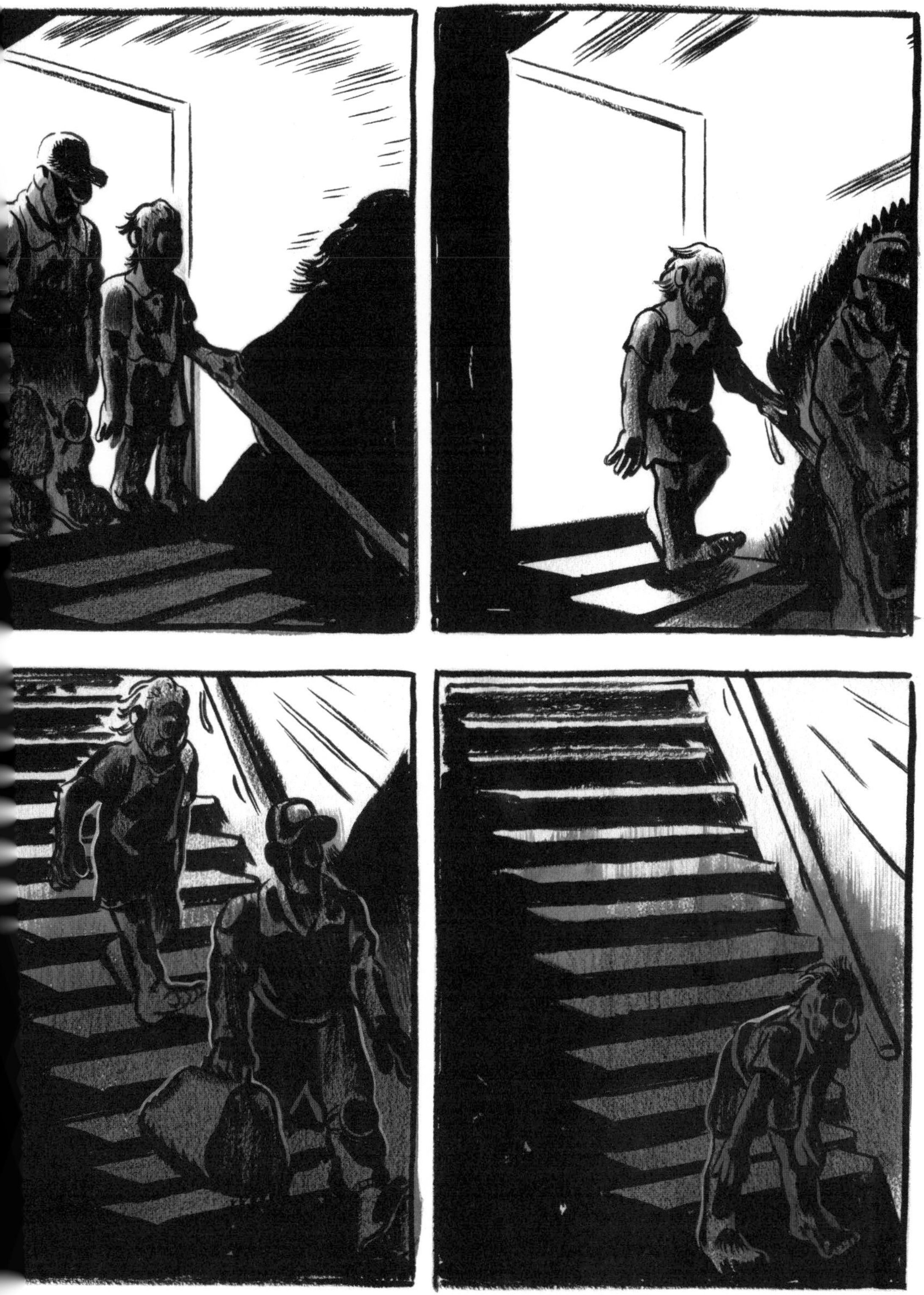

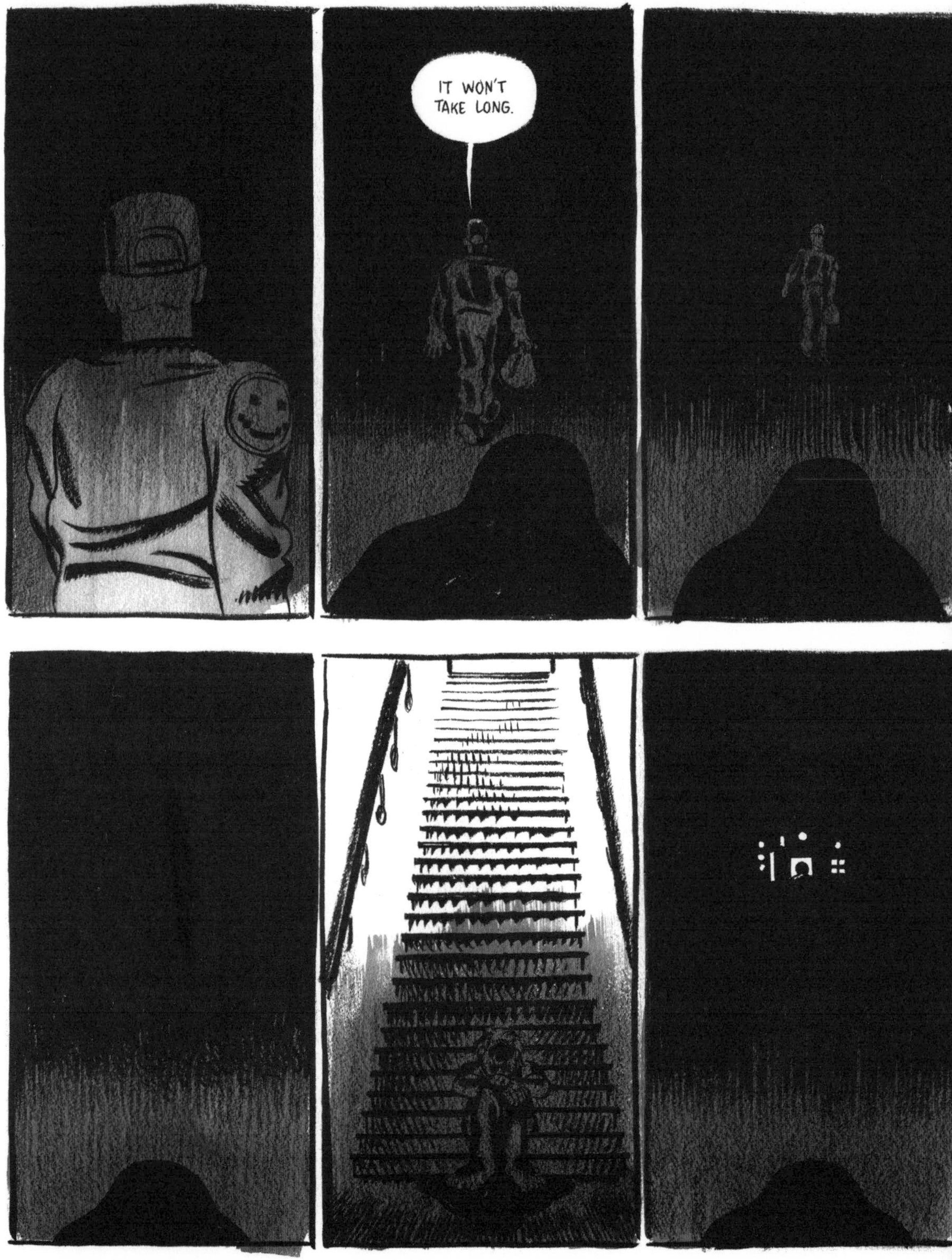
IT WON'T TAKE LONG.

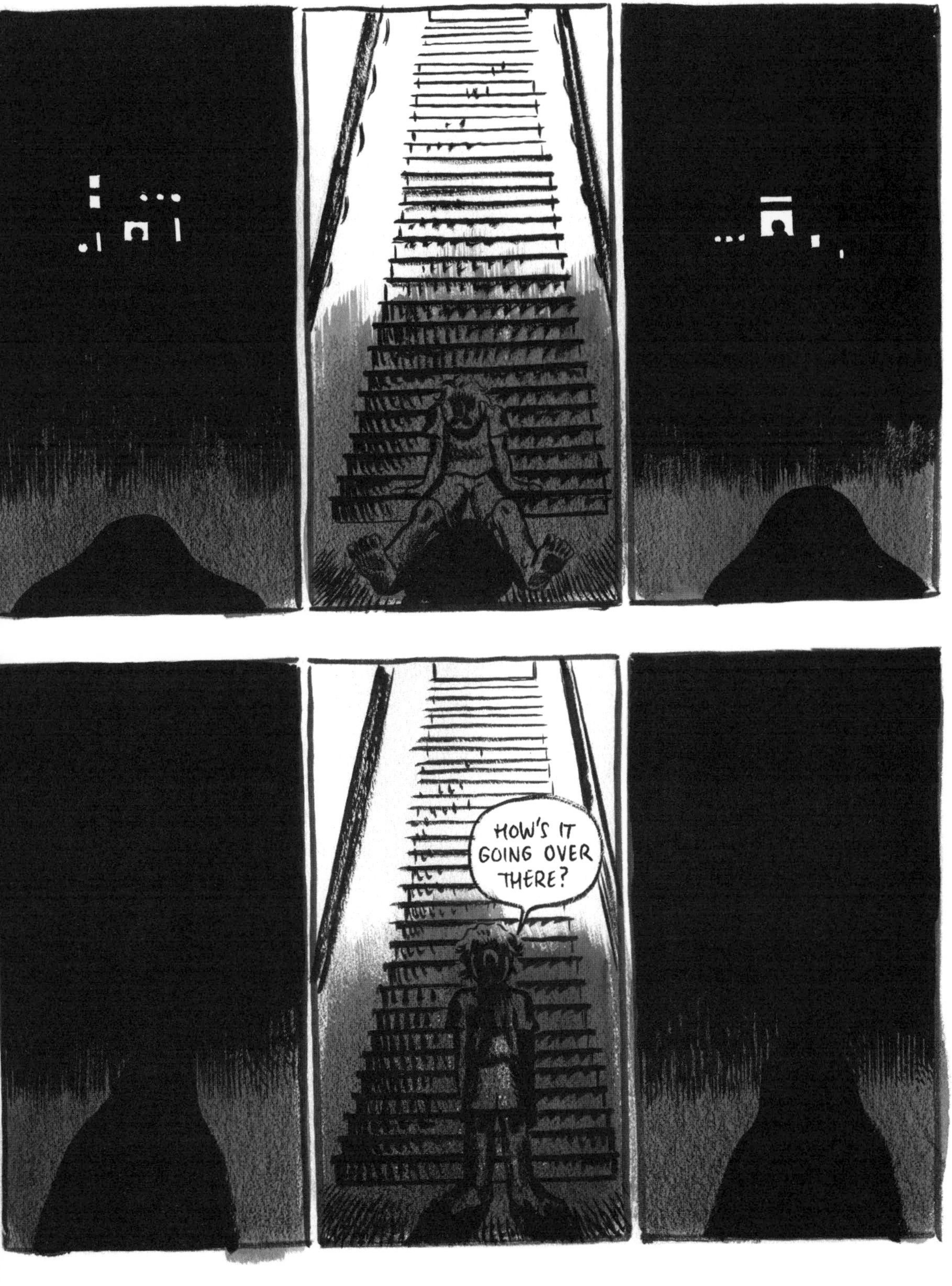
HOW'S IT GOING OVER THERE?

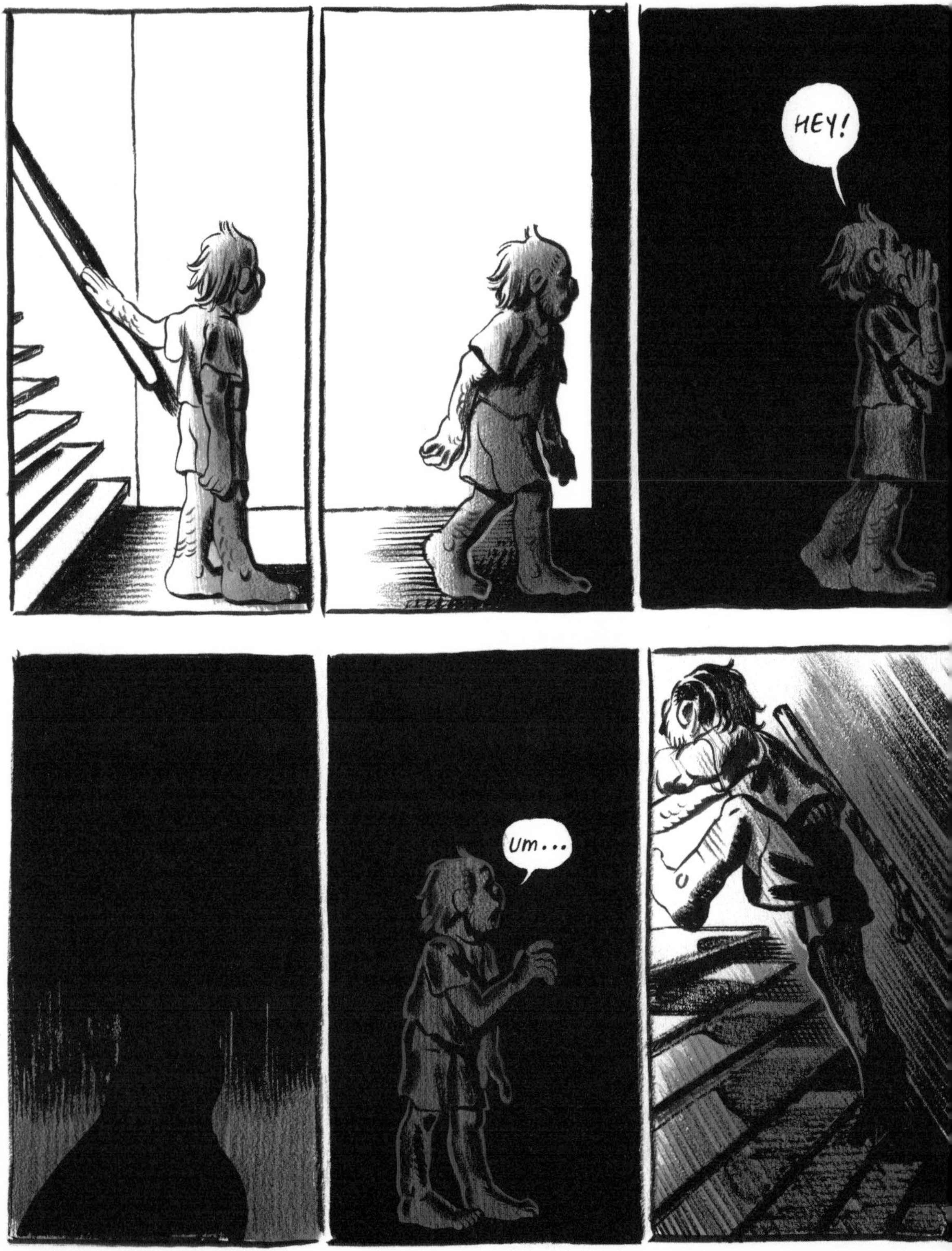
HEY!
UM...

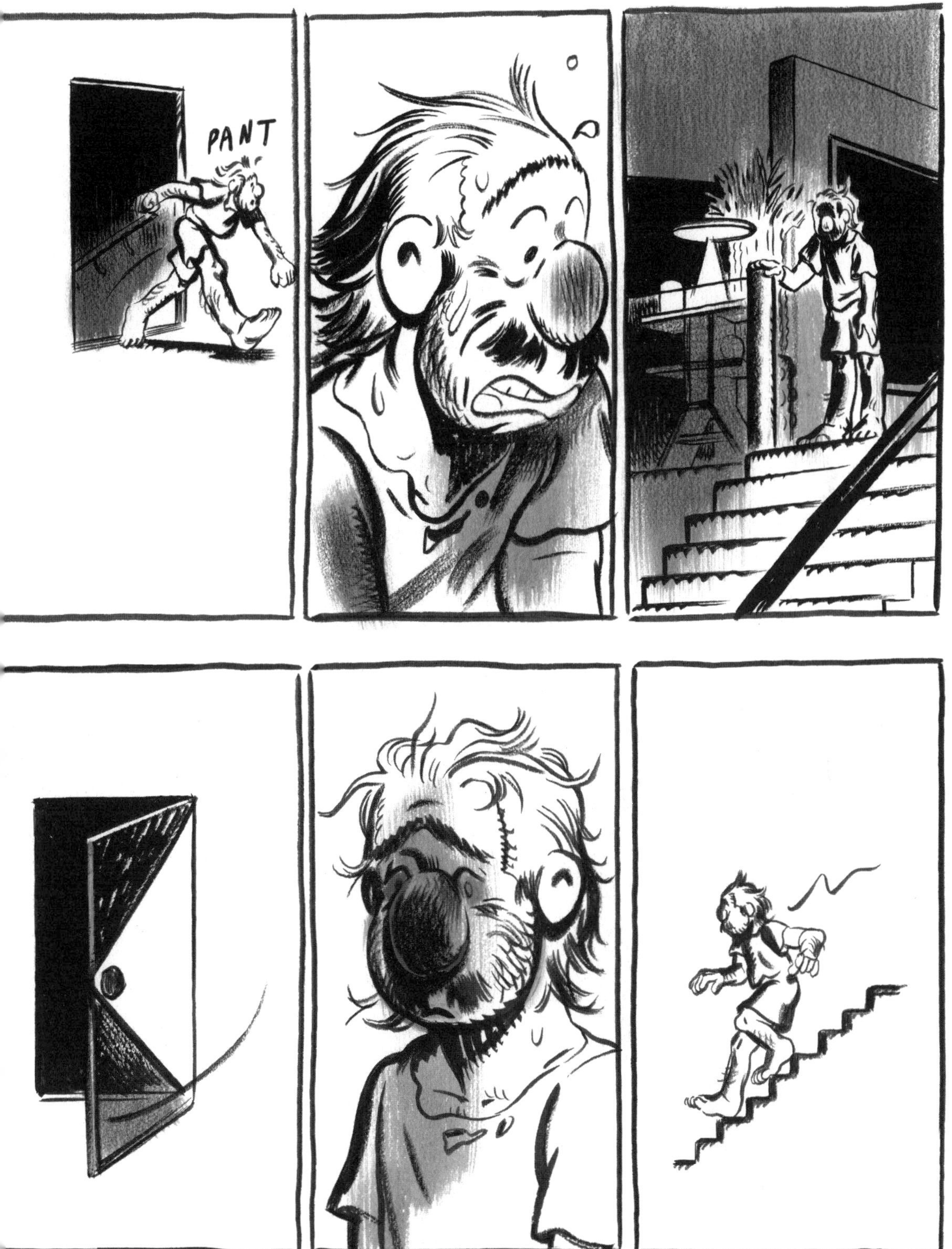
PANT

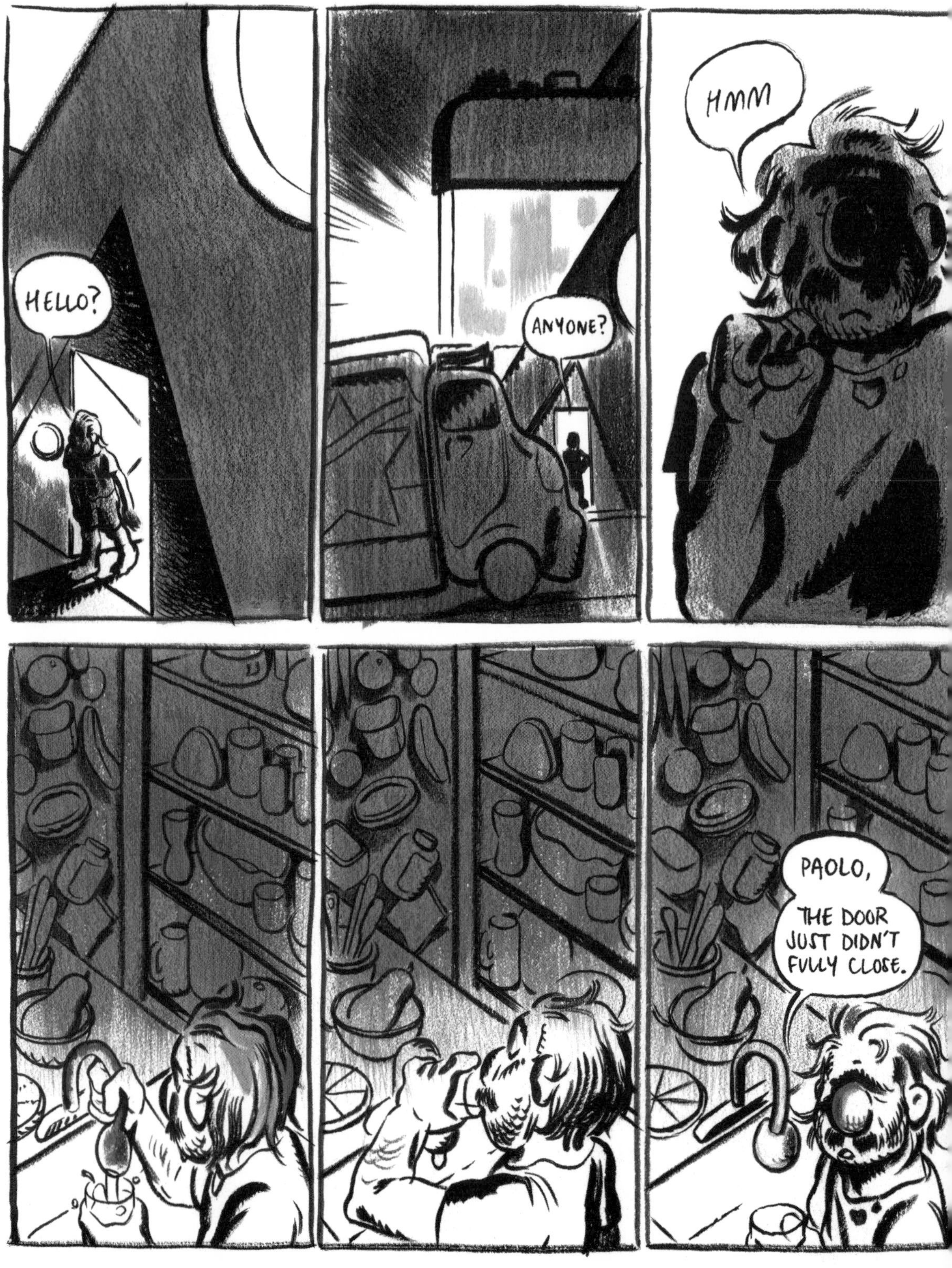
HELLO?
ANYONE?
HMM
PAOLO,
THE DOOR JUST DIDN'T FULLY CLOSE.

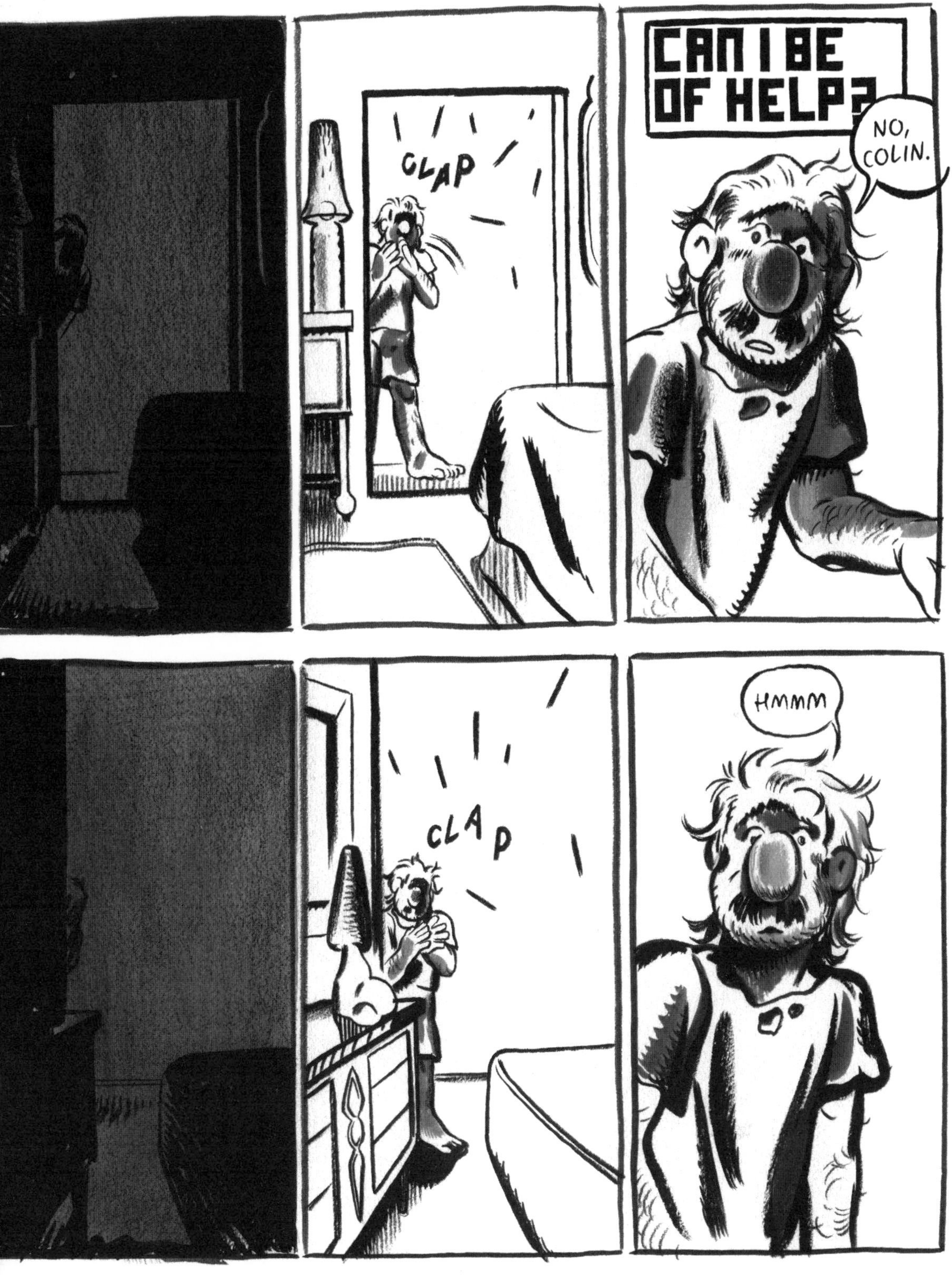
CLAP
CAN I BE OF HELP?
NO, COLIN.
CLAP
HMMM

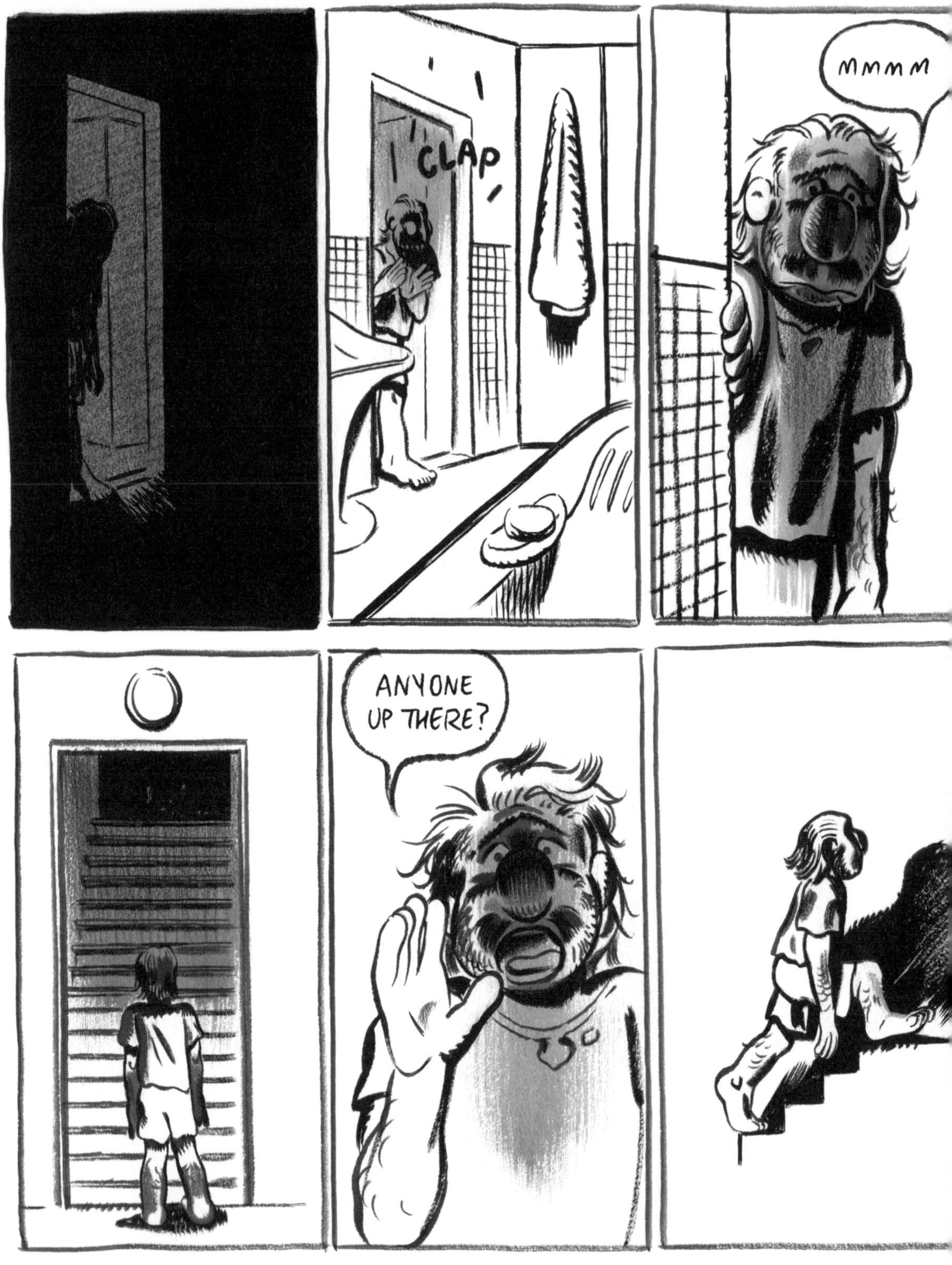
CLAP
MMMM
ANYONE UP THERE?

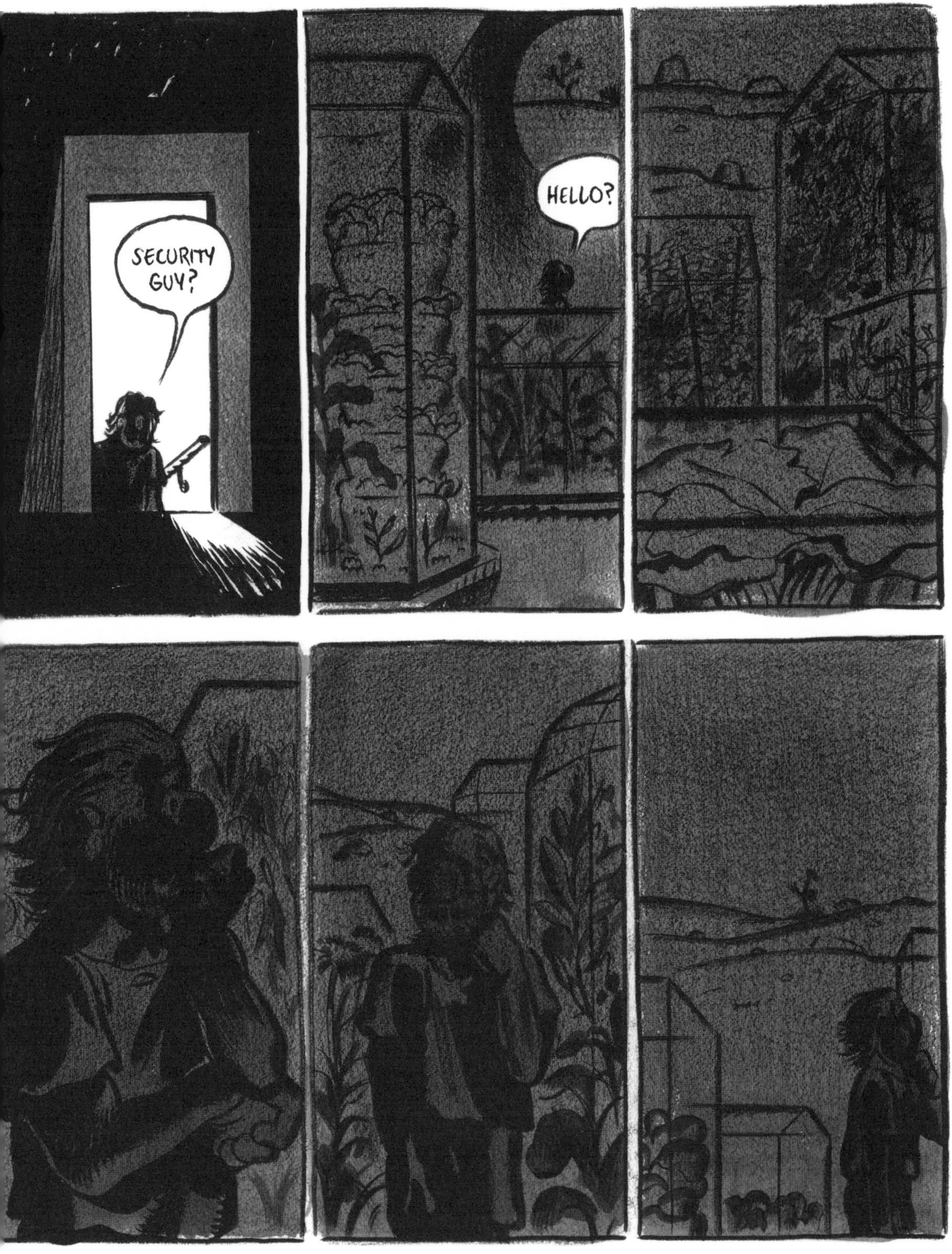
SECURITY GUY?
HELLO?

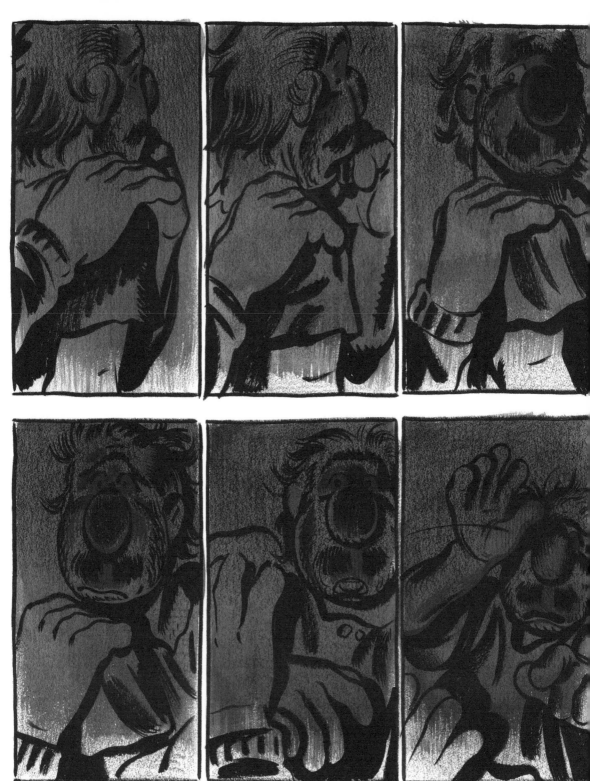

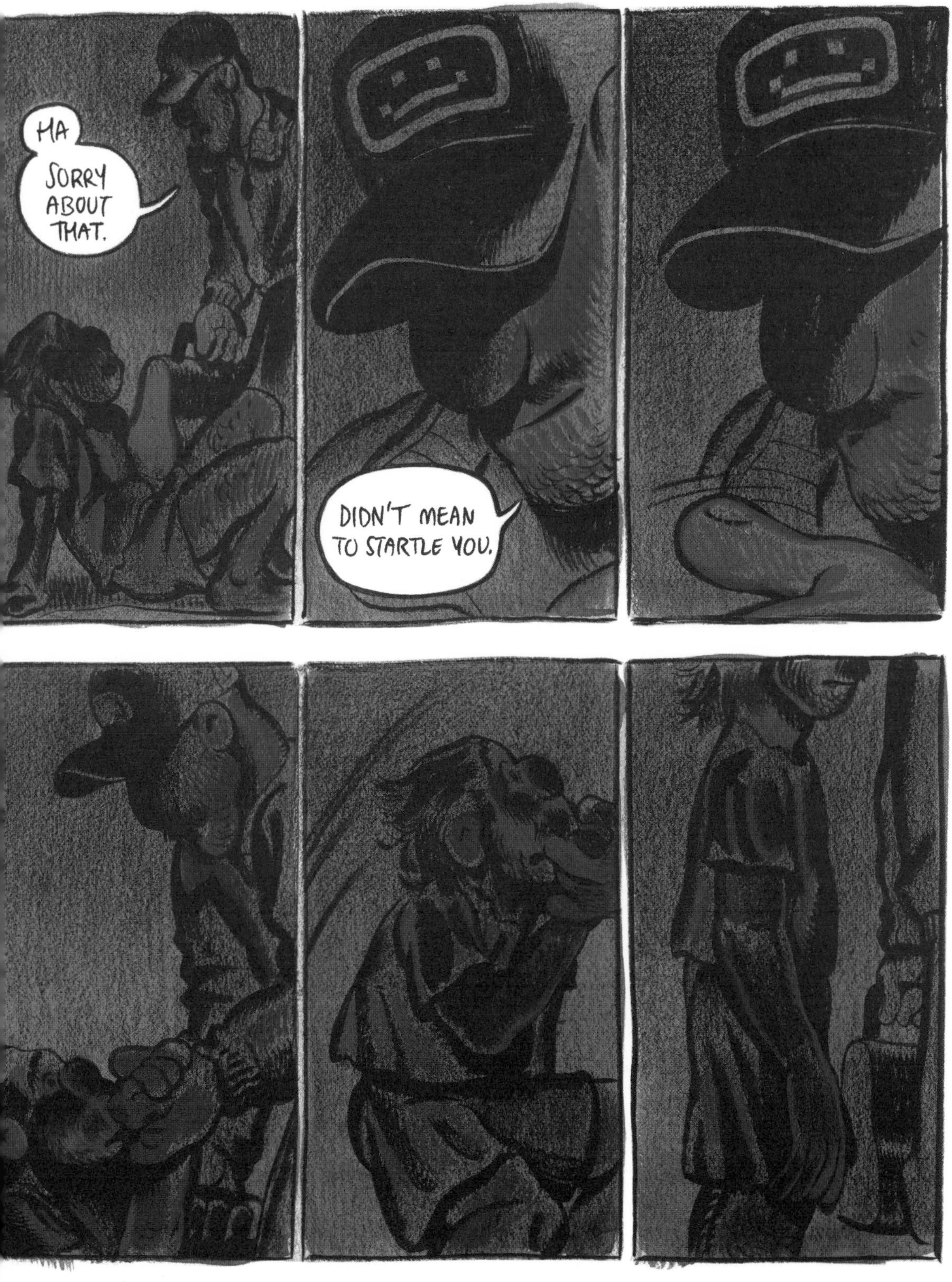
HA
SORRY ABOUT THAT.
DIDN'T MEAN TO STARTLE YOU.

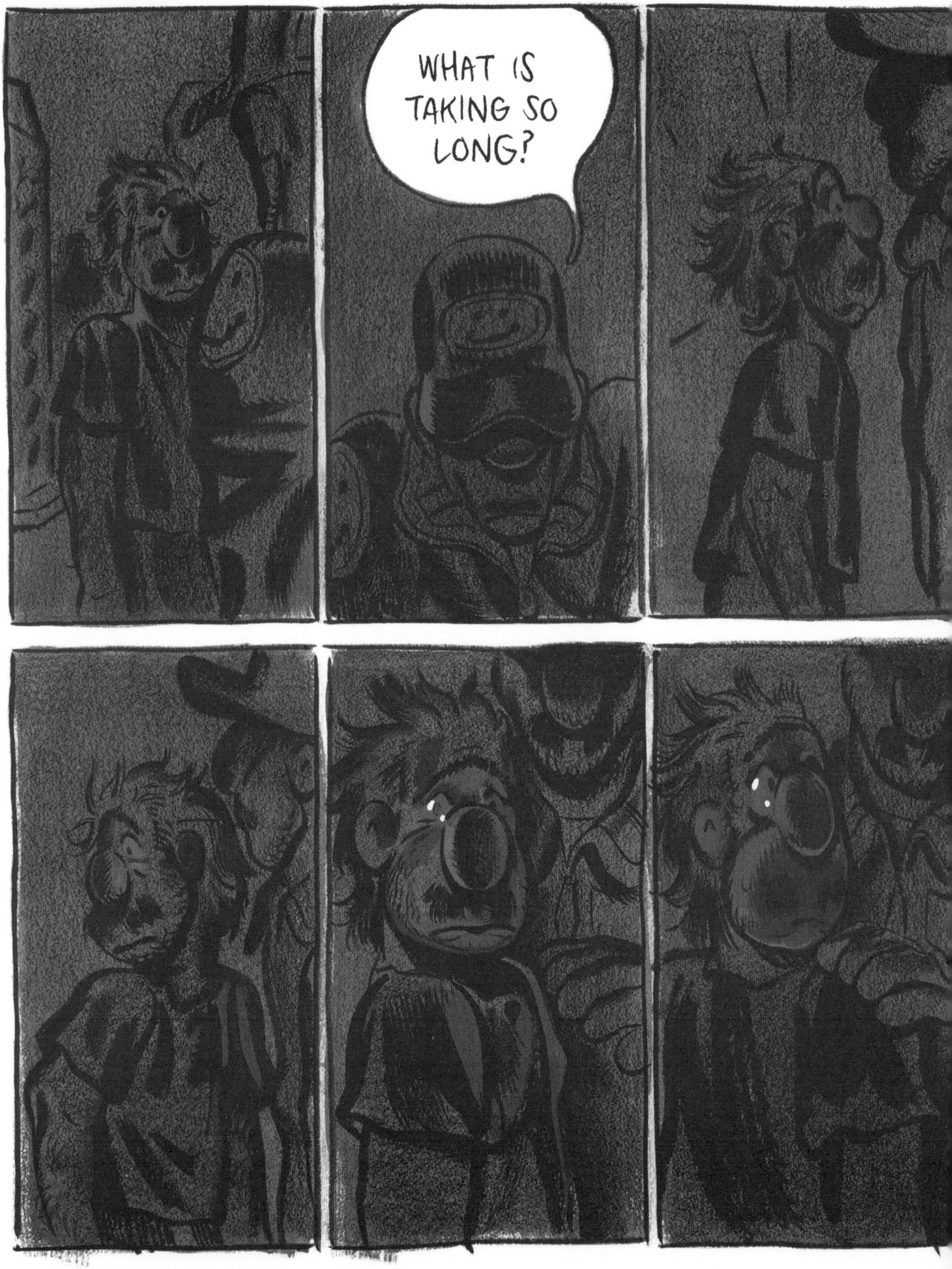
WHAT IS TAKING SO LONG?

WHERE WAS I?

OH, YOUR NEW SECURITY SYSTEM.

WHEN YOU ACTIVATE IT...

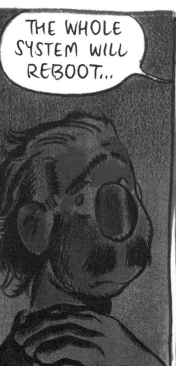

THE WHOLE SYSTEM WILL REBOOT...

SO DON'T BE ALARMED...

IF IT DOESN'T IMMEDIATELY TURN BACK ON.

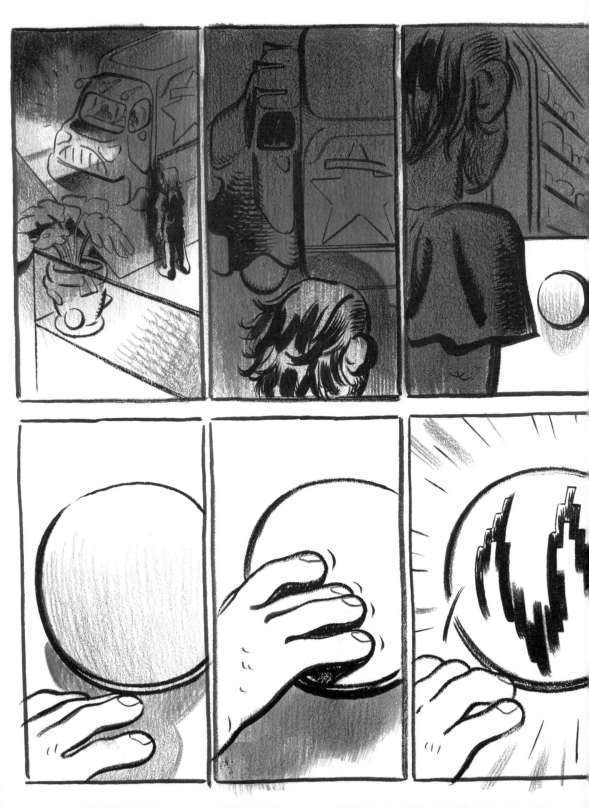

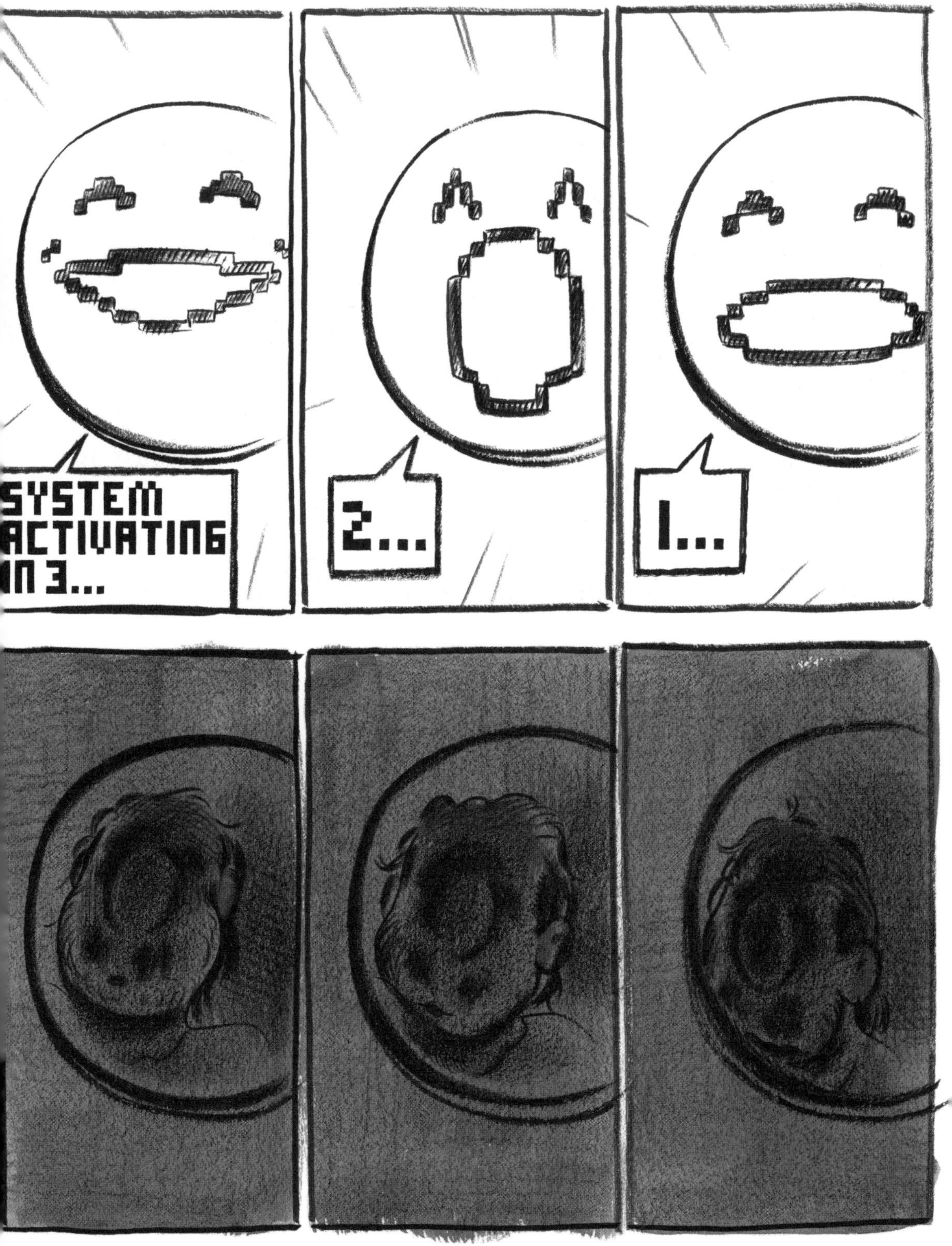
SYSTEM ACTIVATING IN 3...
2...
1...

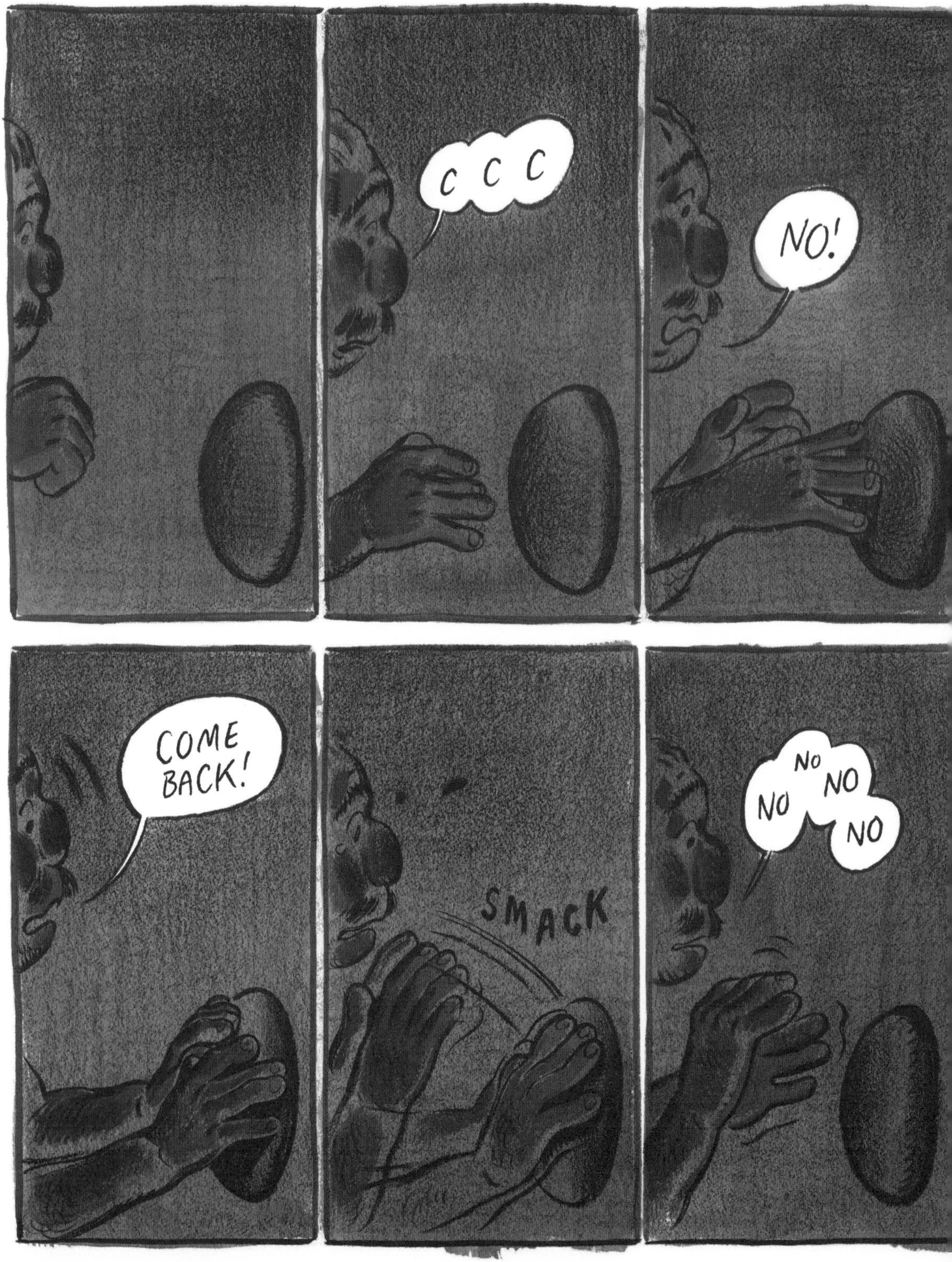
C C C
NO!
COME BACK!
SMACK
NO NO NO NO NO

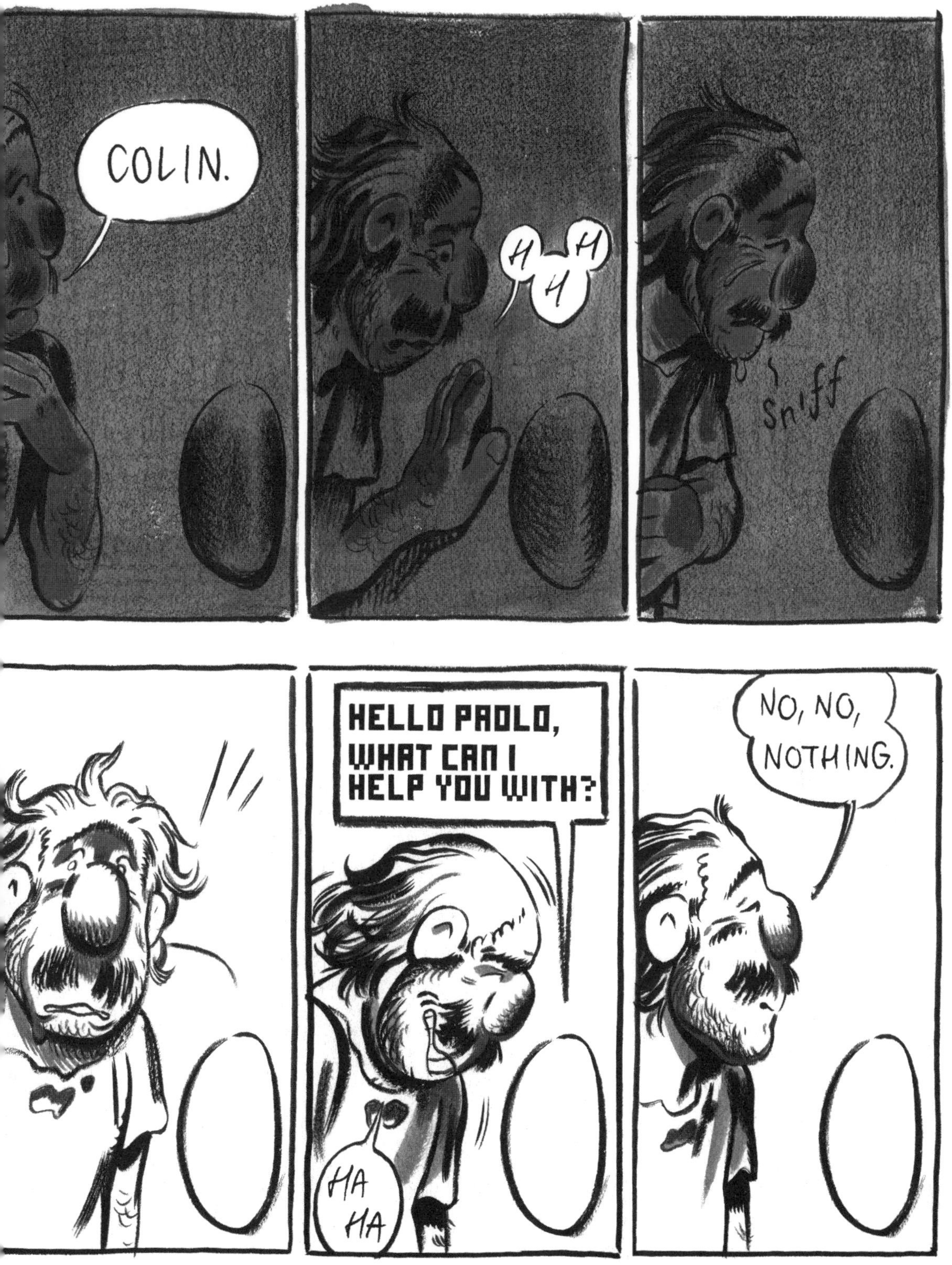
COLIN.
H H H
Sniff
HELLO PAOLO, WHAT CAN I HELP YOU WITH?
HA HA
NO, NO, NOTHING.

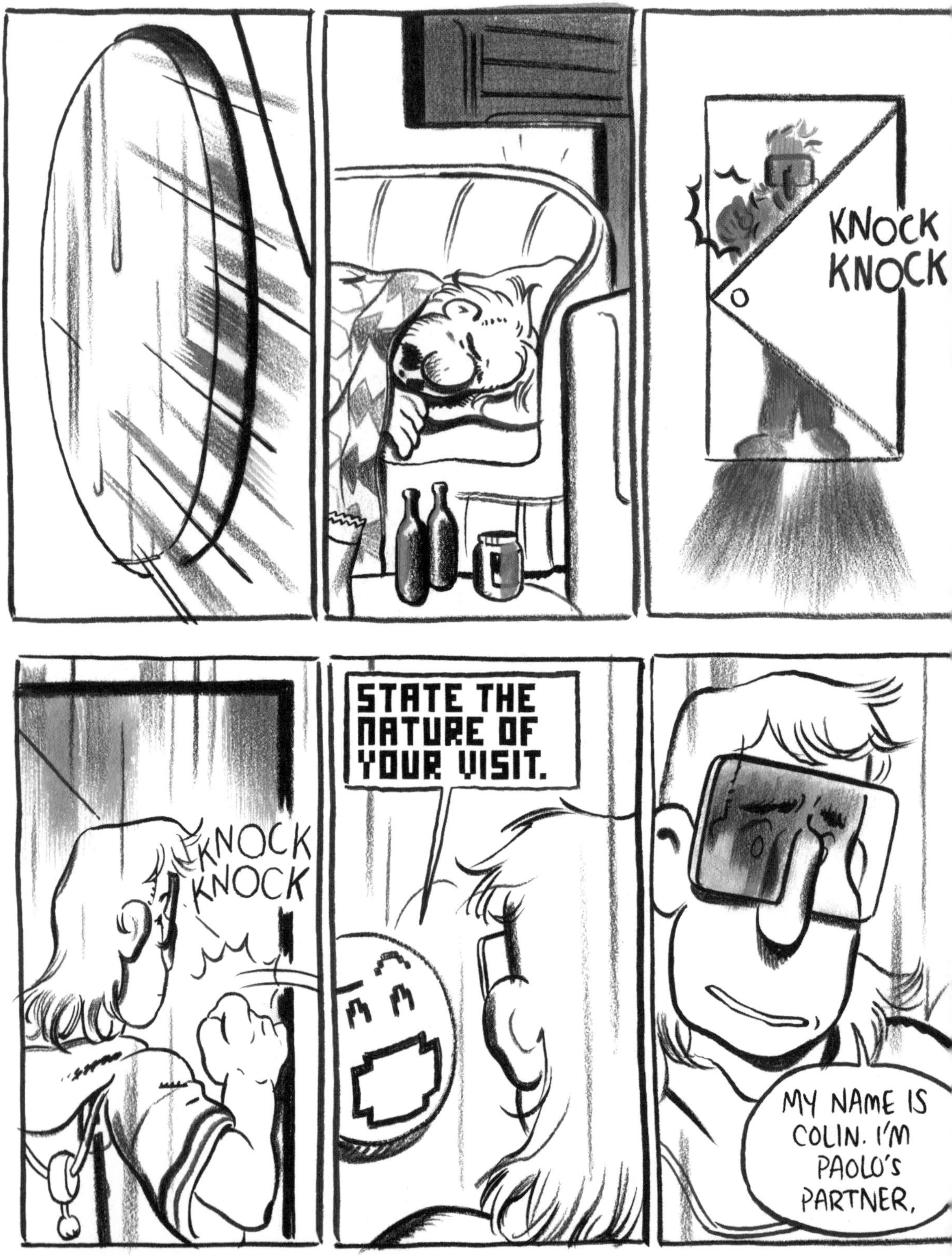
KNOCK KNOCK
KNOCK KNOCK
STATE THE NATURE OF YOUR VISIT.
MY NAME IS COLIN. I'M PAOLO'S PARTNER.

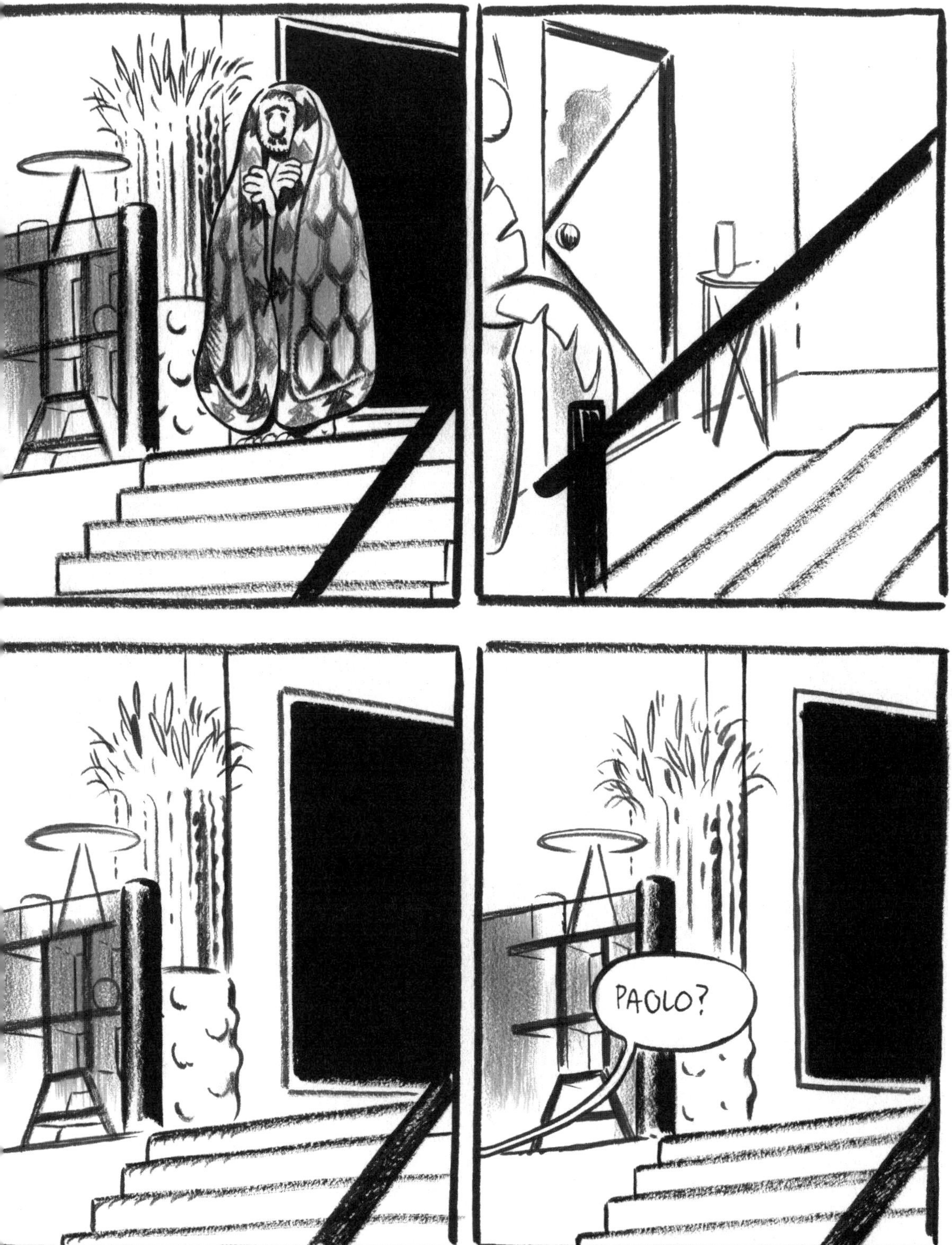
PAOLO?

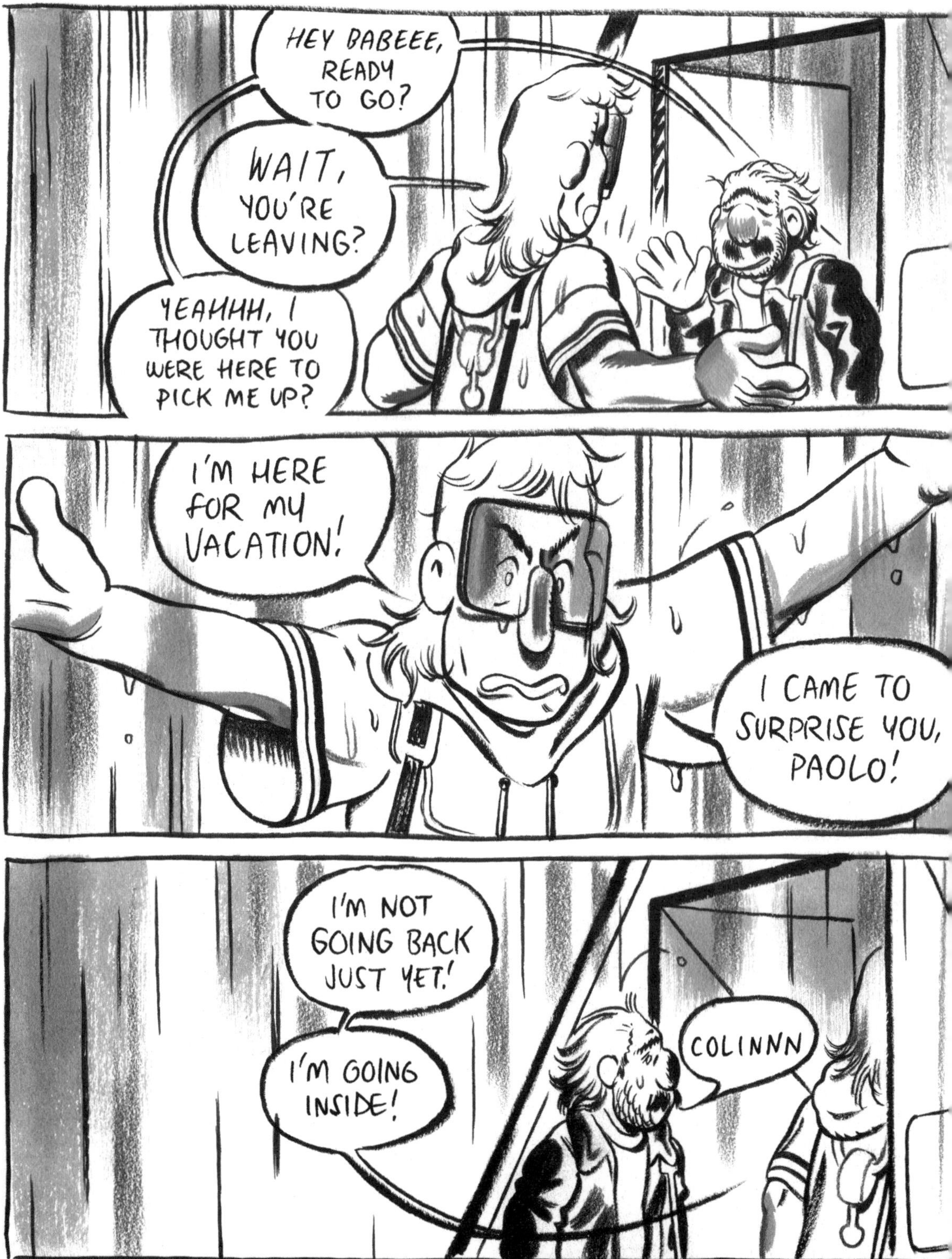
HEY BABEEE, READY TO GO?
WAIT, YOU'RE LEAVING?
YEAHHH, I THOUGHT YOU WERE HERE TO PICK ME UP?
I'M HERE FOR MY VACATION!
I CAME TO SURPRISE YOU, PAOLO!
I'M NOT GOING BACK JUST YET!
I'M GOING INSIDE!
COLINNN

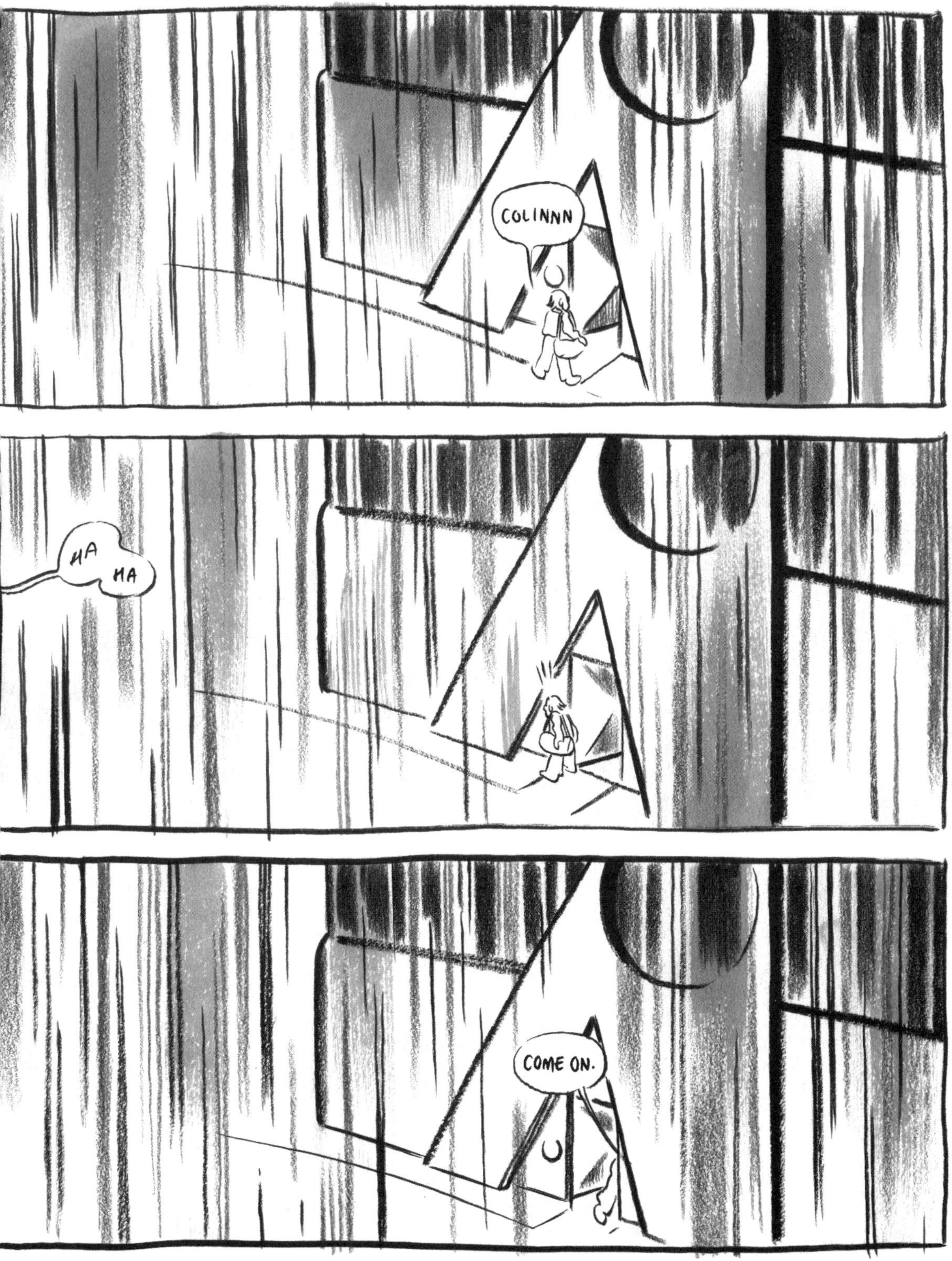
COLINNN
HA HA
COME ON.

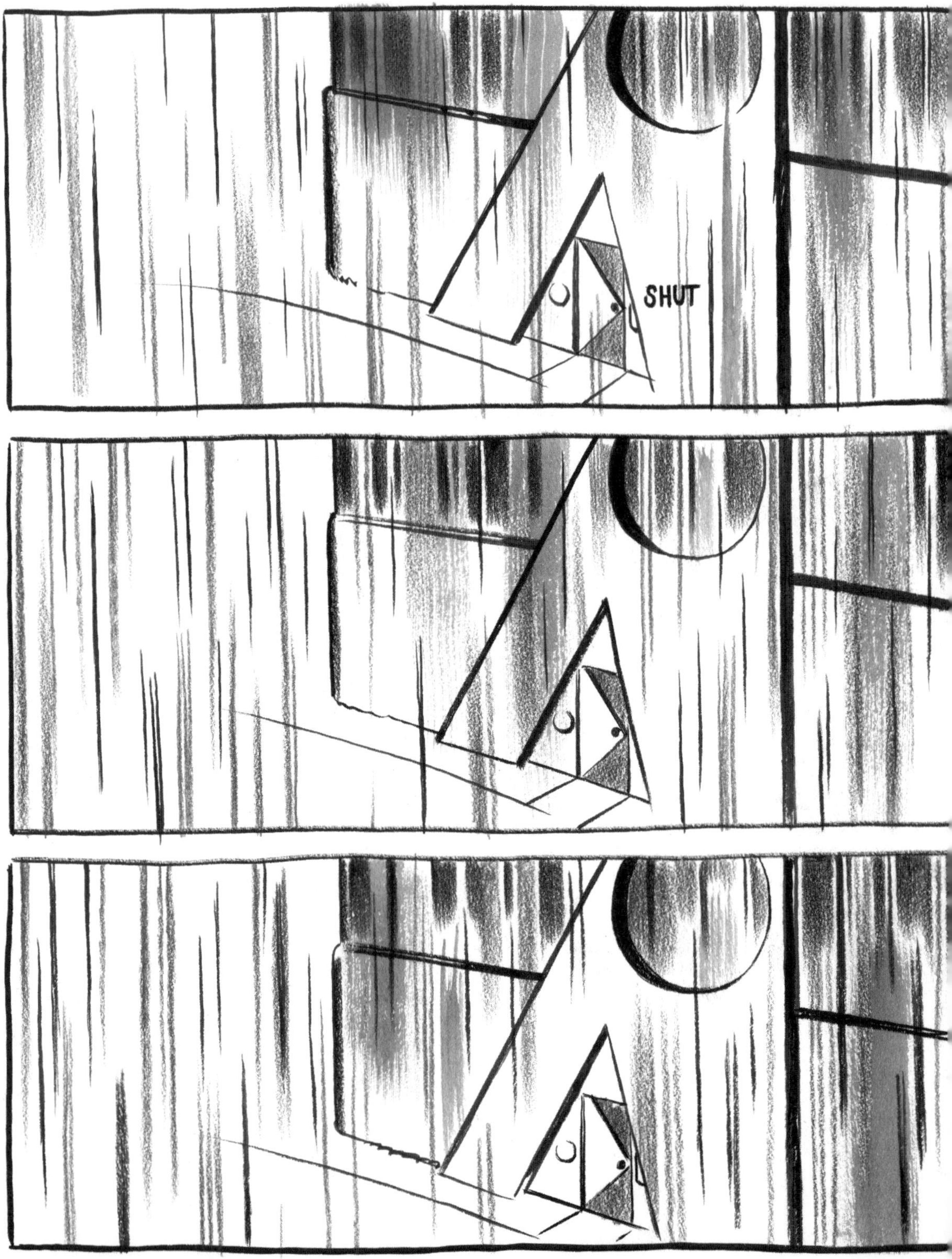
SHUT

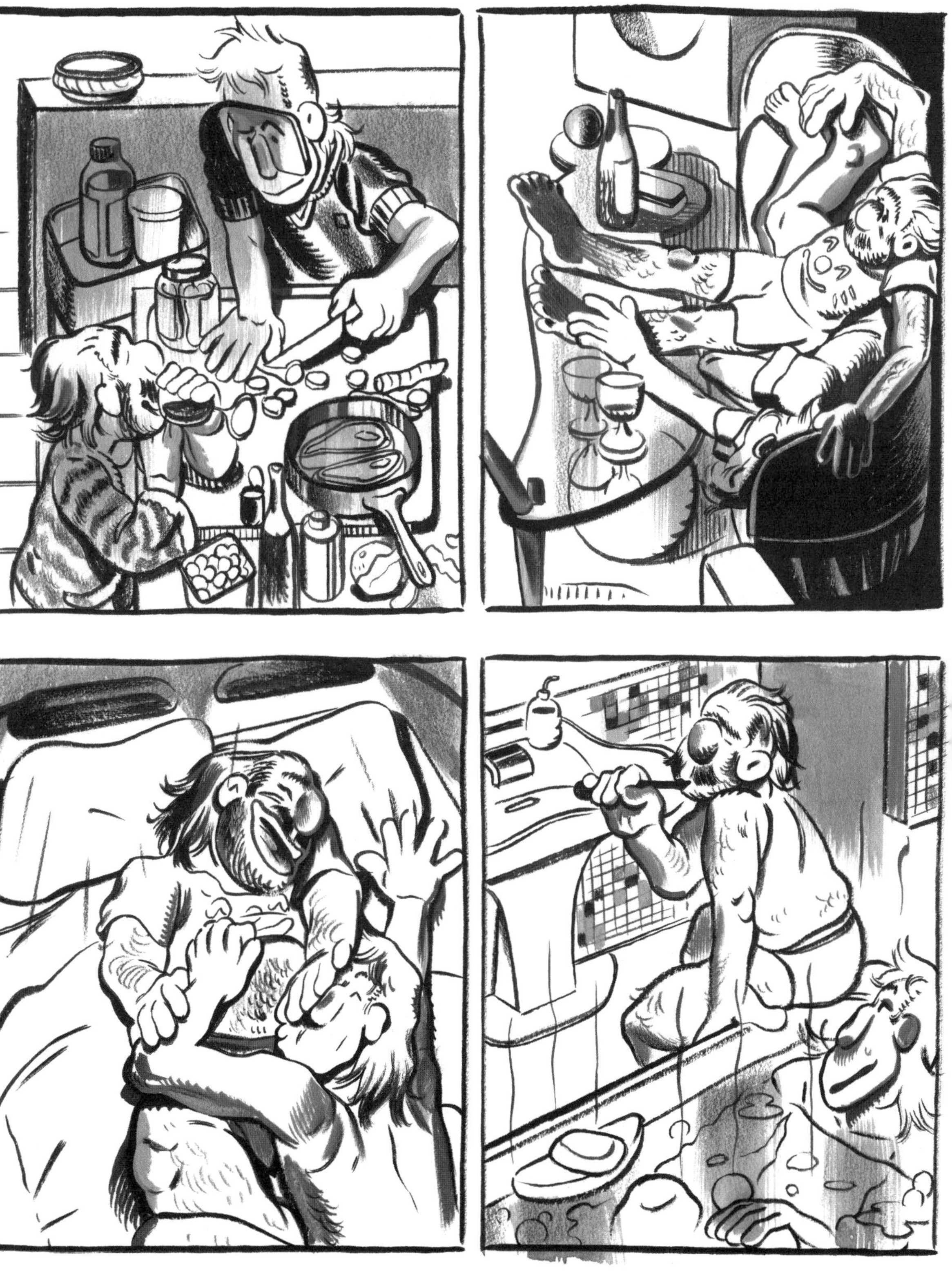

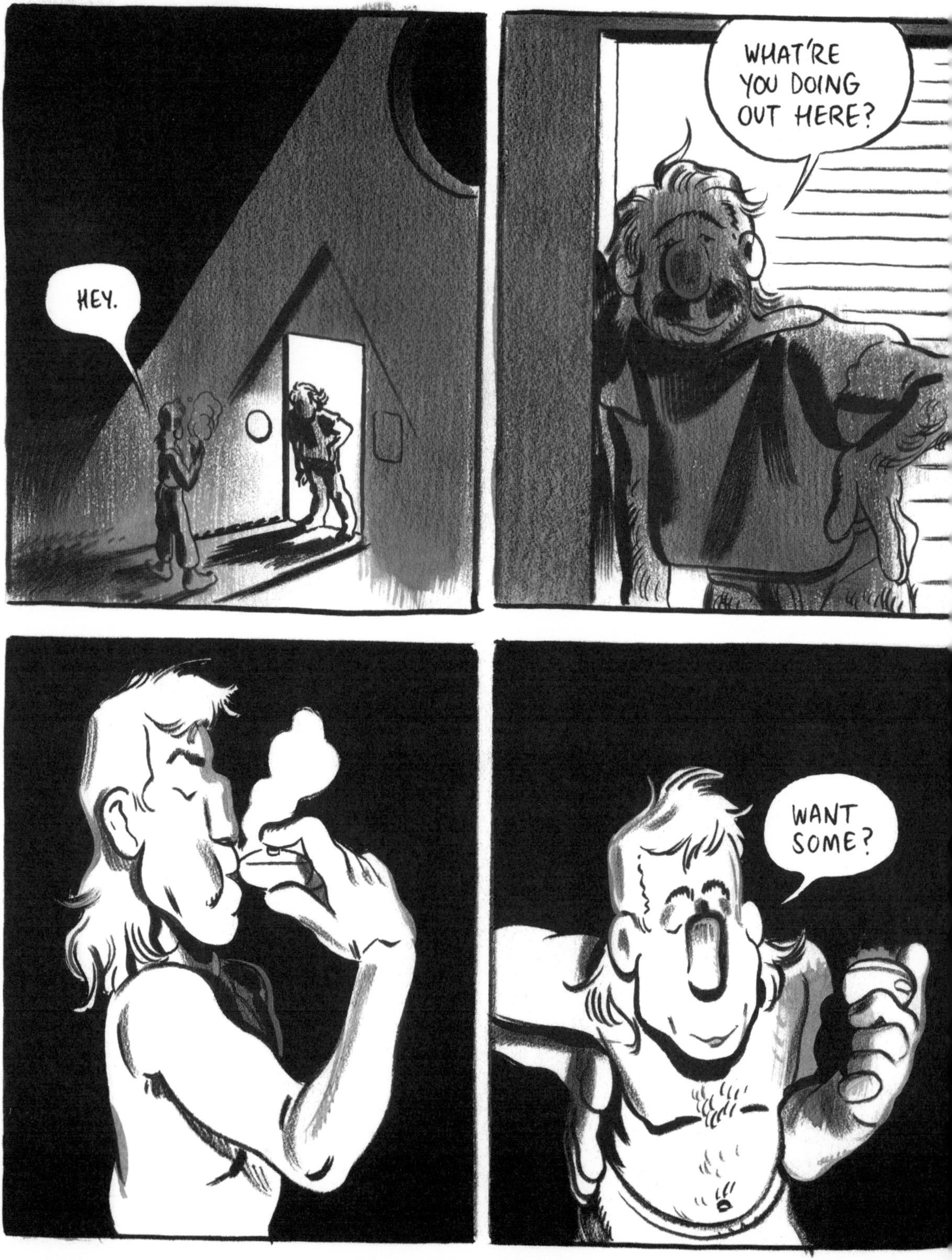
HEY.
WHAT'RE YOU DOING OUT HERE?
WANT SOME?

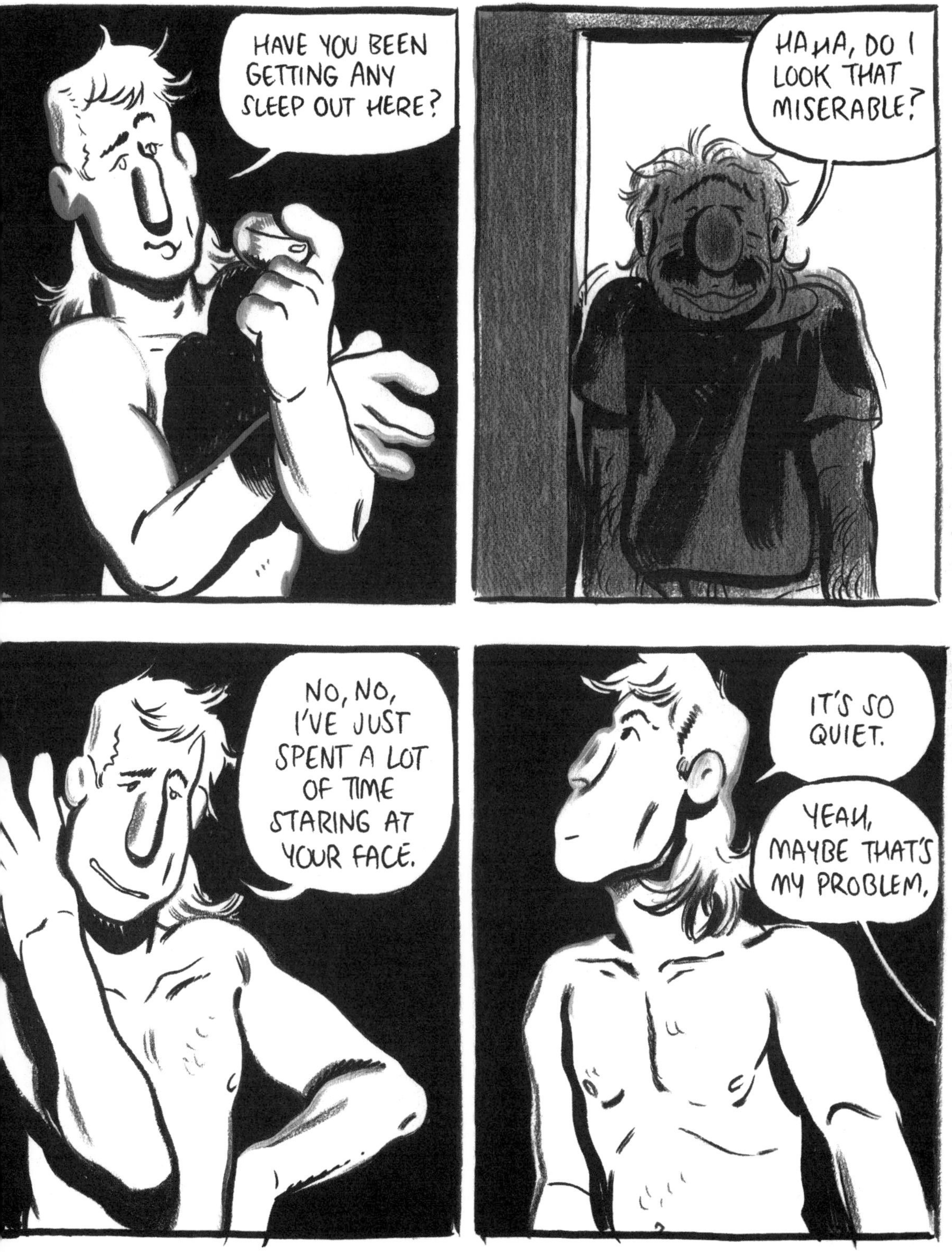
HAVE YOU BEEN GETTING ANY SLEEP OUT HERE?
HAHA, DO I LOOK THAT MISERABLE?
NO, NO, I'VE JUST SPENT A LOT OF TIME STARING AT YOUR FACE.
IT'S SO QUIET.
YEAH, MAYBE THAT'S MY PROBLEM.

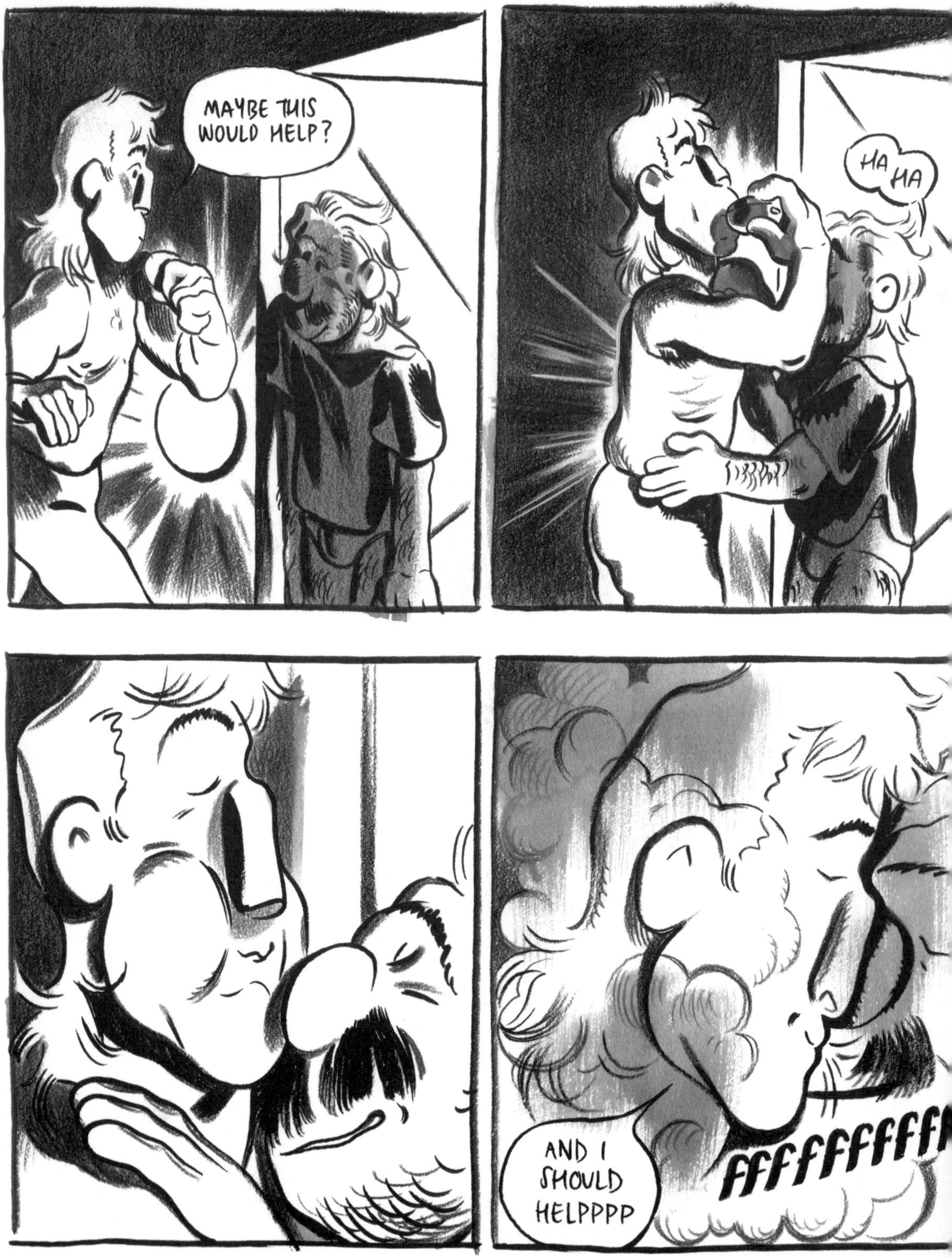
MAYBE THIS WOULD HELP?
HA HA
AND I SHOULD HELPPPP
fffffffff

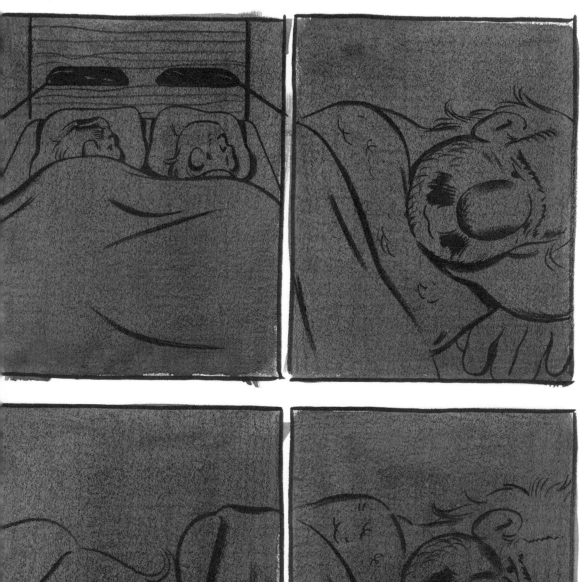
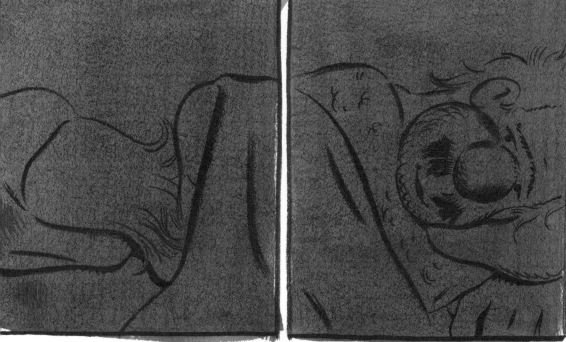

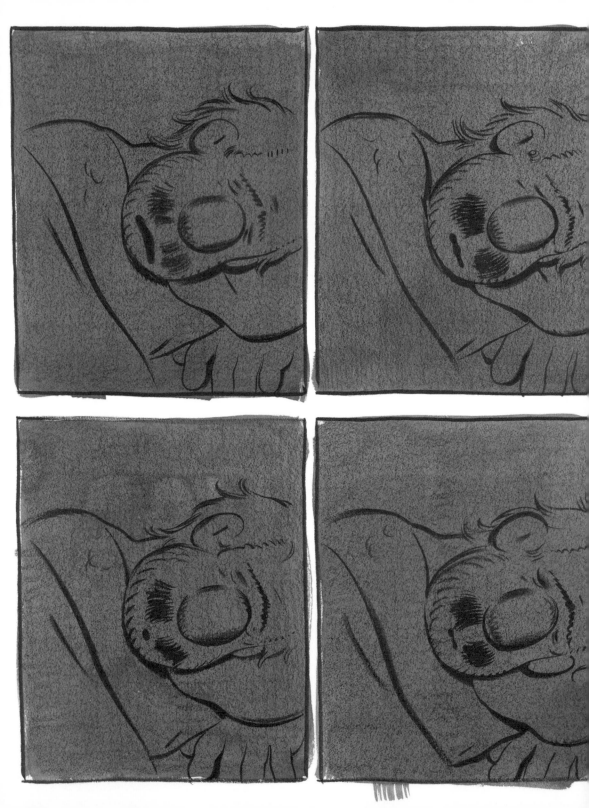

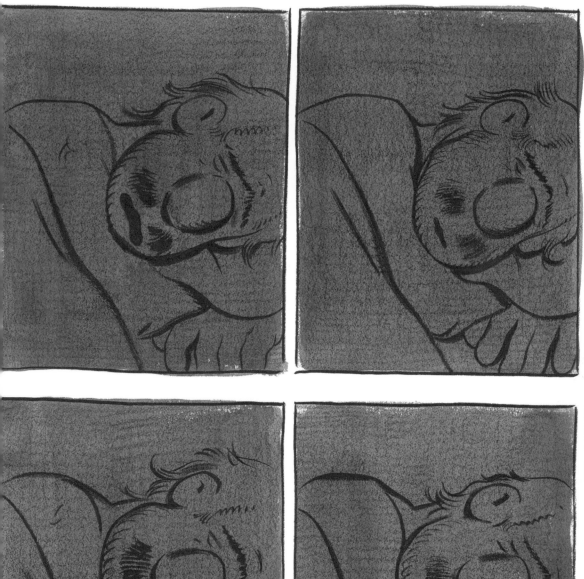
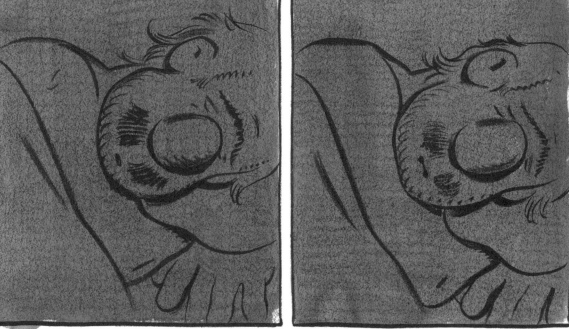

STAY QUIET

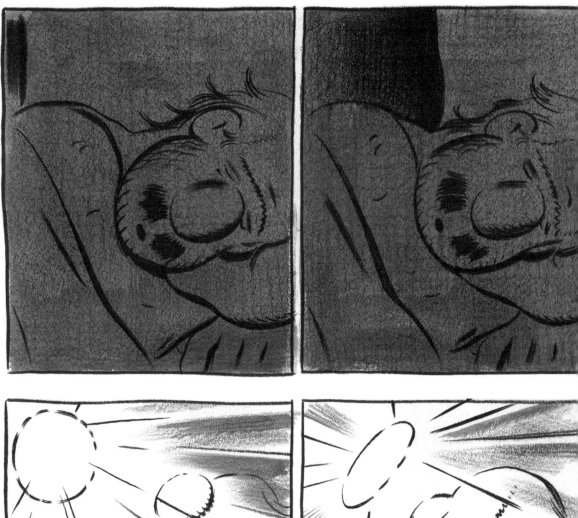

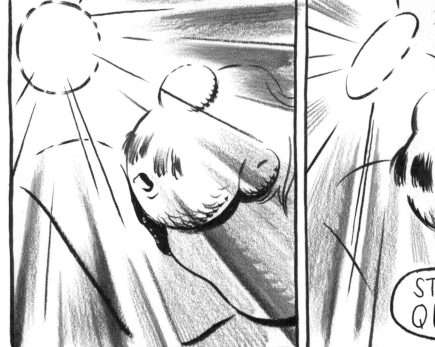

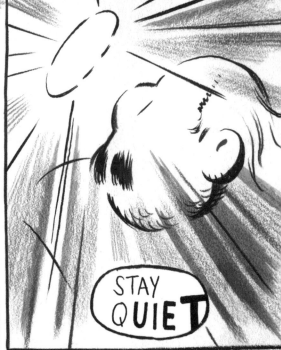

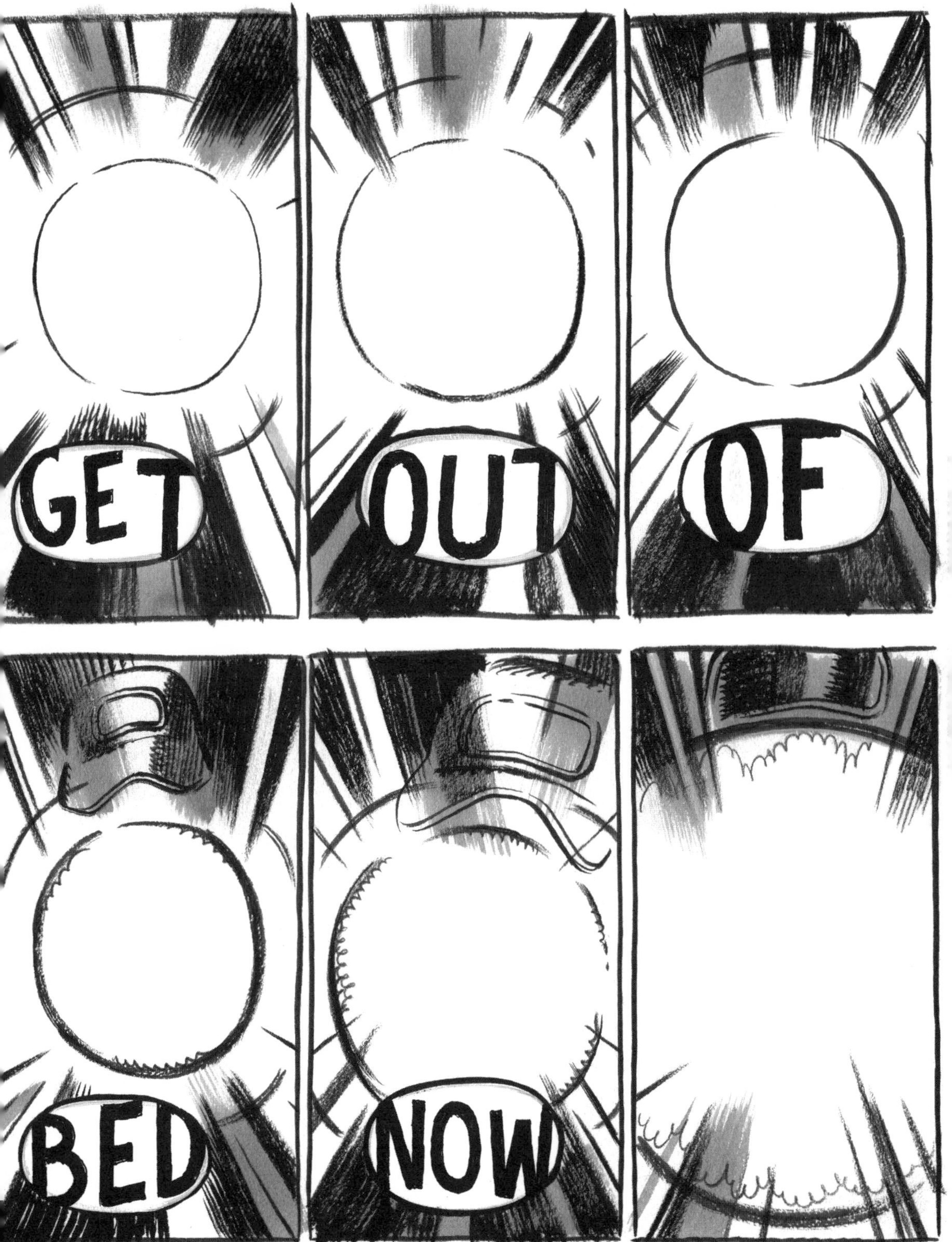
GET
OUT
OF
BED
NOW

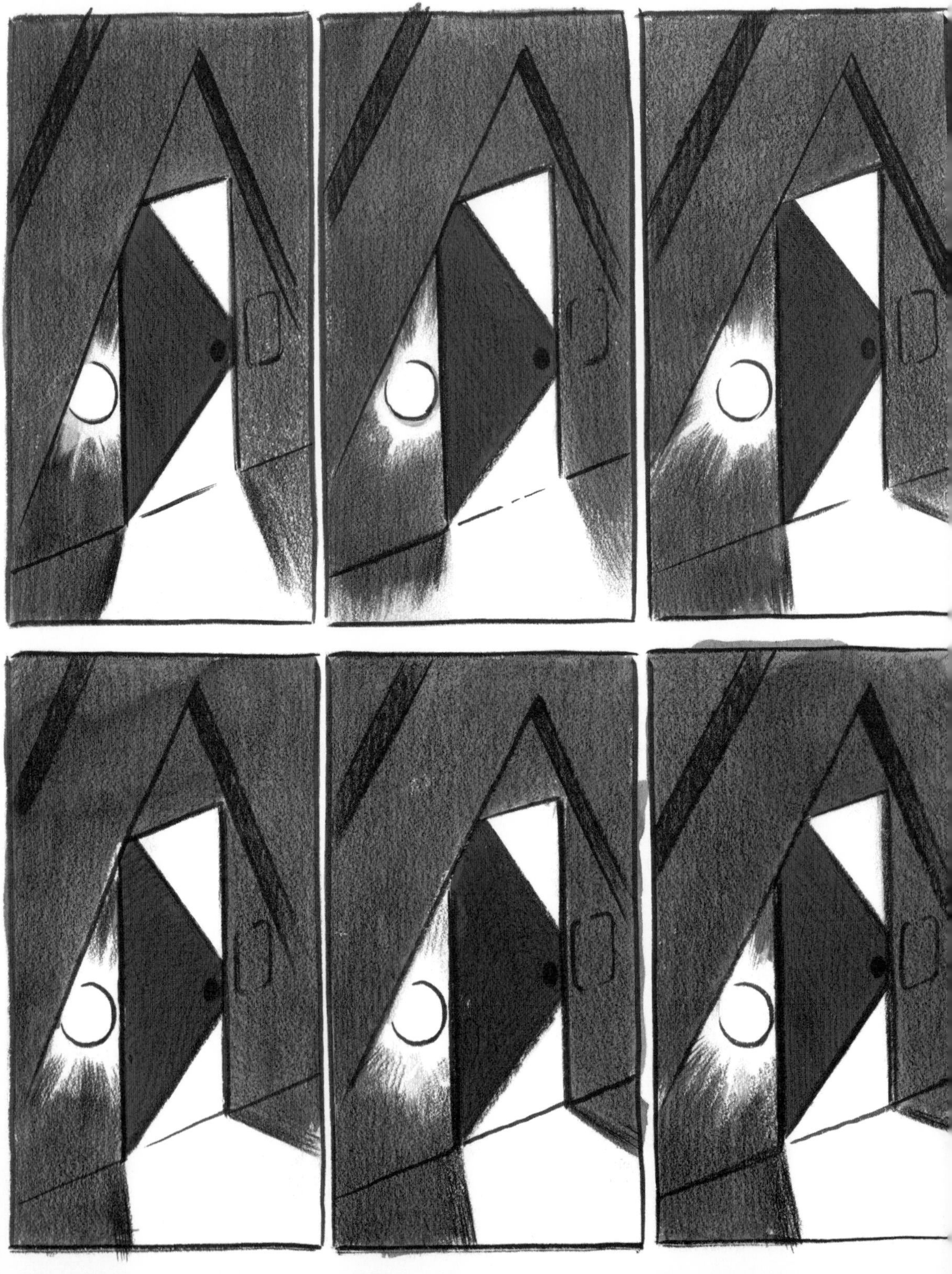

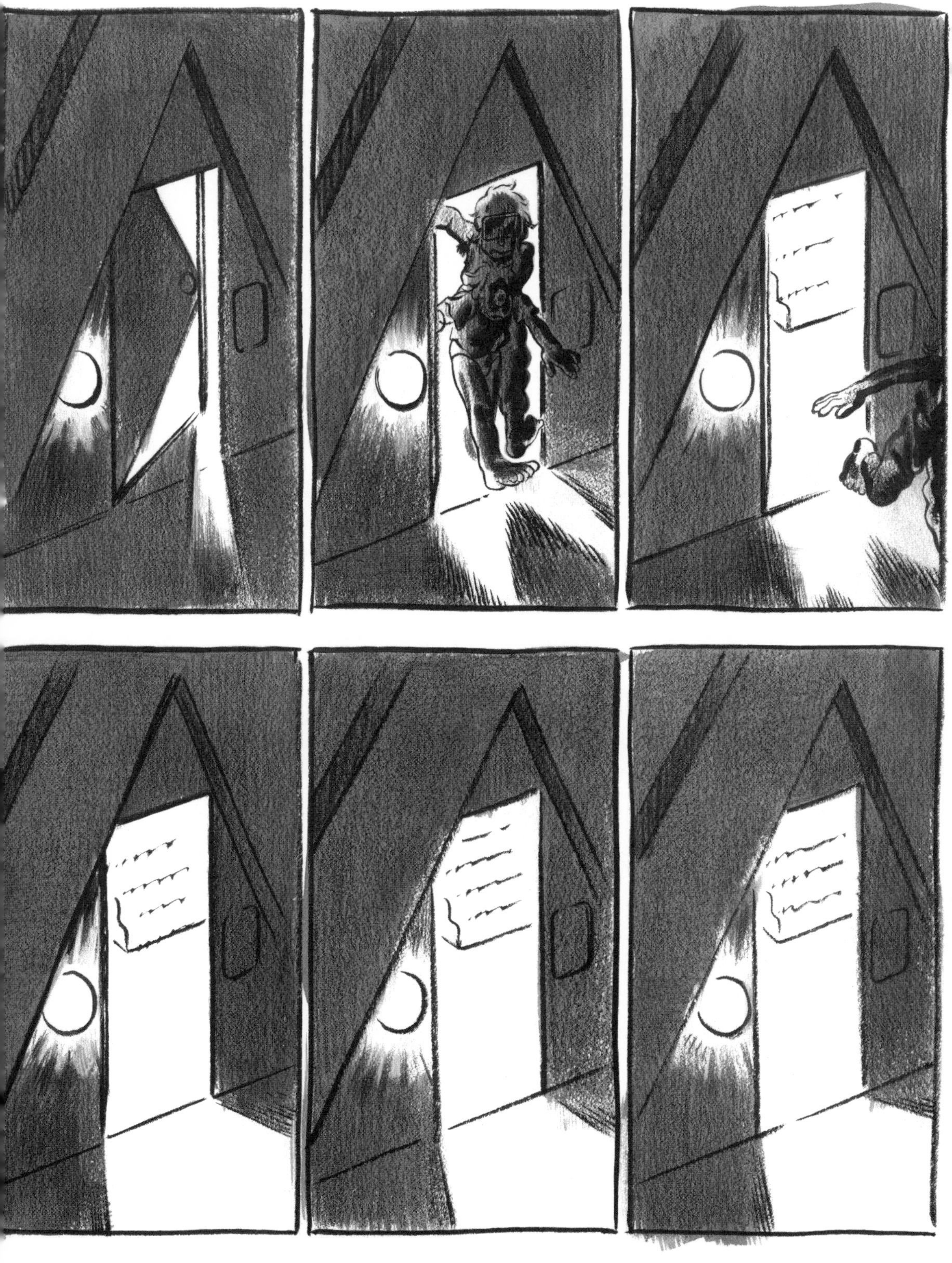

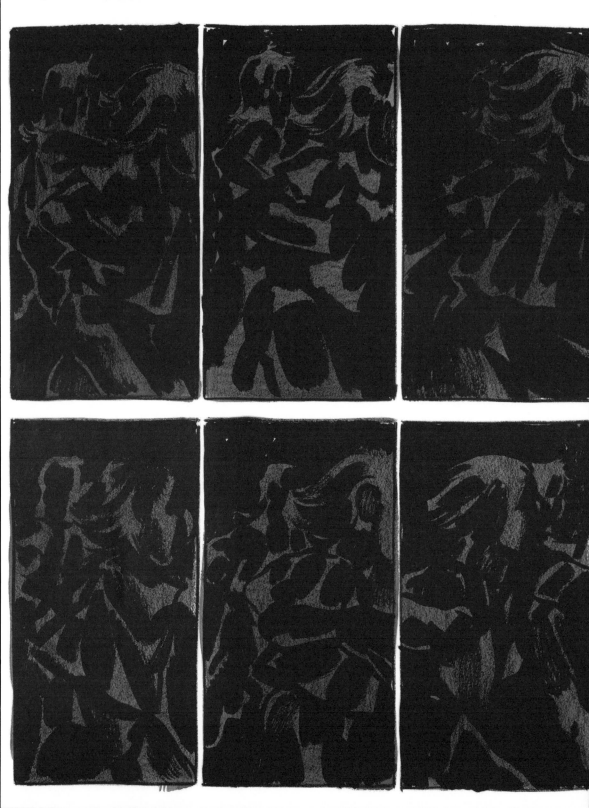

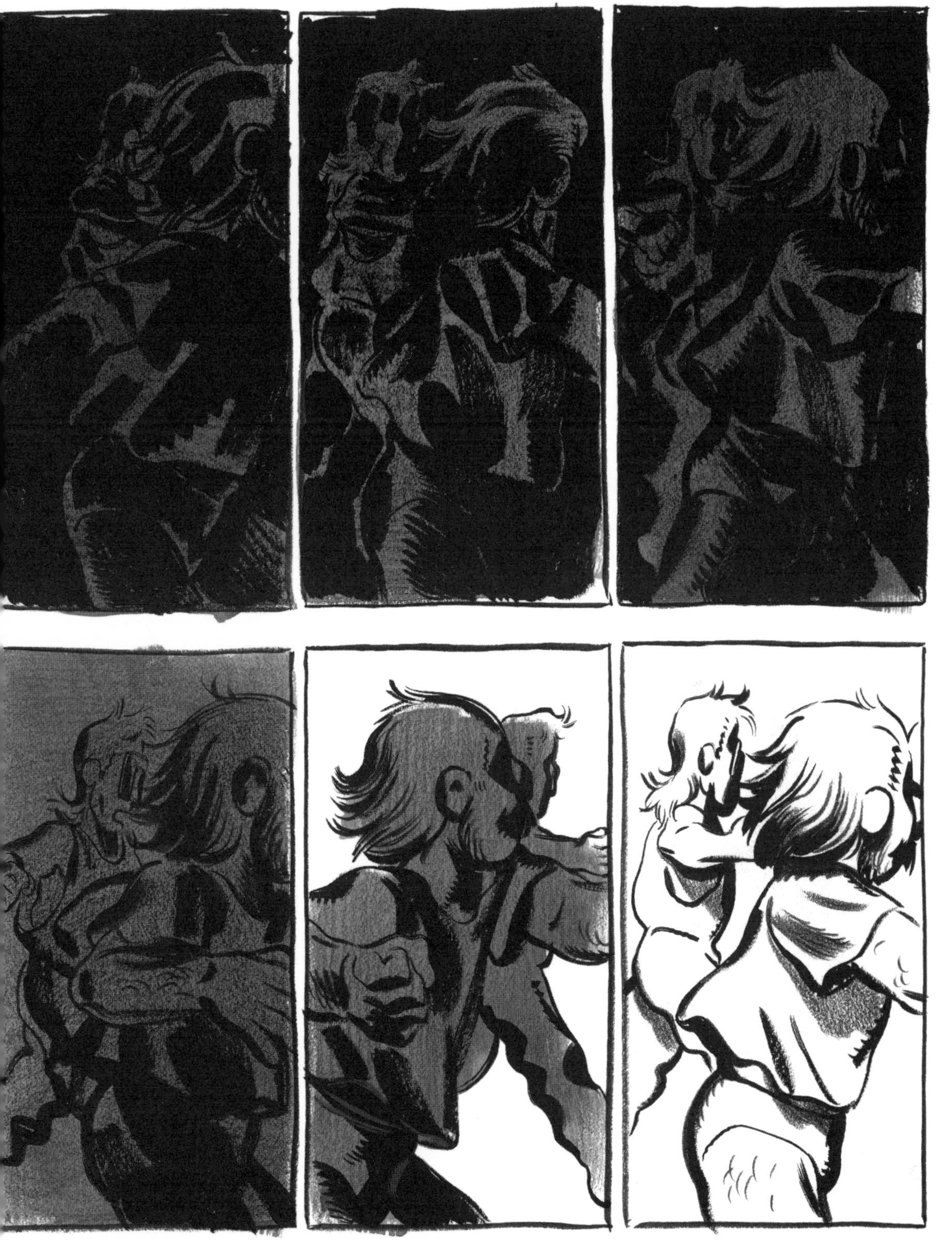

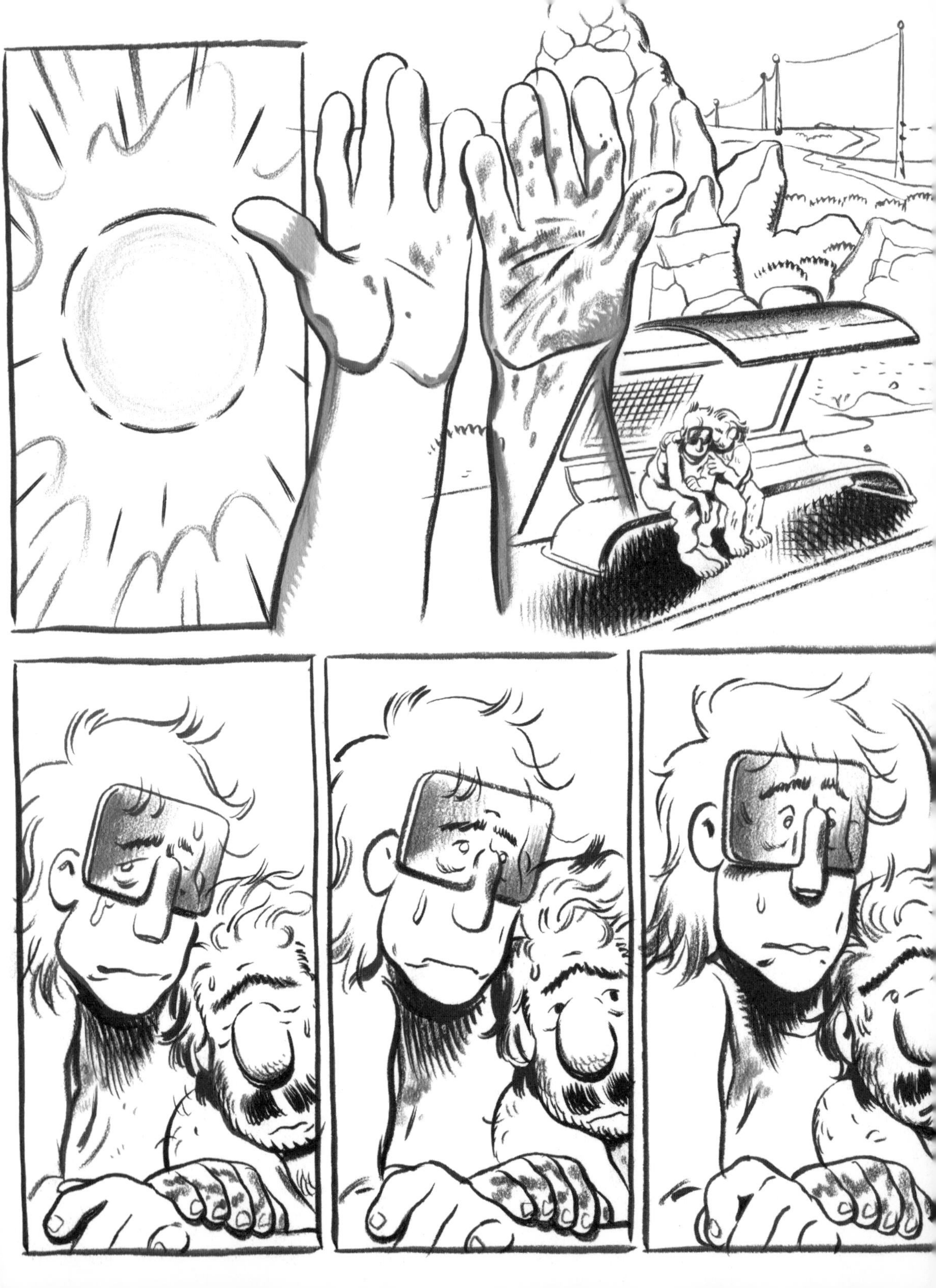

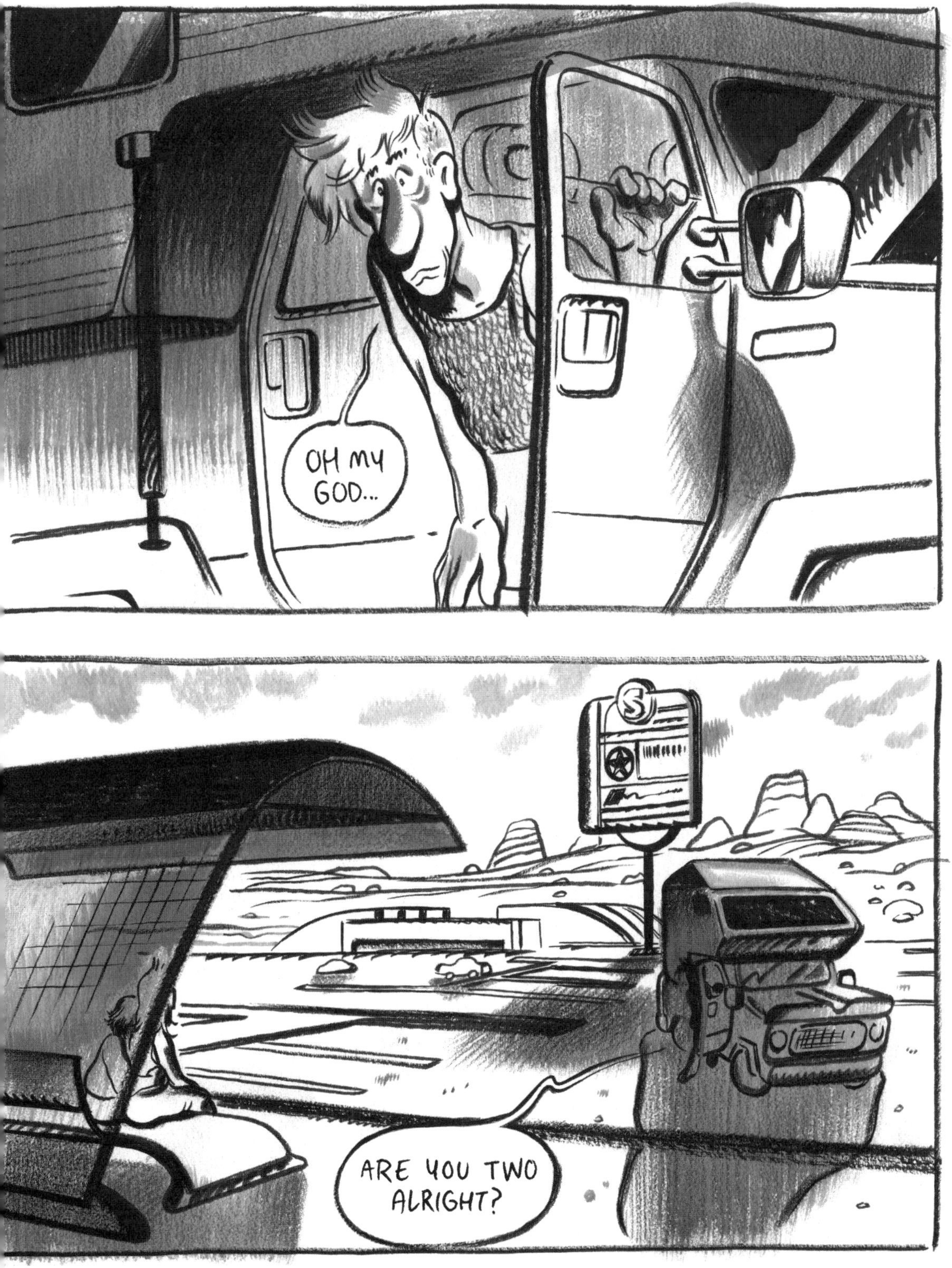
OH MY GOD...
ARE YOU TWO ALRIGHT?

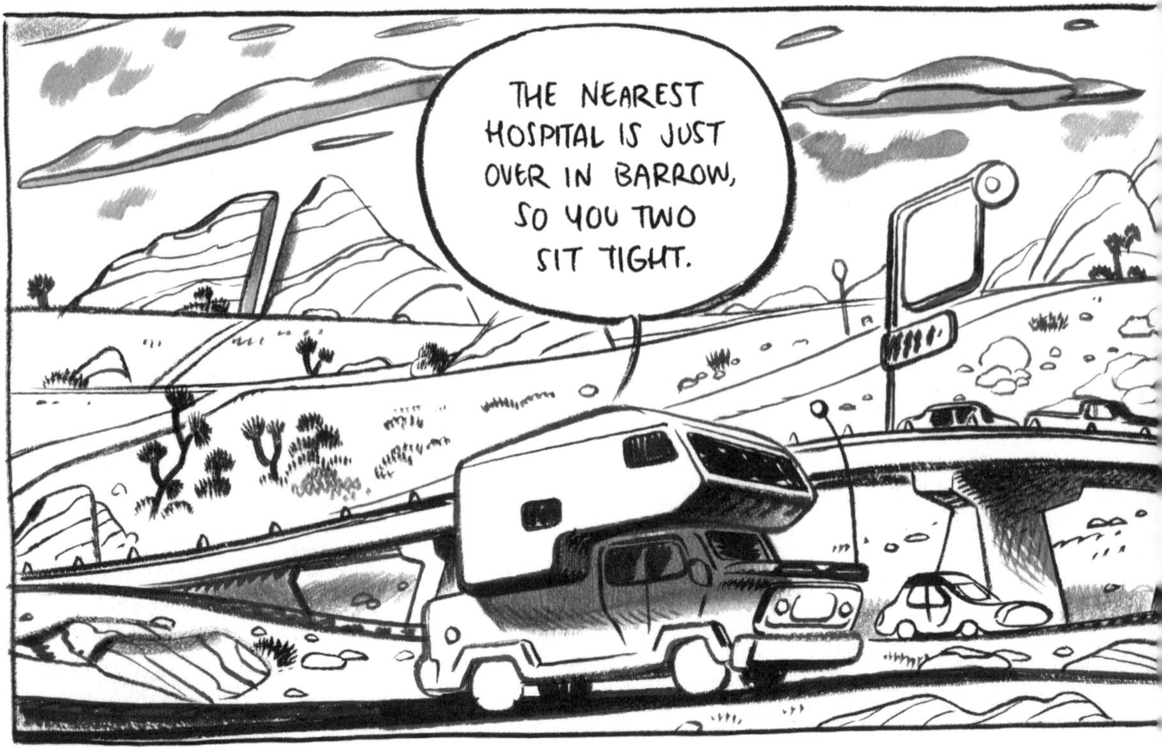
THE NEAREST HOSPITAL IS JUST OVER IN BARROW, SO YOU TWO SIT TIGHT.

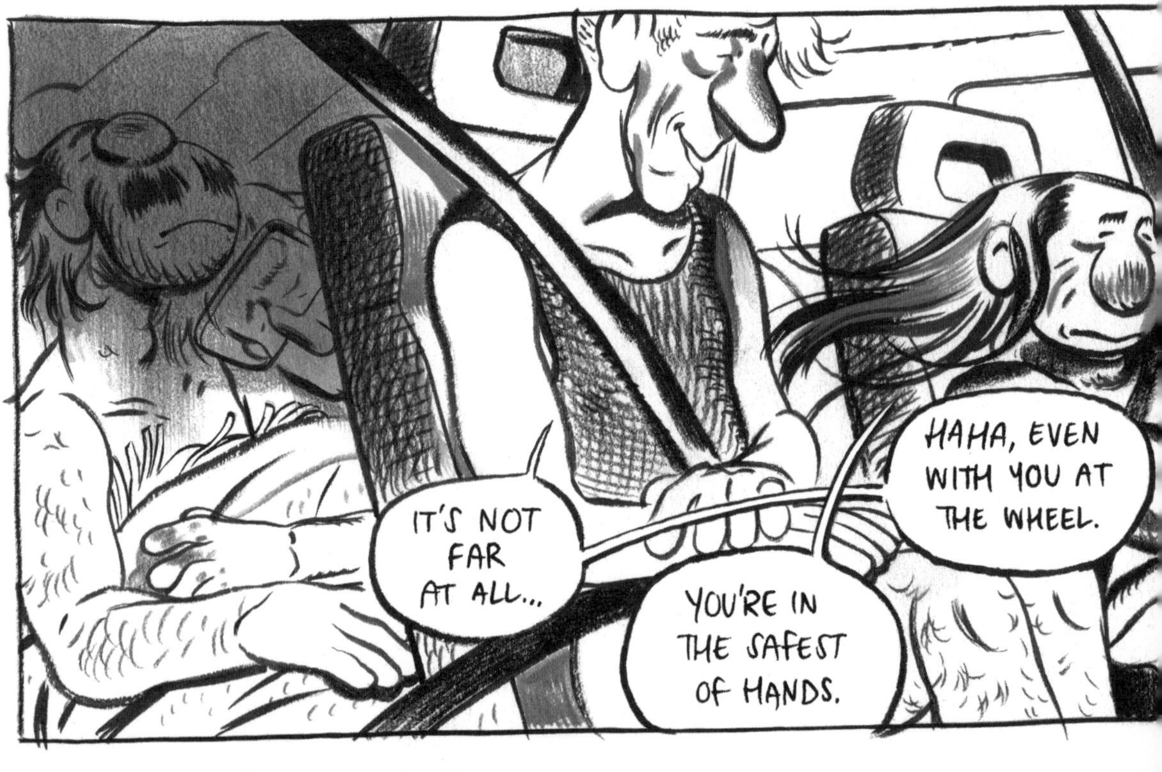
IT'S NOT FAR AT ALL...
YOU'RE IN THE SAFEST OF HANDS.
HAHA, EVEN WITH YOU AT THE WHEEL.

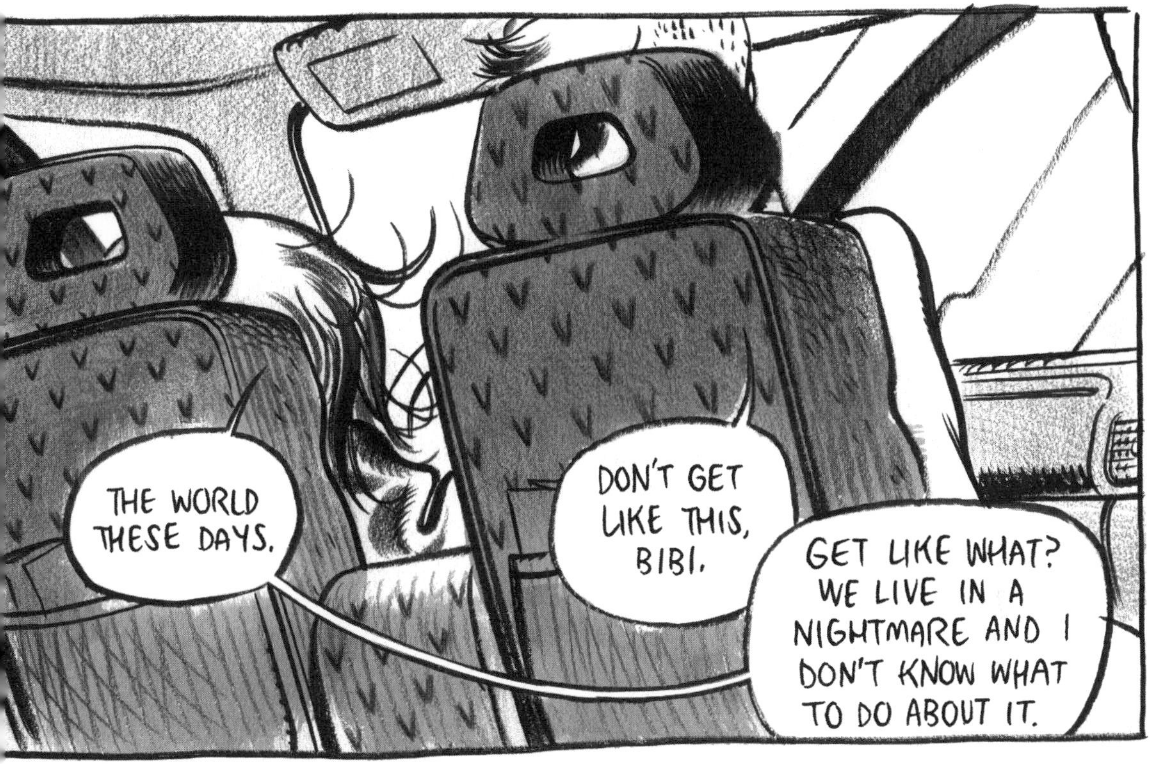
THE WORLD THESE DAYS.
DON'T GET LIKE THIS, BIBI.
GET LIKE WHAT? WE LIVE IN A NIGHTMARE AND I DON'T KNOW WHAT TO DO ABOUT IT.

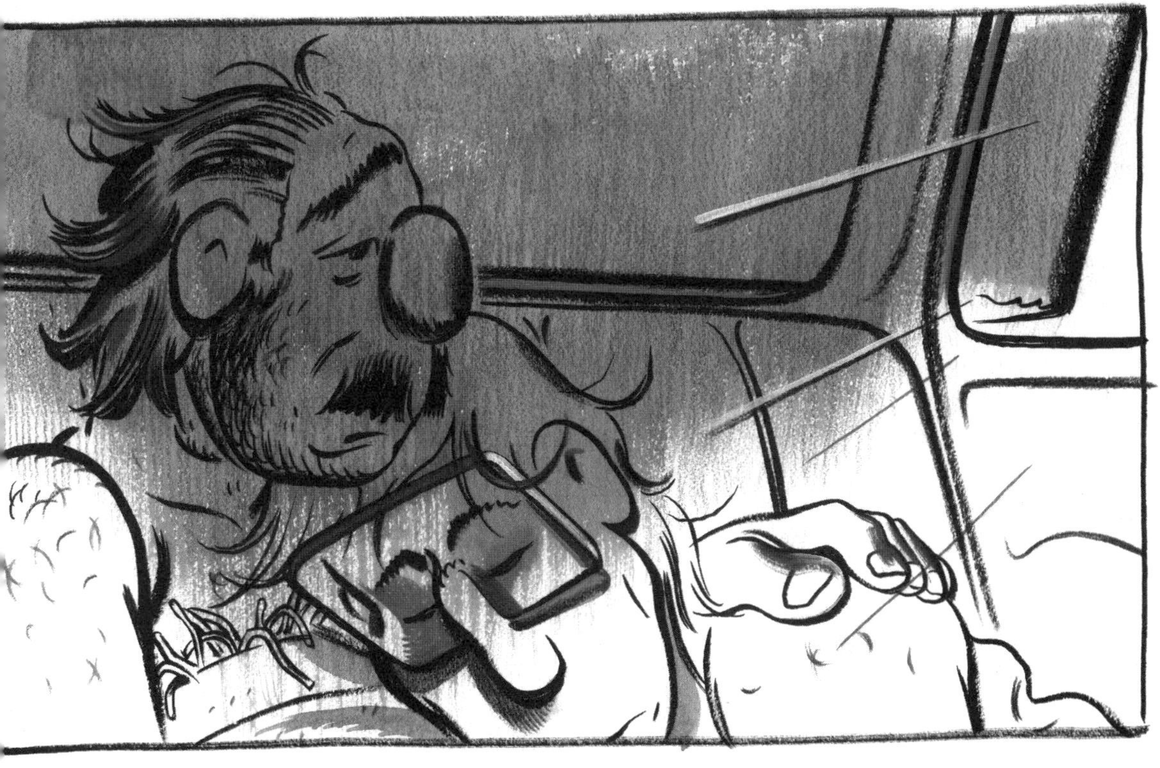

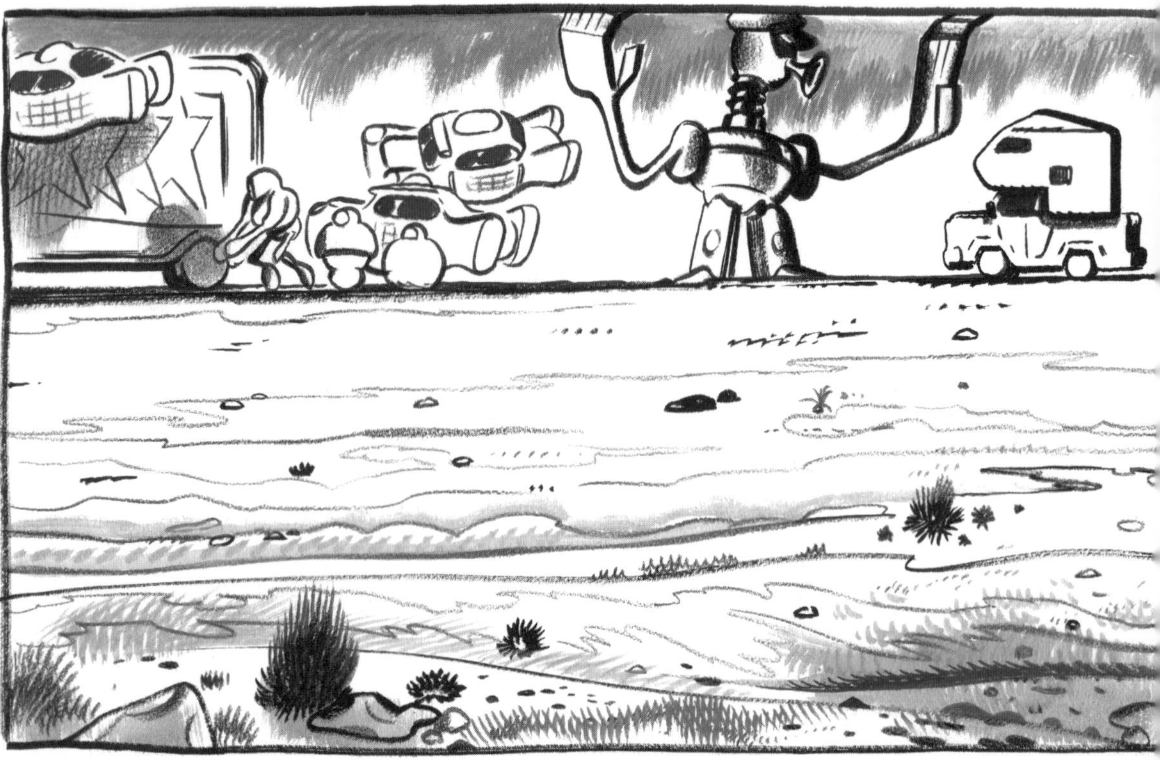

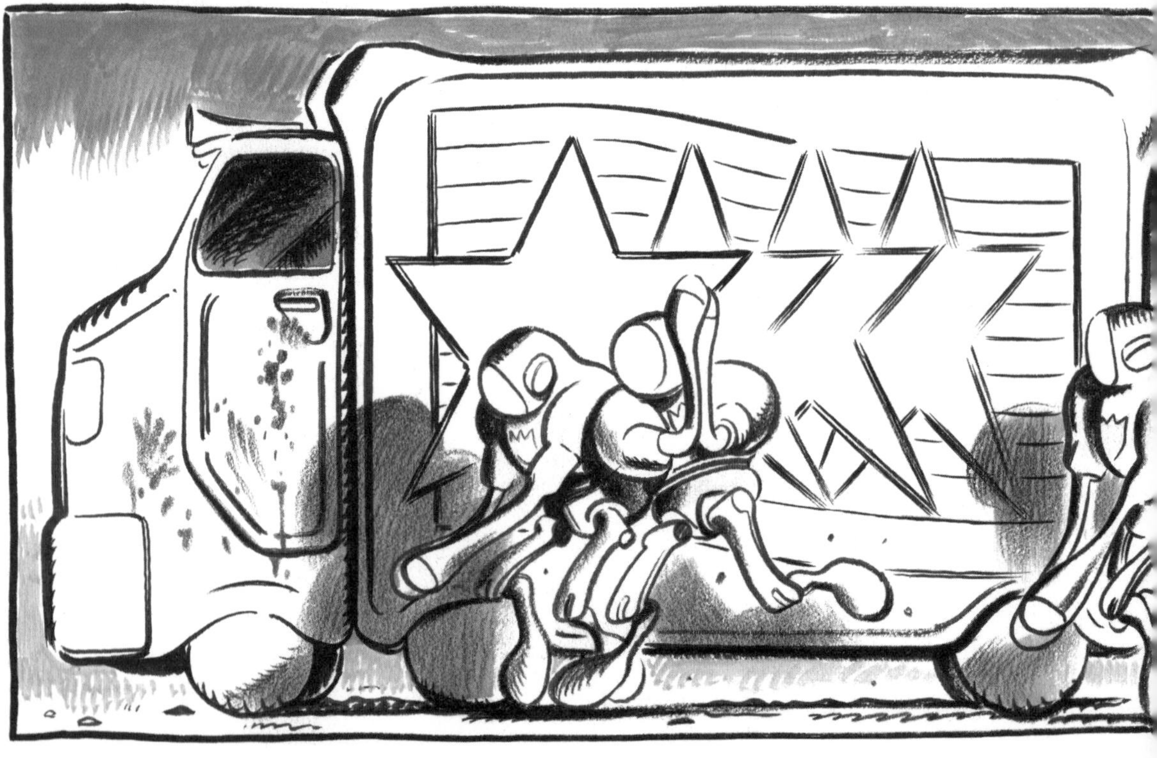

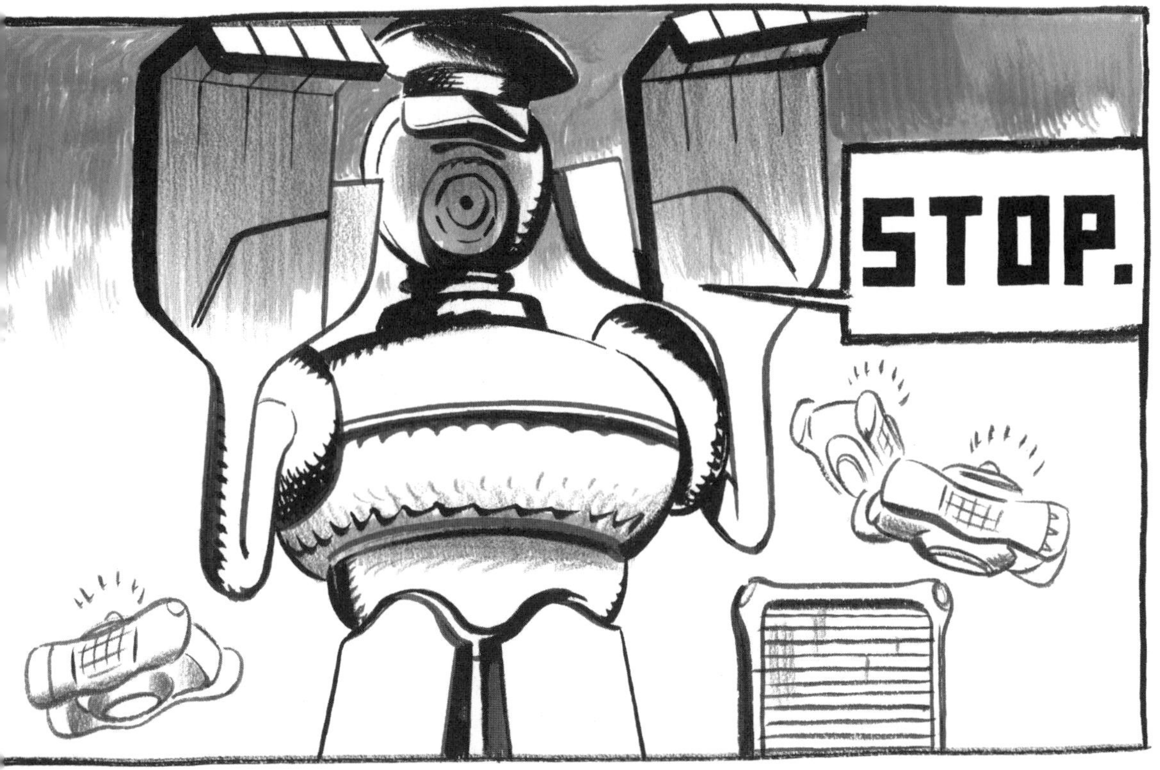
STOP.

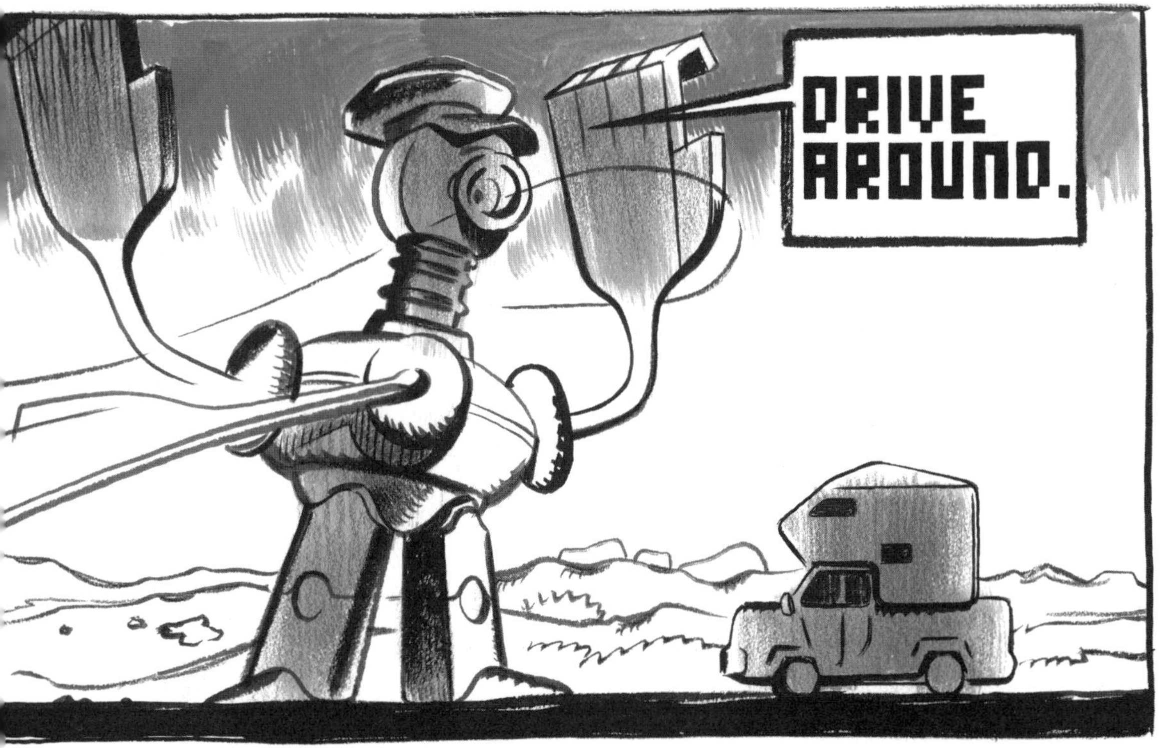
DRIVE AROUND.

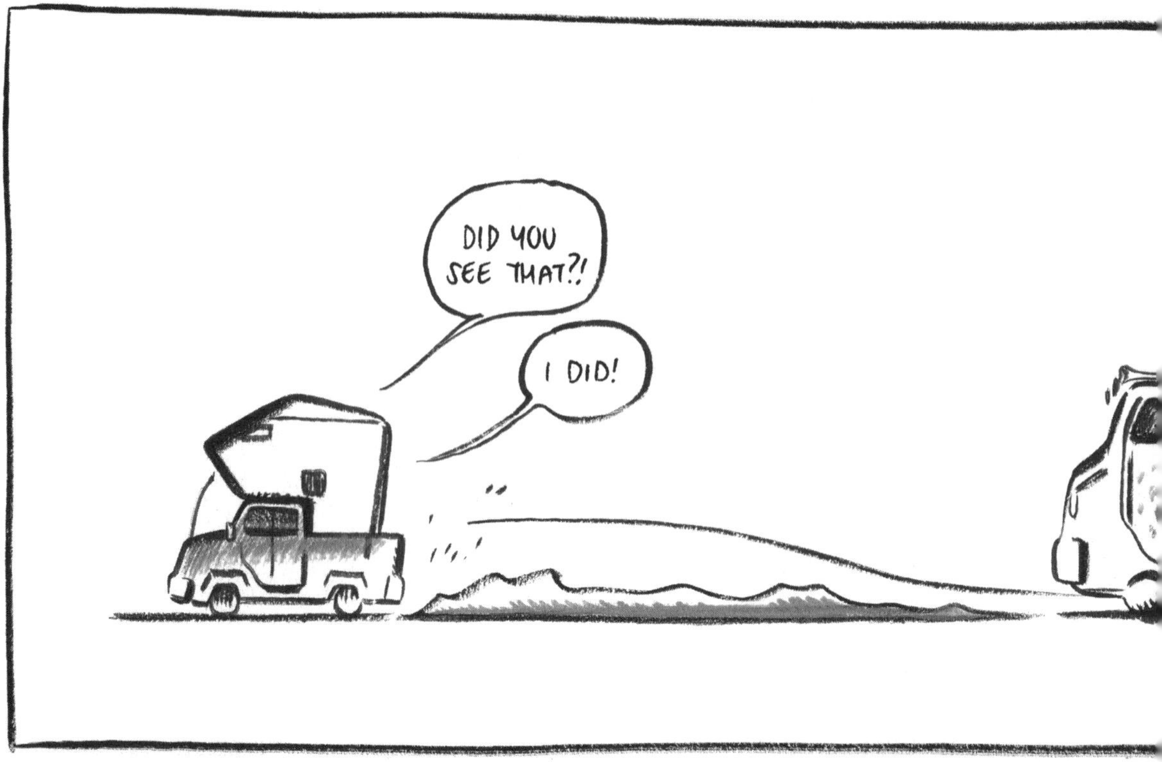
DID YOU SEE THAT?!
I DID!
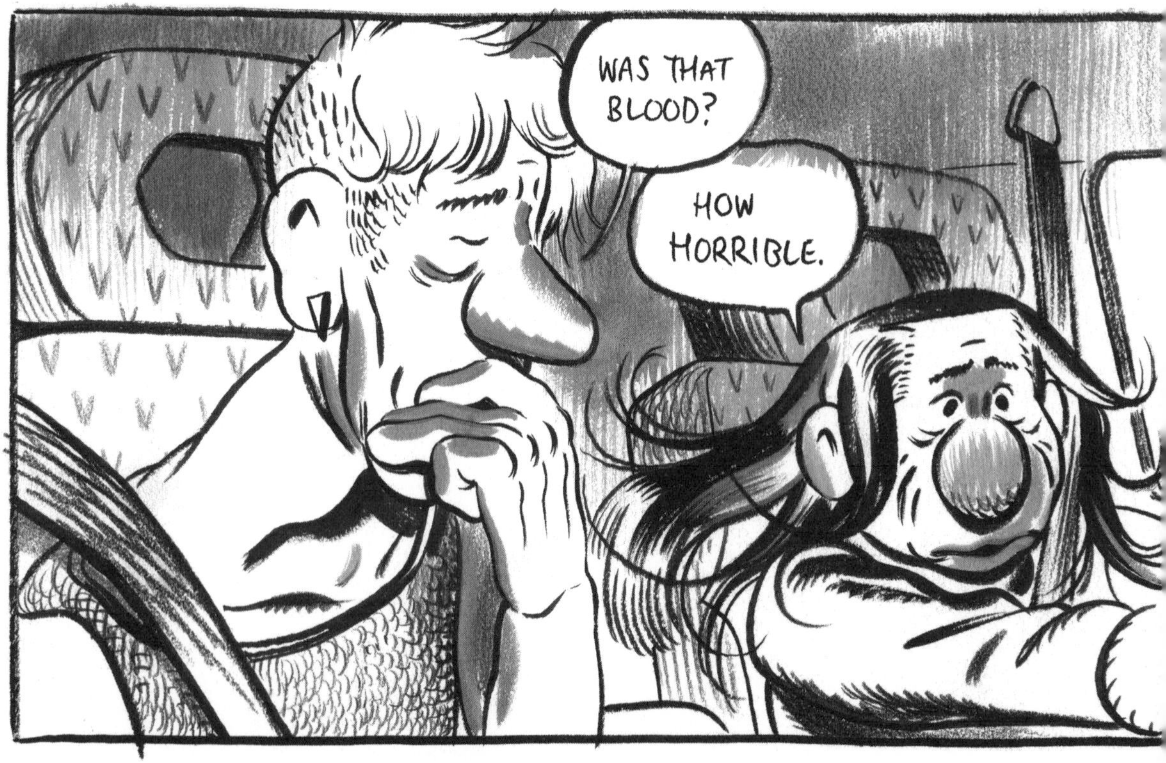
WAS THAT BLOOD?
HOW HORRIBLE.

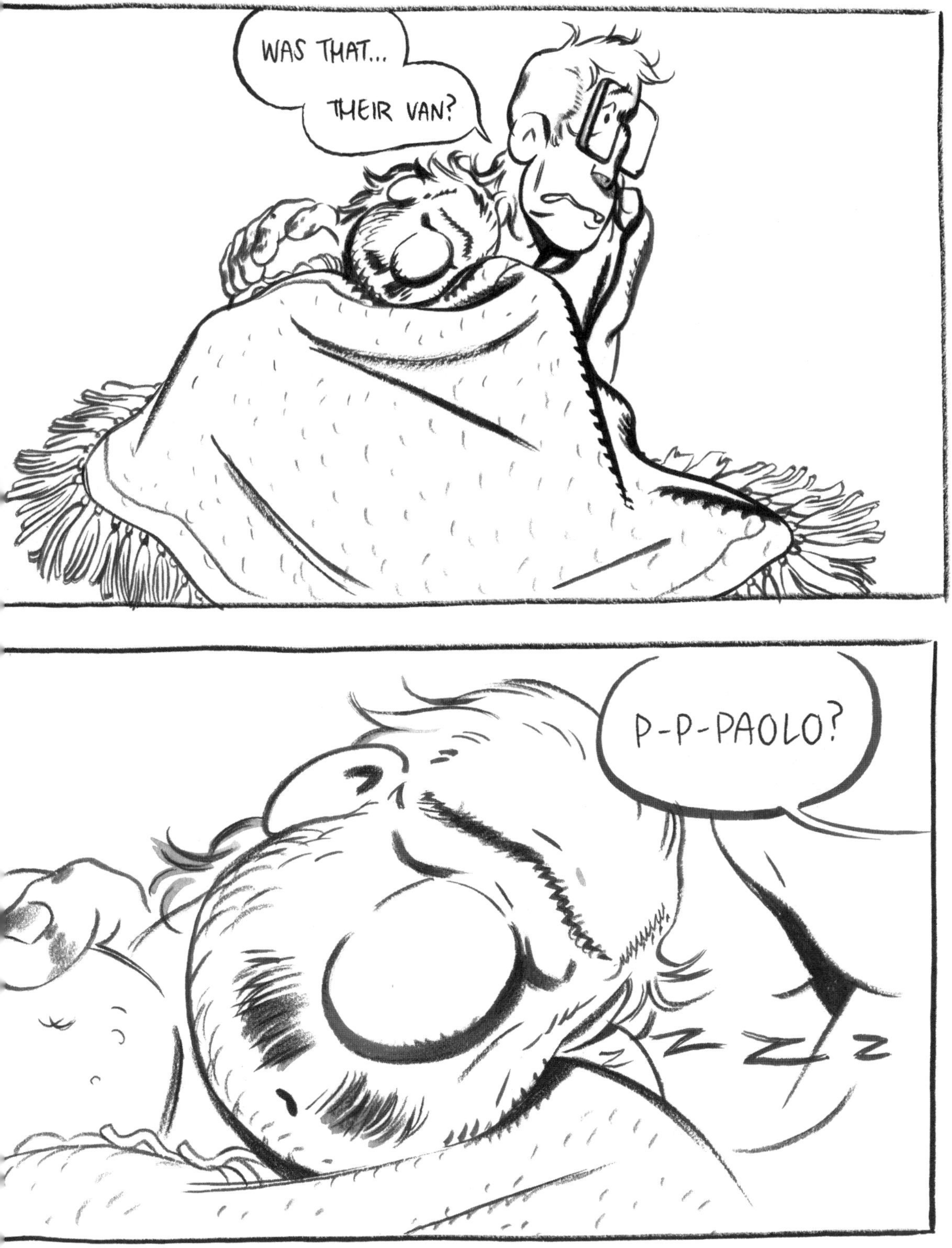
WAS THAT...
THEIR VAN?
P-P-PAOLO?
ZZZ

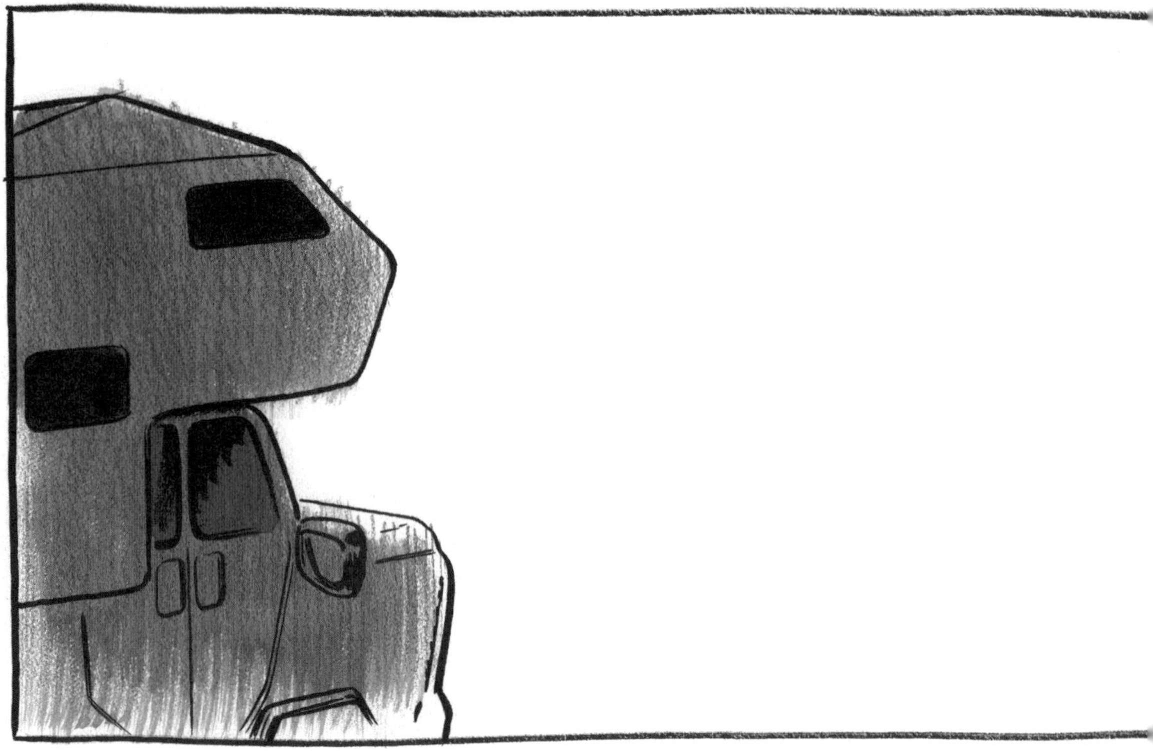

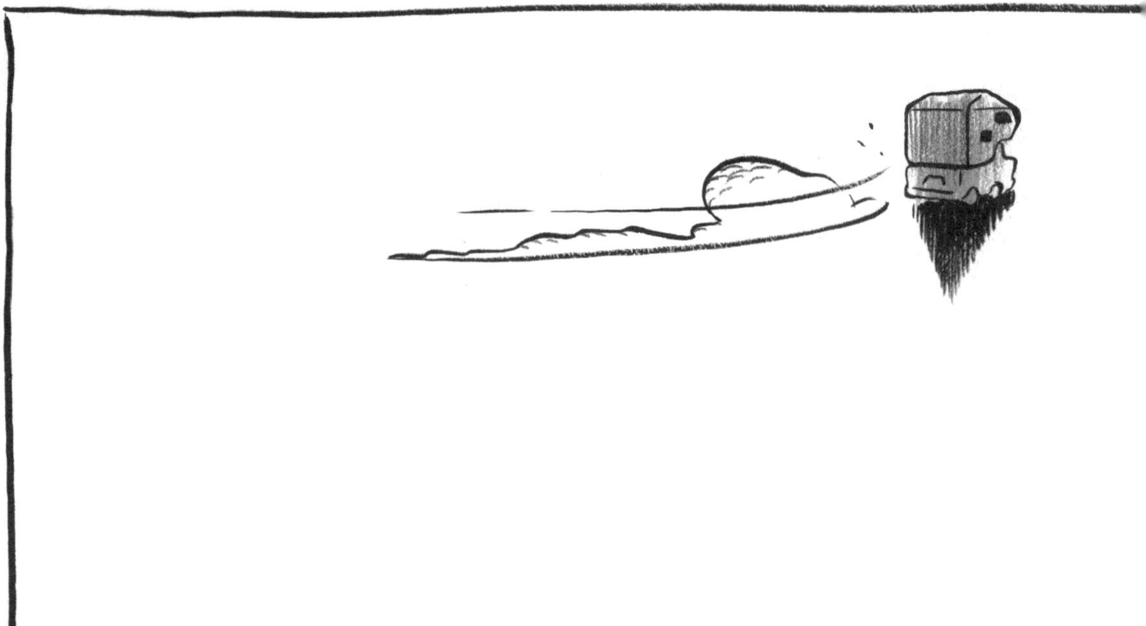

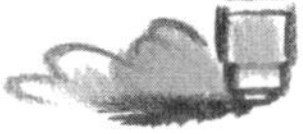

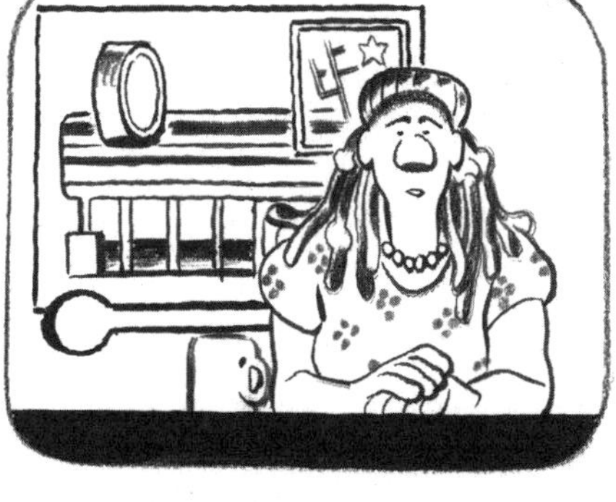

Authorities were called to a Nite Owl convenience store earlier today.

Blood had been detected inside the premises, setting off an alarm system that alerted local authorities to the possibility of a robbery resulting in physical violence.

Inside, authorities found Frank Bradbury covered in the blood of Raymond T. Herbert (both shown here). Herbert had been stabbed during an attempted robbery of a local home. He was found nearby in the passenger's seat of a service truck, alive but in critical condition.

Authorities say they found the two victims, Paolo Sordesto and Colin Preston, at a nearby hospital.

Sordesto had a minor stab wound, which has been treated.

Authorities have begun their investigation into what transpired earlier today.

Sources indicate that both Bradbury and Herbert may be linked to a string of burglaries throughout the area, which authorities have yet been unable to more fully investigate.

With the increase of building projects in what has colloquially been referred to as "The Wastes," authorities have only just begun to extend their policing into this previously uninhabitable area.

Next up, we will be joined here in the studio by a local man who claims to have kept an actual snowball from the last naturally occurring snow storm in this area thirty-five years ago. Stayed tuned after this commercial break.

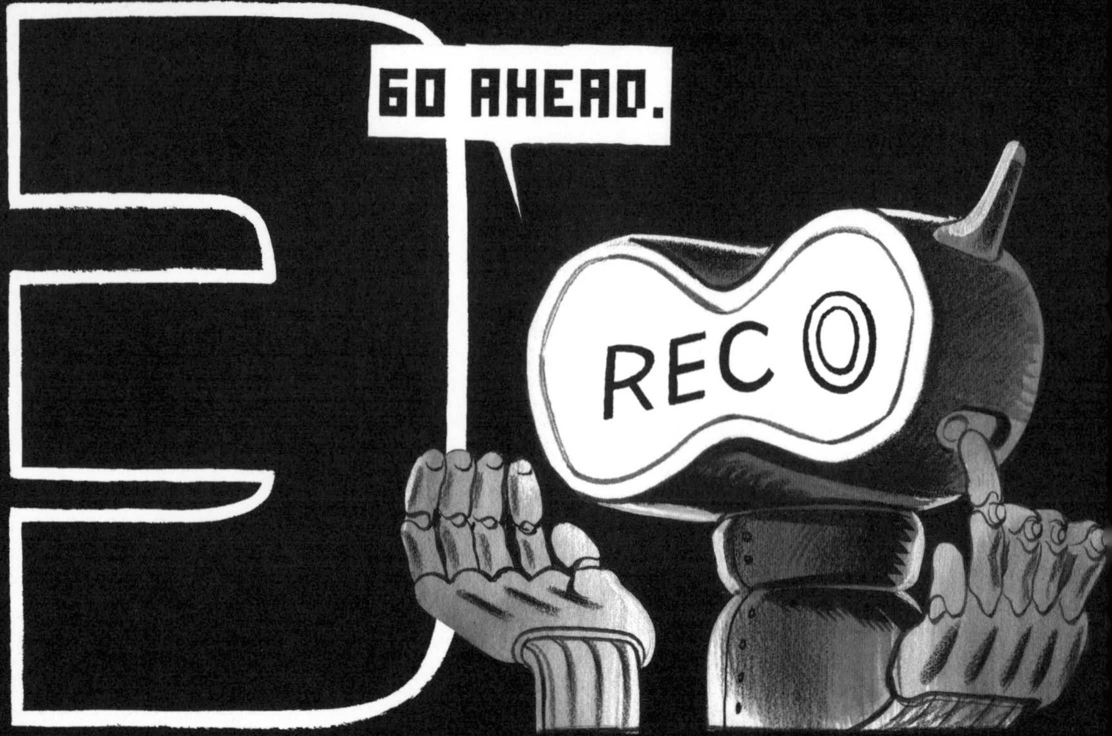
GO AHEAD.
REC

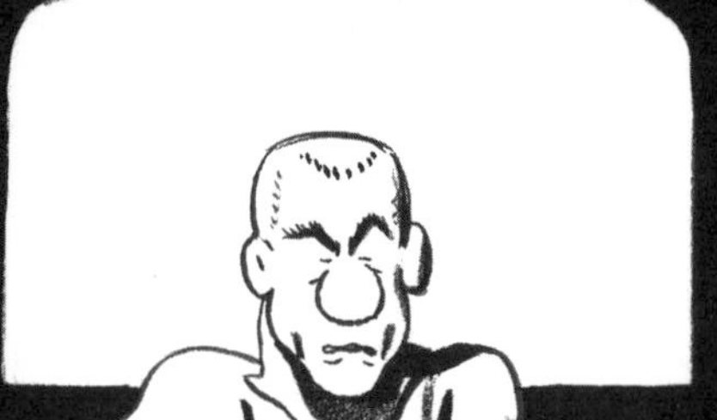

Frank: You already know what we did.

Robot: Sentences are rendered only after a confession has been made.

Frank's lawyer: My client has the right to not say something that may incriminate him during this ongoing investigation.

Frank: Whatever, we did it! This is a waste of my time.

Frank: Besides, I'm sure Ray is next door confessing everything.

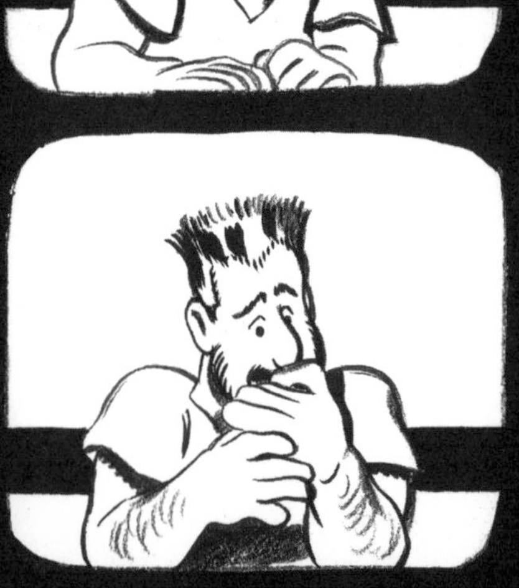

Raymond: I just...I'm sure he thinks I'm going to confess everything, doesn't he?

Robot: We cannot disclose anything about your partner's current interrogation at this time.

Robot: You can take as much time as you would like.

Frank: Fine by me. Clearly I'm not going anywhere.

Raymond's lawyer: You don't have to say anything you don't want to.

Raymond: I know, but I will, because this is how it's always worked between us.

Raymond: I was the violent one initially.

Frank: Whatever, Ray killed that other guy first. He's going to say it was an accident and I'm sure you'll all believe him because he's the nice one.

Raymond: But that came later, after everything else. Frank had lost his job right before we met so he ended up moving in with me. It seems…childish to mention love right now, but…anyway, I was taking care of him financially, too. He had been working at a Power Relay Station, and all he said was that there was an altercation. Anyway, I was helping him out, but I think he was pissed he couldn't take care of himself.

Raymond: It started with petty theft. Smaller stuff. Usually from his ex-boyfriends. He got arrested the first time after he got caught beating up Bruce over those speakers.

Frank: They were mine! No one ever believes that Bruce stole them from me!

Raymond: So, Frank went away for anger management…

Frank: That place was such a crock! Rolling Brooks or Steaming Meadows, whatever it was called....The State decided I was a threat to public safety, but you already know that. Lotta good that place did me.

Raymond: ...and I kept working to pay for his treatment and our...or well, my apartment...and I just waited, which I guess is what you do when you're in love. He got out and still couldn't get a job. Then there was that weekend we met Jens...

Frank: Ray met this guy while we were out drinking who installed security systems for a living. He came over to our place, and I offered to pay him for his employee identification card since he could easily get another job. I mean, he sounded like he didn't even like his job! We were all pretty drunk at that point and I think he was mad—not Ray, but this guy— that we weren't having sex yet...Ray did it, not me.

Raymond: He attacked Frank, so I hit him with this...I guess it was a planter. Hard. We left his body out in the Wastes, out past the Highway 4 onramp. I was just scared and didn't know what to do, and no one goes out there anyway.

Frank: That was Ray! Not me. That's what happened. Honest truth.

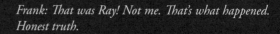

Raymond: So, Frank tried to make good. He had Jens's job installing security systems which he taught himself how to do by watching training modules at the library. Jens was technically a freelancer, so Ray could get the new jobs using Jens's phone... but then he got bored. One day, he came home with all of this stuff, stuff we didn't need that he said he could sell.

I didn't say anything at first because the money was good. I could finally just work my one job and I was grateful I didn't have to donate body tissue each week.

Raymond: Then the local pawn shops stopped buying the stuff Frank was stealing, so he started going out into the Comb Over...

Robot: The Comb Over?

Raymond: Oh, um, it's what people call that outer band of broken-down buildings between the City Center and the Wastes. There were all these efforts to fix it up, but they didn't really do anything...hence the name, "Comb Over."

Raymond: I think the drive out there is what got to him. All those big, beautiful homes between our cramped place and his new dealer. He'd show up in the Security Systems truck and just pretend to be legit, which I guess he was…he just wasn't being entirely honest with the clients about why he wanted inside their homes. I don't know what happened out there. He didn't even come back with the stolen goods at that point. Just the money, after he had already sold them.

We left town once he killed our landlord. He sold anything of Clover's that was valuable and then we were gone.

Robot: Please clarify. Frank murdered your landlord?

Frank: Where does he get off raising our rent?! On that dump?! Ray and I were good tenants! End of discussion.

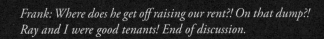

Raymond: We put a mattress in the back of Jens's truck and lived out of it. It was better than it sounds. Out in the Wastes, no one cares who you are or what you've done. If anything, the anger that people out there felt towards the new housing developments was a good cover for us. They know that land is all unusable, but it's theirs. I think Frank started feeding off the frustrations of the locals we'd meet in bars and started taking his anger out on those new homes. Besides, no one who was already living out there had anything for him to steal.

Most of the new homes were empty—not of stuff, but of people, which made his job easy. Most of these places are second homes, so their owners only come out sporadically.

Frank: Don't let Ray put all the blame on me! He was out there with me in that truck! He and I! Door to door!

Raymond: Most of our heists…haha heists…no one was harmed. There was that one woman who lived alone. That was an accident. I think she died from the shock of us waking her up. I was there for that one.

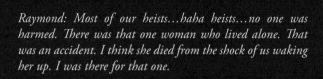

Frank: Ray is going to say, oh, I was the sane one, oh, I was the nice one. I was the one who didn't know how to stop him.

Raymond: Frank got really obsessed with that young guy. I mean, it was hard not to notice him. His place was the only one lit up at night.

Robot: Why do you think Frank became fixated on Paolo?

*Raymond: He stuck out. Being out there alone. He was cute. Or…is **still** cute, I should say.*

Robot: What were you thinking at this time?

Raymond: About the guy? Just that it seemed so nice to be a cute guy living in a nice house. It shouldn't be as hard as it is to have that life.

Frank: I'm such an idiot for not knowing that a second guy came out to visit! He should be here, too! He could have killed Ray!

Raymond: Looking back on it now, it all feels so inevitable, but...it was really good for a while. I'm sure talking about love makes me sound like a little kid who got tricked into all of this, but we...or should I say, I...wanted to make a home together. I still do, in a way. Frank had an awful childhood, and I guess mine was okay, but this need to build something substantial as an adult felt...well, impossible, but also desperately important. But it shouldn't be! It should feel easy to be alive.

Raymond: In stories like this, people always act like crimes of passion happen one morning, randomly. Some stressed out housewife just so happens to smash her husband's head in with a frying pan over breakfast...but, in my experience, it takes a long time to lift that pan.

Raymond: Months. Years, even. Every day it gets a little lighter...and then, suddenly, you feel like you're out of options.

After our thorough investigation, we have found conclusive evidence that Raymond T. Herbert and Frank Bradbury can be linked to the deaths of six individuals:

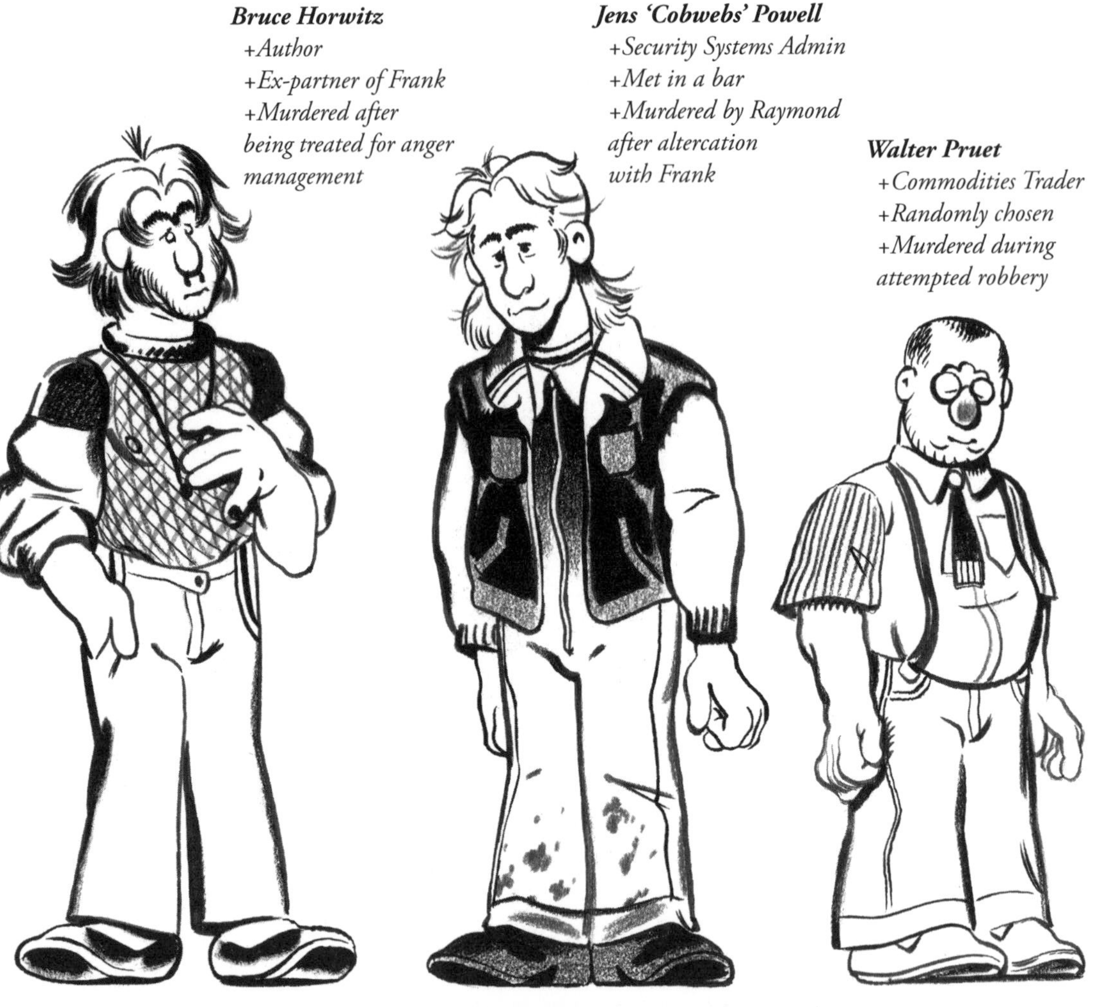
Bruce Horwitz
+Author
+Ex-partner of Frank
+Murdered after being treated for anger management
Jens 'Cobwebs' Powell
+Security Systems Admin
+Met in a bar
+Murdered by Raymond after altercation with Frank
Walter Pruet
+Commodities Trader
+Randomly chosen
+Murdered during attempted robbery

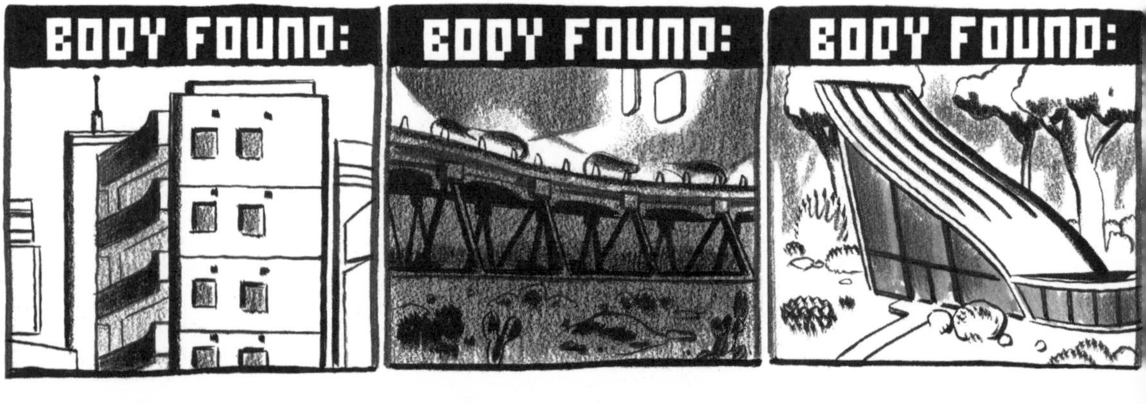
BODY FOUND:
BODY FOUND:
BODY FOUND:

Ashley 'Clover' Donner
+*Lyricist / Landlord*
+*Owned Raymond's apartment*
+*Murdered*

Anita Lang
+*Retired social worker*
+*Randomly chosen*
+*Heart attack during attempted robbery*

Cristobal Cristobal
+*Waiter*
+*Randomly chosen*
+*Murdered during attempted robbery*

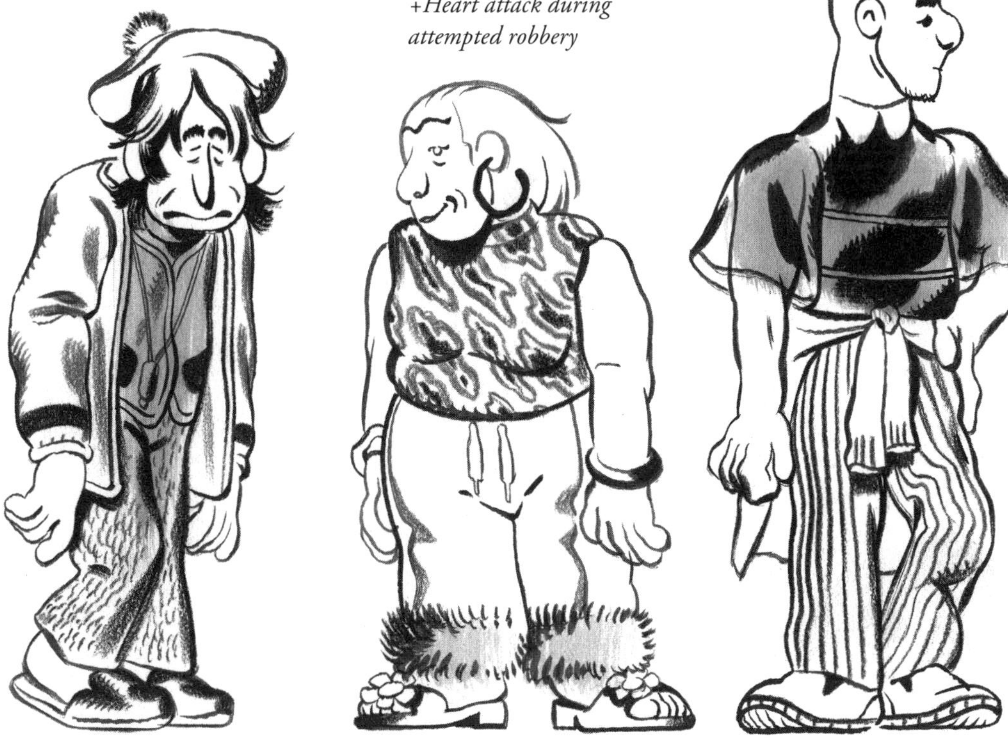

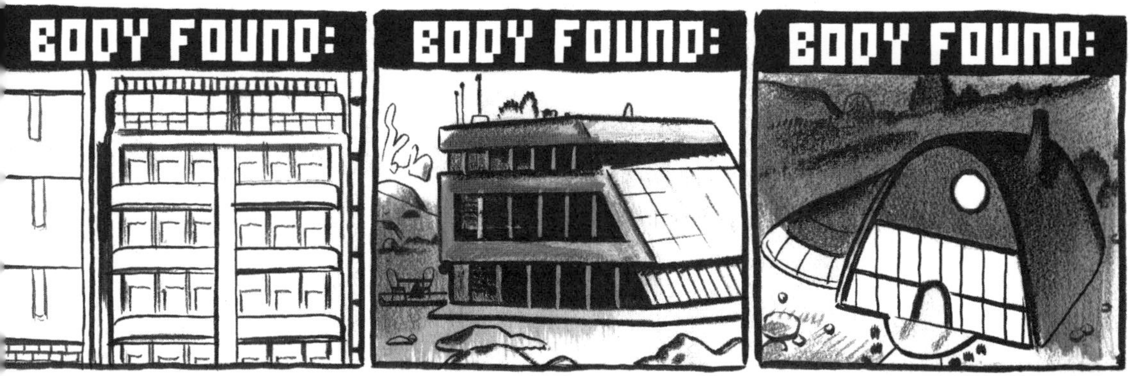
BODY FOUND:
BODY FOUND:
BODY FOUND:

The total number of individual stolen items is currently estimated at 2,451. The number of items found in the back of the truck, at the time of arrest, is 943. Locating each stolen item that has been sold by Frank and Raymond and returning them to their respective owners has been deemed impossible by the current investigation.

The investigation has estimated the total value of the stolen goods to be less than $100,000. Most, if not all, of the items are relatively inexpensive household goods, many of which were being rented from Central Furnishing at the time of robbery. These rented items have since been returned to Central Furnishing. Because losing a piece of rented furniture violates the contract clients make with Central Furnishing at the time of rental, those who have had rented goods stolen, and are still living, are required to pay a fine.

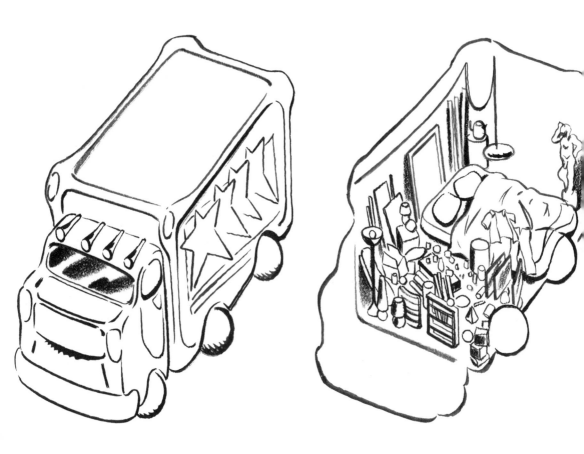

(Stolen security vehicle)

(Cut-away to show Frank and
Ray's modifications)

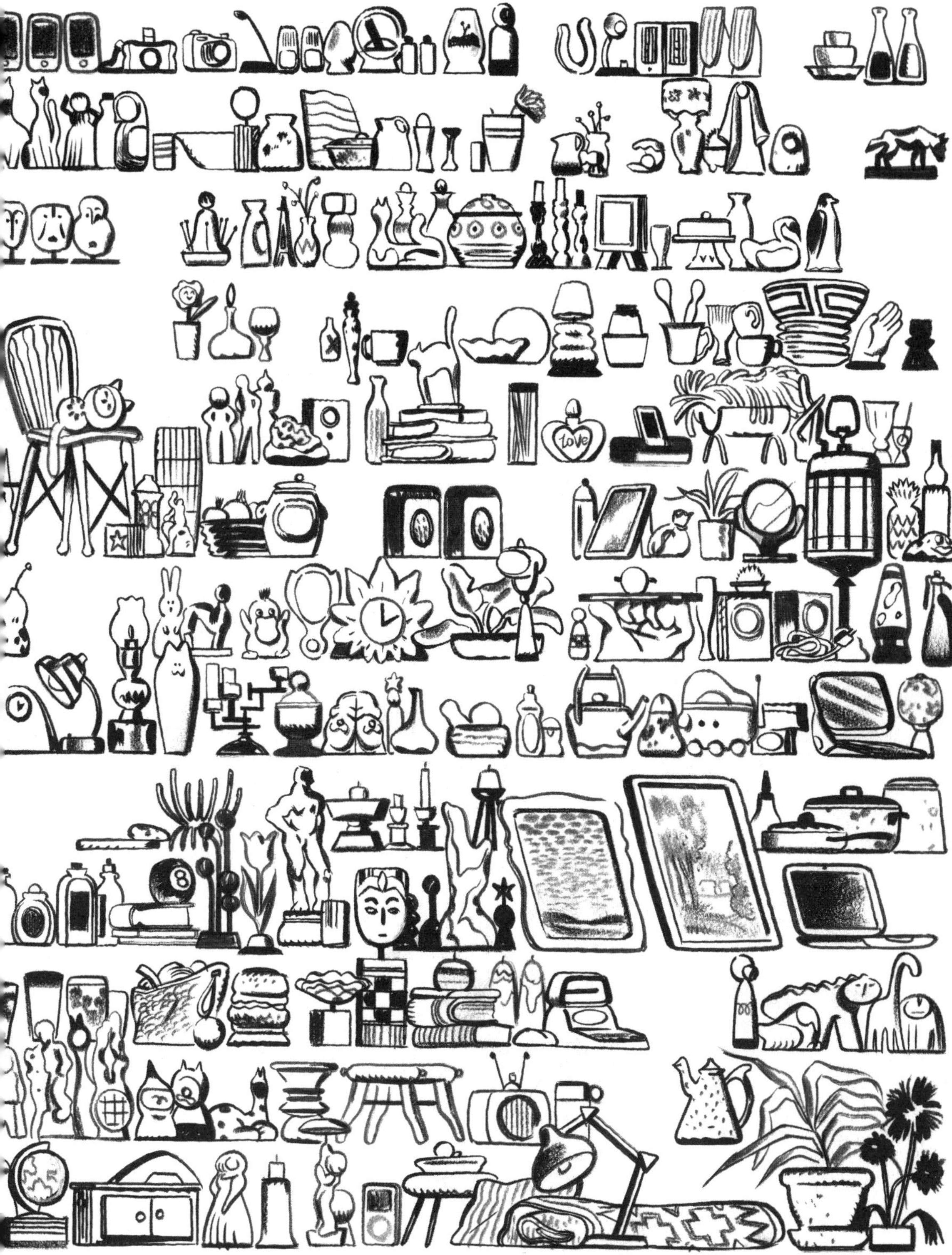
Love
8

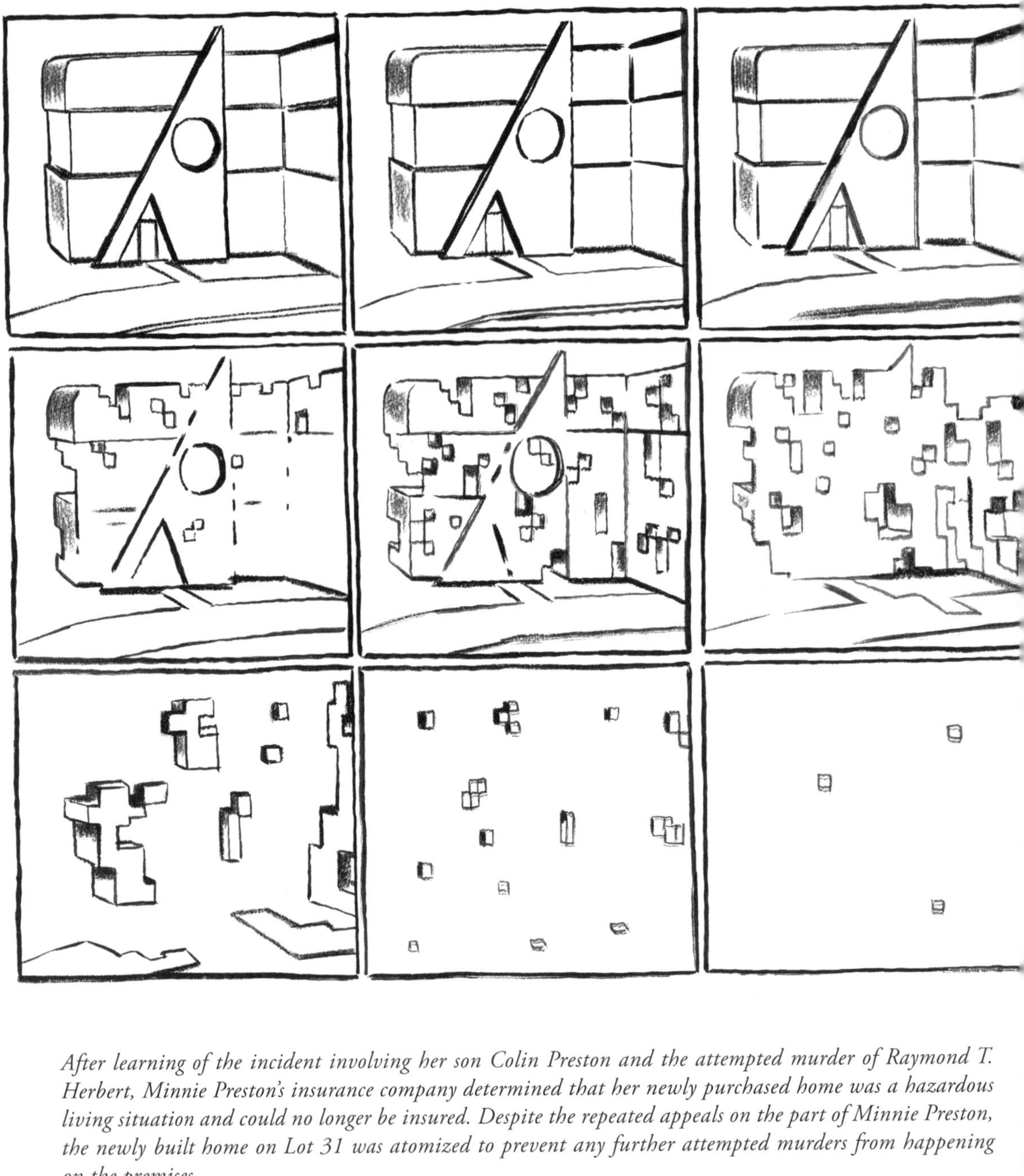

After learning of the incident involving her son Colin Preston and the attempted murder of Raymond T. Herbert, Minnie Preston's insurance company determined that her newly purchased home was a hazardous living situation and could no longer be insured. Despite the repeated appeals on the part of Minnie Preston, the newly built home on Lot 31 was atomized to prevent any further attempted murders from happening on the premises.

Lot 31 has stayed empty, although it was later adopted by local teenagers who have since turned it into a small park for skateboarding. There is a pending motion by the local Homeowners Association to level the unsanctioned skate park on Lot 31 to make space for additional parking. The local teenagers have been protesting this pending motion. No compromise has been reached as of this reporting.

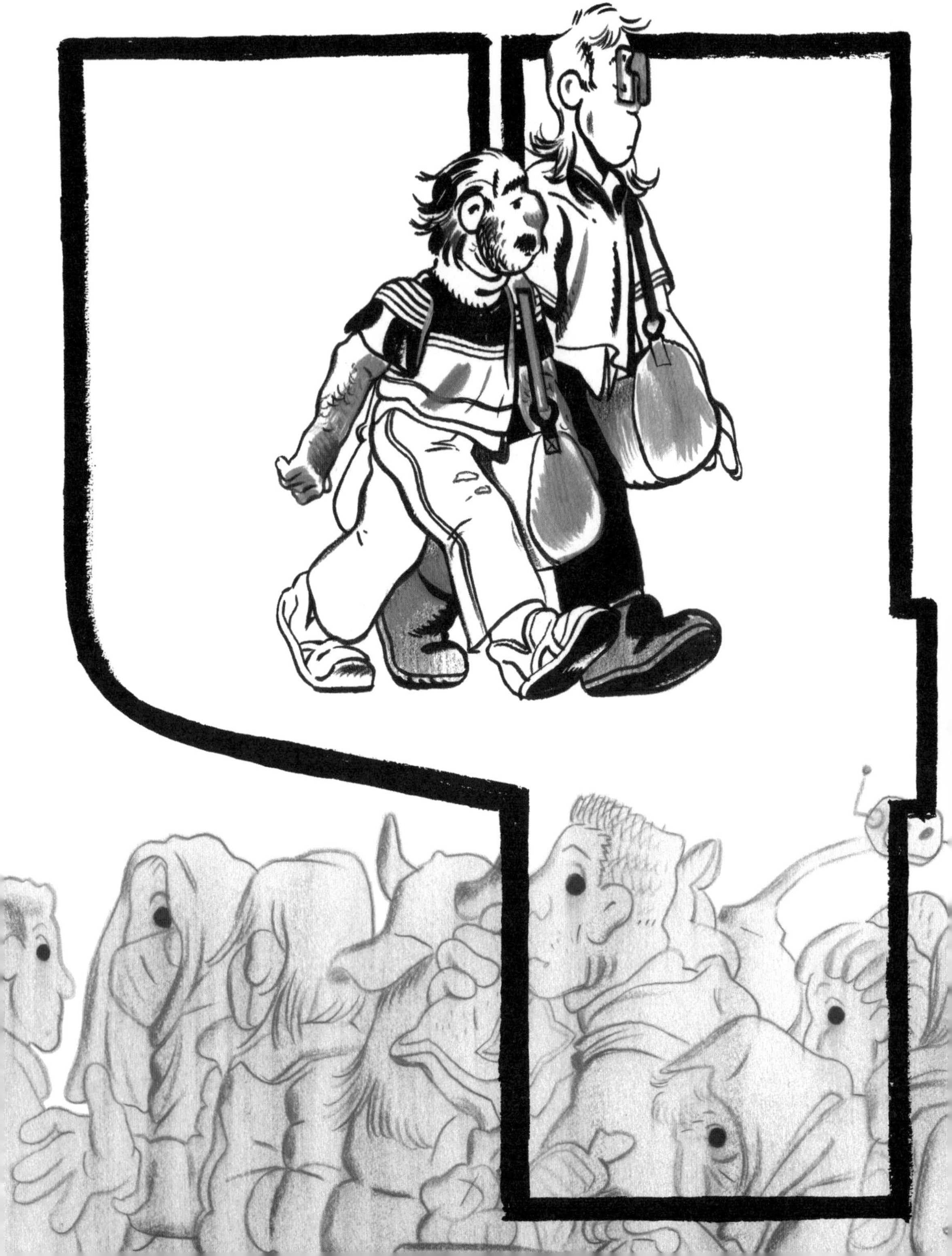

When they returned to the city, Colin and Paolo were certain that everyone knew what had happened to them.

News within the hub of the city circulated quickly. Attempted burglary by two men with a history of similar crimes, a stabbing with a kitchen knife…Surely their story, if only for a moment, had reached the eyes and ears of those back home.

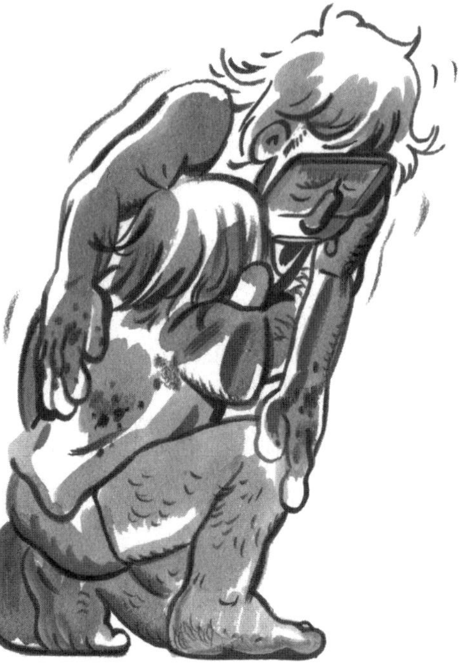

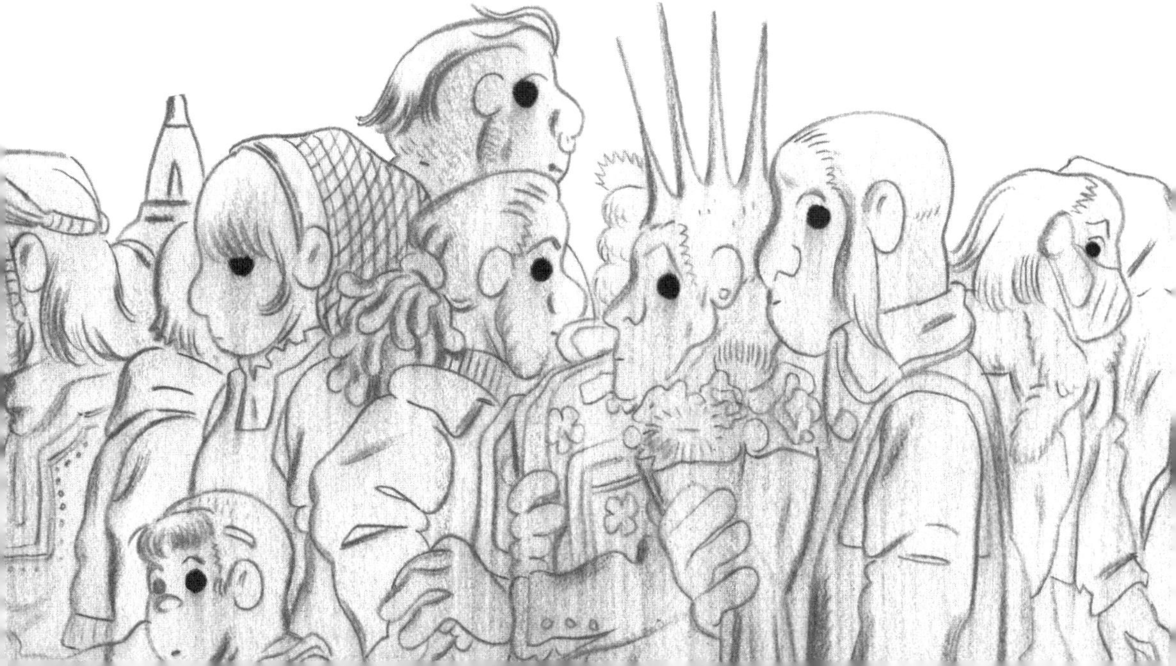

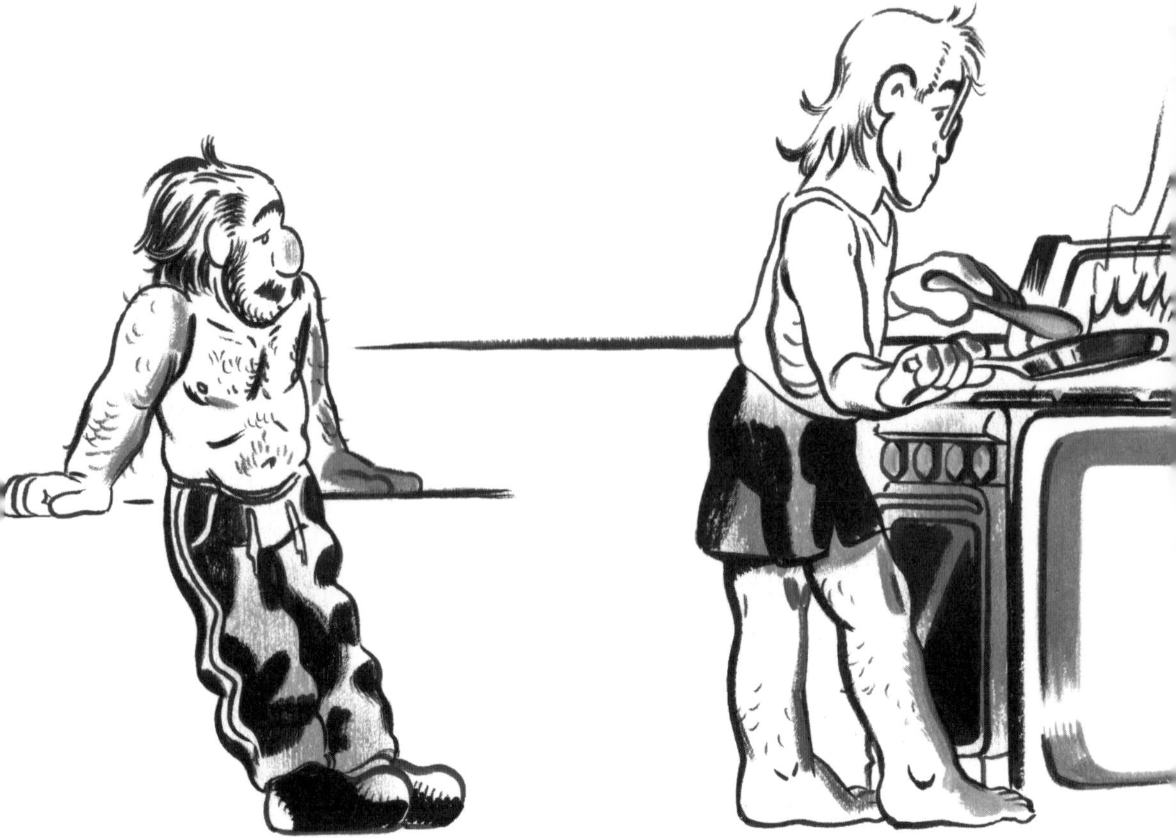

Together, they attempted to pick up their lives where they had left off. In many ways, everything still functioned as it once had, but Paolo couldn't deny that some intangible quality of who they were beforehand had ceased to exist.

When people asked, Paolo had a hard time articulating how Colin was doing. He would say that Colin was fine, which was true. But Paolo struggled with whether he should mention how he felt there was just less of Colin than there had been before, as if his body was having a harder time than usual of hiding what it kept deep inside.

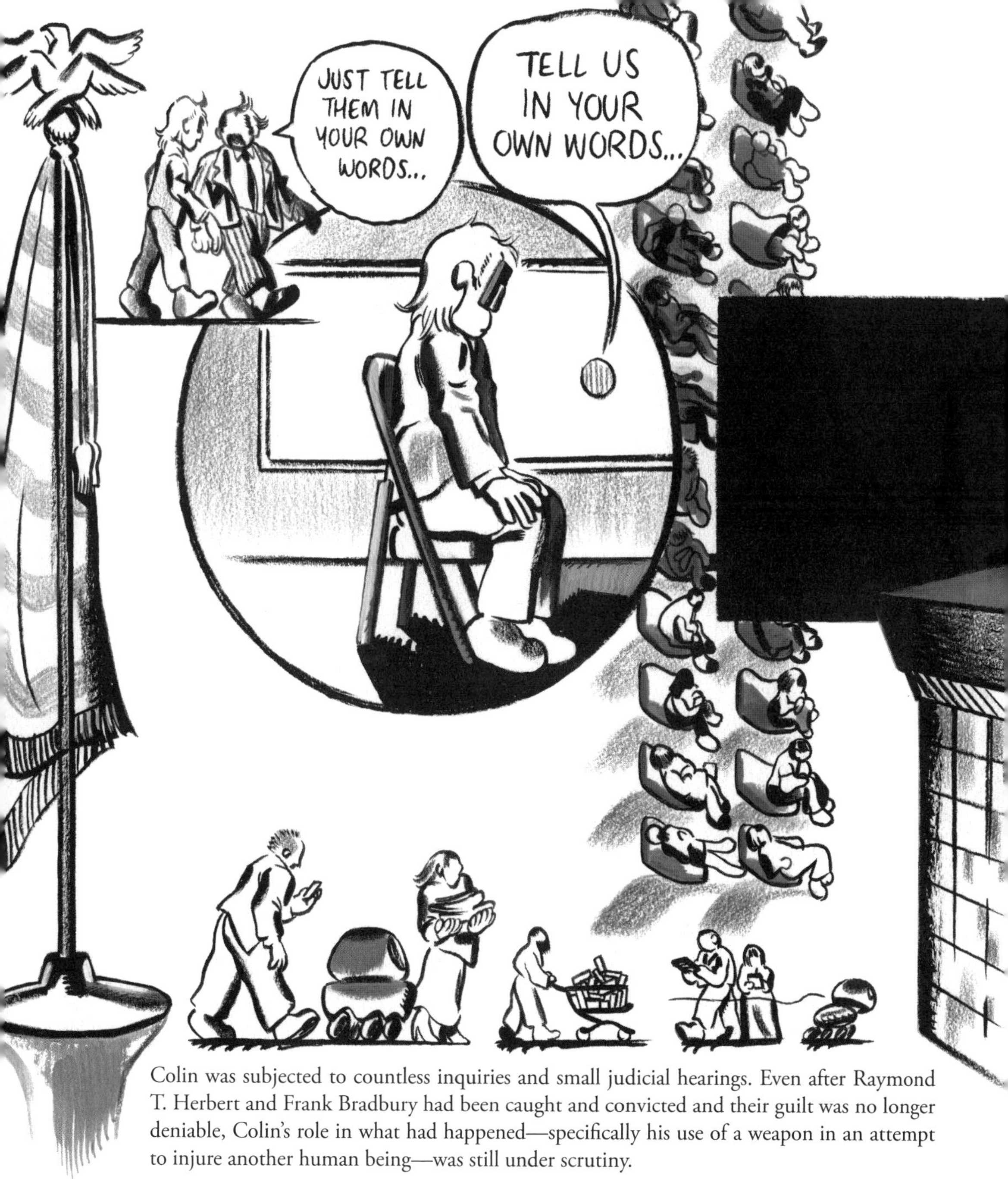
TELL US IN YOUR OWN WORDS...
JUST TELL THEM IN YOUR OWN WORDS...

Colin was subjected to countless inquiries and small judicial hearings. Even after Raymond T. Herbert and Frank Bradbury had been caught and convicted and their guilt was no longer deniable, Colin's role in what had happened—specifically his use of a weapon in an attempt to injure another human being—was still under scrutiny.

The current judicial branch of the government prided itself on having a truer sense of justice than the Administration had. Because all were equal in the eyes of the law, anyone's individual reasons for why they committed a crime were less important than whether or not the suspected criminal was successful in their attempt to commit said crime. The lawyer assigned to Colin's case had one point to stress at each of his hearings—that yes, Colin had used the knife in an act of self-defense, but more importantly, the defendant had not successfully killed the man he had stabbed. A more nuanced reason for Colin's actions wasn't necessary.

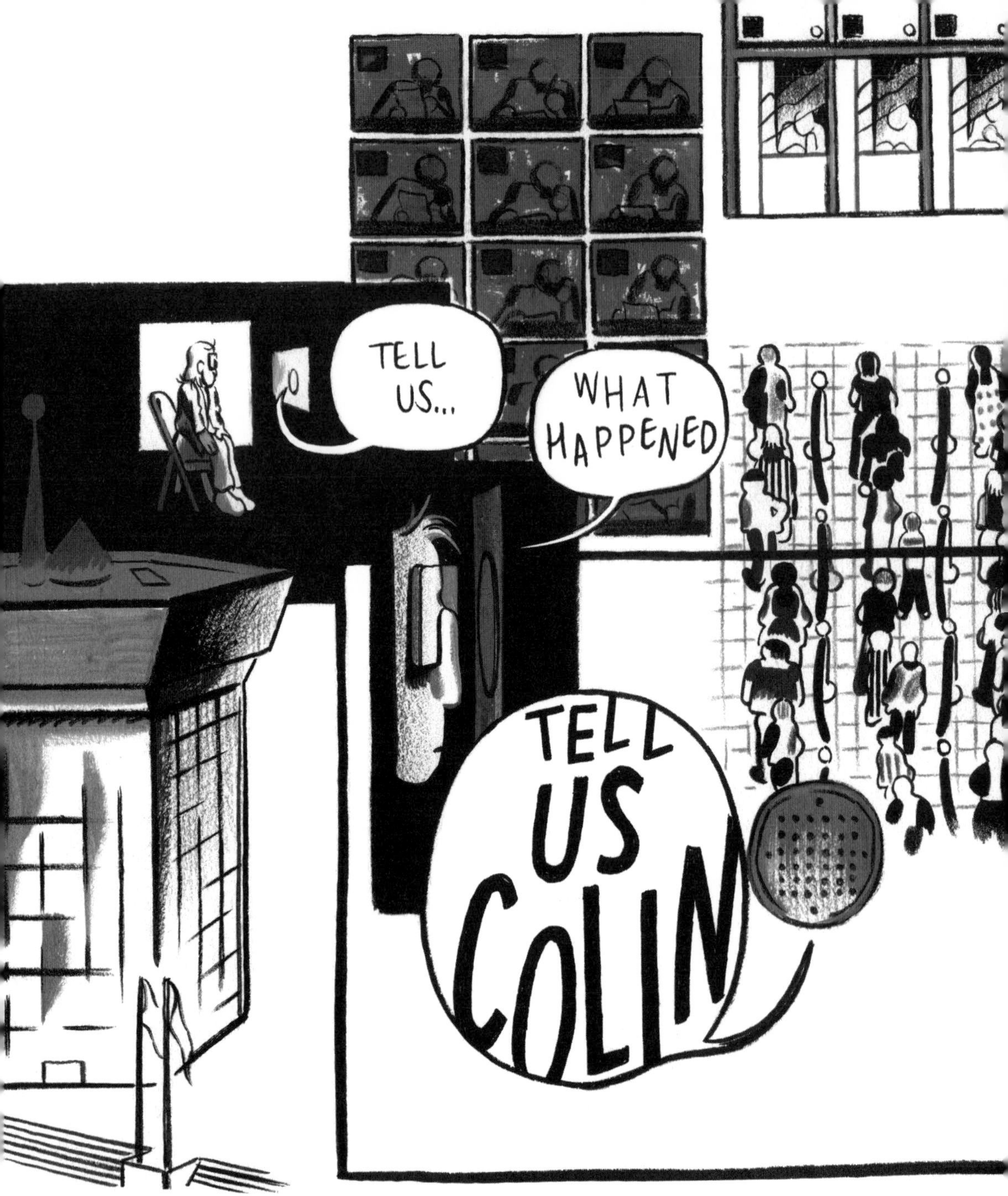
TELL US...
WHAT HAPPENED
TELL US COLIN

Each hearing Colin attended took place in a series of smaller and smaller rooms, deep inside the labyrinth of the Capitol building. Though the current government had done its best to hide the details of the Administration's sinister past, Colin knew, through his work at the Mayor's office, exactly what these rooms had once been used for. However, he was proud of his job, and felt secure in the knowledge that the federally funded murals and affordable in-building daycare center were helping everyone else forget their history, even if it was difficult for him to forget why he was there.

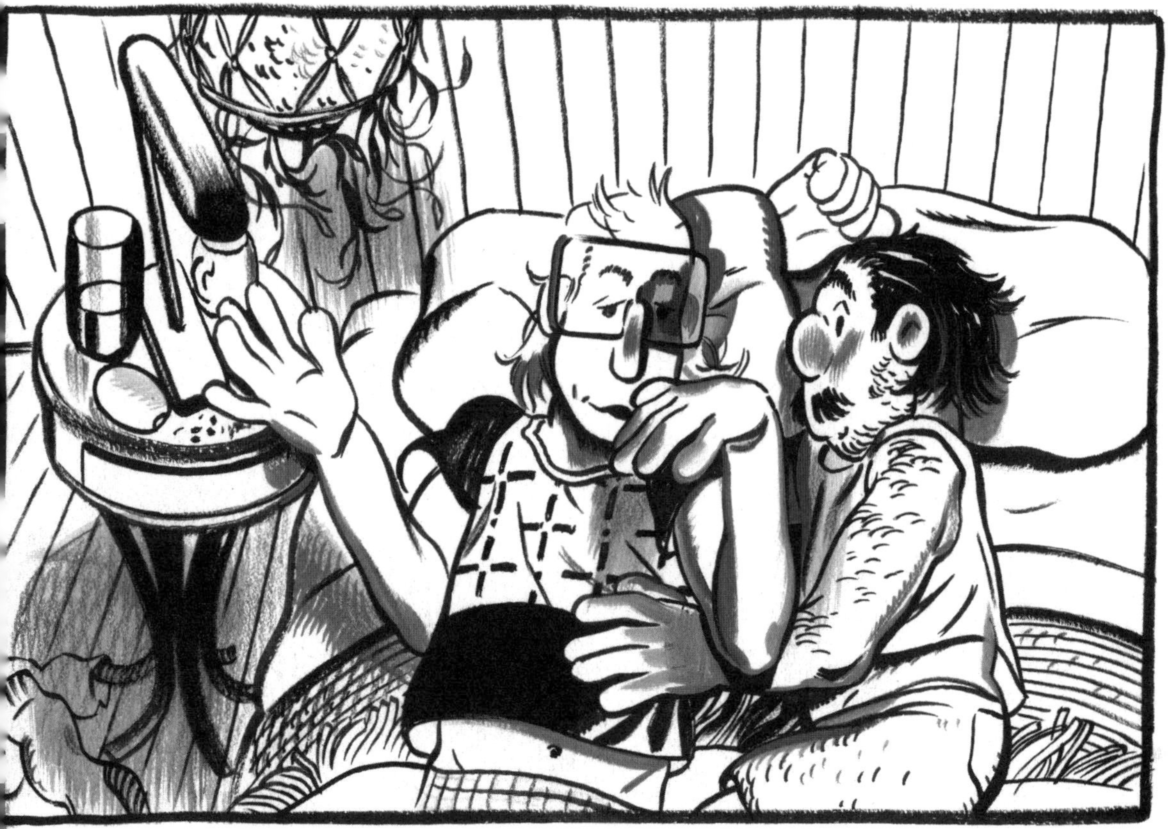

Ever the optimist, Colin would fill Paolo in on all he had witnessed in the Capitol that day, stretching the conversation to make the endless bureaucratic shuffling seem almost worthwhile. At the same time, Paolo was unsure of what to do for his boyfriend besides being supportive and engaged, as Colin had been countless times for him.

They were spending each night at Paolo's, which Paolo never seemed to question. Thinking back months later, it would seem so obvious that Colin had been slowly drifting away.

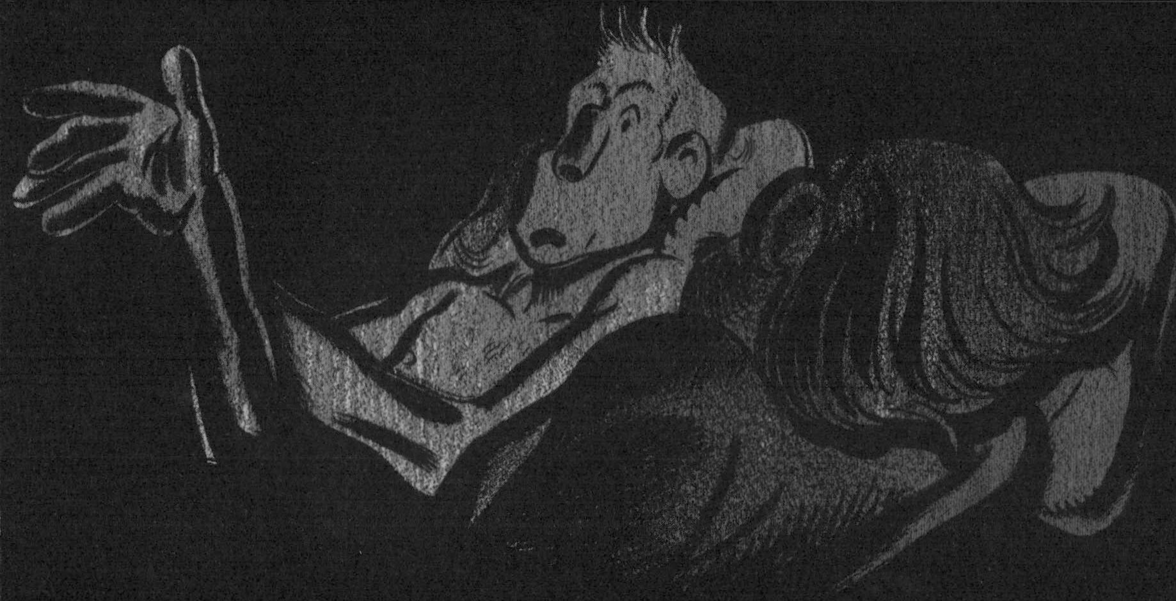

During what would be their last night together, Colin told Paolo the story of how one summer, back when he was a kid, a frog had kept everyone on their cul-de-sac awake for weeks. Each night, the frog's bellowing would come in through their open windows, rattling dishes and sliding furniture around. They tried their best to ignore it, accepting the frog as just another part of their lives, spending their nights marathoning old movies then sleeping the day away.

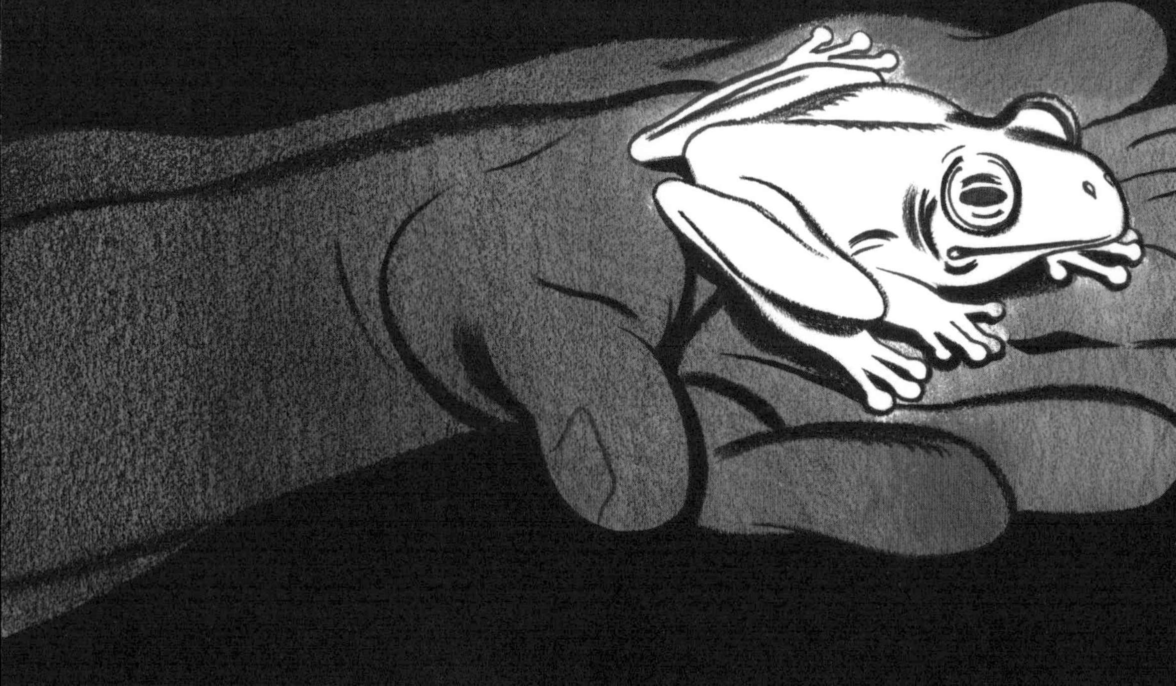

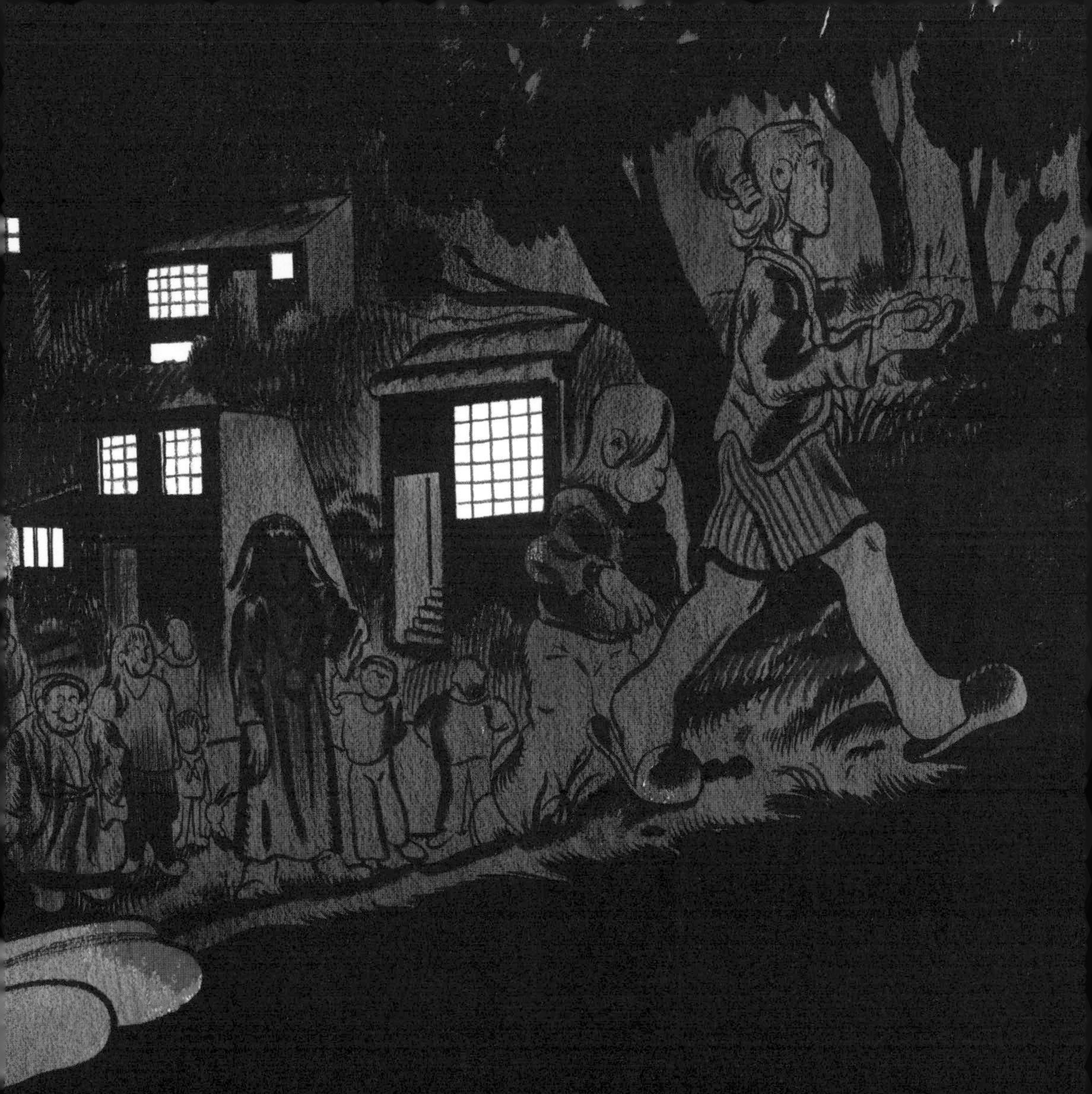

One night, feeling fed up and exhausted, Minnie found the frog, nestled in the brambles of a bush beside their split-level home. In Colin's story, she had walked the frog as far away as she could, followed by a small procession of weary neighbors. He remembered the frog vividly—a creature no larger than a bar of soap, white and smooth in the butterflied palms of Minnie's hands.

They had done their best to make space for it, rearranging their whole lives rather than dealing with the problem itself, no matter how small. But the frog had to go.

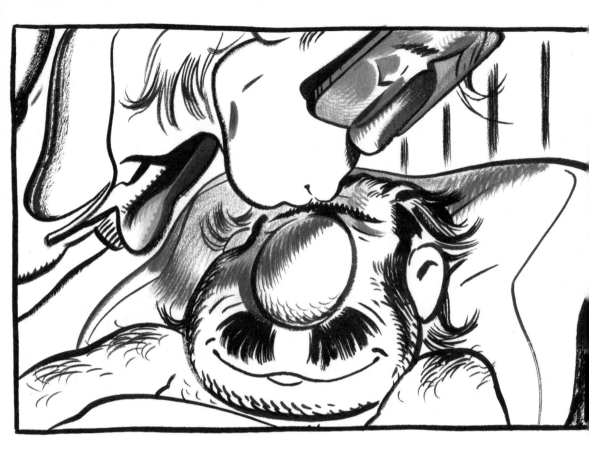

In the morning, Colin got out of bed, readied himself for work, and left.

He never returned to Paolo's apartment, that night or any other night that week.

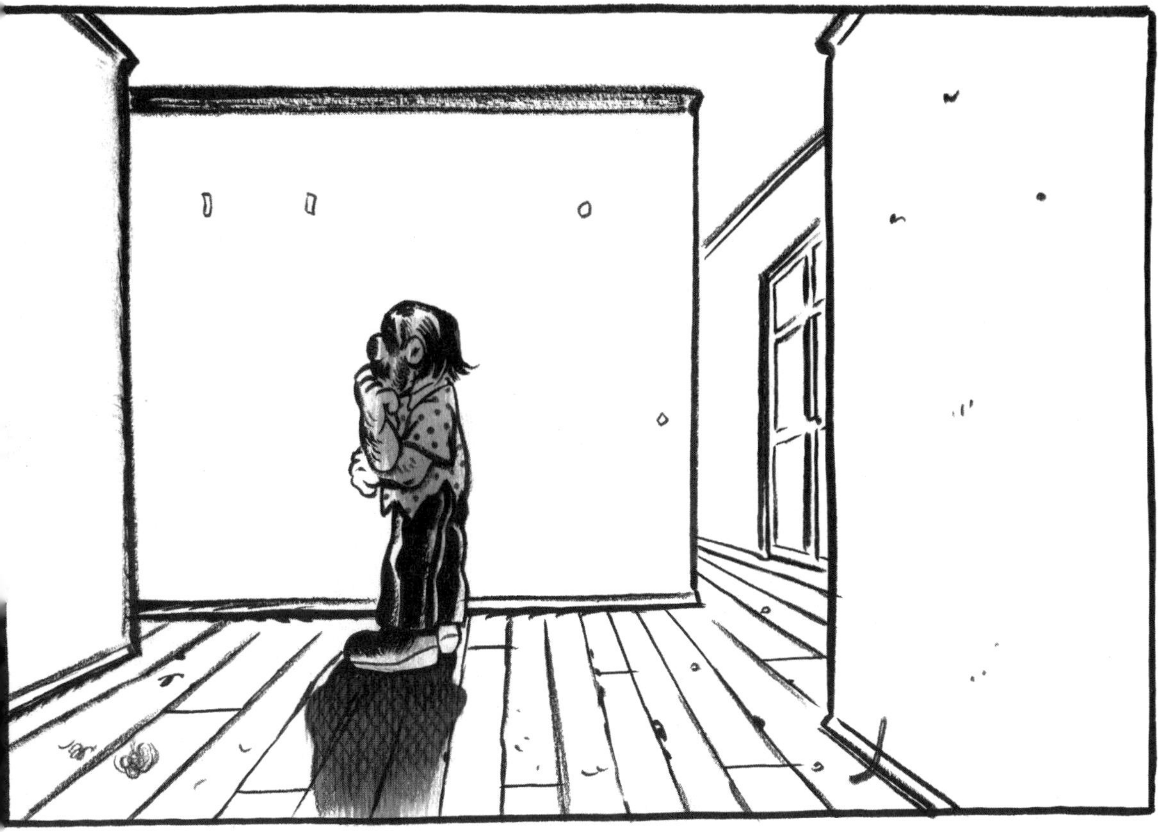

Two days later, and after asking the doorman to let him in, Paolo discovered Colin's empty apartment. Paolo hadn't known that his boyfriend had taken an indefinite leave of absence from work. That instead of going to work each day, he had been cleaning out his apartment. (Paolo assumed he had done so with the help of Avery, though he never asked them to confirm.)

Paolo felt an urgent need to find Colin, but in remembering his story about the frog, he knew that this had been Colin's way of avoiding conflict. He was fine—or at least, he wanted Paolo to think he was. This didn't change the hurt Paolo felt, standing alone in the barren apartment, knowing that Colin had decimated whatever life they had started to build together. He didn't fully understand it, but he knew that Colin had a desperate need to maintain the appearance of stability, and by protecting that need, he had negated Paolo's role as his partner.

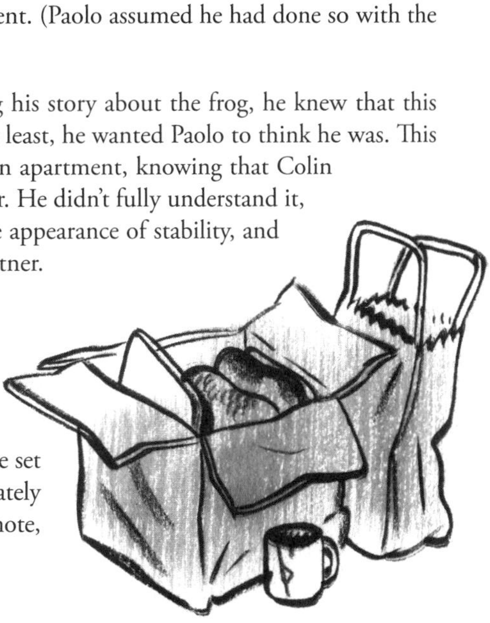

The belongings Paolo had left behind in Colin's apartment were set aside in a box by the door. Everything had been folded and delicately placed, waiting to be found and taken home. There was no note, and Paolo felt foolish wishing one would miraculously appear.

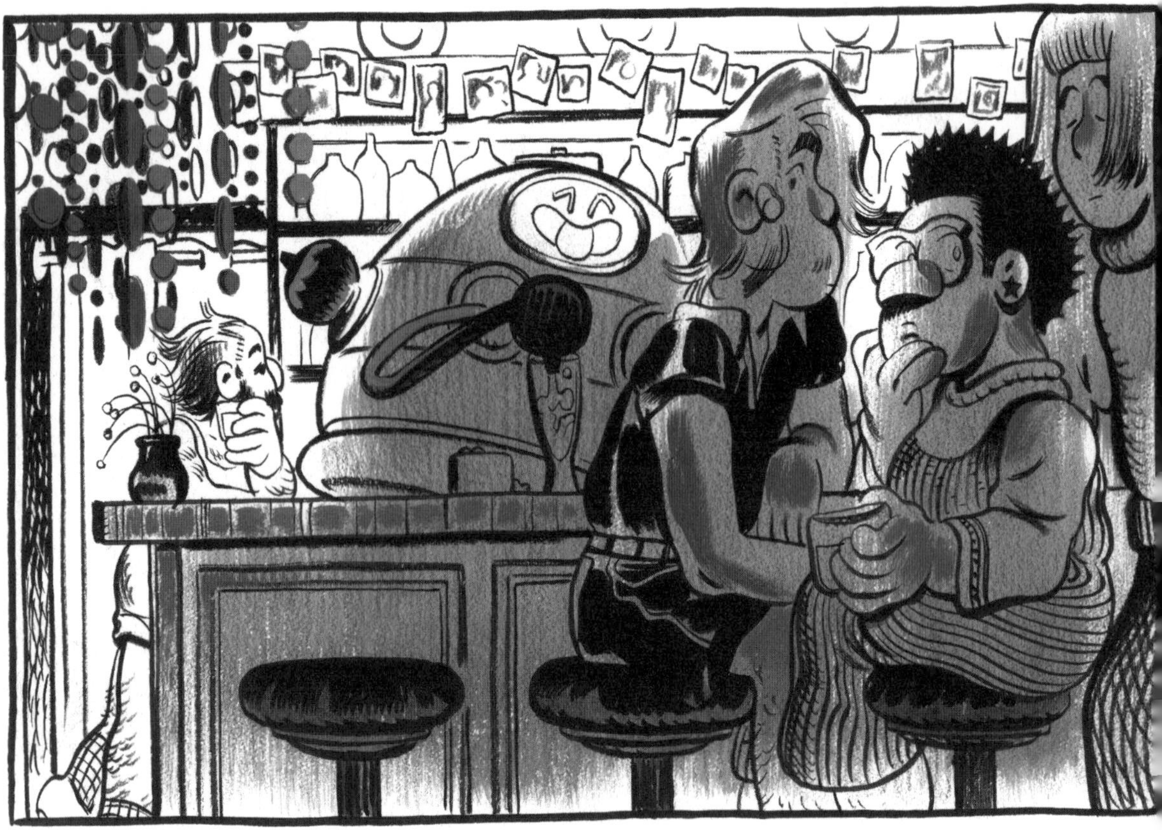

Unemployed, and with too much free time, Paolo started going out more. Colin had felt uncomfortable with their sudden visibility after the incident, unsure if the glimmer in someone's eye was one of recognition or nothing more than a flirty glance. Paolo didn't mind, though. In fact, it made going out easier, pulling men toward him with very little effort.

He stopped going to what had been his usual spots with Colin. The exchanges with Avery and their roommate Jacqueline were too awkward without Colin by his side.

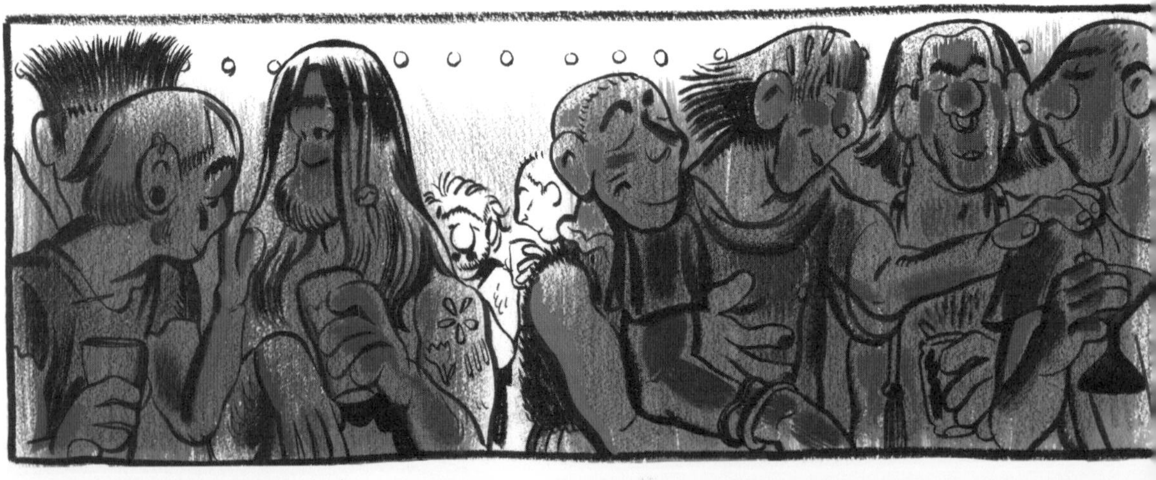

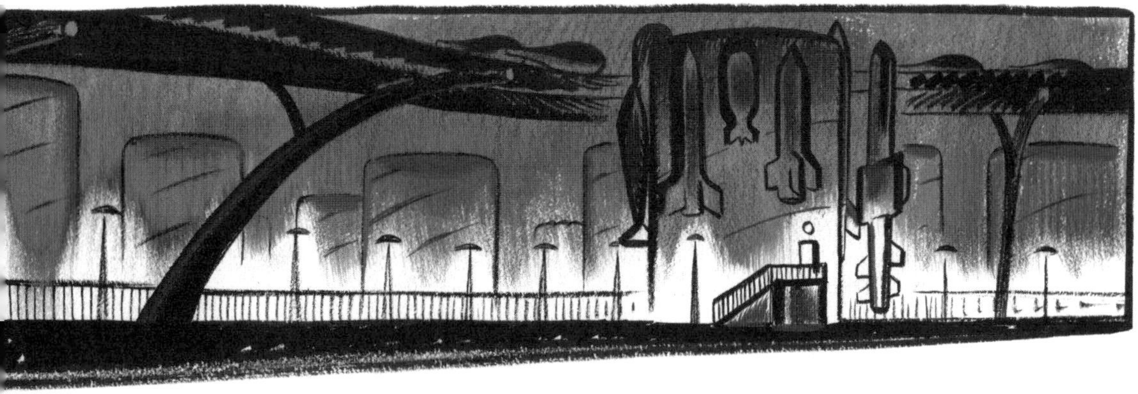

He found new places to go, bars that were older, less popular, harder to find. Places where men had hidden out during less supportive times. The Pit, situated at the bottom of a now-defunct missile silo, still had a Looker—a local navigation system originally devised to keep bars in contact with one another, alerting each other of any possible trouble from the Administration. It also had a search function to help men find other men in the area. A quick photo of the "looker" was taken and added to a map of other men available for whatever it was someone was looking for at the time. The system was color-coded and efficient, even if it had been largely replaced by mobile devices.

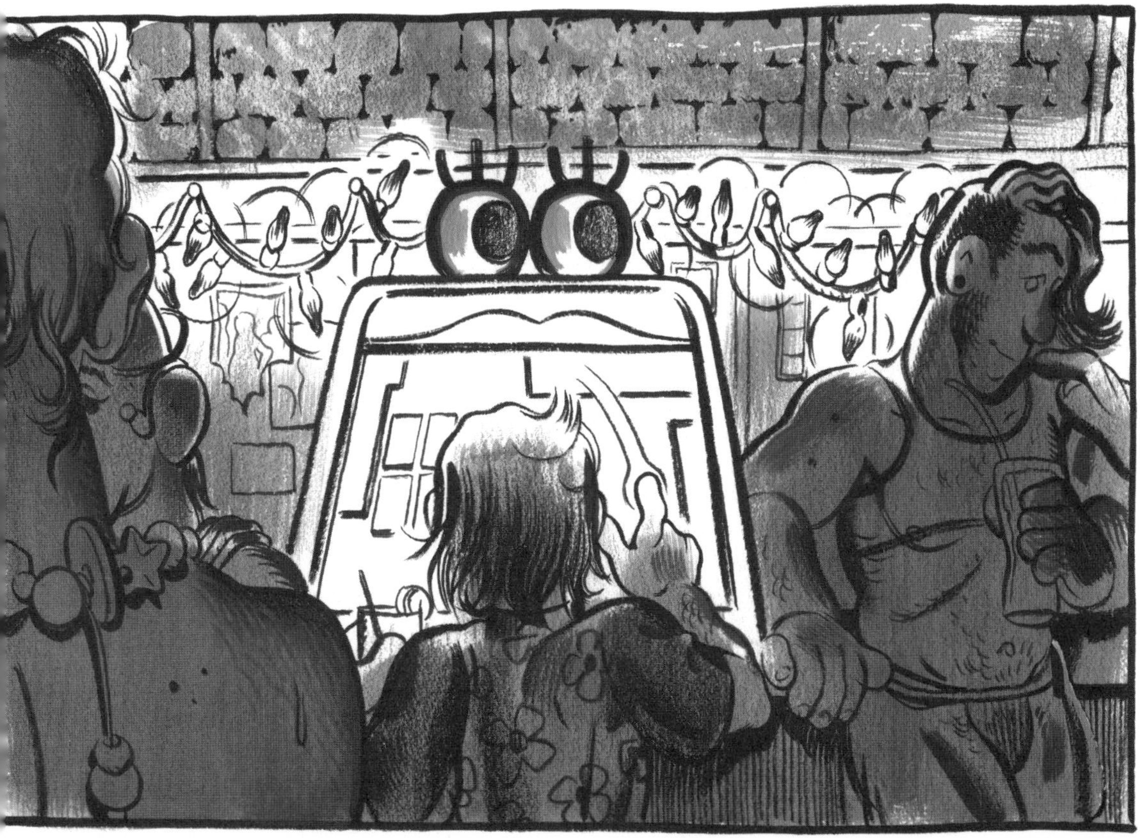

This was how Paolo found Arbor again.

Colin was the one who had originally met Arbor and brought him into their relationship. He also was the one who had first mentioned finding a third. He would be the first to blush over any mention of sex, but much like his mother, he was the biggest flirt Paolo had ever known. Colin was overly generous by nature, and that extended to his romantic interactions. His desire to please those around him was bottomless.

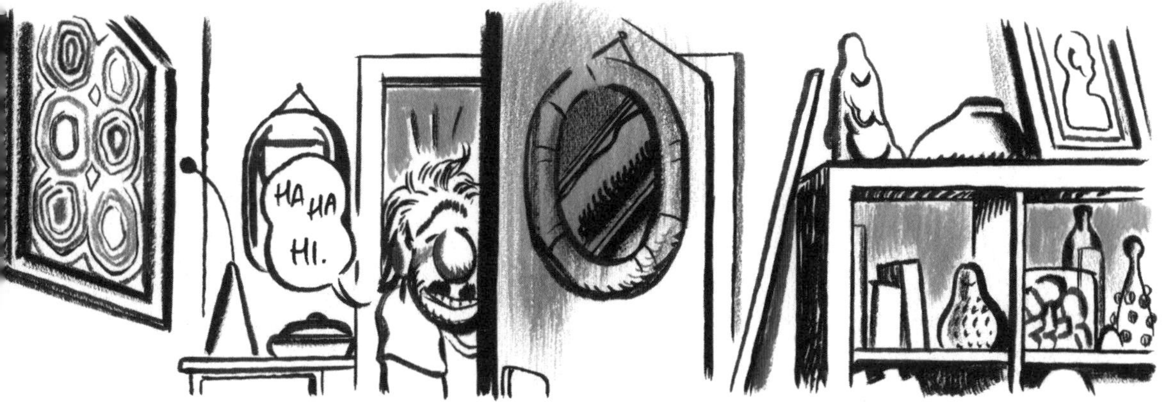
HA HA HI.

Paolo still remembered when he first met Arbor, standing in the doorway of Colin's apartment. Arbor was laughing as he attempted to fill three wine glasses at once, flirting with his half-naked boyfriend who had urged Paolo to drop everything and come over immediately.

Arbor was the *most* of everything—Biggest. Tallest. Loudest. Kindest. Paolo learned that there could be no jealousy over Arbor because there was just no comparing yourself to him. There was only ever going to be one Arbor on this planet, and here he was, filling the room from floor to ceiling.

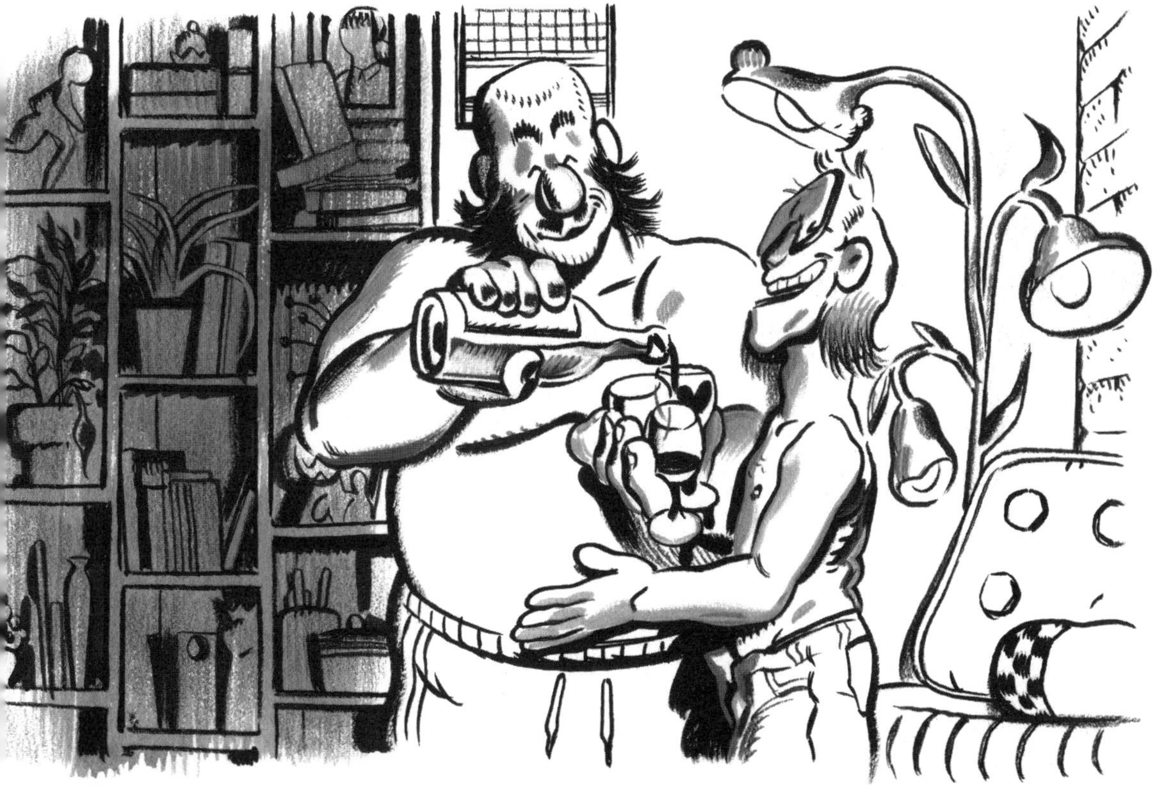

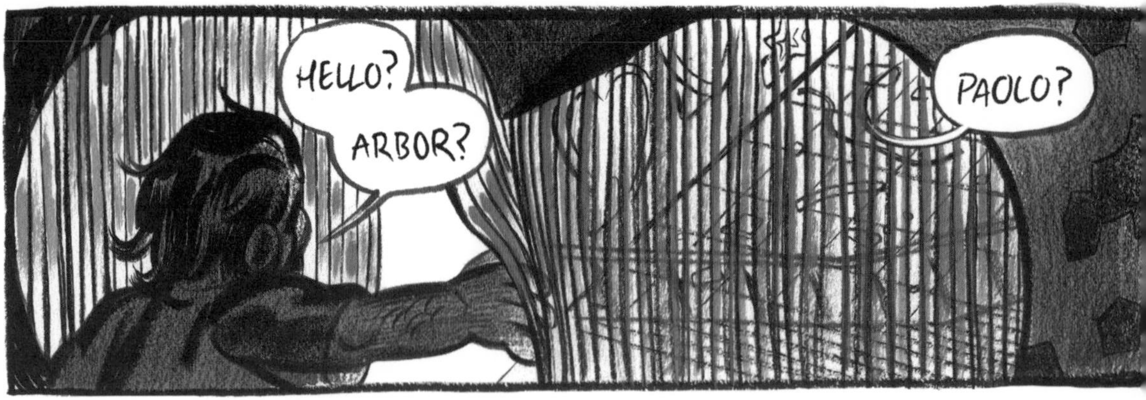
HELLO?
ARBOR?
PAOLO?

In the months since they had last seen each other, Arbor had purchased (that word being used in the most general sense) a run-down, subterranean restaurant that had once been called Fanny's. It had sat vacant for nearly six decades until Arbor accidentally found it while scrolling through a Looker at a nearby bar one night. Its digital marker was still blinking despite having no patrons inside.

It was clear Fanny's had once been grand—everything that could be in the shape of a heart was, from its raised dance floor to its three bars. Even the doorway onto the street was a heart, hidden beneath decades of faded posters, paint, and grime.

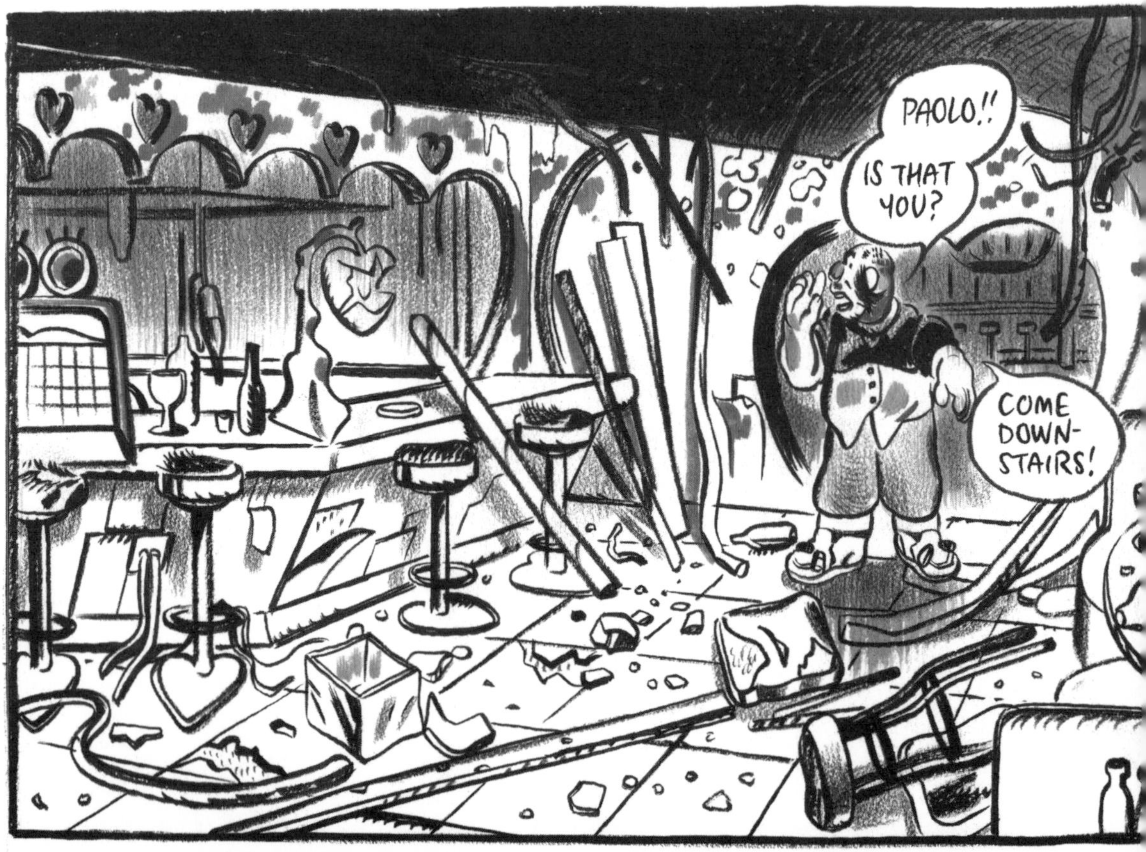
PAOLO!!
IS THAT YOU?
COME DOWN-STAIRS!

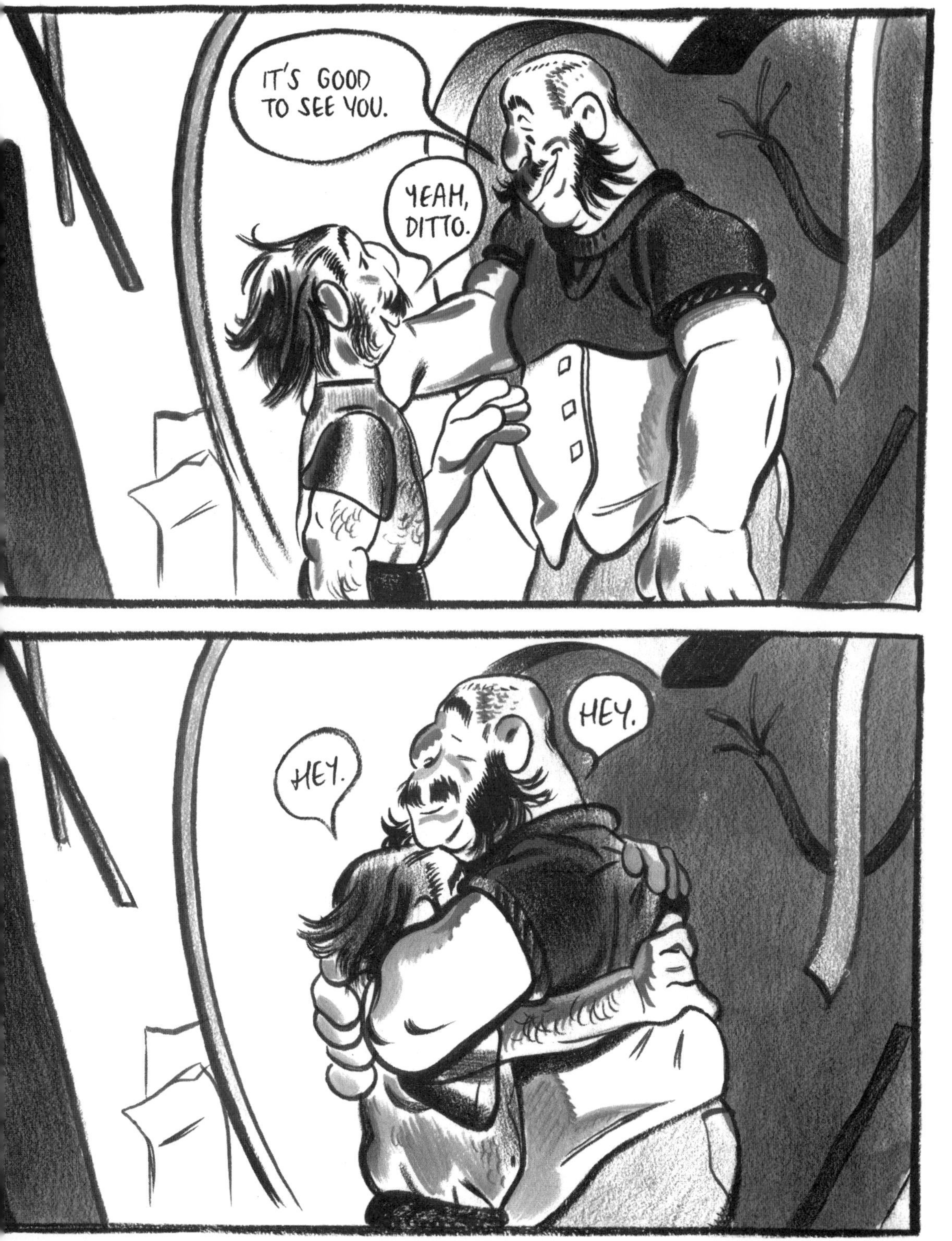
IT'S GOOD TO SEE YOU.
YEAH, DITTO.
HEY.
HEY.

Arbor grew up in a home purchased entirely from a model in a department store catalog. His parents, Cliff and Constance Dacanay, had started their lives over once they fell in love, wiping away any signs of who they were or where they had come from before they had met. His grandparents on both sides had emigrated west due to rising sea levels nearly a century before. If his parents felt any shame over their roots, Arbor never knew. Their eagerness for a comfortable life they felt they had earned just by existing frustrated him deeply. He ached to feel alive, and a home with wax fruit sitting in decorative bowls wasn't what he dreamed of.

Arbor spent his teen years living against the grain in various communal warehouse spaces as a greasy punk. The older punks he met and looked to for guidance warned him against complacency, permanently changed into cautious, practical survivalists, having themselves emerged from such a life after years under the Administration. They were determined to live their own way, without societal expectations, no matter how needlessly difficult that caused their lives to become.

The decision to renovate Fanny's made sense to Arbor—this was a space all his own to live the life he wanted. Although he'd never admit it to himself, it was not unlike the plans made by his parents to build spare bedrooms and walk-in closets.

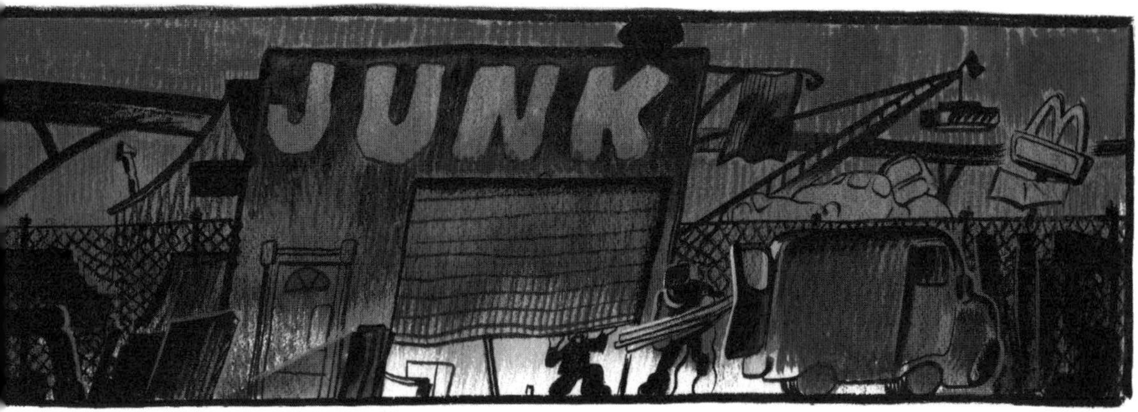
JUNK

Fanny's was slow to reopen. Since legal permits hadn't been secured, most of the work happened during the middle of the night to avoid suspicion. Building supplies were either salvaged from the various abandoned buildings found in the Comb Over or unapologetically stolen. Arbor enlisted his roommates (who, to Paolo—who had once been called "bite-sized" by an ex-boyfriend—all seemed to be overwhelmingly large) to help with the build-out. He tried his best to stay out of their way.

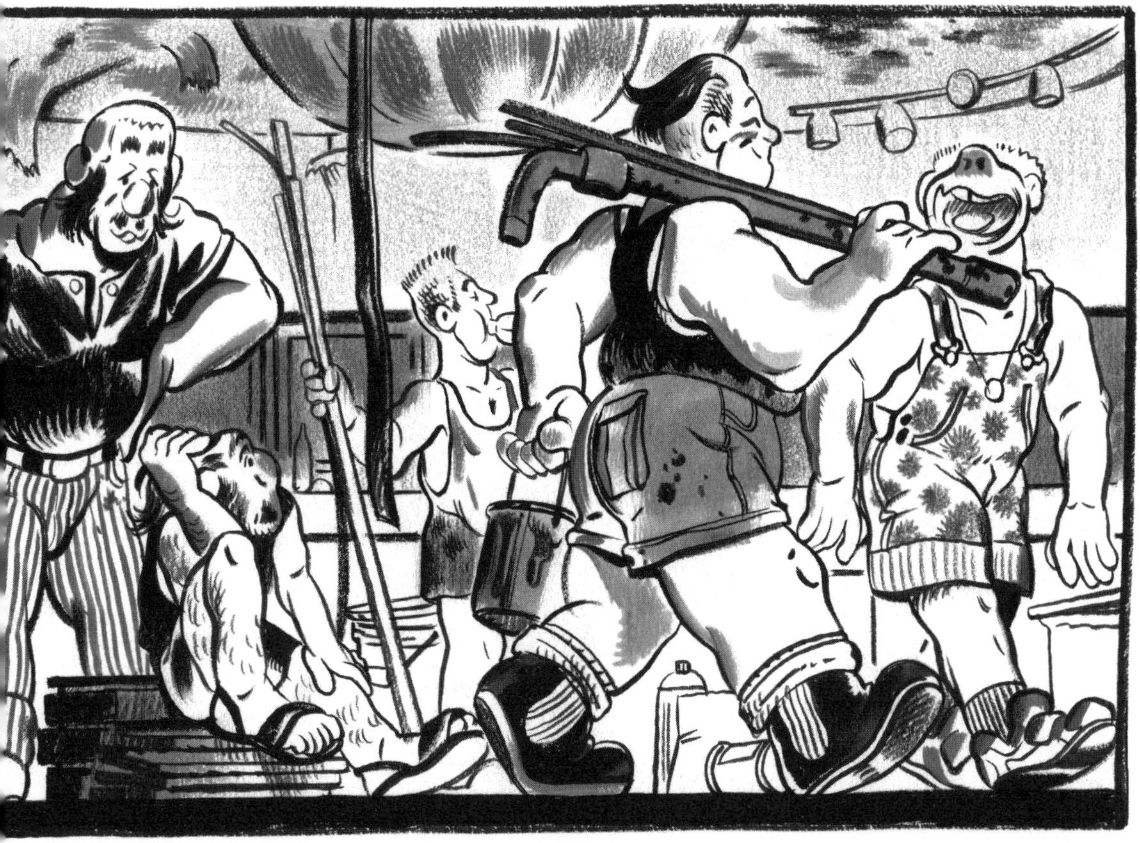

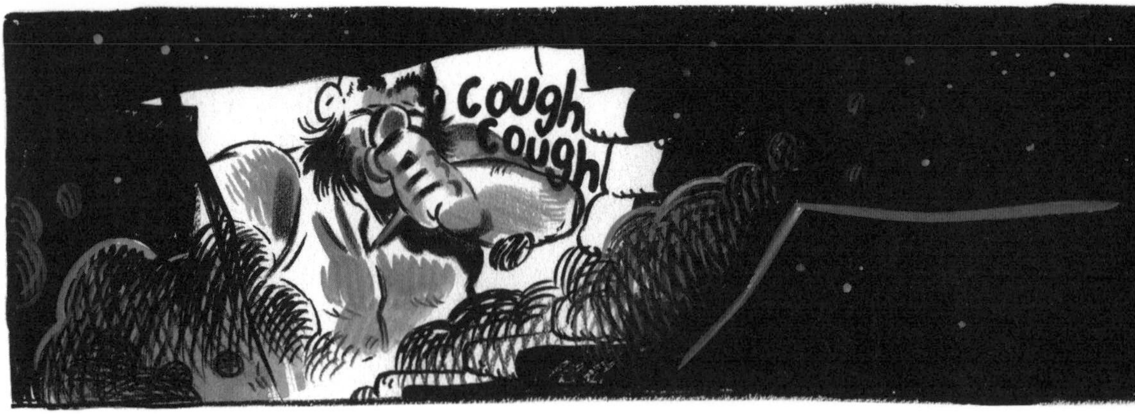
cough
cough

One night, while removing a crumbling, water-damaged wall, Arbor found a room full of outdated Facilitators. Many of them were still intact, covered in a thick coating of dust, patiently waiting for further instructions.

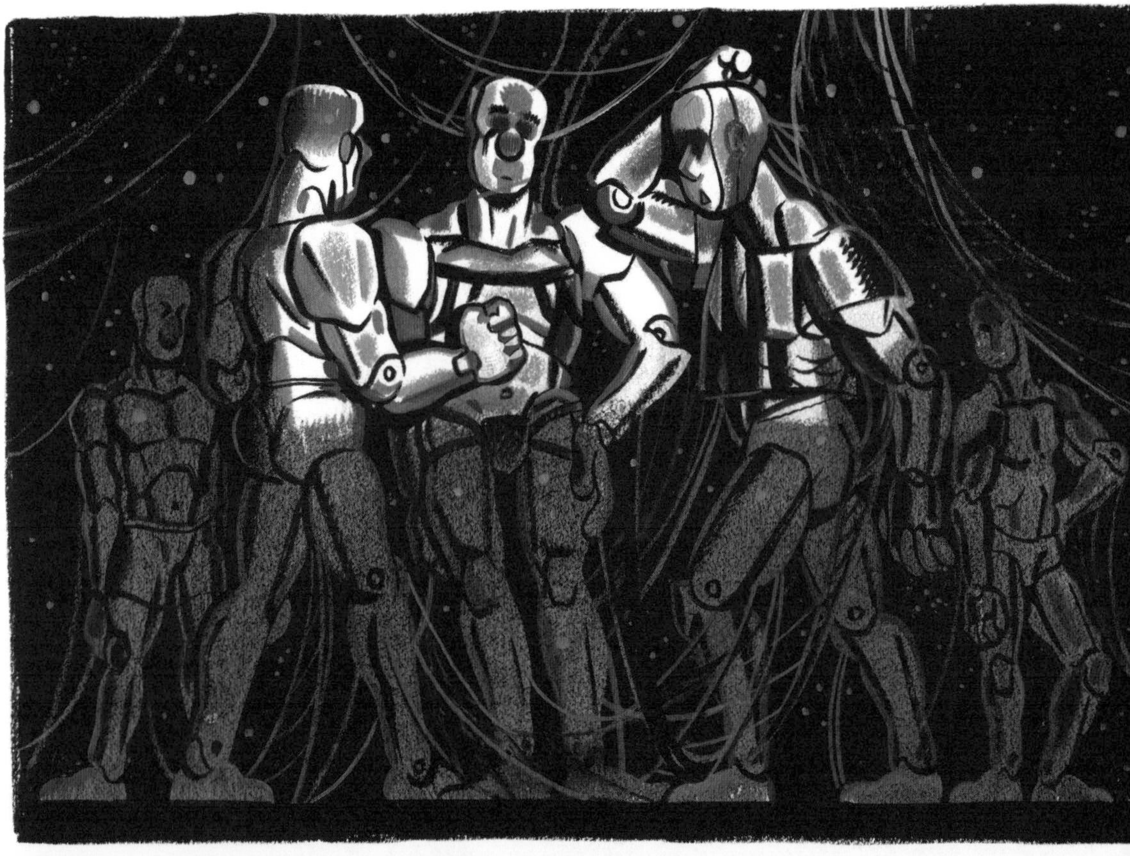

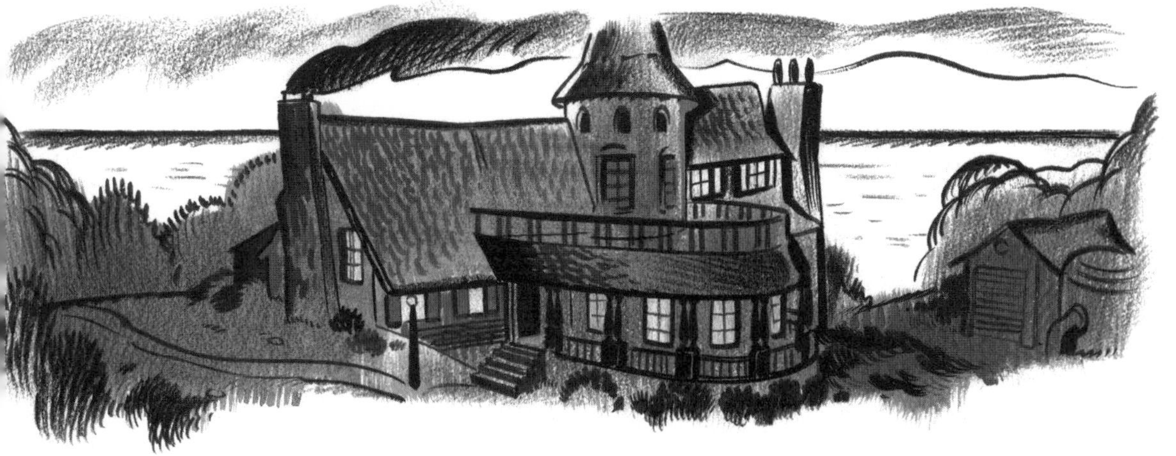

Earlier that spring, back when Arbor had first met Colin and Paolo, one of Colin's coworkers had rented a mansion overlooking the ocean to celebrate their thirtieth birthday. Colin had invited Arbor to join them, partially out of kindness but also to show him off to his coworkers. He would never openly brag about his boyfriends in casual conversation, but bringing them around as proof of his robust sex life felt like the most demure way to mention it.

They spent their weekend eating and drinking and dancing with the fifteen other guests in every one of the mansion's six bedrooms and four-and-a-half bathrooms. They wore wigs. Took turns cooking large meals. Napped anywhere they could find a sunny spot. Had sex in every nook of the four-storied manor. It was perfect.

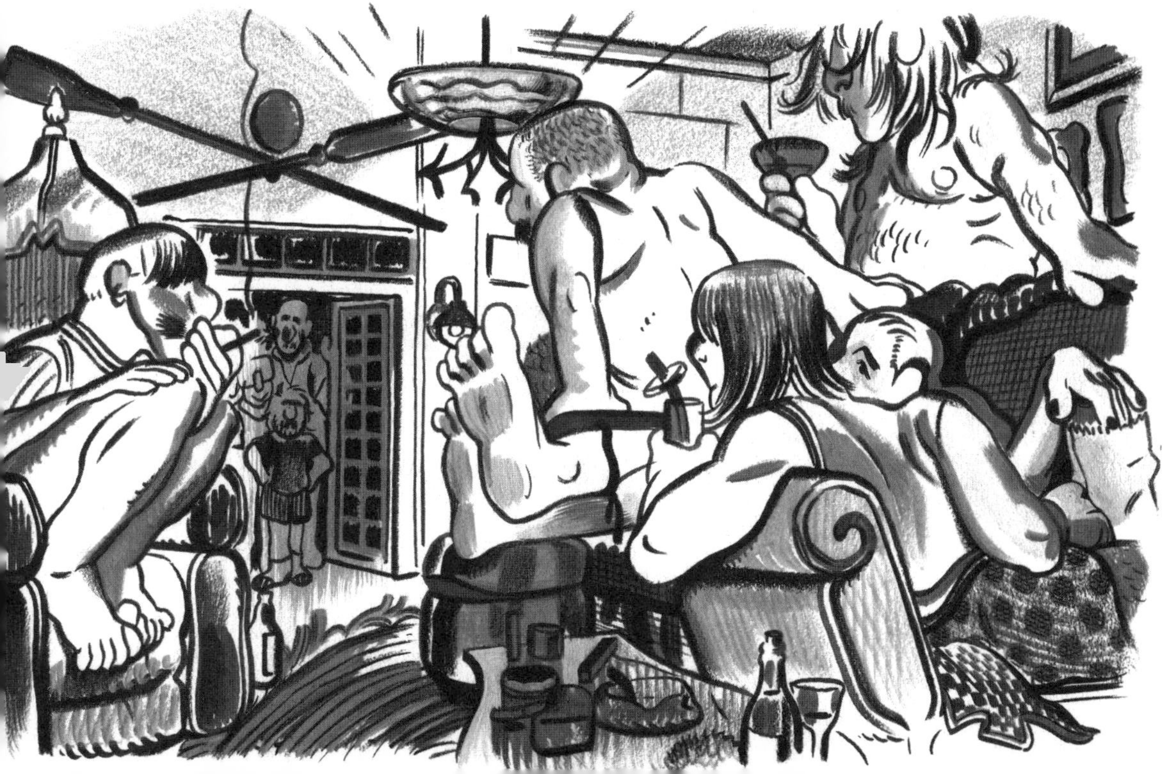

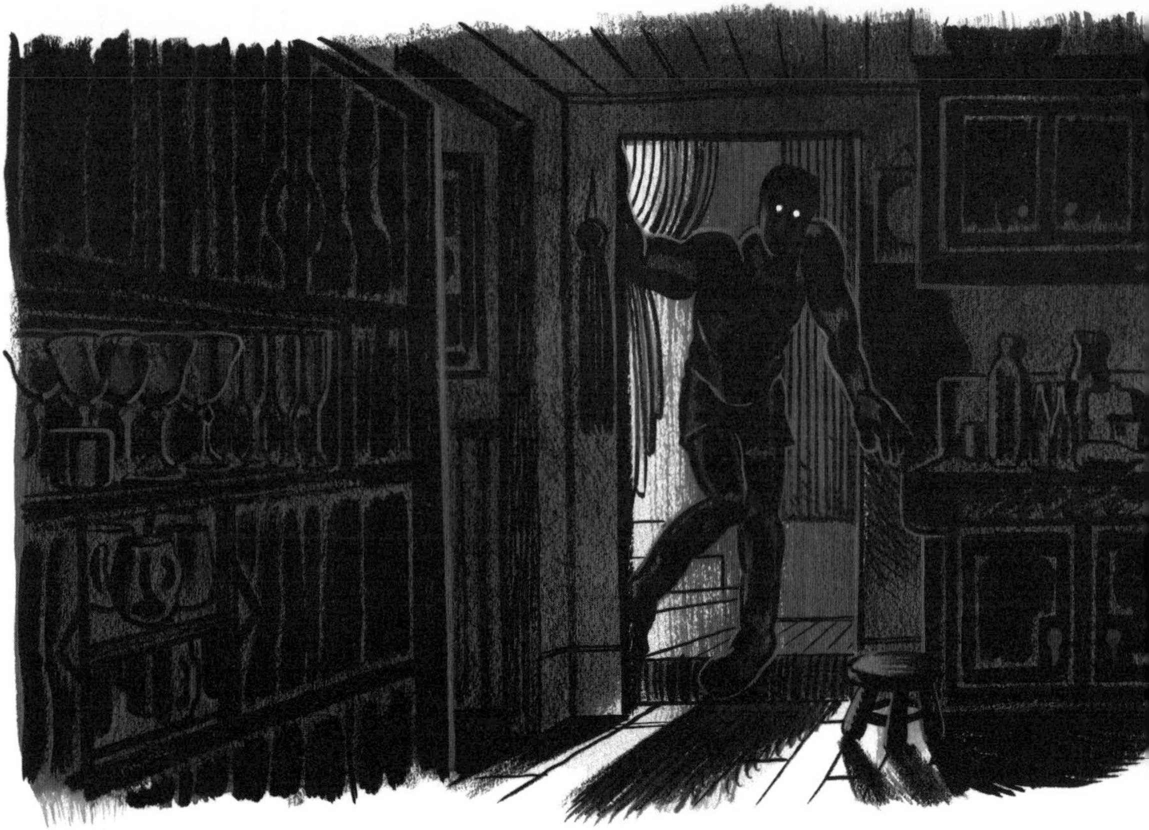

On their second night, two guests ran screaming from a linen closet on the second floor. Stumbling out behind them was an old Facilitator, bare-chested, in a pair of gold lamé boxer shorts and a single, diamond-studded earring. Whoever owned the mansion hadn't kept up with the maintenance of their antiquated sex robot, which lumbered clumsily down the back stairwell, its left leg struggling to keep up with its right. It was quickly ushered outside.

For the rest of the weekend, guests would gather at the wide, ocean-facing windows to stare at the half-naked robot peering back at them from the mansion's well-kept lawns.

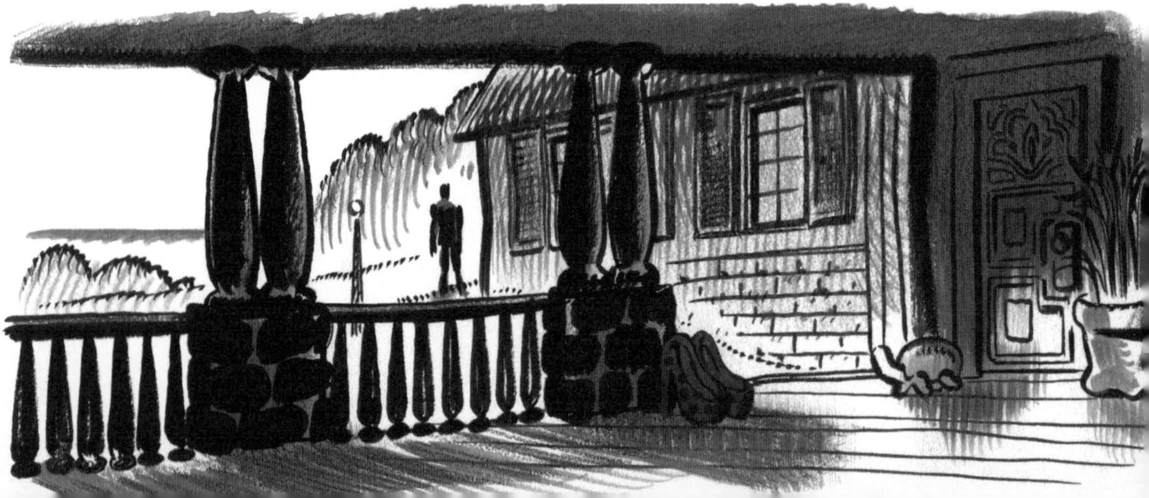

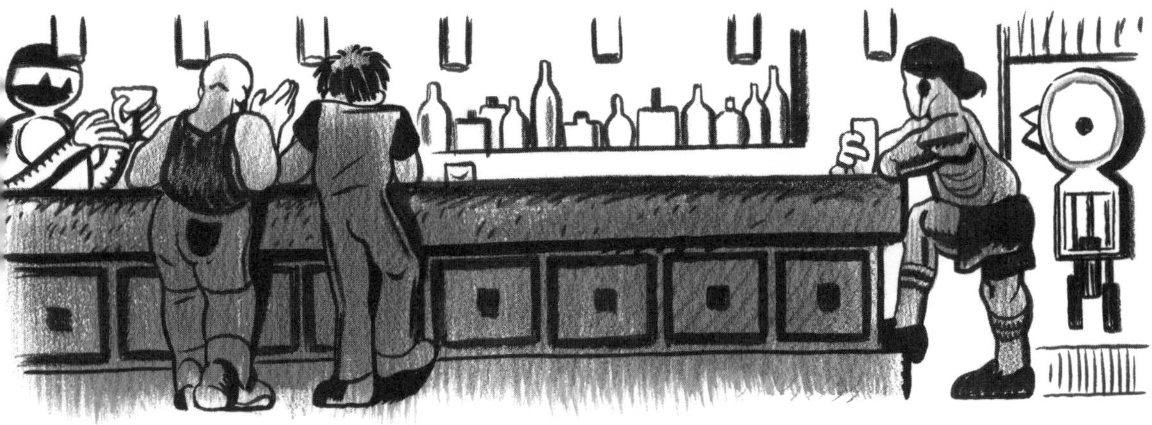

With the increased ferocity of sexually transmitted infections, the Administration had produced a line of robots known as Facilitators intended as a public safety precaution. The Administration embraced automation as a way of removing chance and thereby danger from the lives of its citizens, and in this specific case, its homosexuals. Most bars, regardless of sexual demographic, provided Facilitators of some kind who would be of service if their patrons wanted company that was unquestionably safe.

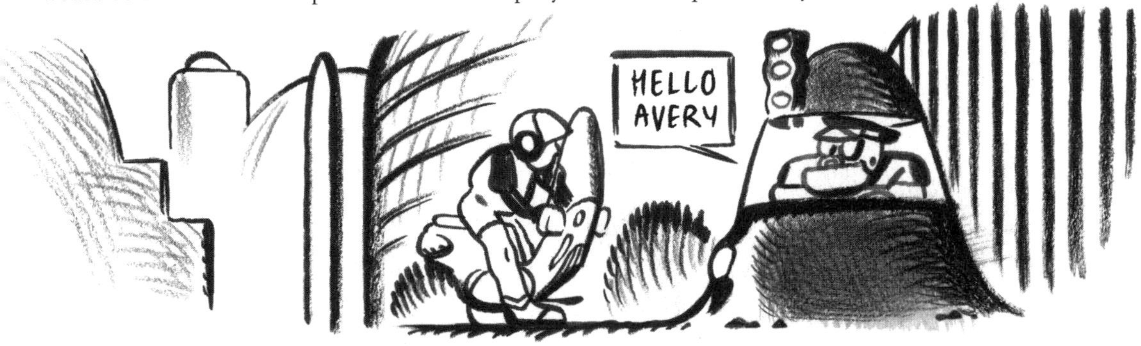
HELLO AVERY

At first, the Facilitators were seen as something good. But what was sold as protection was just another way to control. History has shown that this was how the Administration slowly stripped away rights, framing constraints as gentle suggestions without allowing for alternatives.

After the fall of the Administration, the new government did away with most automation as a precaution against back-sliding into an oppressive state once again. The automation left behind was mostly seen as just novelty. There were a string of late-night talk shows hosted by Facilitators. A Facilitator had written a bestselling detective audio-novella.

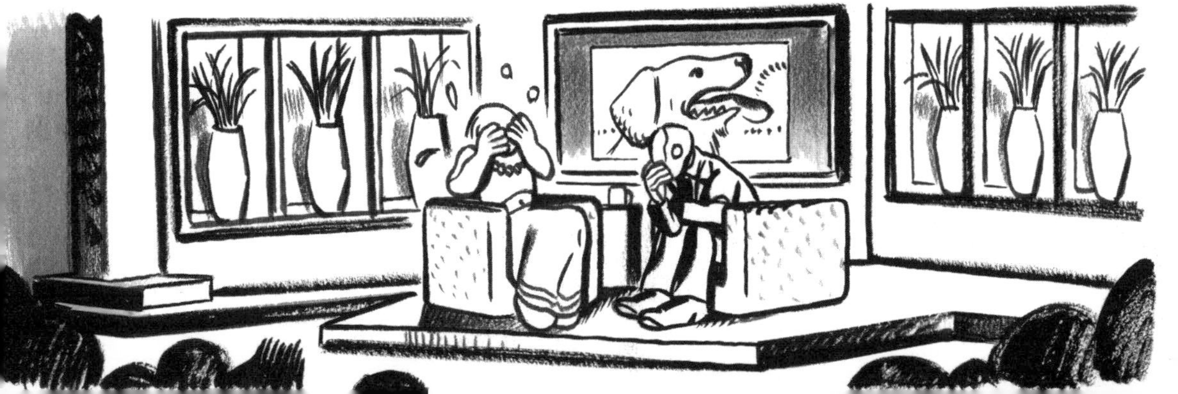

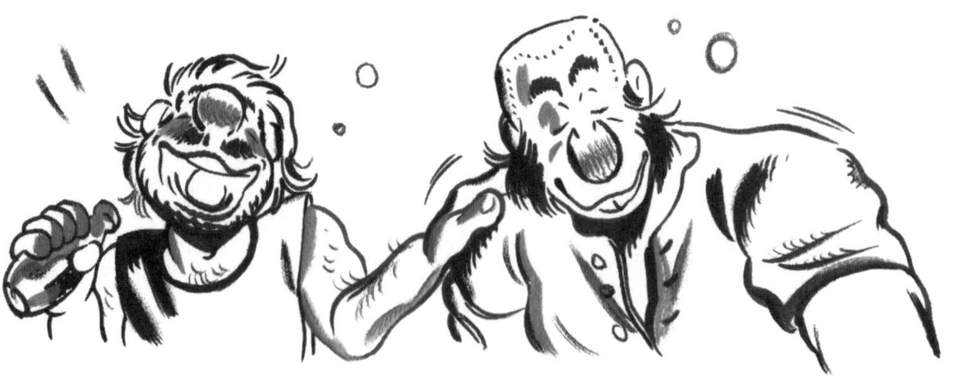

Most of the Facilitators were gone now—decommissioned, broken down into scrap, and recycled into numerous other things. Removing them from civilian use had fallen under the same branch of government that funded Colin's advisory committee. Most of the planning for that effort came from Central Intelligence, the organization Paolo's sisters Karoline and Karolina worked for.

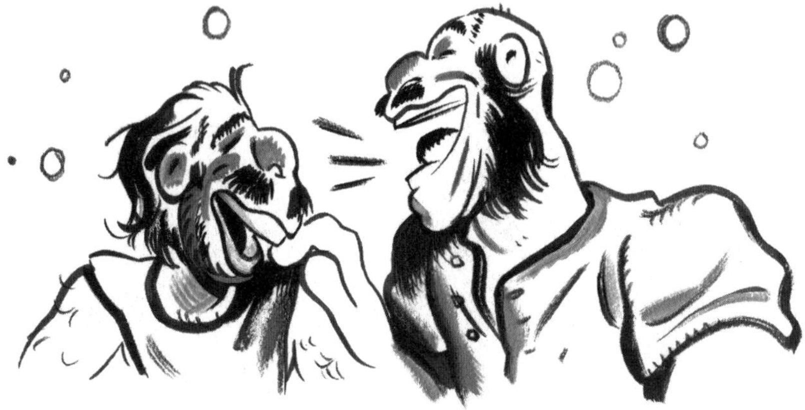

Arbor remembered hearing the older punks he knew in his youth speak about what their sex lives were like when Facilitators were more common. It wasn't that the Administration openly discriminated against any of their individual desires, but through widespread paranoia, it did discourage queer people from following their impulses. The Administration would have never openly admitted that it favored low-risk, monogamous sex between state-sanctioned partners (regardless of orientation), but it worked secretly to curb any complicated personal arrangement that may undermine its vision of the future.

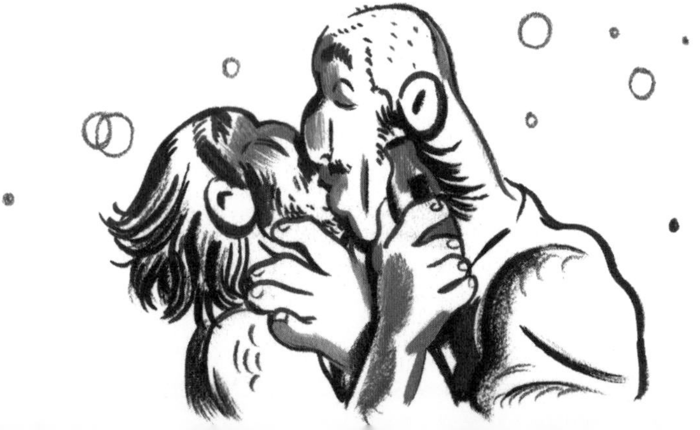

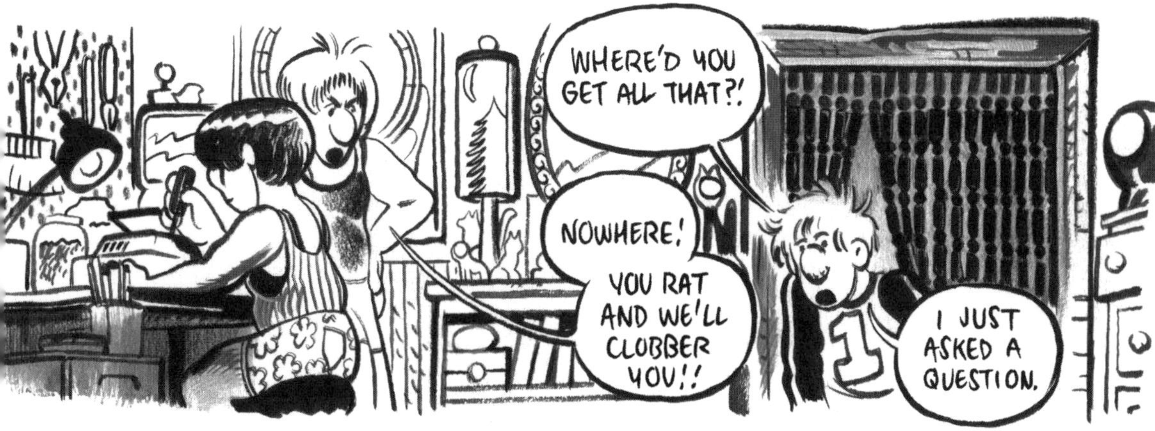
WHERE'D YOU GET ALL THAT?!
NOWHERE!
YOU RAT AND WE'LL CLOBBER YOU!!
I JUST ASKED A QUESTION.

It was Paolo's idea to recommission the abandoned Facilitators into laborers to help expedite the rebuilding of Fanny's. For someone who often claimed to be without any real skills, Paolo was adept at tinkering with the mechanical men. He had watched his older sisters reprogram outdated appliances with kits they ordered from the back of engineering magazines, and had picked up more from them than he realized.

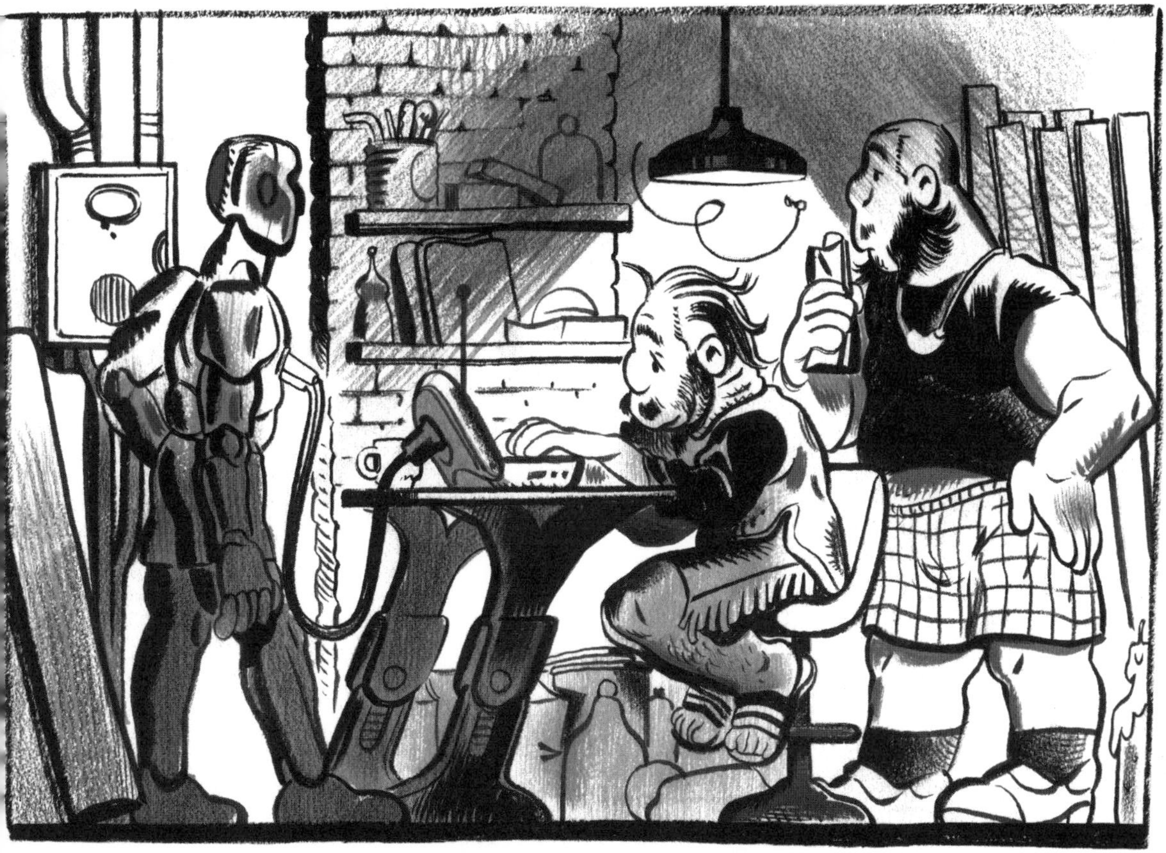

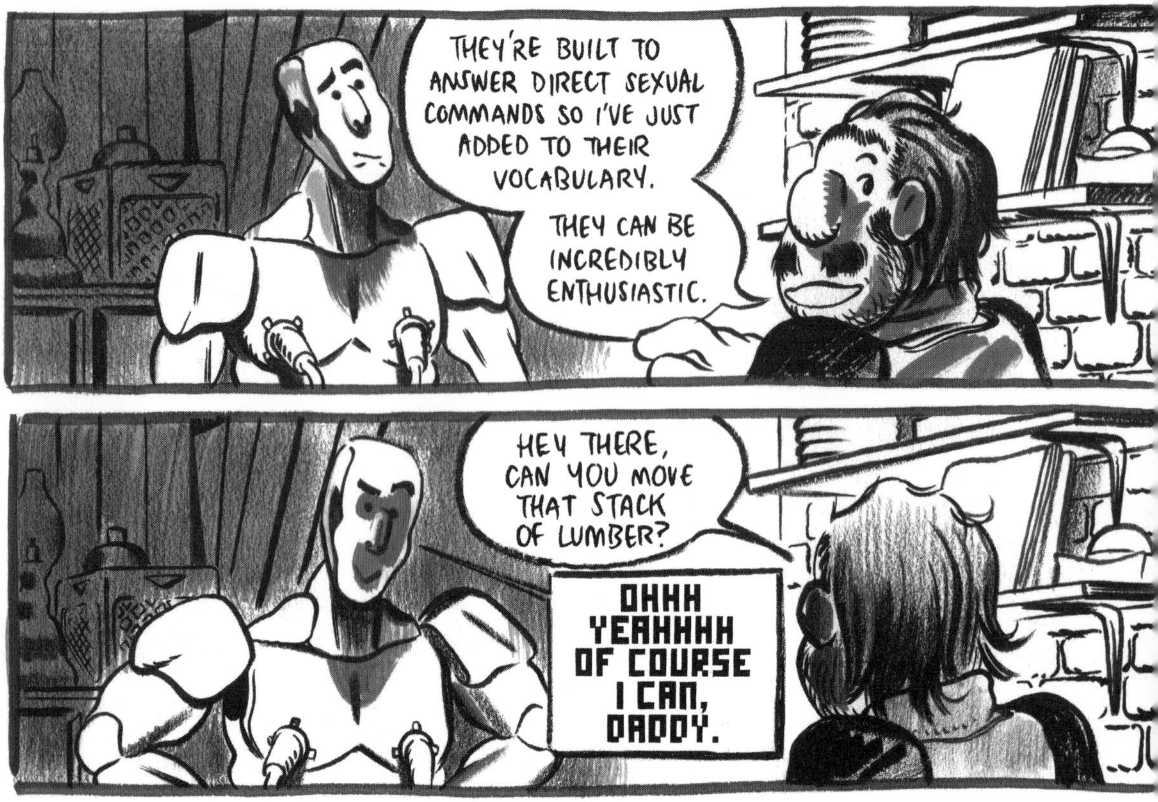
THEY'RE BUILT TO ANSWER DIRECT SEXUAL COMMANDS SO I'VE JUST ADDED TO THEIR VOCABULARY.
THEY CAN BE INCREDIBLY ENTHUSIASTIC.
HEY THERE, CAN YOU MOVE THAT STACK OF LUMBER?
OHHH YEAHHHH OF COURSE I CAN, DADDY.

Growing up after his parents' generation of liberation, Arbor spent his adolescence feeling embarrassed by advertisements full of handsome men buying engagement rings, traveling to tropical locales together, and driving off into sunsets in luxury sports cars. Even then, he knew that would never be his life. The identical faces of the men on billboards weren't the faces he saw at the basement shows he snuck into while underage, standing beside him in a crowd of sweaty people, screaming in unison. Who cared if they looked good in a bathing suit? He would not be one of those people. The Facilitators, in their cold, perfectly sculpted bodies, brought all of those long-forgotten feelings back to the surface.

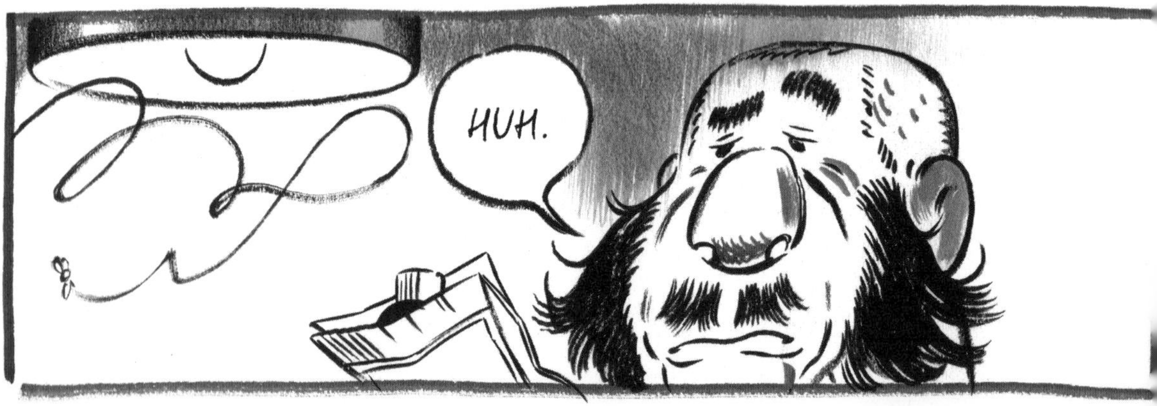
HUH.

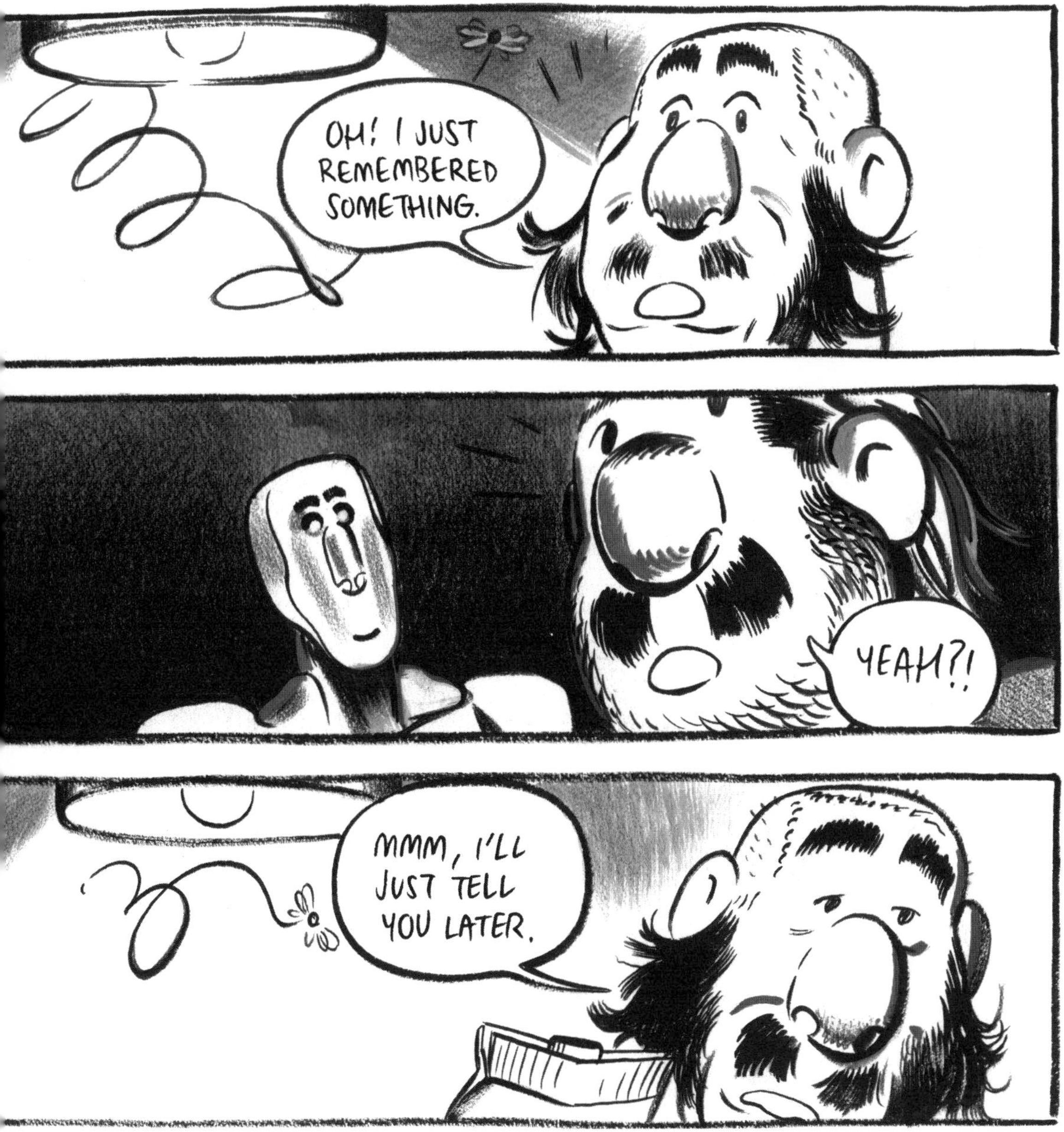
OH! I JUST REMEMBERED SOMETHING.
YEAH?!
MMM, I'LL JUST TELL YOU LATER.

Paolo's work updating the Facilitators quickly outgrew his modest equipment. Their preprogrammed sexual phrases were cute at first, but were now a distraction, slowing down work on the renovations.

Paolo decided to visit his sisters for help.

After both Karoline and Karolina abruptly left their husbands, they purchased a twin Solar Unit just outside of the city center together. They grew a genetically modified kudzu on each roof of their shared home in an effort to cut down on cooling costs, but found that it couldn't be stopped from consuming both buildings. After months of fighting with the members of their local Homeowners Association, even allowing the H.O.A. to attempt—and fail—to quell the spreading vine themselves, the sisters accepted that despite making careers out of spying on others, they had accidentally made their home the most noticeable one in their neighborhood.

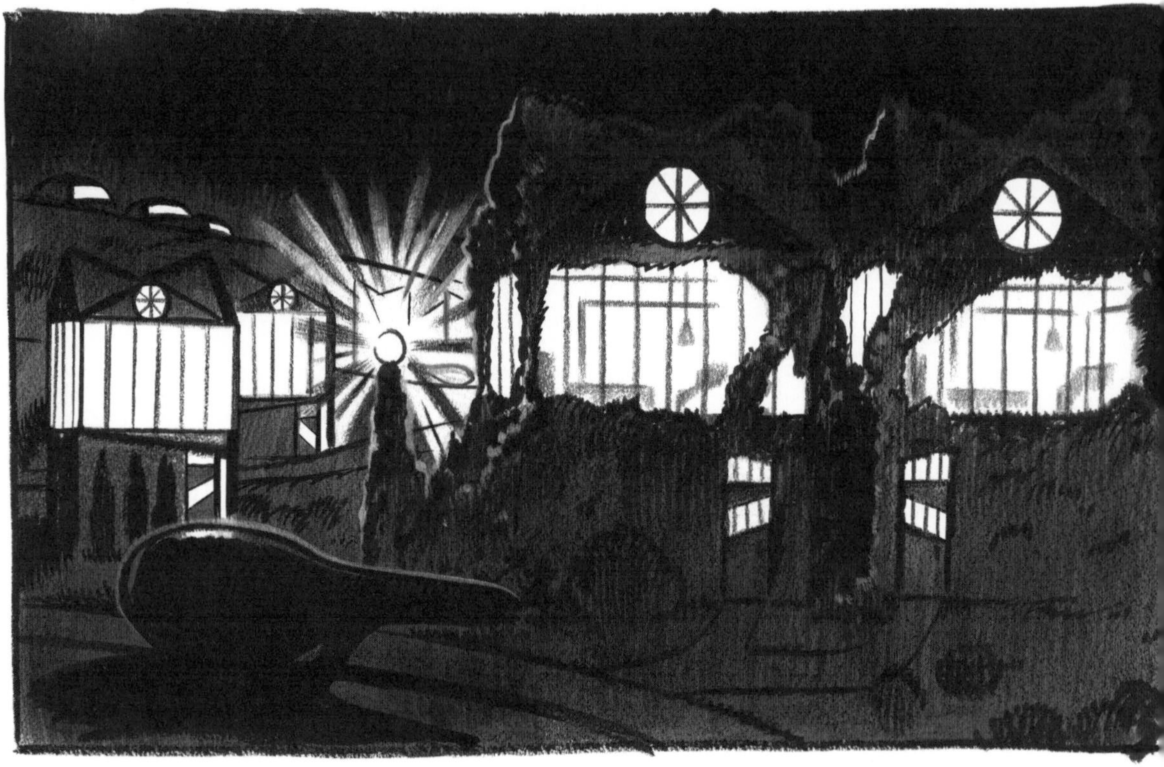

Karoline and Karolina had hoped their boys would follow in their engineering footsteps, but each one was failing to match the potential seen in them. Unlike Paolo, who had ached for the approval of his older sisters, his nephews did not care what their mothers thought. Kory was busy bulking up through various muscle supplements, Korrie was saving up for a used moped, Koren worked the night shift at an artificial fish hatchery, and Karl would simply disappear for days at a time.

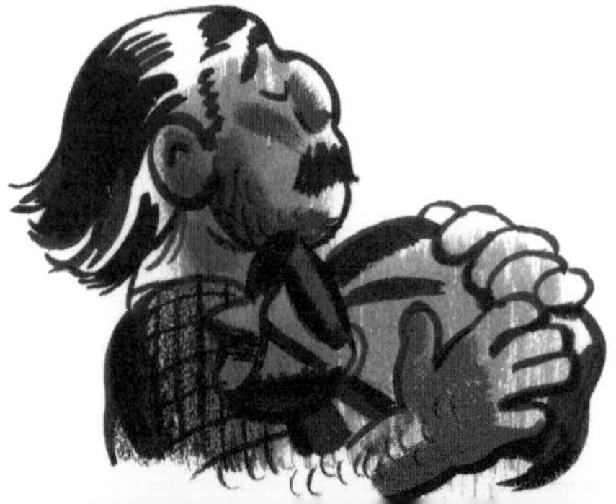

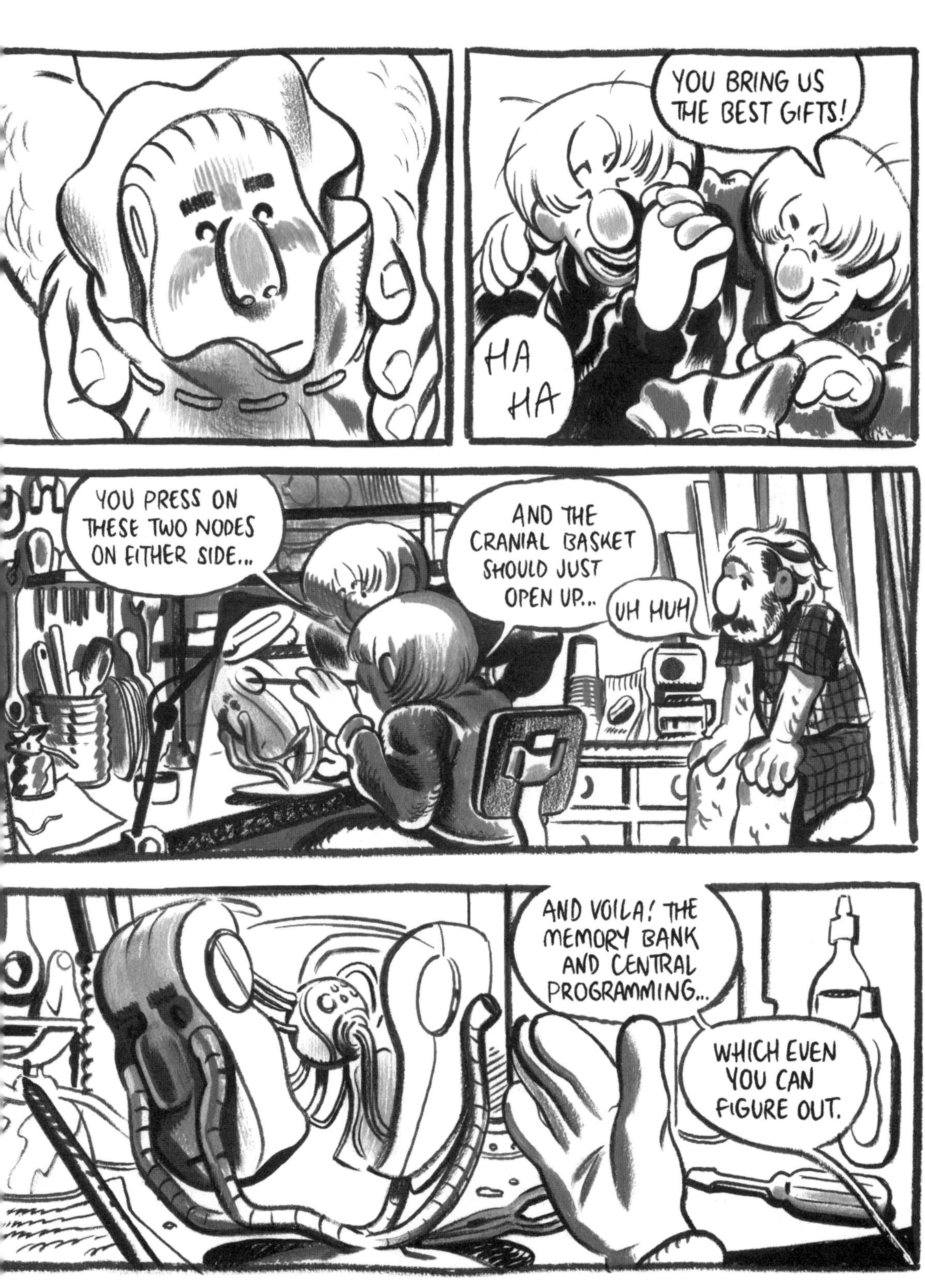
YOU BRING US THE BEST GIFTS!
HA HA
YOU PRESS ON THESE TWO NODES ON EITHER SIDE...
AND THE CRANIAL BASKET SHOULD JUST OPEN UP...
UH HUH
AND VOILA! THE MEMORY BANK AND CENTRAL PROGRAMMING...
WHICH EVEN YOU CAN FIGURE OUT.

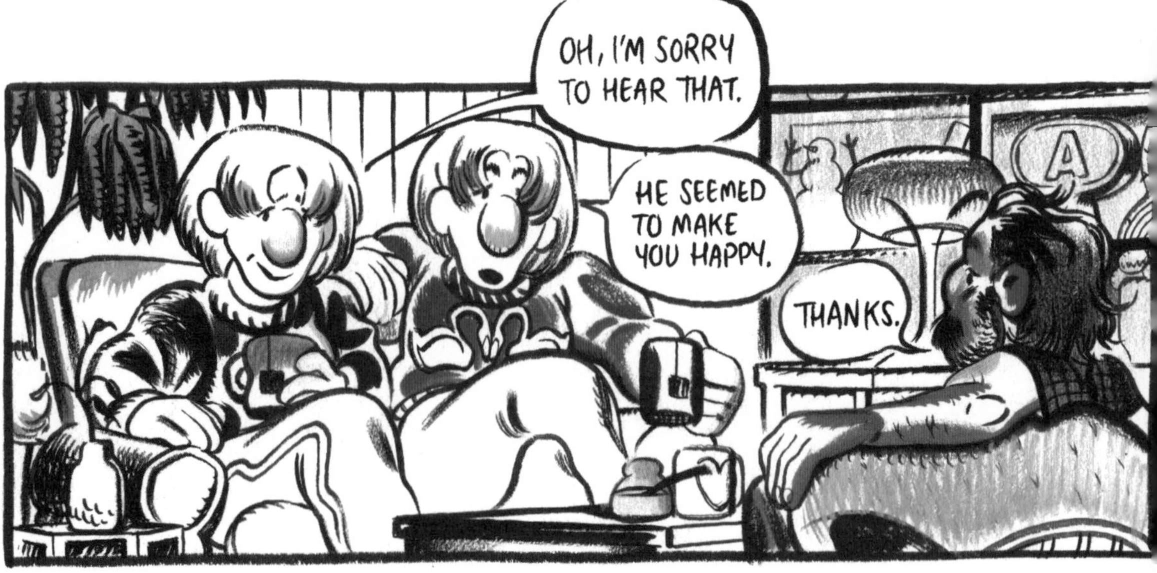
OH, I'M SORRY TO HEAR THAT.
HE SEEMED TO MAKE YOU HAPPY.
THANKS.

Karoline and Karolina were nearly giddy over their baby brother's newfound purpose. This made sense to Paolo, who knew his sisters only ever cared about something if it also involved them. He tried his best to downplay the real reason he needed their expertise—instead of dwelling on how he had brought the head of an antiquated sex robot over in a bag, Paolo shifted the conversation to Colin and his unexpected leaving. The last thing Paolo wanted was for him to be the reason Fanny's got busted, for either their lack of a business license or from harboring a potentially illegal fleet of Facilitators.

As both mothers and professional snoops, Karoline and Karolina had gotten good at not letting their suspicions show. But when Paolo left, they agreed to place their brother on a higher tier of their precautionary watch list. They had placed everyone they knew on this list when they first started working for Central Intelligence, and placement on said list changed according to their perceived level of concern. It gave them peace of mind to know that everyone in their life was being followed. They were never concerned over Karl disappearing each night, because they knew that on most nights he did nothing more than go down to the nearby drainage ditch to throw cinder blocks into it and yell.

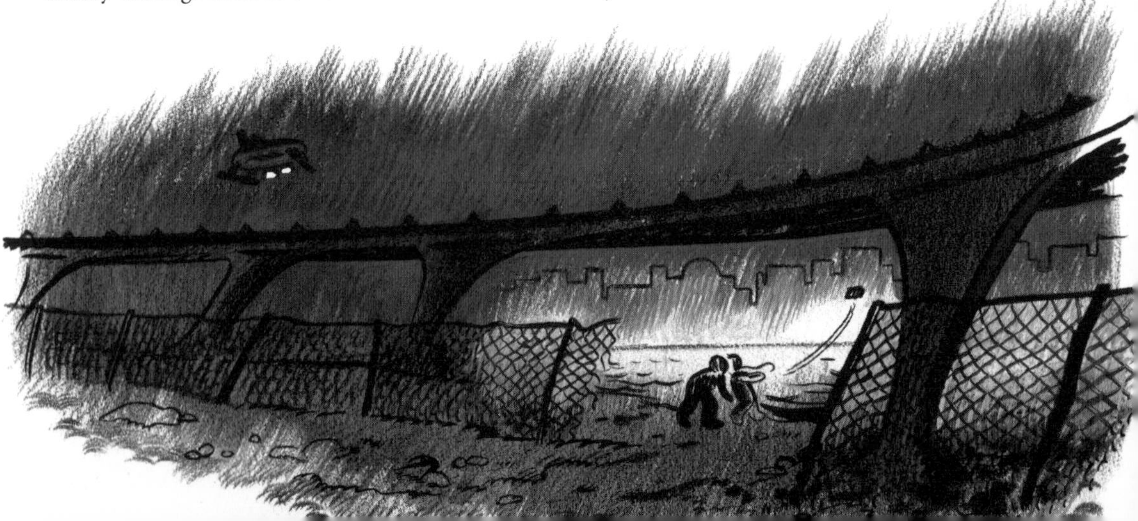

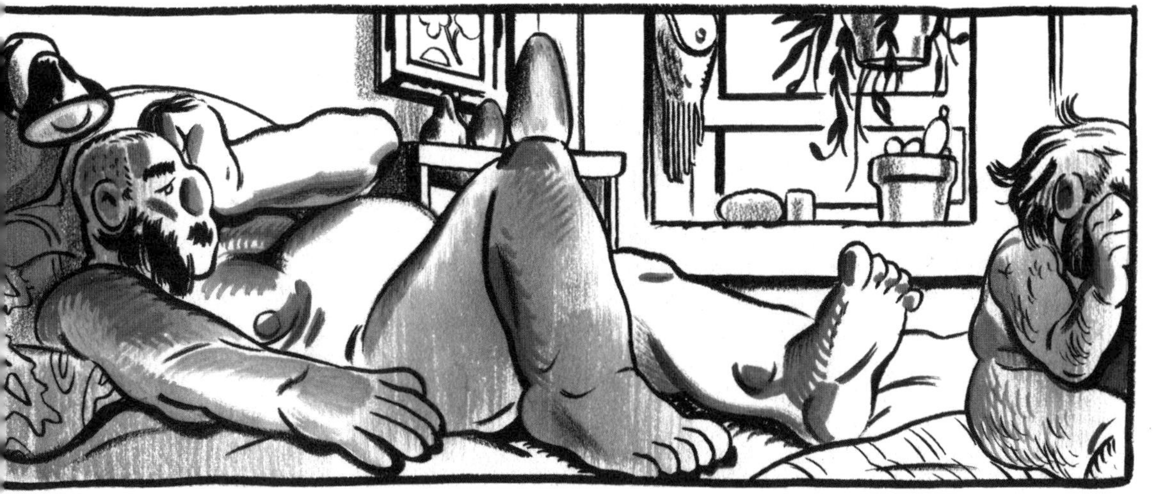

Neither Paolo nor Arbor spoke about how they were regularly sleeping together. They would wait until the rest of the crew had left Fanny's after working all night, then move seamlessly from a working relationship to a more intimate one.

One afternoon, as Paolo was getting ready to go back to his own place, Arbor asked,

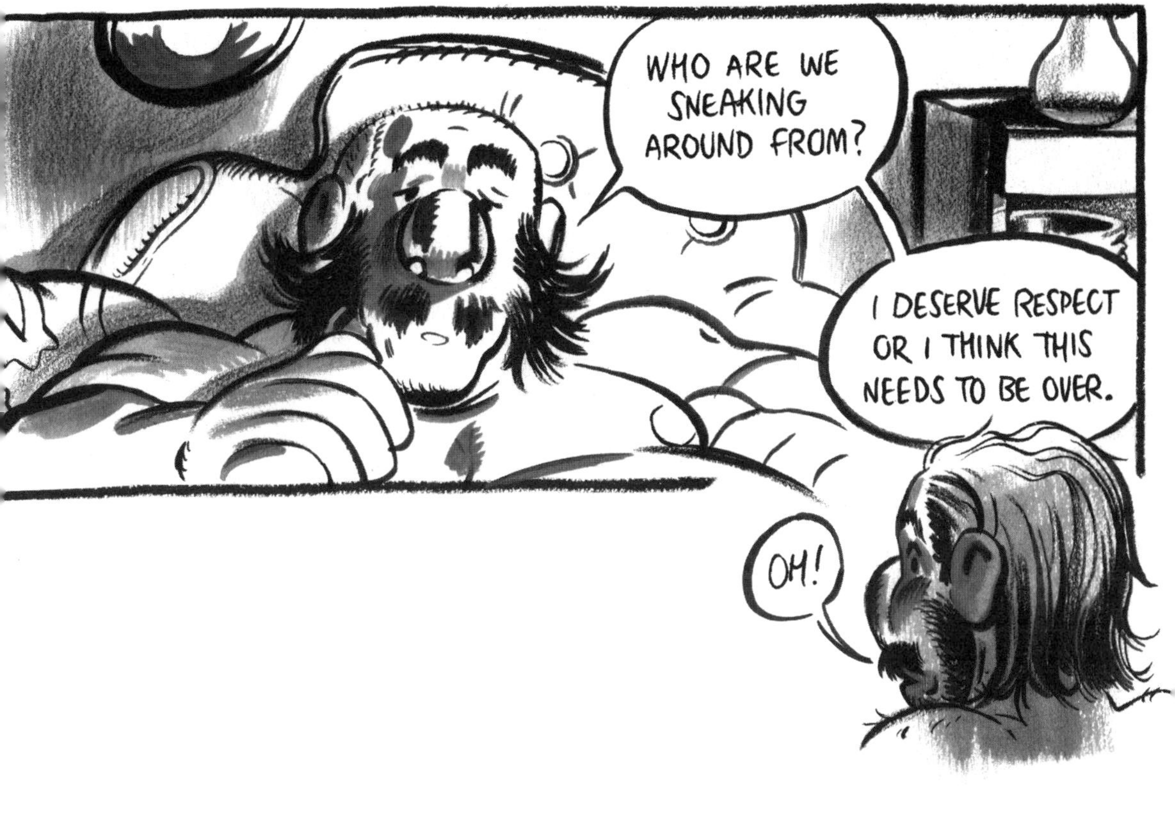
WHO ARE WE SNEAKING AROUND FROM?
I DESERVE RESPECT OR I THINK THIS NEEDS TO BE OVER.
OH!

Their relationship wasn't a new one.

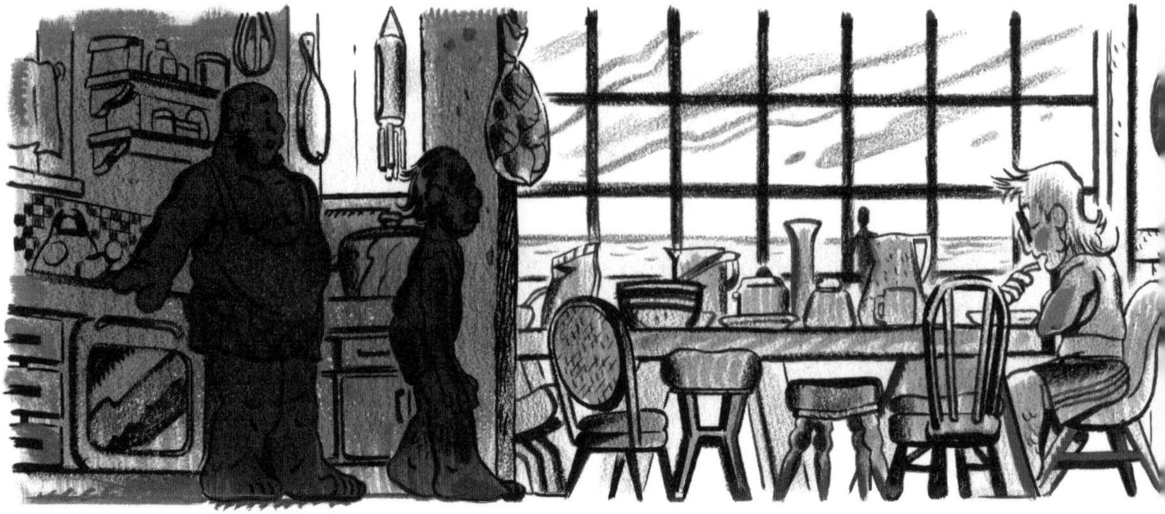

Back when they were still a thrupple and staying in that mansion overlooking the ocean, Colin had taken it upon himself to cook most of the meals for the other guests, unable to let himself fully relax with nothing to do. When Paolo failed to show for breakfast on their last day, Colin went room to room looking for his partner. He had finally found Paolo, not alone, but with Arbor—even though part of their agreement was that all encounters with Arbor were to be enjoyed as a couple.

Colin was rarely despondent, but when he was, Paolo knew it was over something he had done. Colin reeked of disappointment each time Paolo didn't rise to the expectations of who Colin thought he could be.

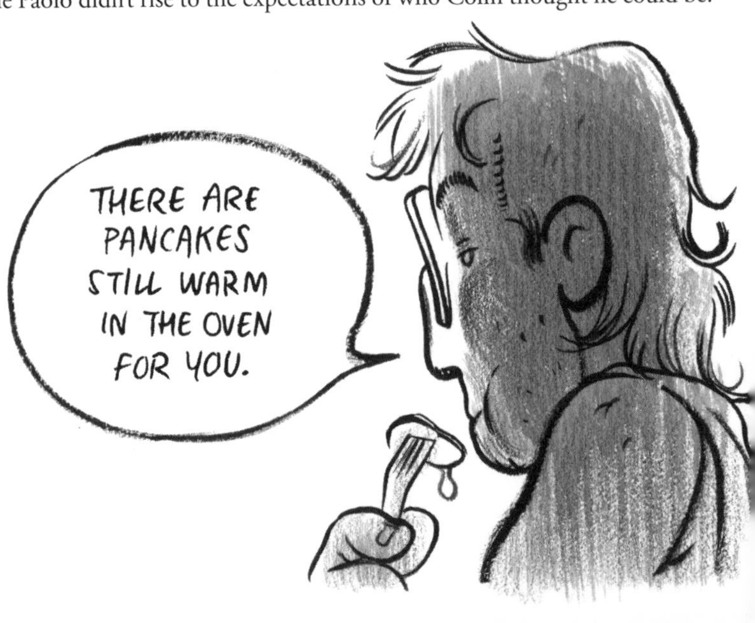
THERE ARE PANCAKES STILL WARM IN THE OVEN FOR YOU.

Arbor had been in several open relationships before, and his role in each one was similar. He'd come to accept that it was easy for people to think they loved him without actually seeing him as a complete person. No matter how generous the couple thought they were being by inviting him into their lives—and inevitably their beds—there was no denying that Arbor maintained a certain otherness. They loved what he represented within their monogamy. From the distance of their own primary relationships, they couldn't see past his broad shoulders and booming voice to the whole of his person.

On the awkward train ride home from their weekend in the rented mansion, Colin's hushed anger was directed solely at Paolo, his boyfriend, his partner, his other half. Arbor was blameless for the betrayal of trust, but sitting quietly across the aisle, Arbor thought about how he had known exactly what he was doing when he pulled Paolo into the spare bedroom that morning. After years of being an accessory to the relationships of others, Arbor was eager for something of his own. He'd be the first to say that trying to claim someone in love was futile, but deep down he craved nothing less than *forever*.

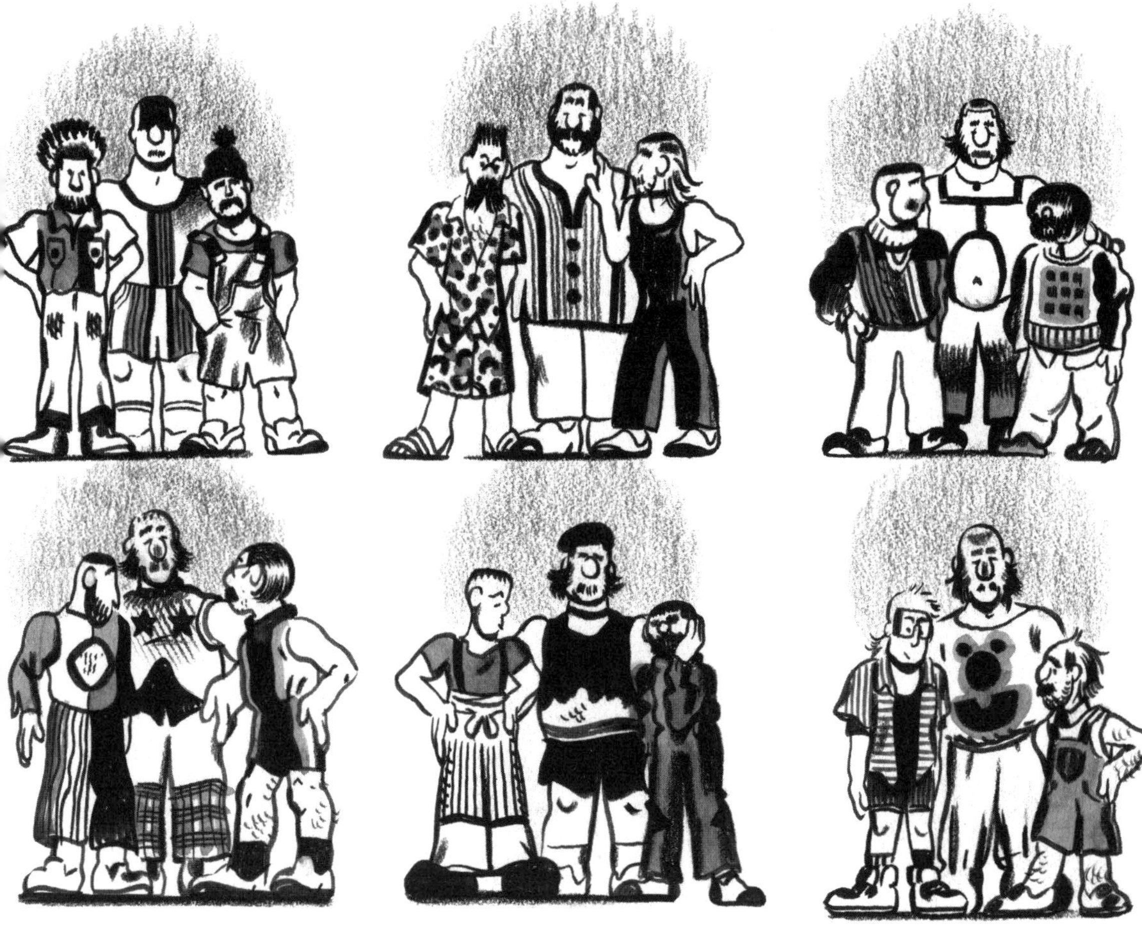

And with that, Paolo moved in with Arbor.

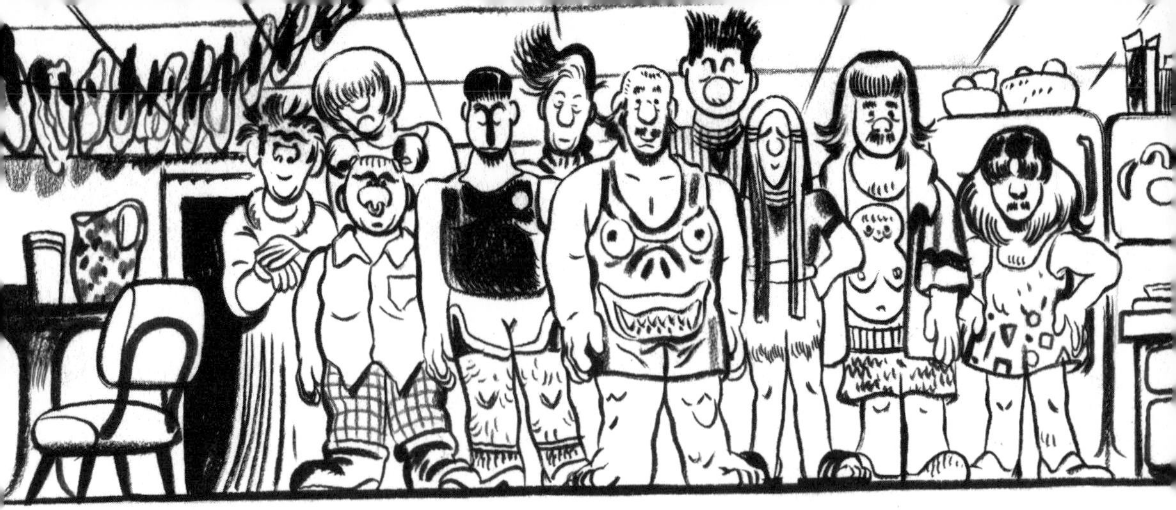

Arbor lived with eleven other people in what had once been the offices of a tech startup spread across two floors of a high-rise. Each member of the household was allowed to build out a section of either floor to do with as they pleased, creating an environment that was constantly evolving. The first floor opened onto a large, outdoor patio used to grow food and dry their clothing in the afternoon sun. At night, Paolo watched the lights flicker on in neighboring buildings, each populated by another similarly-minded group of people living collectively in the dilapidated ruins of a long-forgotten corporation. In the plaza that linked each of the nearby buildings, monthly swap meets were held, as well as the occasional movie screening, badminton game, and sliding scale yoga class.

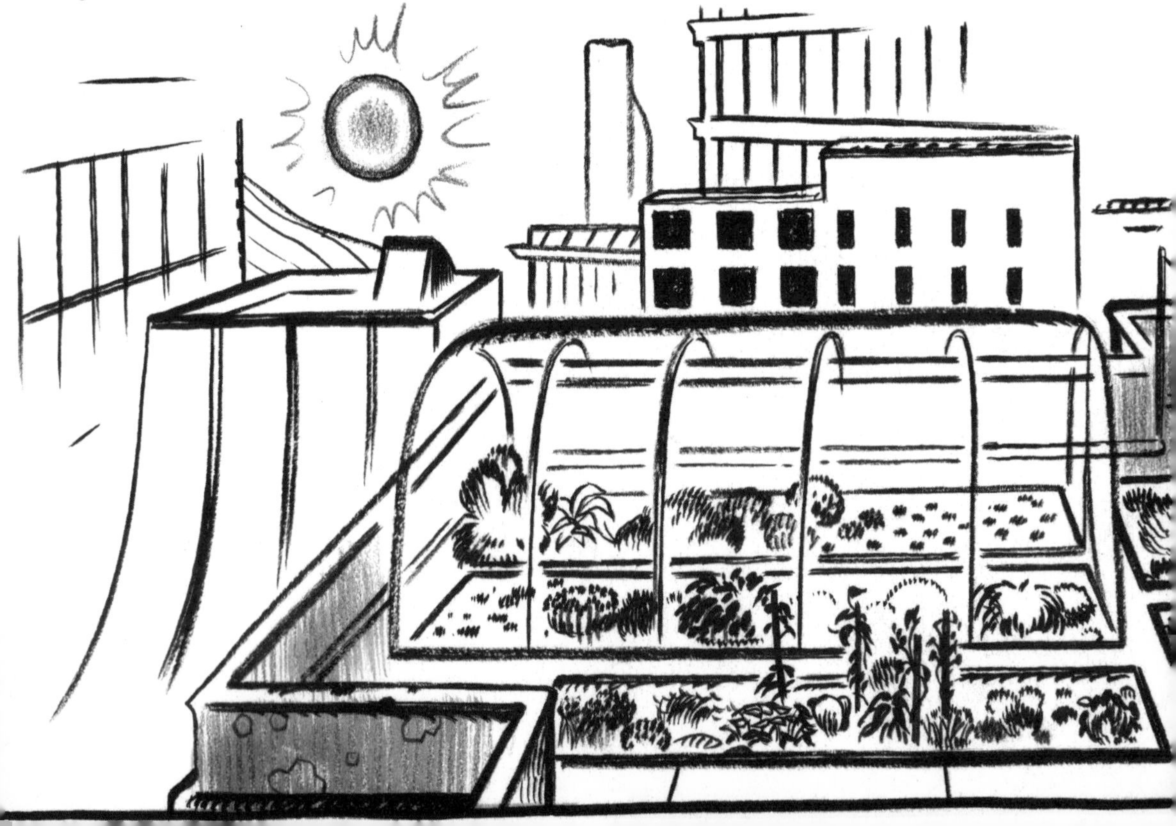

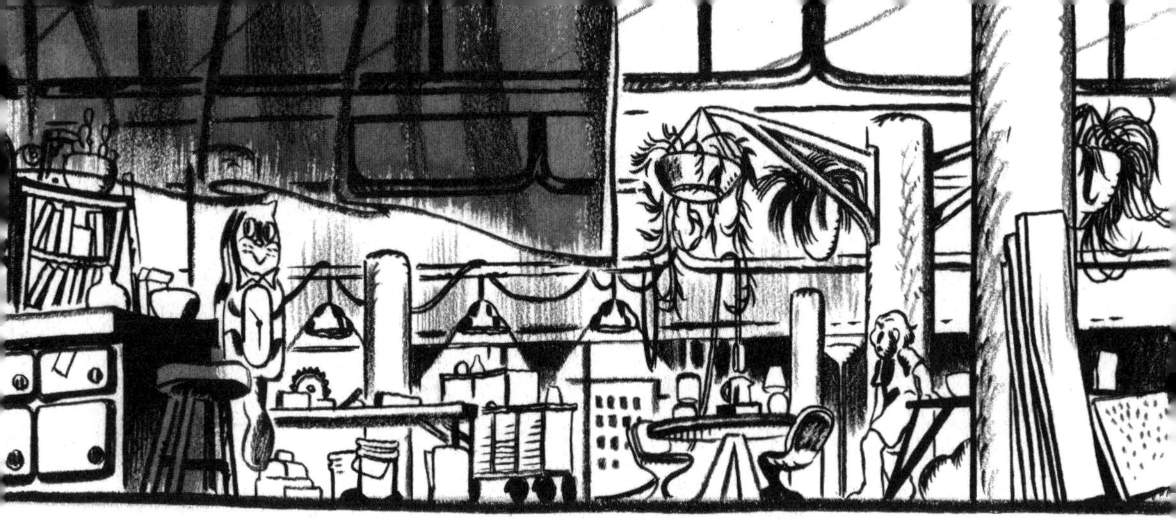

Paolo didn't realize how lonely he was until he found himself living with eleven roommates. Even when Arbor wasn't around, there was always someone who wanted company or needed someone to taste test a recipe or share newly-heard gossip with. He was finally getting to know what it was like to live with a family, the way he had always imagined it to be. Despite the enormity of his new home, Paolo never felt isolated.

With most of their energy going toward realizing Arbor's vision of Fanny's, Paolo's new home sat unfinished. Most of the walls were nothing more than plastic tarp, which would gently flap in the breeze. Large swaths of carpet had been ripped up, revealing the irregular zigzag of industrial glue, which was still tacky in certain places. But Paolo couldn't deny that he felt a certain excitement regarding what a space like theirs could eventually become. He often thought of Minnie's new house, about her own excitement to move in and make a fresh start. But the rigidity of each room being built with a specific purpose in mind saddened him now. He suddenly found himself full of opinions about how he could decorate that he was eager to share.

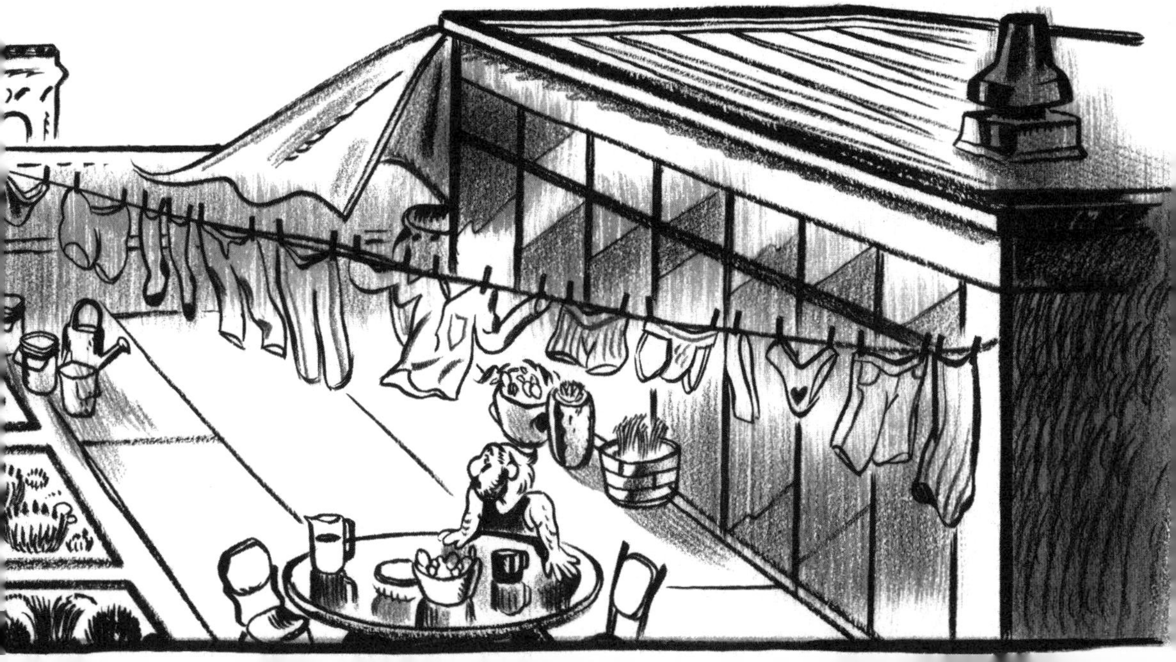

Arbor had constructed a shotgun-style apartment with a living room, a reading room, and a bedroom out of what had once been a row of interconnected conference rooms, creating a massive space just for himself.

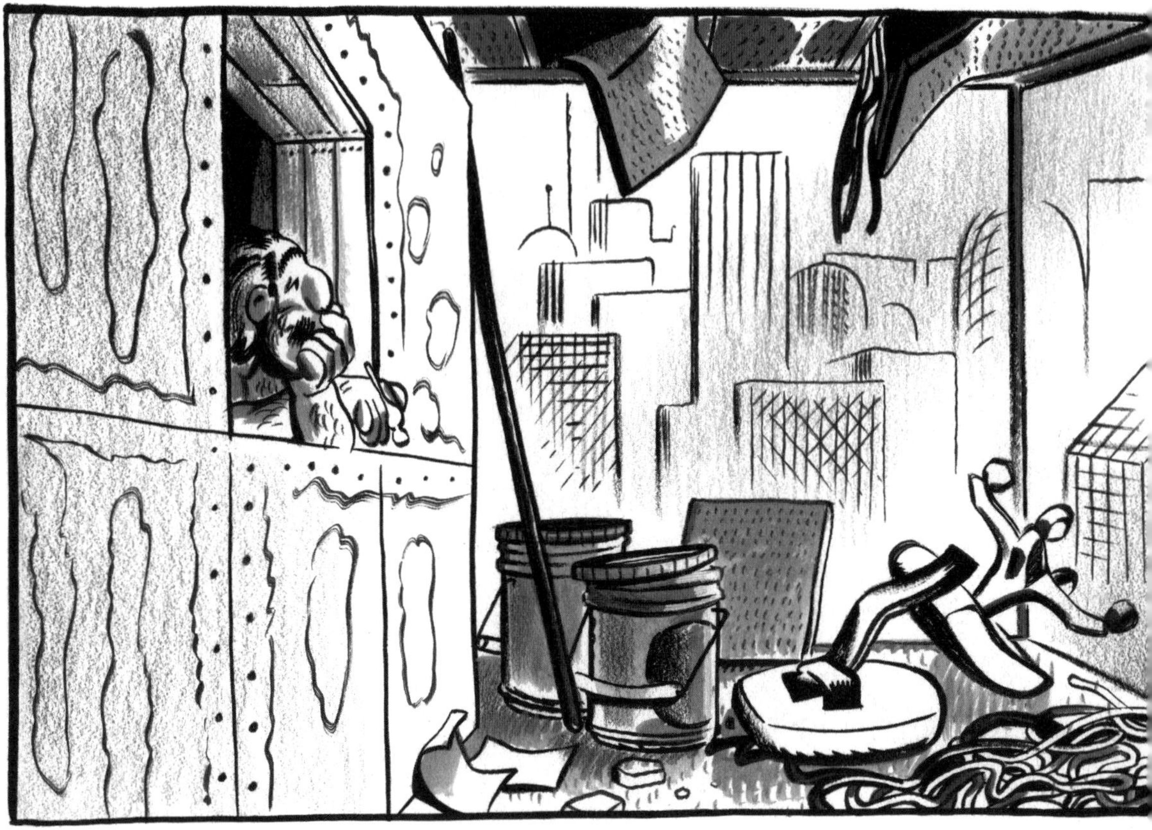

Paolo's favorite feature was the fake window built into the wall beside his bed. It was impossible to open a window on the seventeenth floor of a skyscraper, and Arbor missed some of the normalcy that came with living in a traditional home. In some ways, the window was practical—the conference rooms originally had glass walls that, after being replaced with drywall, didn't let in natural light. The window made Paolo feel as if they were miniatures living in an oversized dollhouse, which for him was oddly comforting. Each morning, the sun would arrive uninterrupted, streaming through the floor-to-ceiling glass walls, piercing a square of sunlight onto the ceiling of their bedroom. Through that window, Paolo could start his day by watching the few people who still worked in the area, which were mostly custodians endlessly sterilizing the countless floors of un-rented offices.

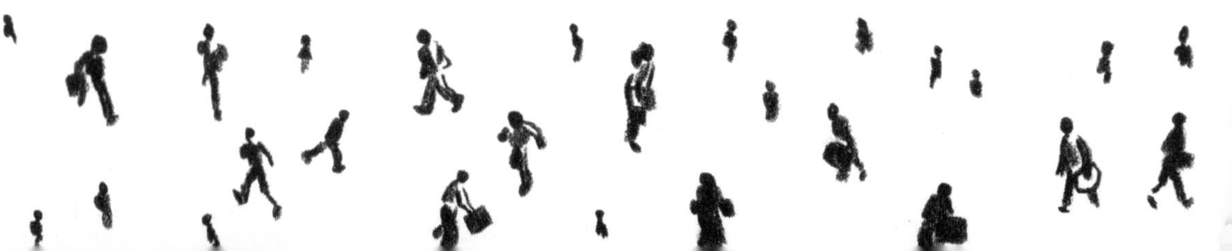

Though it had been Arbor's idea, actually living with a partner was an unbelievable shock to him. He had so easily rejected many of life's expectations that doing *without* had become a major part of how he defined who he was. Everything was done his own way, if only to ensure that nothing ever hurt him too badly.

Now, he found himself randomly bursting into laughter.

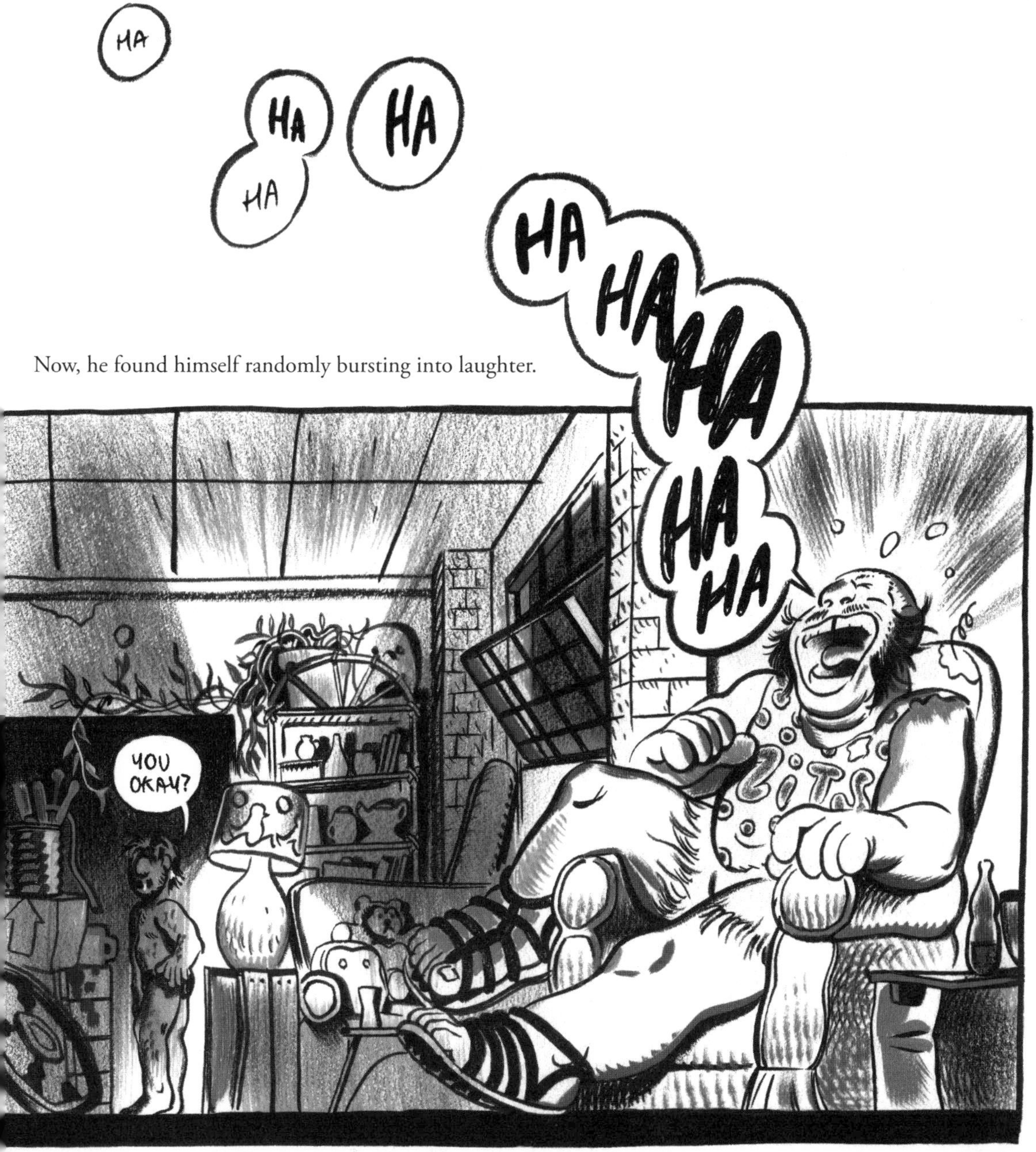
HA
HA
HA
HA
HA HA HA HA HA HA HA
YOU OKAY?

With the work on Fanny's nearing completion, Paolo began to transition the Facilitators from construction to wait staff. Despite Arbor's reluctance, he agreed that their novelty could temporarily be a worthwhile gimmick to get customers in the door. He was insistent that their clothing be non-sexual, though, wary of the connotations many people still had about Facilitators and conscious of wanting to make an inclusive space for more than just gay men.

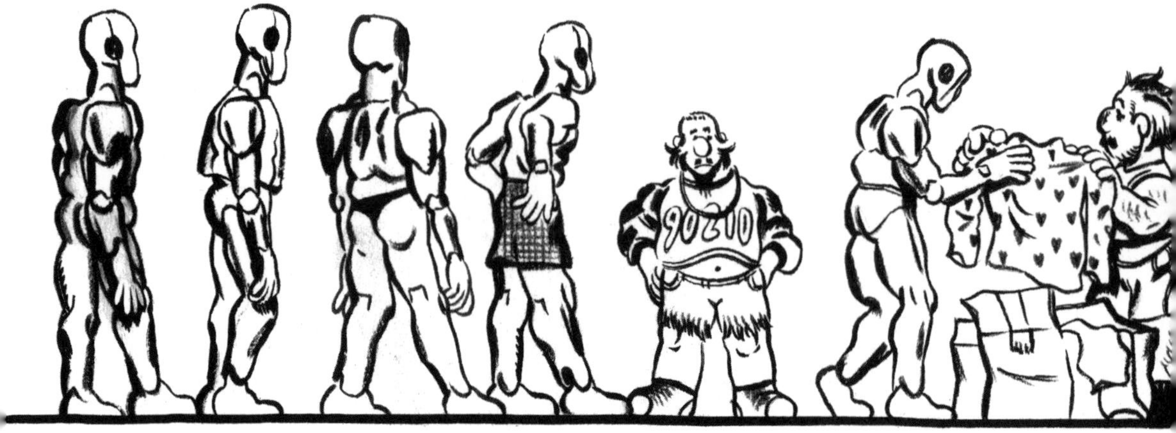
90210

Inevitably, everything Paolo dressed the robots in read as provocative. The work he had done reprogramming them had delivered mixed results, leaving some of the robots with strange sexual affectations that quickly tainted whatever outfit they were wearing. Despite his best efforts to hide his frustration, Arbor's patience had grown thin. Neither Arbor nor Paolo could admit how they felt about the situation, and for the first time since they became re-entangled, they found themselves avoiding each other.

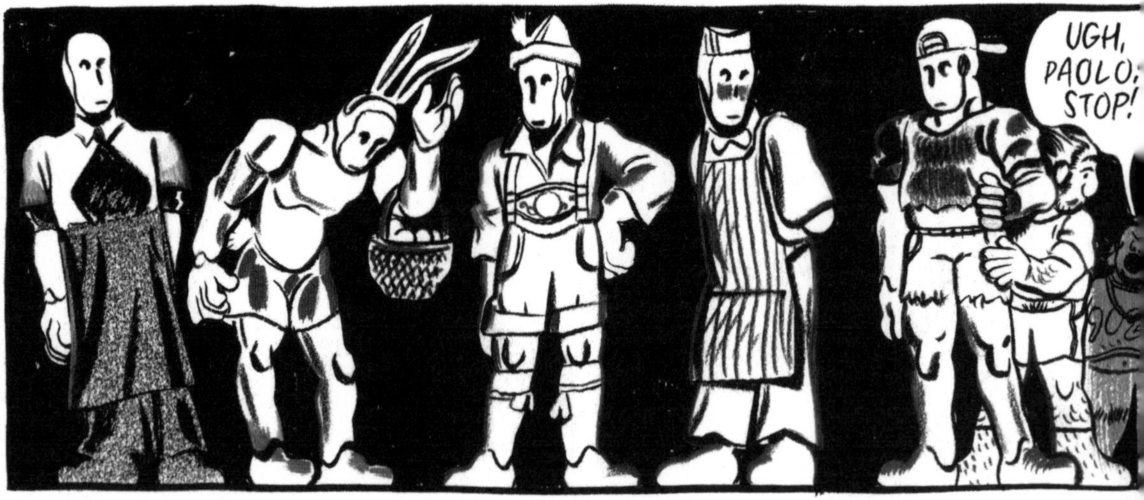
UGH, PAOLO, STOP!

Determined to make things right, Paolo began working long hours trying to fix whatever remained of the Facilitators original programming.

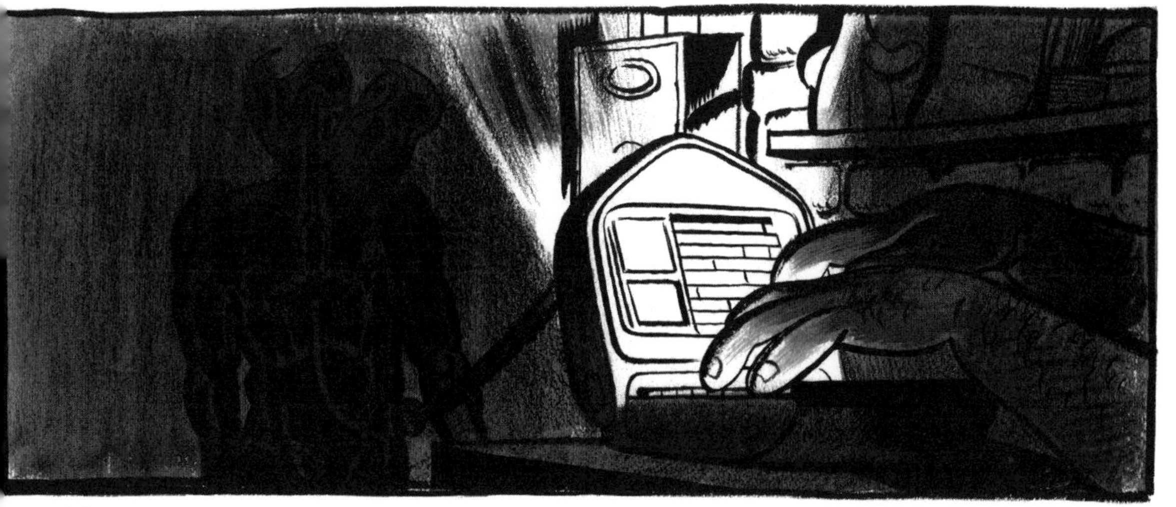

The problem with the Facilitators was that each of their individual memory banks were difficult to gain access to. Then, once inside, their hard drives were full of unnecessary files, which made deciding what was actually important tedious. Paolo found hours and hours of footage recorded by the Facilitators themselves, back when Fanny's was still a functioning bar. He learned that they often took photos with drunk patrons, the palms of their hands doubling as cameras. Paolo would often play random videos of young men enjoying themselves, dancing to music he had never heard before, to keep him company through the late nights of scrubbing software.

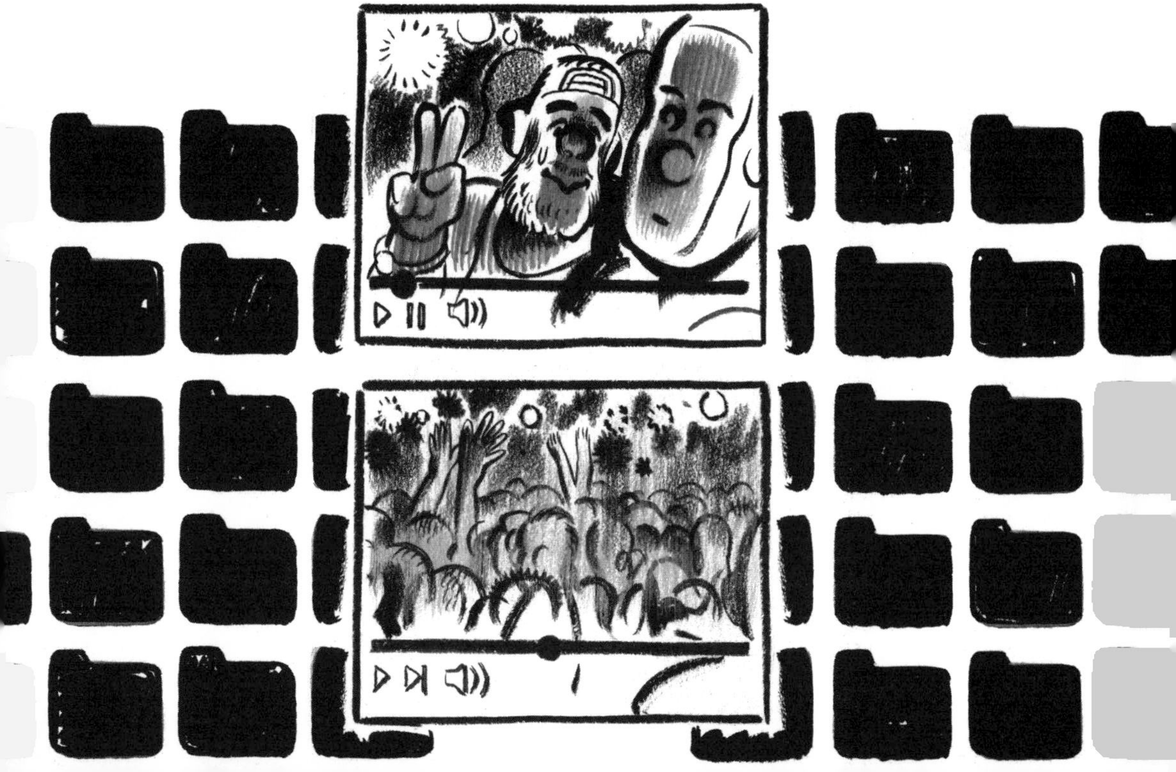

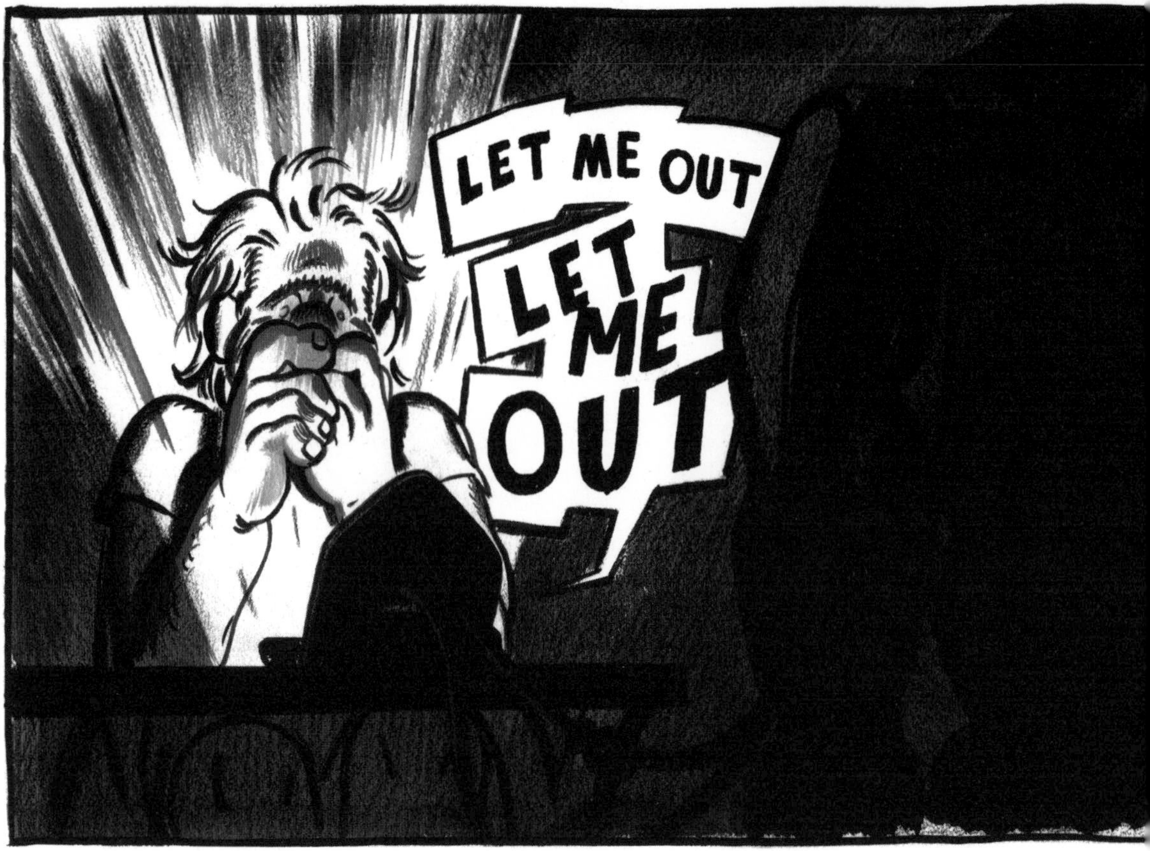
LET ME OUT
LET ME OUT

Late one evening, when his eyes had just begun to droop from the strain of staring at his monitor, Paolo was horrified to hear screams on one of the recorded videos. Scrubbing through, Paolo learned it was a video of a man who, after being invited to a back room for what can only be assumed as something sexual, was then trapped behind a door locked from the outside. The Facilitator who was recording stood outside the door, immobile, as the man's pleas went unanswered, lost in the pulse of thumping nightclub music. After a few minutes of this, the video continued to show the Facilitator walking back into the main room of the bar, moving through the crowd of men, all of whom were unaware of what had happened.

After he found the first video, Paolo quickly discovered other nearly identical videos, recorded in different bars: A man, usually drunk, excitedly talking about something pointless, following a Facilitator to some space deep within the bar, only to realize he had been duped as a door was locked behind him. Some men sobbed. Others were eerily silent.

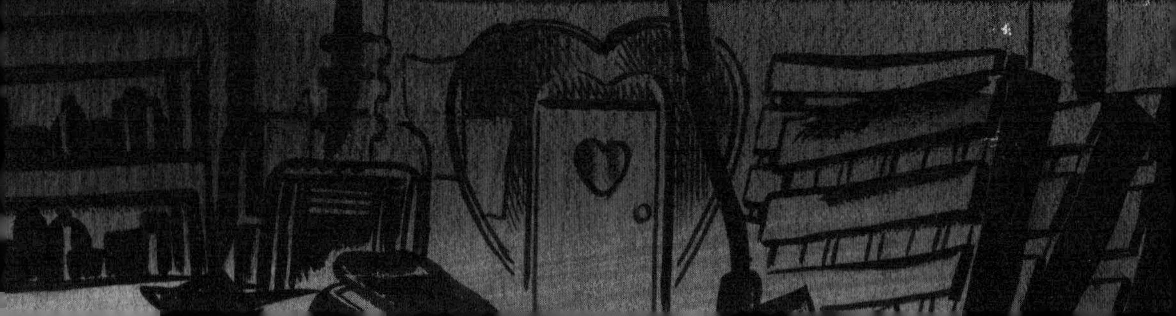

For Paolo, removing the libido programming from each robot became secondary to combing through hours of recorded video, looking for an explanation.

Arbor wasn't surprised by what he saw on the tapes. He had heard stories just like this when he was younger from the older queers and punks he and his friends idolized. At the time, he would never admit that he hadn't fully believed them, but now the evidence was undeniable.

During the early days of construction at Fanny's, while cleaning out the piles of crumbled plaster, rotting seat cushions, and shattered glass, someone found a locked door. Like every other door, it was heart-shaped. A few people tried their best to pry it open but soon gave up, distracted by more productive uses of their time.

Paolo awkwardly asked a Facilitator to help. With one swift tug, the Facilitator pulled the old door completely out of its frame. Inside was a private lounge, complete with curving satin sofas—each in the shape of a heart—unused heart-shaped sconces, a mirrored stage, and a pole for dancing. And there, curled into himself like a wood shaving, was the man Paolo had heard screaming.

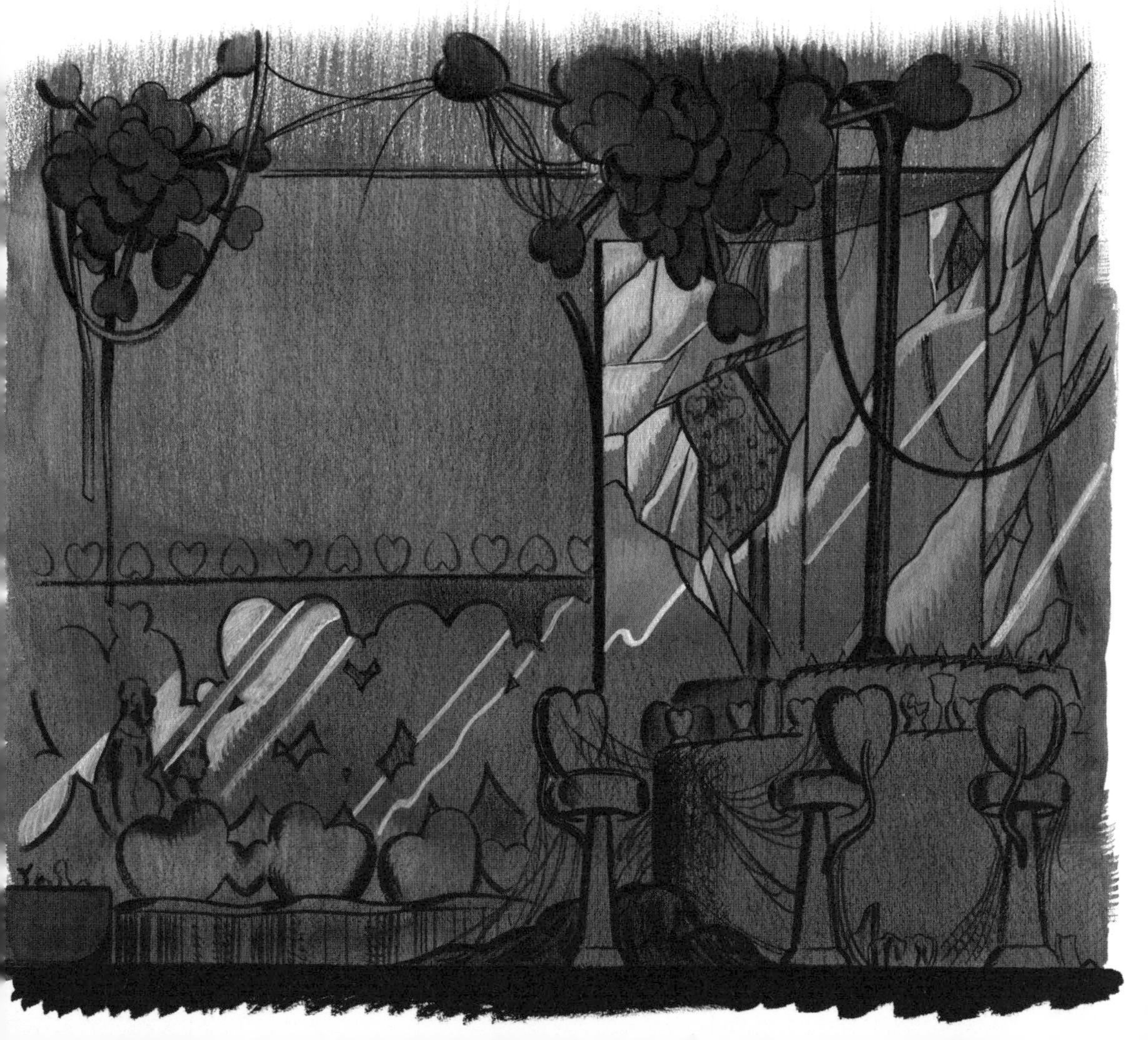

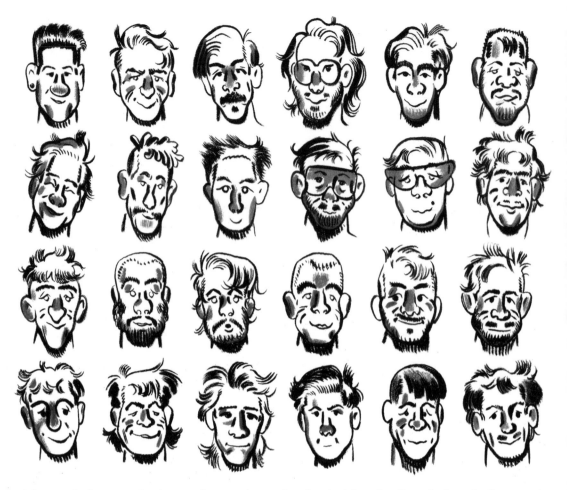

Arbor reached out to other bars in the area about what they had found at Fanny's. A total of twenty-six bodies were uncovered, each one in a similarly forgotten back room only accessible by the Facilitator found in that bar. None of these current bar owners had ever questioned that their new business came with a Facilitator. They had just been excited to have a space of their own, to repopulate these spaces that had been neglected under the Administration.

Through inconclusive investigative reports published at the time, Paolo discovered a series of nearly identical Missing Persons cases. In each one, a man had gone missing after a night out. They were often alone, either looking to pick someone up on their way home or making a quick stop before meeting up with friends later. Though there was no way of knowing how many other men still lay undiscovered in the back rooms of bars outside of their own neighborhood, the number of additional reports Paolo found seemed endless, eclipsing the twenty-six bodies they had found many times over.

The question Paolo couldn't understand was: *Who would still go out to bars after hearing about disappearing men?* The public's assumption was that if the Administration had deployed Facilitators to prevent the spread of disease, then these disappearances couldn't possibly be linked to the Facilitators themselves. It was easy to see now that the Administration wanted to use fear to separate its population of civilly disobedient youth by forcing them all to stay home. The only problem was: they hadn't realized there's no better protest to growing hysteria than continuing to live your life unperturbed.

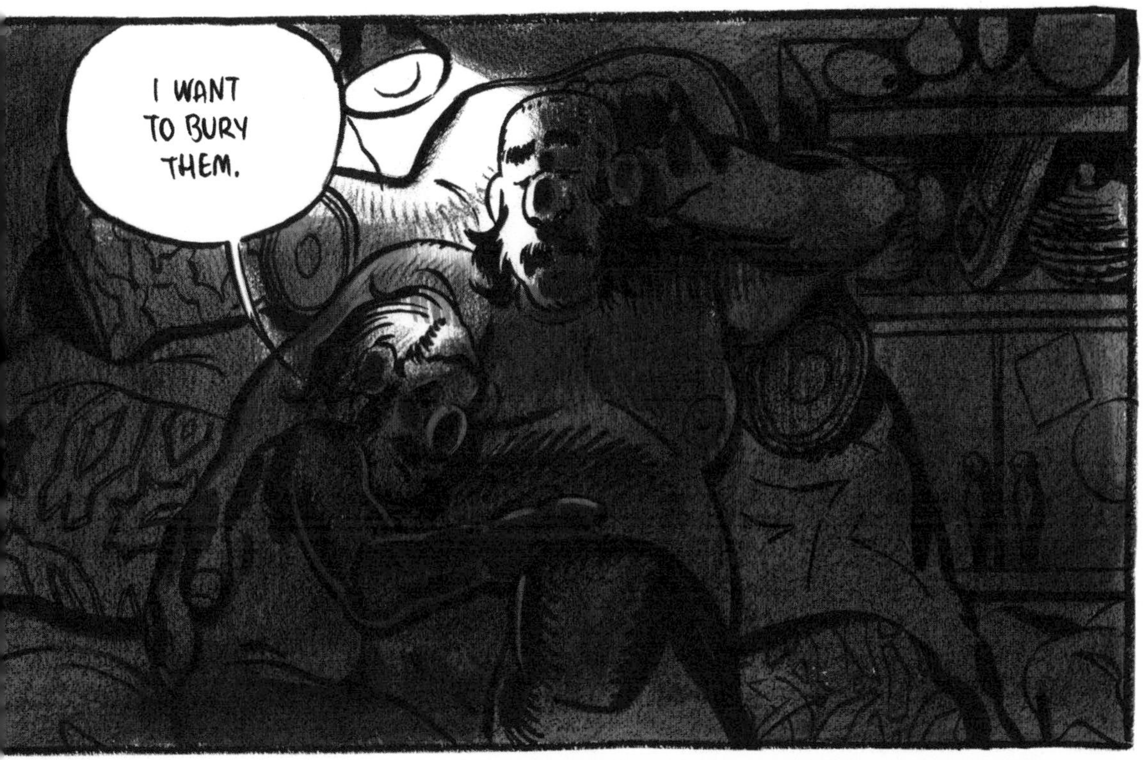
I WANT TO BURY THEM.

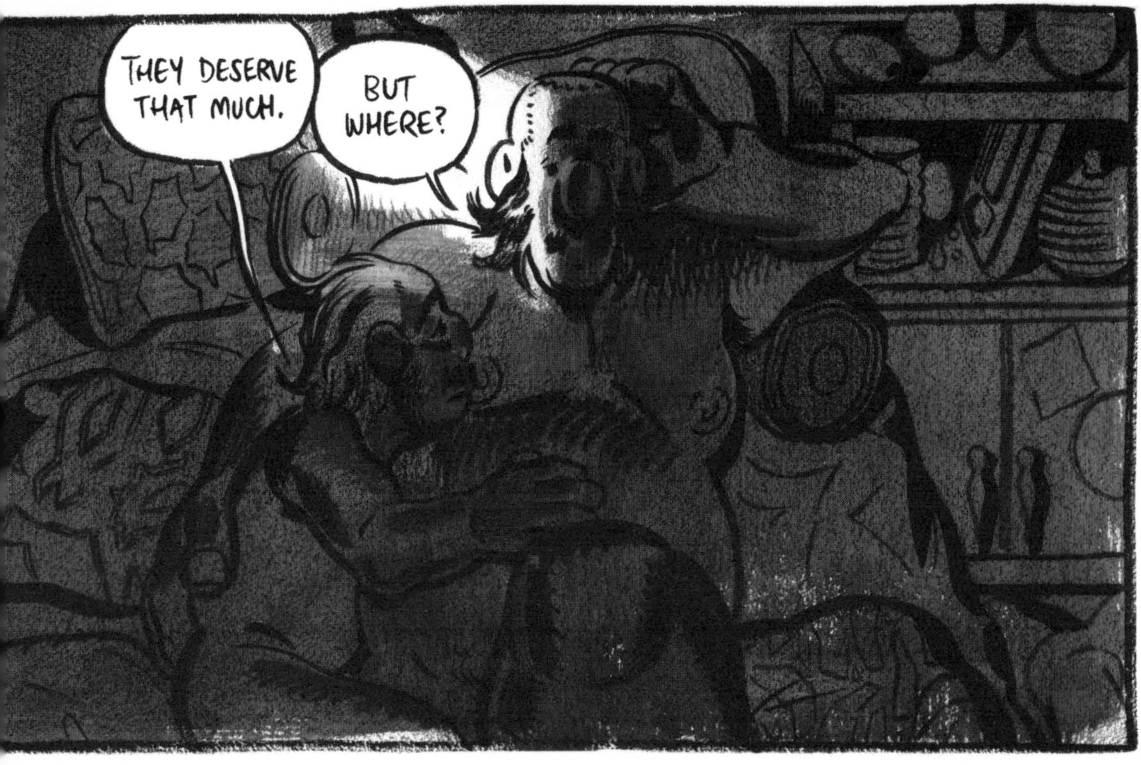
THEY DESERVE THAT MUCH.
BUT WHERE?

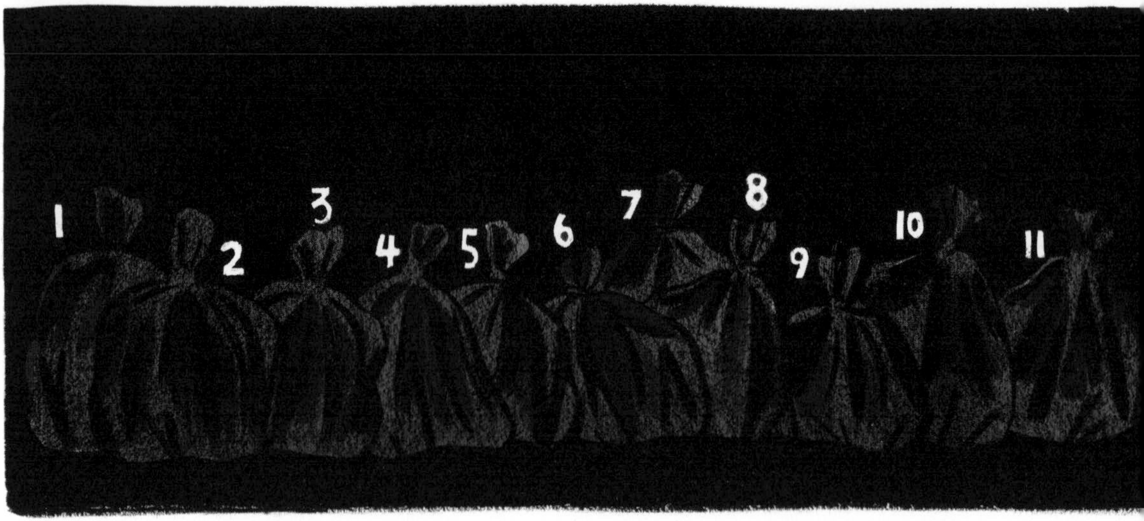
1
2
3
4
5
6
7
8
9
10
11

A long time ago, the Wastes had once been the sprawl that people spread out into when their lives in the city began to feel too cramped. It held the promise of contentment, the dream of having a space all your own: A backyard. A two car garage. Somewhere to raise a family the way a family ought to be raised. But after decades of diminishing levels of rainfall causing wind erosion, resource scarcity, and plumes of dust-filled air, this once-lush landscape became uninhabitable for close to a century. Most of the buildings Paolo and Arbor drove past had crumbled into nothing, the life beaten out of them after years of lying abandoned beneath the blistering sun.

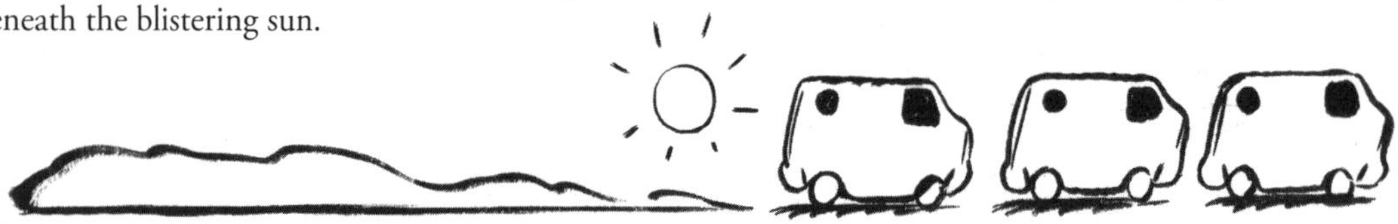

Paolo rented three vans to transport the bodies out into the Wastes for burial. Because of their limited budget, each body was placed in a black trash bag. A few of his roommates did the lifting for him, but Paolo could tell that after spending decades in the stale air of the lounges they died in, each body barely weighed anything at all.

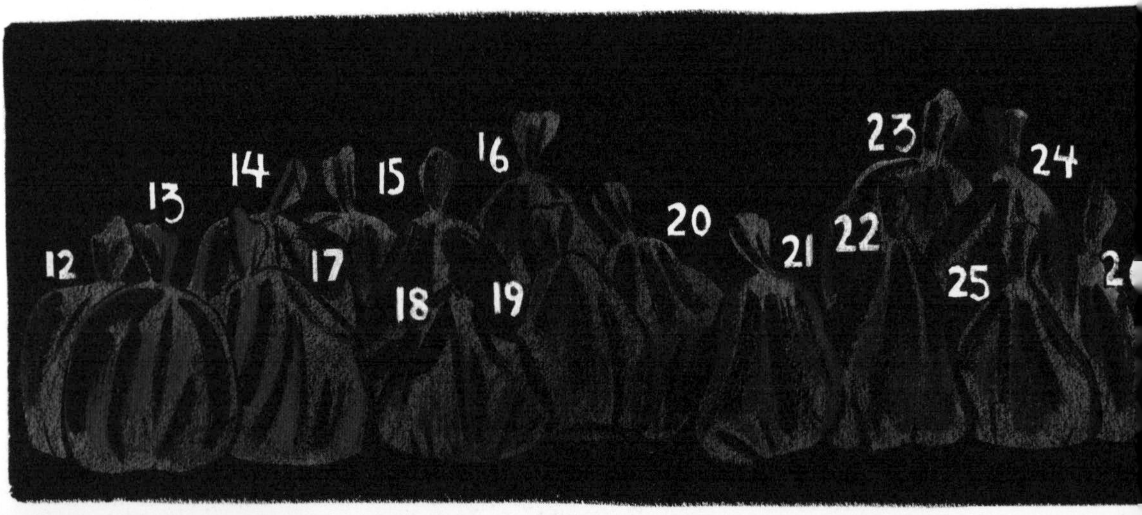
12
13
14
15
16
17
18
19
20
21
22
23
24
25
2

Since Paolo never got the chance to modify the programming for all of the Facilitators, there were still a few capable of doing manual labor. Arbor felt it was tasteless to have the murderers bury their own victims, but there was no other way to dig that many graves without help.

All twenty-six graves were dug just as the sun dipped below the horizon and continued on below their feet. Arbor asked Paolo to say a few words, but he was unable to come up with anything besides "I'm sorry." Most of the men still had identification on them, but information wasn't as easily available nowadays as it had once been. The thought of nonchalantly presenting individual I.D. cards at Central Information for twenty-six Missing Persons was laughable. Paolo decided he would investigate them one at a time to avoid suspicion.

All he knew was that the man found in the back of Arbor's bar was named Oliver Ashley Walsh, age thirty-three, height 5'11", green eyes. His birthday was August 11th. Arbor was thinking of changing the name of the bar to O's, but he was nervous about having to explain what the name meant to patrons.

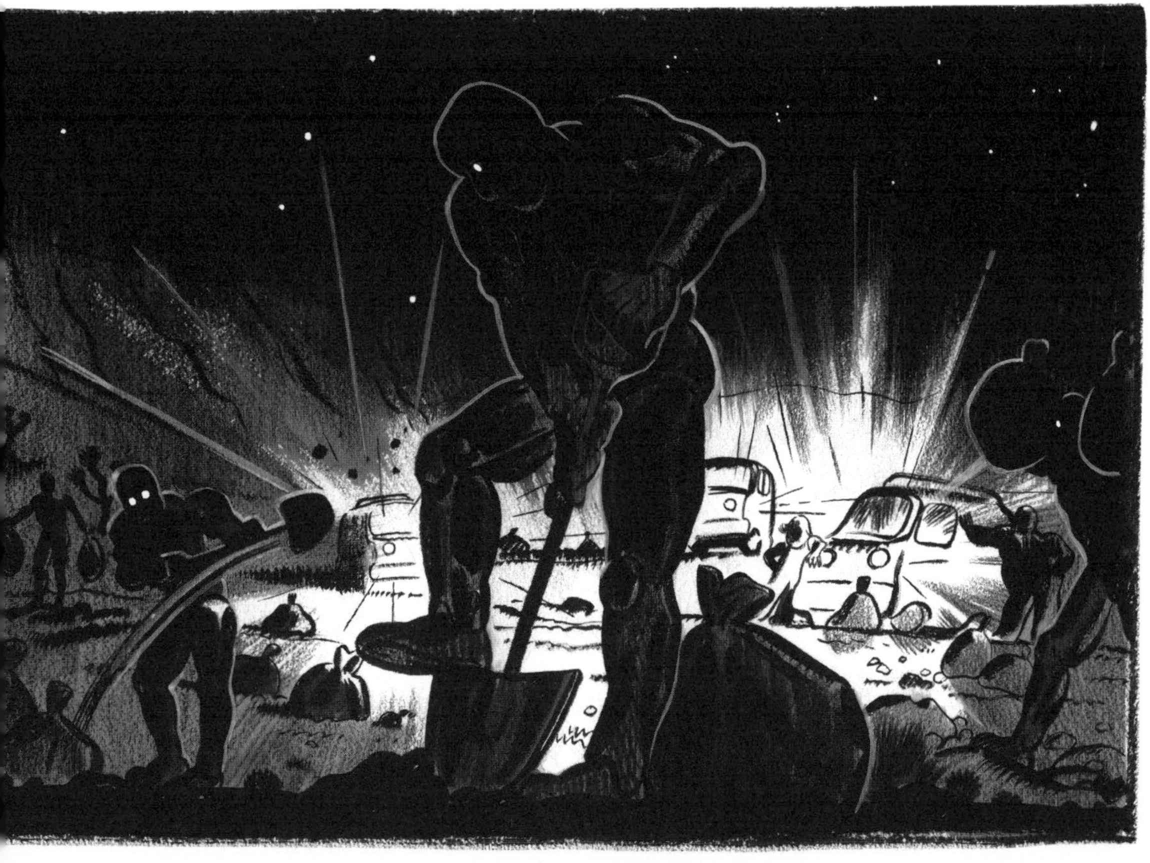

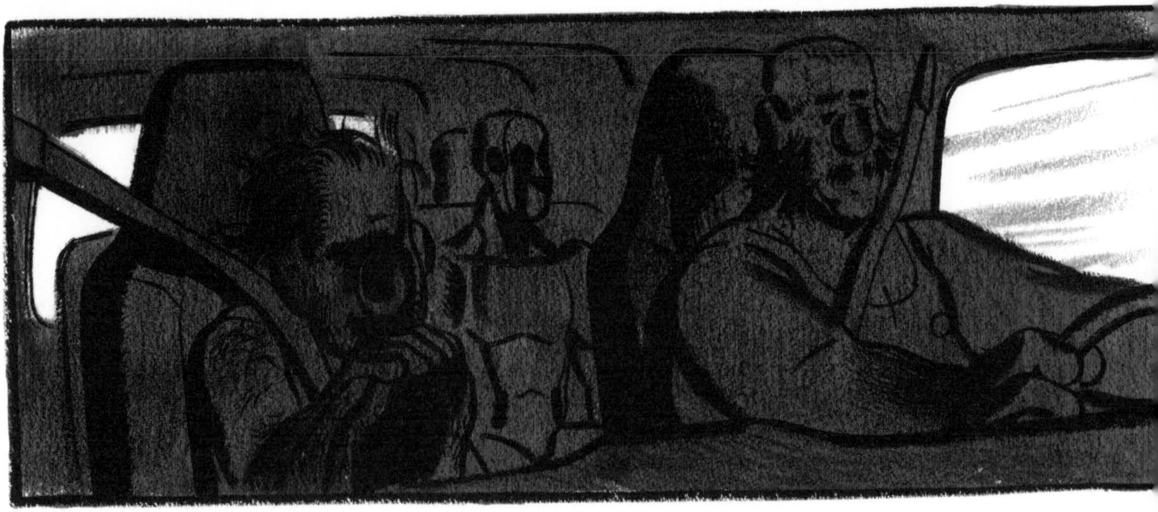

The buried plastic bags made Arbor think of his grandfather. Lolo Abe had liked to think of himself as a gardener, though he wasn't a particularly good one. He'd throw seeds wherever there was open soil, causing the lawn surrounding his home to grow untamed and wild. His neighbors hated him.

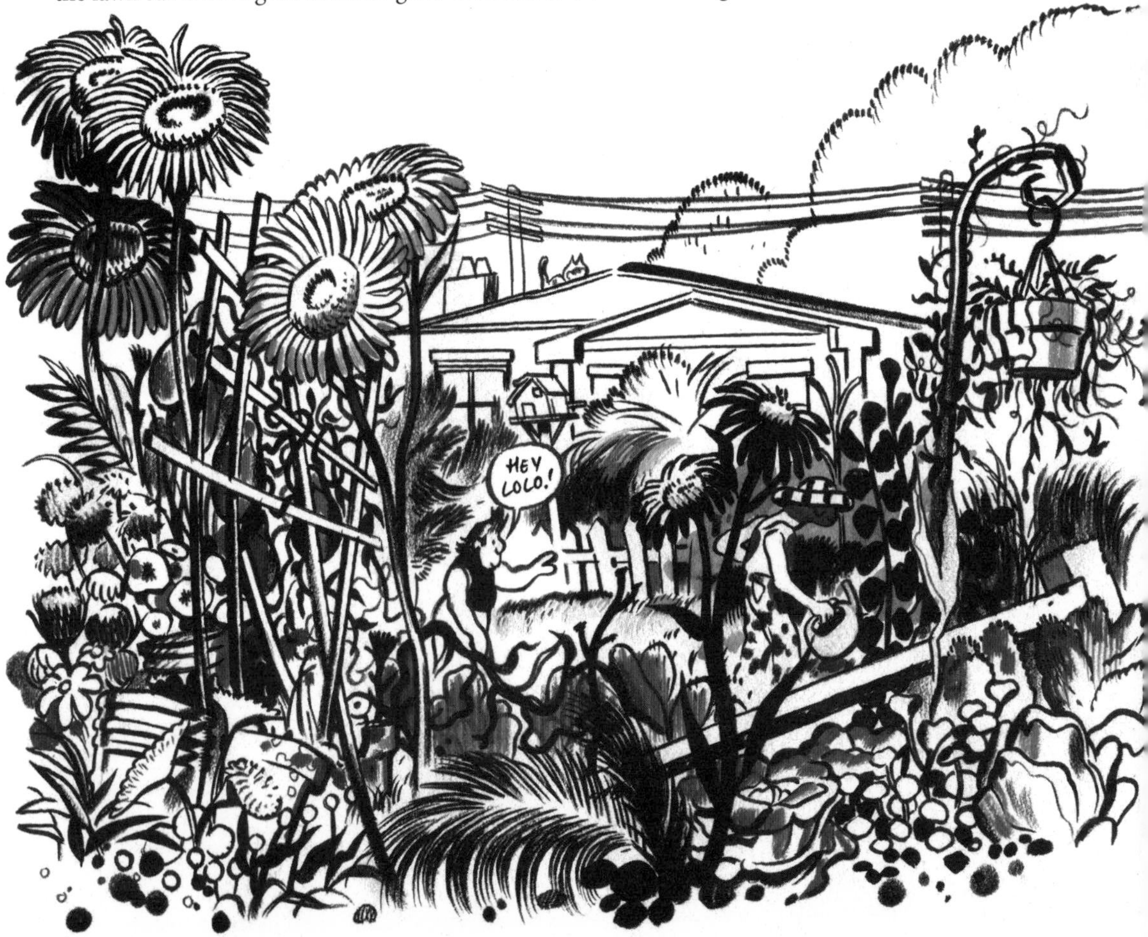
HEY LOLO!

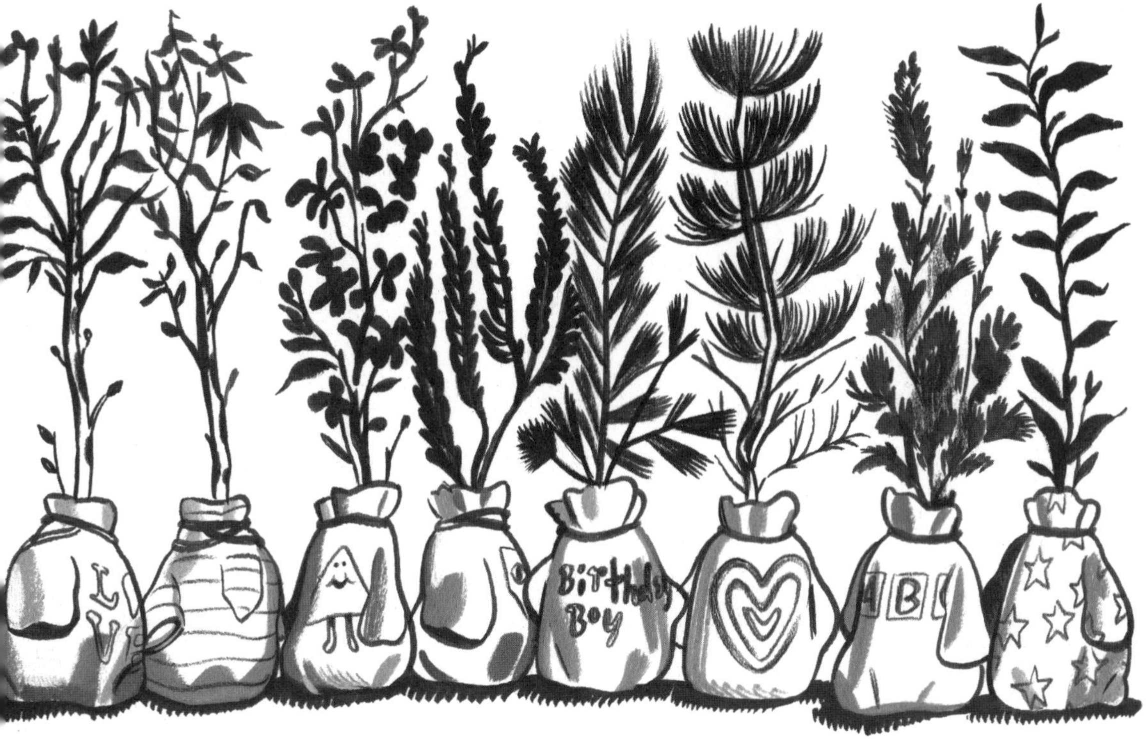
Birthday
Boy

One day, Lolo Abe arrived with a truck full of saplings ready to be planted. He had gathered each bundle of roots up in an old t-shirt. Arbor asked him why, and Lolo Abe told him (in Tagalog) that it was so that each tree would have something to wear when it grew up big and strong, just like him. Together, they spent their day driving around and planting the saplings wherever they could find free soil, avoiding security cameras and overprotective home owners. Arbor wondered if any of those trees had done well for themselves. The thought of a tree wearing a novelty t-shirt was, yes, unbelievable. But thinking of his grandfather, and the trees they had planted, made Arbor yearn for a less complicated time in his life.

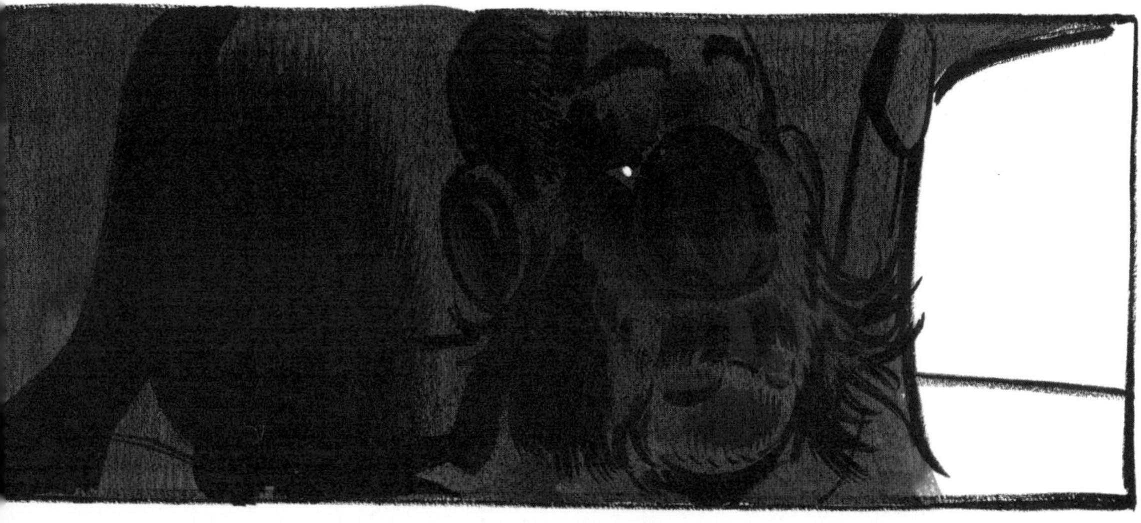

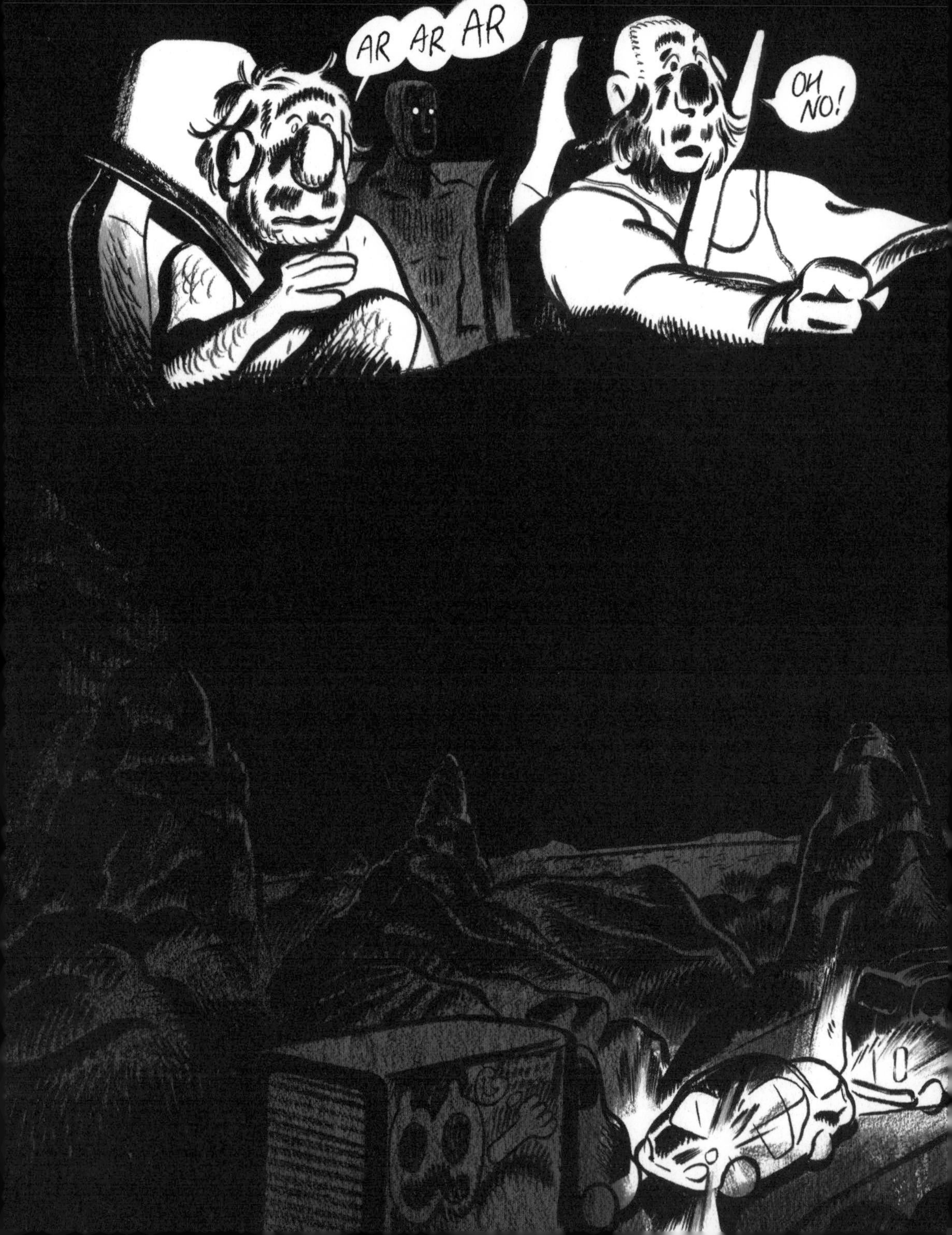
AR AR AR
OH NO!

Traffic began to slow ahead of them, and Arbor remembered what he had meant to tell Paolo.

Frank Bradbury's date of execution had been set, and after the horror of their recent discovery, Arbor had forgotten that it was taking place today. With nowhere to turn off the highway, Paolo was stuck staring straight ahead, watching this man's last moments of life play out on the large digital display above their heads.

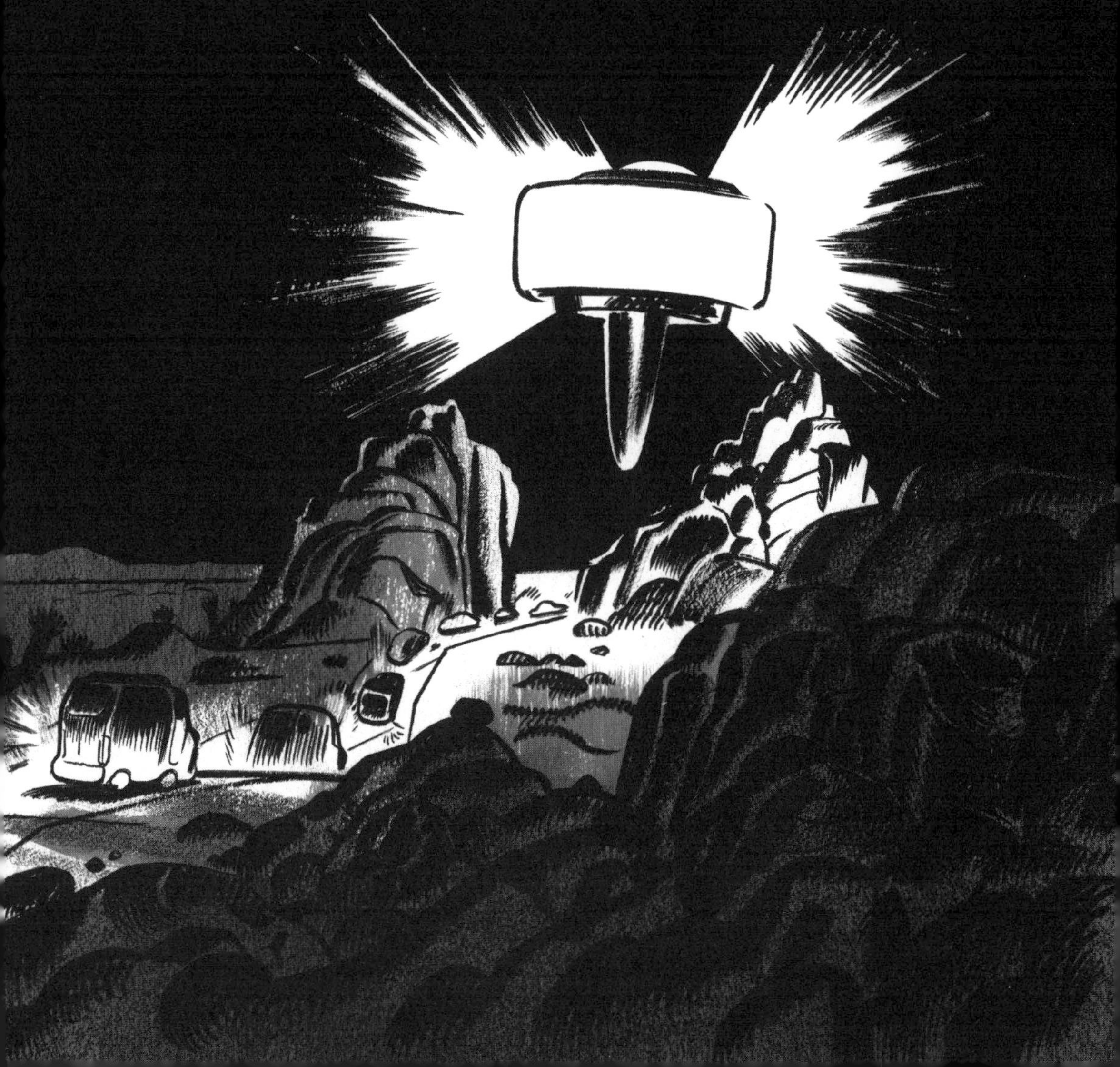

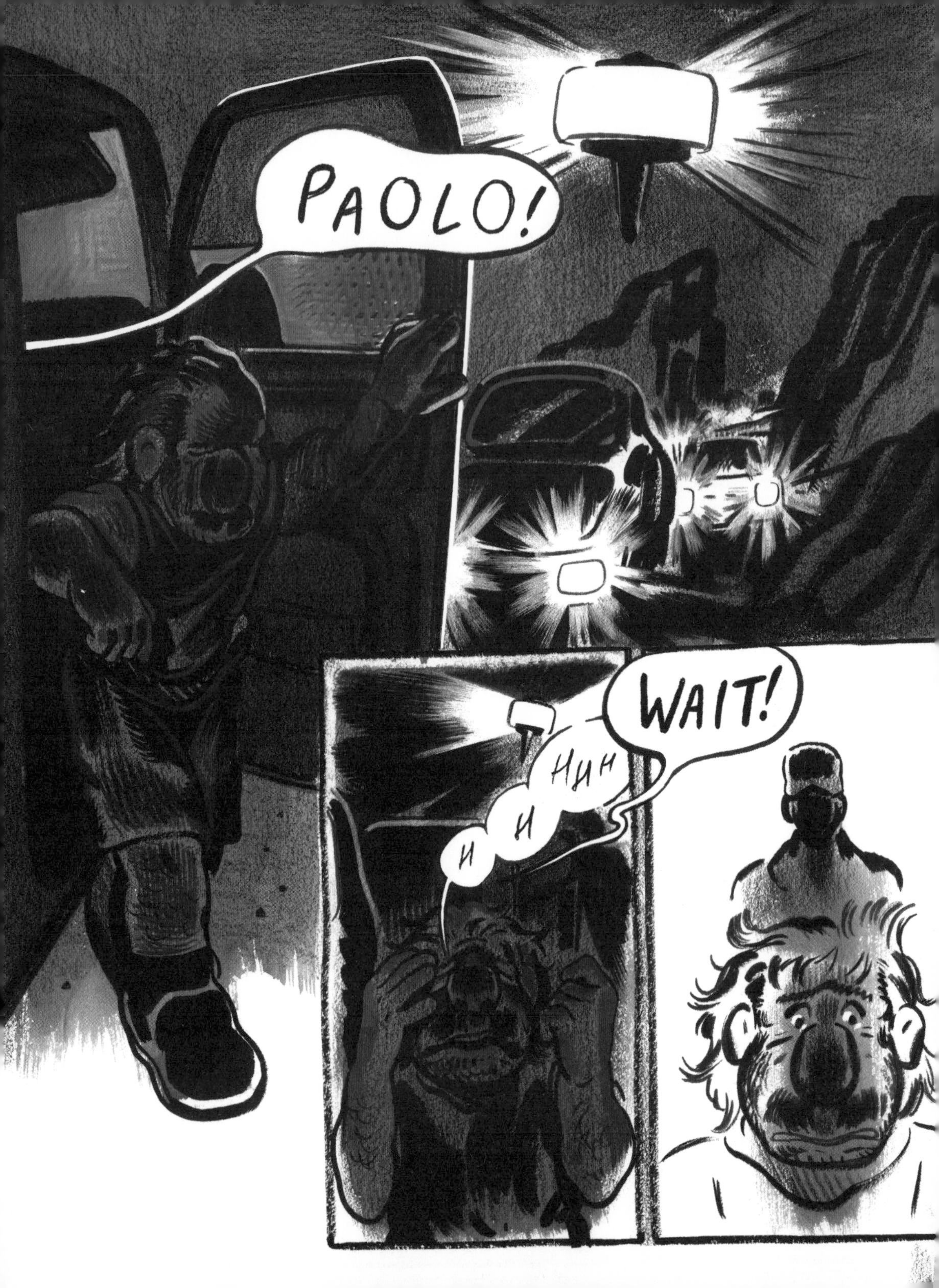
PAOLO!
H
H
HUH
WAIT!

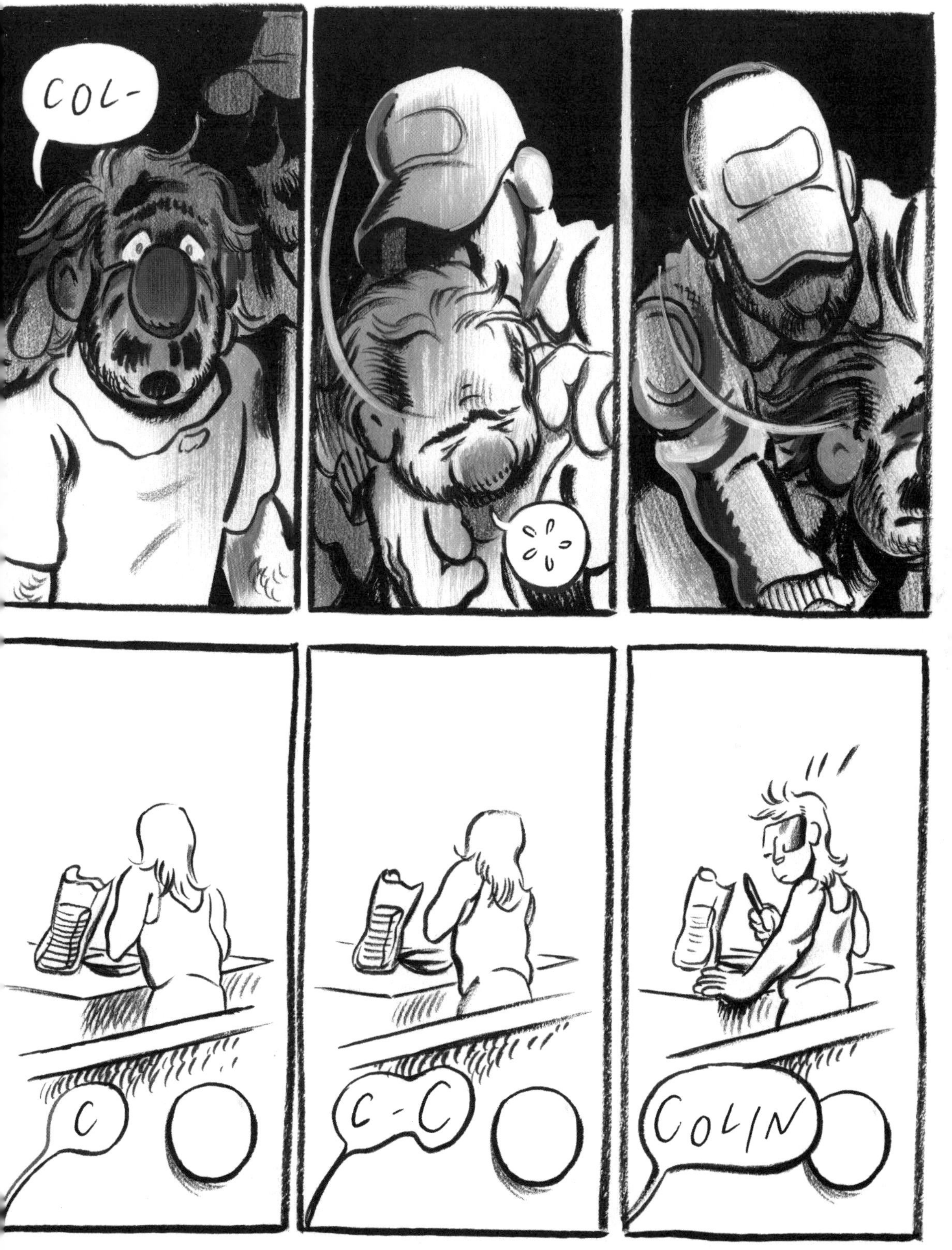
COL-
C
C-C
COLIN

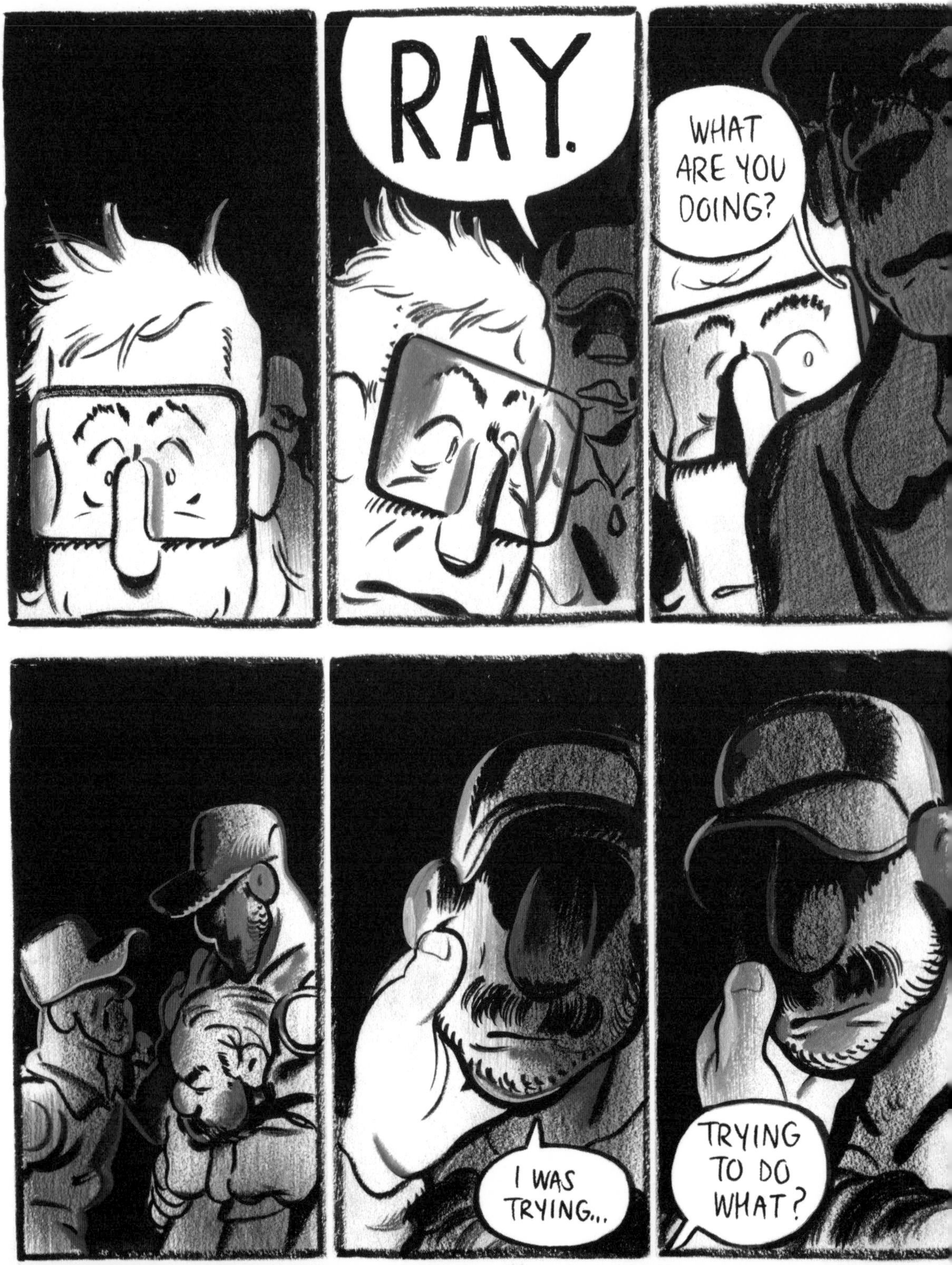
RAY.
WHAT ARE YOU DOING?
I WAS TRYING...
TRYING TO DO WHAT?

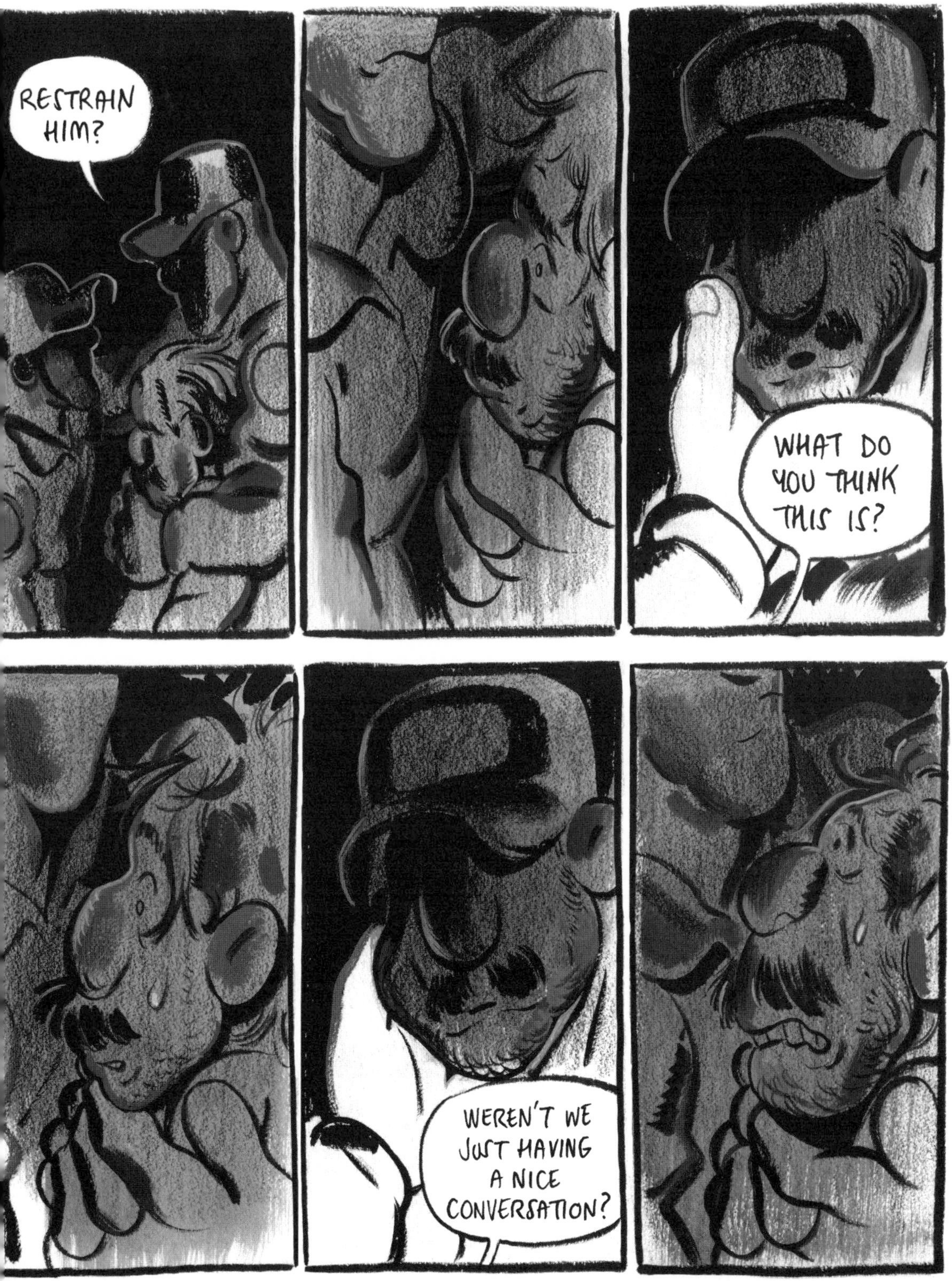
RESTRAIN HIM?
WHAT DO YOU THINK THIS IS?
WEREN'T WE JUST HAVING A NICE CONVERSATION?

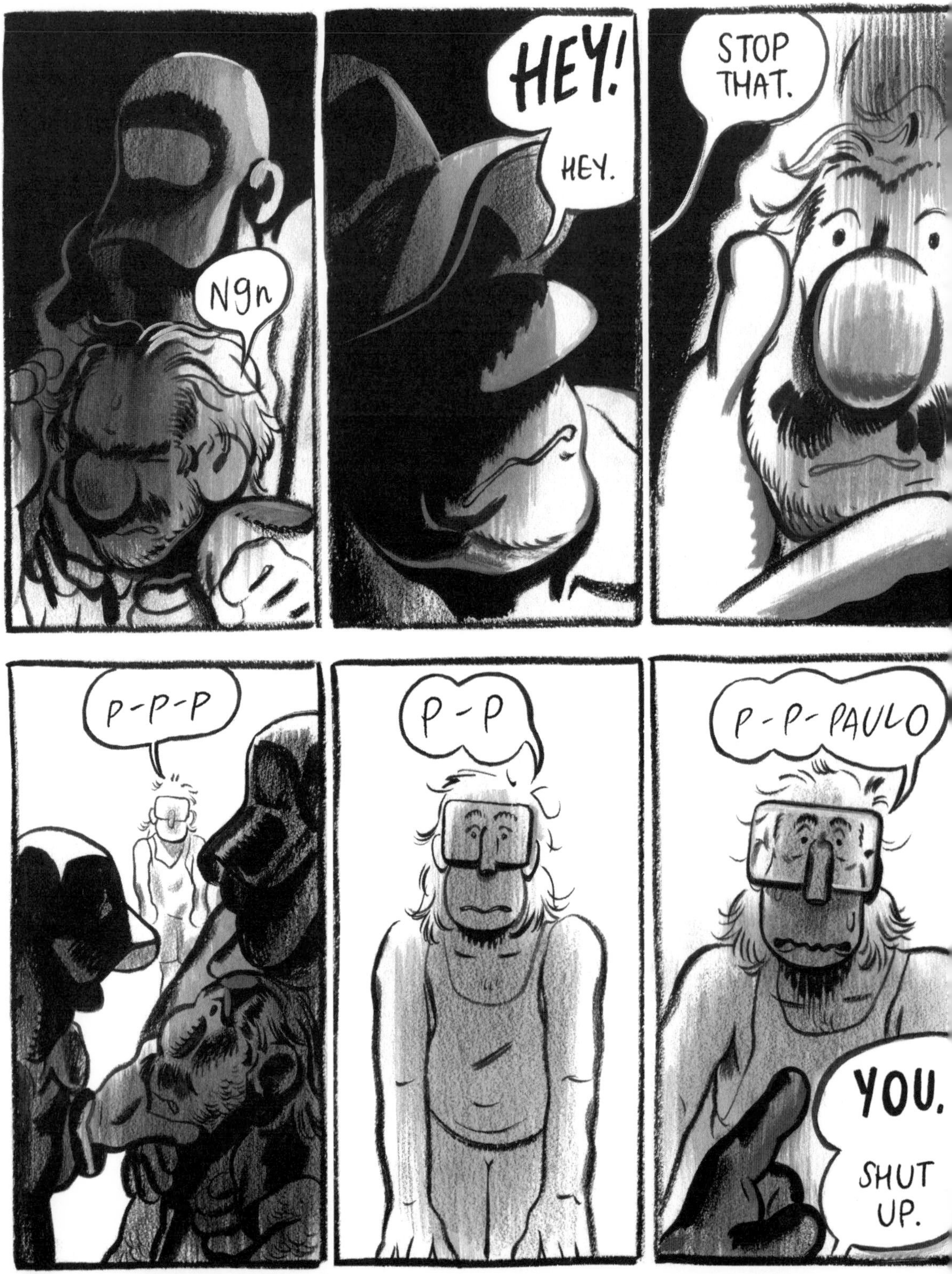
Ngn
HEY!
HEY.
STOP THAT.
P-P-P
P-P
P-P-PAULO
YOU.
SHUT UP.

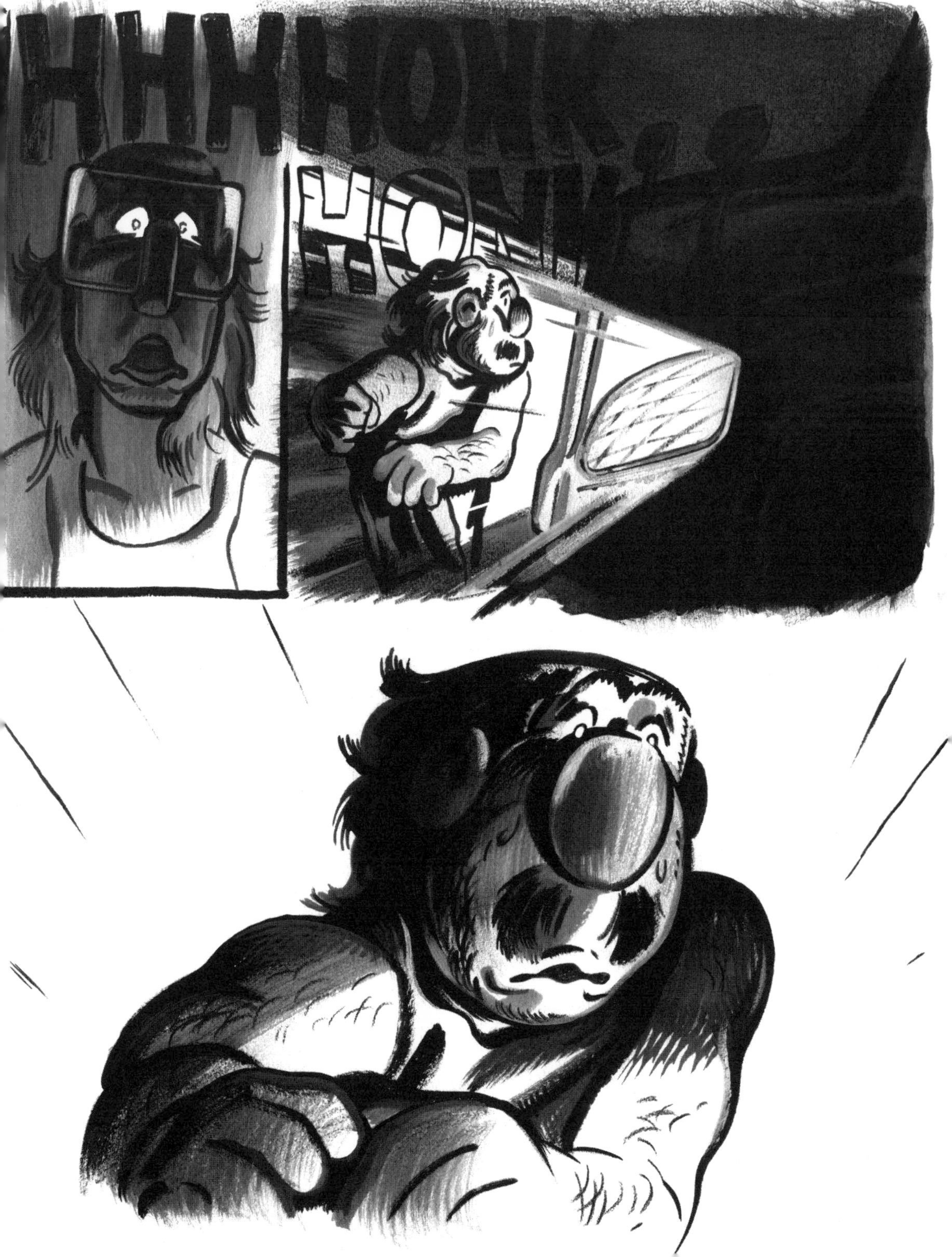
HHHHONK

Paolo and Arbor were stopped just inside the city limits by a small group of federal agents. What started as a routine traffic stop quickly escalated, as Arbor was asked to open his van for a more thorough search. In the back seat, the agents found a Facilitator buckled up like any other passenger. The two other vans were searched, and each Facilitator was clumsily dragged out into the chilly night air.

Paolo and Arbor were taken into custody for further questioning. Before they could make a call, Karoline and Karolina showed up looking genuinely concerned about their brother's safety. Paolo knew it was suspicious when his sisters showed up too quickly, but that had always been their way. They forced themselves into his life to try and fix it even if, more often than not, it meant they were the ones responsible for whatever was happening to him in the first place.

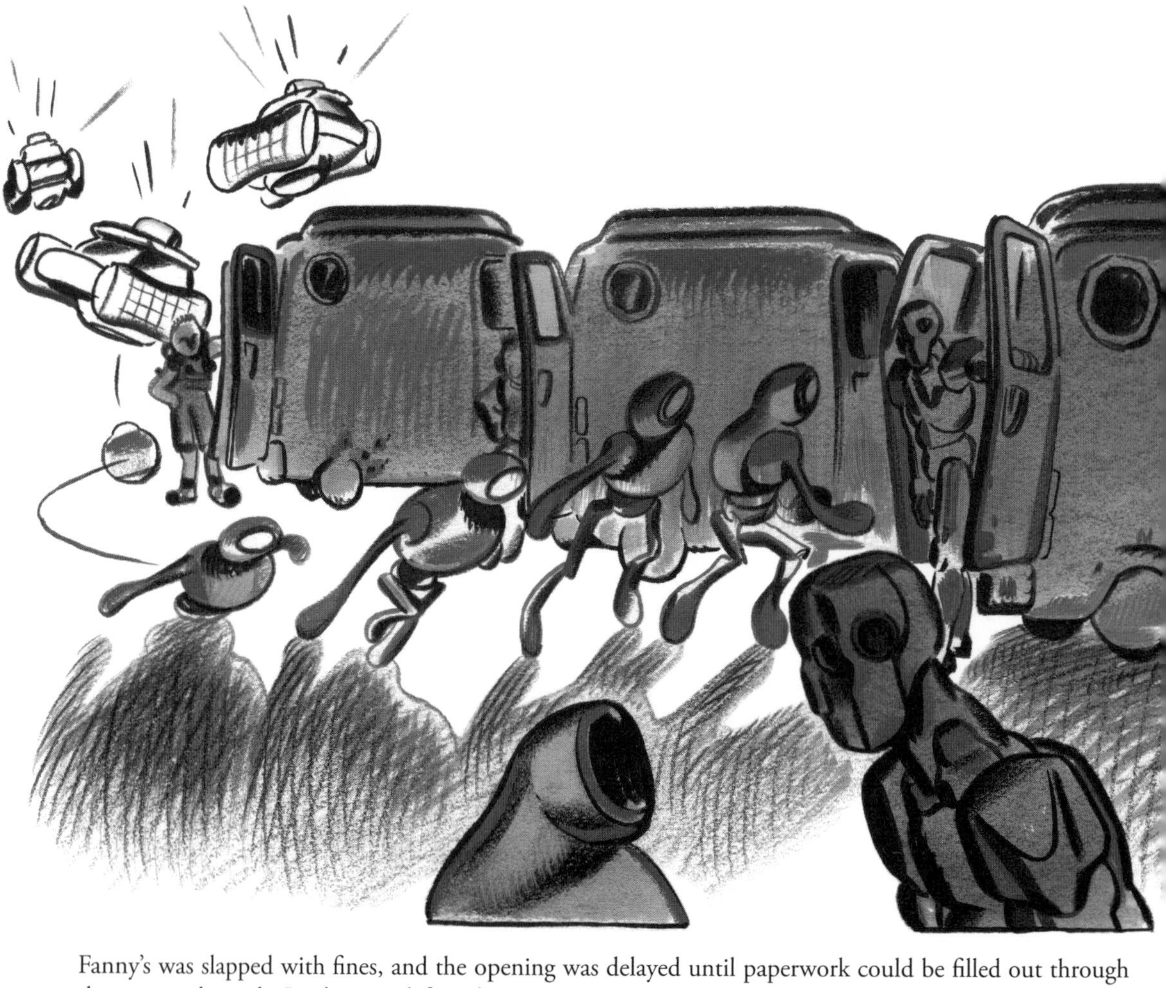

Fanny's was slapped with fines, and the opening was delayed until paperwork could be filled out through the proper channels. Looking to defuse the strange situation, Arbor brought everyone over to Fanny's for a nightcap. He knew it was only a matter of time before the authorities came for the rest of the Facilitators, and he wanted them gone. He coyly pretended to not know where the robots had come from, and instead focused his energy on making polite small talk and smoothly refilling drinks.

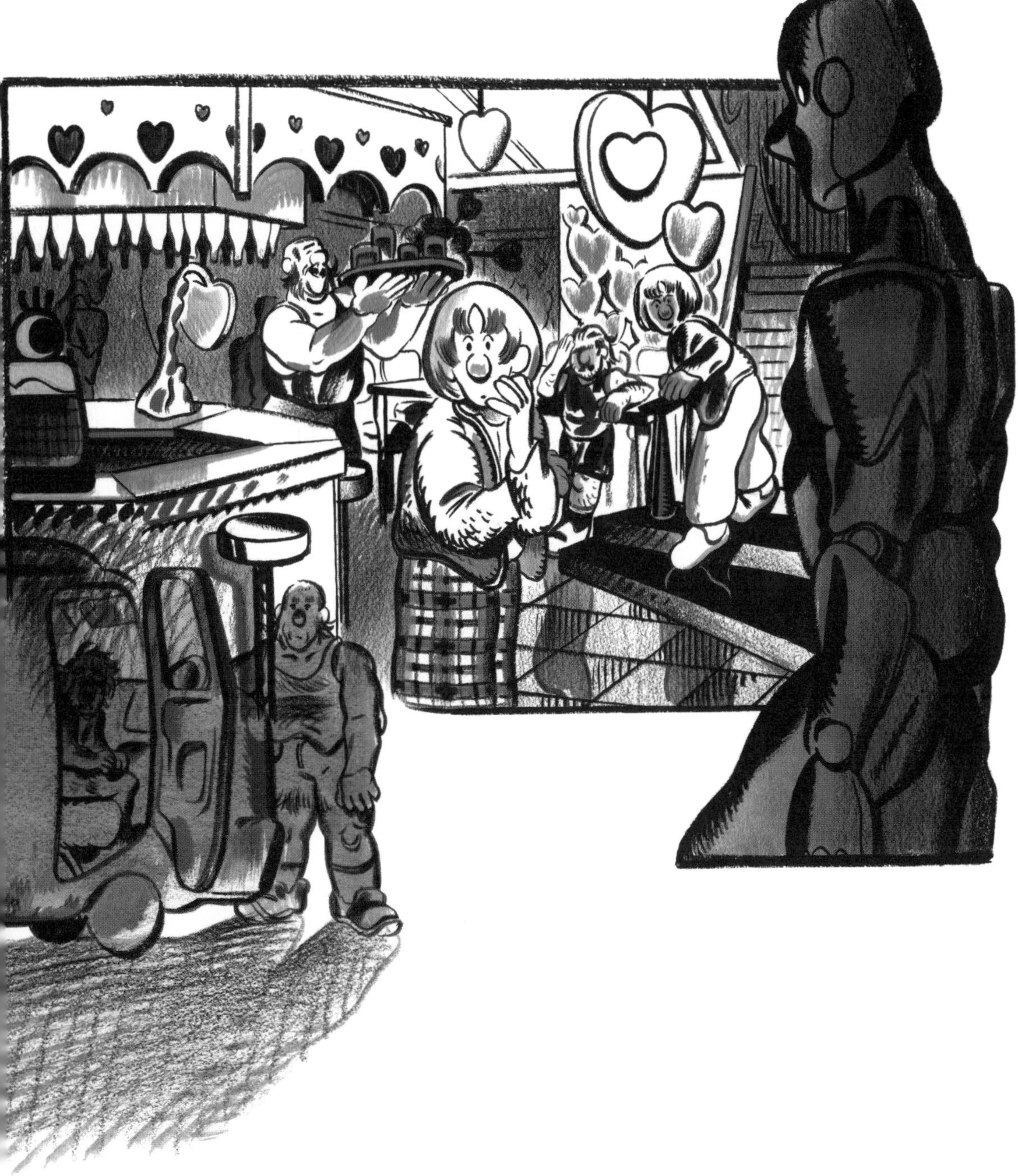

Karoline and Karolina took the Facilitators from Paolo to properly clear their memory banks. They would eventually return three of the six, claiming that the missing ones didn't survive the cleaning. The ones that did return were more distracted than before, and were soon returned to the room they had been found in and forgotten for a second time. Paolo never mentioned the bodies they had discovered, and his sisters never let on if they had learned about them from clearing the memory banks.

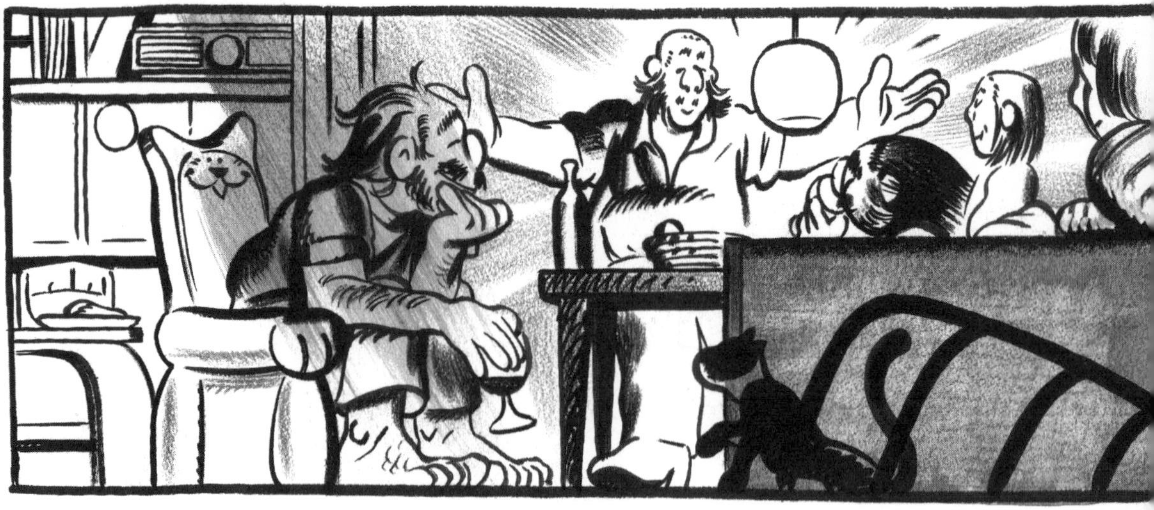

It only made sense that Arbor would be brought around to meet the entire Sordesto family after meeting Paolo's older sisters.

Watching Arbor move through the room was intoxicating. It was surprising how at home he was; a gracious guest. Paolo would never be the center of attention in his family, especially now that he was sharing them with someone like Arbor. But that didn't matter. Paolo was happy.

Paolo and Arbor spoke about Colin often. After all, he was the reason they had met. They would wonder what he was up to. How he was doing. If he had seen the execution, too. When he spoke about Colin, Paolo could feel warmth spread across his chest. There was a genuine love for someone he had once known.

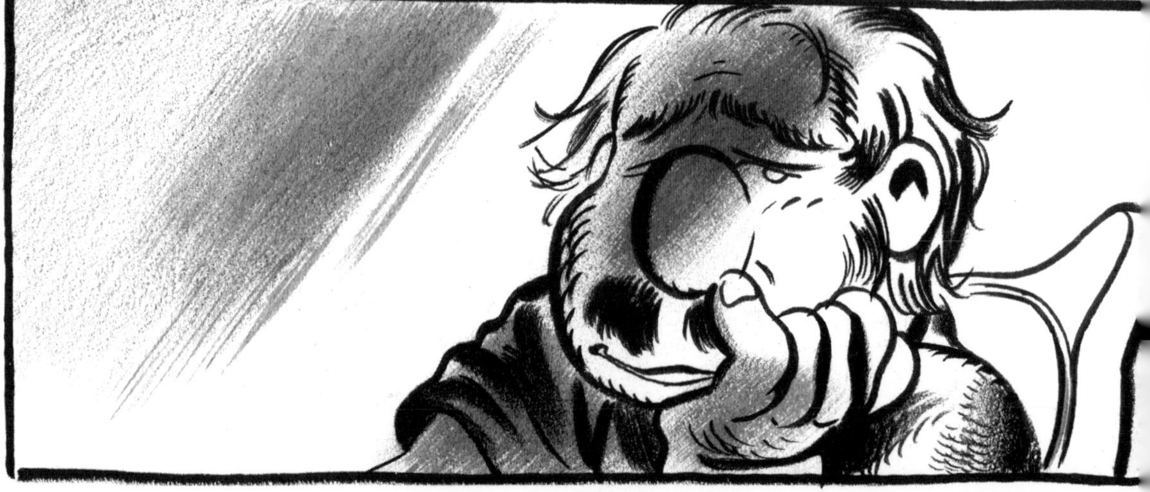

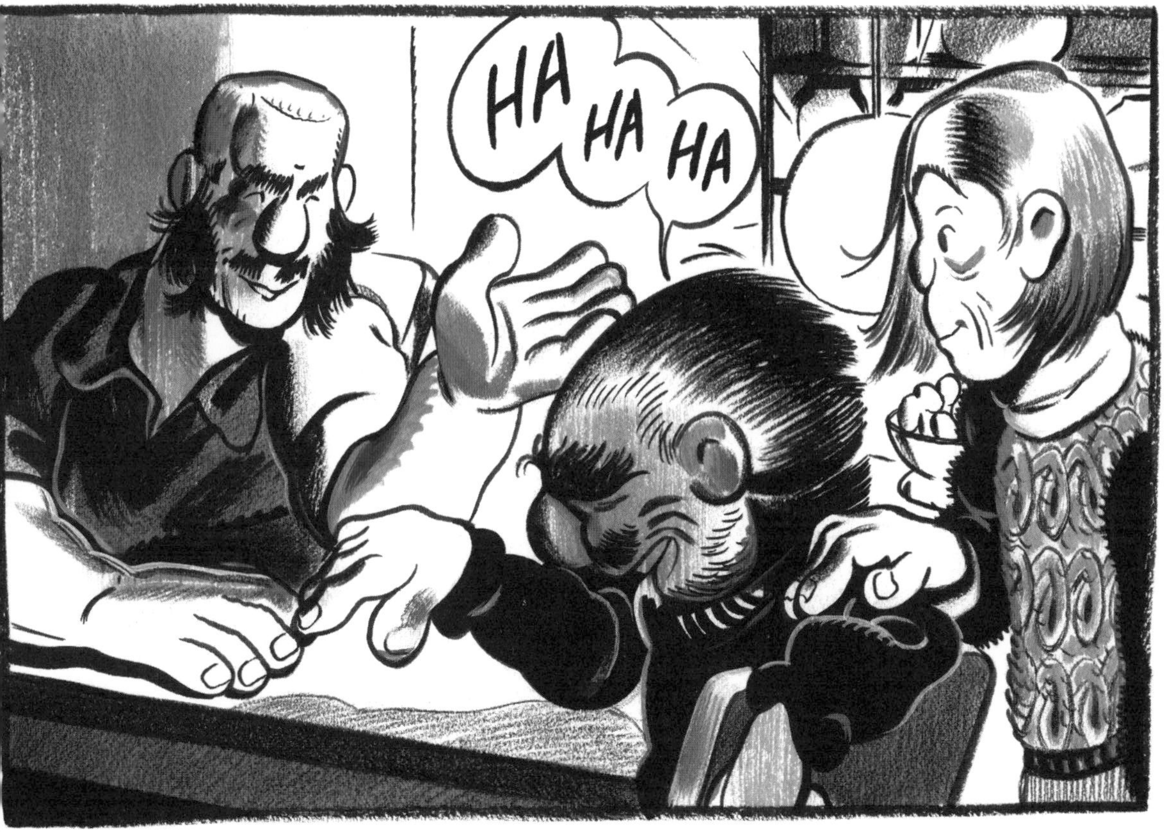
HA HA HA

But watching Arbor challenge his father to arm wrestling—his father instantly immobilized by his own laughter at the absurdity of it all—knocked Paolo right out.

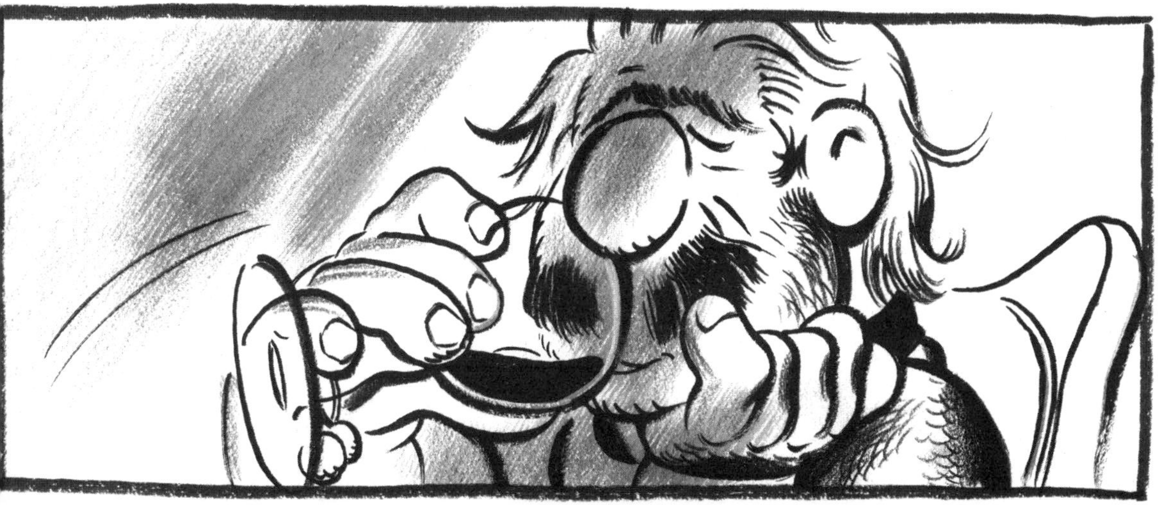

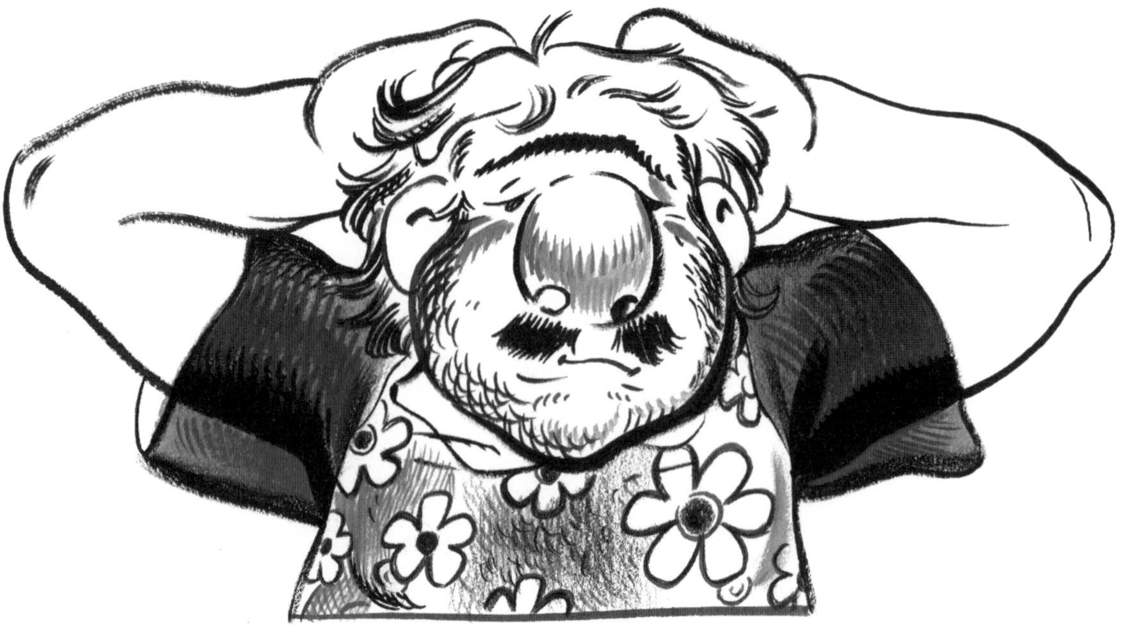

Paolo thought about the Facilitators a lot. He could understand Arbor's distrust of them but knew in his heart that he didn't agree, even after he was confronted with the reality of their programming.

He could never admit that the Facilitators reminded him of his sisters' dolls.

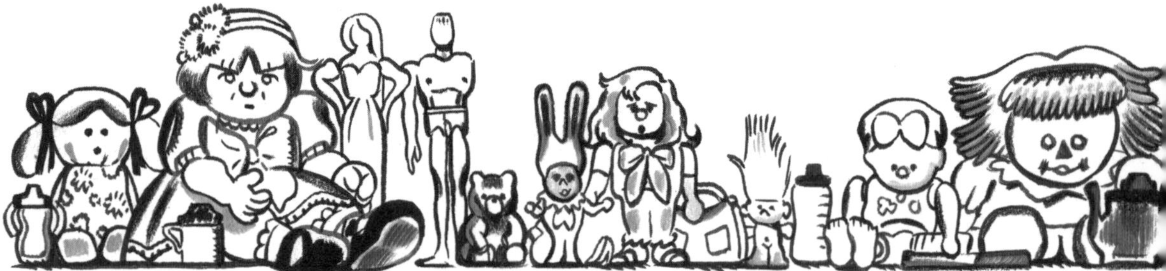

The gift of choice for every birthday and major holiday was always a doll of some kind. And because of their parents' anxiety about having children who are ungrateful for all that they had sacrificed, Karoline and Karolina never felt comfortable explaining just how uninterested in the dolls they were. For years the dolls sat ignored, beneath beds and in cramped closets, while his sisters pursued engineering, robotics, and real human boys.

That is, until Paolo discovered them.

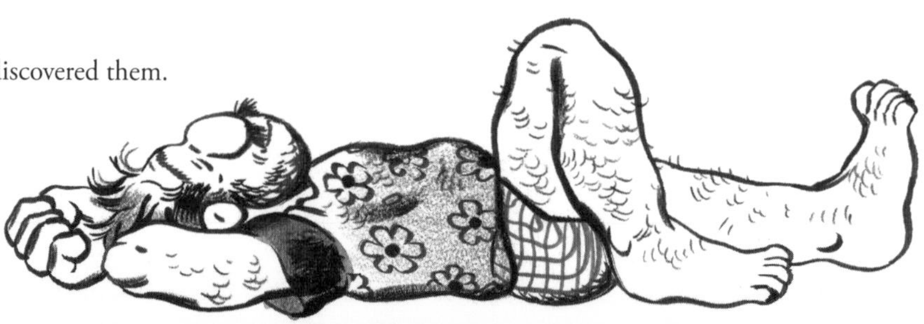

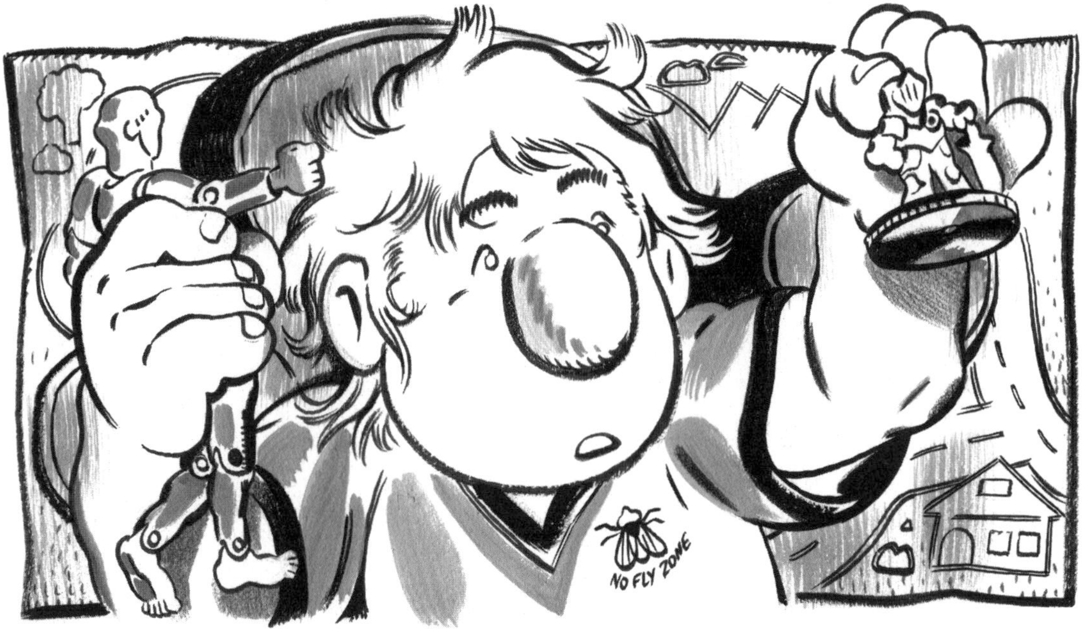
NO FLY ZONE

It wasn't that the dolls felt like friends, exactly, but having been a lonely child gave the dolls a certain magic. Their rapt attention was intoxicating. They waited for Paolo to make a decision about their lives, and what they would do with their tiny shoes and plastic accessories. Paolo had accepted early on that he was seen as, and in many ways was, a passive person. He waited for others to tell him what they needed from him. But the Facilitators, much like the dolls, were nothing without him. He and his slowly accumulating thoughts gave them a purpose, and in turn allowed him to take up space safely.

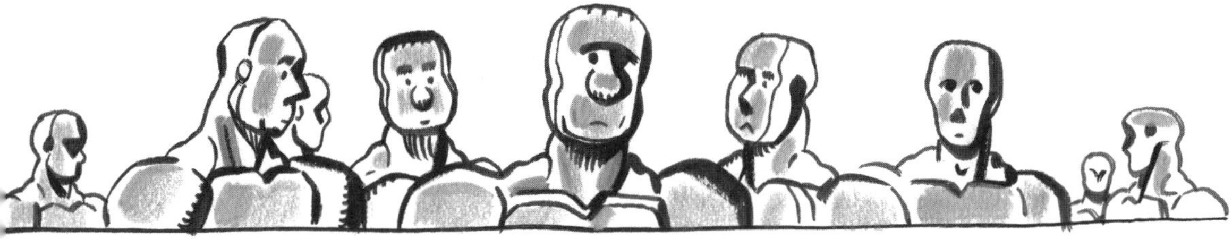

It didn't hurt that the Facilitators were inhumanly attractive. Their chiseled, unchanging bodies made his face flush in the same way that taking the clothing off a male doll had done years before. He often worried that Arbor wouldn't be happy knowing how turned on he was by something Arbor stood so firmly against.

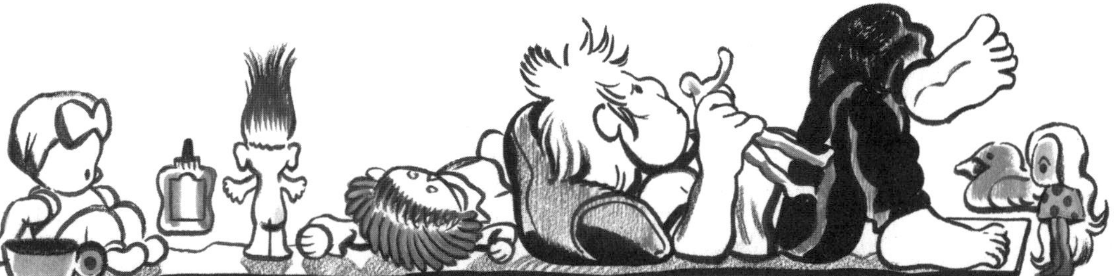

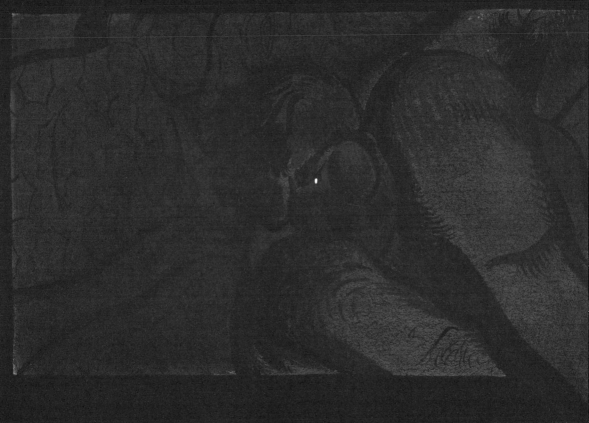

Unable to sleep until Arbor came home, Paolo had gotten good at pretending to be asleep when Arbor slid himself into their bed, slowly opening his eyes as if he had just noticed his boyfriend was even there. Arbor would try his best to recount all that had happened during his shift at Fanny's, but his exhaustion always got the best of him, the stories making less and less sense as he drifted off. Whatever happened would have to wait till the morning over a late breakfast.

Nestled against his sleeping boyfriend, Paolo would lay there, his head still full from the day, contemplating the endless list of things he needed to remember to do; things that, over time, had accumulated over the course of their life together. With Fanny's now fully operational, they could continue renovations on their own home—what needed replacing, updating, a good cleaning.

Despite all the things that needed to get done, he knew their bed was perfect. It had been stolen from a forgotten showroom by Arbor, one of those Seen On T.V. Made From Foam Intended For The Space Station mattresses that came with a certificate and a lifetime guarantee. Arbor had called it a Goldilocks bed. Soft, but not too soft. Firm, but not too firm. Just right.

Paolo knew, though, that even with how much of the bed they took up together, there was no denying there'd always be space for one more.

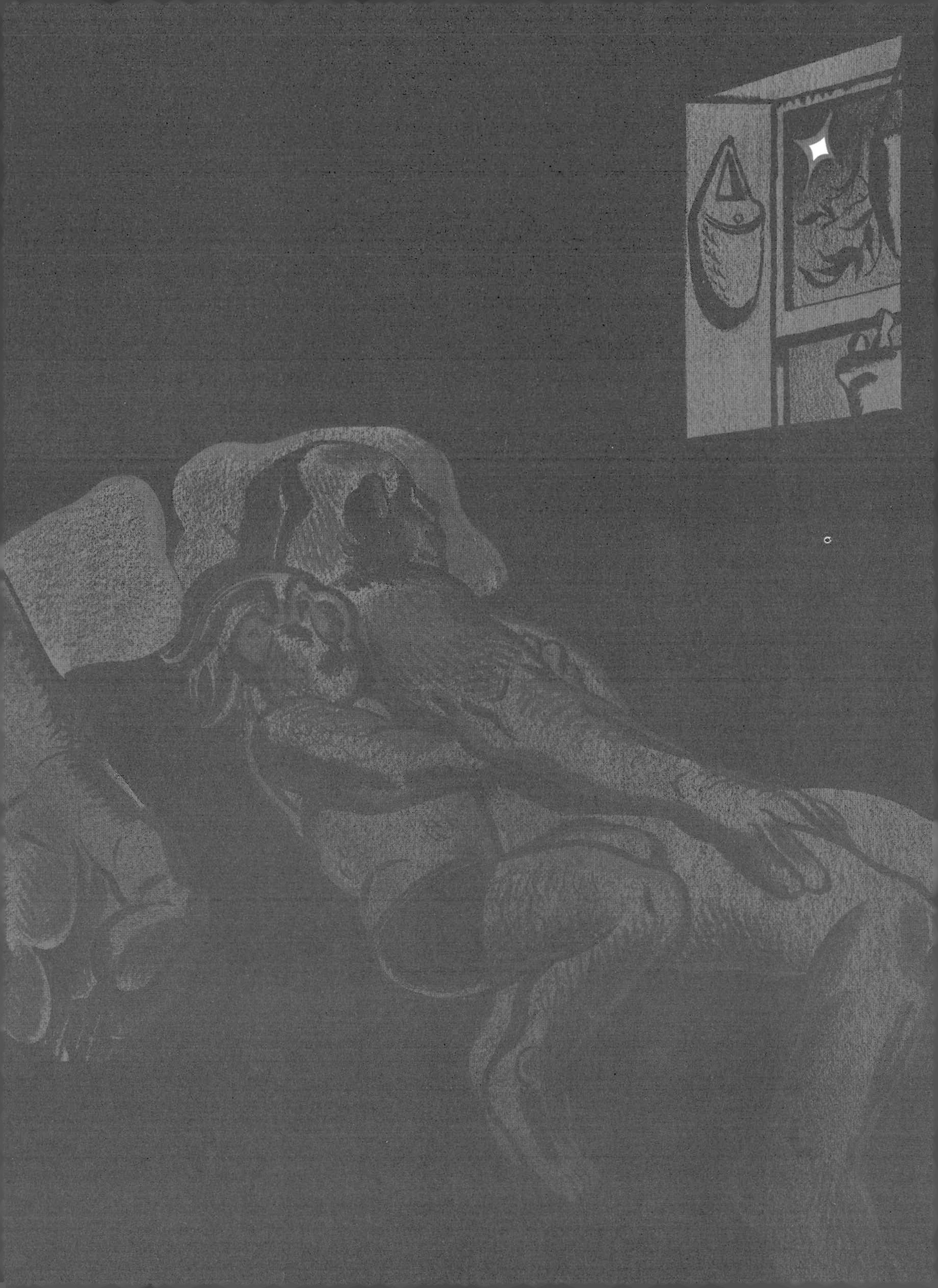

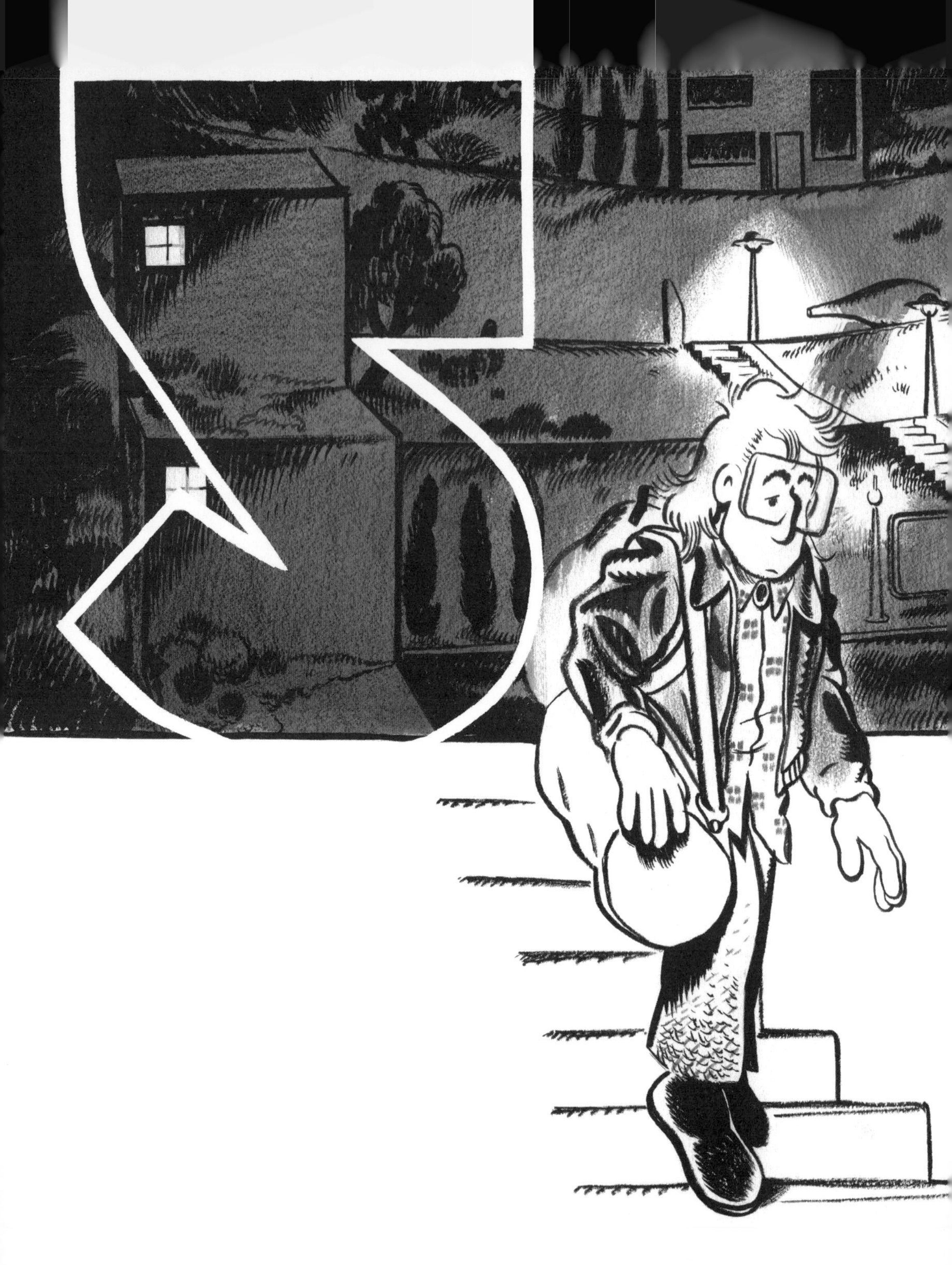

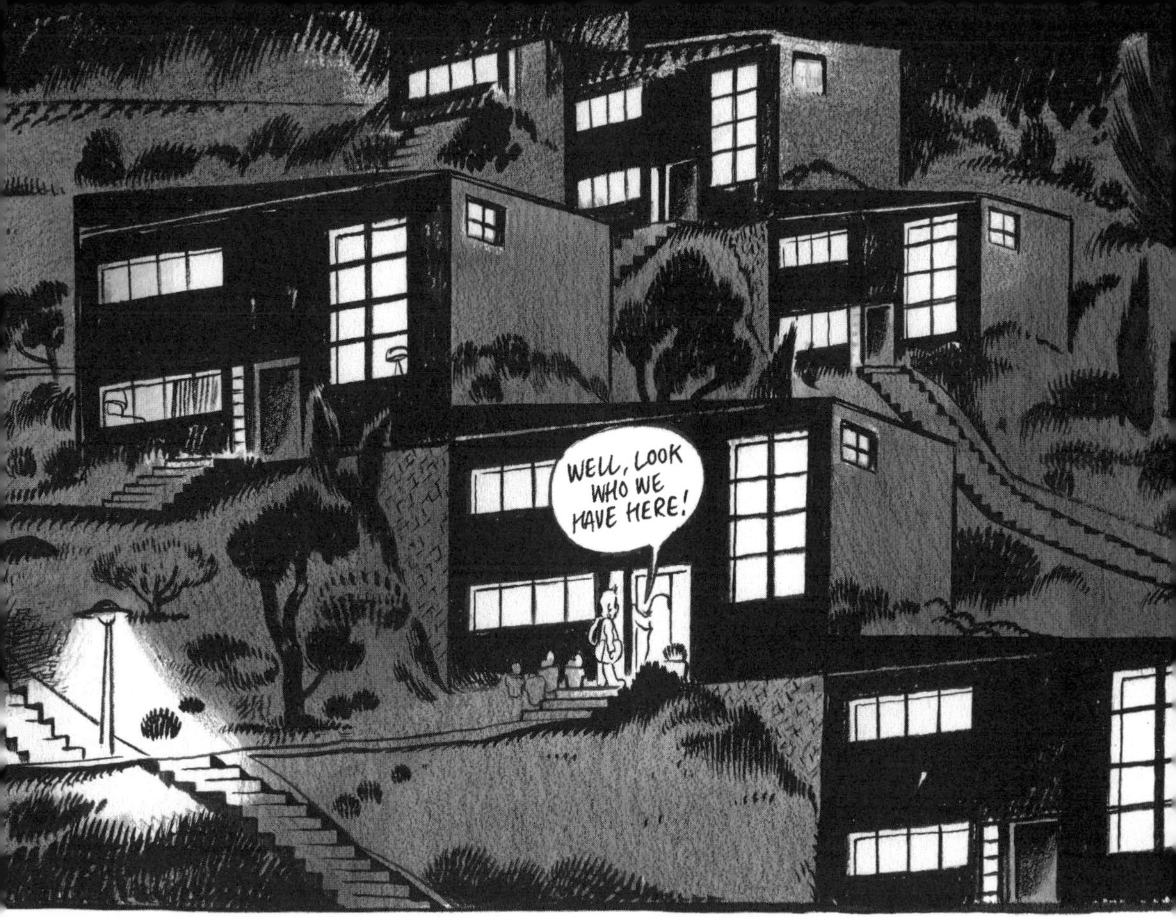
WELL, LOOK WHO WE HAVE HERE!

Bag in hand, Colin arrived at Minnie's door unannounced. He had made this trip countless times before, but this was his first since the stabbing. They hadn't spoken since then, either.

Minnie's partner David opened the door, welcoming him in with a big smile.

All of the newly purchased furniture Minnie had delivered to the home she almost moved into had already been returned to her. The belongings she'd spent weeks packing up had all been moved out—and then, unexpectedly, been moved back in—without her. She hadn't spent a single night in her new place.

Colin arrived to find Minnie deciding what to do with her second couch, which she had bought for her new home. She had planned on donating the older couch once she moved out, but now the old couch and the new couch sat awkwardly pressed together in the overcrowded living room.

It wasn't too long ago that Colin had laid down on the new couch while watching television with Paolo. But standing there in Minnie's living room, he had trouble believing that had ever happened.

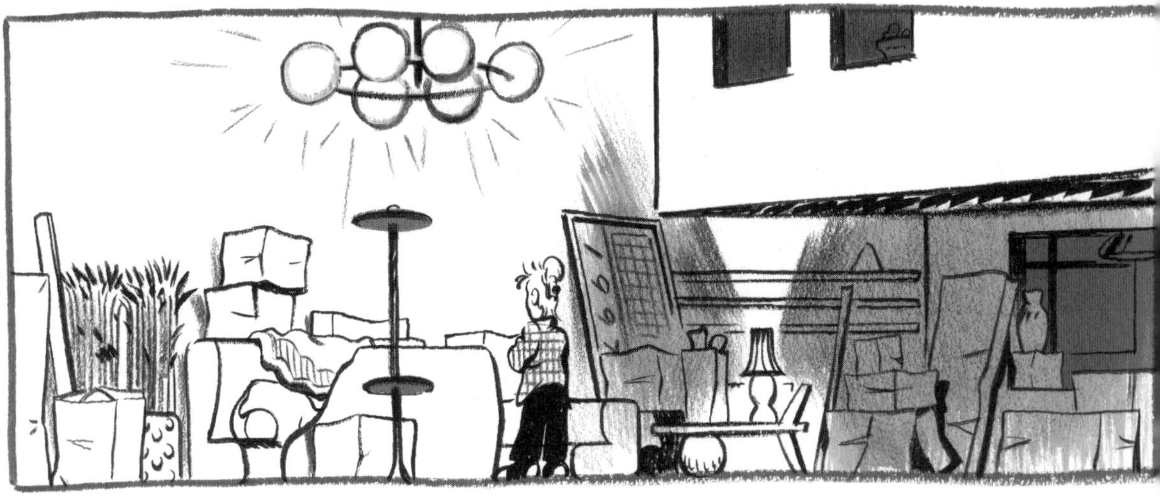

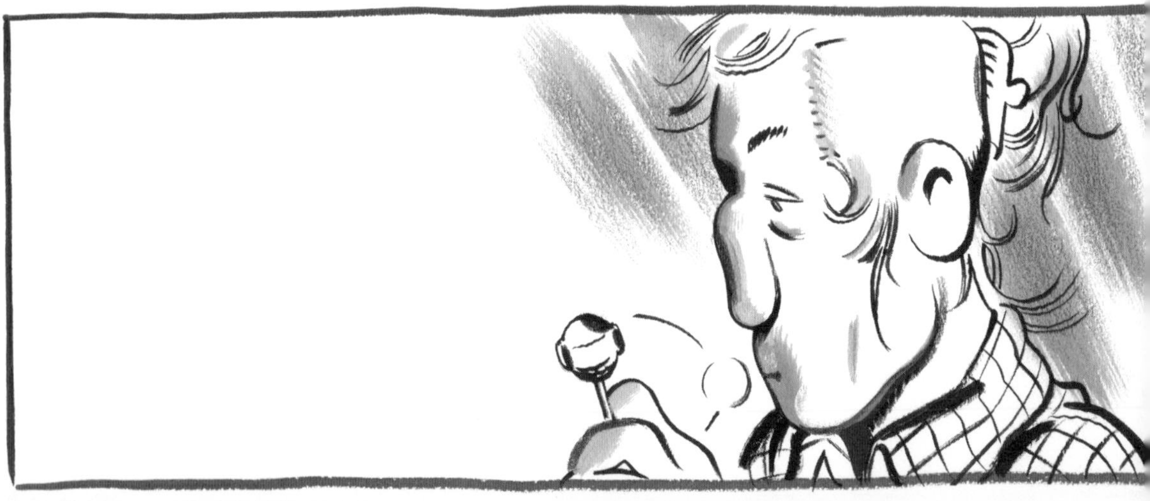

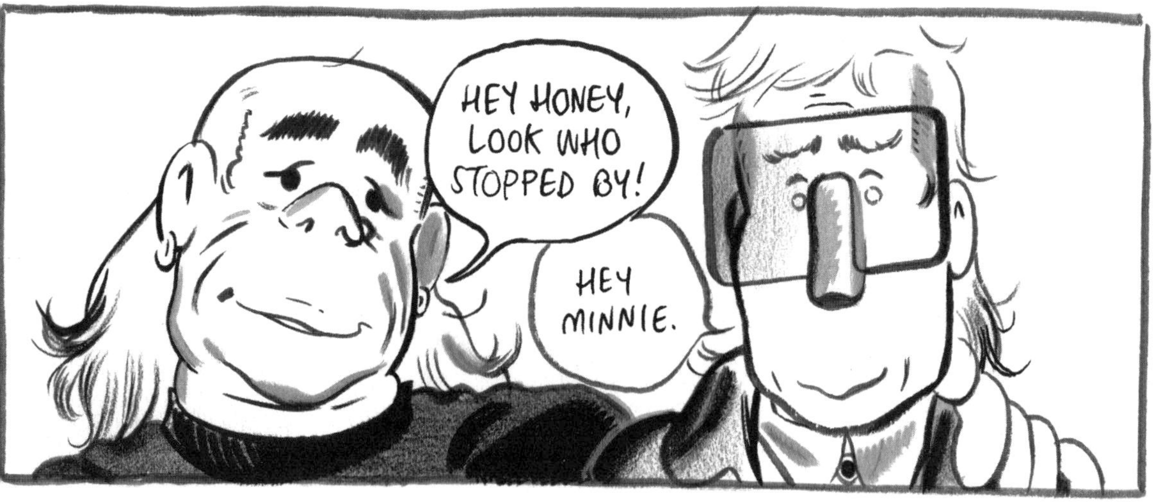
HEY HONEY, LOOK WHO STOPPED BY!
HEY MINNIE.

Minnie didn't acknowledge Colin's arrival; her gaze was focused unceasingly on the couches. David made a string of suggestions in an attempt to be useful, but Minnie didn't respond.

Minnie and David had met at a convention for Dancers the year before last. David wasn't a Dancer but had attended to help his cousin (who *was* a Dancer) sell herbal supplements at a booth. Minnie saw their meeting as an example of all that *The Dance* could teach us, and David, who loved romantic comedies, told everyone that it was serendipity. Unassuming and kind, he quickly folded his life into Minnie's without so much as a wrinkle. Colin had no idea what they talked about when he wasn't there, but David was agreeable, and he supposed that was enough.

He often spoke to Colin about the men he used to date back when he used to date men. He would reminisce about how much the city had changed, talk about what bars he used to frequent, and recount the palpable joy he felt coming of age after the fall of the Administration. But he never talked about any of this in front of Minnie, which made these conversations feel more uncomfortable than Colin felt they needed to be.

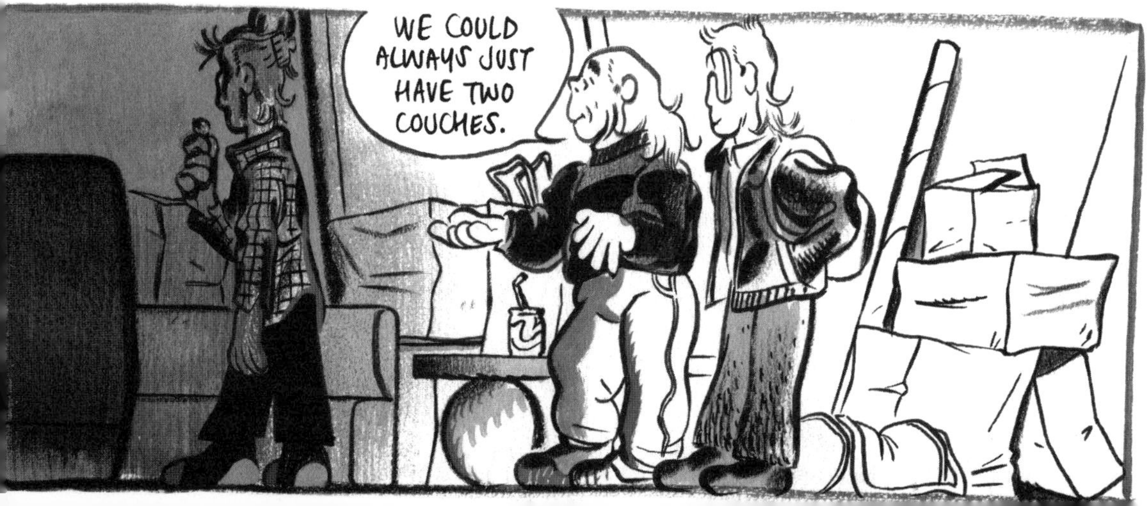
WE COULD ALWAYS JUST HAVE TWO COUCHES.

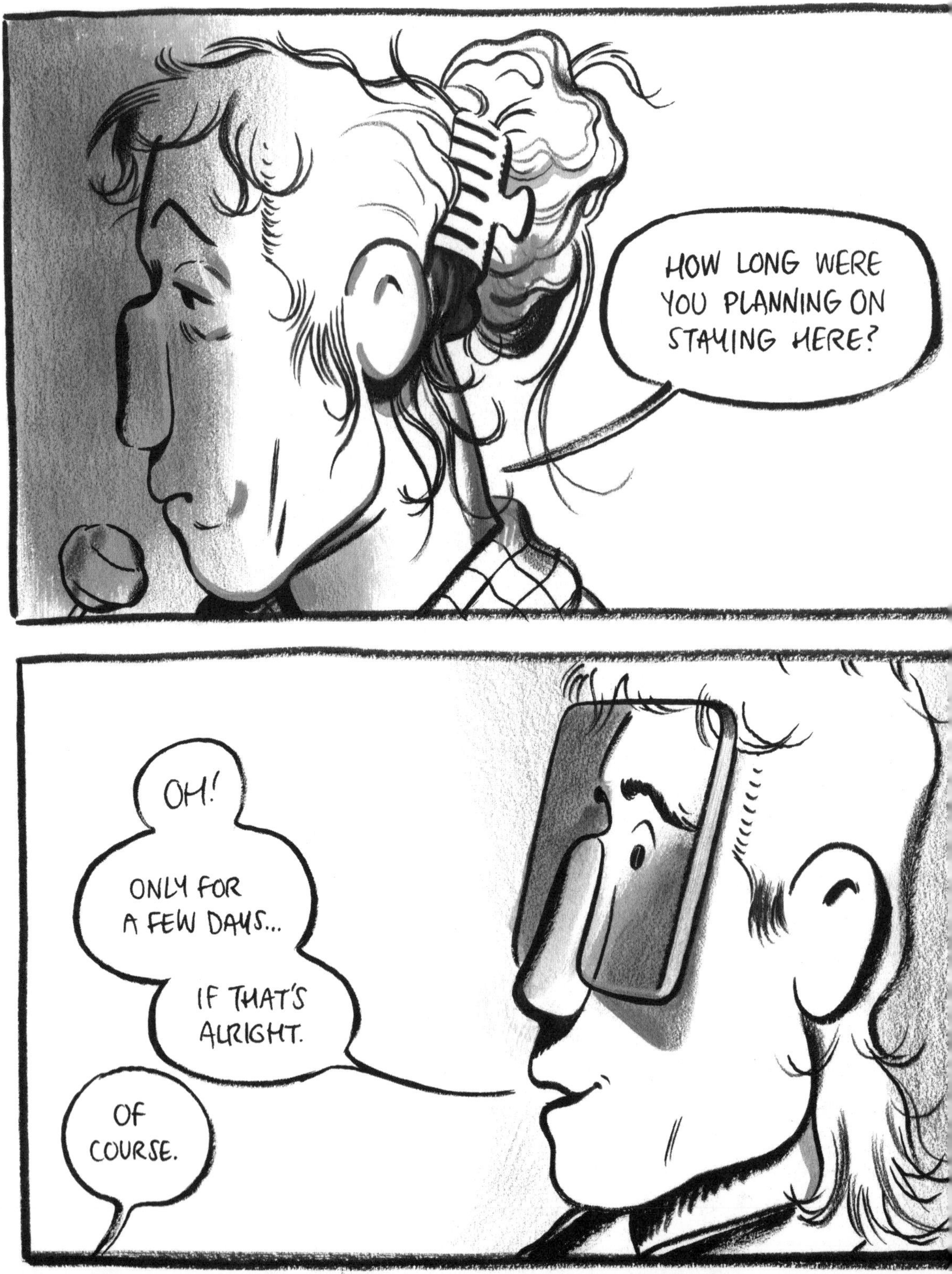
HOW LONG WERE YOU PLANNING ON STAYING HERE?
OH!
ONLY FOR A FEW DAYS...
IF THAT'S ALRIGHT.
OF COURSE.

After the incident, while Colin and Paolo were being treated in a local hospital, Minnie didn't come out to see them. The attending nurse gave her a call while Paolo was being stitched up, and then Colin himself called again after Paolo came through the surgery without complications. Their phone call was brief and to the point. Minnie sounded distant, as if she had just woken up from a nap that had lasted too long.

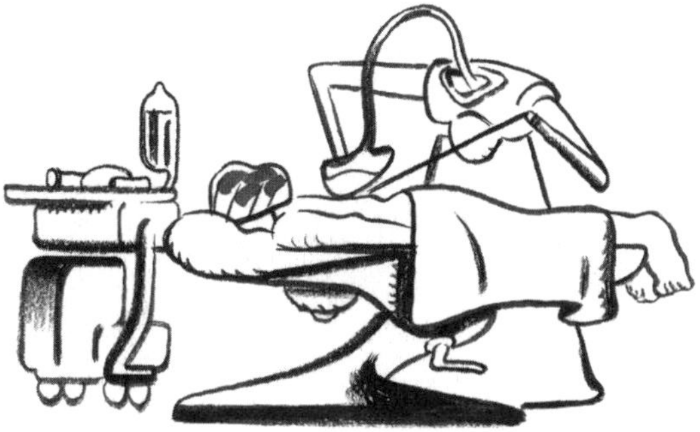

Despite having just met Colin and Paolo—seated at a bus stop and covered in blood—Bibi and Susan stayed with them that morning. Just as a nurse was administering a sedative to Colin and Paolo to help them fall asleep after their ordeal, they gave Colin a transport card with their information and address printed on it. And then they left.

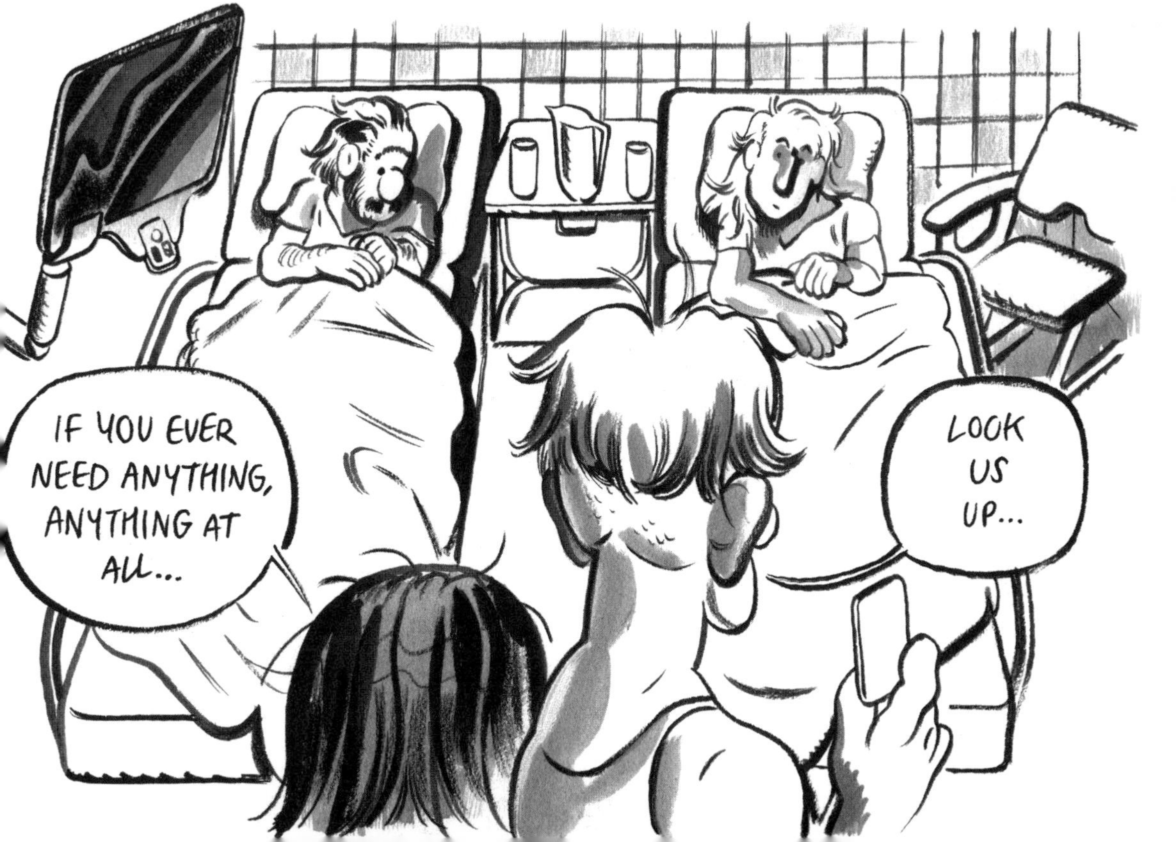
IF YOU EVER NEED ANYTHING, ANYTHING AT ALL...
LOOK US UP...

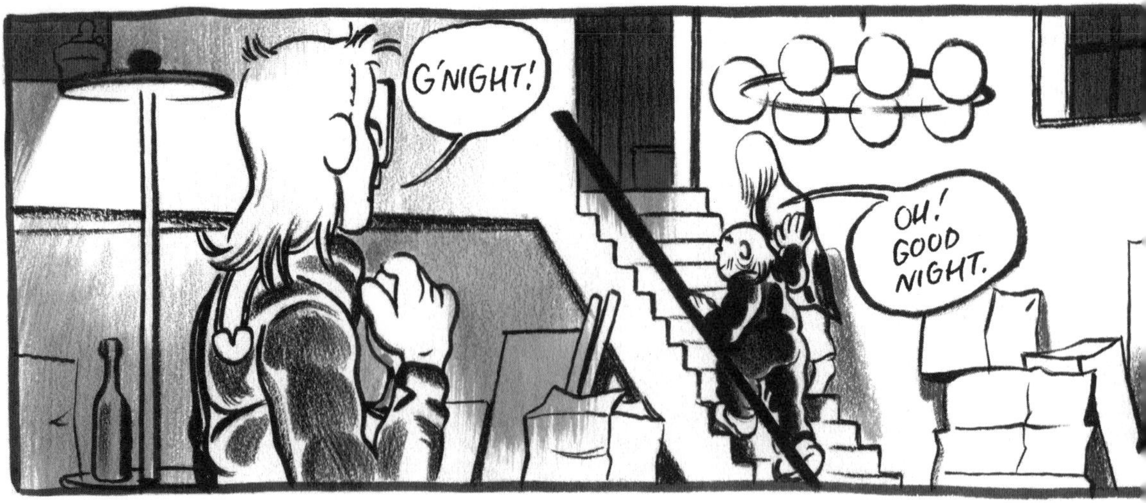
G'NIGHT!
OH! GOOD NIGHT.

There was no denying that the whole ordeal had been hard on Minnie. Sure, it had been difficult for everyone—here was Colin, fleeing his own life, unable to cope with the aftermath—but for Minnie, the effect on her was physical. She spoke of vague body aches, sudden forgetfulness, and constant headaches. Unable to sleep at night, she would unpack boxes, and then, exhausted, she would sleep through most of the day.

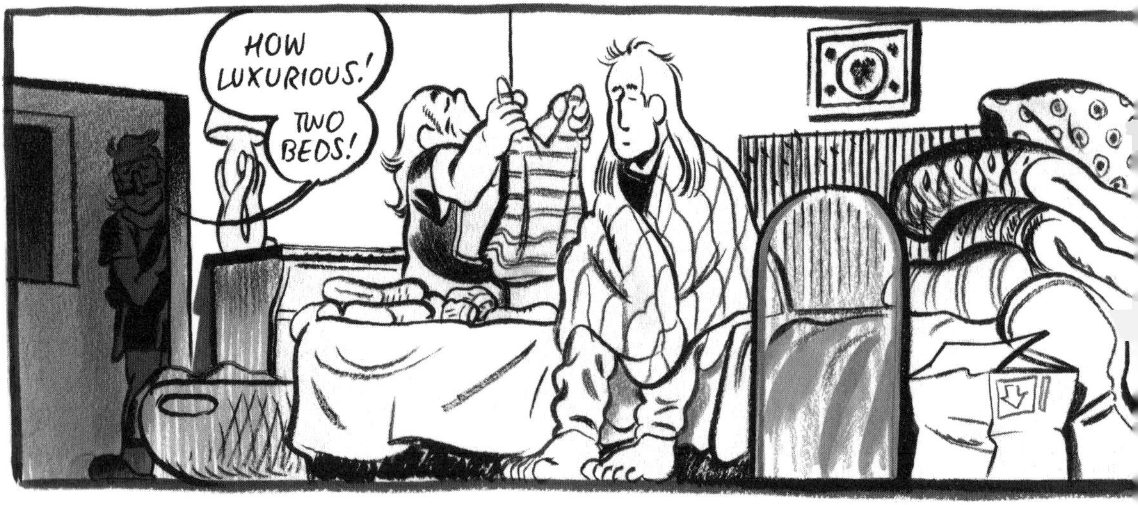
HOW LUXURIOUS!
TWO BEDS!

Although Minnie was Colin's mom, their relationship had always felt like something closer to a friendship. Suddenly, it felt more age appropriate. It was hard for Colin to think of Minnie as older, like moms often were. Like Minnie had never been.

Each day of his visit continued on like this until one morning, Colin woke to find that Minnie had left without saying goodbye.

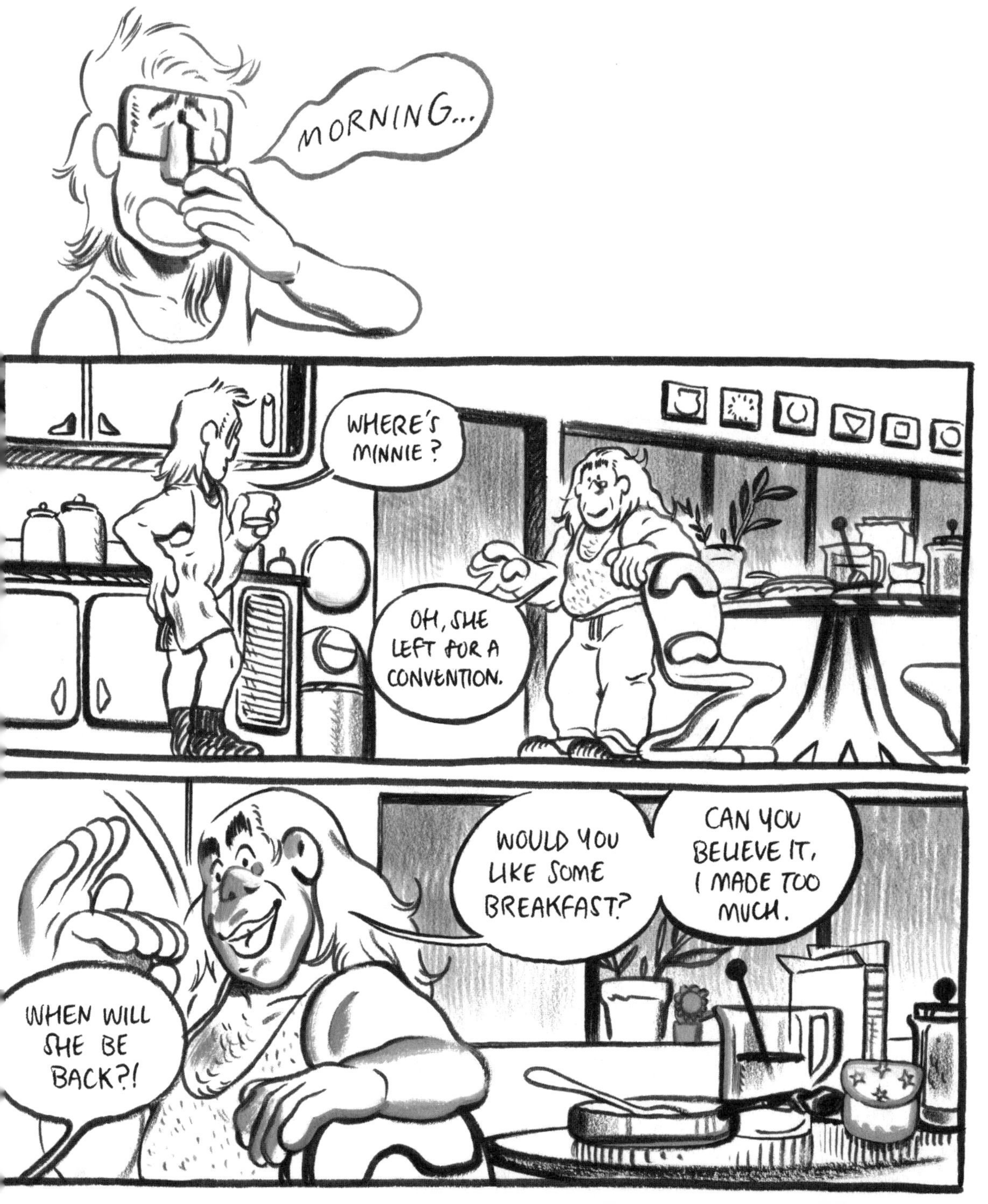
MORNING...
WHERE'S MINNIE?
OH, SHE LEFT FOR A CONVENTION.
WOULD YOU LIKE SOME BREAKFAST?
CAN YOU BELIEVE IT, I MADE TOO MUCH.
WHEN WILL SHE BE BACK?!

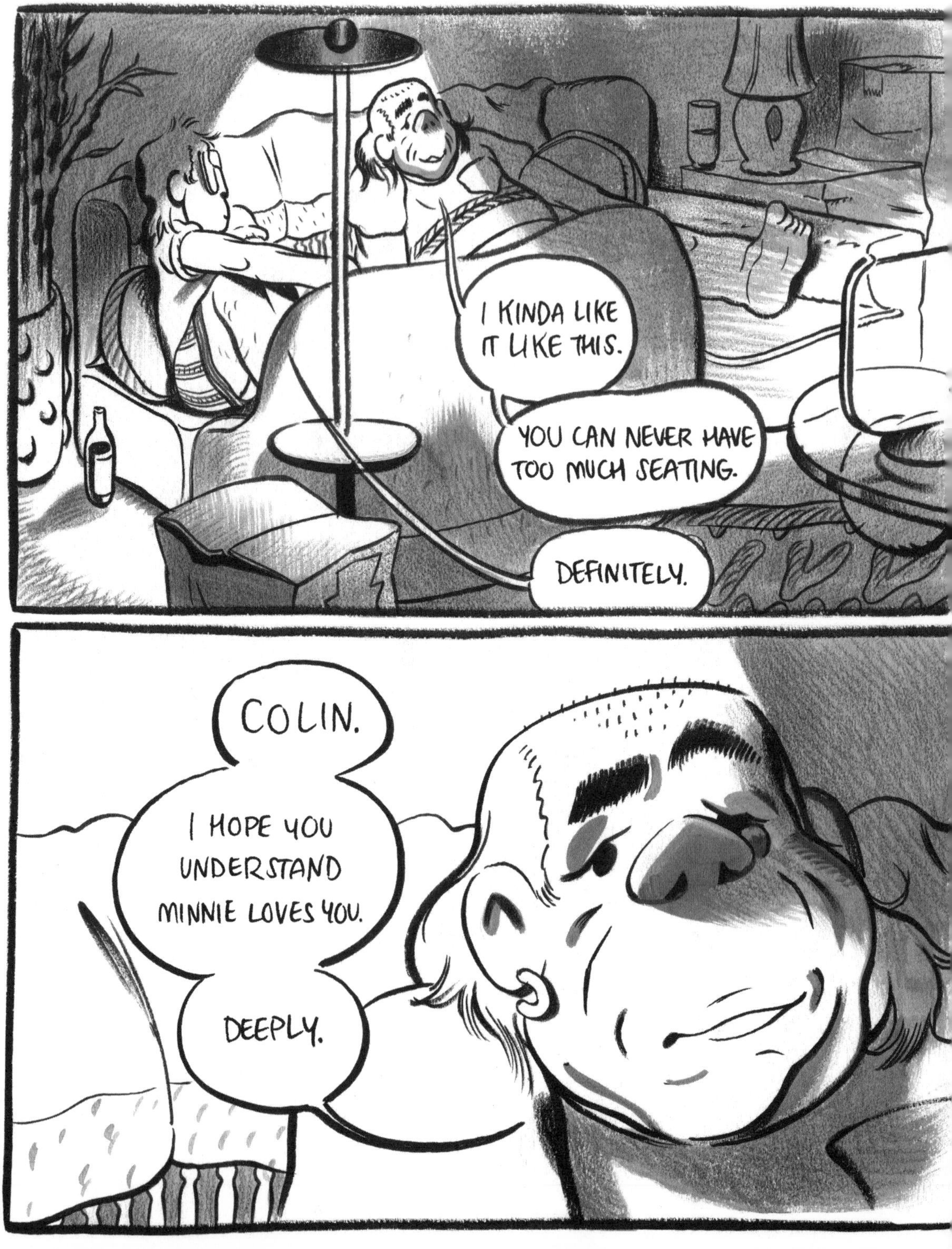
I KINDA LIKE IT LIKE THIS.
YOU CAN NEVER HAVE TOO MUCH SEATING.
DEFINITELY.
COLIN.
I HOPE YOU UNDERSTAND MINNIE LOVES YOU.
DEEPLY.

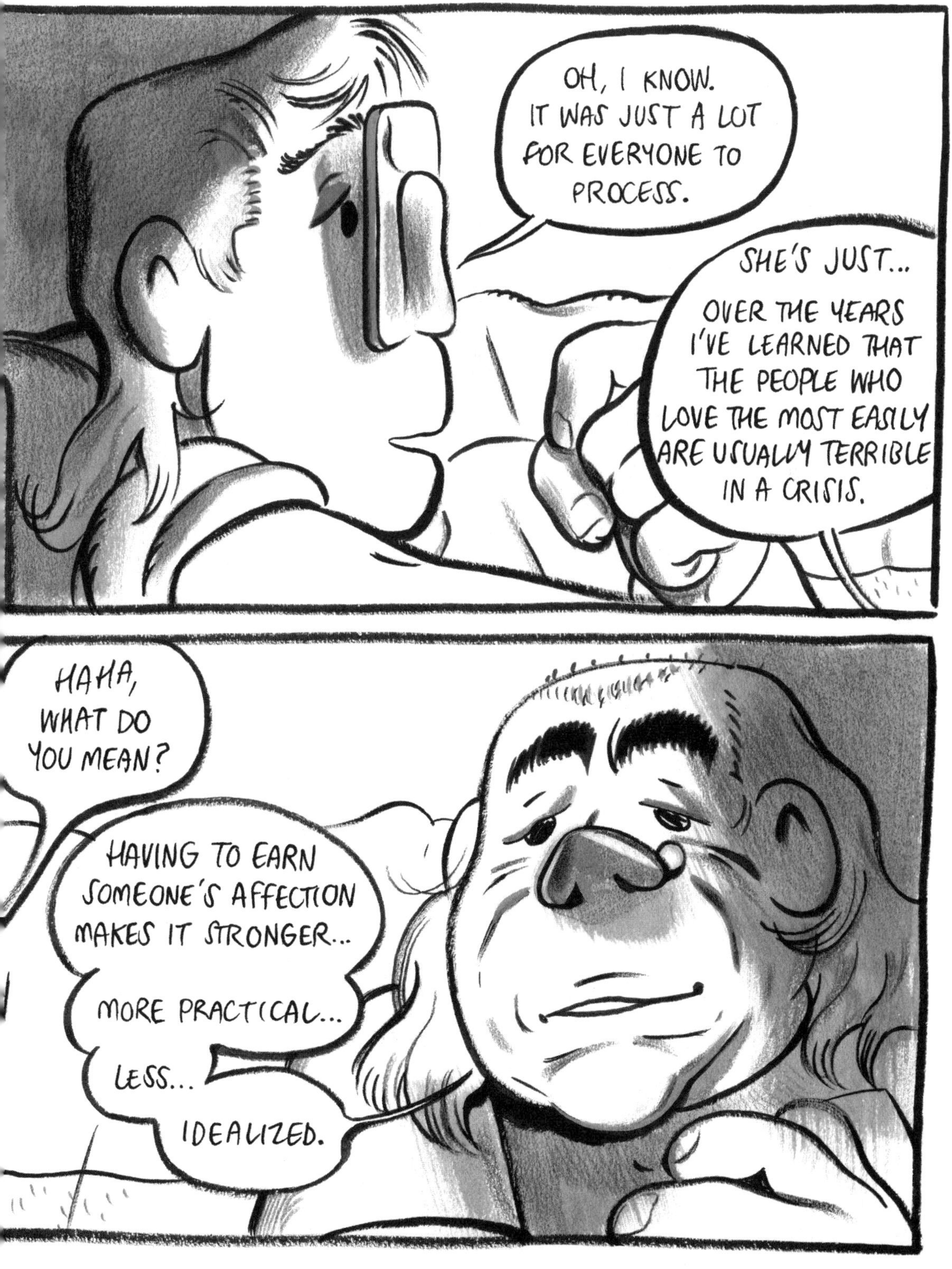
OH, I KNOW. IT WAS JUST A LOT FOR EVERYONE TO PROCESS.
SHE'S JUST...
OVER THE YEARS I'VE LEARNED THAT THE PEOPLE WHO LOVE THE MOST EASILY ARE USUALLY TERRIBLE IN A CRISIS.
HAHA, WHAT DO YOU MEAN?
HAVING TO EARN SOMEONE'S AFFECTION MAKES IT STRONGER...
MORE PRACTICAL...
LESS...
IDEALIZED.

The next morning, Colin left as well.

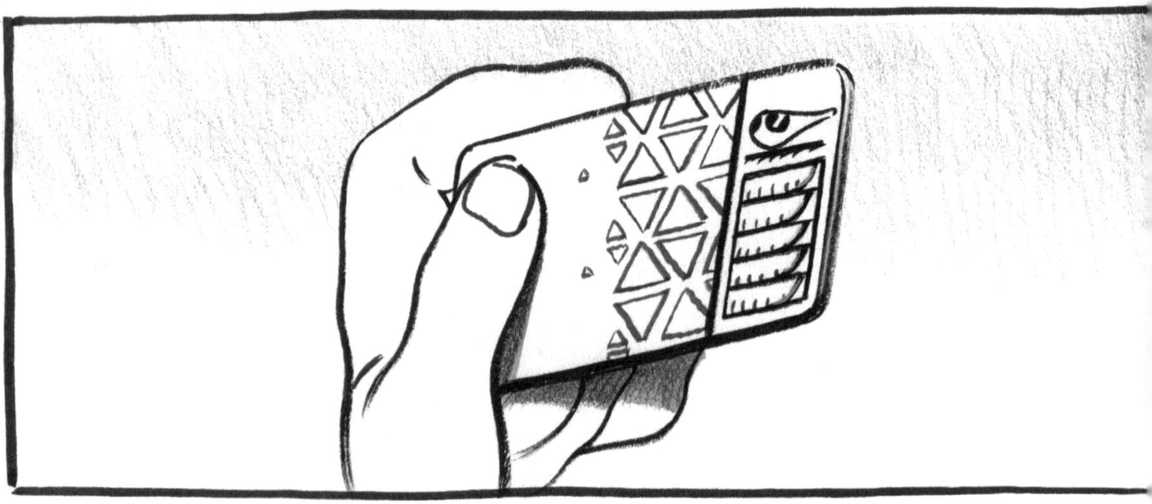

He wasn't entirely sure of his plan, but taking Bibi and Susan up on their offer felt like as good an idea as any. The card they had given to him—well, to Colin and Paolo—was used for Commuters, a network of automated vehicles originally intended to help travelers come in and out of the city center. Each card contained a single route for the vehicle to follow, allowing the Commuter, and its passenger, to move across the vast network of interconnected rail lines.

Unfortunately, due to their connection to the Administration, their popularity had been waning for decades. Most of the routes had fallen into disrepair or had been scrapped entirely, the decommissioned rails being melted down for other underfunded municipal projects. That, as well as their use of the same renewable energy that caused a string of disasters a few years prior—colloquially referred to as The Bolt Revolt—caused people to return to more self-reliant modes of transportation, like cars.

Colin enjoyed the Commuters, though. They felt like the dream of a more perfect future, even if that dream was tied up with everything else the Administration had done. (He wasn't aware of any atrocities the Commuters had been used for, since the committee in charge of that revitalization was part of an entirely different department than his—Transportation, not Culture).

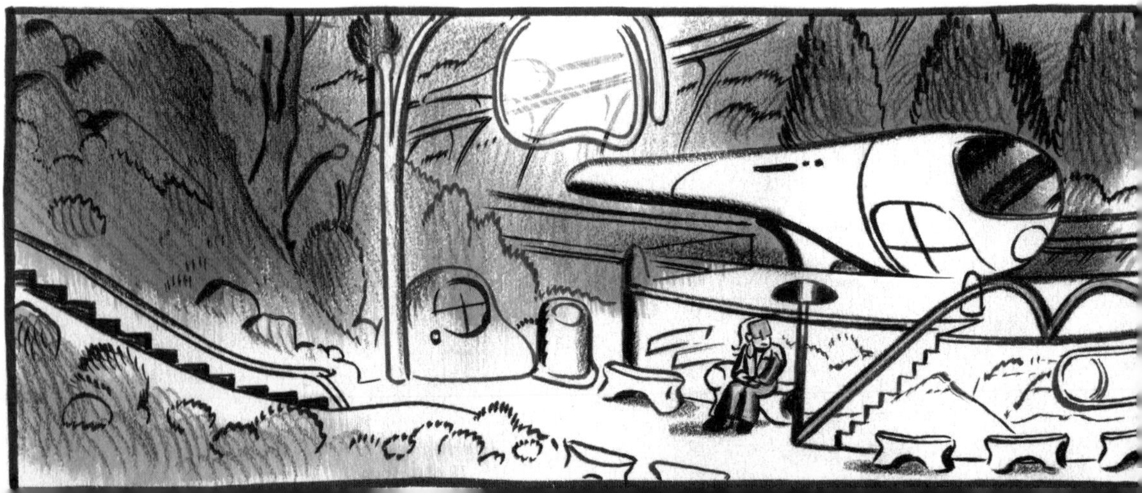

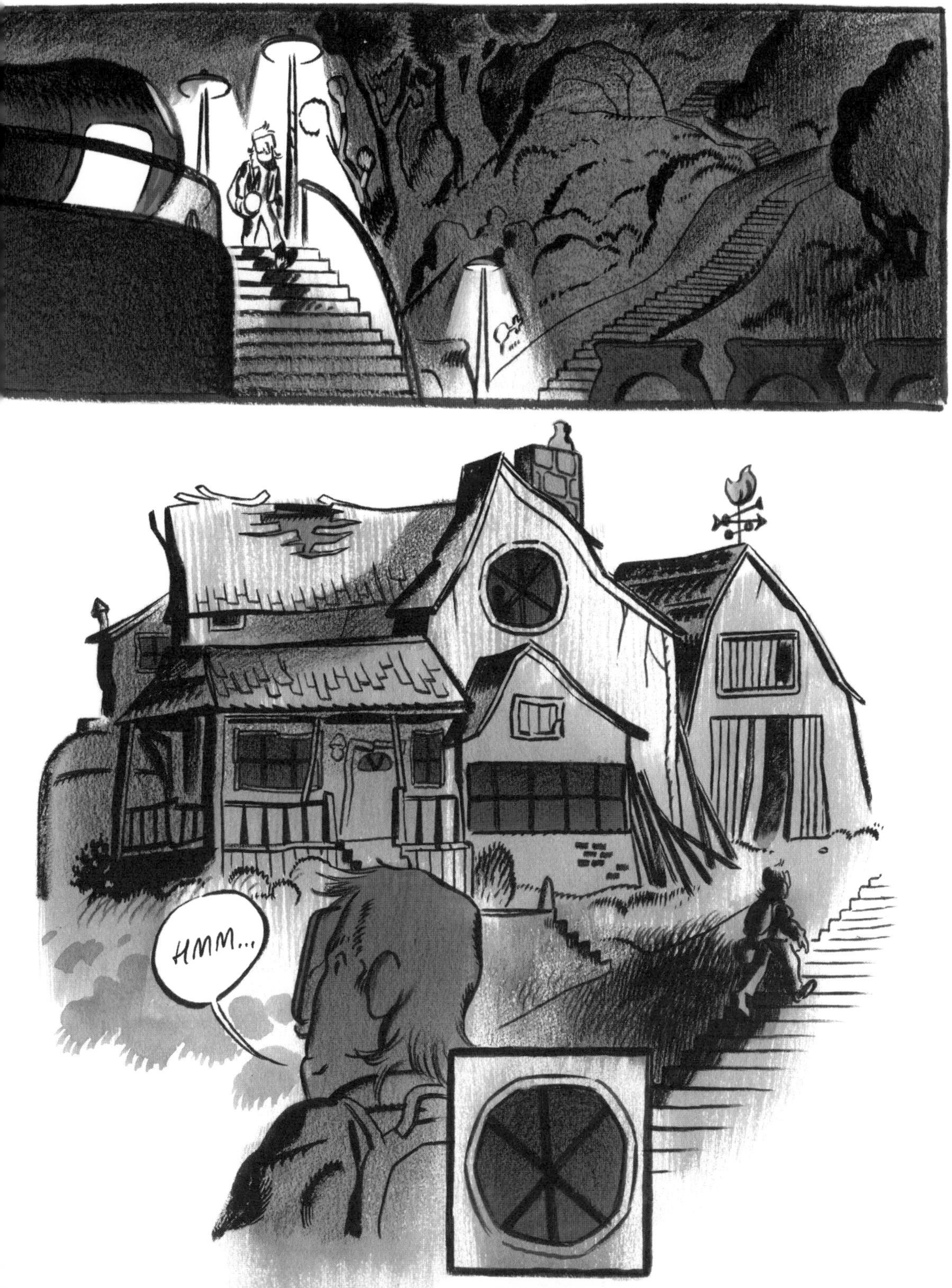
HMM...

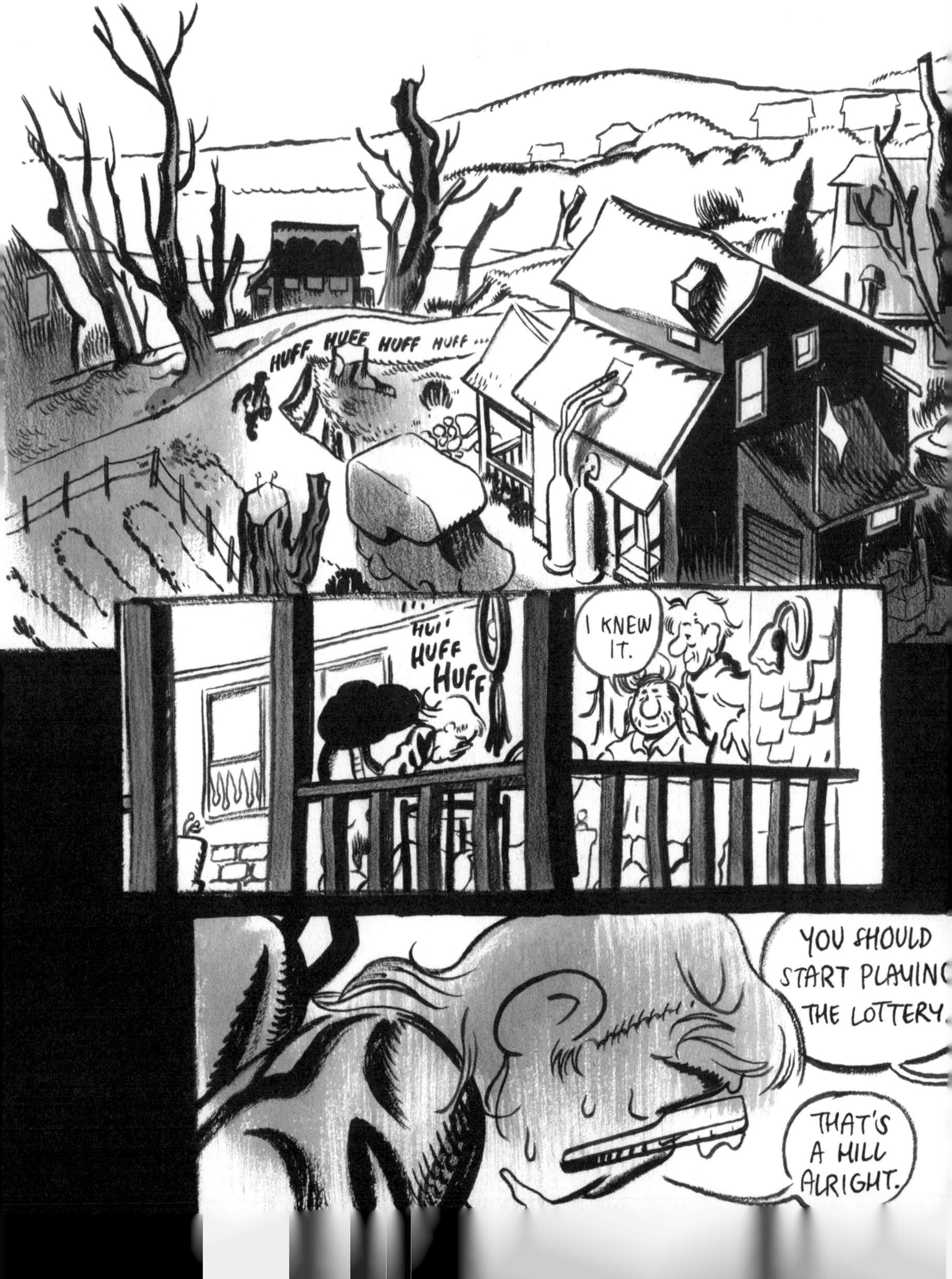
HUFF HUFF HUFF HUFF...
HUF HUFF HUFF
I KNEW IT.
YOU SHOULD START PLAYING THE LOTTERY.
THAT'S A HILL ALRIGHT.

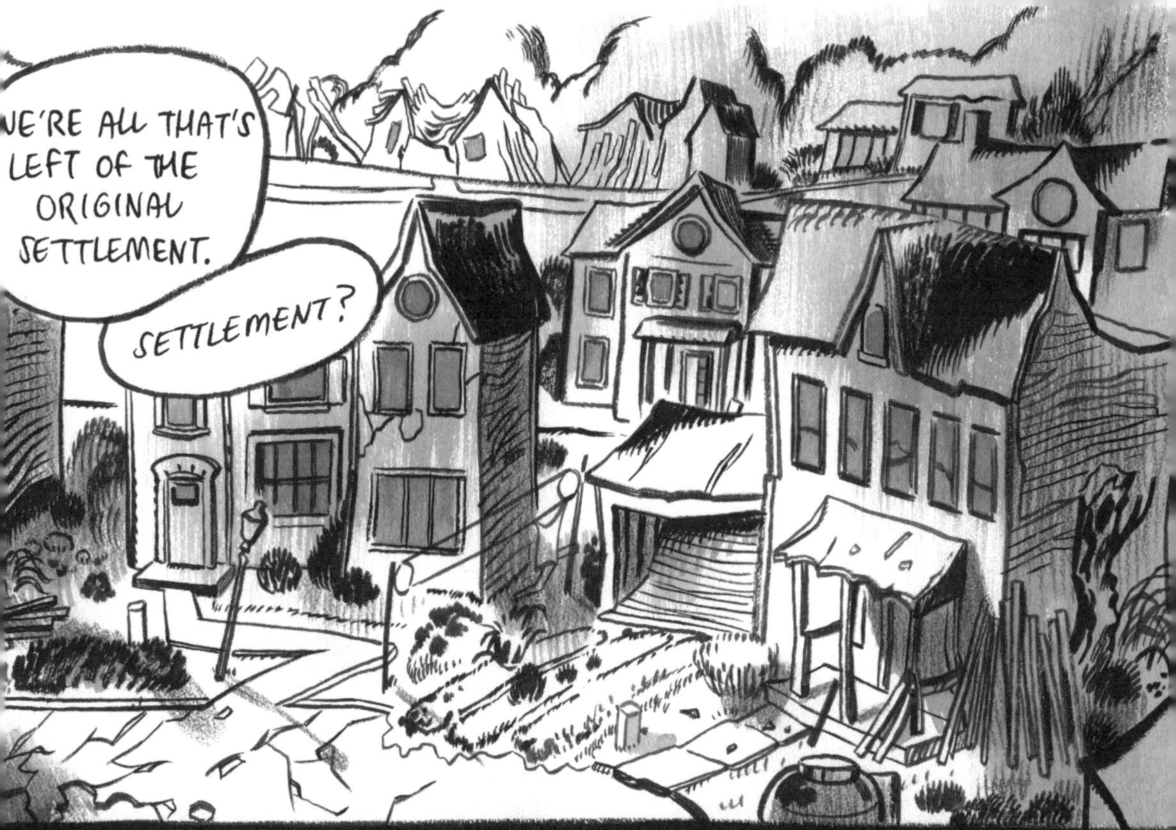
WE'RE ALL THAT'S LEFT OF THE ORIGINAL SETTLEMENT.
SETTLEMENT?

The farmhouse that Bibi and Susan resided in sat on the top of a huge incline, overlooking the sweeping valley below. Living on the windward side of the mountain range, their land was lush and green, drastically different from the scorched leeward side that bordered the Wastes.

Colin passed nearly a dozen homes—all abandoned—on his long trek up the hill. All of the homes were large, two-story suburban models built around a cul-de-sac, with vinyl siding and two-car garages. Jutting out between them were all kinds of rough, man-made structures—garden sheds made from salvaged materials, basins for collecting rainwater, stables for housing animals. Most of the asphalt driveways had been ripped up and converted into overgrown vegetable gardens.

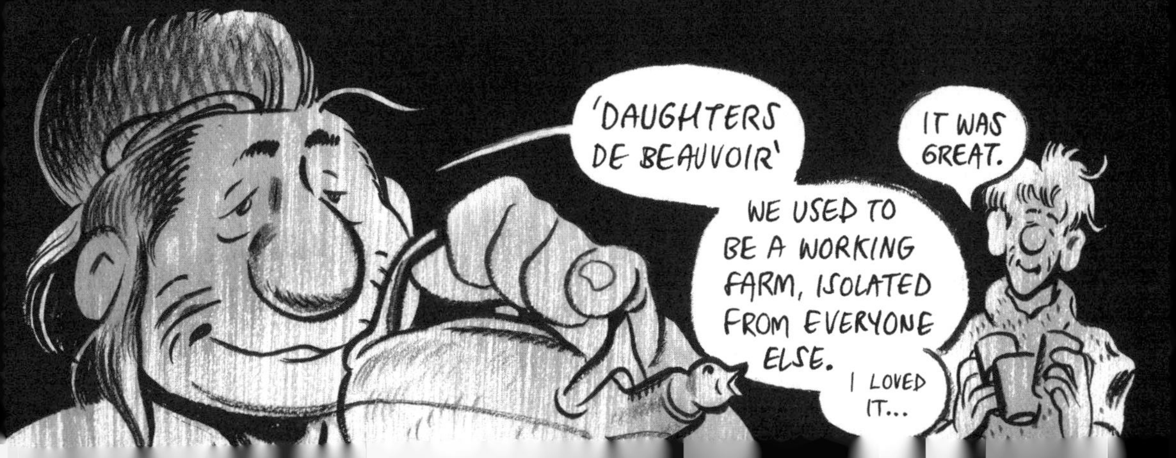
'DAUGHTERS DE BEAUVOIR'
WE USED TO BE A WORKING FARM, ISOLATED FROM EVERYONE ELSE.
IT WAS GREAT.
I LOVED IT...

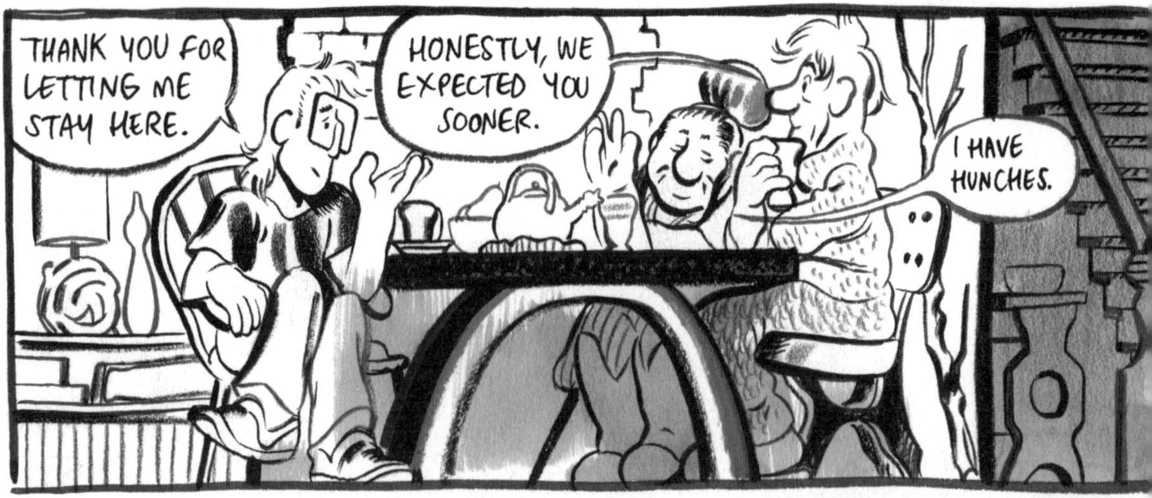
THANK YOU FOR LETTING ME STAY HERE.
HONESTLY, WE EXPECTED YOU SOONER.
I HAVE HUNCHES.

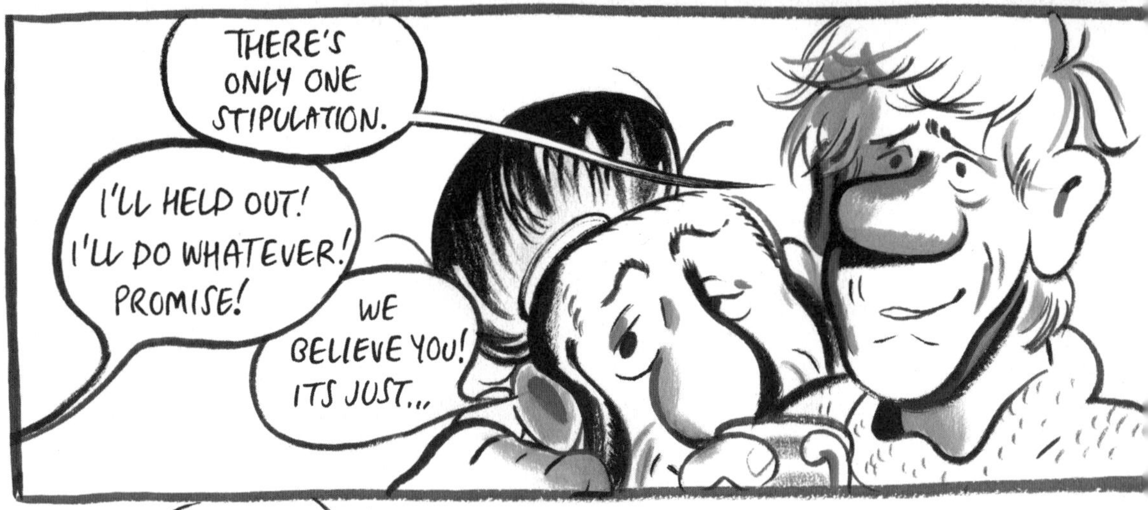
THERE'S ONLY ONE STIPULATION.
I'LL HELP OUT! I'LL DO WHATEVER! PROMISE!
WE BELIEVE YOU! ITS JUST...

As part of the original pact the settlement had been founded on, back when Susan was Colin's age, no men were allowed inside any of the homes.

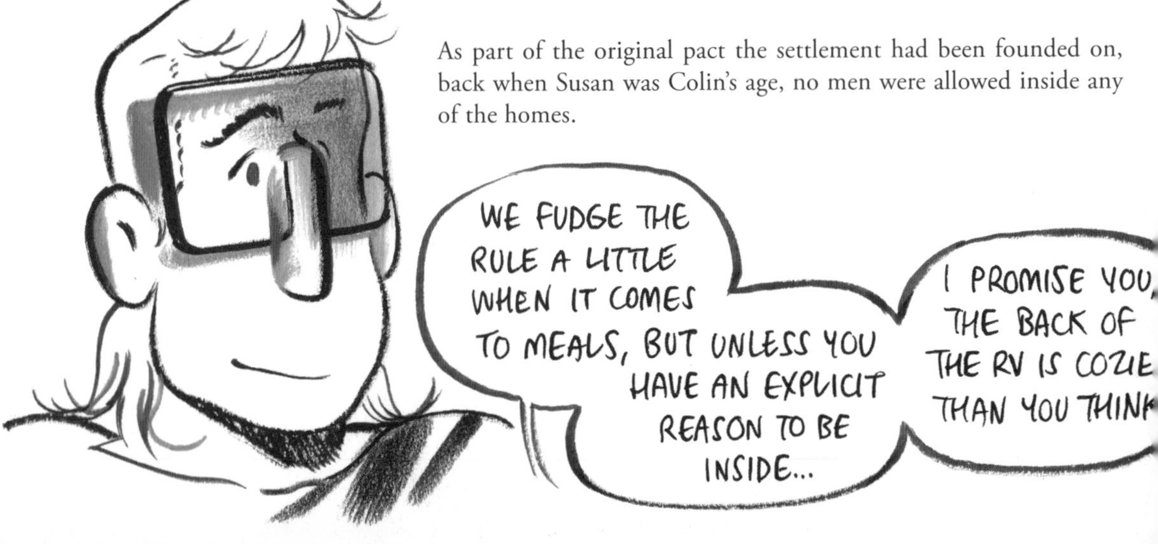
WE FUDGE THE RULE A LITTLE WHEN IT COMES TO MEALS, BUT UNLESS YOU HAVE AN EXPLICIT REASON TO BE INSIDE...
I PROMISE YOU, THE BACK OF THE RV IS COZIE THAN YOU THINK

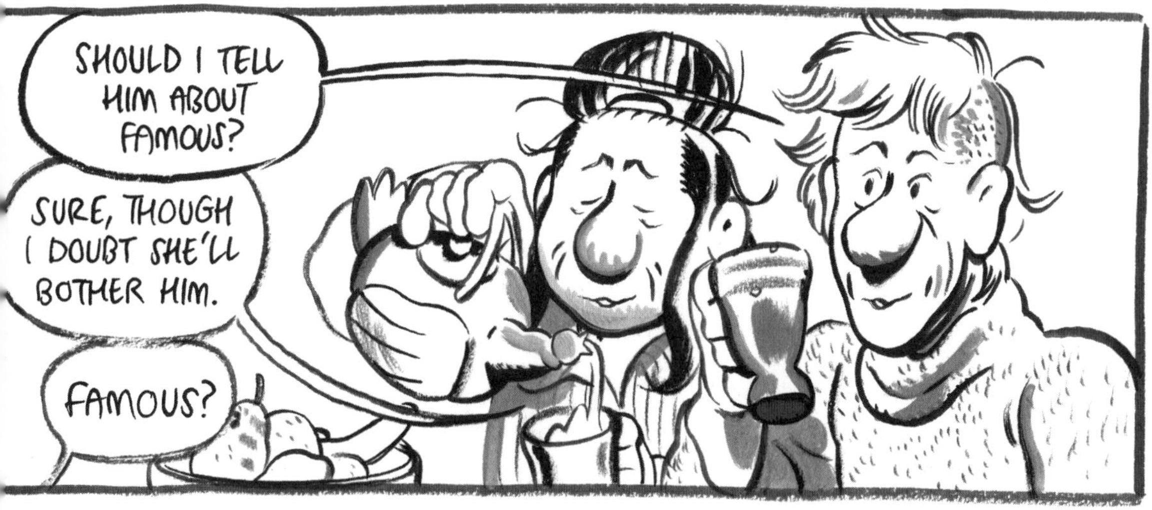
SHOULD I TELL HIM ABOUT FAMOUS?
SURE, THOUGH I DOUBT SHE'LL BOTHER HIM.
FAMOUS?

Susan and her former partner Famous had created the intentional community they named *The Daughters de Beauvoir*. They drafted up the original charter, discovered the unoccupied neighborhood while out on a hike, and broke up the streets into what would become tracts of farmland. Together.

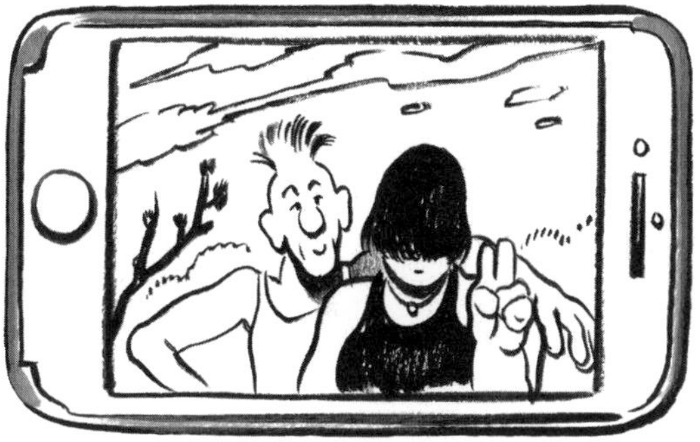

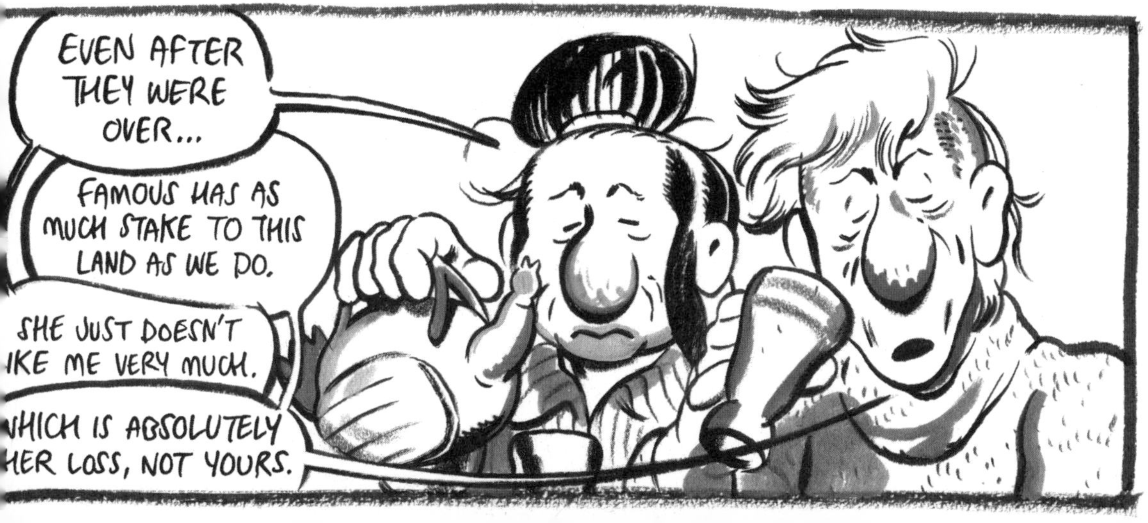
EVEN AFTER THEY WERE OVER...
FAMOUS HAS AS MUCH STAKE TO THIS LAND AS WE DO.
SHE JUST DOESN'T IKE ME VERY MUCH.
VHICH IS ABSOLUTELY HER LOSS, NOT YOURS.

Bibi was right. It wasn't half bad in the back of the RV. It smelled a little musty, as if the whole truck had been packed away in storage for too long, but he could open the small window, which helped.

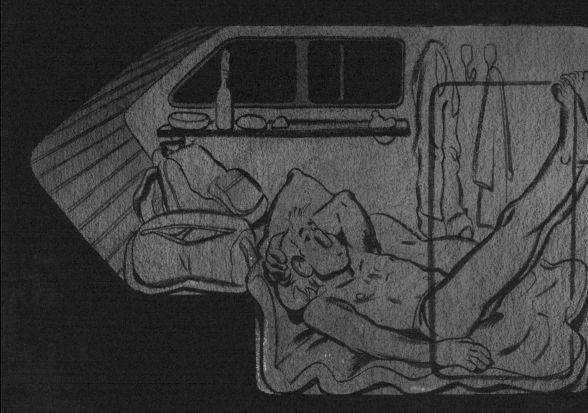

As Colin dozed off, the musk of the room made him think of a boy he had once kissed. It wasn't his first kiss, but it was the first he remembered really liking. He and the boy had grown up in the same neighborhood. One time he told Colin about how he used to think vapor trails from planes were actually asteroids crashing to Earth; he always held his breath, waiting for the impact. He had been wearing a hand-me-down winter jacket that hadn't been properly aired out. Ever since, that particular smell of mildew made Colin's heart race. He remembered just how handsy he got the afternoon he helped Paolo clean out his cluttered apartment.

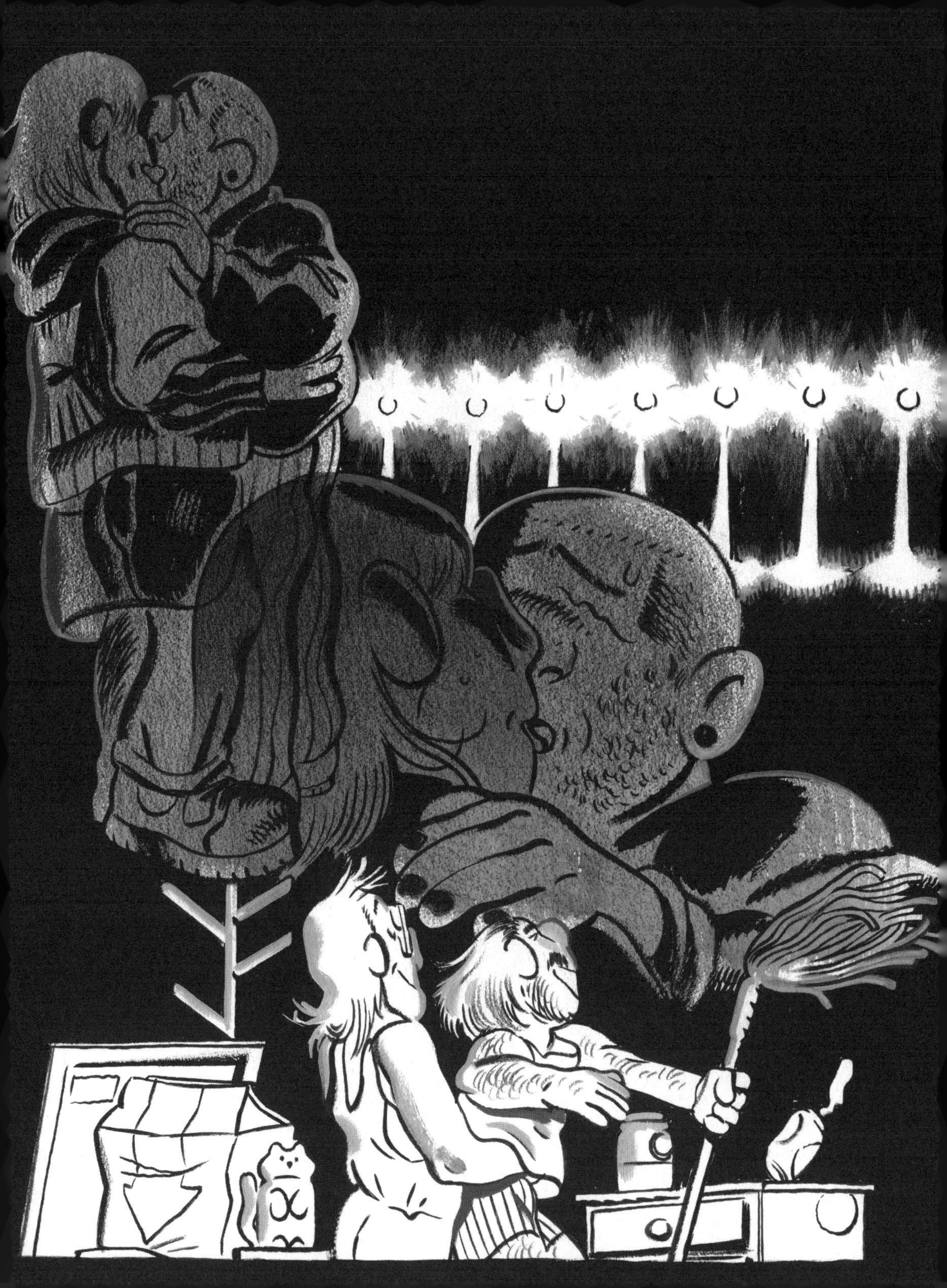

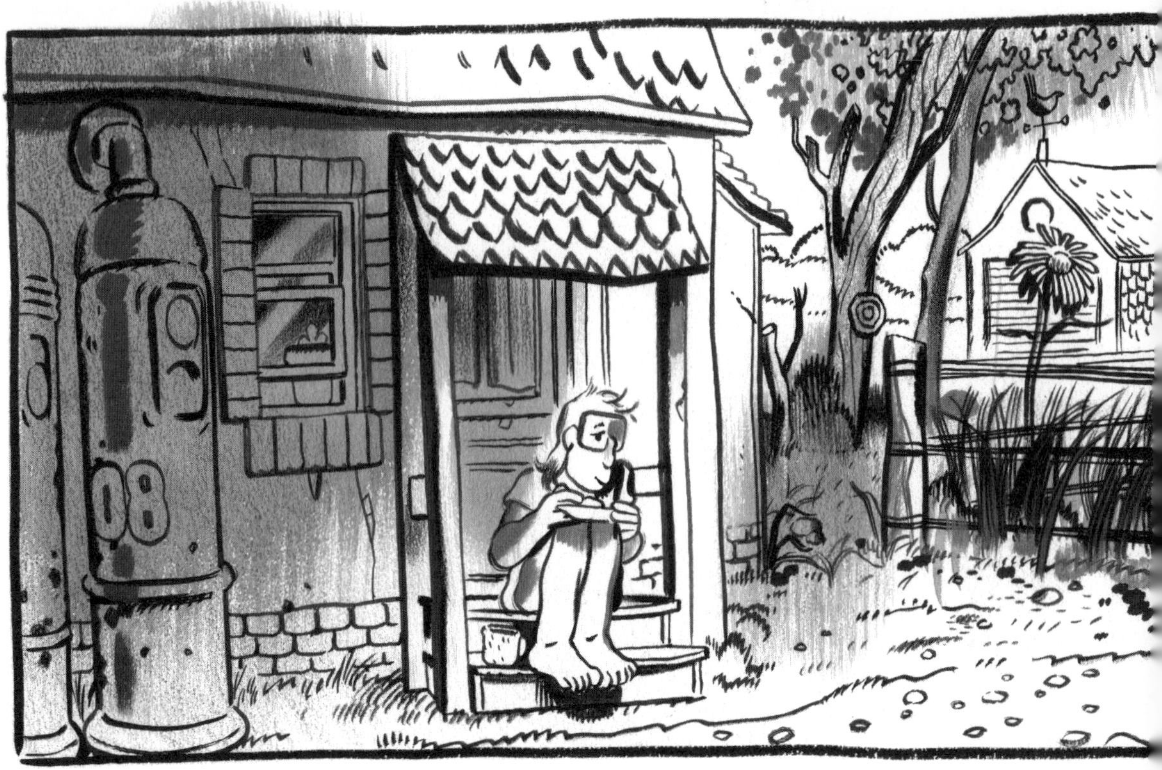
08

Colin was shocked by how beautiful mornings on the farm were. The light felt brighter, more dense—unmistakable in its beauty. He knew he could appreciate it more now that he didn't have obligations like he did back in the city, but…regardless, he felt grateful.

Colin tried to picture what *de Beauvoir* must've been like in its prime. He couldn't really imagine what a community built on a shared goal must have felt like. This didn't seem anything like *The Dance*—most Dancers he met only talked in vague platitudes about Being Positive or how Change Was Good, without any of the practical concerns of how to make that actually happen. He knew Minnie's troupe did community outreach, but as far as he knew, that didn't extend beyond soliciting donations and pamphleting.

Bibi made fresh biscuits, which Colin ate on the back porch. He could tell they came from a stale mix, but they tasted delicious.

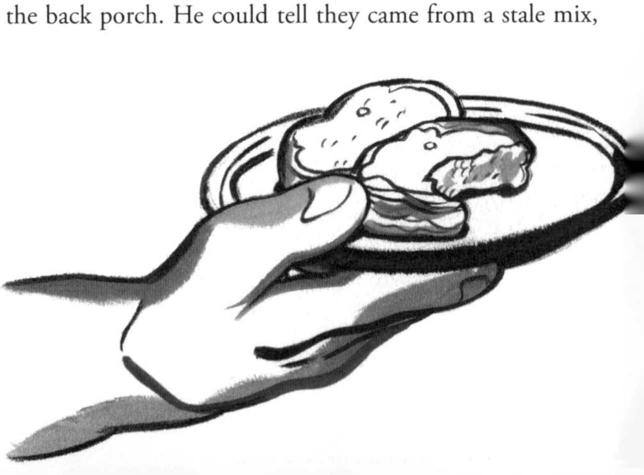

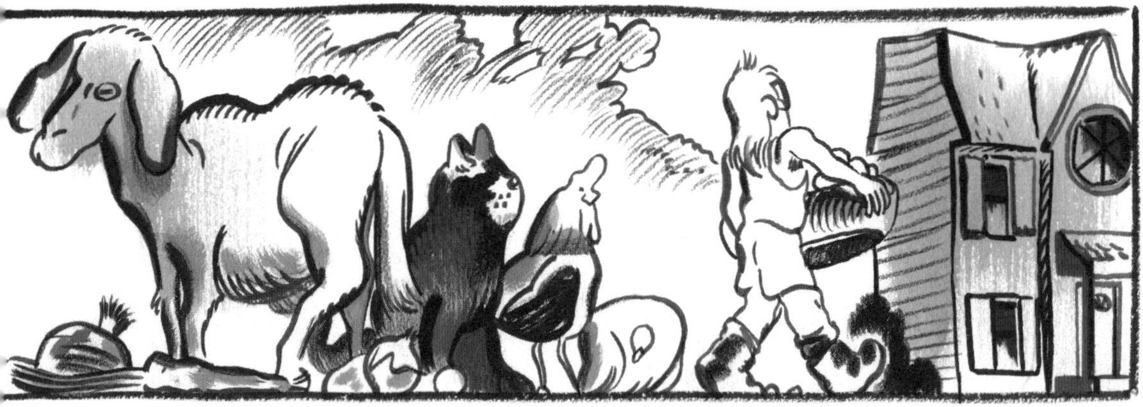

As part of their arrangement, Bibi and Susan gave Colin a list of chores to take care of each day. For example, he'd feed the few animals still living there: three chickens, a scraggly, one-eyed goat named Eileen, and an old cat Colin named Opie. Susan wouldn't let him near any of the gardens, but she let him move heavy baskets of vegetables into one of the neighboring homes they set aside as their root cellar.

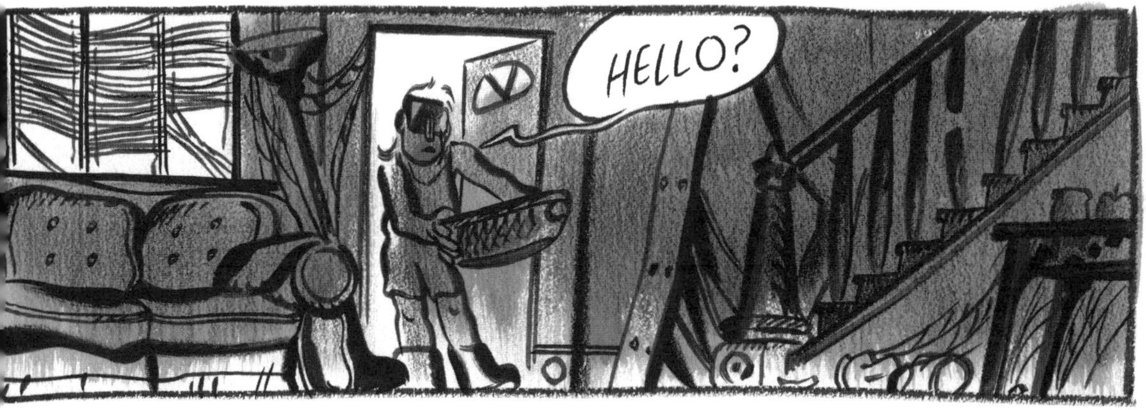
HELLO?

Occasionally, Colin would be sent to look through the other homes to find anything that could still be of use. The homes had long been stripped of anything worth any money, but occasionally he'd find something salvageable, if not interesting: a broken, stringless harp; a jacquard loom that took up most of a living room; an old, rusted out motorcycle with a bumper sticker that said "A woman needs a man like a fish needs a bicycle." Despite knowing that all of the homes were empty, Colin would still announce himself whenever he walked inside, his voice echoing through the long-neglected rooms.

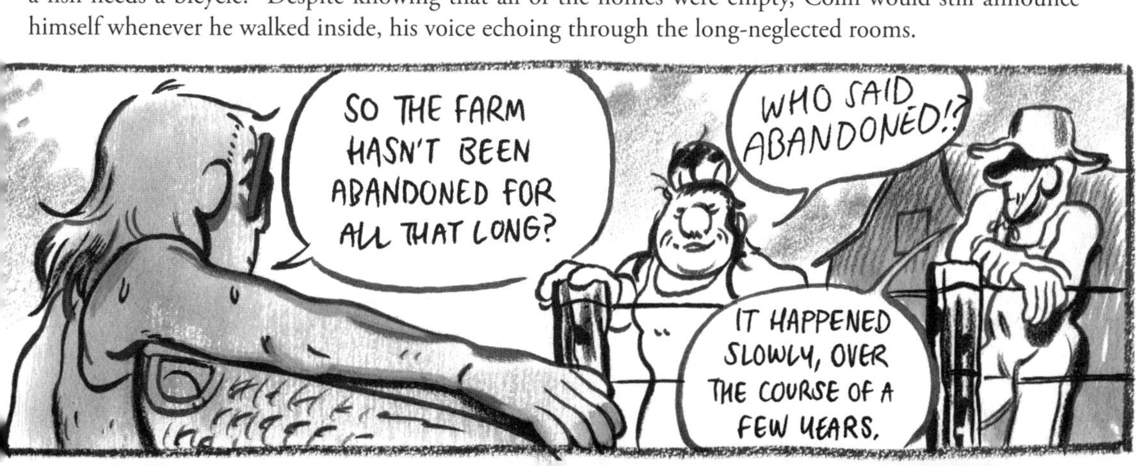
SO THE FARM HASN'T BEEN ABANDONED FOR ALL THAT LONG?
WHO SAID ABANDONED!?
IT HAPPENED SLOWLY, OVER THE COURSE OF A FEW YEARS.

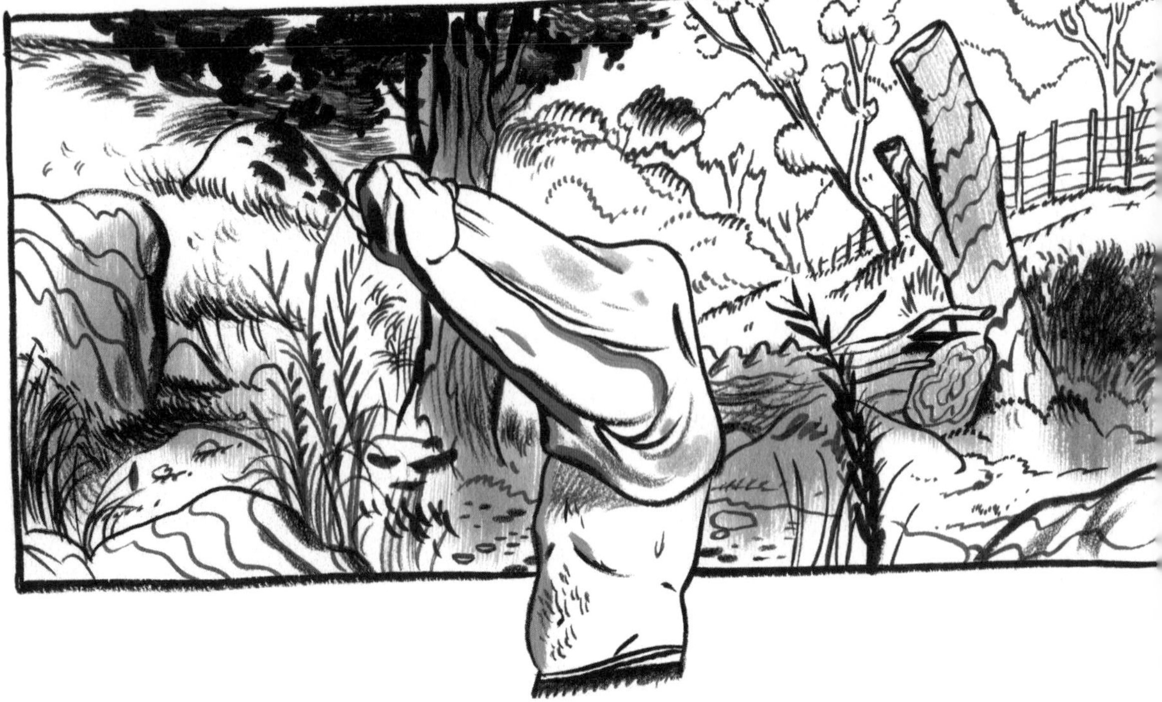

Without the obligations of his old life, Colin could finally recognize how stressed he had been these past few months. Even before Paolo was assaulted, Colin had carried his entire life on his shoulders, and now, standing in the warm embrace of the sun, he could feel his body unclench. He felt comfortable enough to shed his sweaty shirt, something he rarely felt relaxed enough to do. Standing there in the dappled light, he didn't have to be strong enough to support anyone or anything with his optimism and his patience.

Before he met Paolo, Colin struggled to indulge the way people his age were expected to. He spent his nights out overthinking everything. Having sex was a way to give Colin's body a purpose, and to distract himself from his insecurities about it. Paolo was always more comfortable around other men than Colin ever was, but Colin did find it easier to open up by having someone there by his side.

When Colin's doubts flared up, Paolo was quick to flatter him, but Colin mentioning his insecurities would also always make Paolo laugh. He couldn't help it. To him, Colin was overwhelmingly attractive, and his inability to recognize that was silly. Paolo always enjoyed Colin's eagerness for intimacy without realizing he was the one bringing it out in him. The safety of already having a boyfriend gave Colin permission to unselfconsciously be himself.

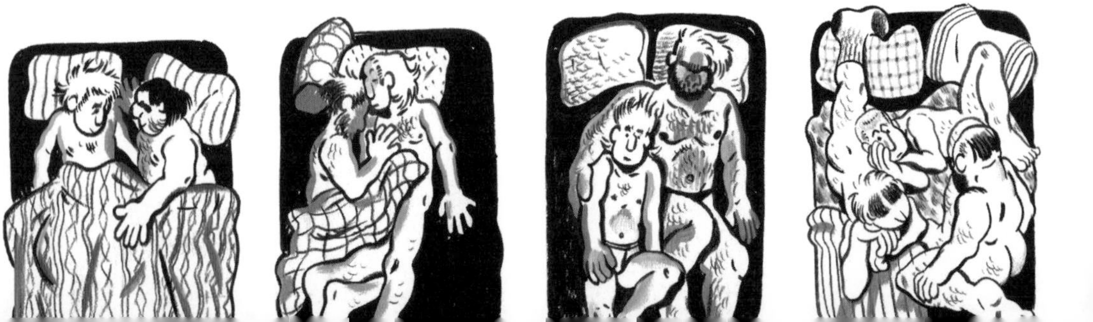

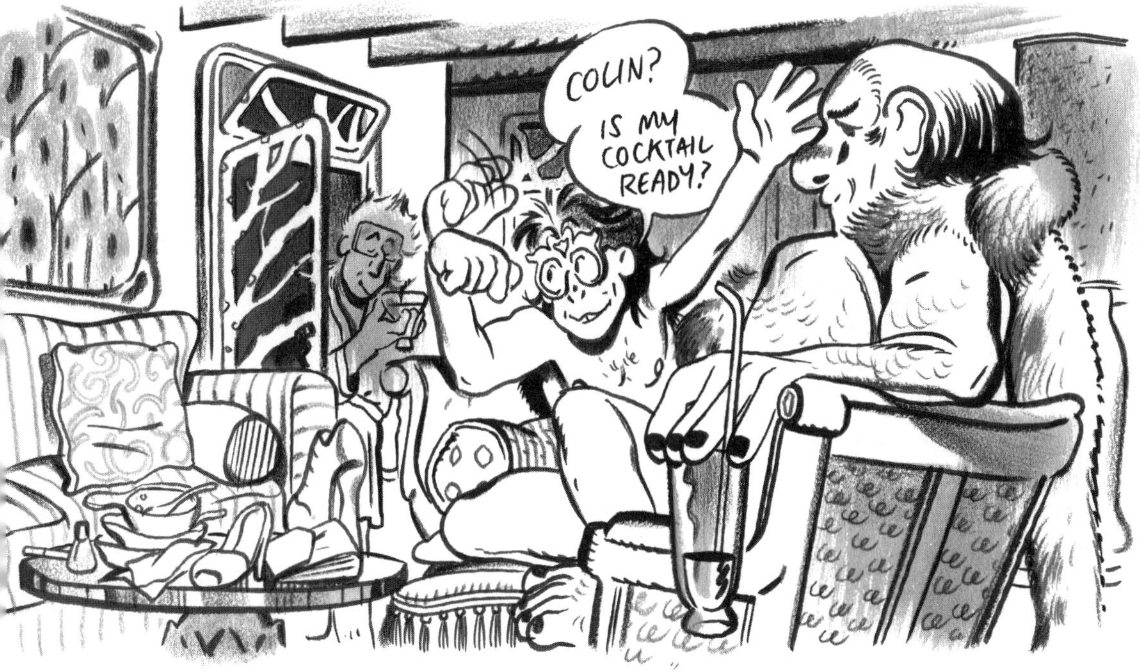
COLIN?
IS MY COCKTAIL READY?

Colin's coworker Hank, the person who rented that seaside mansion to celebrate his birthday, was a notorious flirt. His sexuality was prominent and leading, like the prow of a ship. Everyone was attracted to him, including Colin, though he detested admitting that even to himself. Hank occupied a confusing space in Colin's brain—did he want to *be* him? Have sex with him? Mimic his sense of ease? Prove to him he was just as sexual? Or just benefit from being within his orbit?

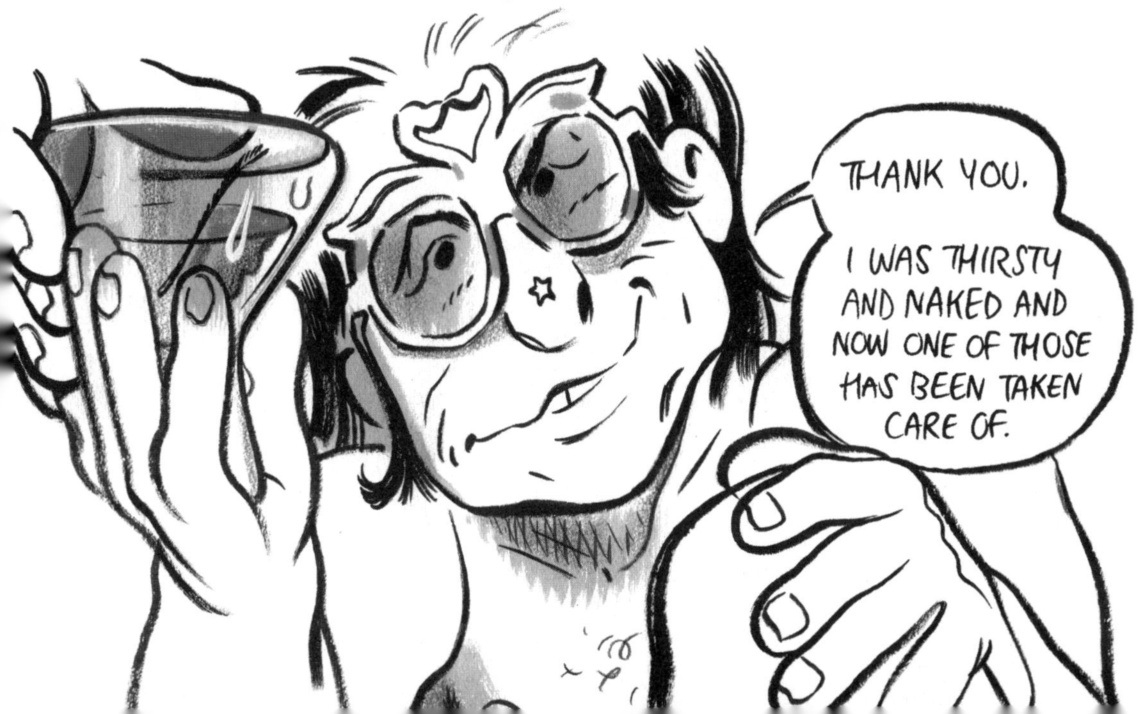
THANK YOU.
I WAS THIRSTY AND NAKED AND NOW ONE OF THOSE HAS BEEN TAKEN CARE OF.

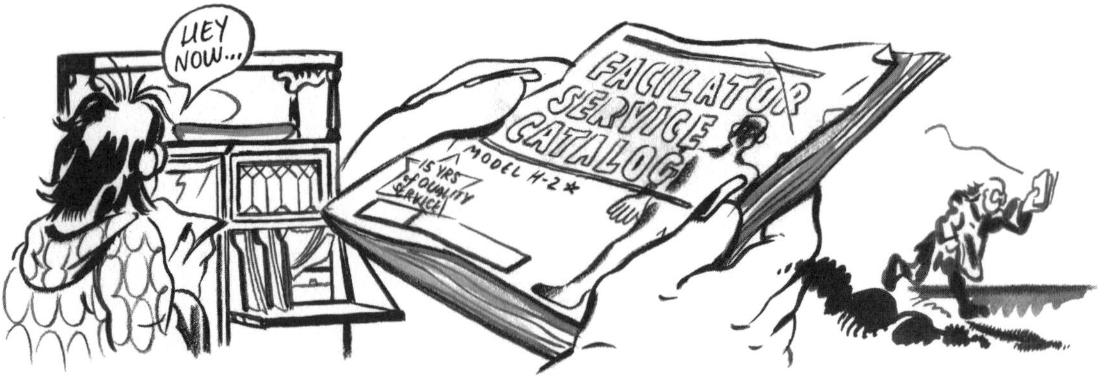
HEY NOW...
FACILATOR SERVICE CATALOG
MODEL H-2*
15 YRS of QUALITY SERVICE!

Hank had found the Facilitator's operating manual while trying to locate napkins to set the table with. In a flurry of excitement, he had run out across the lawn to pull down the Facilitator's gold lamé boxer shorts because earlier someone had wondered if the Facilitator's equipment was adjustable. Hank discovered that it was—there was a dial on the inner thigh.

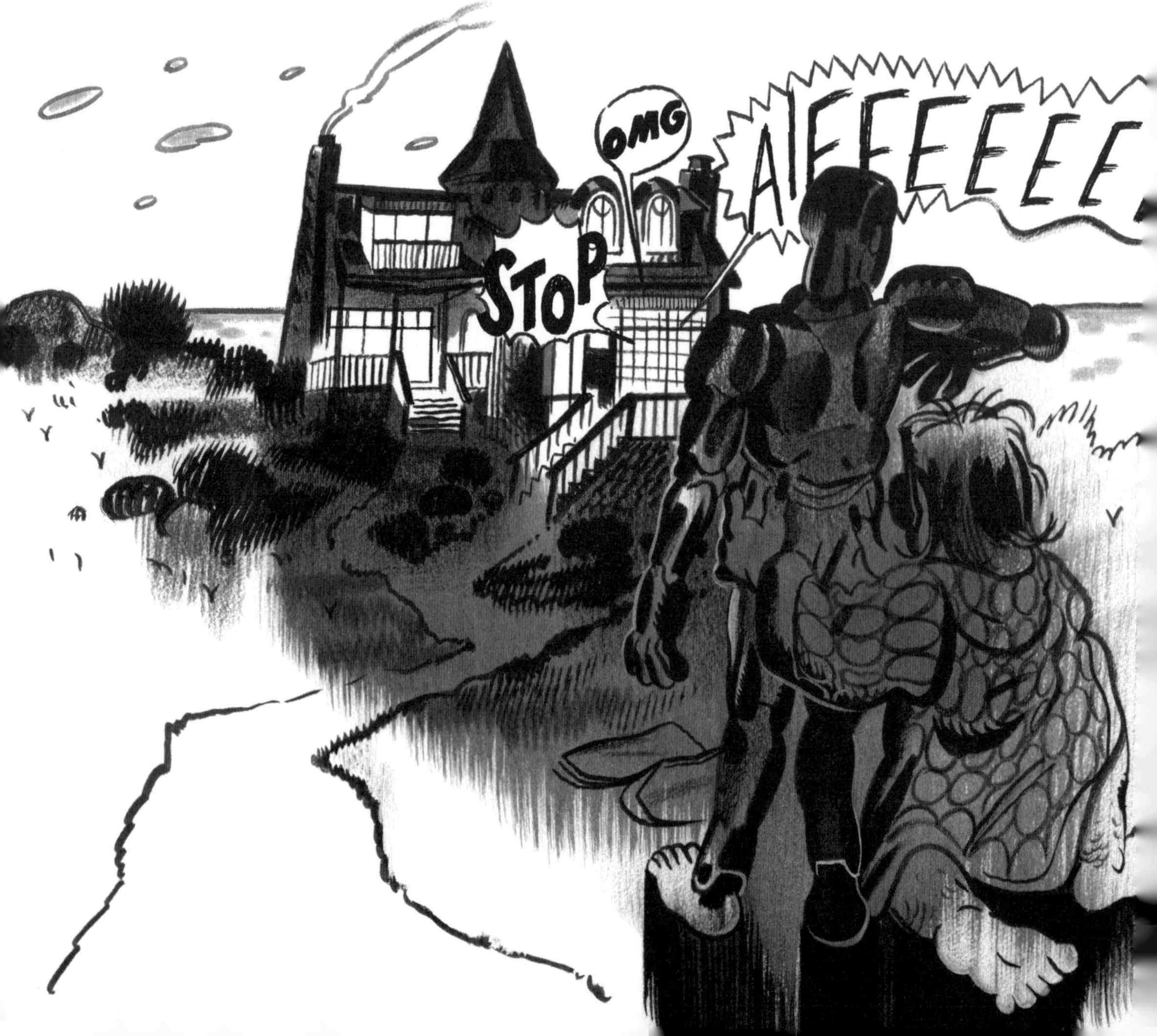
OMG
STOP
AIEEEEEE

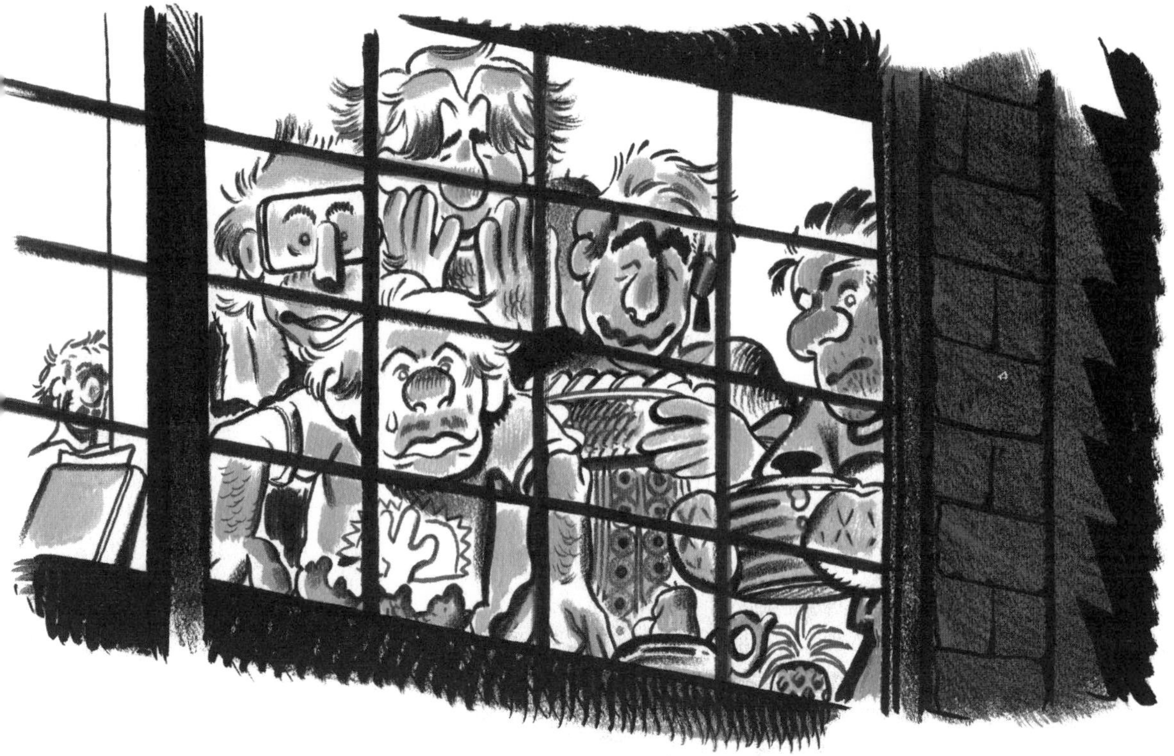

In the month he had been with Bibi and Susan, Colin had absorbed every story they told him about *de Beauvoir* and the women who had once called this place home. Nearly every story focused primarily on arguments—arguing about whether or not to sell their vegetable harvests each season, discussions on whether or not to kill a wasp nest that moved into someone's attic, the struggle to find a local livestock veterinarian who wasn't a man…and so on. Although Colin could do without the bickering, there was something enticing about living a life full of other people. Maybe the reason he had felt so often overwhelmed in his life was because it had just been him. Maybe Hank was so captivating because he was someone Colin could simply follow. Colin was never going to be someone who cavorted in quite *that* way, but he could follow after Hank if Hank tested those waters for him first.

Having spent his life as an only child, Colin was starting to realize that maybe there was solace in not going it alone.

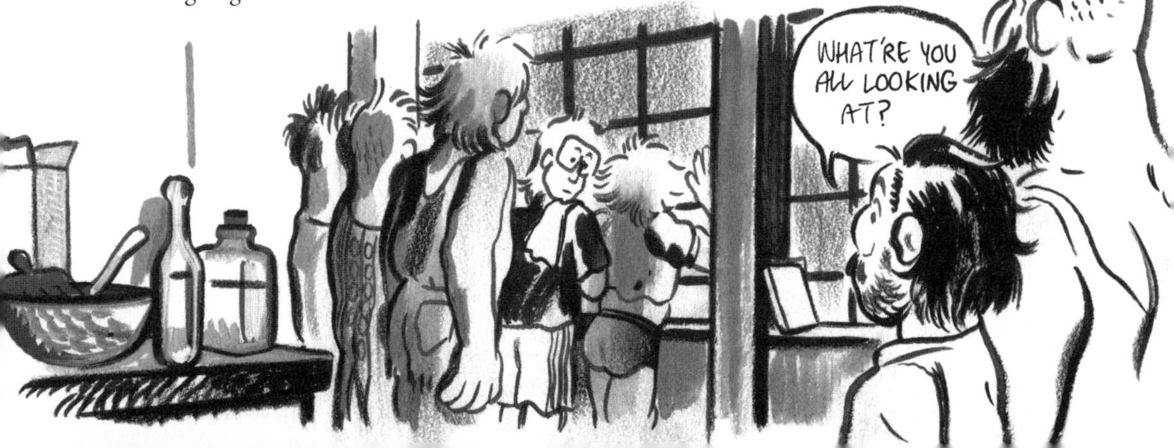
WHAT'RE YOU ALL LOOKING AT?

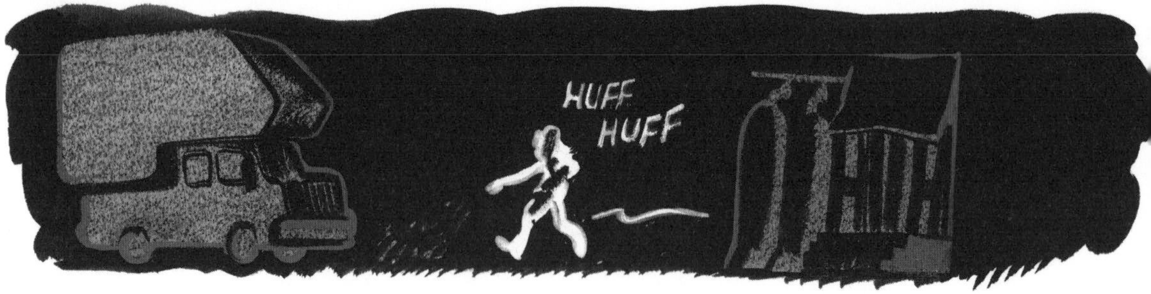
HUFF
HUFF

The distance from the kitchen door to the RV wasn't very far, but Colin would run it every night. Once inside the safety of the camper, he'd laugh at how silly he had been, but he couldn't help himself. He knew there was nothing out there in the dark besides Famous, and the thought of this mysterious ex-lover wandering the woods alone at night was ridiculous, even as Colin's heart pounded in his chest.

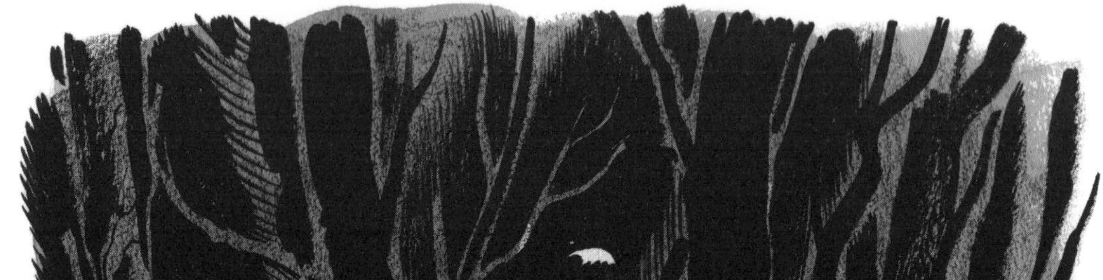

To think that not that long ago he had walked out of Minnie's house, shirtless, to smoke in the middle of the night. How safe he had felt.

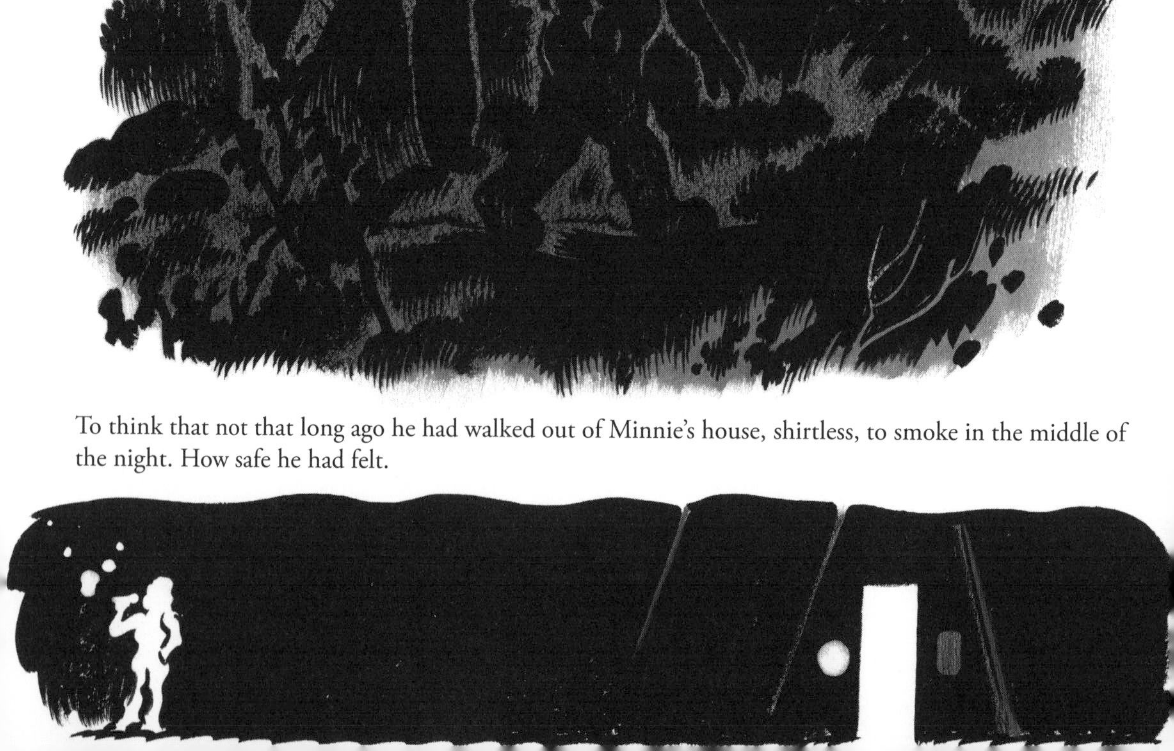

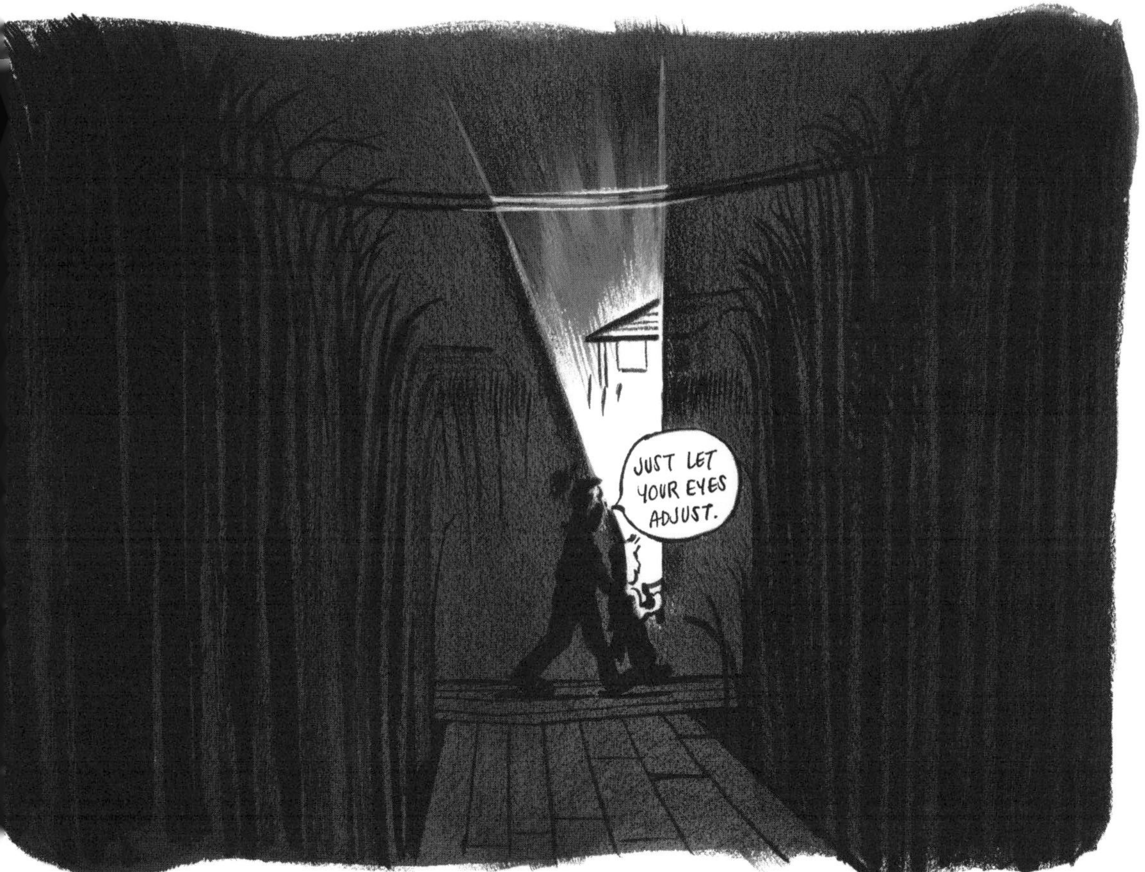
JUST LET YOUR EYES ADJUST.

When he was a kid, Minnie would always bring Colin to the same secluded beach community on vacations. He could vividly remember how walking along the darkened boardwalks at night had terrified him. Minnie would urge him not to use his flashlight, to enjoy standing alone beneath a sky full of stars and decommissioned satellites. Reassuring him that there was nothing out there besides the revelling gay men at the nearby clubs.

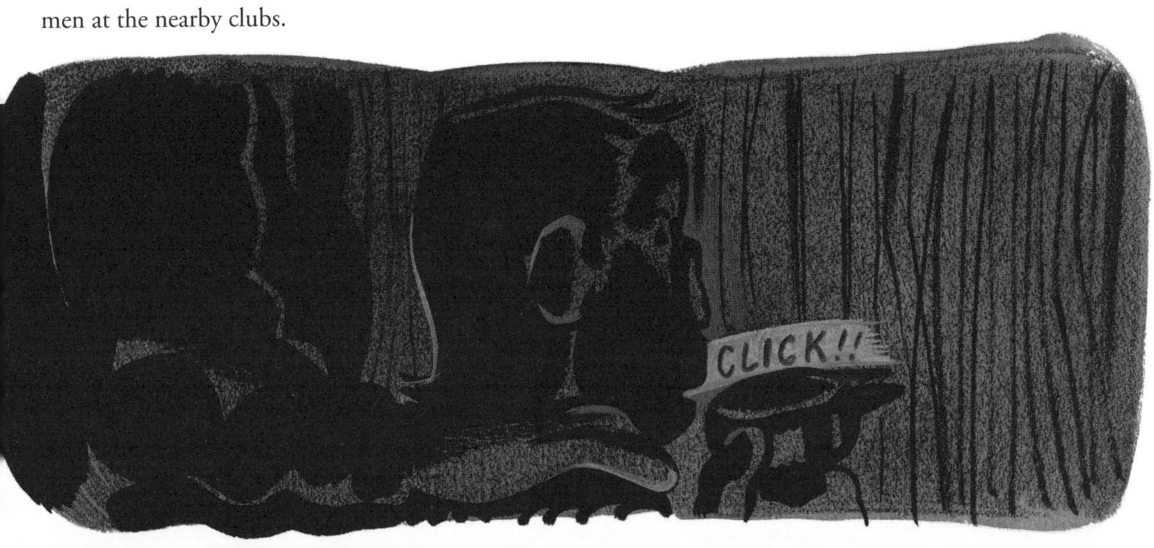
CLICK!!

It wasn't uncommon to catch Opie making her way back from the bottom of the hill. Colin had a hunch that she had found a way to get fed every meal twice—once from him, and then again from Famous.

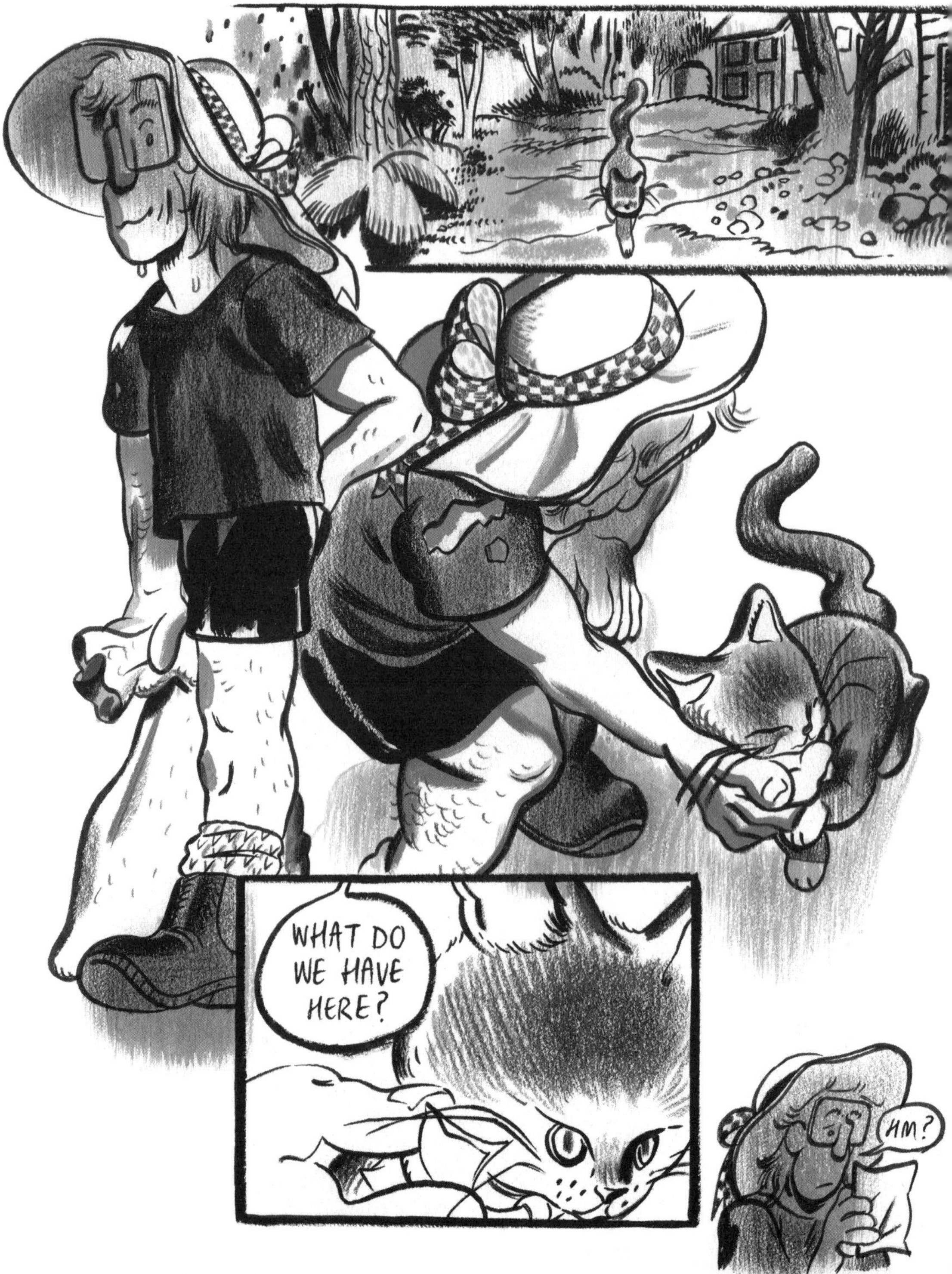
WHAT DO WE HAVE HERE?
HM?

He wanted to know what had happened to the rest of *The Daughters* but was reluctant to ask. The note gave him his opportunity.

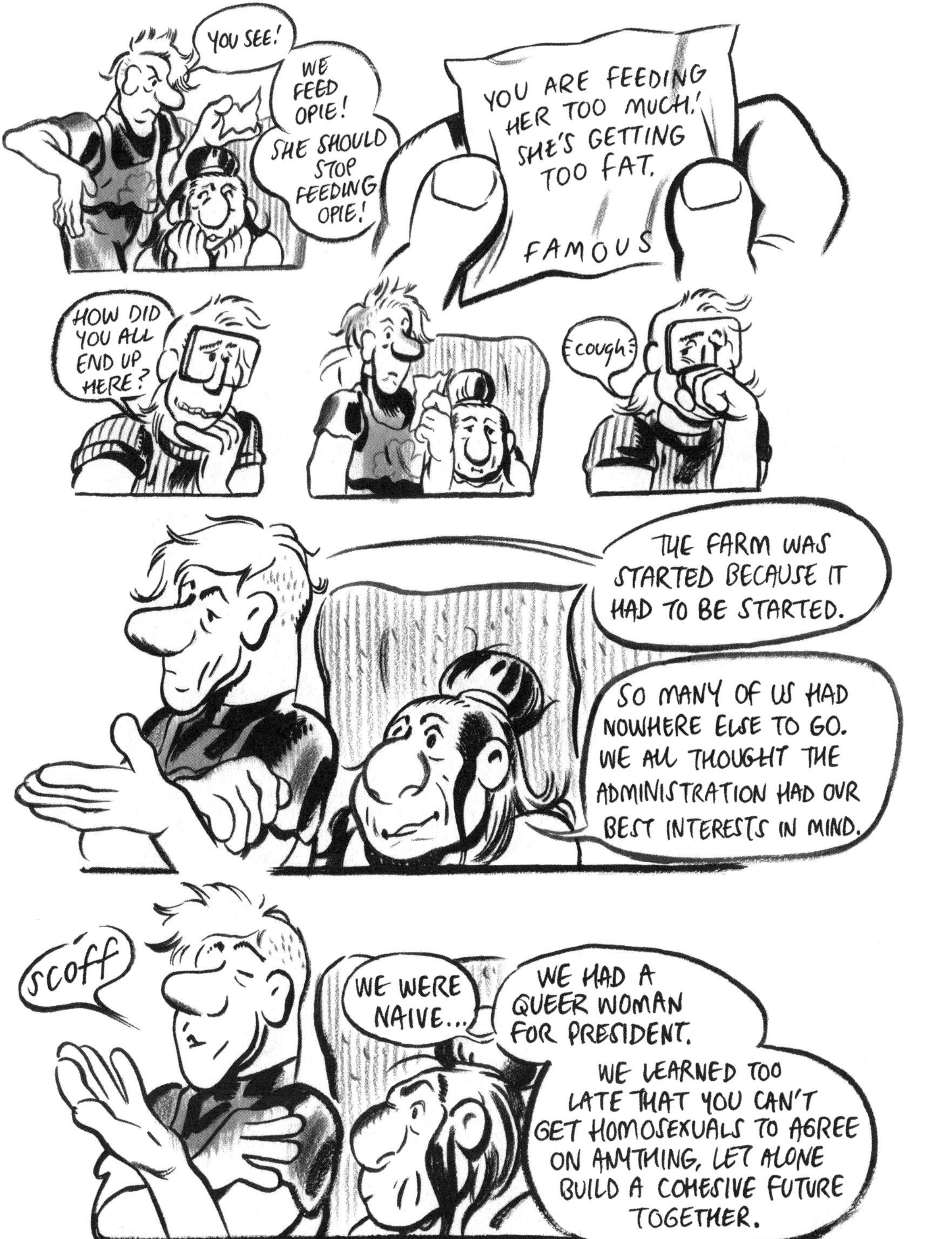
YOU SEE!
WE FEED OPIE!
SHE SHOULD STOP FEEDING OPIE!
YOU ARE FEEDING HER TOO MUCH! SHE'S GETTING TOO FAT.
FAMOUS
HOW DID YOU ALL END UP HERE?
cough
THE FARM WAS STARTED BECAUSE IT HAD TO BE STARTED.
SO MANY OF US HAD NOWHERE ELSE TO GO. WE ALL THOUGHT THE ADMINISTRATION HAD OUR BEST INTERESTS IN MIND.
scoff
WE WERE NAIVE...
WE HAD A QUEER WOMAN FOR PRESIDENT.
WE LEARNED TOO LATE THAT YOU CAN'T GET HOMOSEXUALS TO AGREE ON ANYTHING, LET ALONE BUILD A COHESIVE FUTURE TOGETHER.

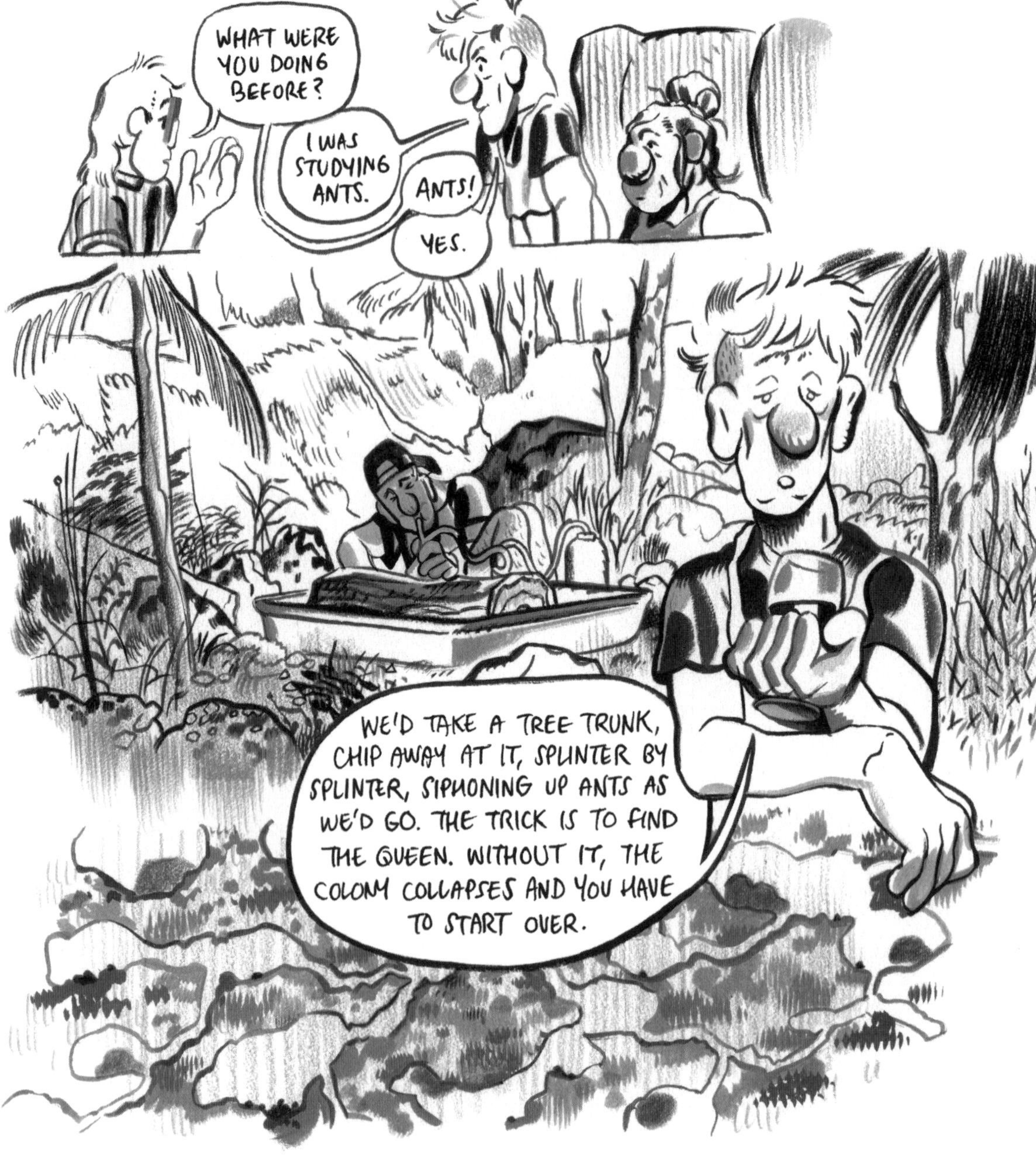
WHAT WERE YOU DOING BEFORE?
I WAS STUDYING ANTS.
ANTS!
YES.
WE'D TAKE A TREE TRUNK, CHIP AWAY AT IT, SPLINTER BY SPLINTER, SIPHONING UP ANTS AS WE'D GO. THE TRICK IS TO FIND THE QUEEN. WITHOUT IT, THE COLONY COLLAPSES AND YOU HAVE TO START OVER.

Susan had been working with a team of scientists to study the ways in which individual ants pass information along to the colony as a whole. She spent her twenties out in the field researching, harvesting ant colonies hidden deep within fallen trees to bring back to her lab to study in isolation.

Susan had developed a deep love for ants. Their efficiency. The way in which a colony functioned without any one ant, not even the queen, making decisions that governed the whole. Even the fact that the labor necessary to run the colony was all done by female worker ants was exciting to her.

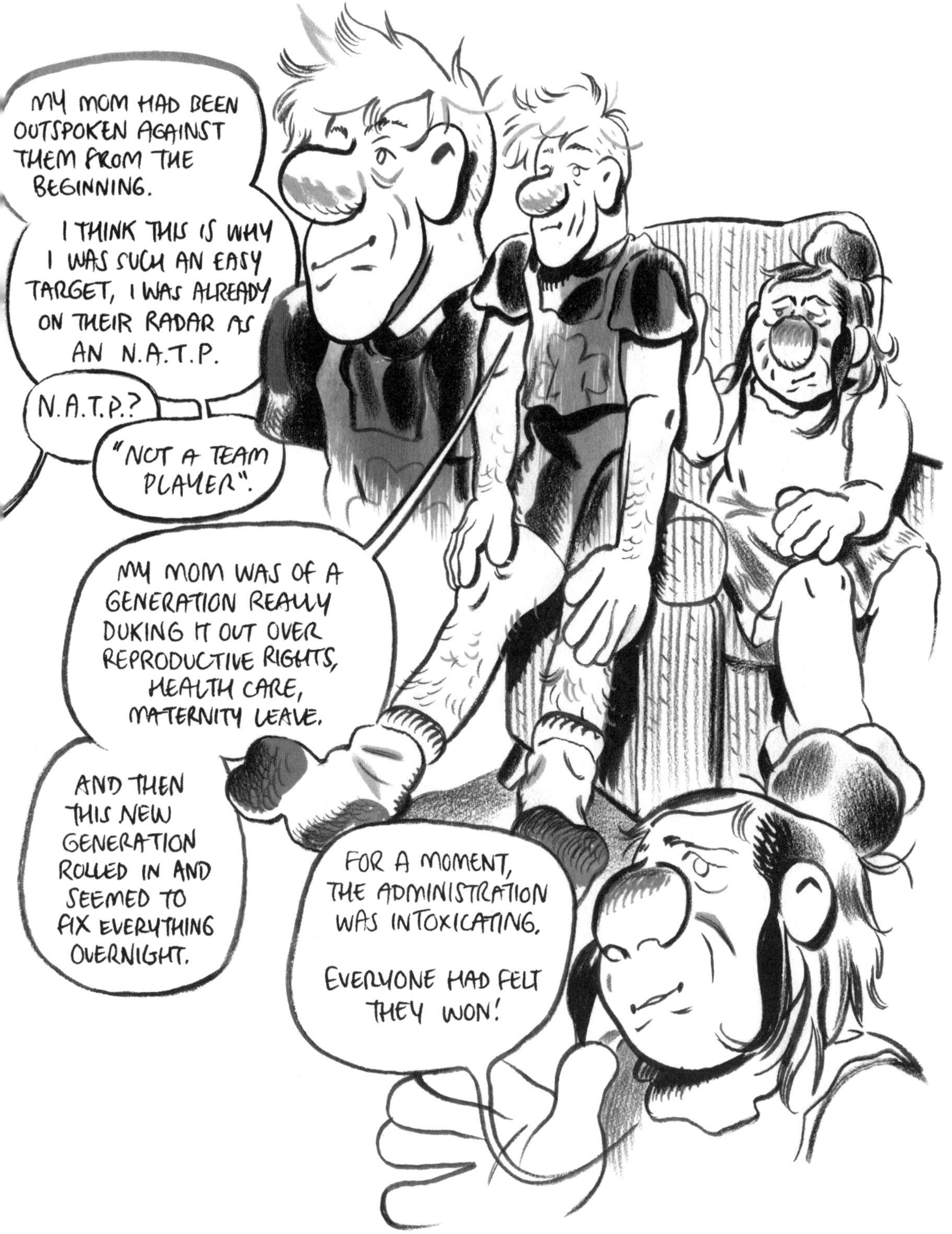
MY MOM HAD BEEN OUTSPOKEN AGAINST THEM FROM THE BEGINNING.
I THINK THIS IS WHY I WAS SUCH AN EASY TARGET, I WAS ALREADY ON THEIR RADAR AS AN N.A.T.P.
N.A.T.P.?
"NOT A TEAM PLAYER".
MY MOM WAS OF A GENERATION REALLY DUKING IT OUT OVER REPRODUCTIVE RIGHTS, HEALTH CARE, MATERNITY LEAVE.
AND THEN THIS NEW GENERATION ROLLED IN AND SEEMED TO FIX EVERYTHING OVERNIGHT.
FOR A MOMENT, THE ADMINISTRATION WAS INTOXICATING.
EVERYONE HAD FELT THEY WON!

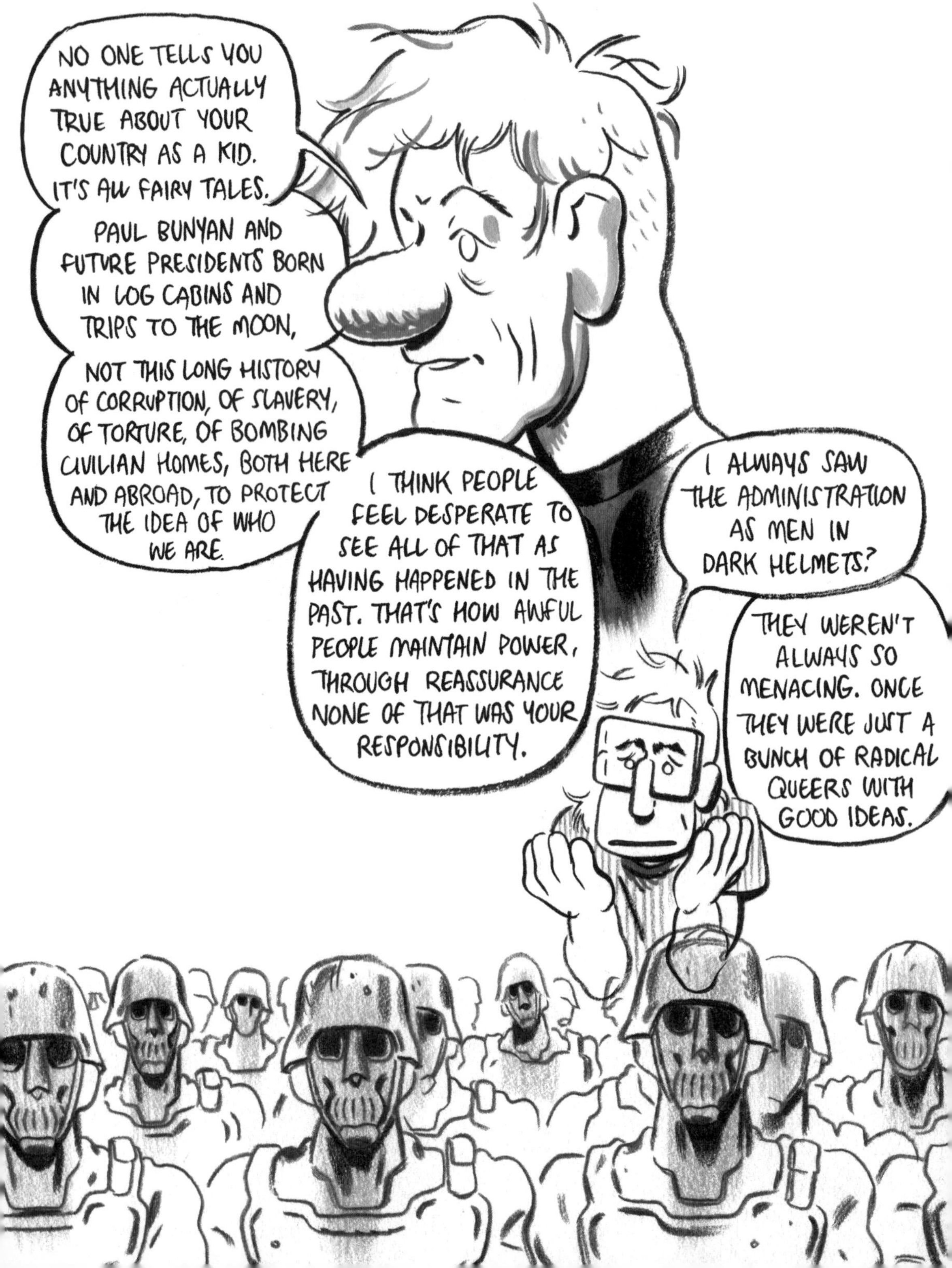
NO ONE TELLS YOU ANYTHING ACTUALLY TRUE ABOUT YOUR COUNTRY AS A KID. IT'S ALL FAIRY TALES.
PAUL BUNYAN AND FUTURE PRESIDENTS BORN IN LOG CABINS AND TRIPS TO THE MOON,
NOT THIS LONG HISTORY OF CORRUPTION, OF SLAVERY, OF TORTURE, OF BOMBING CIVILIAN HOMES, BOTH HERE AND ABROAD, TO PROTECT THE IDEA OF WHO WE ARE.
I THINK PEOPLE FEEL DESPERATE TO SEE ALL OF THAT AS HAVING HAPPENED IN THE PAST. THAT'S HOW AWFUL PEOPLE MAINTAIN POWER, THROUGH REASSURANCE NONE OF THAT WAS YOUR RESPONSIBILITY.
I ALWAYS SAW THE ADMINISTRATION AS MEN IN DARK HELMETS?
THEY WEREN'T ALWAYS SO MENACING. ONCE THEY WERE JUST A BUNCH OF RADICAL QUEERS WITH GOOD IDEAS.

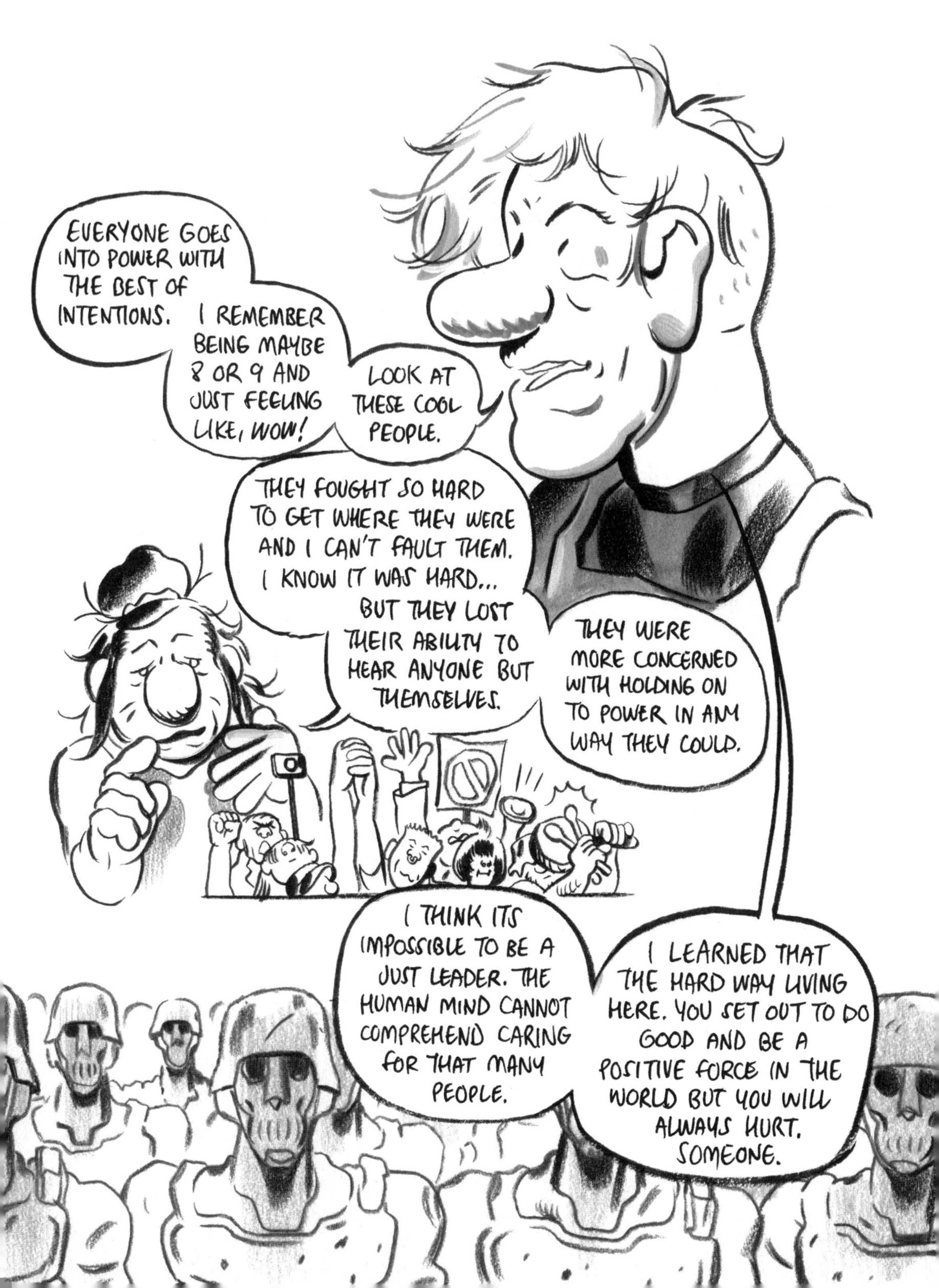
EVERYONE GOES INTO POWER WITH THE BEST OF INTENTIONS.
I REMEMBER BEING MAYBE 8 OR 9 AND JUST FEELING LIKE, WOW!
LOOK AT THESE COOL PEOPLE.
THEY FOUGHT SO HARD TO GET WHERE THEY WERE AND I CAN'T FAULT THEM. I KNOW IT WAS HARD...
BUT THEY LOST THEIR ABILITY TO HEAR ANYONE BUT THEMSELVES.
THEY WERE MORE CONCERNED WITH HOLDING ON TO POWER IN ANY WAY THEY COULD.
I THINK ITS IMPOSSIBLE TO BE A JUST LEADER. THE HUMAN MIND CANNOT COMPREHEND CARING FOR THAT MANY PEOPLE.
I LEARNED THAT THE HARD WAY LIVING HERE. YOU SET OUT TO DO GOOD AND BE A POSITIVE FORCE IN THE WORLD BUT YOU WILL ALWAYS HURT. SOMEONE.

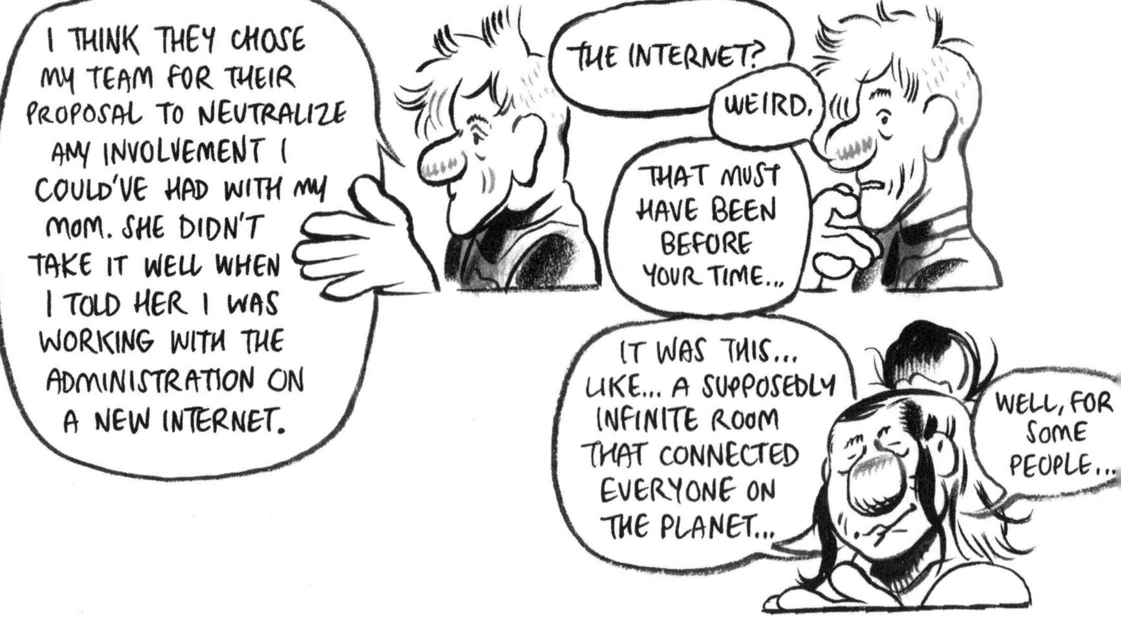
I THINK THEY CHOSE MY TEAM FOR THEIR PROPOSAL TO NEUTRALIZE ANY INVOLVEMENT I COULD'VE HAD WITH MY MOM. SHE DIDN'T TAKE IT WELL WHEN I TOLD HER I WAS WORKING WITH THE ADMINISTRATION ON A NEW INTERNET.
THE INTERNET?
WEIRD.
THAT MUST HAVE BEEN BEFORE YOUR TIME...
IT WAS THIS... LIKE... A SUPPOSEDLY INFINITE ROOM THAT CONNECTED EVERYONE ON THE PLANET...
WELL, FOR SOME PEOPLE...

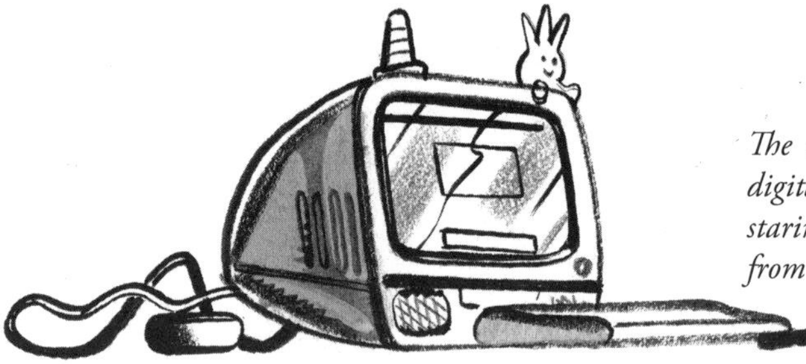

The original Internet had been built around a digital interface where each person worked by staring at a screen all day, disconnected physically from those on the other side.

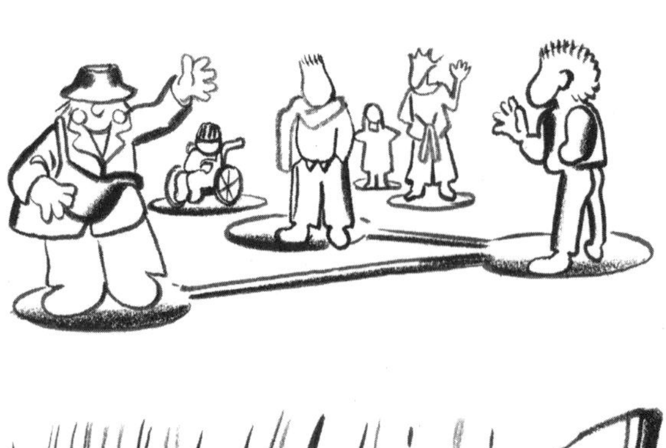

One day, representatives from the Administrati approached Susan and her team with a proposal— share their expertise on ant colonies with a new proje they had in development.

Their proposal hoped to create an Internet th strengthened interpersonal connections between peop by removing the distance created by the screen itself.

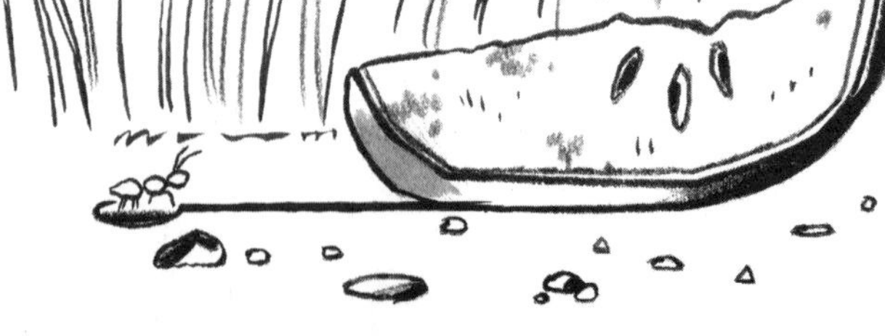

Ants communicate by sense of smell—when a ant finds a food source, it leaves behind a trail pheromones, alerting other ants to the food they foun As other ants come along and harvest that food, th strengthen that trail with more pheromones. But on the food is gone, they stop, and the trail disappears, n longer serving its purpose.

The Administration hoped this new version of th Internet would function in the same way.

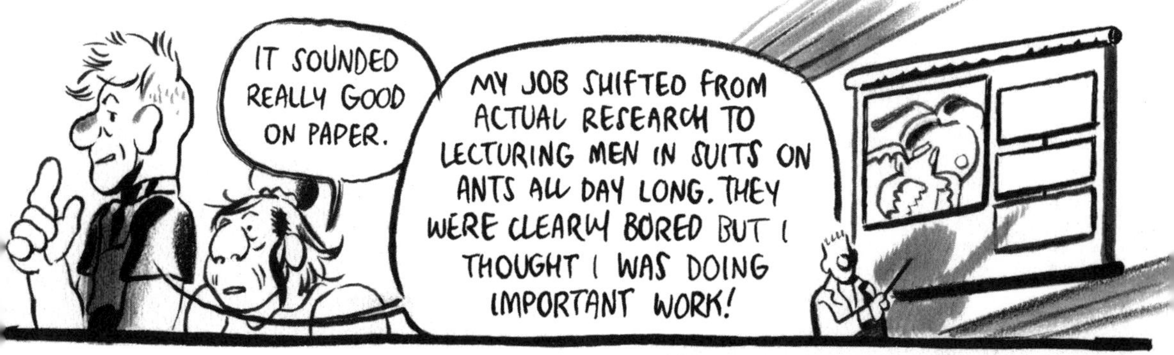
IT SOUNDED REALLY GOOD ON PAPER.
MY JOB SHIFTED FROM ACTUAL RESEARCH TO LECTURING MEN IN SUITS ON ANTS ALL DAY LONG. THEY WERE CLEARLY BORED BUT I THOUGHT I WAS DOING IMPORTANT WORK!

The Administration argued that the horrors experienced on the original Internet had occurred because of a lack of limitations—rampant consumerism, an inability to adequately filter horrific imagery, and an endless capacity to direct cruelty anonymously at strangers.

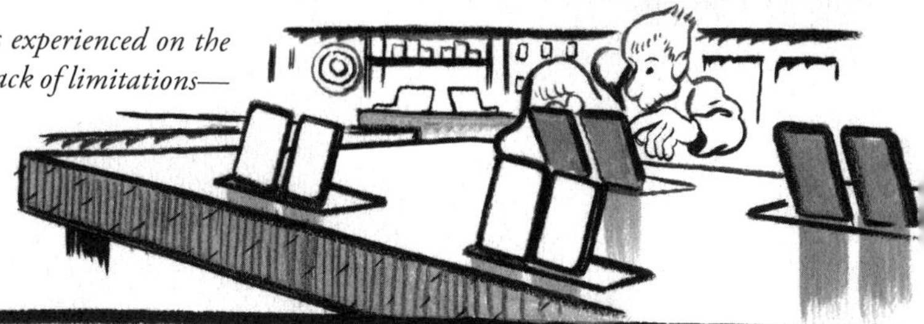

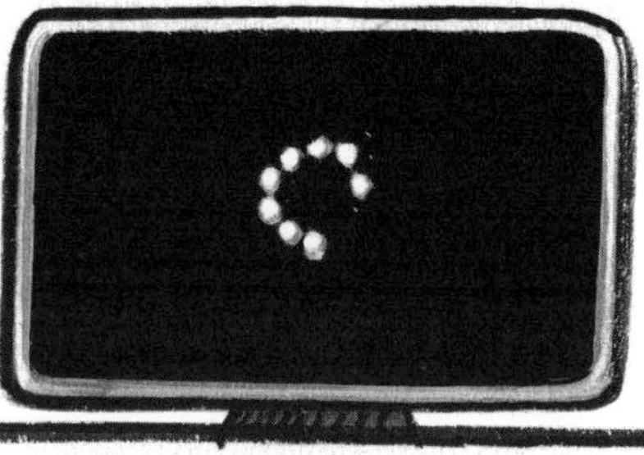

What my team and I didn't know at the time was that the Administration just wanted to dismantle the Internet entirely rather than create something better. Here were all these once-radical thinkers desperate to solidify their power by denying everyone access to the tools they had used to get there in the first place.

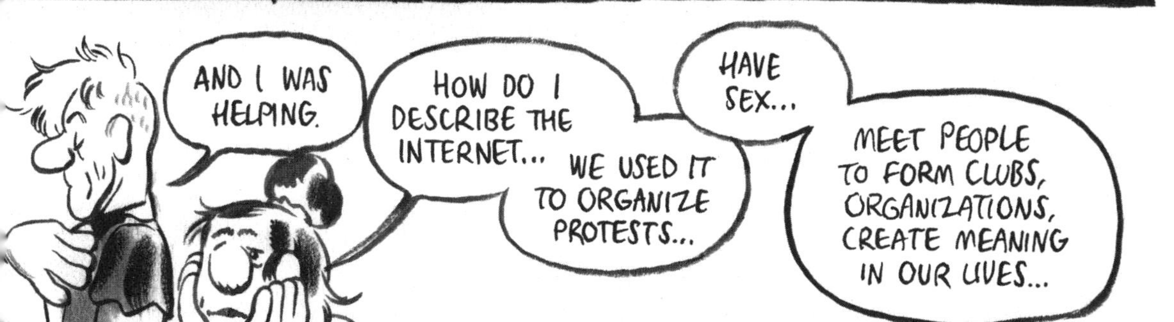
AND I WAS HELPING.
HOW DO I DESCRIBE THE INTERNET...
WE USED IT TO ORGANIZE PROTESTS...
HAVE SEX...
MEET PEOPLE TO FORM CLUBS, ORGANIZATIONS, CREATE MEANING IN OUR LIVES...

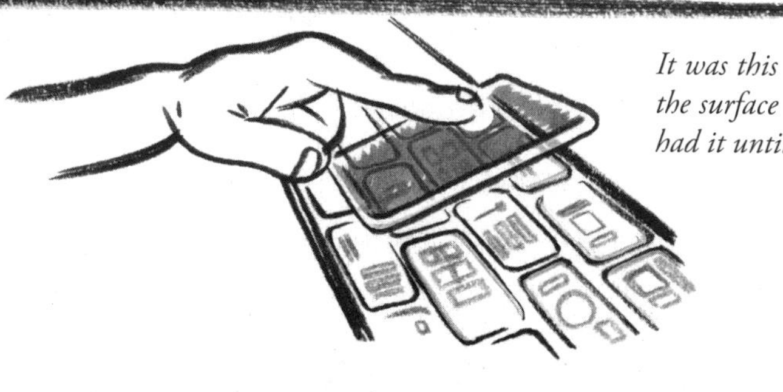

It was this whole secondary world existing just below the surface of our own. We didn't know how good we had it until it was too late.

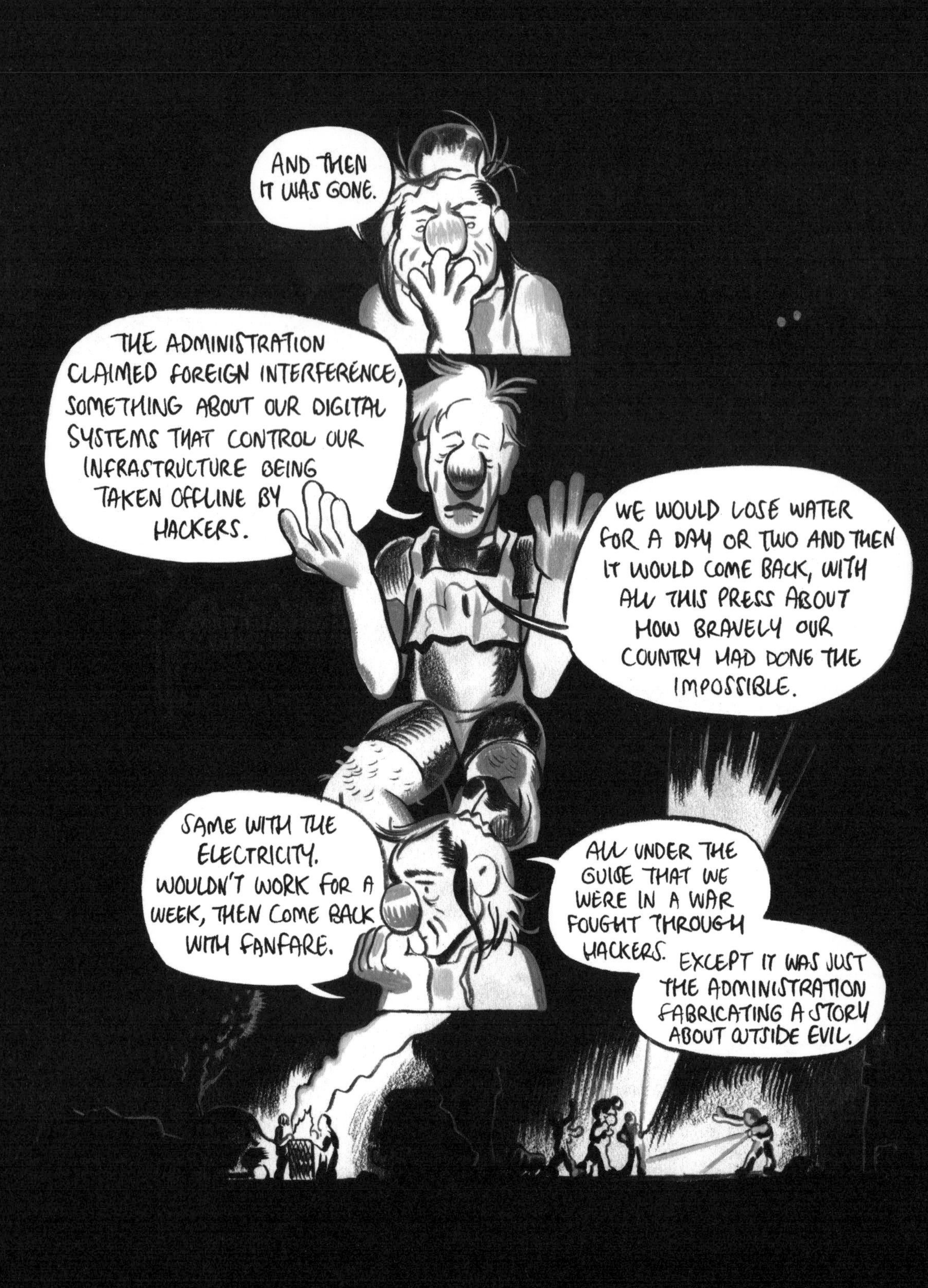
AND THEN IT WAS GONE.
THE ADMINISTRATION CLAIMED FOREIGN INTERFERENCE, SOMETHING ABOUT OUR DIGITAL SYSTEMS THAT CONTROL OUR INFRASTRUCTURE BEING TAKEN OFFLINE BY HACKERS.
WE WOULD LOSE WATER FOR A DAY OR TWO AND THEN IT WOULD COME BACK, WITH ALL THIS PRESS ABOUT HOW BRAVELY OUR COUNTRY HAD DONE THE IMPOSSIBLE.
SAME WITH THE ELECTRICITY. WOULDN'T WORK FOR A WEEK, THEN COME BACK WITH FANFARE.
ALL UNDER THE GUISE THAT WE WERE IN A WAR FOUGHT THROUGH HACKERS.
EXCEPT IT WAS JUST THE ADMINISTRATION FABRICATING A STORY ABOUT OUTSIDE EVIL.

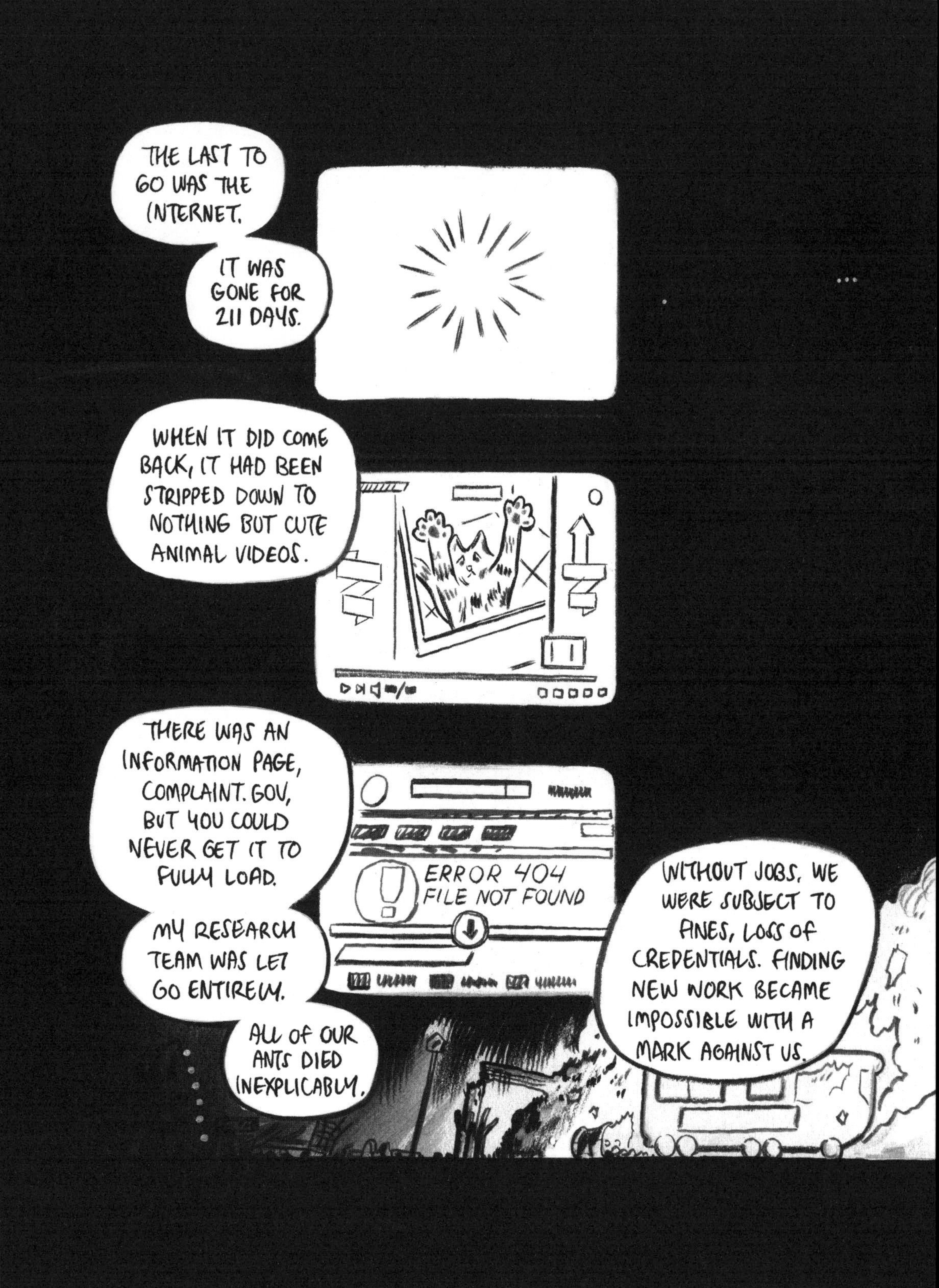
THE LAST TO GO WAS THE INTERNET.
IT WAS GONE FOR 211 DAYS.
WHEN IT DID COME BACK, IT HAD BEEN STRIPPED DOWN TO NOTHING BUT CUTE ANIMAL VIDEOS.
THERE WAS AN INFORMATION PAGE, COMPLAINT.GOV, BUT YOU COULD NEVER GET IT TO FULLY LOAD.
ERROR 404
FILE NOT FOUND
MY RESEARCH TEAM WAS LET GO ENTIRELY.
ALL OF OUR ANTS DIED INEXPLICABLY.
WITHOUT JOBS, WE WERE SUBJECT TO FINES, LOSS OF CREDENTIALS. FINDING NEW WORK BECAME IMPOSSIBLE WITH A MARK AGAINST US.

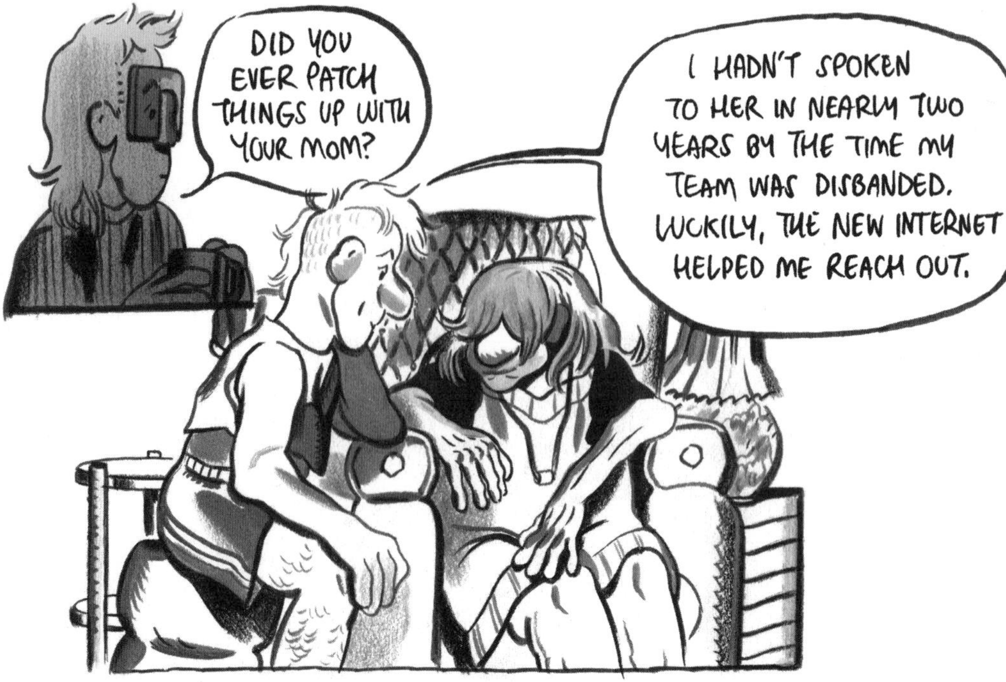
DID YOU EVER PATCH THINGS UP WITH YOUR MOM?
I HADN'T SPOKEN TO HER IN NEARLY TWO YEARS BY THE TIME MY TEAM WAS DISBANDED. LUCKILY, THE NEW INTERNET HELPED ME REACH OUT.

The device didn't use pheromones, like the ants, but it did function similarly enough—treating each person you interacted with as a link along a digital chain, allowing your device to speak to other devices along that chain. Since each person has their own social network—be it their job, their family, or their neighborhood block—you could easily communicate with other people along any chain you had access to.

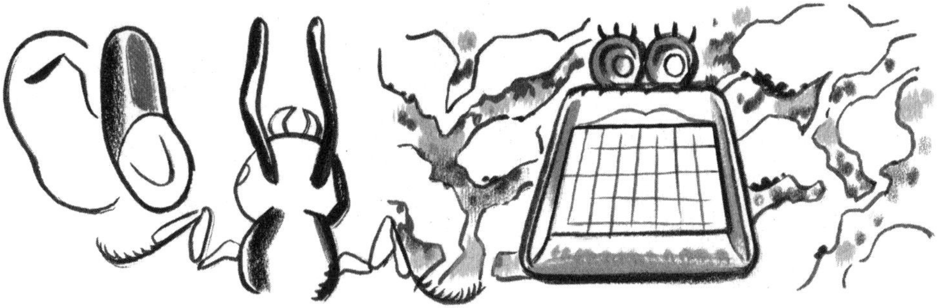

At its best, it was good for things like finding lost pets, locating nearby sexual partners, putting furniture up for sale…things like that. It was a community, but smaller than the Internet, more singular. Less accessible to people without an already robust social network in real life.

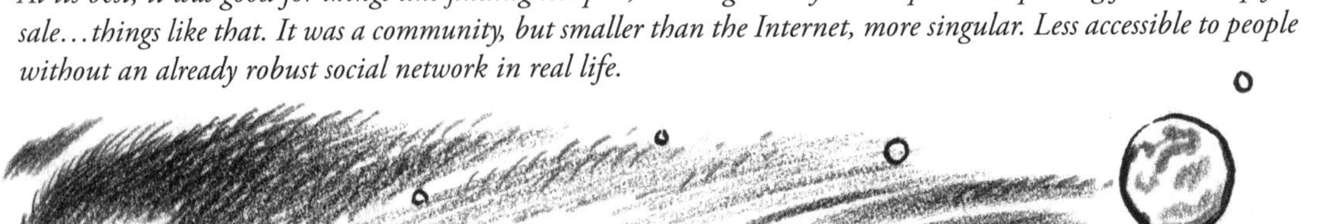

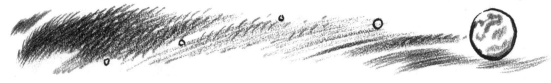

What made the Internet so remarkable was having global access to anyone and anything beyond one's small slice of the world. Yes, it had its problems, but its sudden loss has shaped us.

But the Internet we have now is somehow even more insular than when we were all behind our screens. Audio messages sent between users can be saved in order to bring back specific memories, but they aren't visual, and they can't be easily shared between people.

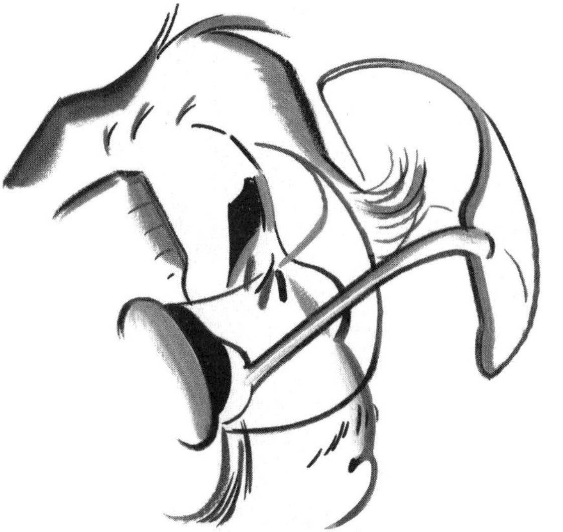

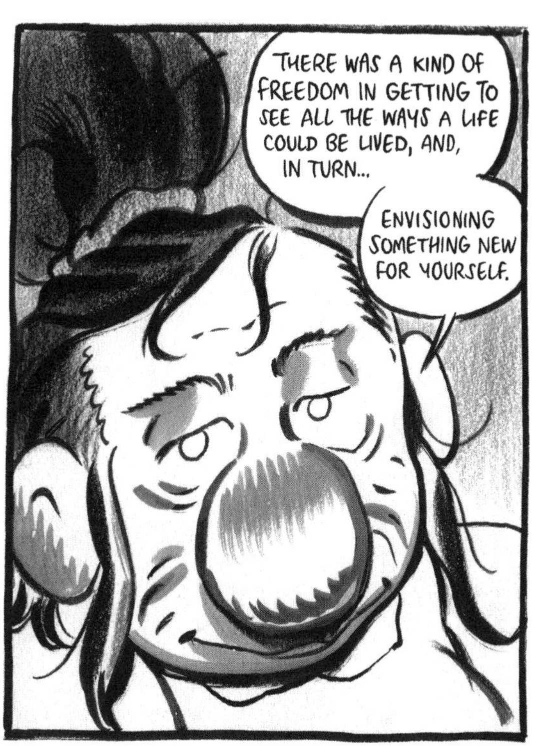
THERE WAS A KIND OF FREEDOM IN GETTING TO SEE ALL THE WAYS A LIFE COULD BE LIVED, AND, IN TURN...
ENVISIONING SOMETHING NEW FOR YOURSELF.

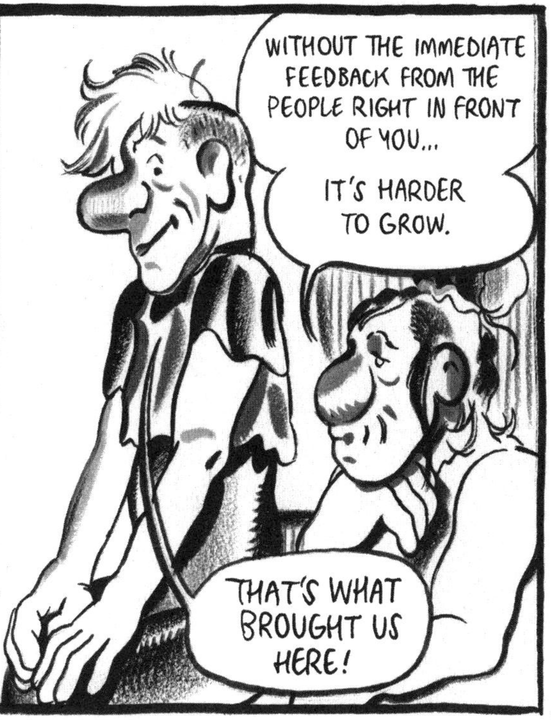
WITHOUT THE IMMEDIATE FEEDBACK FROM THE PEOPLE RIGHT IN FRONT OF YOU...
IT'S HARDER TO GROW.
THAT'S WHAT BROUGHT US HERE!

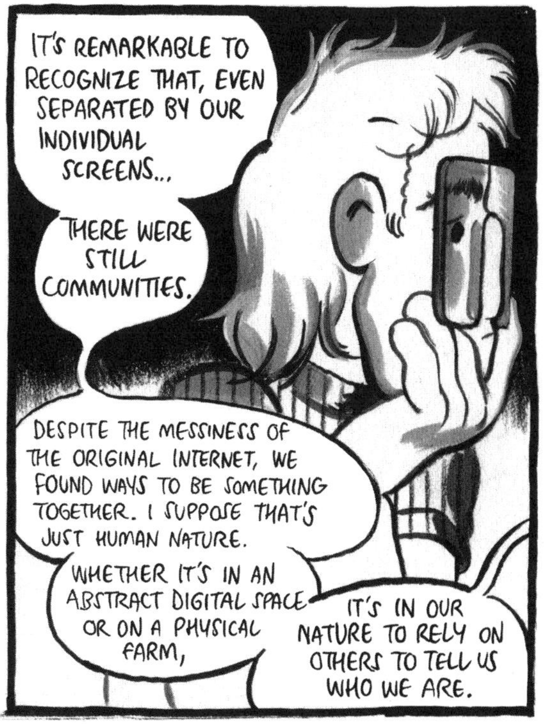
IT'S REMARKABLE TO RECOGNIZE THAT, EVEN SEPARATED BY OUR INDIVIDUAL SCREENS...
THERE WERE STILL COMMUNITIES.
DESPITE THE MESSINESS OF THE ORIGINAL INTERNET, WE FOUND WAYS TO BE SOMETHING TOGETHER. I SUPPOSE THAT'S JUST HUMAN NATURE.
WHETHER IT'S IN AN ABSTRACT DIGITAL SPACE OR ON A PHYSICAL FARM,
IT'S IN OUR NATURE TO RELY ON OTHERS TO TELL US WHO WE ARE.

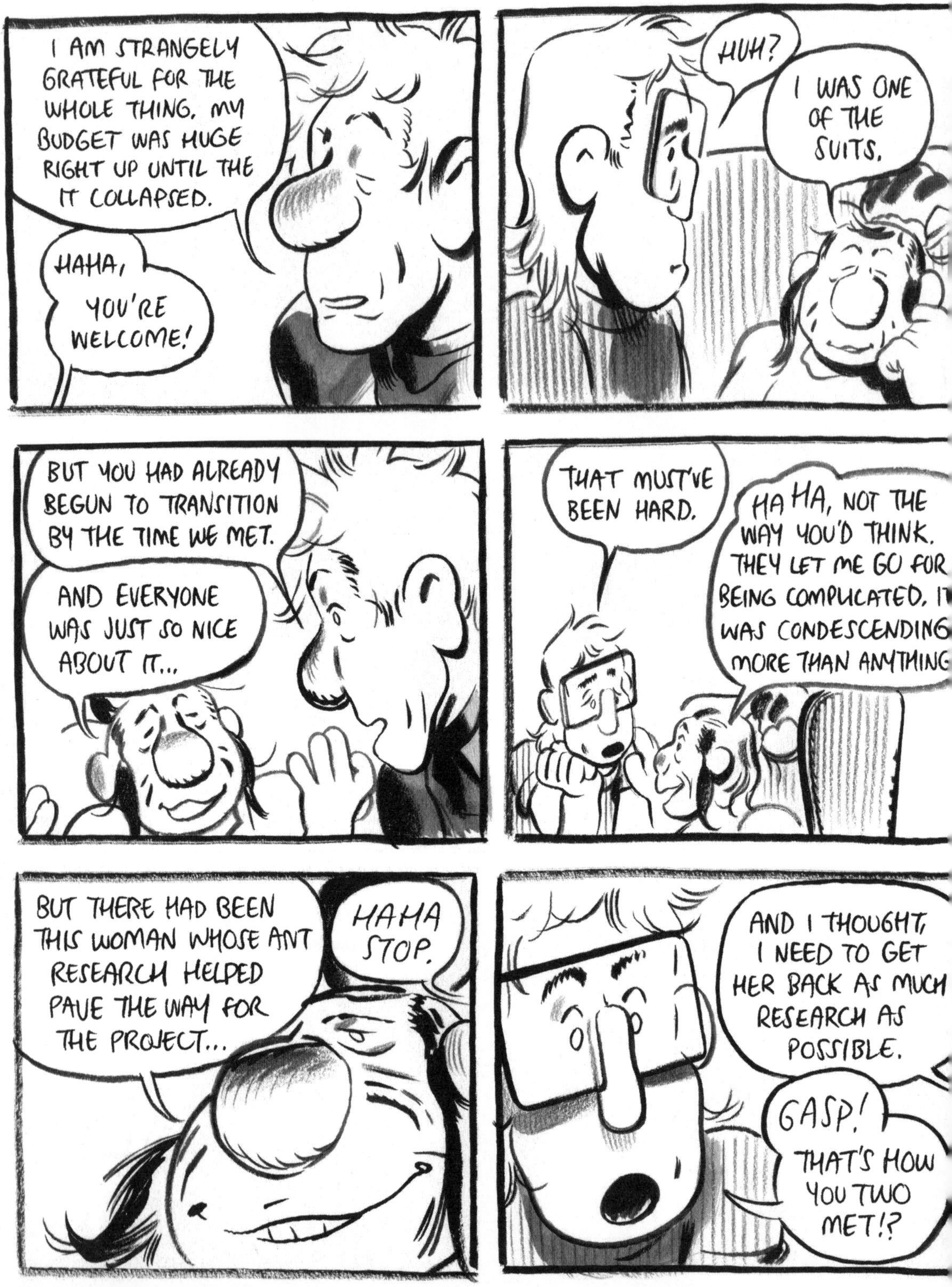
I AM STRANGELY GRATEFUL FOR THE WHOLE THING. MY BUDGET WAS HUGE RIGHT UP UNTIL THE IT COLLAPSED.
HAHA, YOU'RE WELCOME!
HUH?
I WAS ONE OF THE SUITS.
BUT YOU HAD ALREADY BEGUN TO TRANSITION BY THE TIME WE MET.
AND EVERYONE WAS JUST SO NICE ABOUT IT...
THAT MUST'VE BEEN HARD.
HA HA, NOT THE WAY YOU'D THINK. THEY LET ME GO FOR BEING COMPLICATED. IT WAS CONDESCENDING MORE THAN ANYTHING
BUT THERE HAD BEEN THIS WOMAN WHOSE ANT RESEARCH HELPED PAVE THE WAY FOR THE PROJECT...
HAHA STOP.
AND I THOUGHT, I NEED TO GET HER BACK AS MUCH RESEARCH AS POSSIBLE.
GASP!
THAT'S HOW YOU TWO MET!?

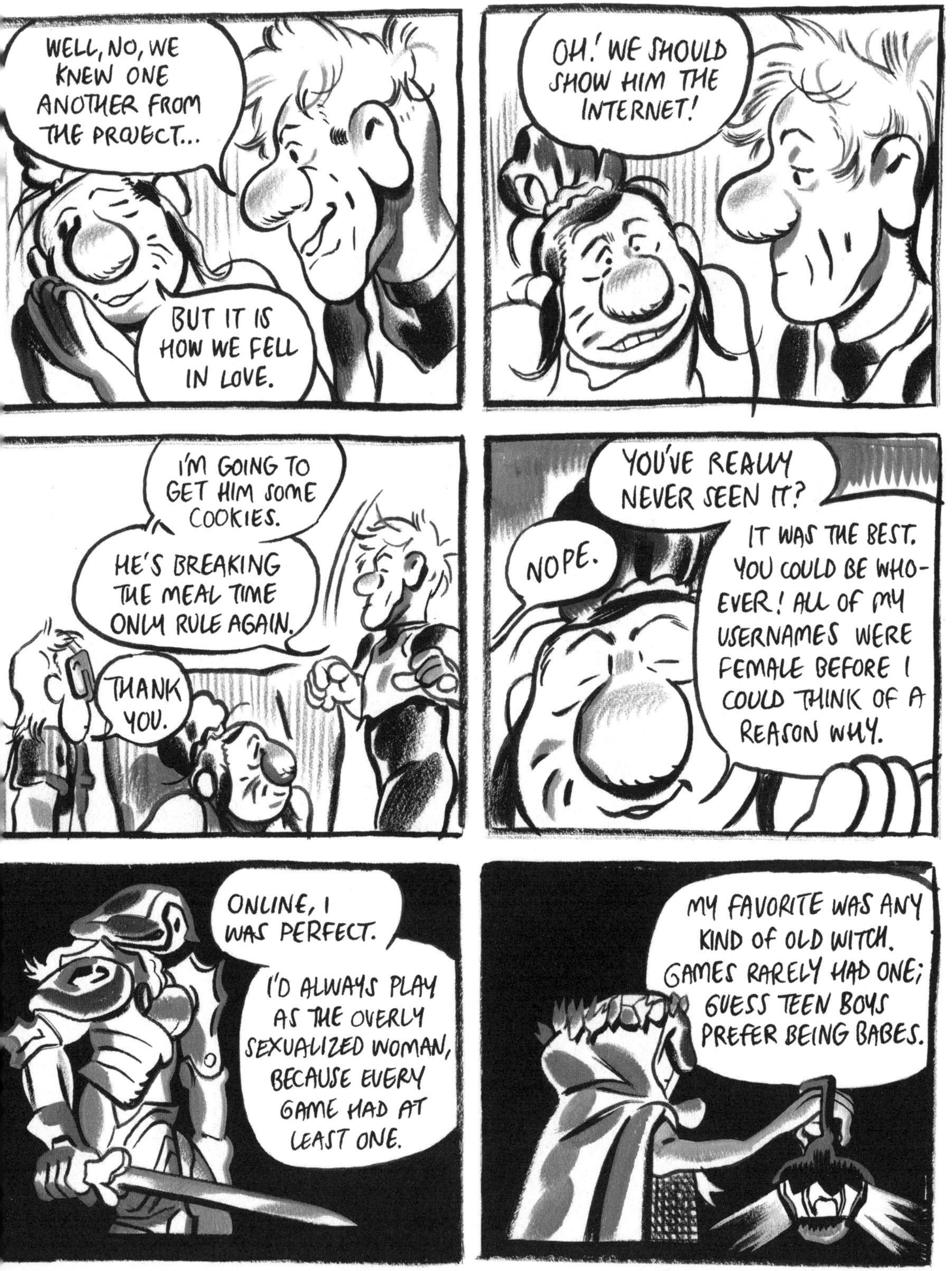
WELL, NO, WE KNEW ONE ANOTHER FROM THE PROJECT...
BUT IT IS HOW WE FELL IN LOVE.
OH! WE SHOULD SHOW HIM THE INTERNET!
I'M GOING TO GET HIM SOME COOKIES.
HE'S BREAKING THE MEAL TIME ONLY RULE AGAIN.
THANK YOU.
YOU'VE REALLY NEVER SEEN IT?
NOPE.
IT WAS THE BEST. YOU COULD BE WHO-EVER! ALL OF MY USERNAMES WERE FEMALE BEFORE I COULD THINK OF A REASON WHY.
ONLINE, I WAS PERFECT.
I'D ALWAYS PLAY AS THE OVERLY SEXUALIZED WOMAN, BECAUSE EVERY GAME HAD AT LEAST ONE.
MY FAVORITE WAS ANY KIND OF OLD WITCH. GAMES RARELY HAD ONE; GUESS TEEN BOYS PREFER BEING BABES.

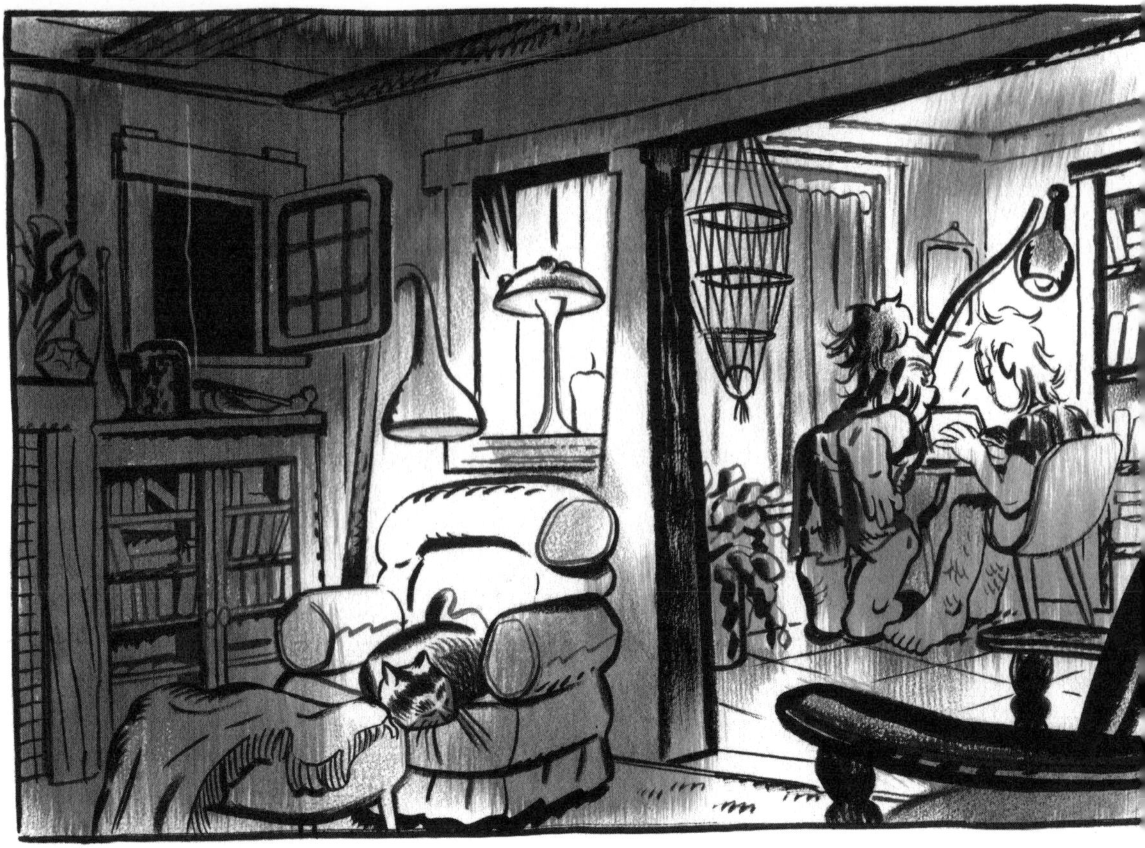

Susan and her team archived a chunk of the Internet for what they claimed were "research purposes" while working for the Administration. The archive wasn't connected to anything beyond their laptops, but clicking through the websites gave them the illusion of what the Internet had once been like.

When Bibi first turned on the computer, she told Colin to search for anything he wanted to, a concept he couldn't comprehend. Over the past decade, books had begun circulating again after being severely restricted during the Administration, but few people can comfortably read the long passages of text. Many see books as a novelty, and most are sold as decoration. Faced with the instant gratification of the Internet, Colin thought it was odd that books had ever existed at all, their information static and unchanging.

He found decades worth of newspaper archives available for anyone to read and a website dedicated solely to facts, covering everything from world history to the biographies of celebrities to the synopses of television shows no one remembered. Could *books* show video after video of animals performing human-like activities, or people accidentally hurting themselves in comedic ways, and still contain what felt like an endless scroll of information to learn from?

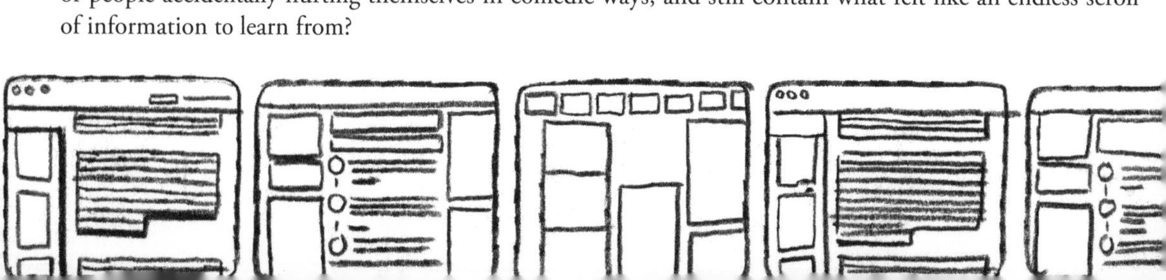

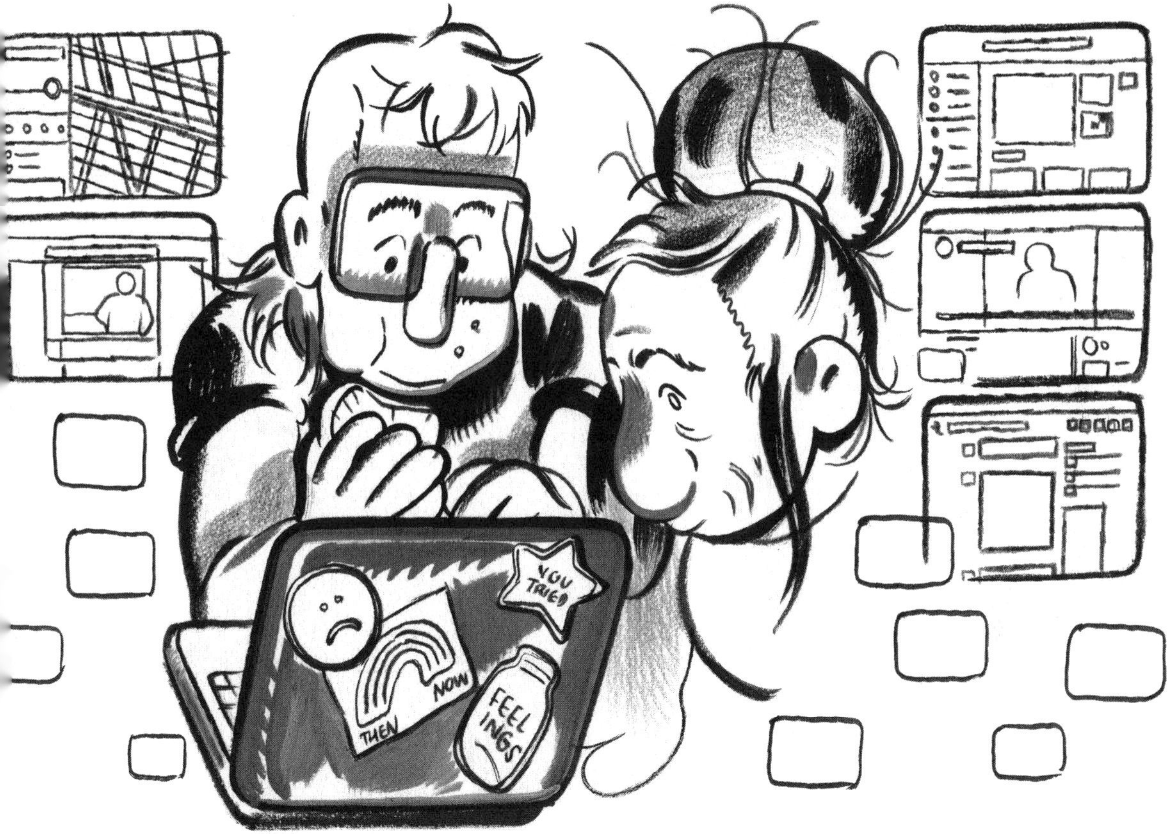
YOU TRIED
NOW
THEN
FEEL INGS

The only thing Colin could equate to using the Internet was digging at the beach as a child. You'd shovel sand for hours until eventually, unexpectedly, something beautiful would appear.

Most of the archive Susan's team had saved was overwhelmed by viruses and neglect, reflecting what the Internet had looked like in its final days. Websites were full of broken links and pop-up ads still attempting to sell you products that didn't exist anymore. Most searches led him nowhere. Occasionally, though, he'd unearth something impossibly beautiful—a photograph taken the moment a seagull dove into an ice cream cone in someone's outstretched hand; a sixty-second clip of men in matching outfits performing a tightly choreographed dance routine on a stage for thousands; even a low-quality audio recording of someone sketching out a song they were writing, saved from another recording device and preserved on the Internet for all time. Colin spent a week transfixed by a series of video makeup tutorials starring a teenage girl who referred to herself as pReCiOuSANGEL4eva. She reviewed various makeup kits and gave advice on how to paint one's face for any occasion, all while talking openly about her dream of one day owning her own line of products. She only made seven videos, the last one ending when her mother walked into her bedroom telling her it was time for dinner.

He structured his day around waking up early, doing whatever chores needed to be done, and then spending the rest of his day exploring the Internet. Over dinner, he'd recount what he found to Susan and Bibi, who'd just nod and smile knowingly.

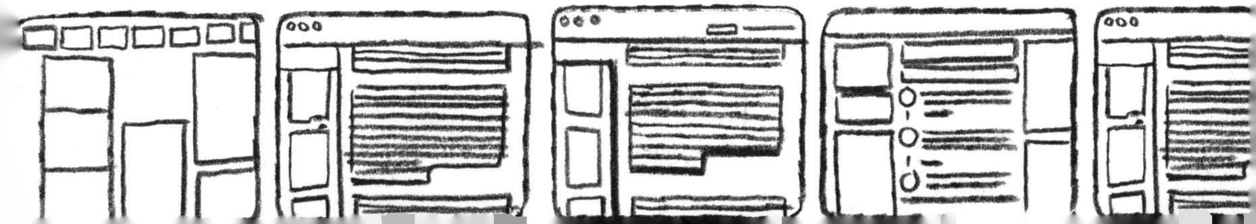

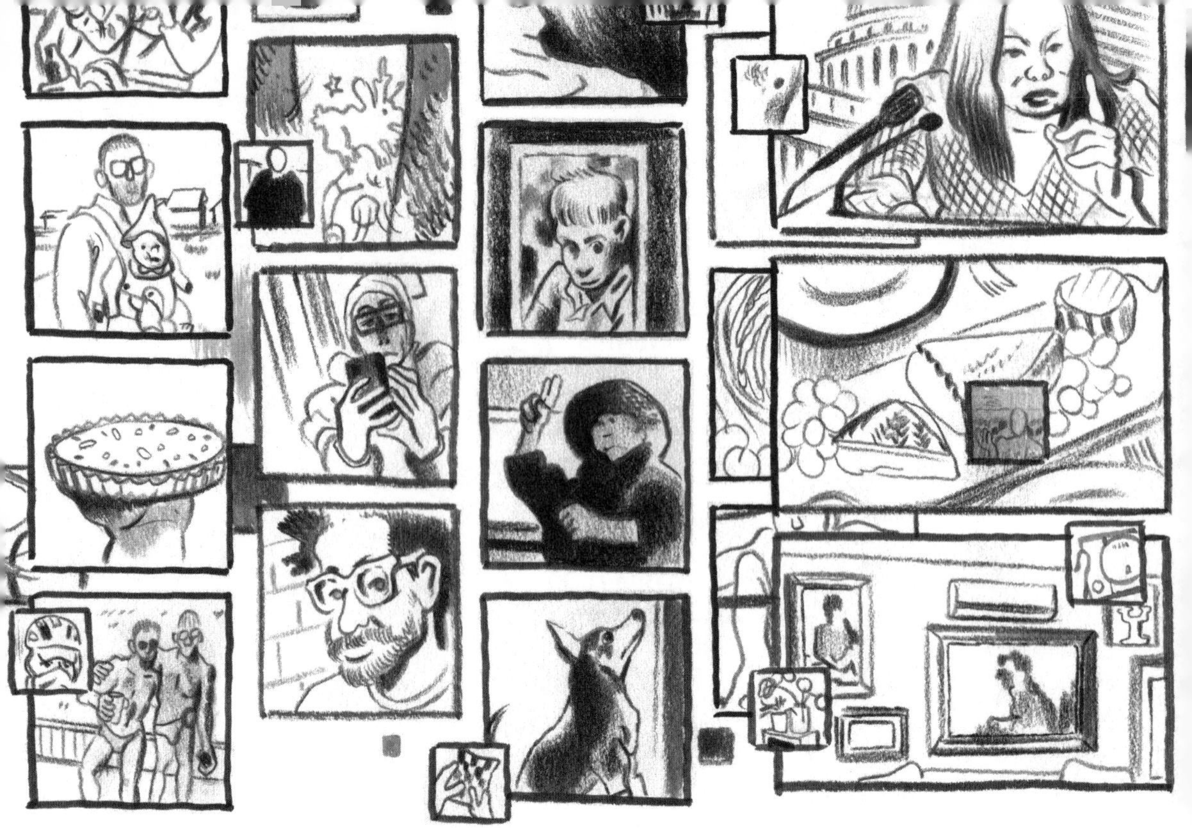

What struck Colin as the most fascinating part of the Internet was how open everyone had been. Even in his small slice of the Internet, there were countless photos to look at, cataloging nearly every part of someone's life—meals they had eaten, outfits they had worn, parties they'd attended, places they had seen, homes they had lived in, and people they had loved.

He found episodes from a television show that followed celebrities around their lavish mansions, penthouses, and vacation homes as they gave a walking tour. Another show where well-deserving people were given the chance to have their homes re-decorated. Sometimes it went poorly. Other times, grown adults would cry unabashedly, standing in front of a home they didn't recognize. It was startling to see someone expose their lives and their person in that way, allowing Colin to walk in and take a look around.

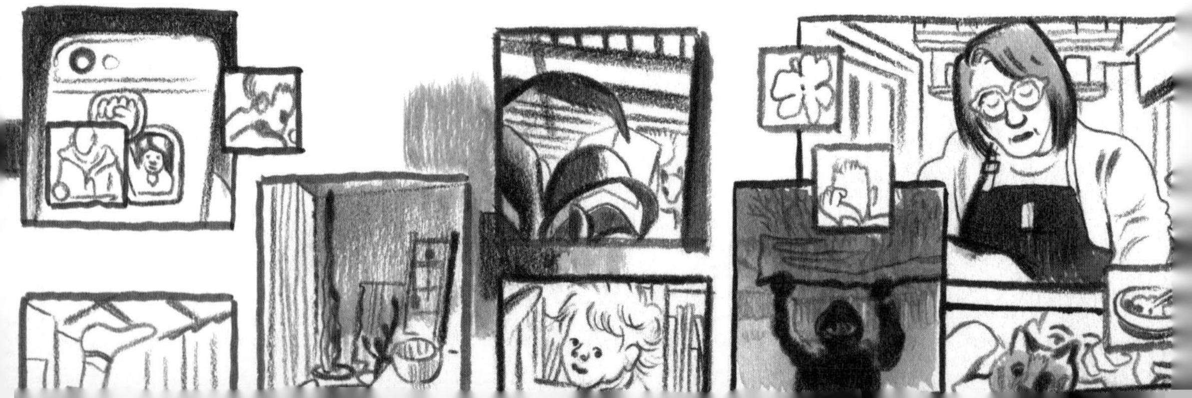

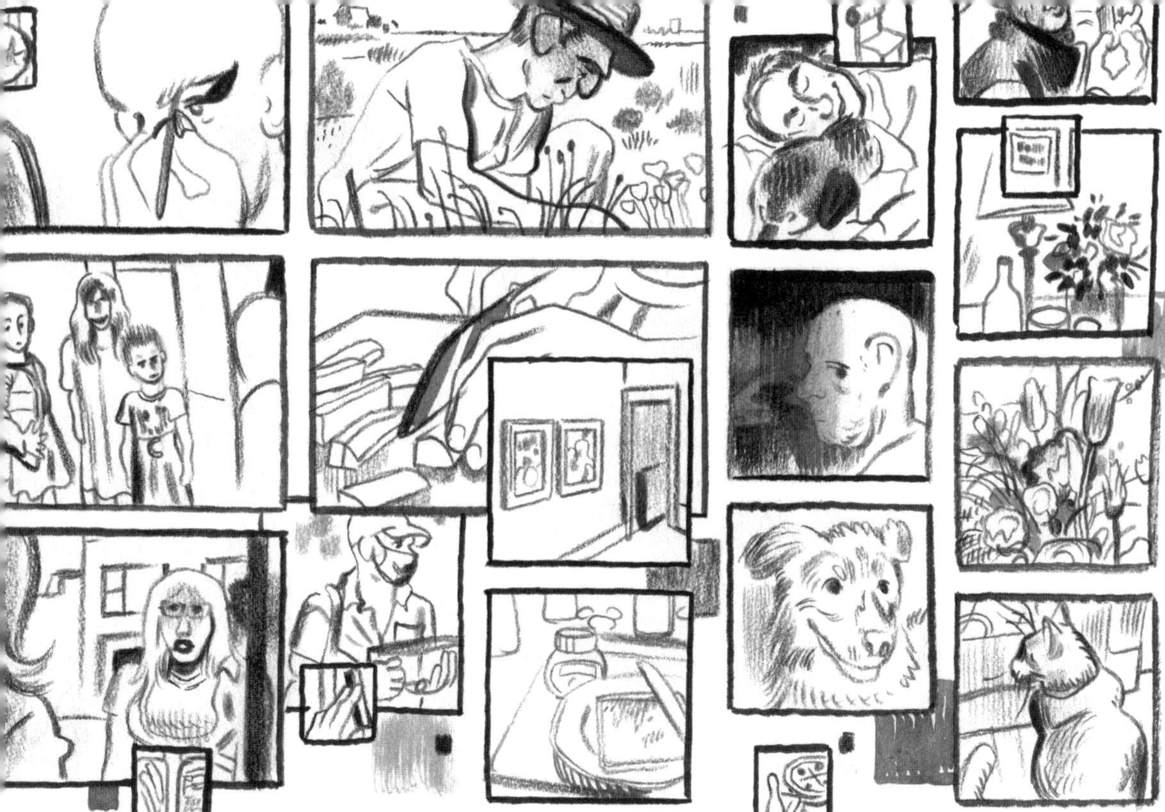

Maybe it was because this experience was new for him, but Colin imagined that watching someone else's life unfold in this way must have been stressful for the viewer. Even from the safe distance of time, he could feel jealousy and anxiety burble up in him while looking through the endless strings of memorable occasions and experiences once shared the whole world over. He was no longer with Paolo, and yet he worried about how they had looked as a couple while comparing himself to the documented lives of the attractive couples he found through his Internet searches.

He ached thinking about the one night they had spent together in Minnie's new home. Who knows what the future would have held for them if that trip hadn't cut short their time together? Wasn't that what made photographs so sad—seeing an oblivious version of yourself preserved for all time,
ignorant to what you know now?

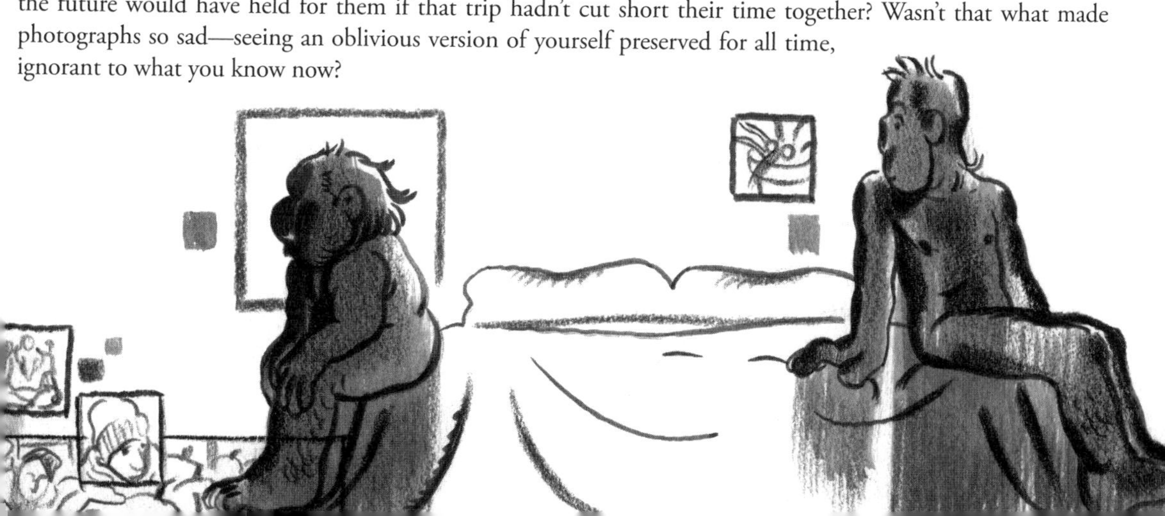

It didn't take long for Colin to discover pornography.

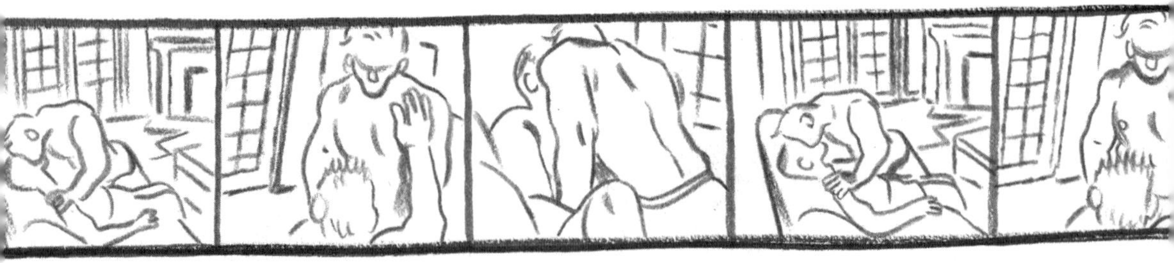

He had known about similar things—Paolo had even written Virtual Reality foreplay games—but not like this. It wasn't so much that the sex was salacious, but that people would choose to record themselves having it—by themselves, with friends, with their romantic partners—preserving it for all time. It made sense that the impulse to document your life for posterity would include *all* parts of it, but the intimacy of these videos—even if it was clear that they were performing—was overwhelming. His face felt flush watching video after video, and he frequently got up to make sure the door was locked.

One time while they were having sex, Paolo had asked Colin to hit him. In the heat of the moment, Colin had hit Paolo with a closed fist, not slapping him with an open palm, which knocked the wind out of him.

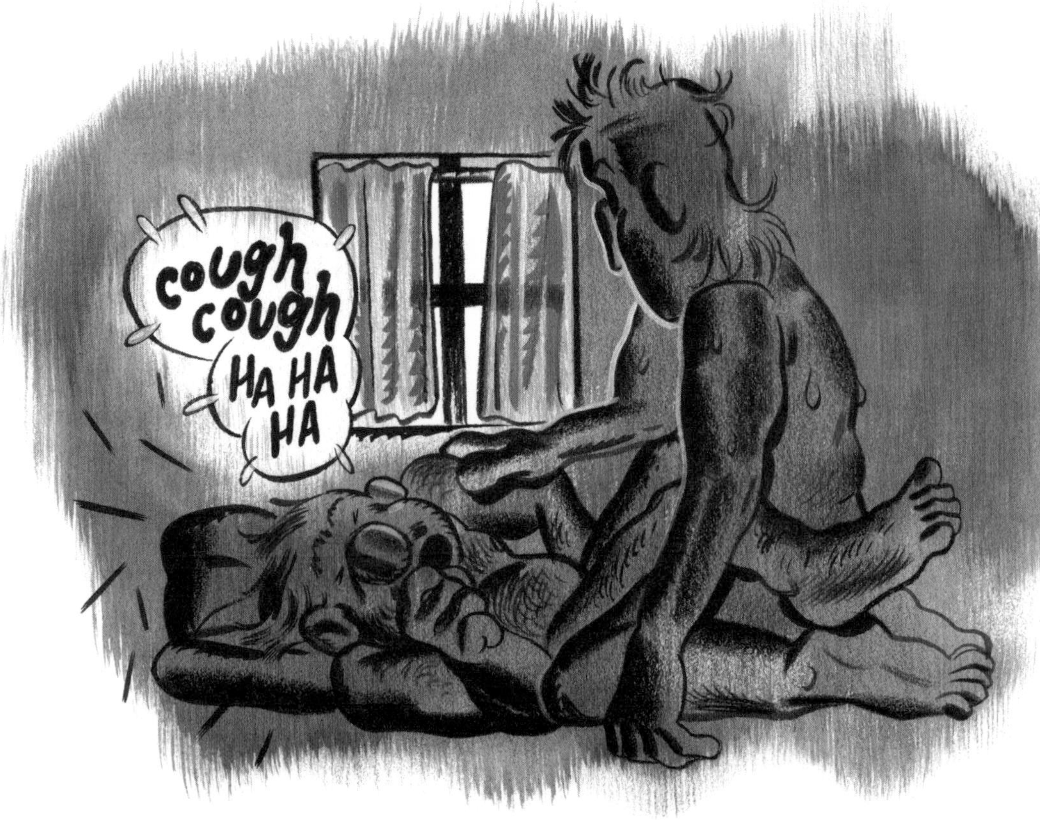
cough, cough
HA HA HA

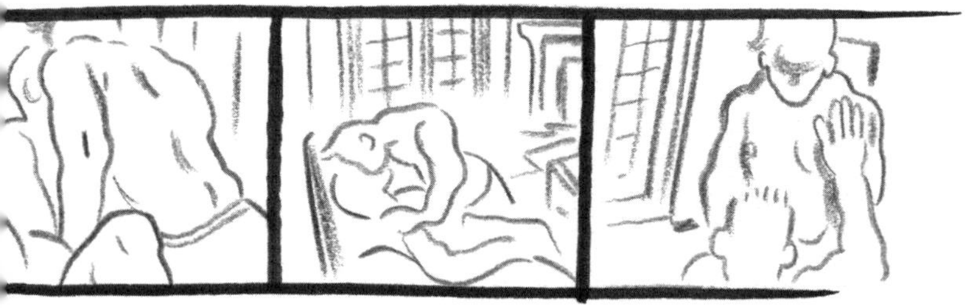

Paolo instinctually tried to save the moment by squeezing in some laughter between his fitful coughs, but Colin was mortified by his mistake. They never spoke about it again, but whenever Colin hit Paolo correctly in the future, the gesture felt too self-aware, almost apologetic, taking them both out of the moment.

Watching these strangers have perfectly orchestrated sex made Colin think of that night he hit Paolo and, in turn, made Colin miss him for the first time since he left.

Colin knew that if he asked, Paolo would say that he had been a great boyfriend. Somehow, this made Colin feel worse, knowing he'd never be able to really believe that. For a moment, he wished this Internet still worked, not so that he could seek out Paolo's reassurance, but just to check in and see that Paolo's life was continuing on, even if it was without him.

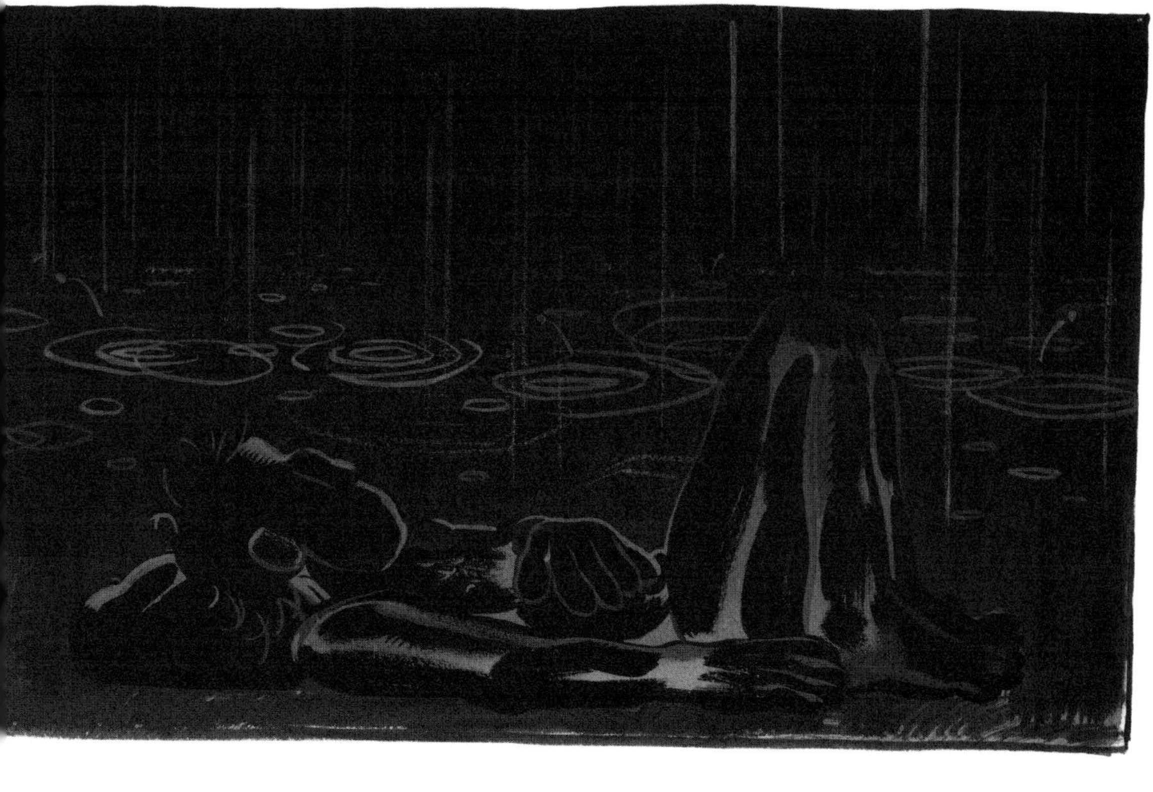

That night it rained.

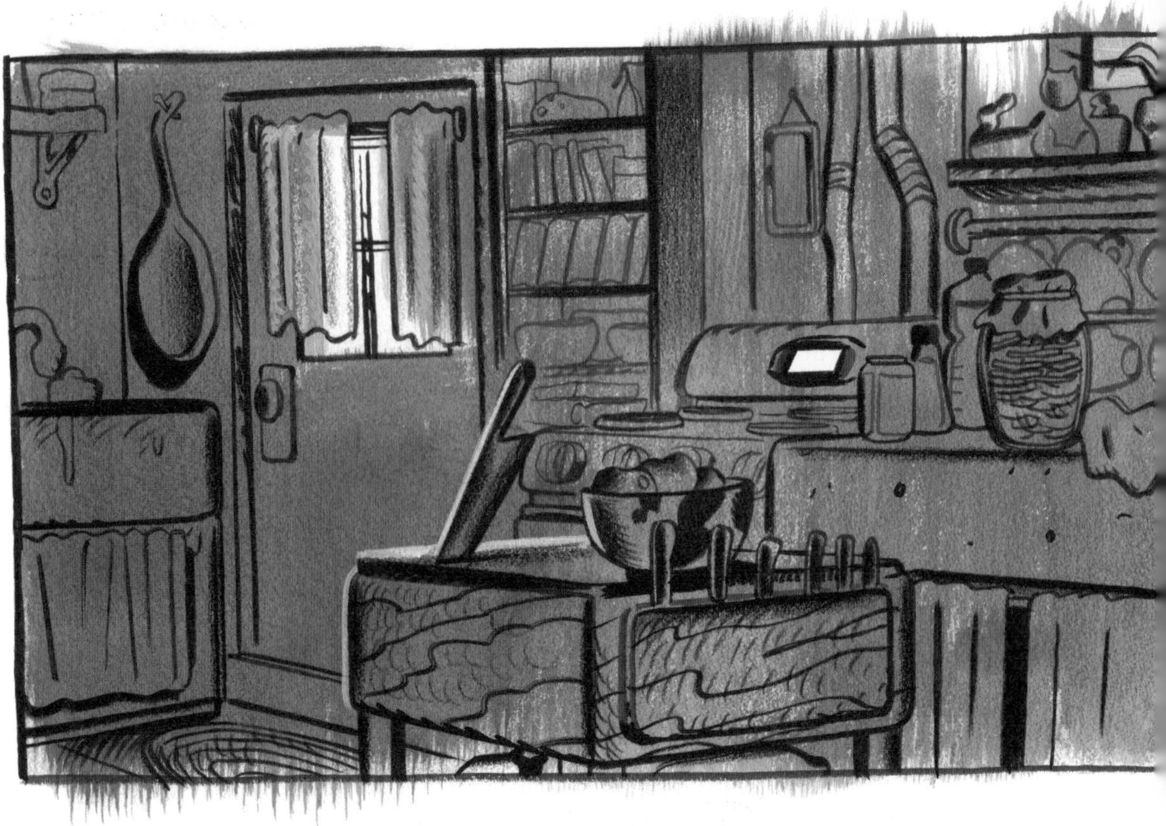

The rain continued on through the morning, preventing Colin from completing any of his outdoor chores. Susan and Bibi left to take their truck into town—with the camper still attached—to resupply. Without anywhere else to take shelter from the rain, Colin was allowed to stay inside the house, spending his day idly surfing the Internet.

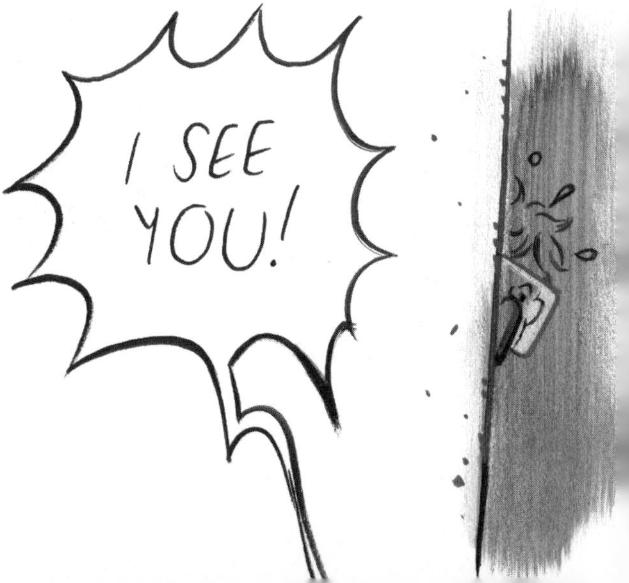
I SEE YOU!

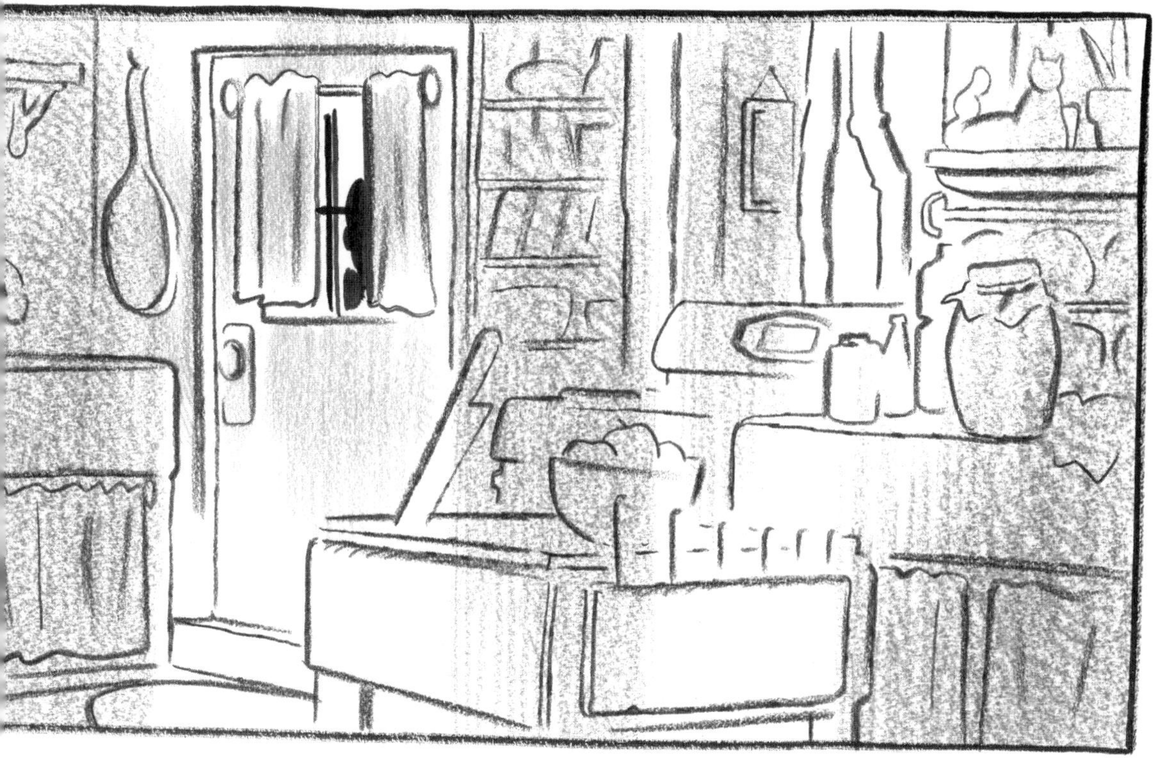

Unexpectedly, Colin heard a knock at the kitchen door. The noise felt louder than usual after two months of quiet.

Colin peeked his head around the door frame of the kitchen, and Famous saw him immediately. Even from a distance, Colin could see Famous's face clench tight in anger.

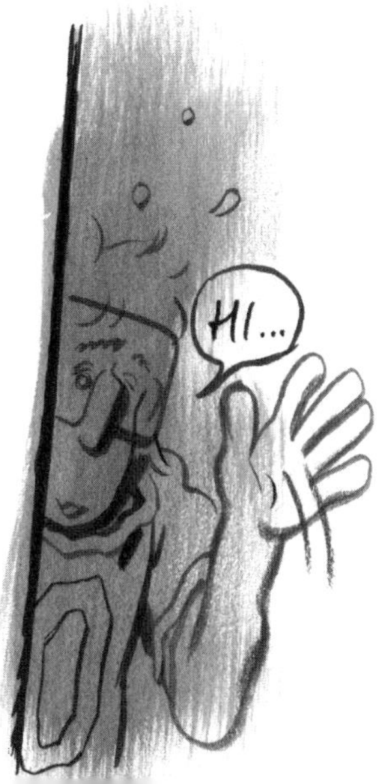
HI...

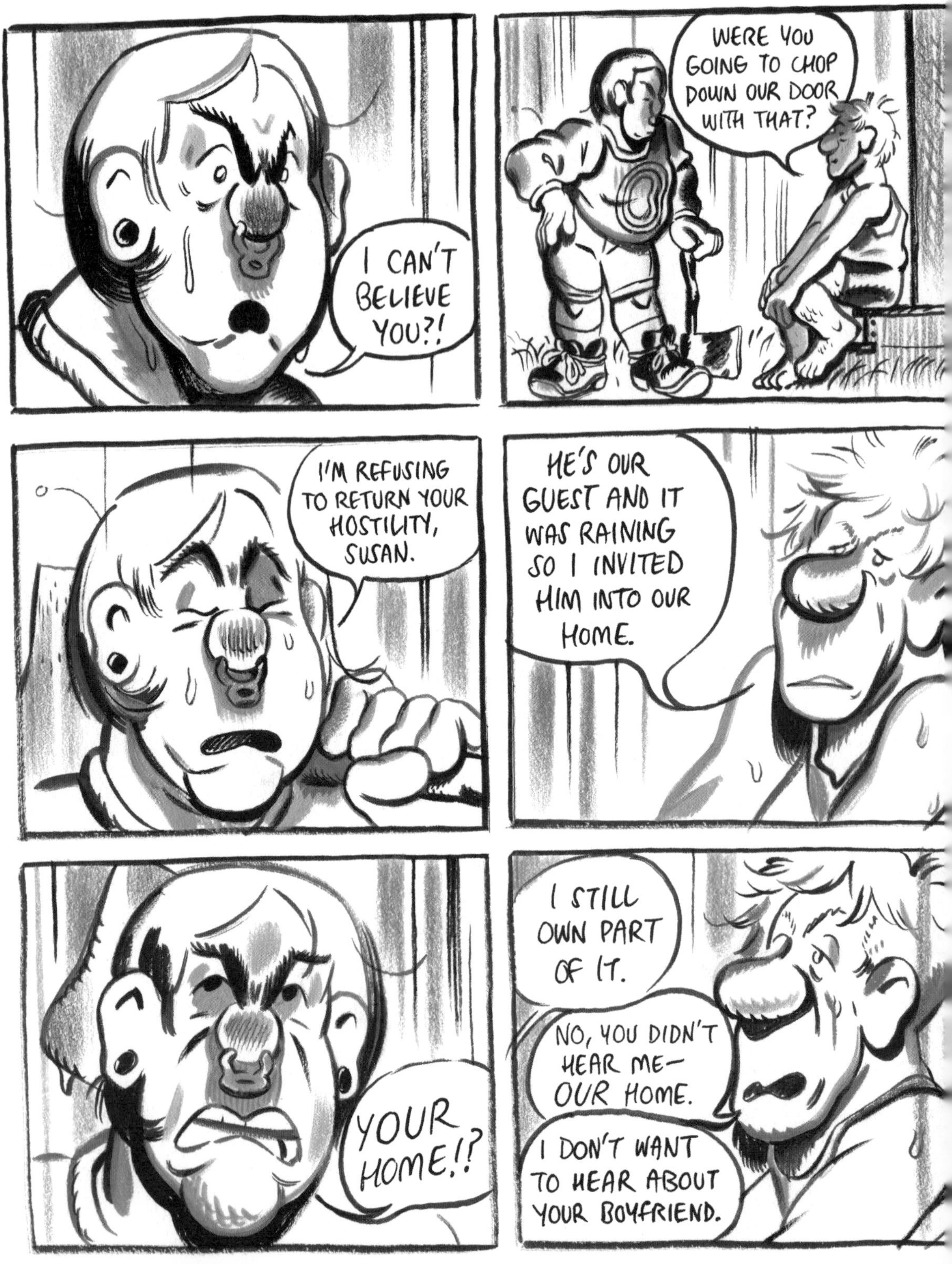
I CAN'T BELIEVE YOU?!
WERE YOU GOING TO CHOP DOWN OUR DOOR WITH THAT?
I'M REFUSING TO RETURN YOUR HOSTILITY, SUSAN.
HE'S OUR GUEST AND IT WAS RAINING SO I INVITED HIM INTO OUR HOME.
YOUR HOME!?
I STILL OWN PART OF IT.
NO, YOU DIDN'T HEAR ME– OUR HOME.
I DON'T WANT TO HEAR ABOUT YOUR BOYFRIEND.

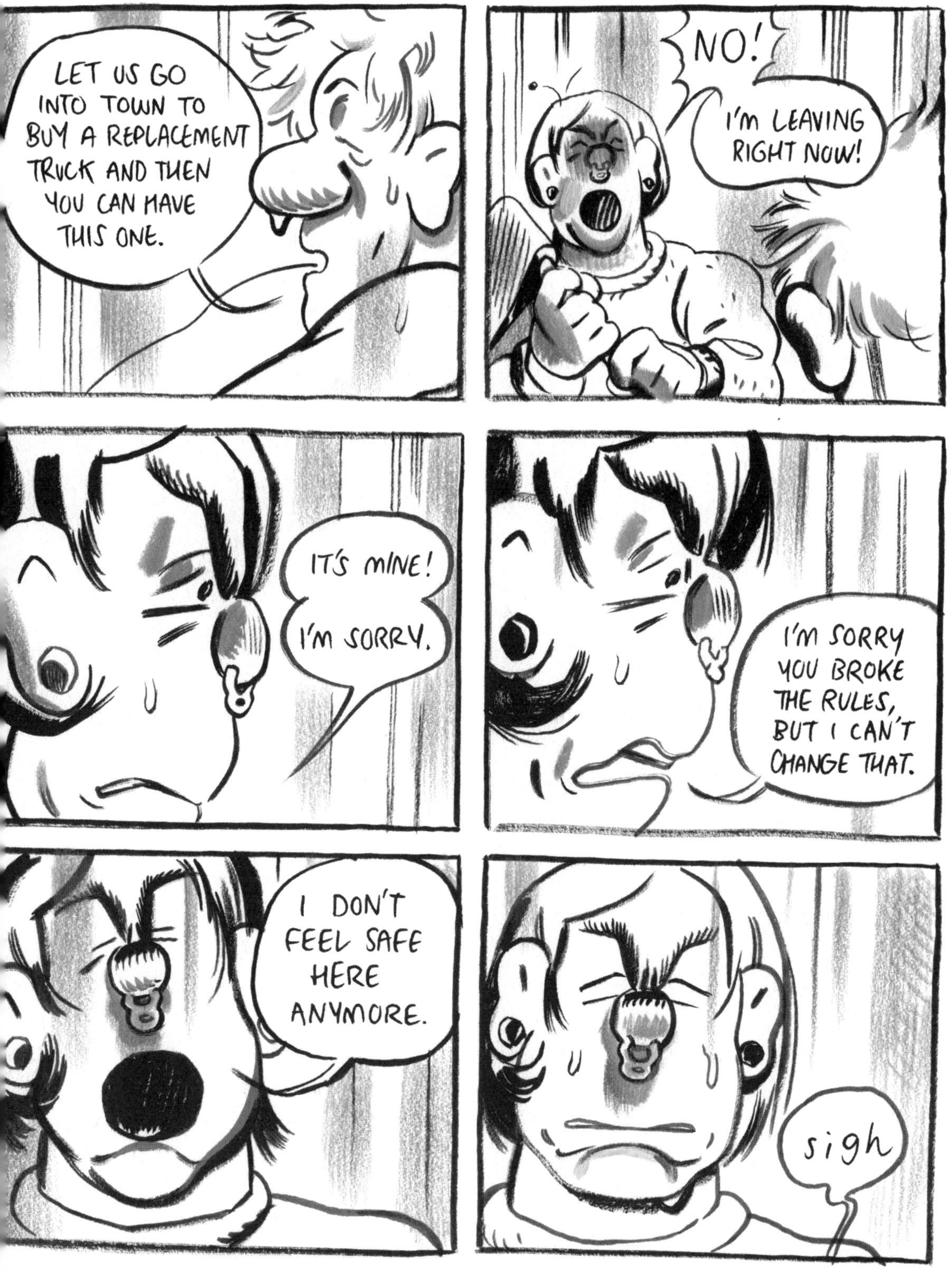
LET US GO INTO TOWN TO BUY A REPLACEMENT TRUCK AND THEN YOU CAN HAVE THIS ONE.
NO!
I'M LEAVING RIGHT NOW!
IT'S MINE!
I'M SORRY.
I'M SORRY YOU BROKE THE RULES, BUT I CAN'T CHANGE THAT.
I DON'T FEEL SAFE HERE ANYMORE.
sigh

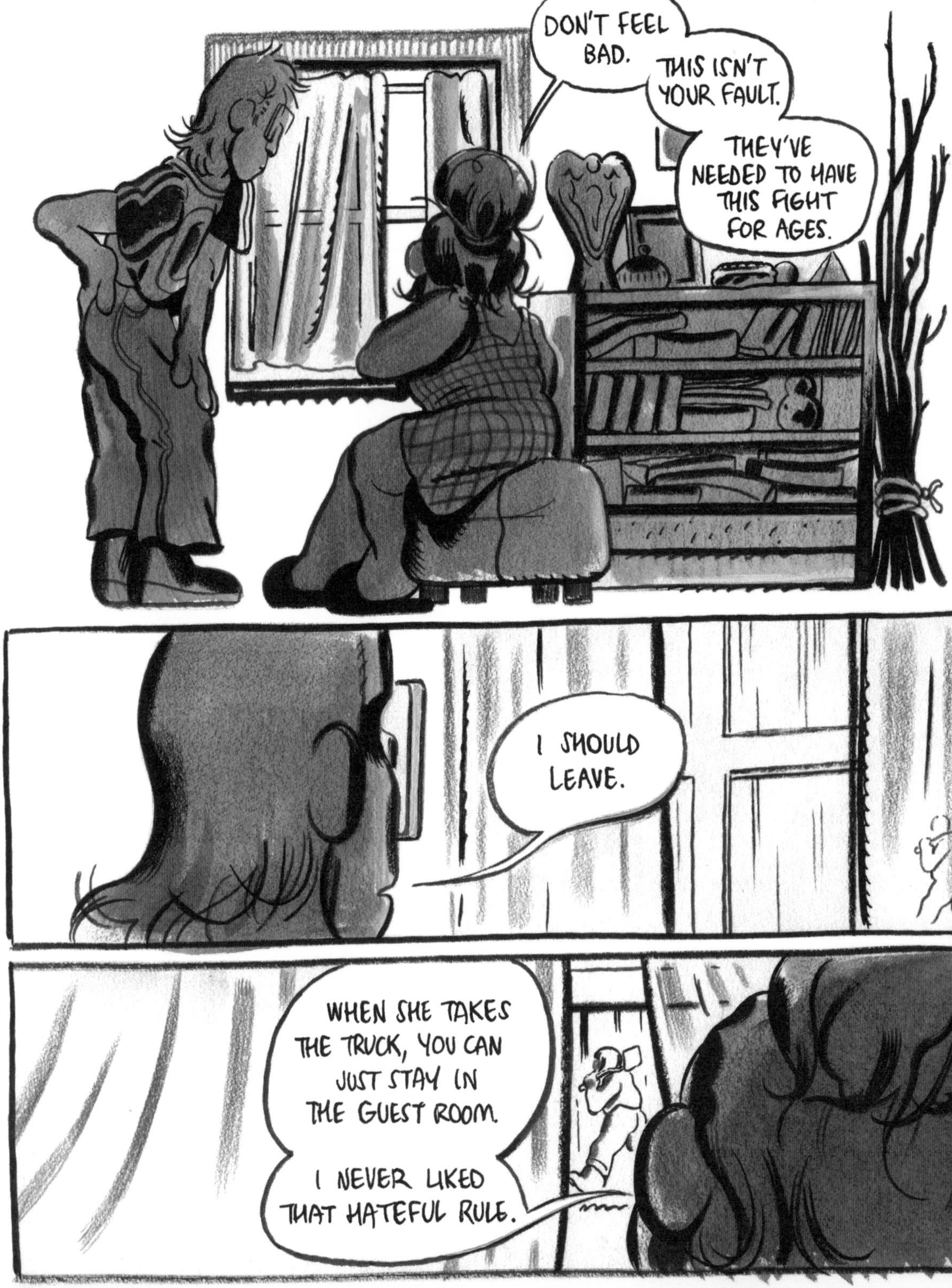
DON'T FEEL BAD.
THIS ISN'T YOUR FAULT.
THEY'VE NEEDED TO HAVE THIS FIGHT FOR AGES.
I SHOULD LEAVE.
WHEN SHE TAKES THE TRUCK, YOU CAN JUST STAY IN THE GUEST ROOM.
I NEVER LIKED THAT HATEFUL RULE.

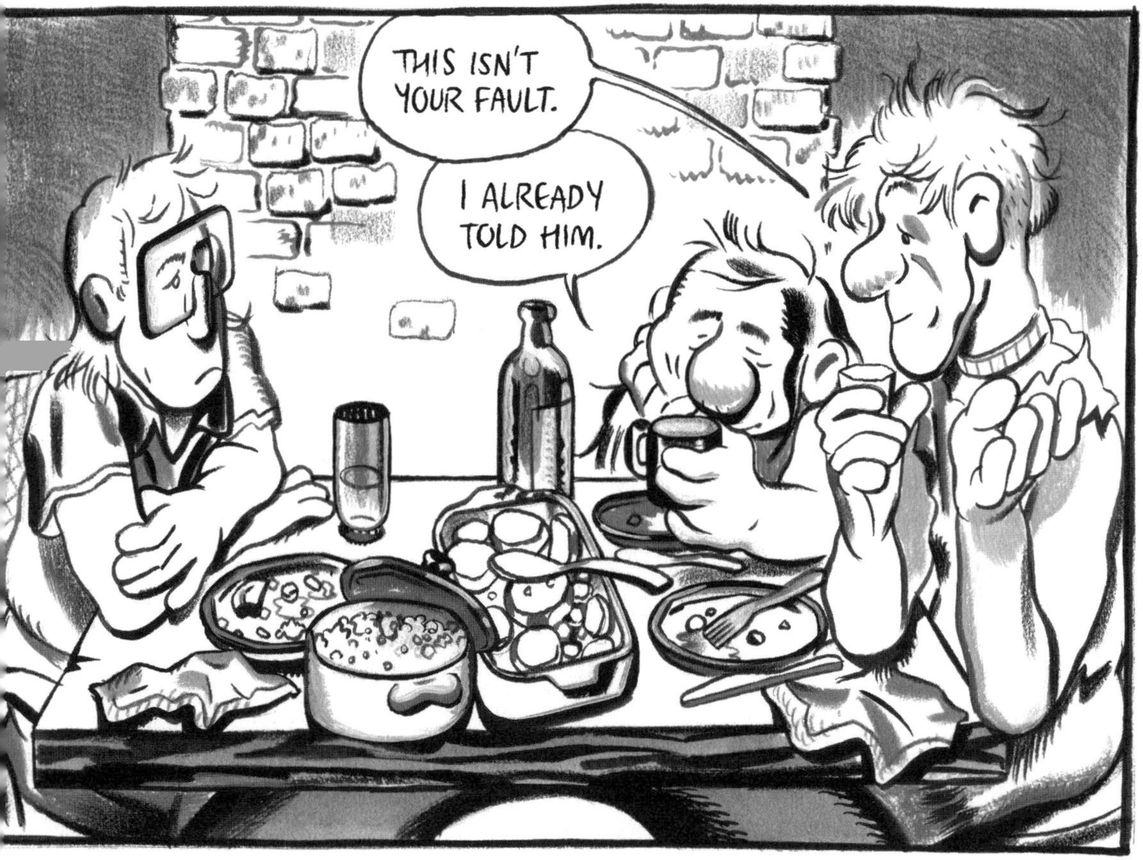
THIS ISN'T YOUR FAULT.
I ALREADY TOLD HIM.

During his brief time living on Susan and Bibi's farm, Colin was staggered by their generosity. They had this incredible ability to intuit his needs. Once, while he was helping them prepare dinner in the kitchen, they caught him looking queasy while holding a carving knife, and quickly moved him to another task. After that, the meals they served never required a knife to eat.

Although there was no denying that Colin was grateful for it, their generosity was beginning to make him feel guilty, despite their reassurances. He couldn't shake the feeling that he had made their lives more difficult by arriving on their doorstep.

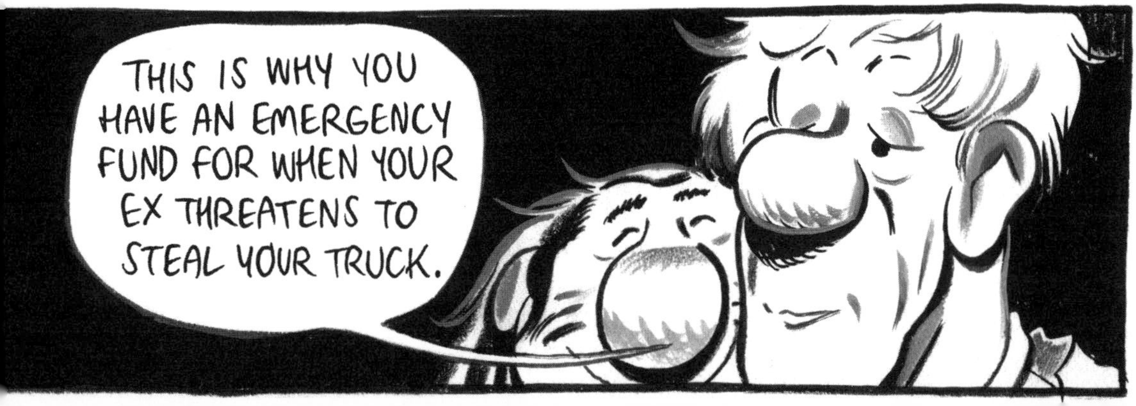
THIS IS WHY YOU HAVE AN EMERGENCY FUND FOR WHEN YOUR EX THREATENS TO STEAL YOUR TRUCK.

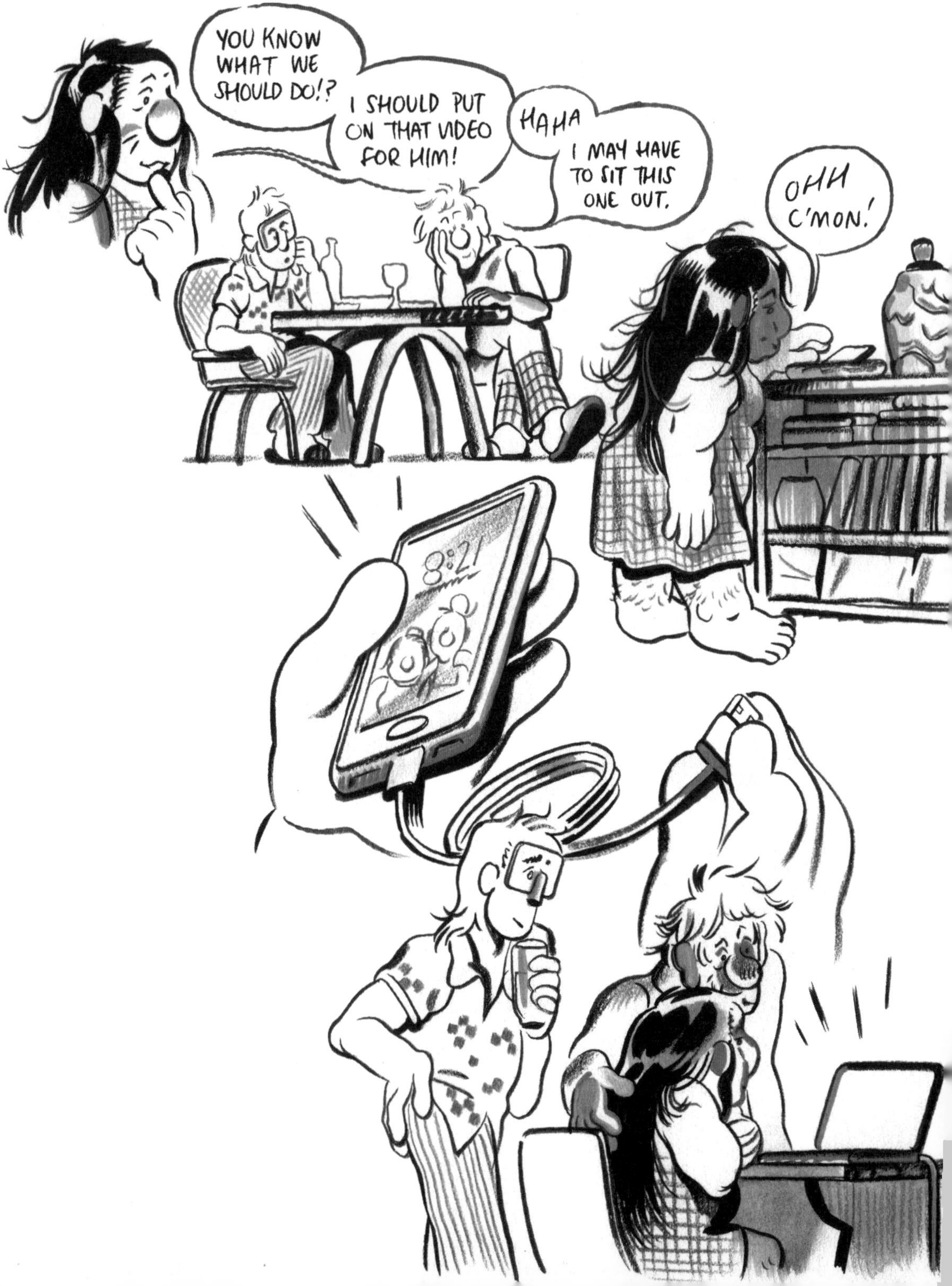
YOU KNOW WHAT WE SHOULD DO!?
I SHOULD PUT ON THAT VIDEO FOR HIM!
HAHA
I MAY HAVE TO SIT THIS ONE OUT.
OHH C'MON!
8:21

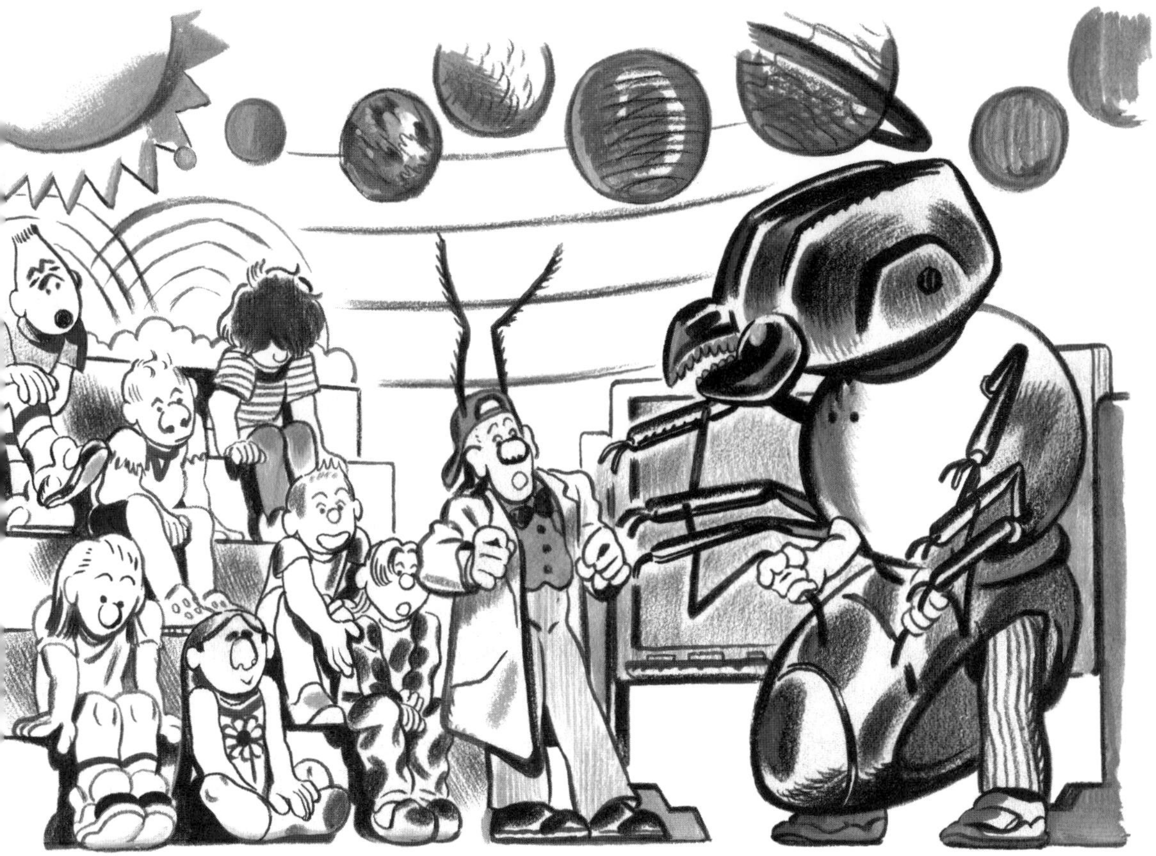

The program, called "The Learning Library," was a low-budget educational television show for children. After the opening credits, Susan came out wearing a long white lab coat and a pair of antennae, and told the kids gathered at her feet everything she knew about ants. She was very young, younger than Colin, back before she had moved out to the countryside. Back before she met Bibi. Even back before Famous.

After Susan relayed some introductory facts about ants, a person wearing a head-to-toe ant costume walked on screen to help the children visualize the different parts of an ant's body. Susan feigned shock for the children, but to any discerning adult it was clear from the gentle, inquisitive inflection in her voice that she knew a giant ant person was about to walk on stage.

Colin, Susan and Bibi re-watched the whole episode together in rapt silence. It was easy to see how much joy Bibi felt watching her partner do what she did best. Colin wondered if Susan was disappointed over having left her life as a research scientist behind. *Did she miss ants? Did she wonder what she would have found if the Administration had just left her team alone?* Colin realized that Bibi hadn't put the show on for him, but to cheer up Susan. To remind her of the joy she had once known, of the good she had accomplished, to help assuage her current stress.

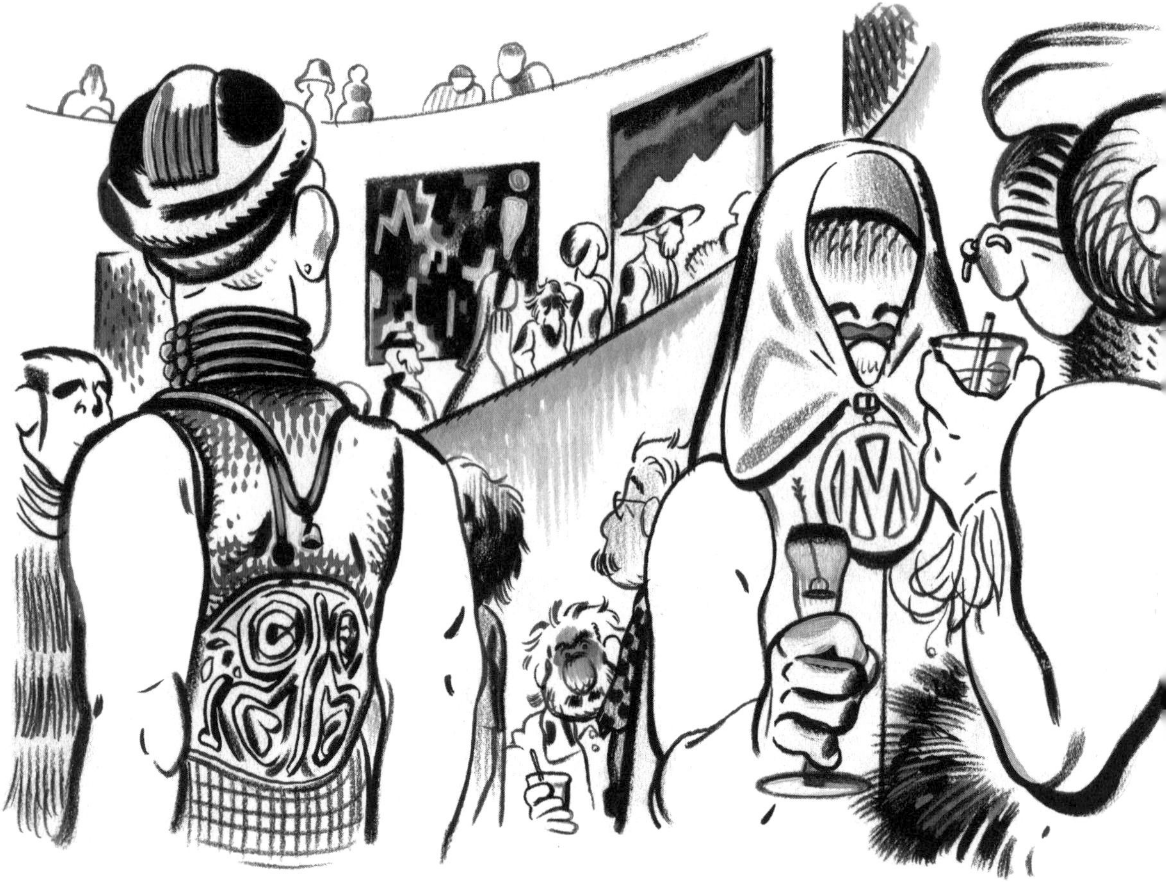

That night in the camper, Colin thought of all the times Paolo had attended the events Colin helped organize for the arts council. He'd be busy working—delegating to the hired waiters about which trays of hor d'oeuvres to bring out when, explaining to some patron with a lot of money what some artist had intended something to mean—when he'd look up and see Paolo from across the room, his boyfriend's eyes already looking his way, smiling widely, soaking up Colin from a distance.

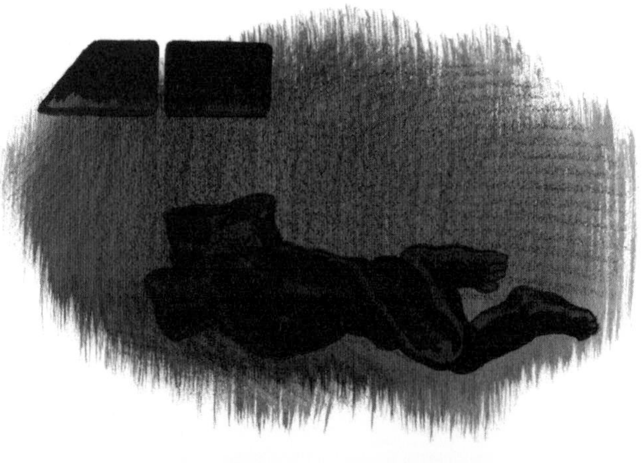

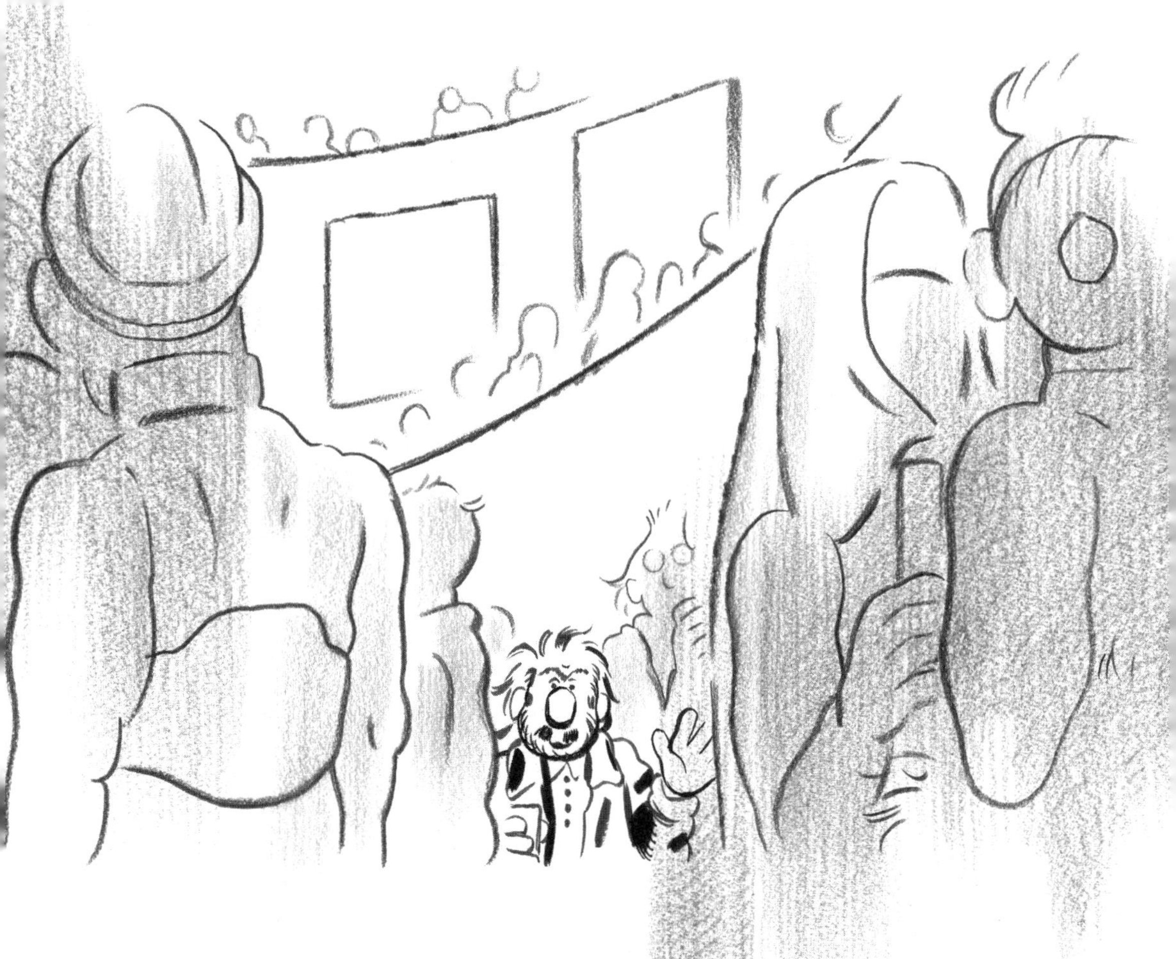

The following morning, Colin didn't get a wake-up knock like he normally did. It was usually Susan who would knock, letting him know breakfast was ready—a meal they ate obscenely early, which he still struggled to wake himself up for even after two months.

The gentle sway of the RV as it was driven down the highway kept Colin asleep longer than usual. When he did wake up, he was nowhere near Susan and Bibi's farm.

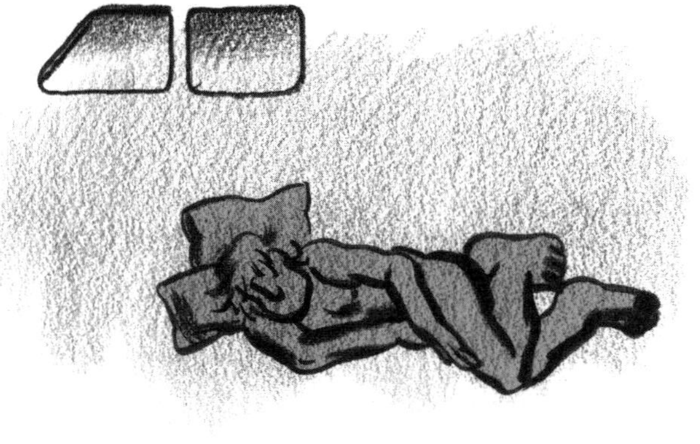

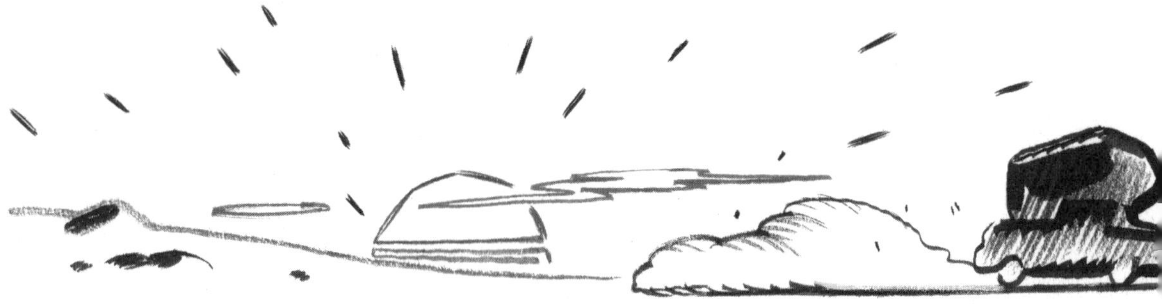

Suddenly terrified of falling off the truck, Colin began to shout. The truck hit potholes and he thrashed about, unable to steady himself in the moving vehicle.

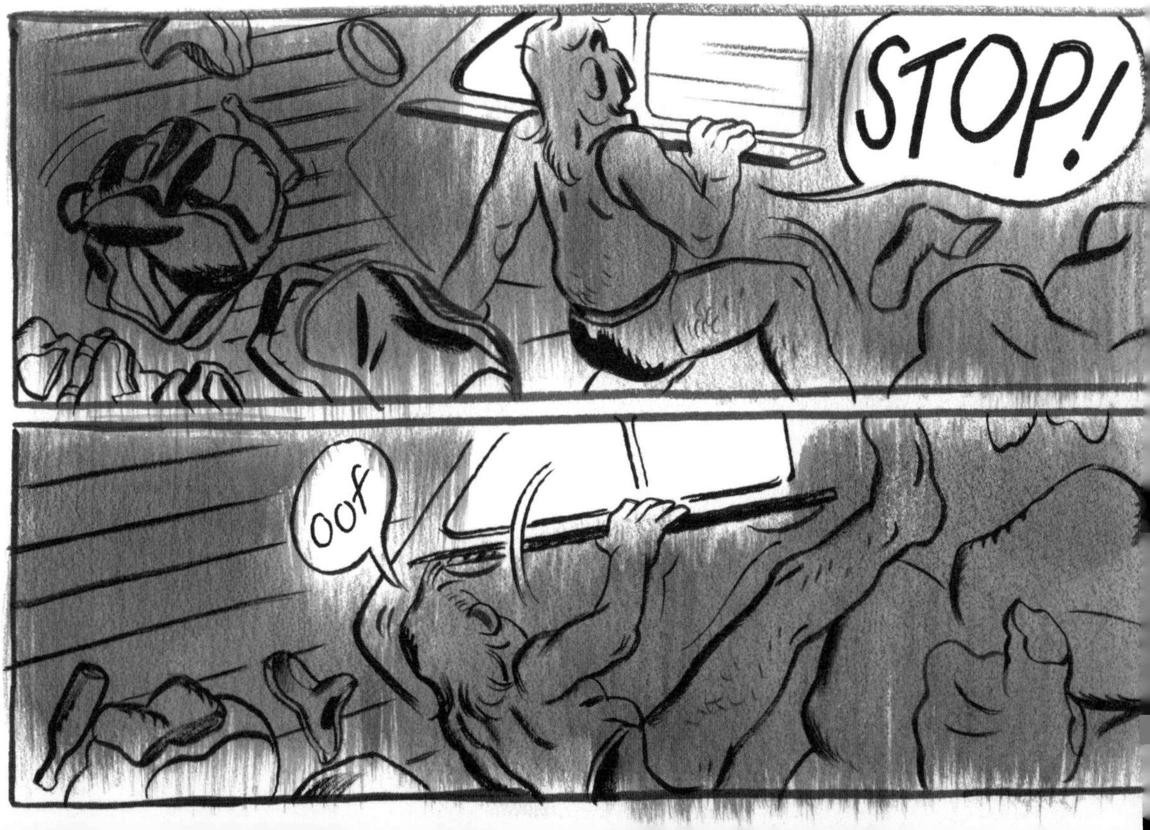
STOP!
oof

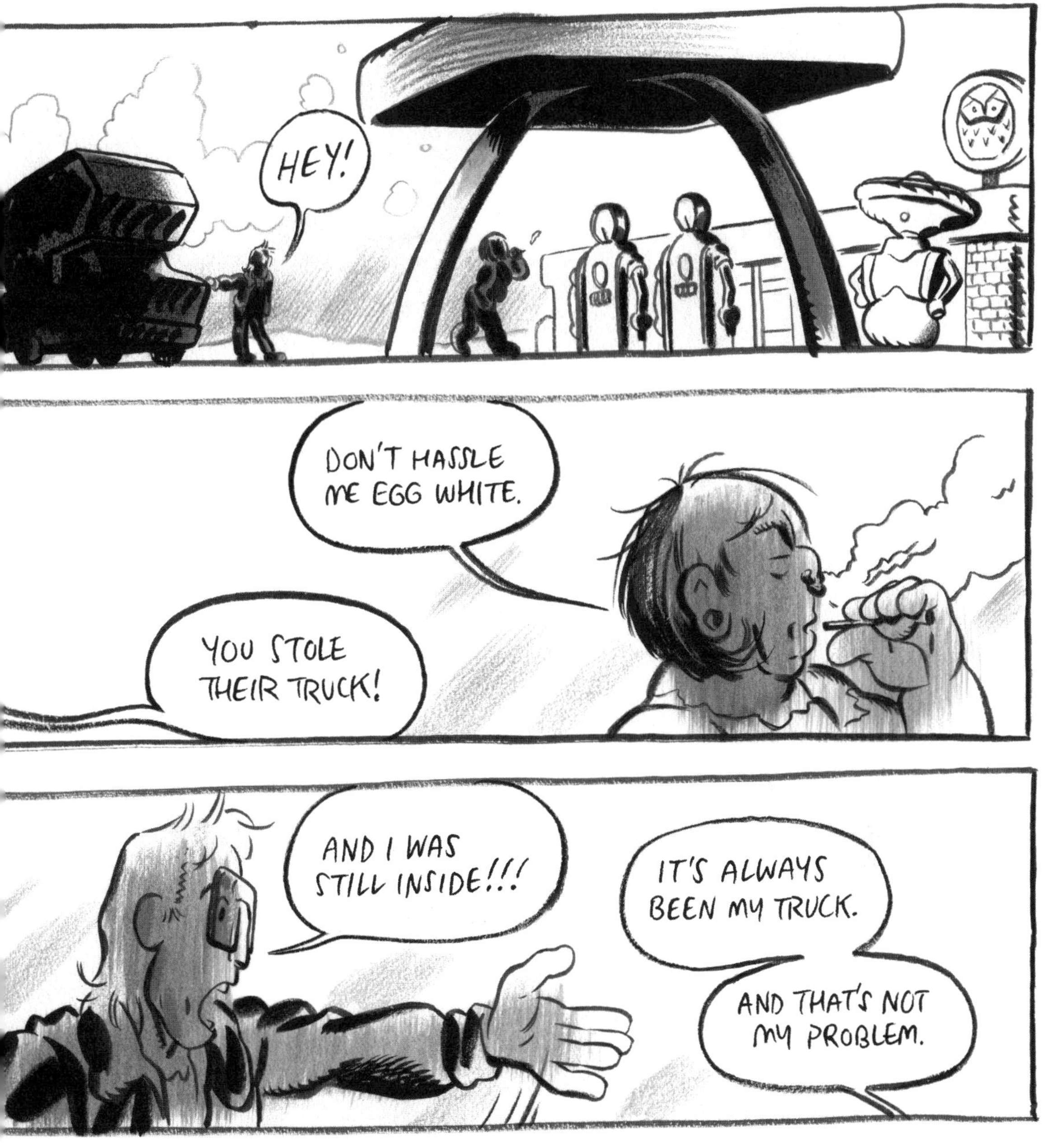
HEY!
DON'T HASSLE ME EGG WHITE.
YOU STOLE THEIR TRUCK!
AND I WAS STILL INSIDE!!!
IT'S ALWAYS BEEN MY TRUCK.
AND THAT'S NOT MY PROBLEM.

The morning was already too hot. He could feel the sweat starting to collect on the inside of his leather jacket.

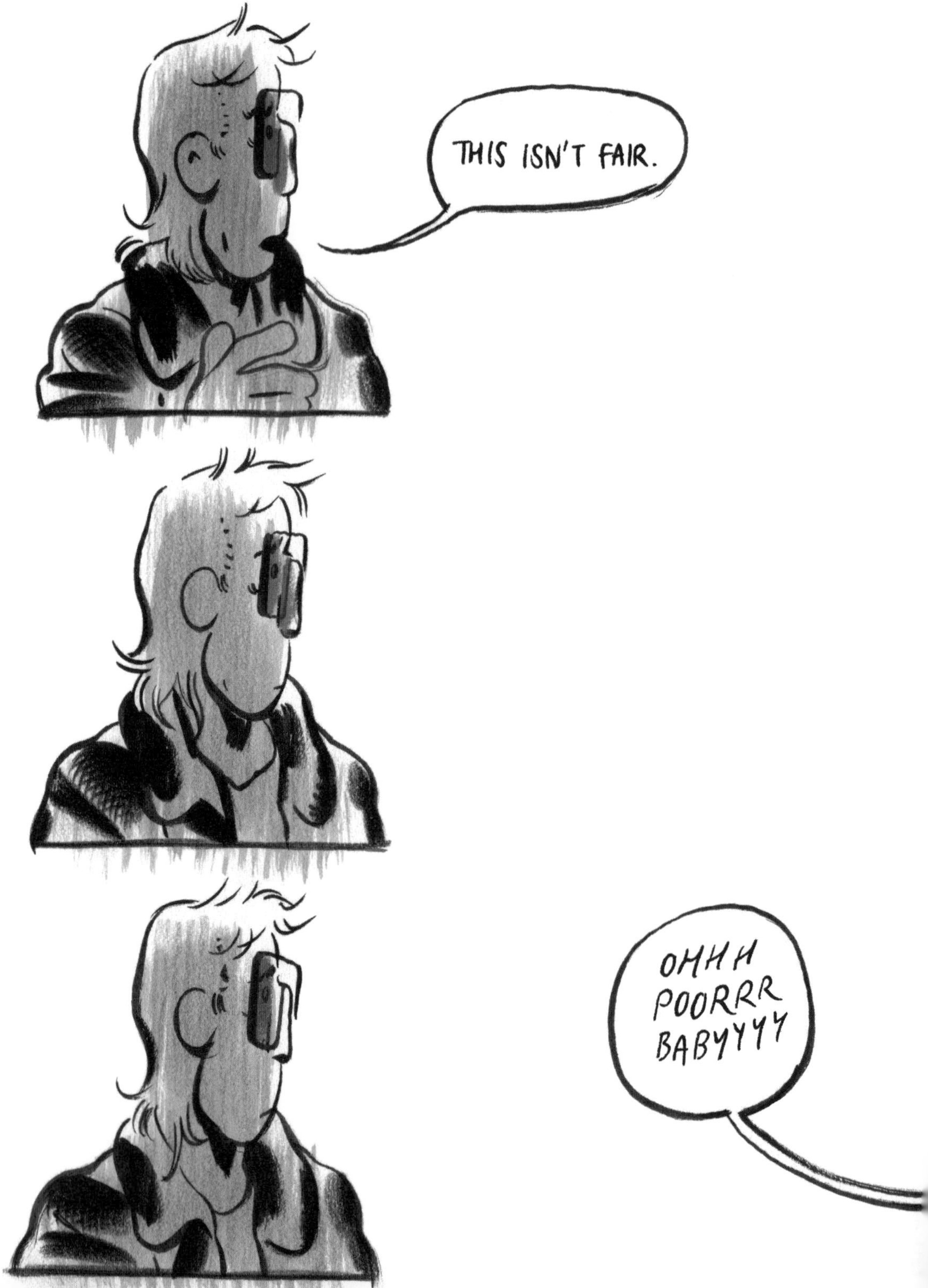
THIS ISN'T FAIR.
OHHH POORRR BABYYYY

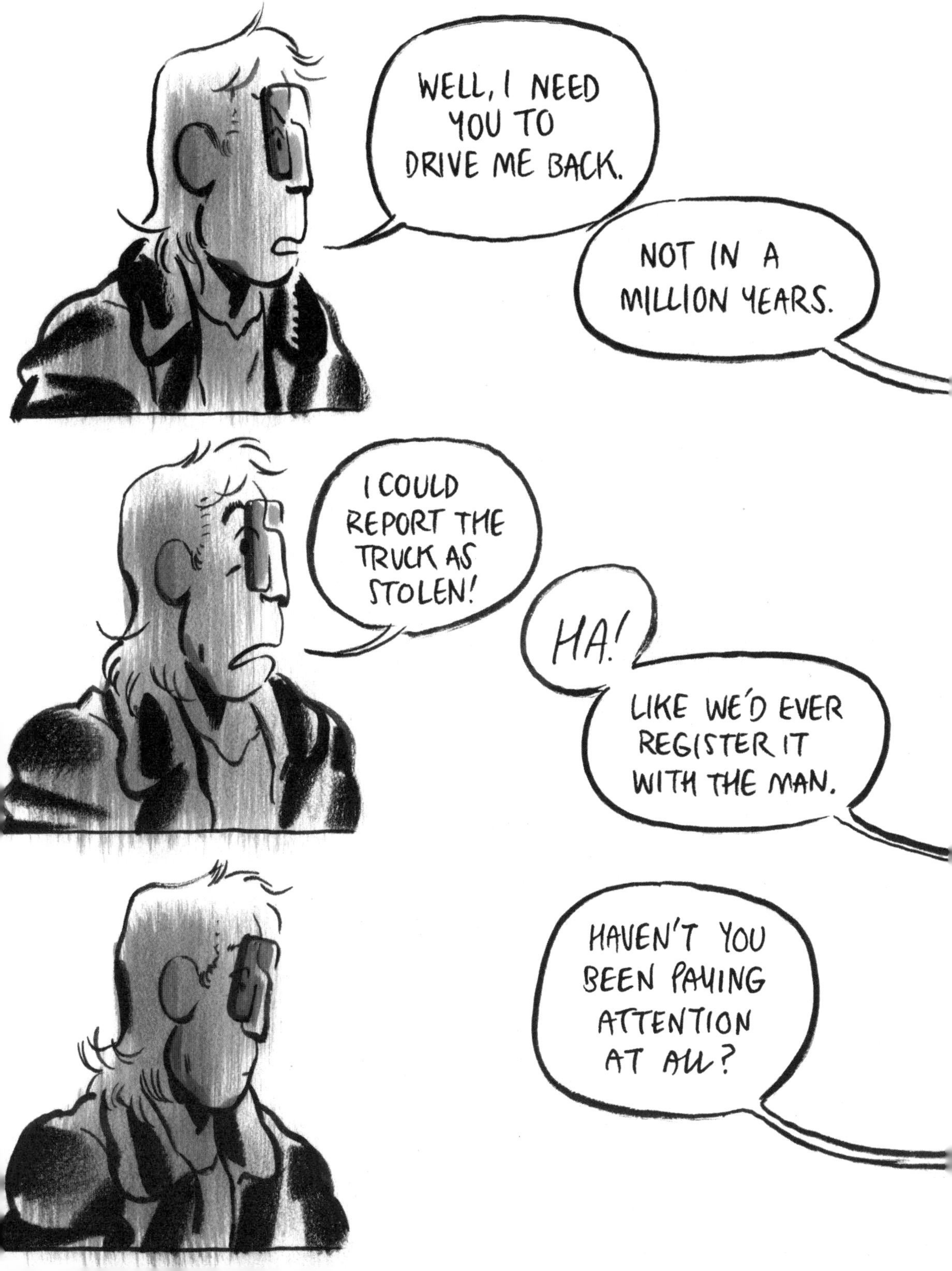
WELL, I NEED YOU TO DRIVE ME BACK.
NOT IN A MILLION YEARS.
I COULD REPORT THE TRUCK AS STOLEN!
HA!
LIKE WE'D EVER REGISTER IT WITH THE MAN.
HAVEN'T YOU BEEN PAYING ATTENTION AT ALL?

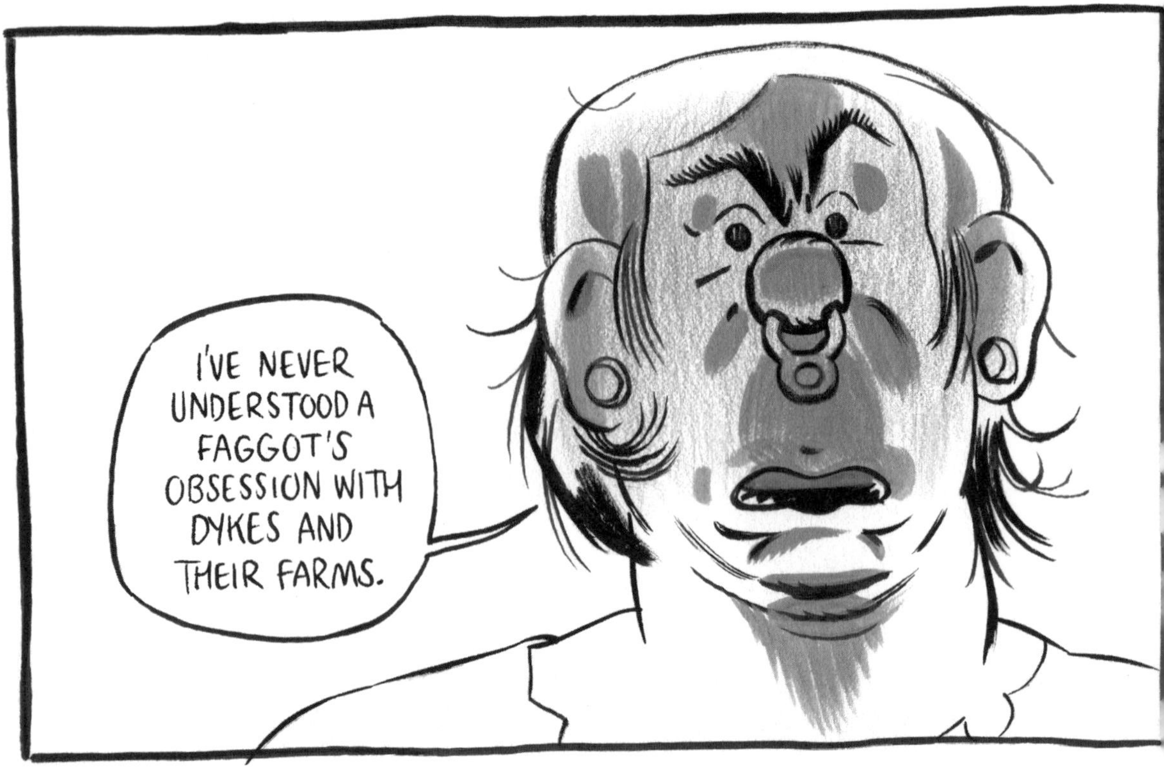
I'VE NEVER UNDERSTOOD A FAGGOT'S OBSESSION WITH DYKES AND THEIR FARMS.
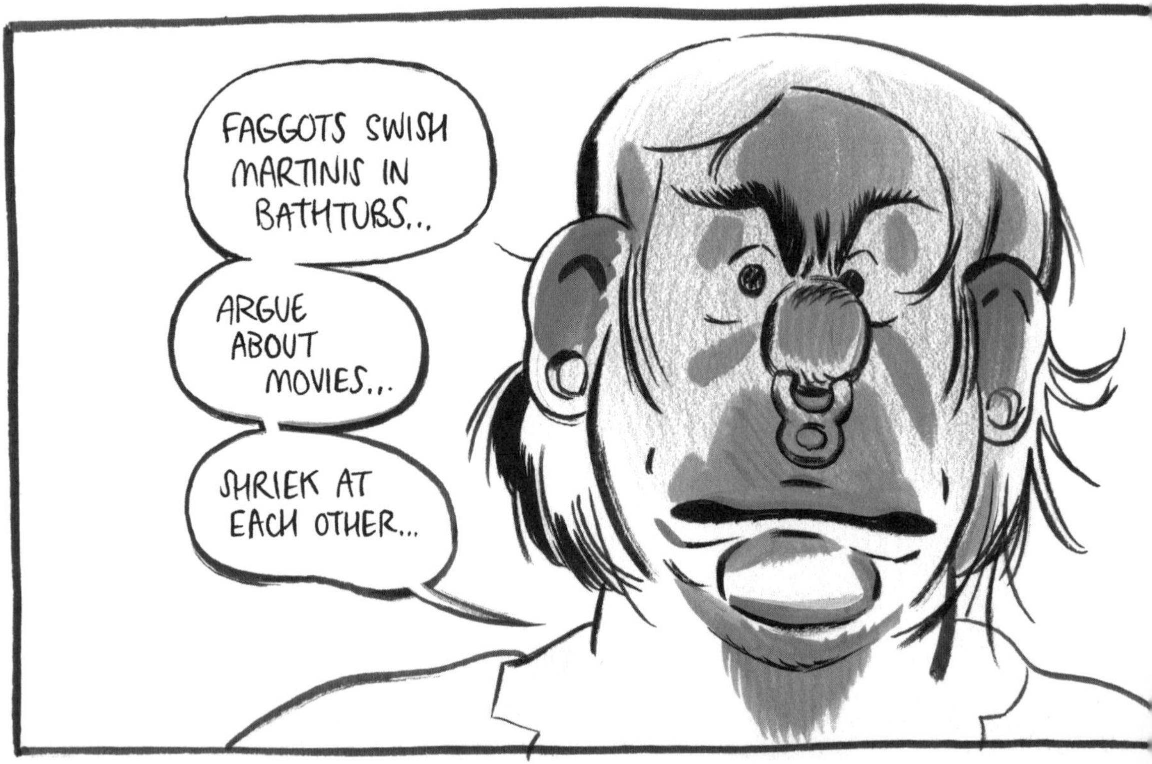
FAGGOTS SWISH MARTINIS IN BATHTUBS...
ARGUE ABOUT MOVIES...
SHRIEK AT EACH OTHER...

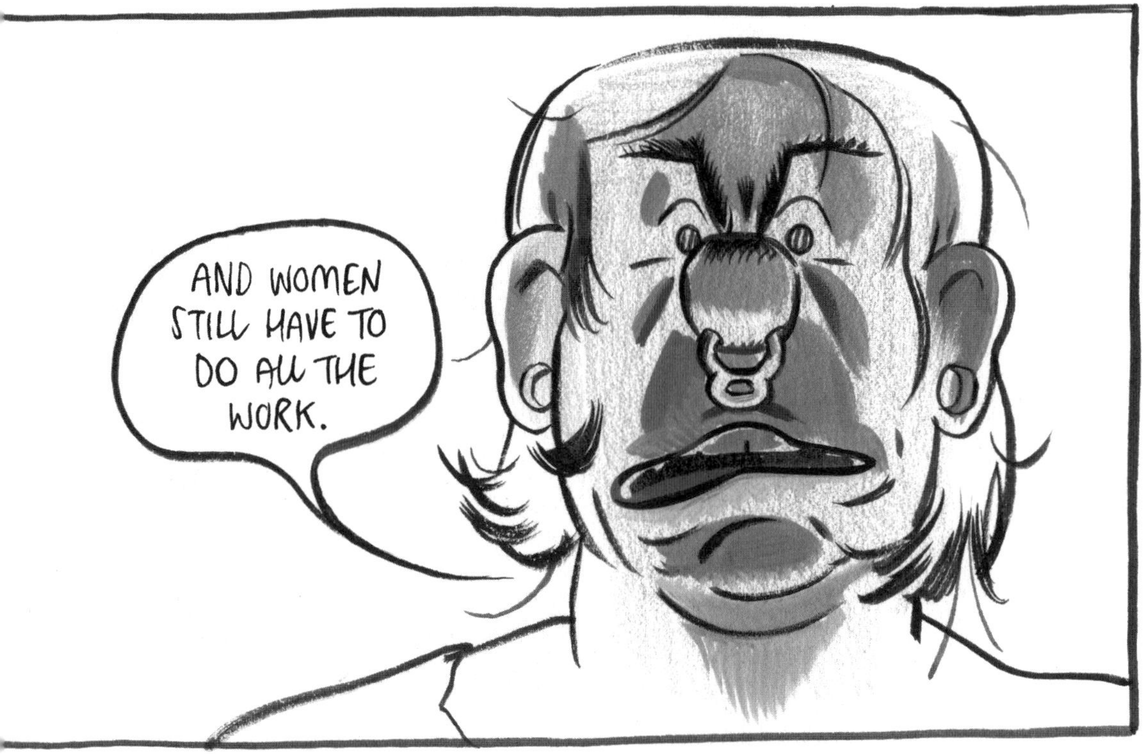
AND WOMEN STILL HAVE TO DO ALL THE WORK.
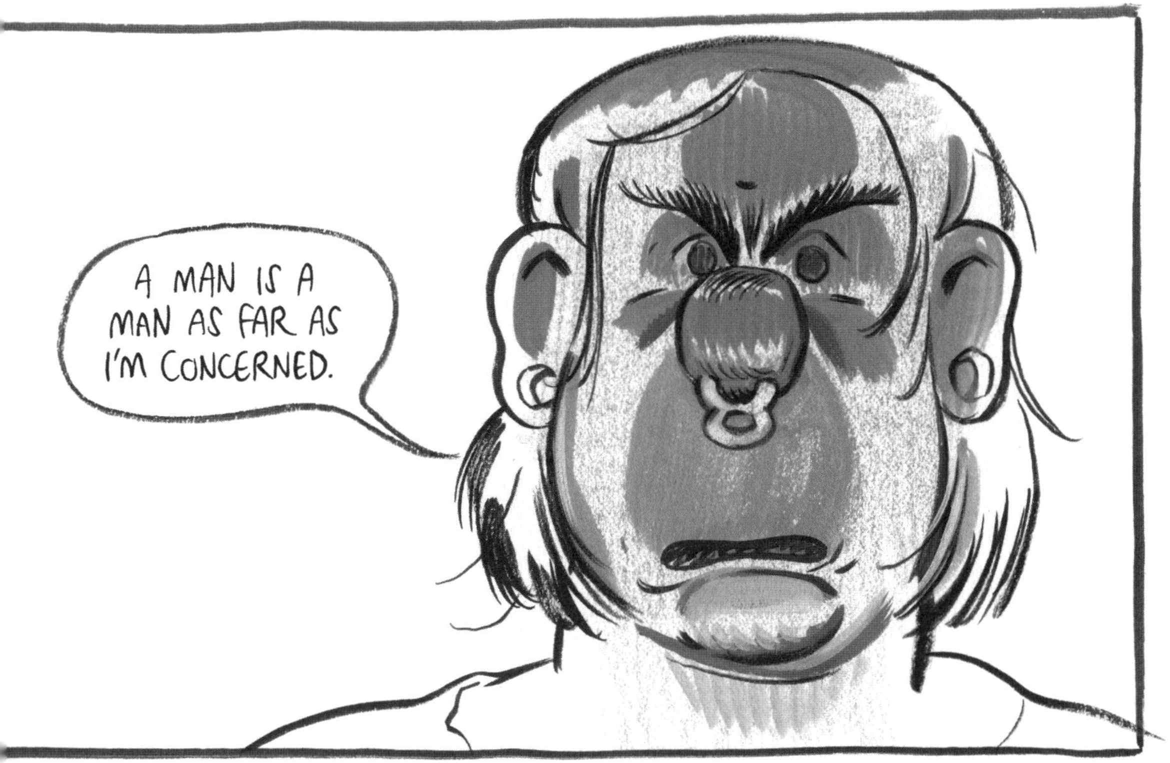
A MAN IS A MAN AS FAR AS I'M CONCERNED.

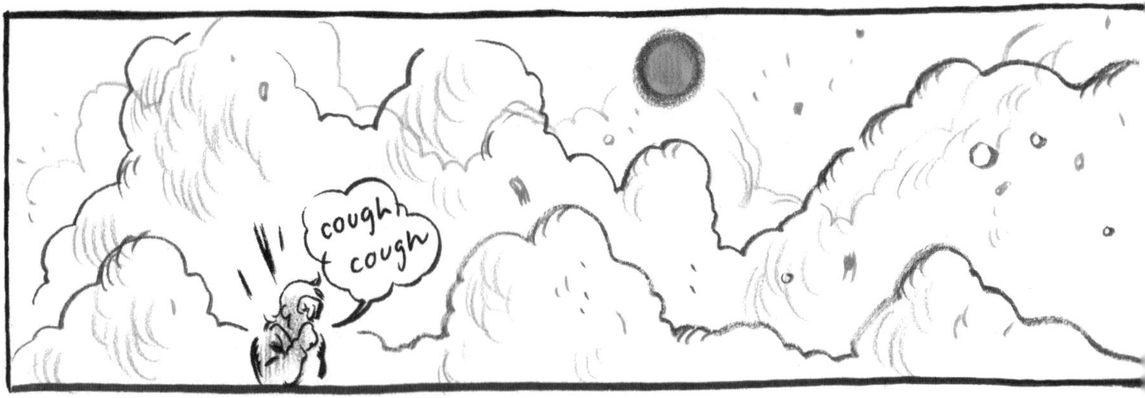
cough cough

And with that, she was gone.

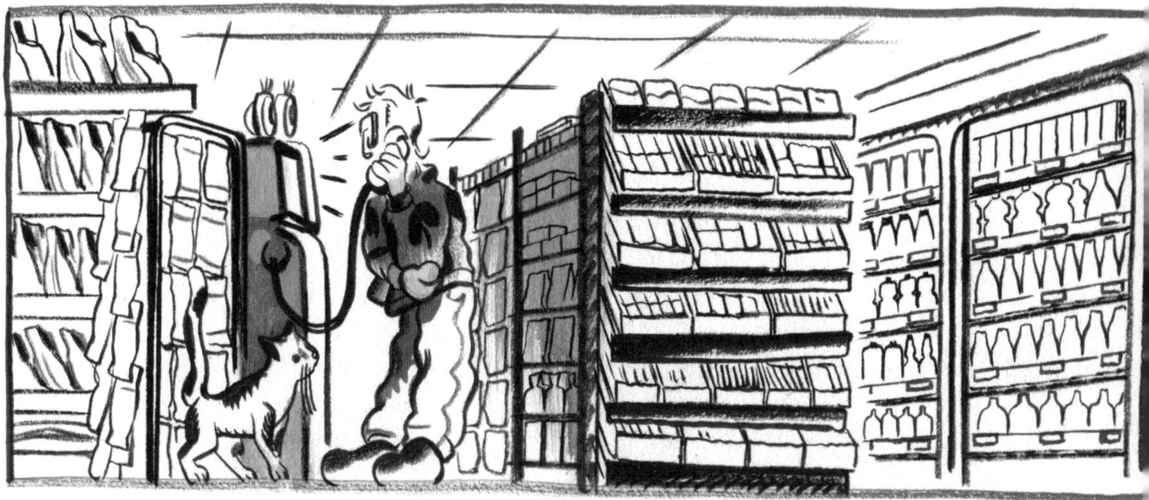

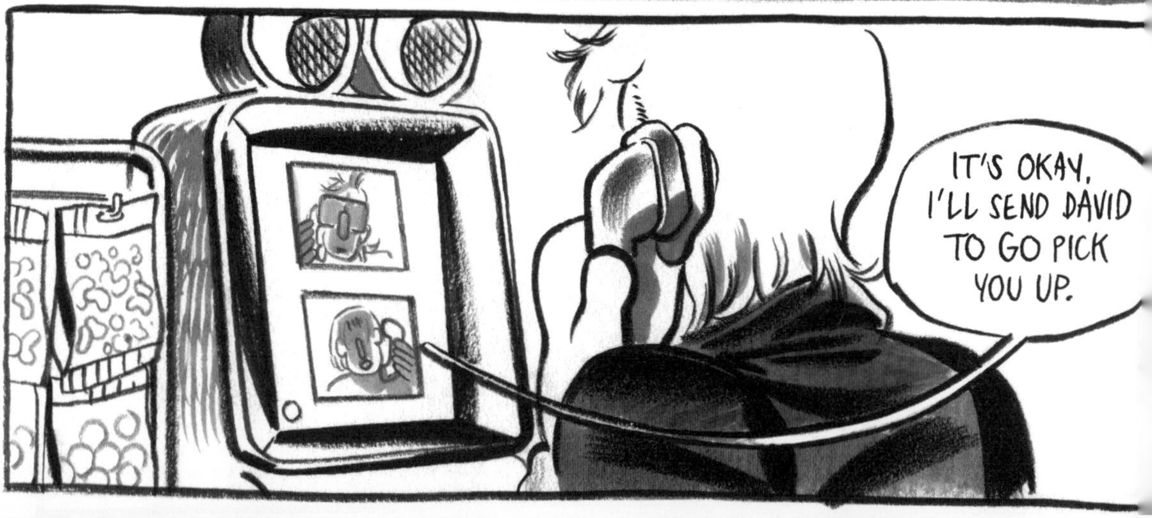
IT'S OKAY, I'LL SEND DAVID TO GO PICK YOU UP.

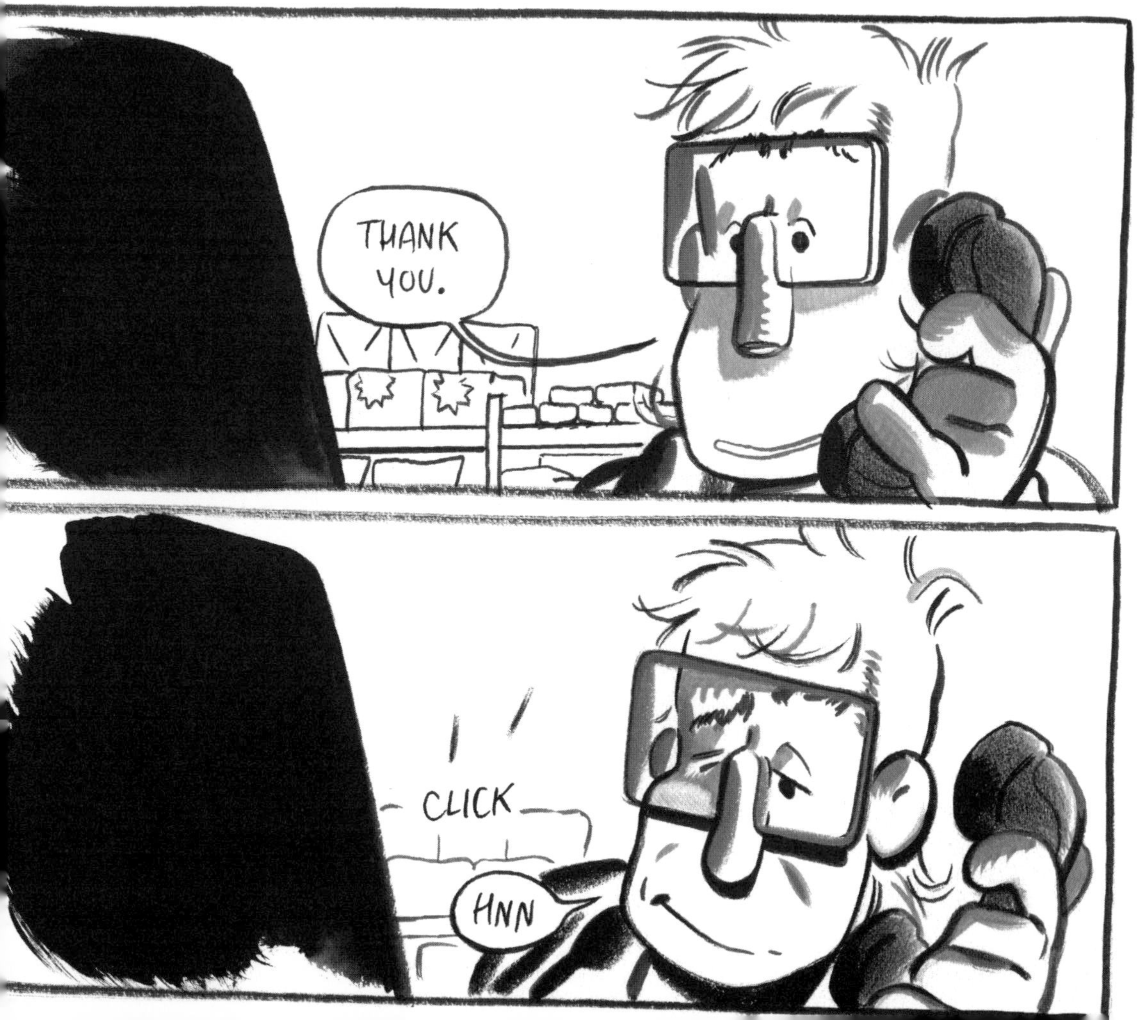
THANK YOU.
CLICK
HNN

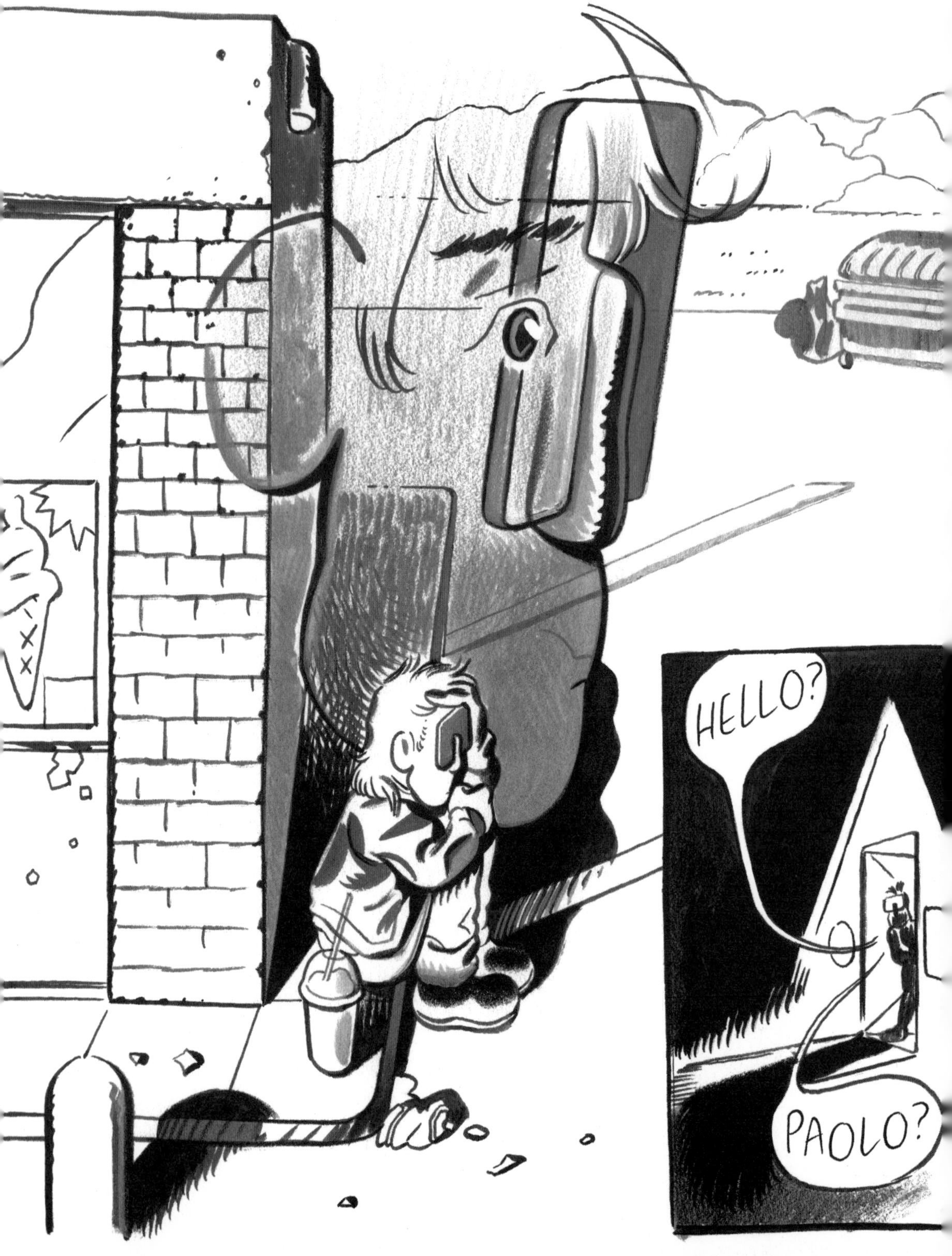
HELLO?
PAOLO?

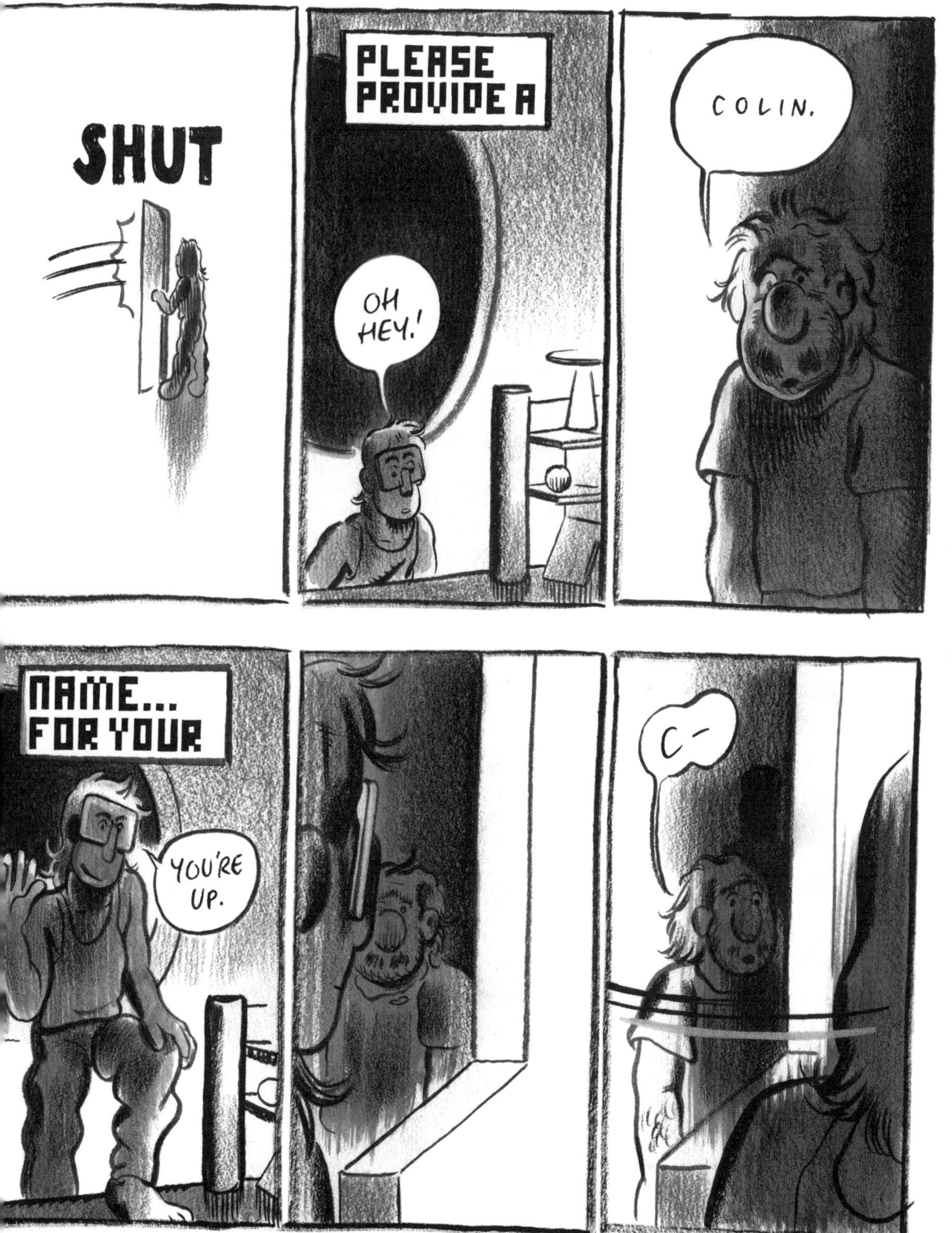
SHUT
PLEASE PROVIDE A
OH HEY.'
COLIN.
NAME... FOR YOUR
YOU'RE UP.
C-

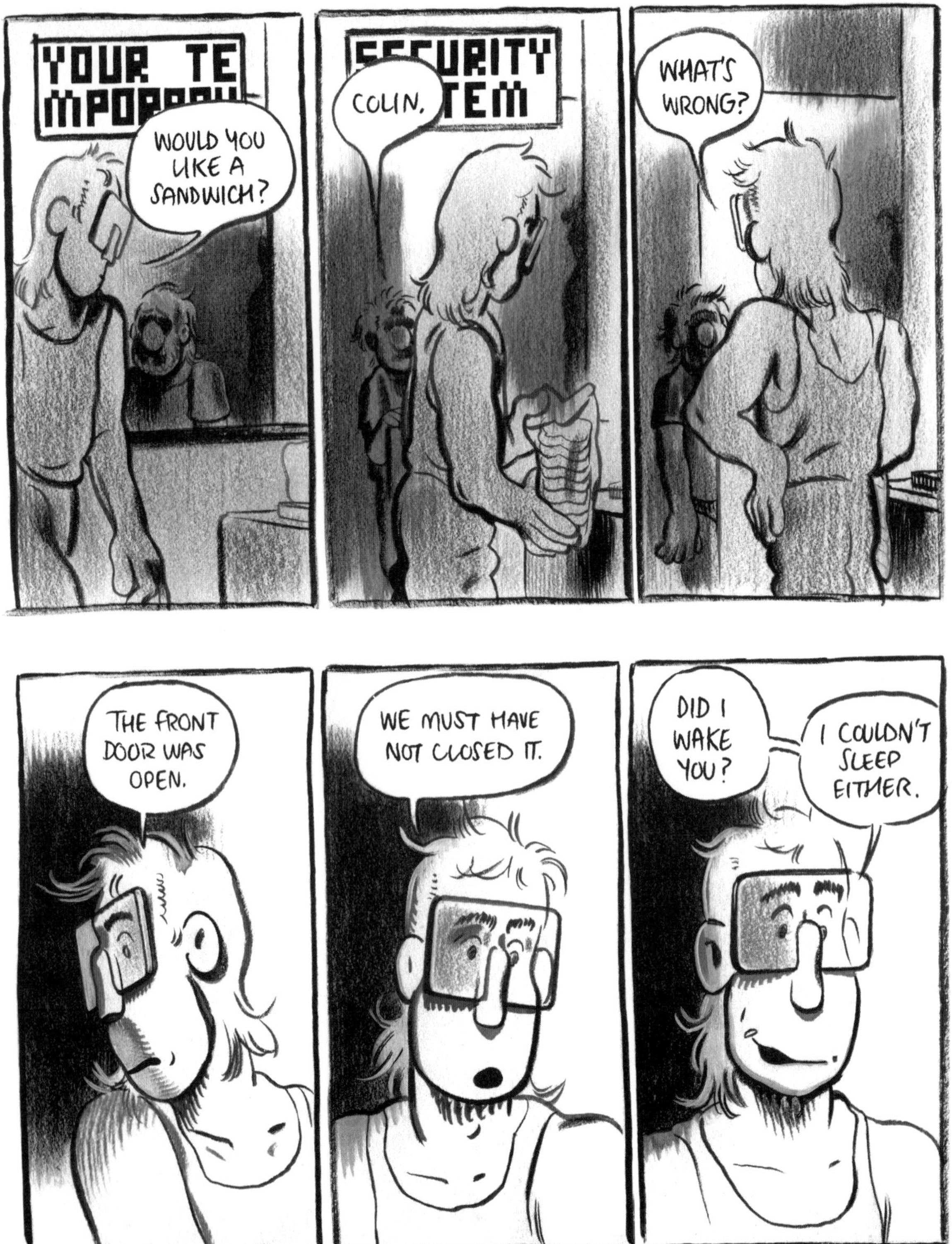
YOUR TE
MPORARY
WOULD YOU LIKE A SANDWICH?
SECURITY
TEM
COLIN.
WHAT'S WRONG?
THE FRONT DOOR WAS OPEN.
WE MUST HAVE NOT CLOSED IT.
DID I WAKE YOU?
I COULDN'T SLEEP EITHER.

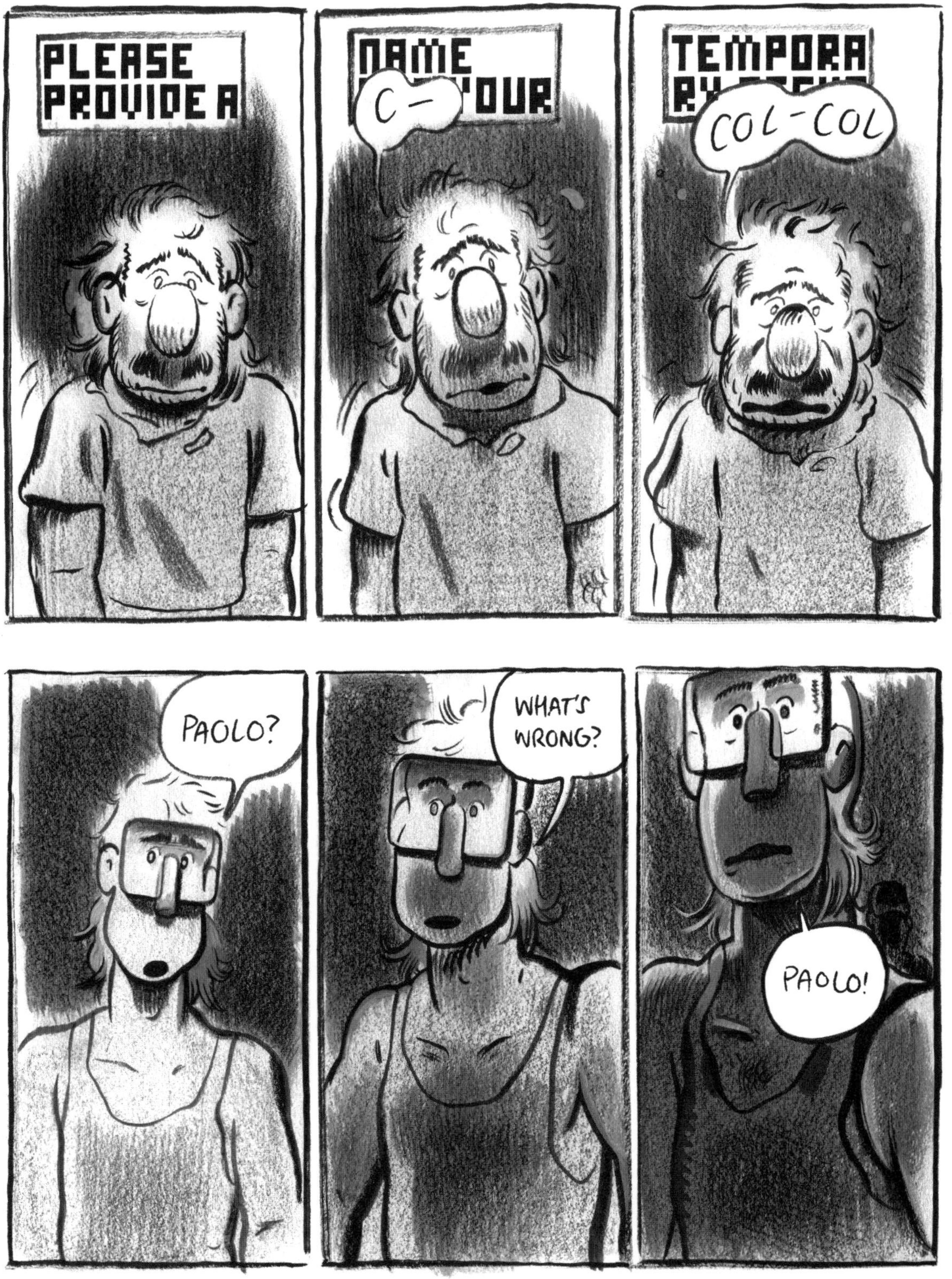
PLEASE PROVIDE A
NAME
C—
YOUR
TEMPORA
COL-COL
PAOLO?
WHAT'S WRONG?
PAOLO!

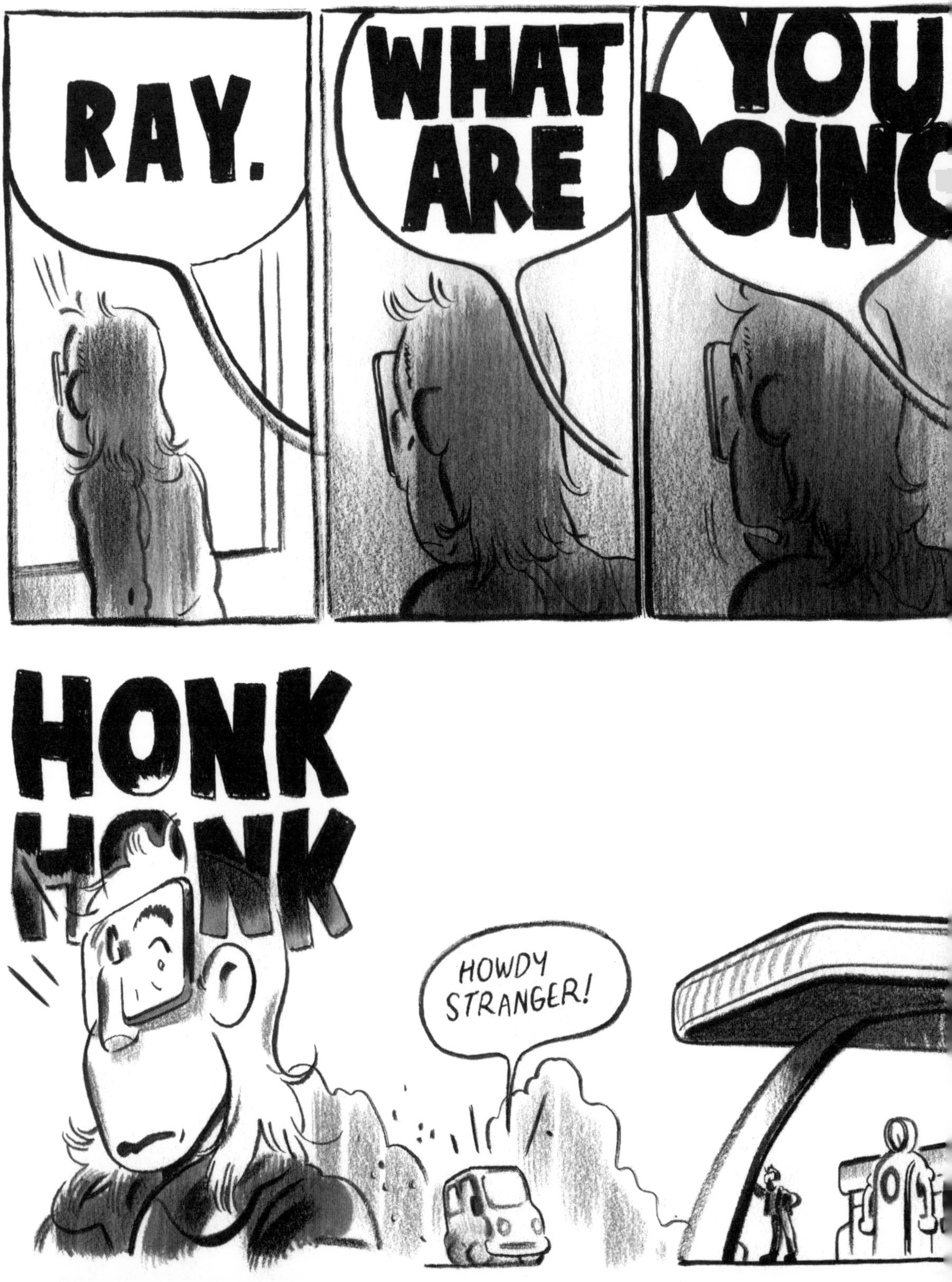
RAY.
WHAT ARE
YOU DOING
HONK HONK
HOWDY STRANGER!

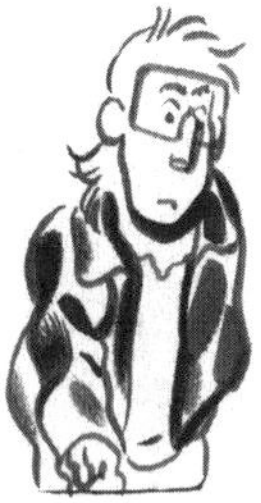

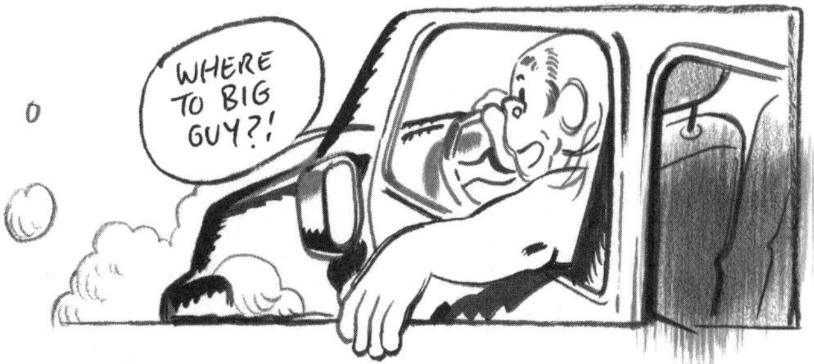
WHERE TO BIG GUY?!

Famous had left with all of his belongings, which he figured were now bouncing around in the back of her truck out on the open road. Even if he knew how to get back to the farm, he was too embarrassed to show up unannounced for a second time, to stretch Susan and Bibi's generosity until it finally snapped.

But the thought of returning to the city—back to his job, back to Paolo, if he would still have him—made Colin queasy. He had spent the day stuck at that refueling station, working up the courage to tell David to take him anywhere, knowing he'd drive him there, regardless of the distance. And yet, in that moment, Colin knew where he had to go.

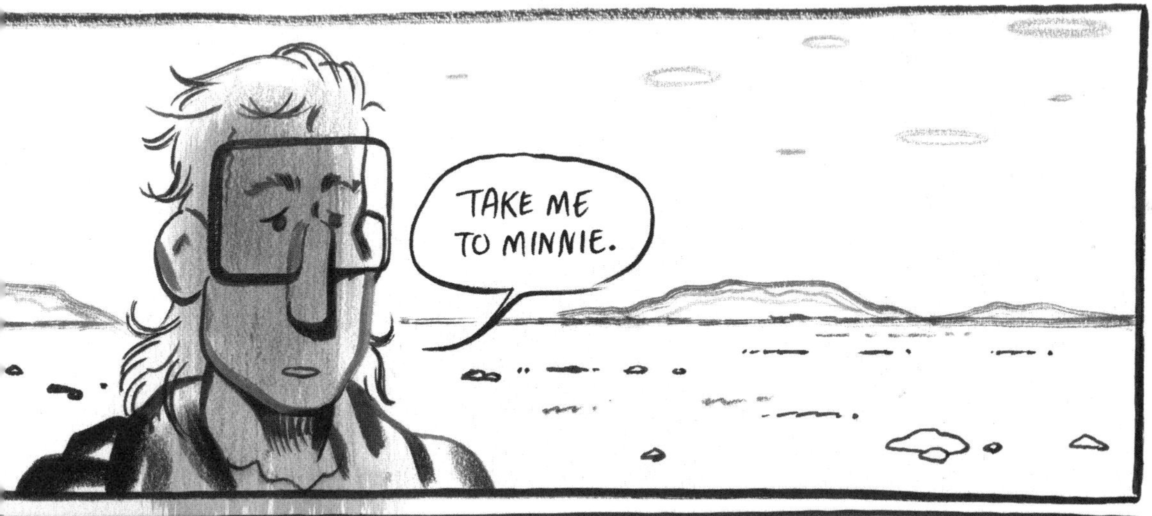
TAKE ME TO MINNIE.

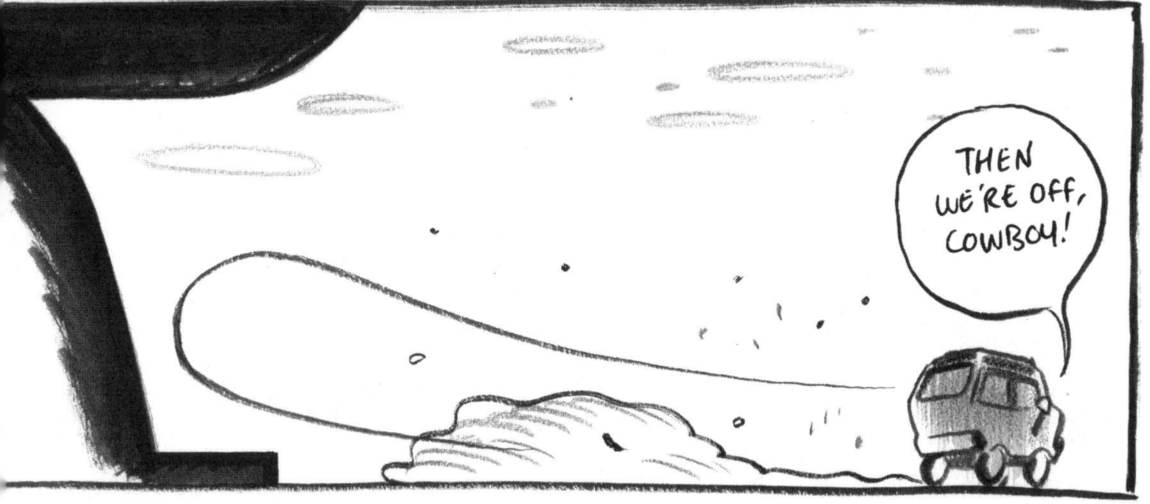
THEN WE'RE OFF, COWBOY!

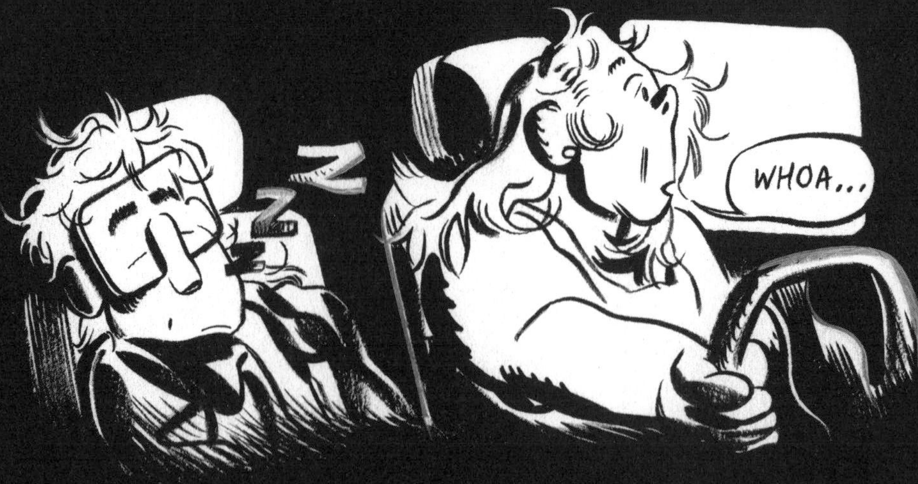
WHOA...

Asleep in David's car, Colin missed the execution of Frank Bradbury. David looked on in sadness, making a blessing against his chest with his free hand. As the cars slowed around them to gawk, David focused on the road ahead, determined to deliver his passenger safely.

When Colin woke up hours later, David decided not to tell him about what he had missed.

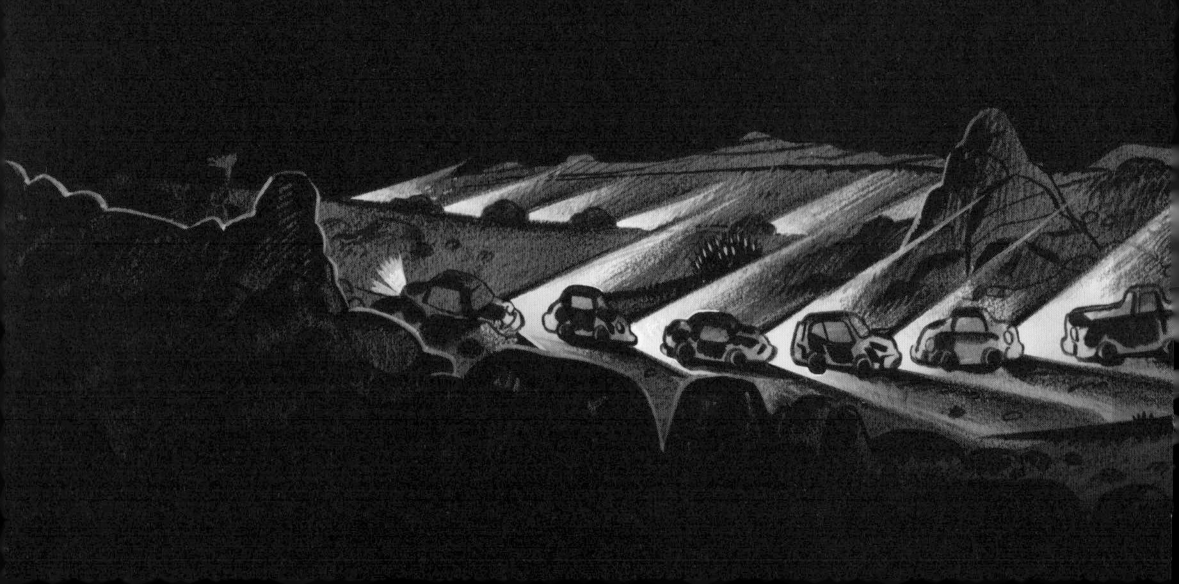

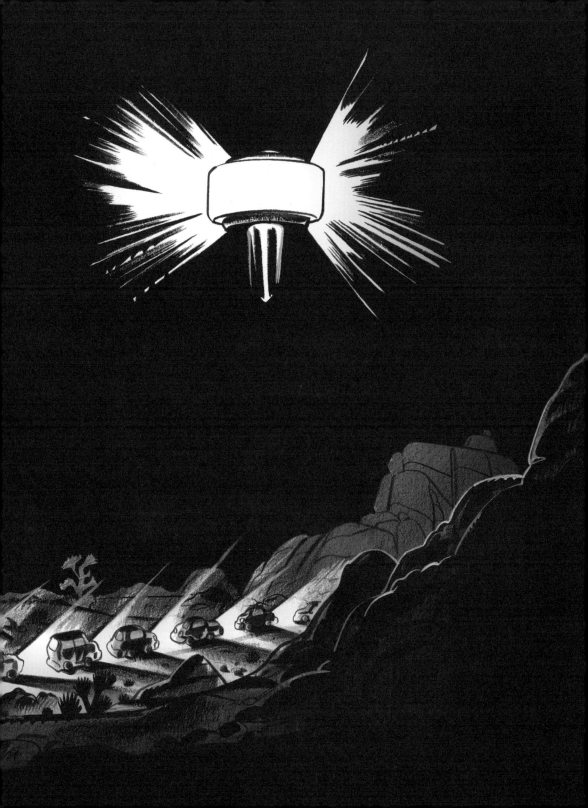

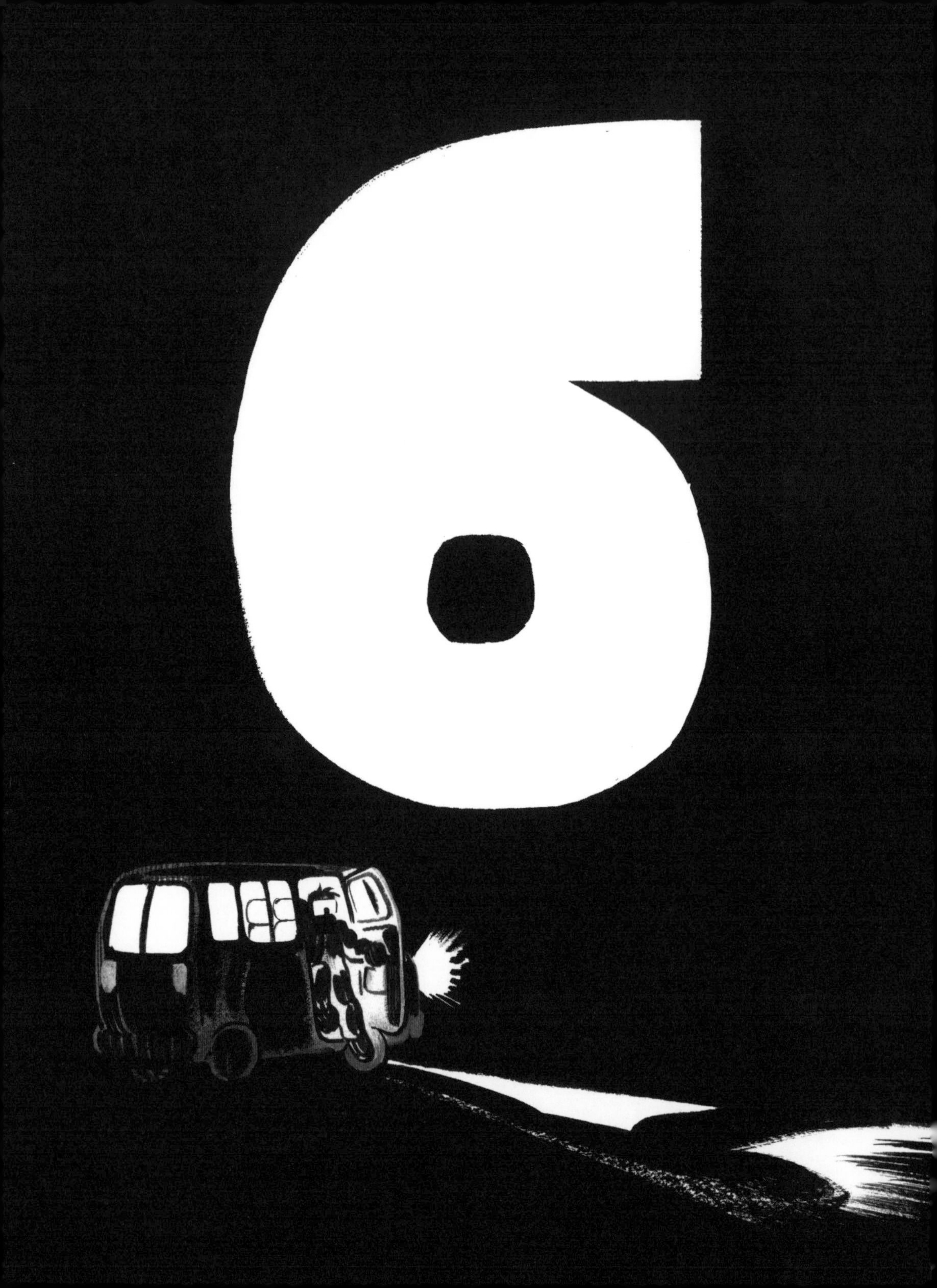
6

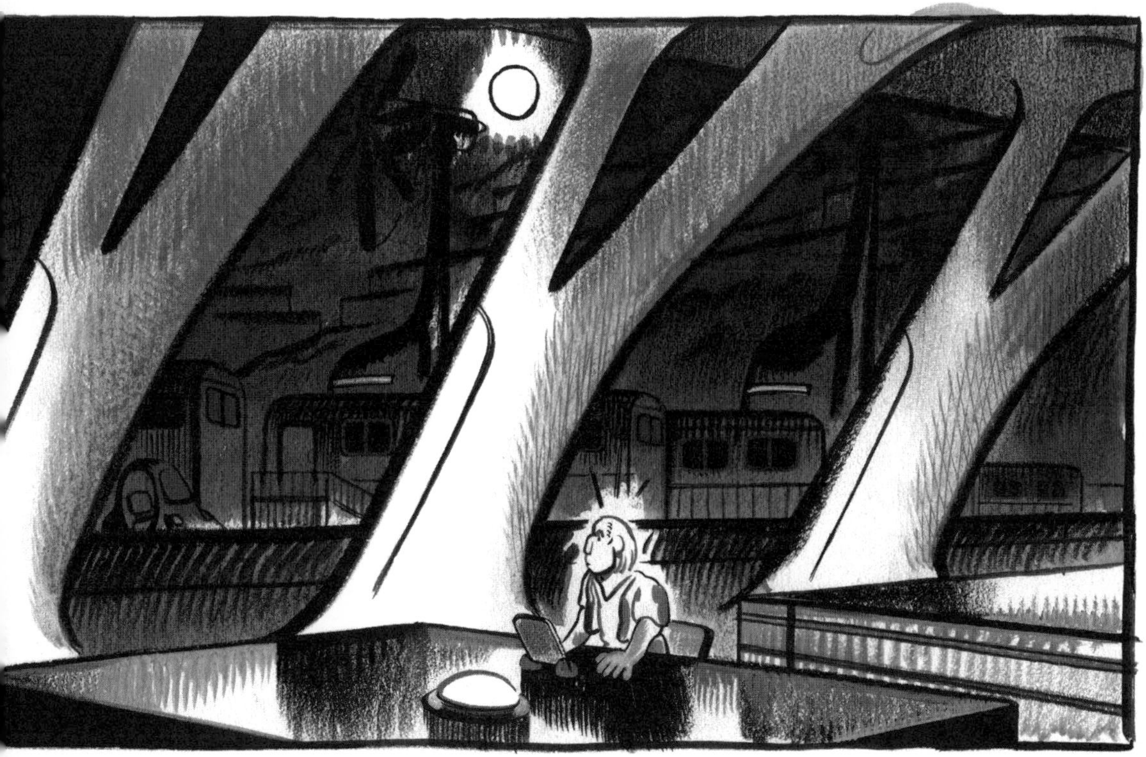

The faint sound of the closing of a distant car door cut through the still night air. Colin had arrived. His arrival wasn't a surprise—Minnie had stayed up to wait for him—but now that he was here, she felt nervous.

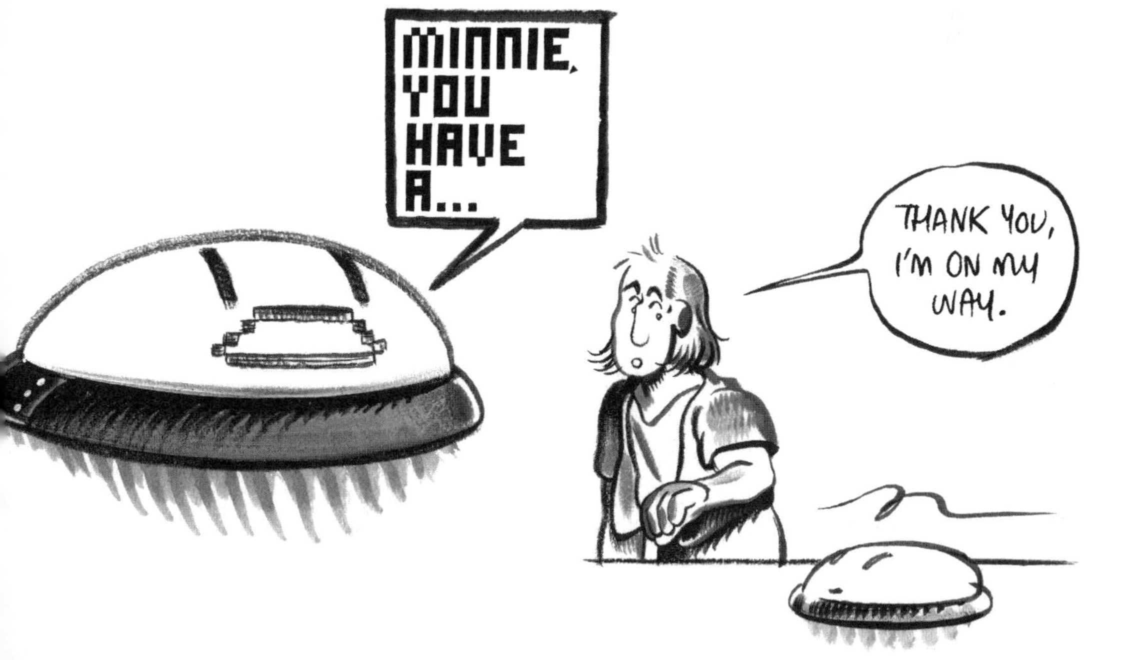
MINNIE, YOU HAVE A...
THANK YOU, I'M ON MY WAY.

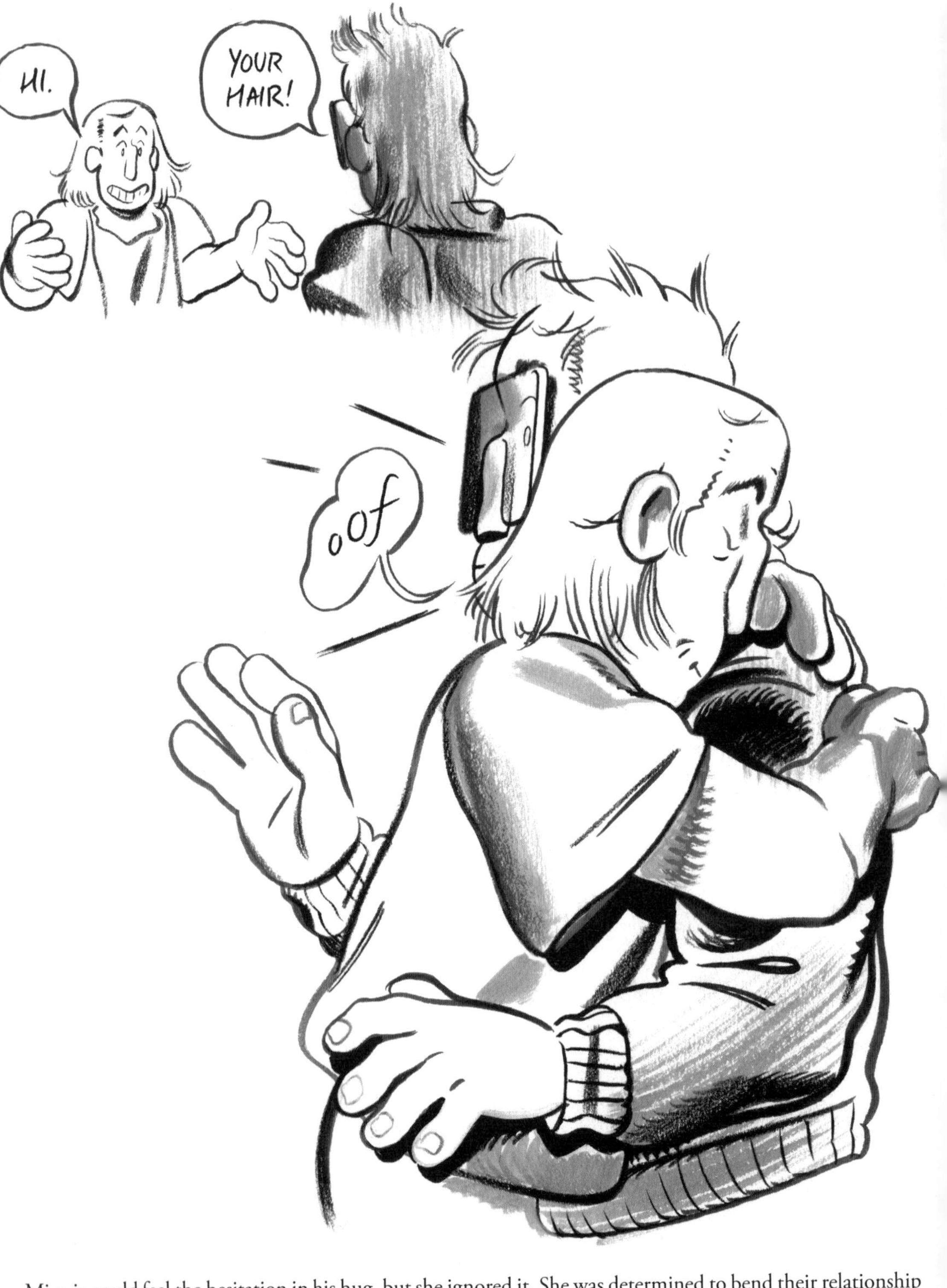
HI.
YOUR HAIR!
oOf

Minnie could feel the hesitation in his hug, but she ignored it. She was determined to bend their relationship back into the shape it had taken for most of their lives.

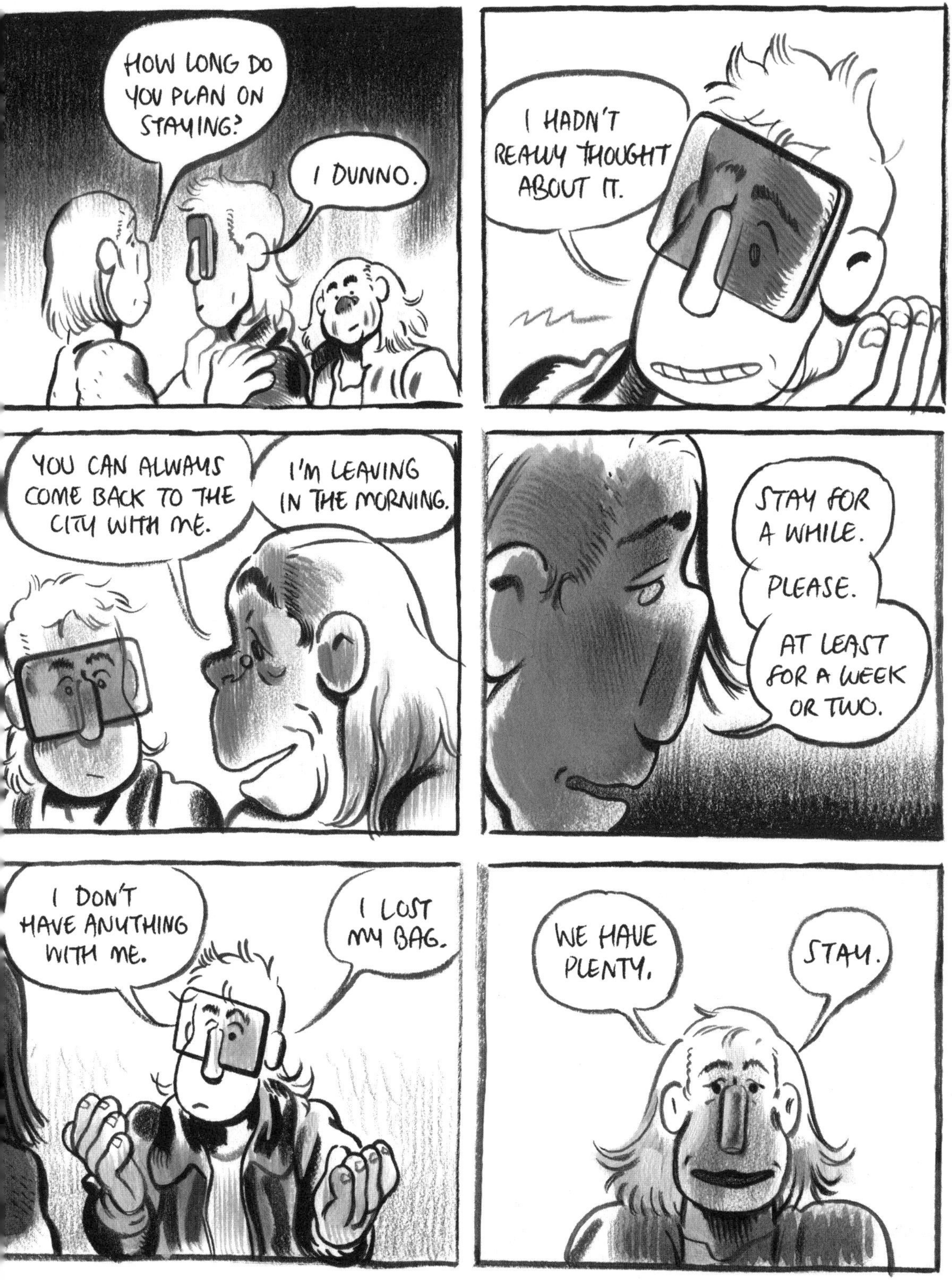
HOW LONG DO YOU PLAN ON STAYING?
I DUNNO.
I HADN'T REALLY THOUGHT ABOUT IT.
YOU CAN ALWAYS COME BACK TO THE CITY WITH ME.
I'M LEAVING IN THE MORNING.
STAY FOR A WHILE.
PLEASE.
AT LEAST FOR A WEEK OR TWO.
I DON'T HAVE ANYTHING WITH ME.
I LOST MY BAG.
WE HAVE PLENTY.
STAY.

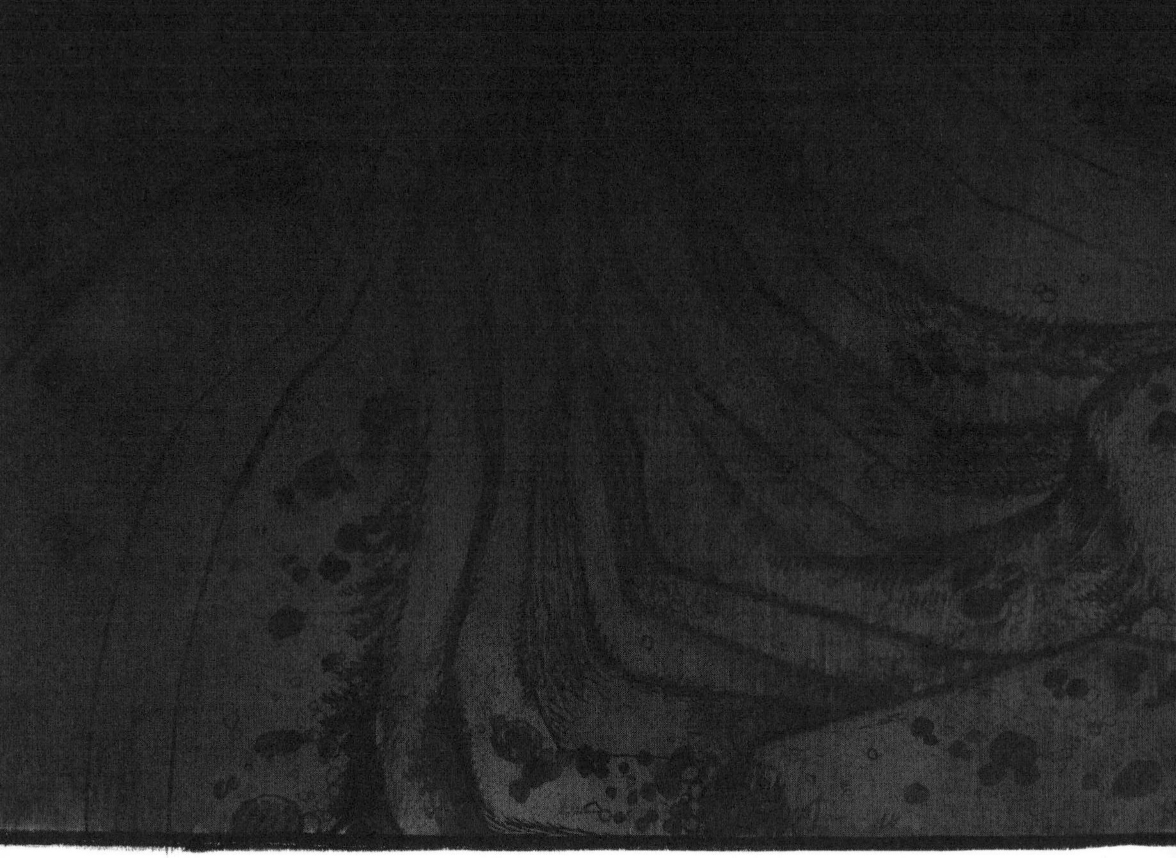

Minnie's dance troupe occupies the abandoned campus of a large telecommunication manufacturer. Since being built, the structure was briefly used as an unmarked military outpost and refueling station, a shelter during natural disasters, and the set of a short-lived reality television series.

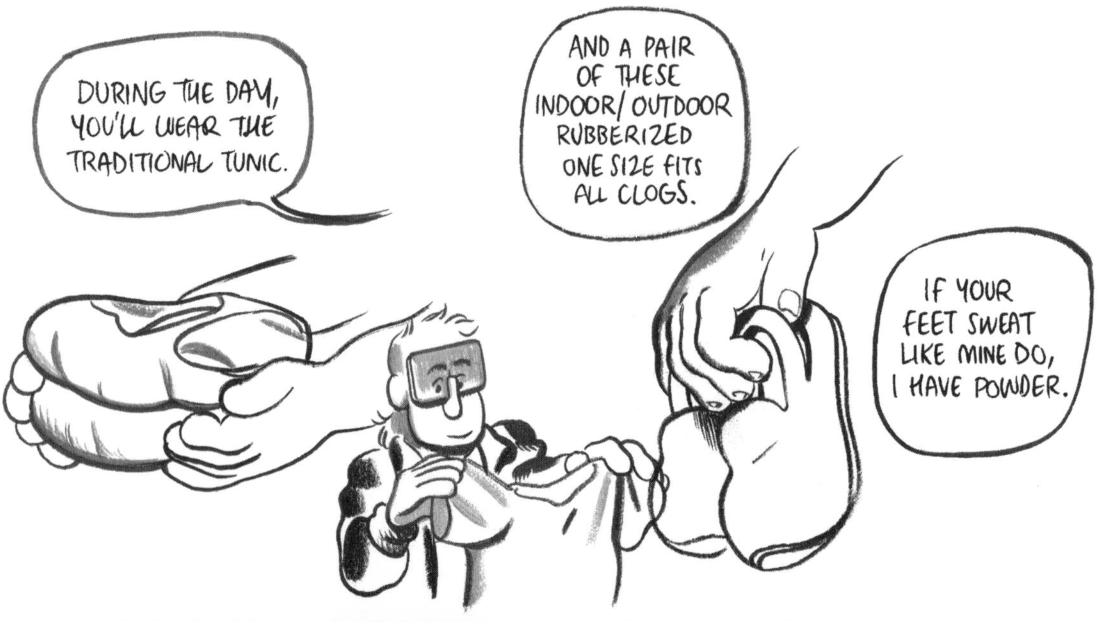

DURING THE DAY, YOU'LL WEAR THE TRADITIONAL TUNIC.
AND A PAIR OF THESE INDOOR/OUTDOOR RUBBERIZED ONE SIZE FITS ALL CLOGS.
IF YOUR FEET SWEAT LIKE MINE DO, I HAVE POWDER.

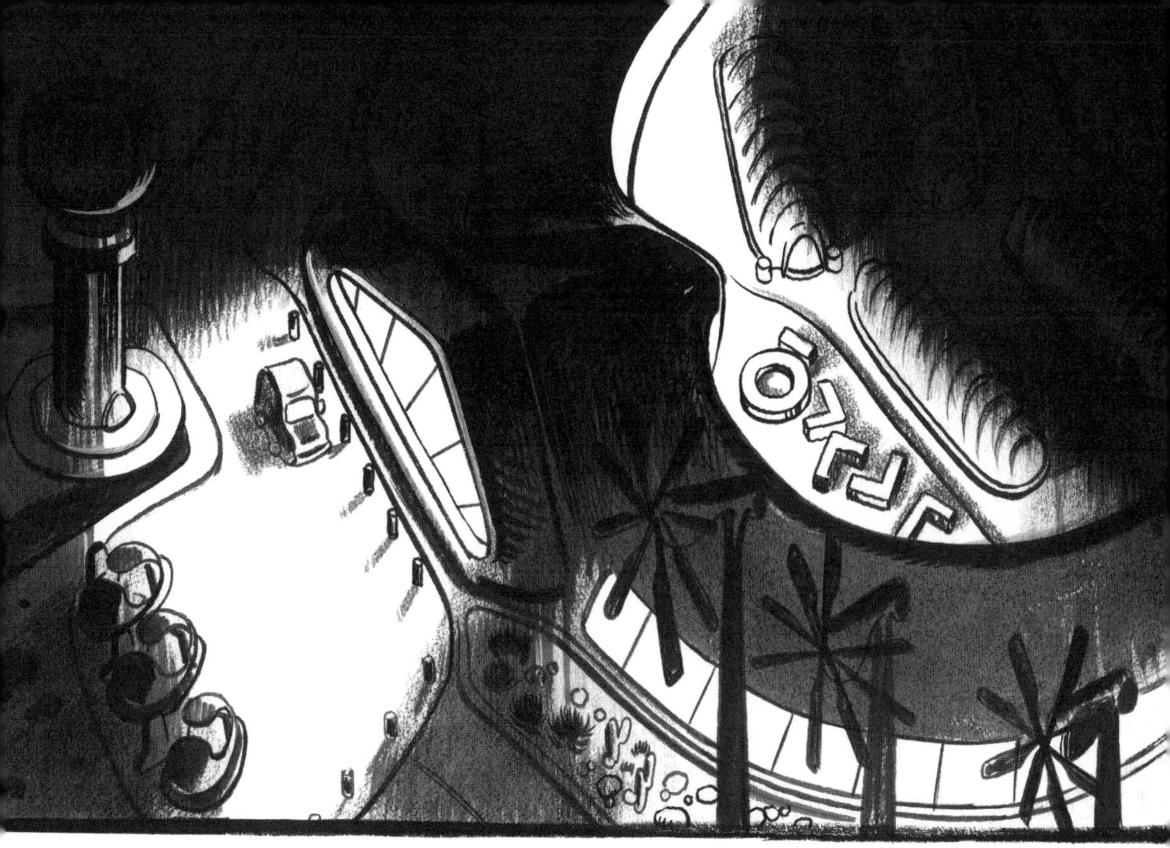

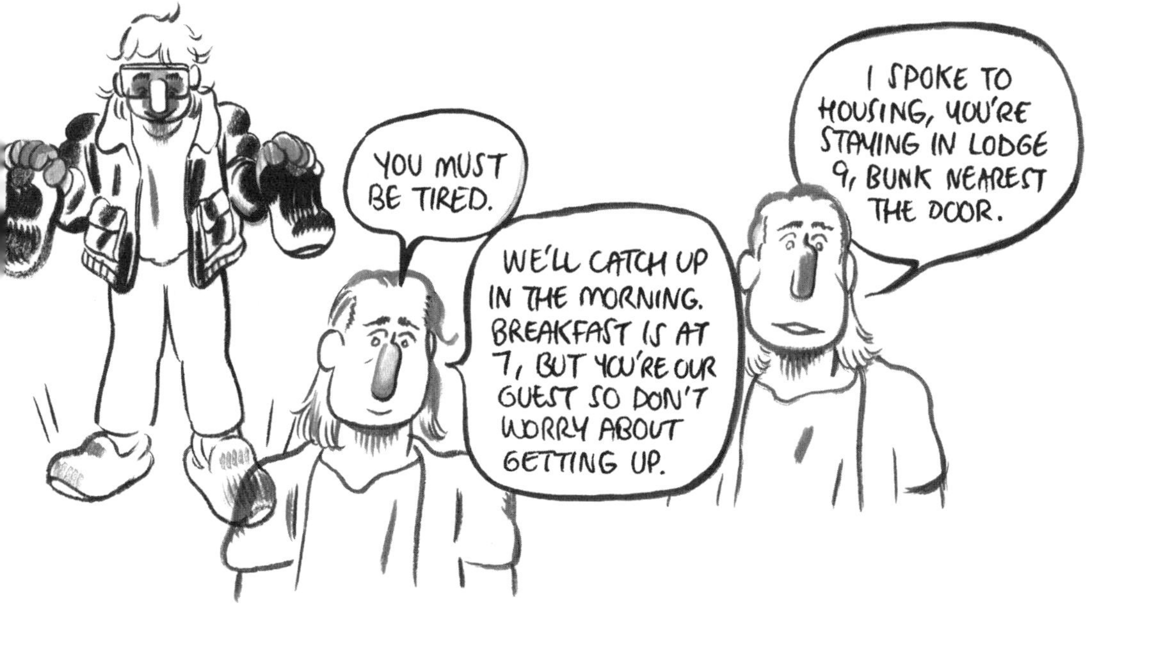
YOU MUST BE TIRED.
WE'LL CATCH UP IN THE MORNING. BREAKFAST IS AT 7, BUT YOU'RE OUR GUEST SO DON'T WORRY ABOUT GETTING UP.
I SPOKE TO HOUSING, YOU'RE STAYING IN LODGE 9, BUNK NEAREST THE DOOR.

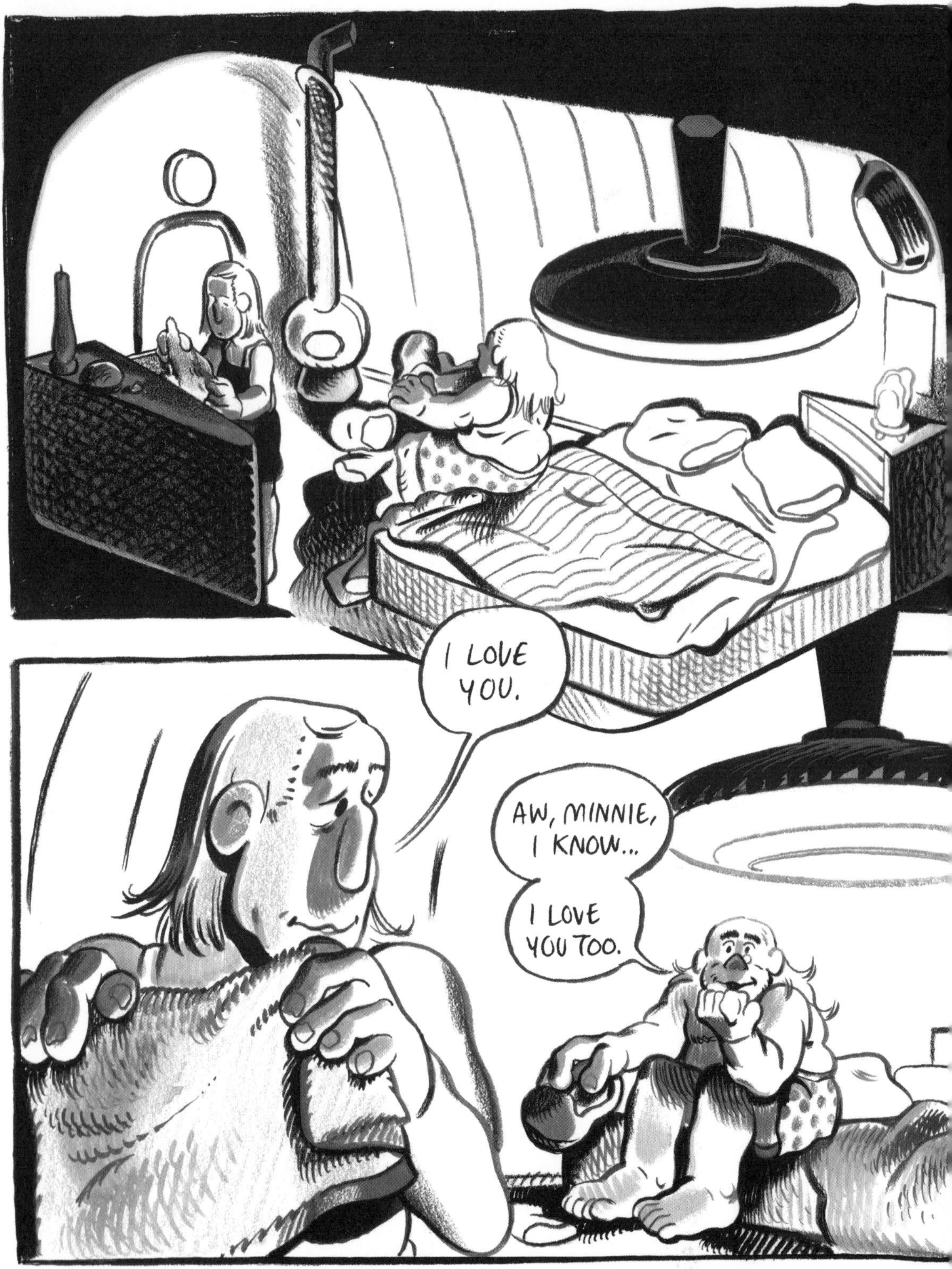
I LOVE YOU.
AW, MINNIE, I KNOW...
I LOVE YOU TOO.

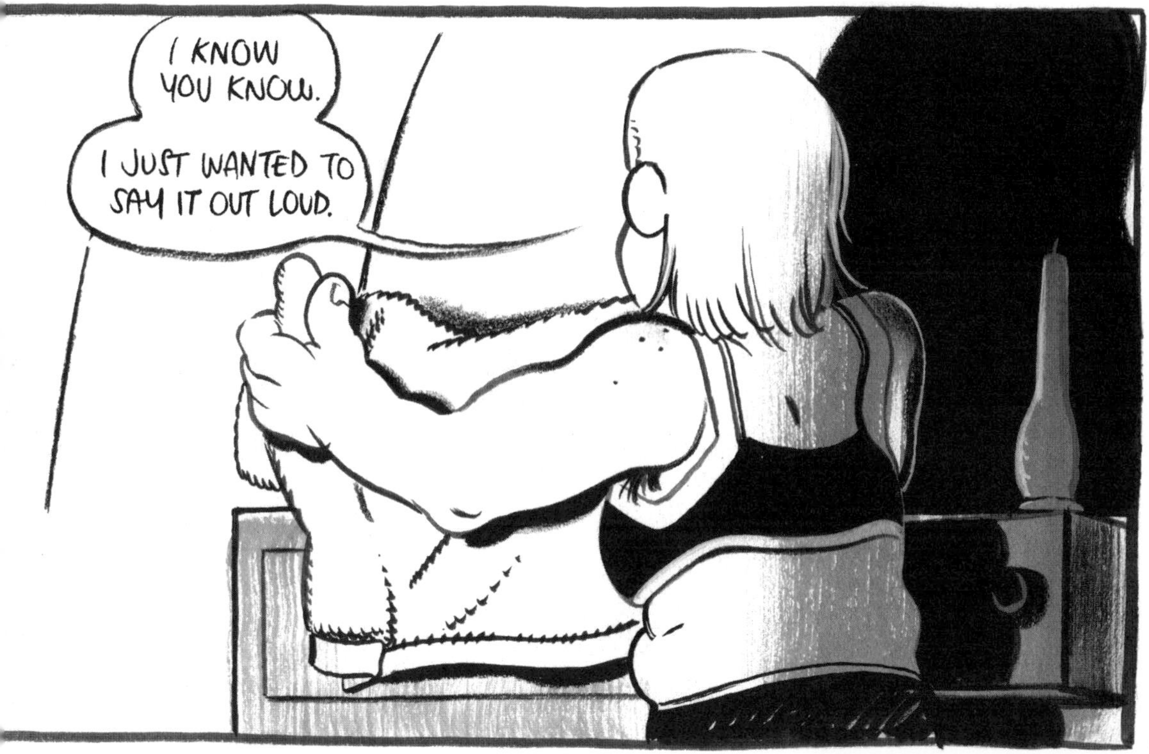
I KNOW YOU KNOW.
I JUST WANTED TO SAY IT OUT LOUD.

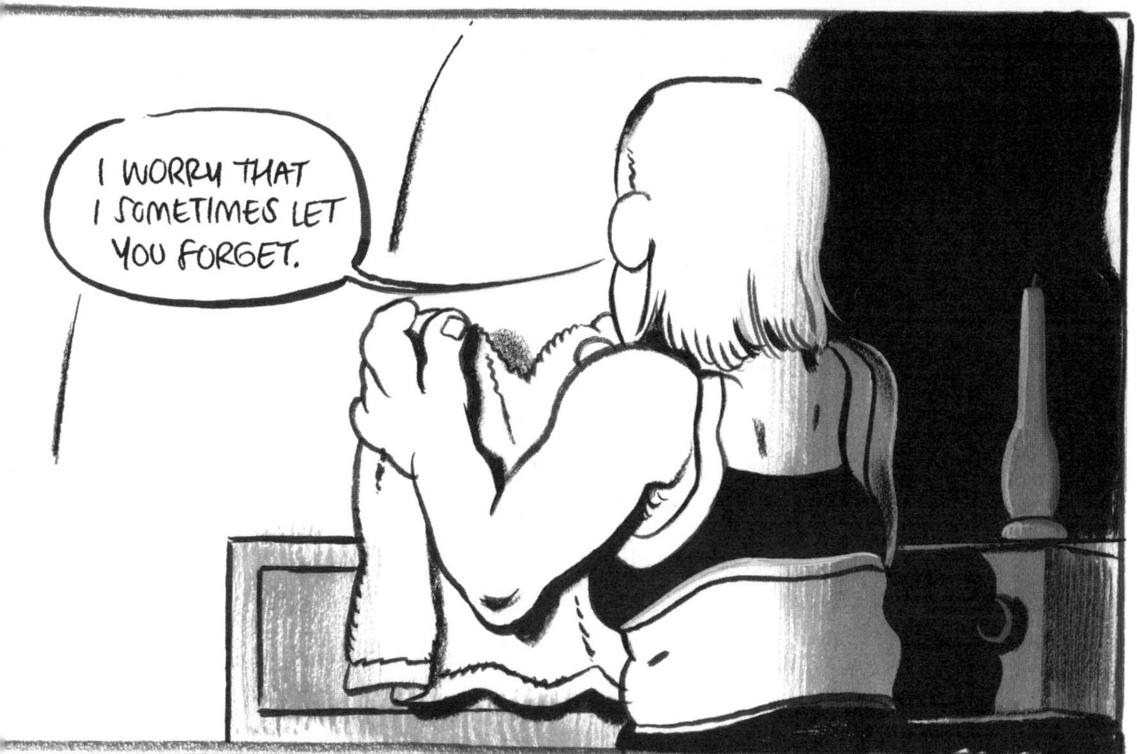
I WORRY THAT I SOMETIMES LET YOU FORGET.

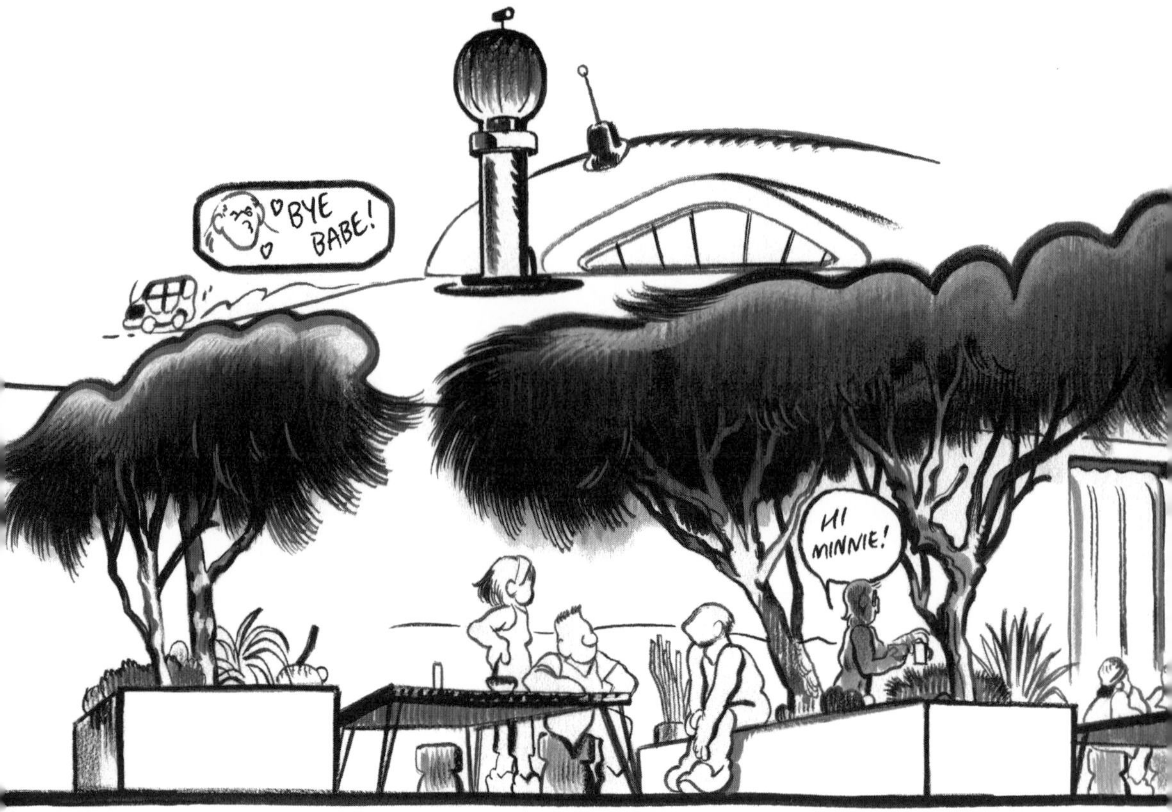
BYE BABE!
HI MINNIE!

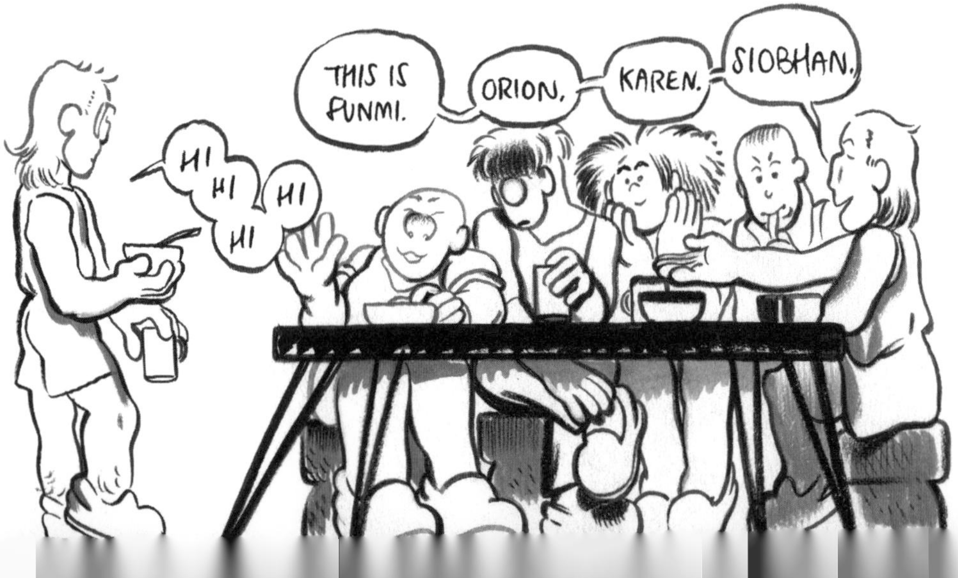
THIS IS FUNMI.
ORION.
KAREN.
SIOBHAN.
HI
HI
HI
HI

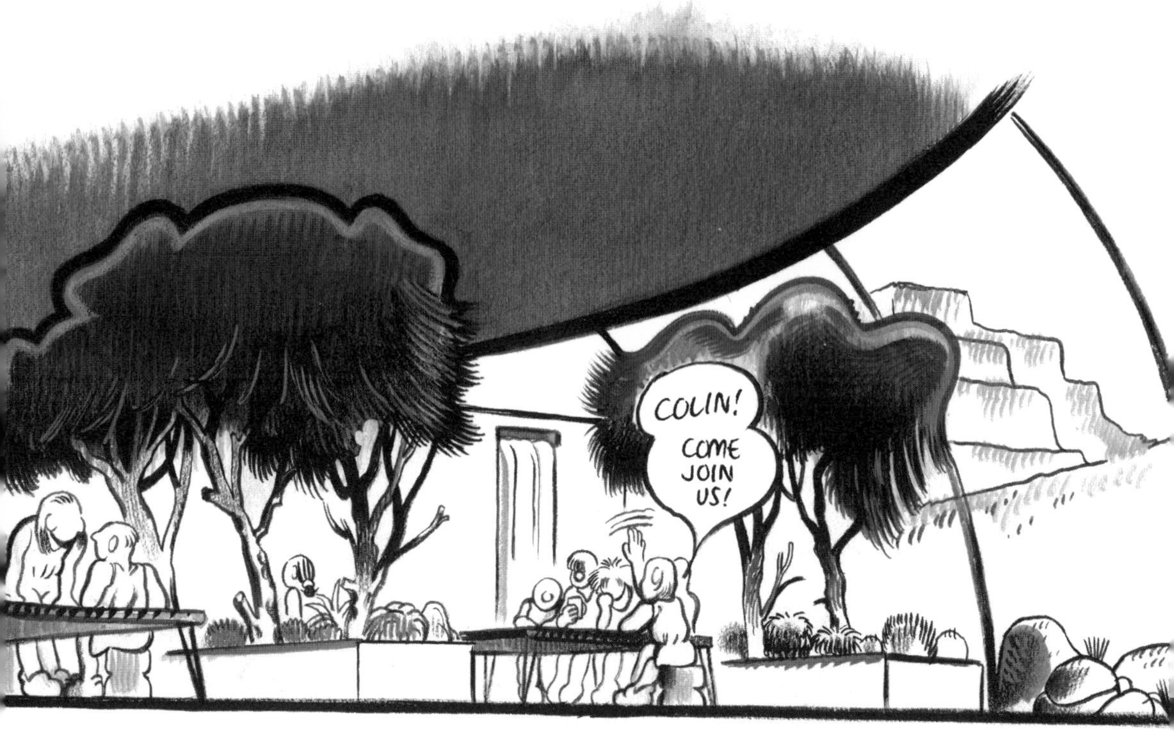
COLIN!
COME JOIN US!

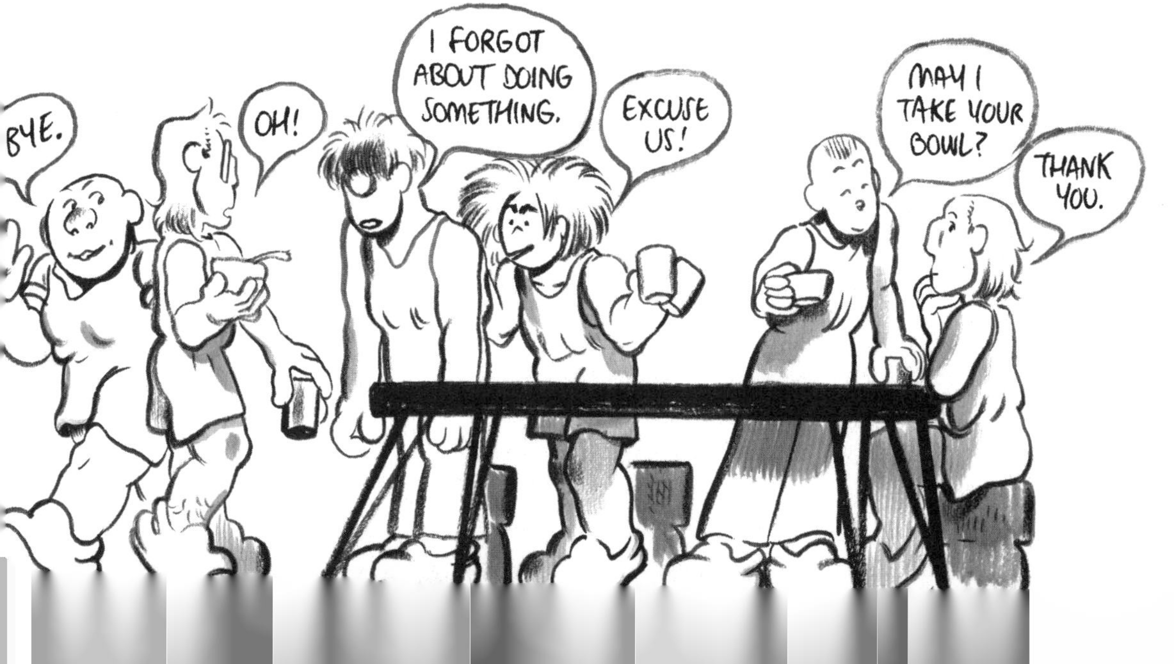
BYE.
OH!
I FORGOT ABOUT DOING SOMETHING.
EXCUSE US!
MAY I TAKE YOUR BOWL?
THANK YOU.

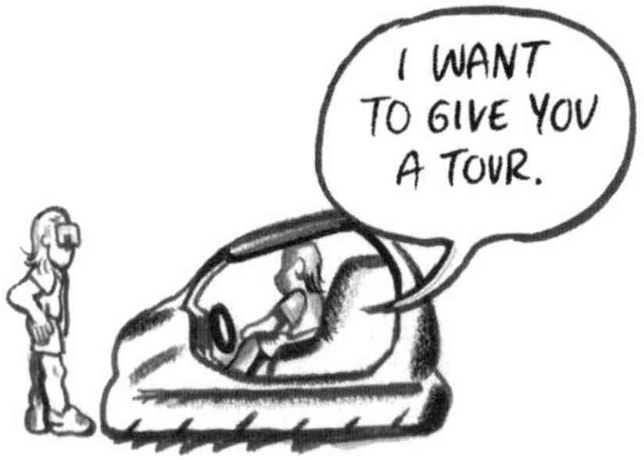
I WANT TO GIVE YOU A TOUR.

Minnie's official troupe, TR-23, is temporarily working in a town called Neon.

Neon was originally established by the Staghorn Coal Corporation, which built a small trading post around their newly constructed coal mine. Though the town was small, it began to flourish as people moved into the area to get work in coal mining. As the demand for coal rose, both the town and the mine expanded, until its expansion abruptly collapsed when alternative forms of energy were introduced, causing the Staghorn Coal Corporation to file for bankruptcy. By that point, the area had been strip-mined into uninhabitability. People still lived in Neon, but the population was dwindling. Life was hard.

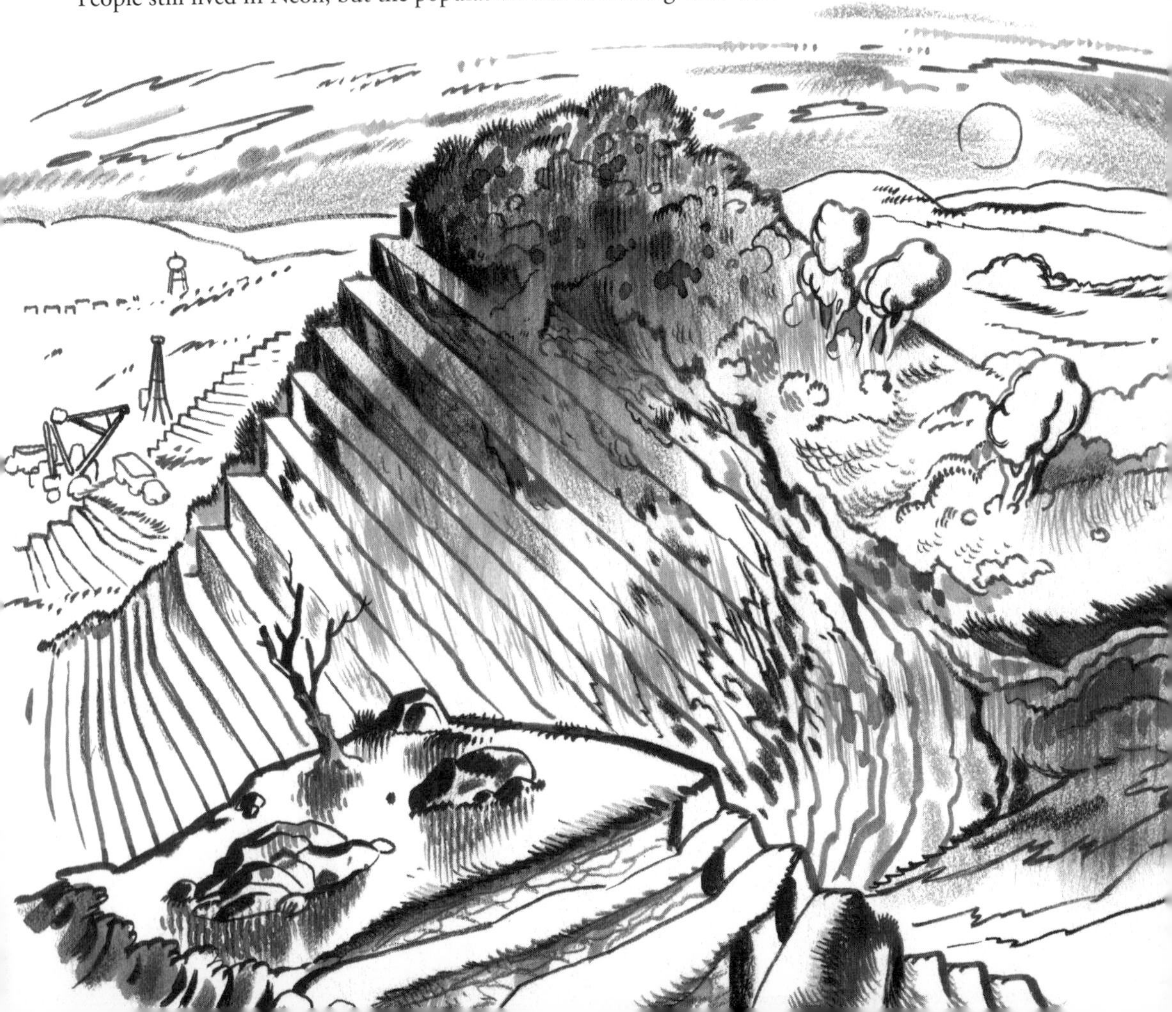

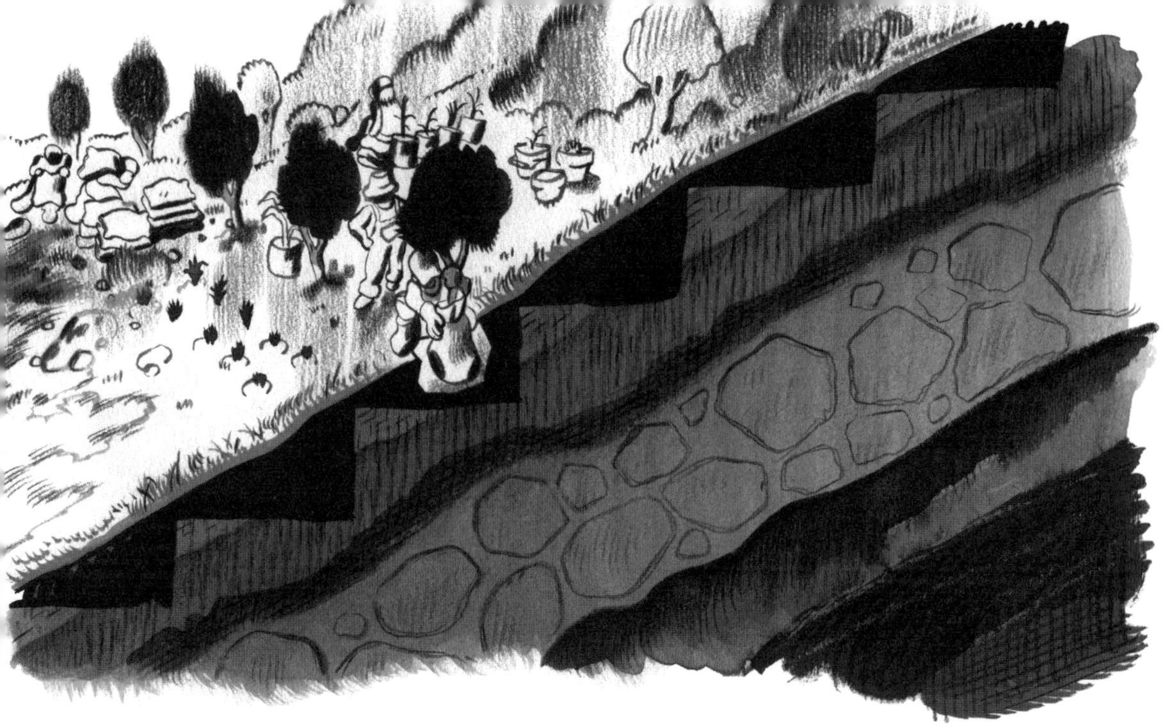

That is, until three decades ago, when the swell of excitement following the fall of the Administration created a trend of conservation and reconstruction within the country. Suddenly, there was interest in restoring the ecosystems surrounding Neon to their former glory. GrowUp!, an organization created by one of the original financiers of the major telecommunications company TeleComCorp, hoped to generate interest in Neon by turning it into a destination for young people who wanted a chance to leave the overcrowded, underserved cities and start a new life for themselves.

Through GrowUp!, young people earned a living wage laying down carbon rich soil, grass seed, and trees into the tracts cut into the strip-mined mountains in the hope of reviving its ecosystem. For a time, it worked. Forests were slowly replenished. Nearby towns that had been abandoned flourished once again, filled with boutiques and restaurants opened by people who couldn't afford to do so in the larger, more expensive cities. Modern homes, equipped with every convenience, were built alongside the older brick buildings as communities grew. New schools. A library. Ground was even broken for a combination sports arena and concert stadium.

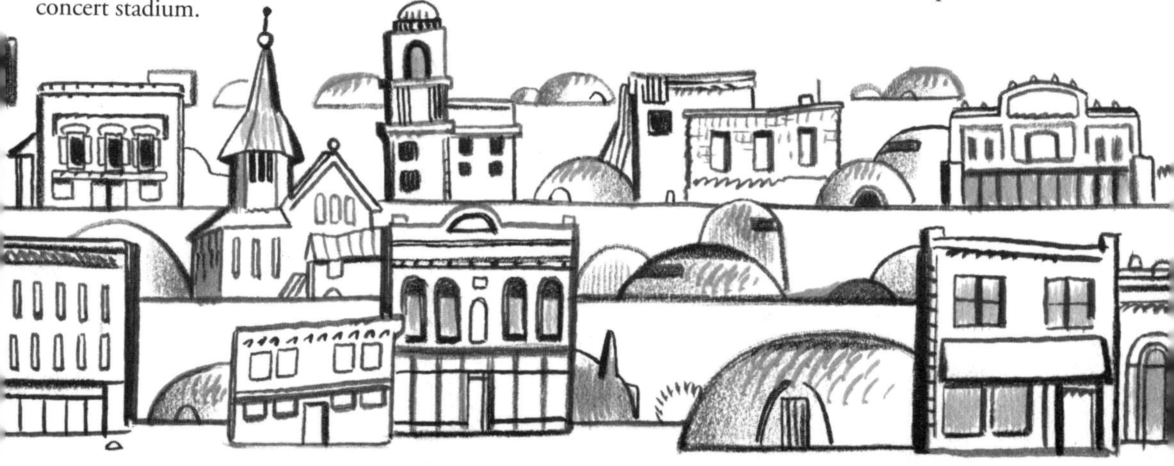

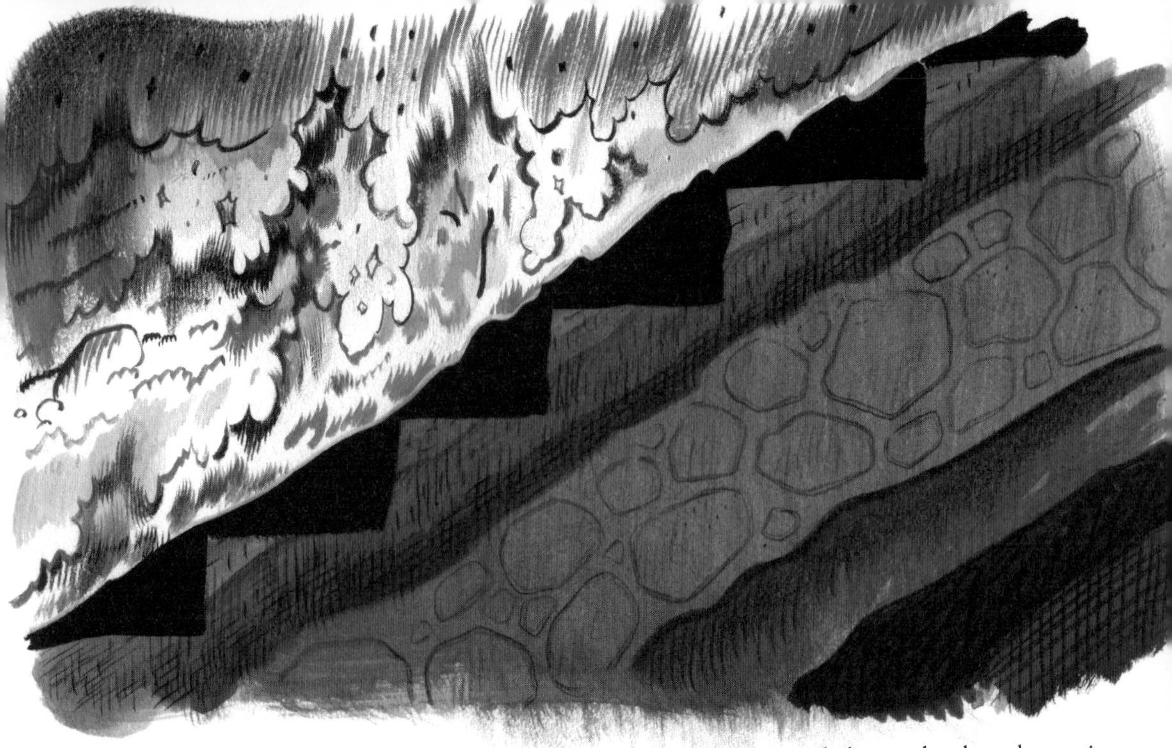

But two arid springs in a row produced substantial droughts that turned the newly planted trees into kindling. The mountain range was soon engulfed in ever-expanding wildfires. GrowUp!'s project management favored photogenic, non-native trees and grasses that were more susceptible to fire, disrupting the ecosystem even further.

During its first period of expansion, when it was still a coal mine, Neon had strip-mined deep into the earth, creating cavernous valleys with no intention of salvaging that land. During its second period of expansion, when it was considered a good real-estate investment, Neon built homes in those valleys. After the forest fires, though, those areas became uninhabitable, the air choked with ash, stagnating in the geologic bowl created by the artificial cliffs of strip-mining. Neon rapidly emptied out and was soon forgotten, save for the few residents who had always lived there.

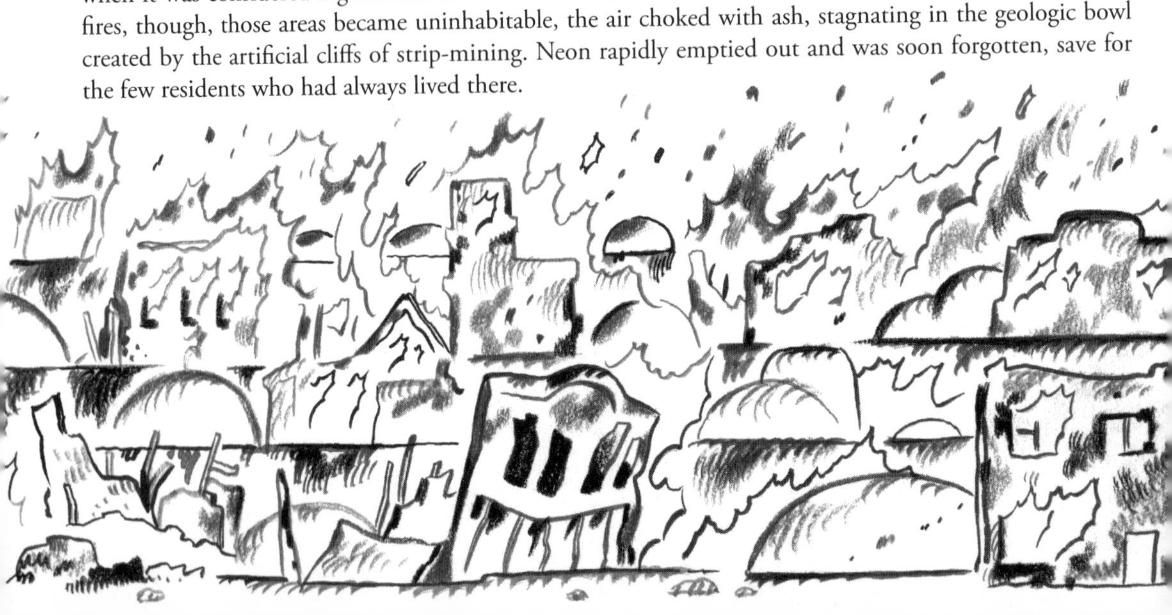

The forest fires destroyed many of the original brick buildings in Neon, but the newly built modular homes remained. These have been nicknamed "shell homes" because of their white, sloping sides and domed roofs.

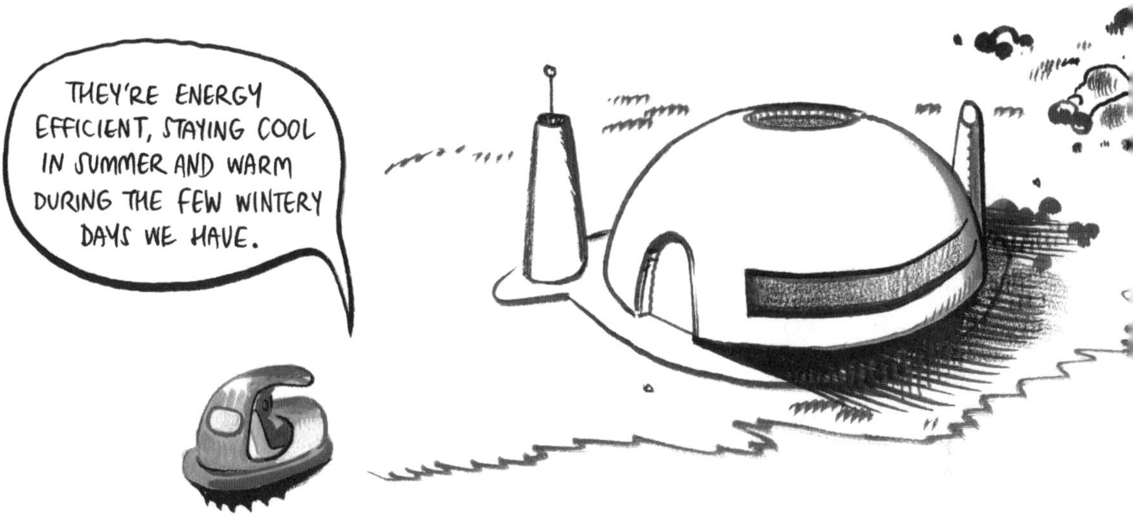
THEY'RE ENERGY EFFICIENT, STAYING COOL IN SUMMER AND WARM DURING THE FEW WINTERY DAYS WE HAVE.

Because these shell homes were built to maximize space and energy efficiency, everything is operated by remote control, which is powered by the electrical grid—not just the lights, but the kitchen appliances, water filtration, heating, cooling and plumbing. Once the relay stations were abandoned, the shell homes became unlivable, and many residents chose to return to what remained of the original buildings.

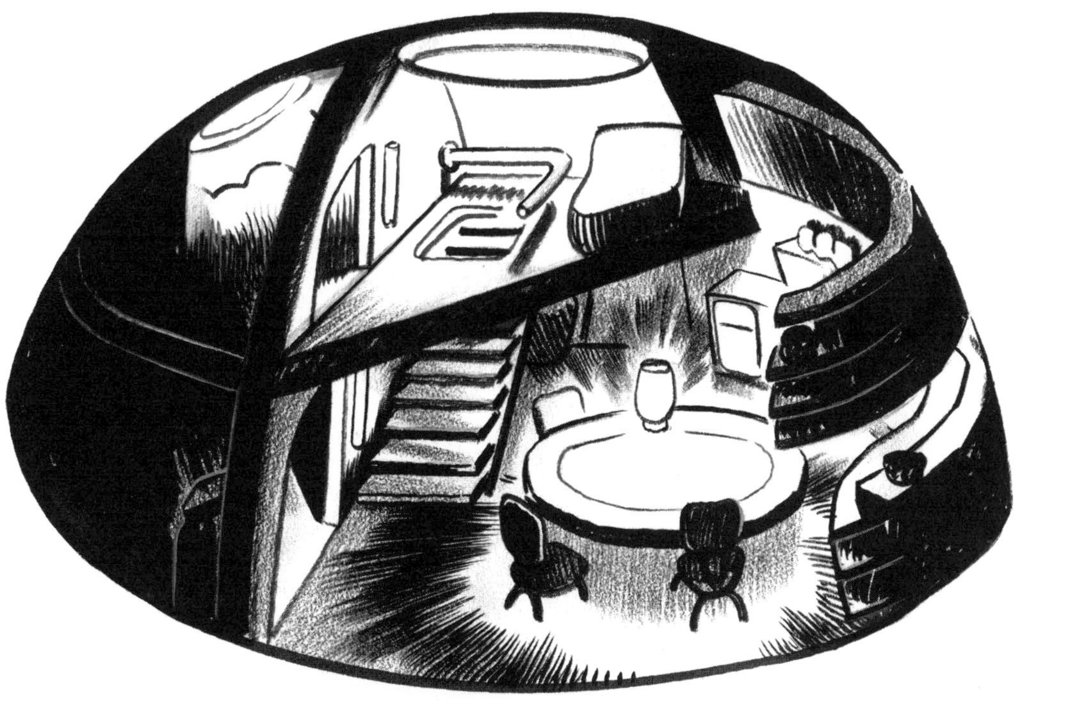

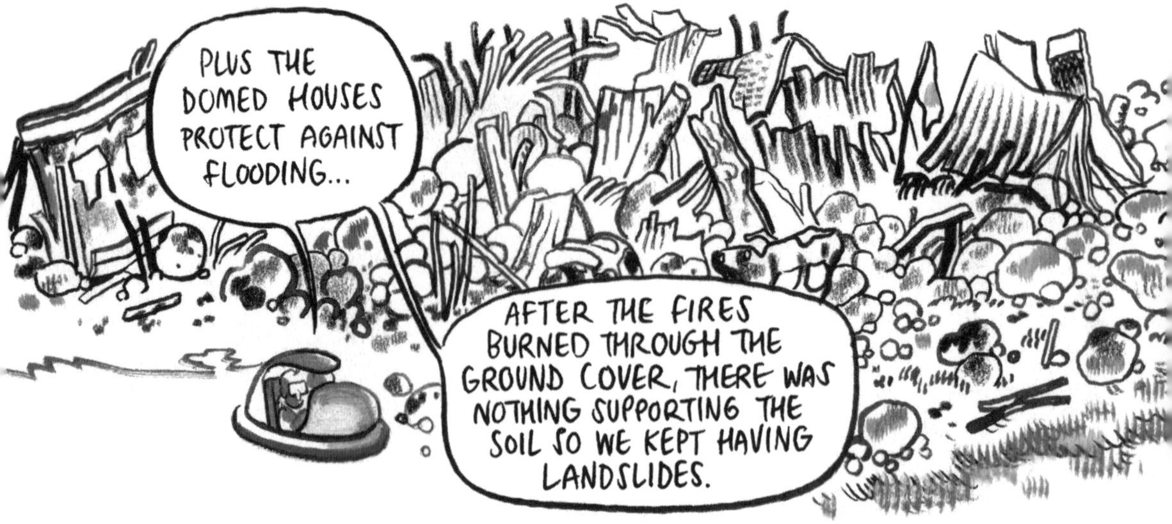
PLUS THE DOMED HOUSES PROTECT AGAINST FLOODING...
AFTER THE FIRES BURNED THROUGH THE GROUND COVER, THERE WAS NOTHING SUPPORTING THE SOIL SO WE KEPT HAVING LANDSLIDES.

When a shell home's power is restored, the home "pops," causing every appliance to turn on simultaneously. Cabinet doors flip open, tele-screens turn on, toilets flush… as if a magician were doing all of their tricks at once.

Convincing residents to move back into the uninhabited shell homes has been difficult. Although they are the few remaining-habitable spaces in Neon, most people distrust them. For those people the Dancers do help move into a shell home, many choose to remain unconnected to the power grid, living as they have always lived. Who can blame a population who has seen nothing but strangers arrive uninvited, looking to help but inevitably causing harm?

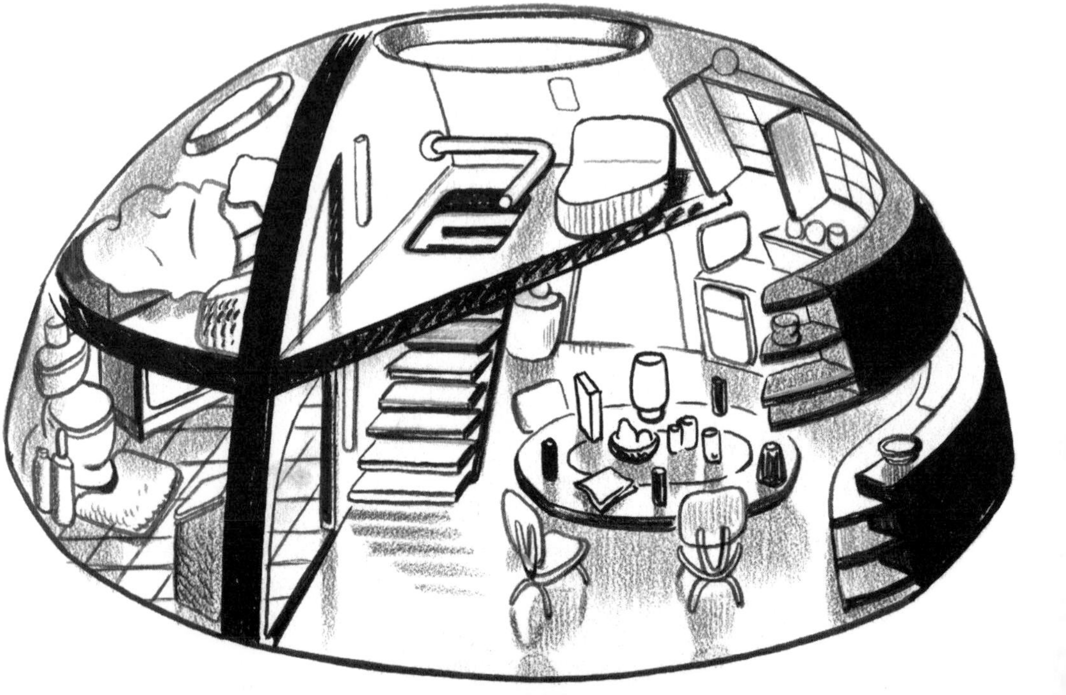

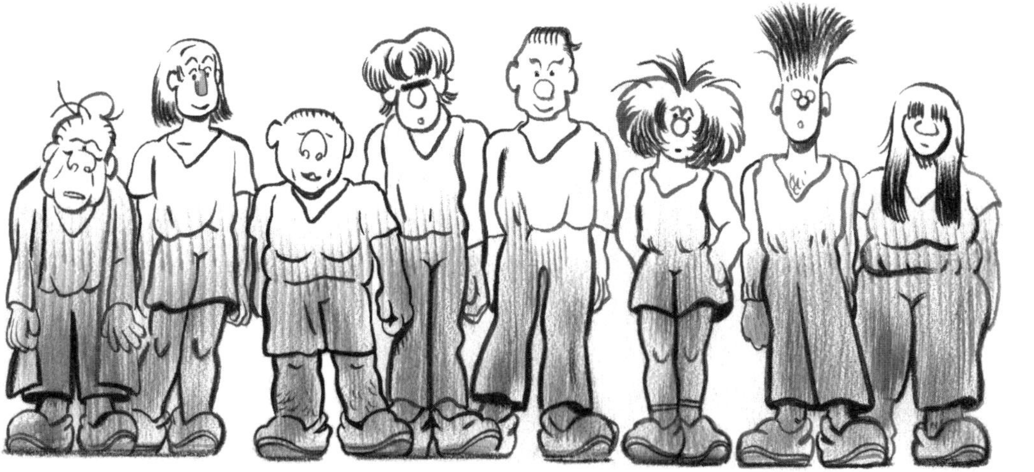

A central tenet of the modern Dancer ideology is the idea of "Good Works"—actively choosing to move through the world in a way that is kind and generous. The organization itself often set up official projects to help achieve this on a larger scale. Minnie's troupe, Troupe 23, was chosen to spearhead the efforts to restore Neon once more.

Under GrowUp!'s leadership, massive relay stations were built all along the valley to bring renewable energy from nearby power stations into Neon. After all, Neon had only one power station that still burned coal. Although this change in energy usage was emotionally charged for the original residents, who had all once made a living mining coal, the town acquiesced to the transition and its power station was decommissioned.

Unfortunately, once GrowUp! left, the newer relay stations were also abandoned, leaving the remaining residents worse off than they had been before. The few people who could afford generators relied on them for electricity, but most people simply lived in darkness.

With the help of TR-23, the relay stations have come back into service. Using this energy, large-scale air filtration stations have been built in an effort to remove harmful matter from the air. Despite all of this, after both the betrayals of the Staghorn Coal Corporation and GrowUp!, the residents of Neon are distrustful of Dancers and their continued efforts are slow going.

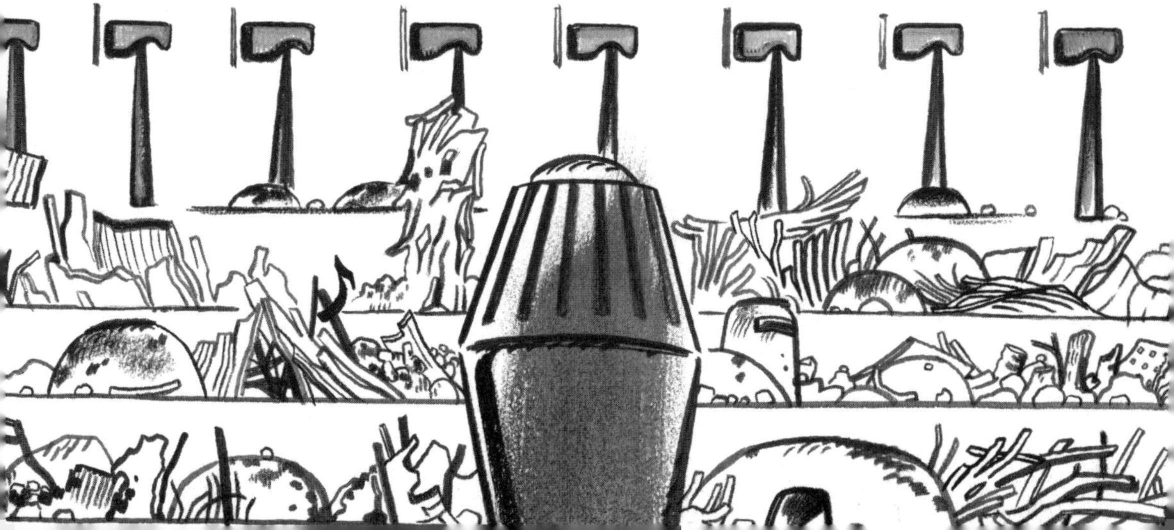

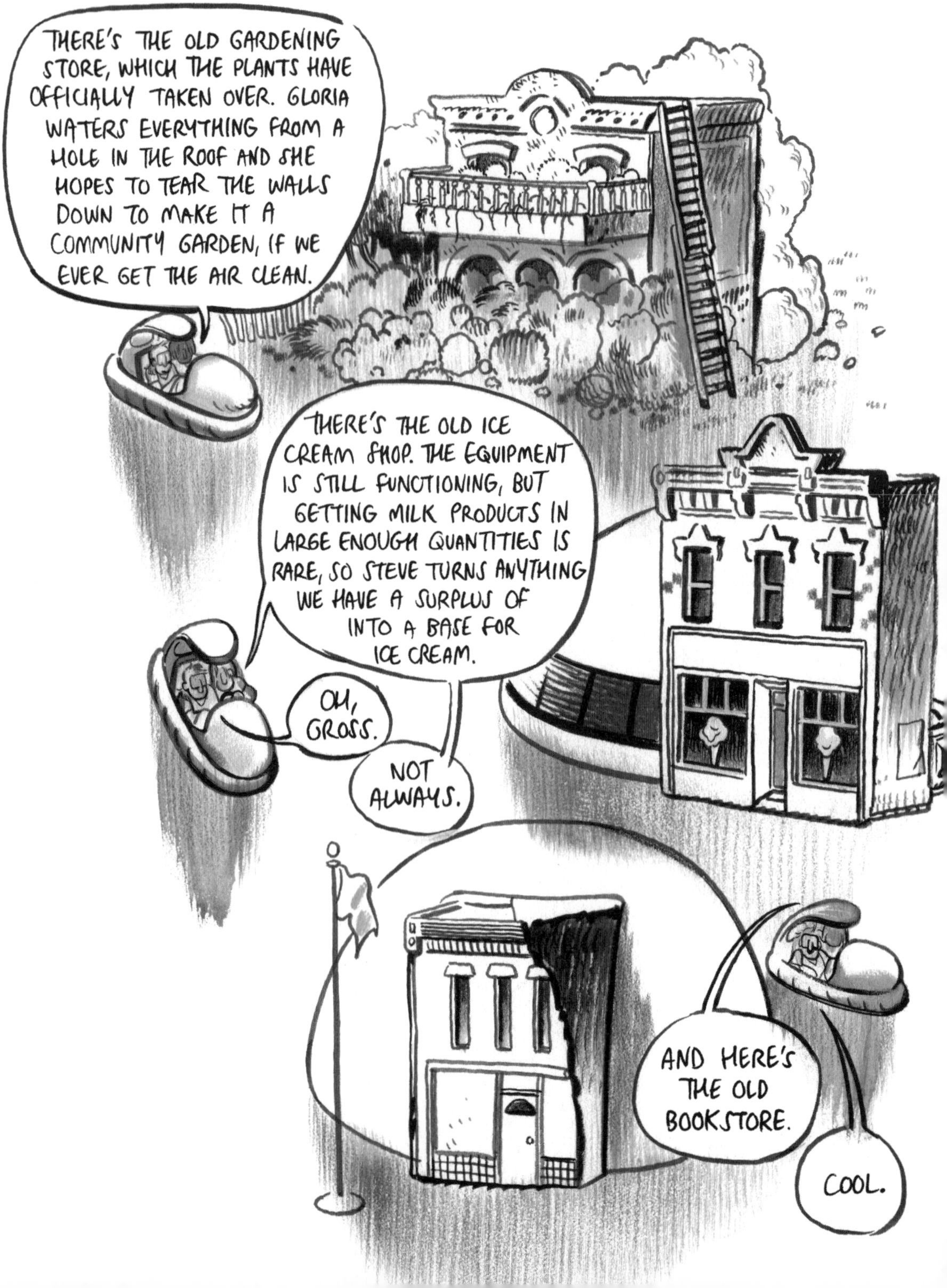
THERE'S THE OLD GARDENING STORE, WHICH THE PLANTS HAVE OFFICIALLY TAKEN OVER. GLORIA WATERS EVERYTHING FROM A HOLE IN THE ROOF AND SHE HOPES TO TEAR THE WALLS DOWN TO MAKE IT A COMMUNITY GARDEN, IF WE EVER GET THE AIR CLEAN.
THERE'S THE OLD ICE CREAM SHOP. THE EQUIPMENT IS STILL FUNCTIONING, BUT GETTING MILK PRODUCTS IN LARGE ENOUGH QUANTITIES IS RARE, SO STEVE TURNS ANYTHING WE HAVE A SURPLUS OF INTO A BASE FOR ICE CREAM.
OH, GROSS.
NOT ALWAYS.
AND HERE'S THE OLD BOOKSTORE.
COOL.

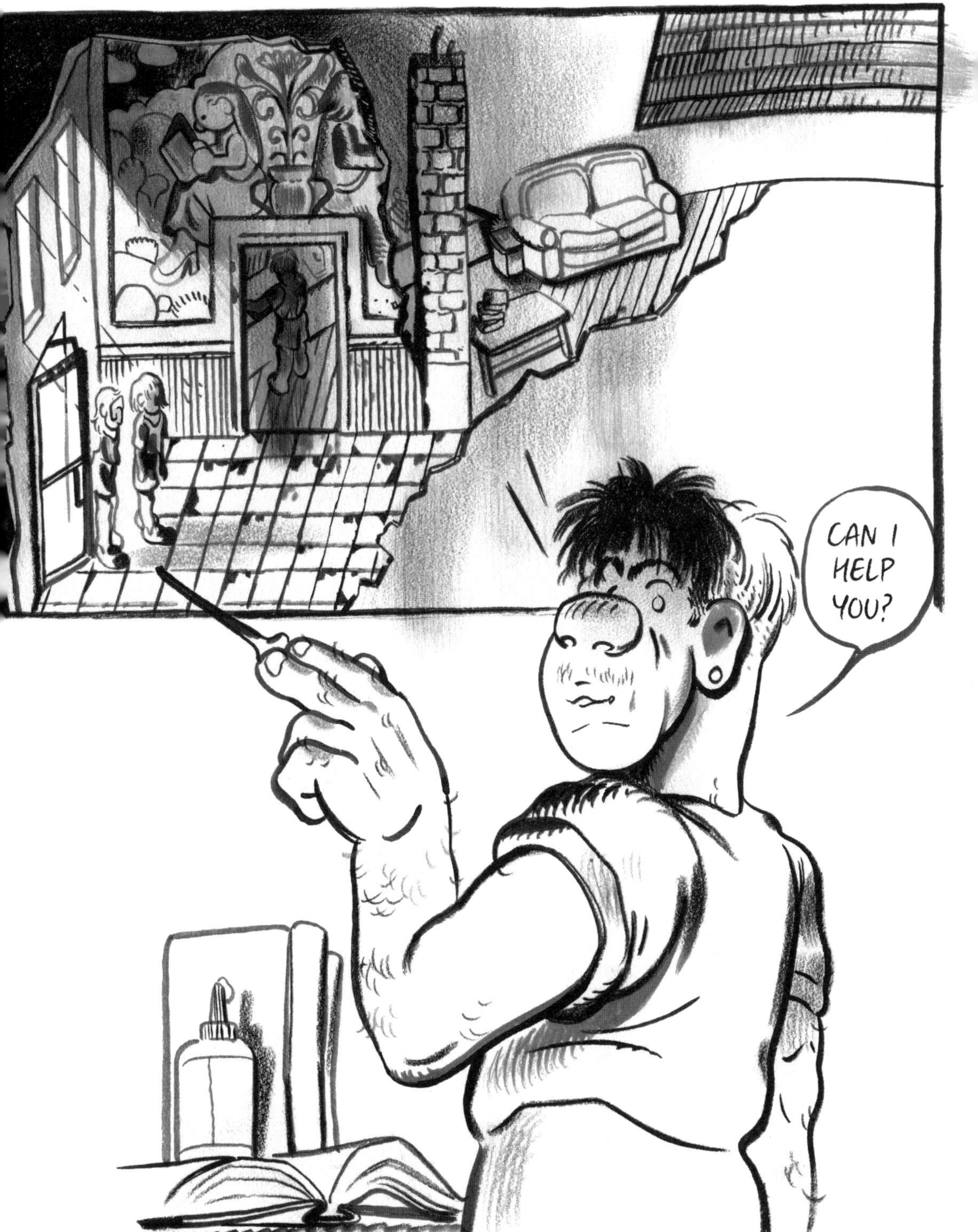
CAN I HELP YOU?

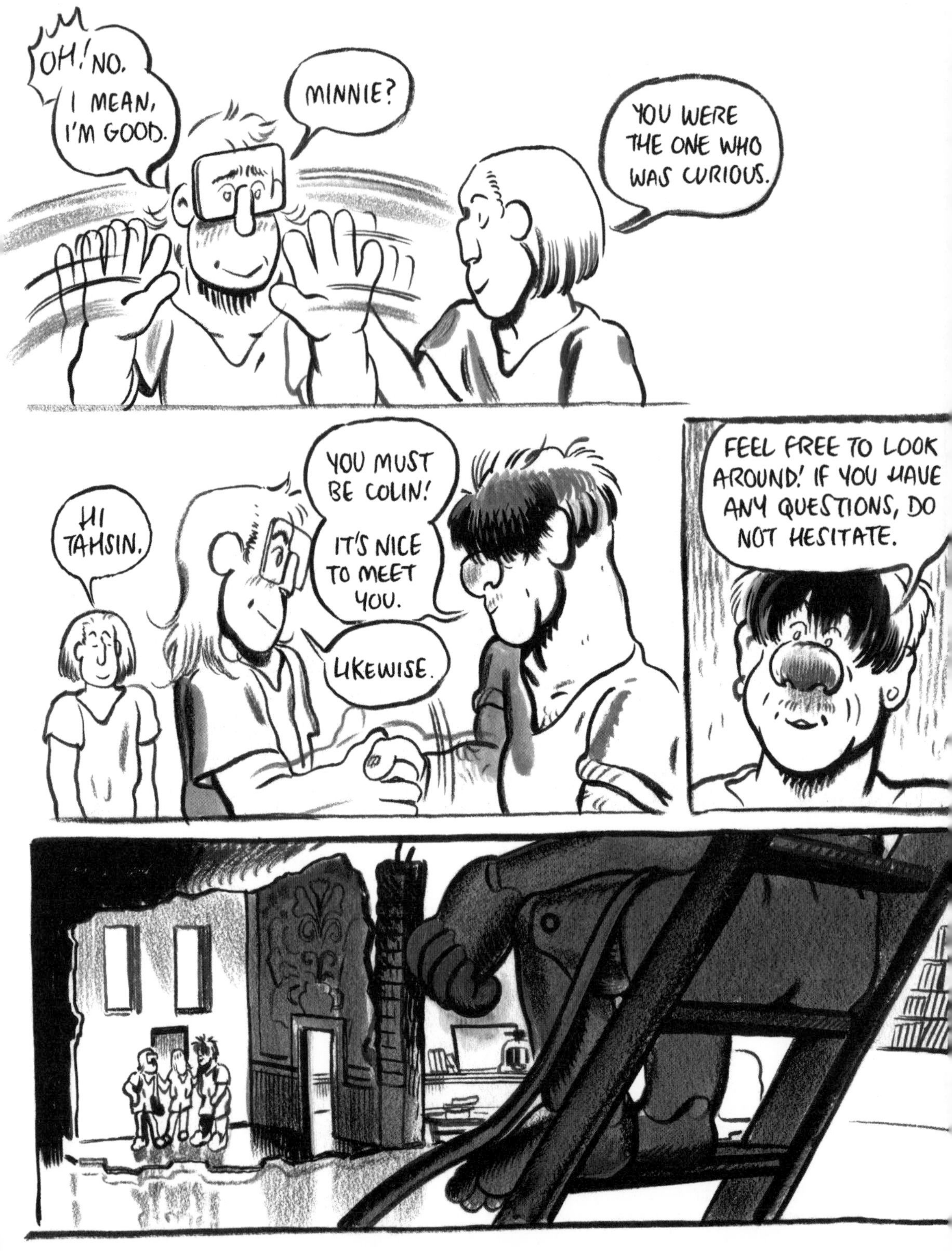
OH! NO.
I MEAN, I'M GOOD.
MINNIE?
YOU WERE THE ONE WHO WAS CURIOUS.
HI TAHSIN.
YOU MUST BE COLIN!
IT'S NICE TO MEET YOU.
LIKEWISE.
FEEL FREE TO LOOK AROUND! IF YOU HAVE ANY QUESTIONS, DO NOT HESITATE.

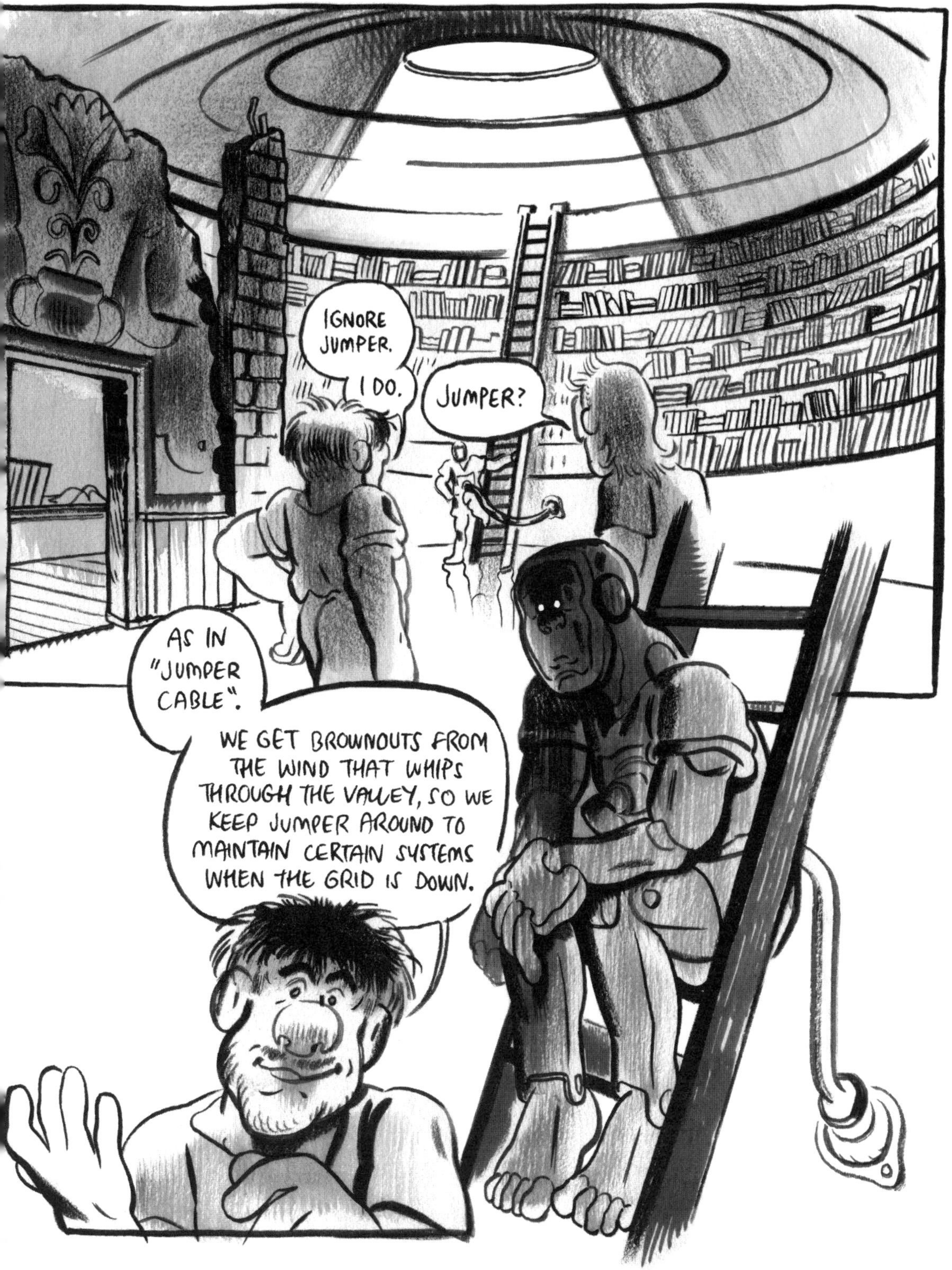
IGNORE JUMPER.
I DO.
JUMPER?
AS IN "JUMPER CABLE".
WE GET BROWNOUTS FROM THE WIND THAT WHIPS THROUGH THE VALLEY, SO WE KEEP JUMPER AROUND TO MAINTAIN CERTAIN SYSTEMS WHEN THE GRID IS DOWN.

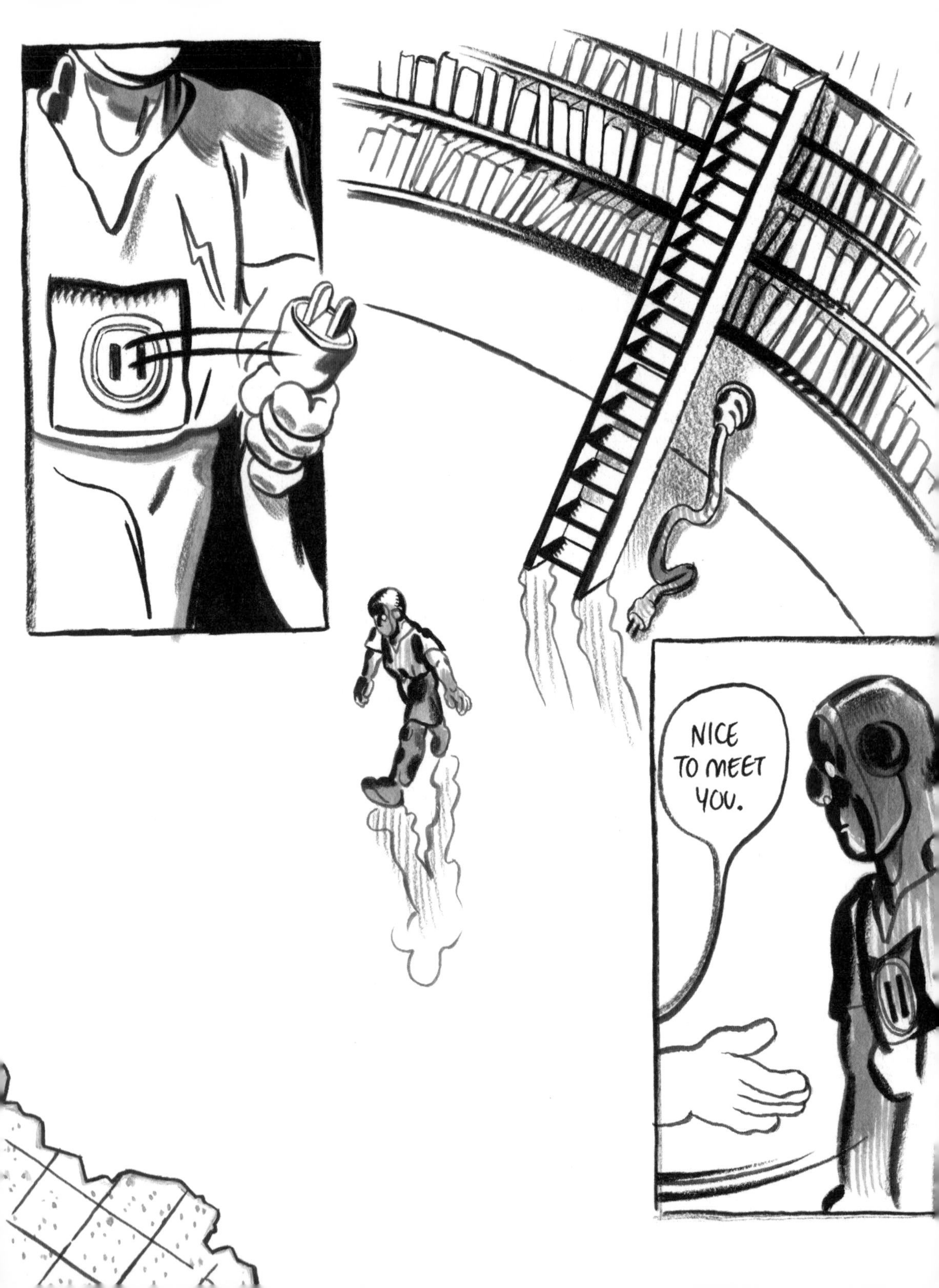
NICE TO MEET YOU.

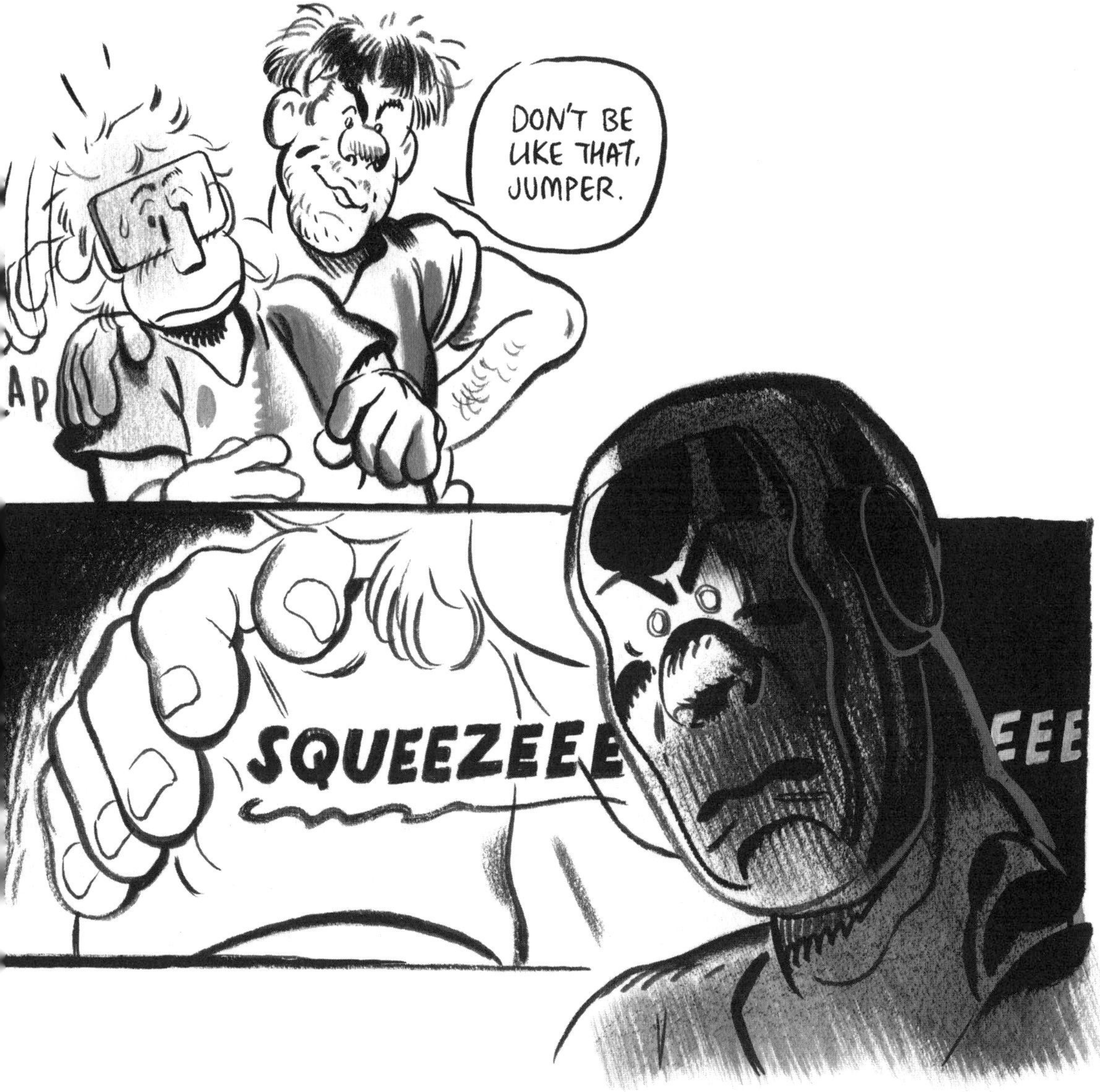
DON'T BE LIKE THAT, JUMPER.
SQUEEZEEE
EEE

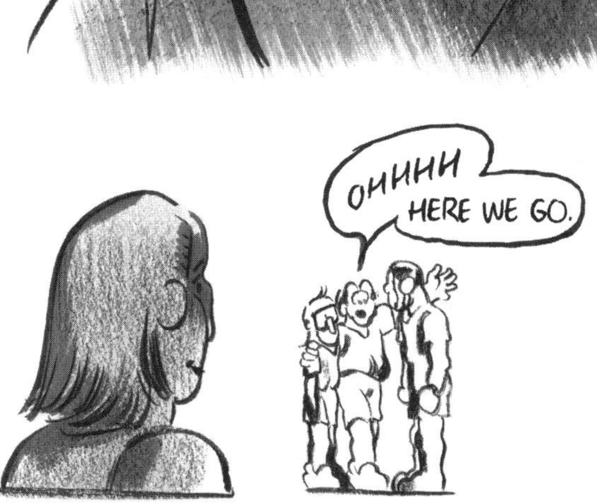
OHHHH HERE WE GO.

Minnie cherished opportunities to see Colin as a complete person. As someone who could be in love.

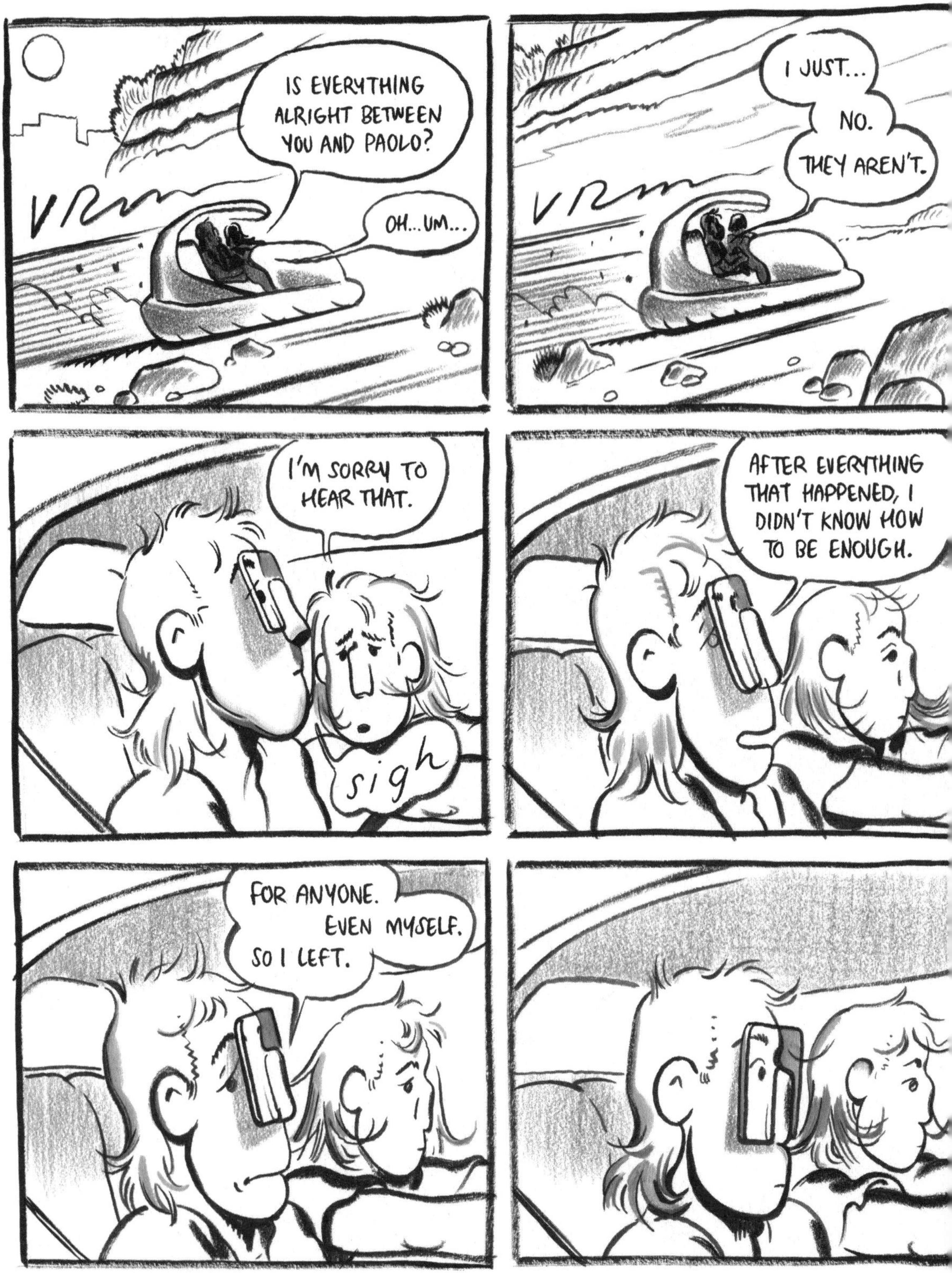
IS EVERYTHING ALRIGHT BETWEEN YOU AND PAOLO?
VRM
OH...UM...
I JUST...
NO.
THEY AREN'T.
VRM
I'M SORRY TO HEAR THAT.
sigh
AFTER EVERYTHING THAT HAPPENED, I DIDN'T KNOW HOW TO BE ENOUGH.
FOR ANYONE.
EVEN MYSELF.
SO I LEFT.

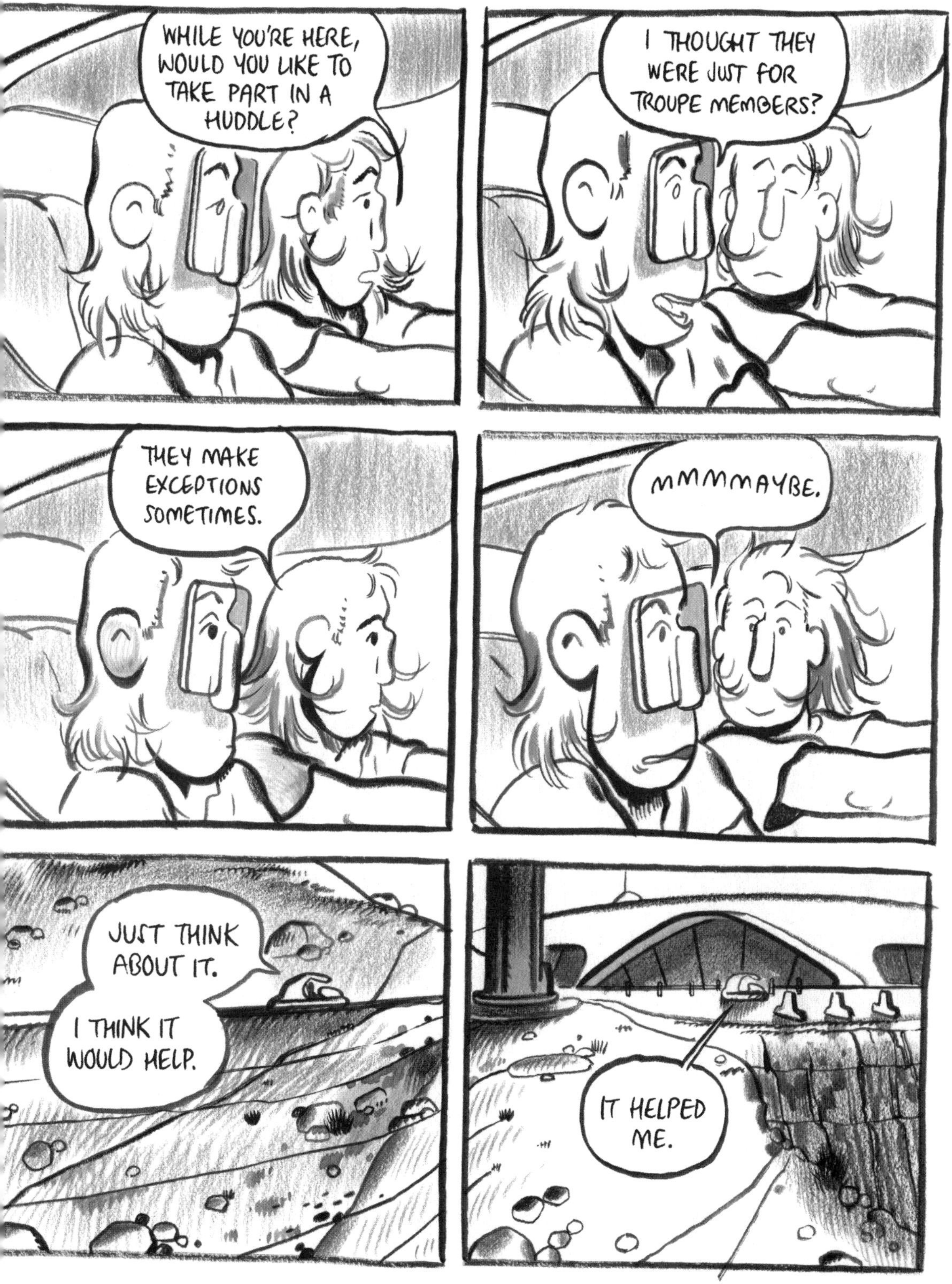
WHILE YOU'RE HERE, WOULD YOU LIKE TO TAKE PART IN A HUDDLE?
I THOUGHT THEY WERE JUST FOR TROUPE MEMBERS?
THEY MAKE EXCEPTIONS SOMETIMES.
MMMMAYBE.
JUST THINK ABOUT IT.
I THINK IT WOULD HELP.
IT HELPED ME.

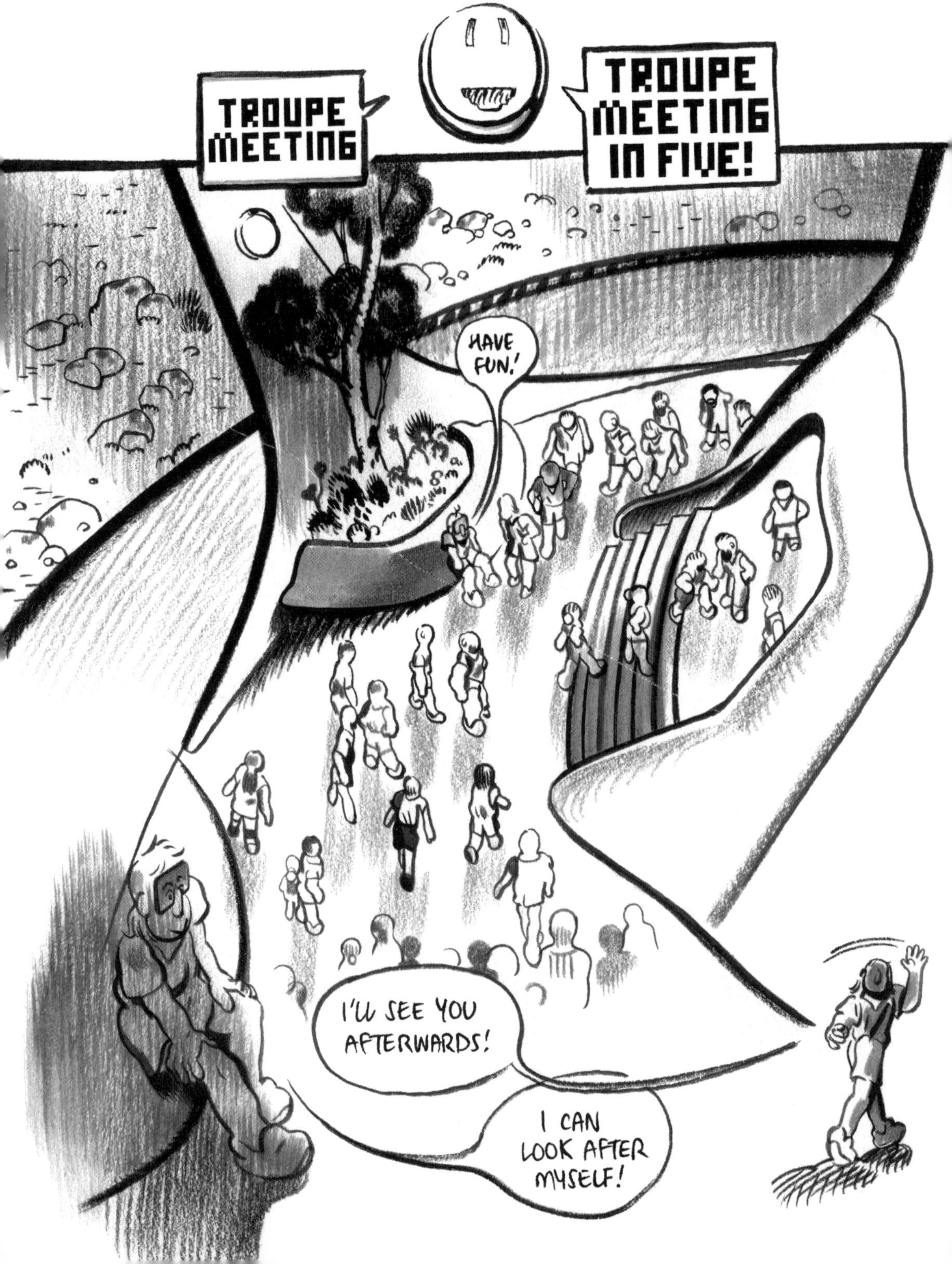
TROUPE MEETING
TROUPE MEETING IN FIVE!
HAVE FUN!
I'LL SEE YOU AFTERWARDS!
I CAN LOOK AFTER MYSELF!

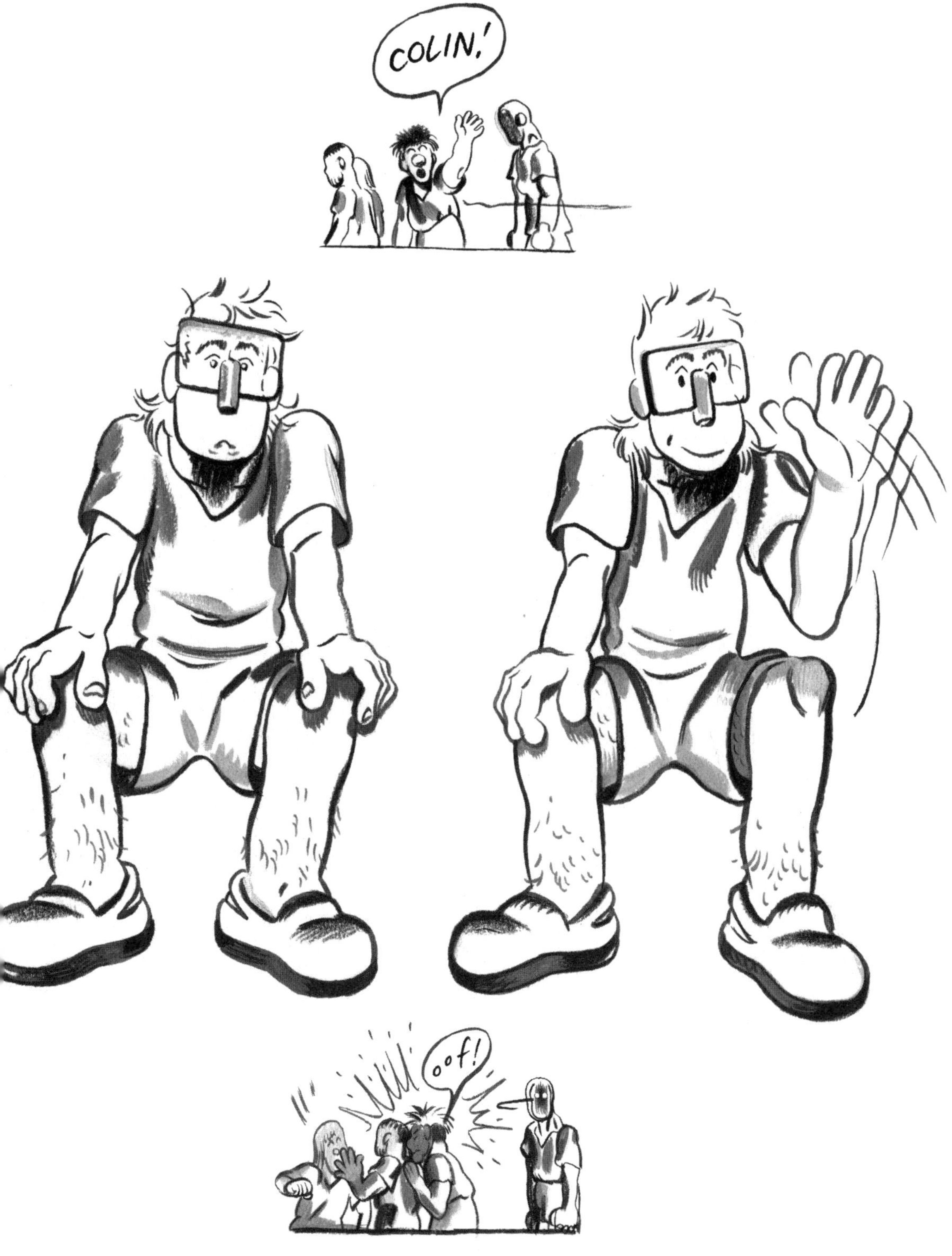
COLIN!
oof!

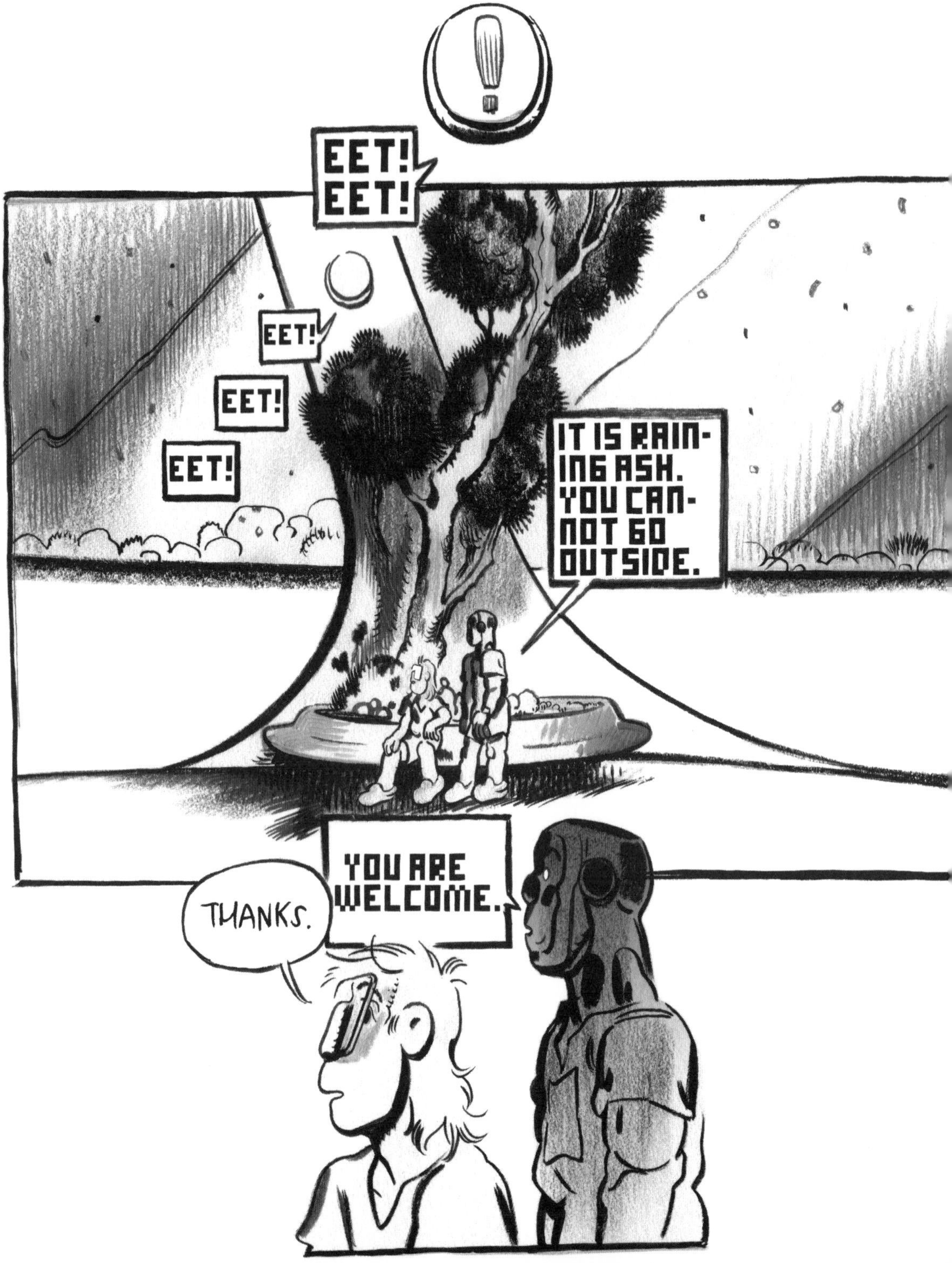
!
EET! EET!
EET!
EET!
EET!
IT IS RAINING ASH. YOU CANNOT GO OUTSIDE.
THANKS.
YOU ARE WELCOME.

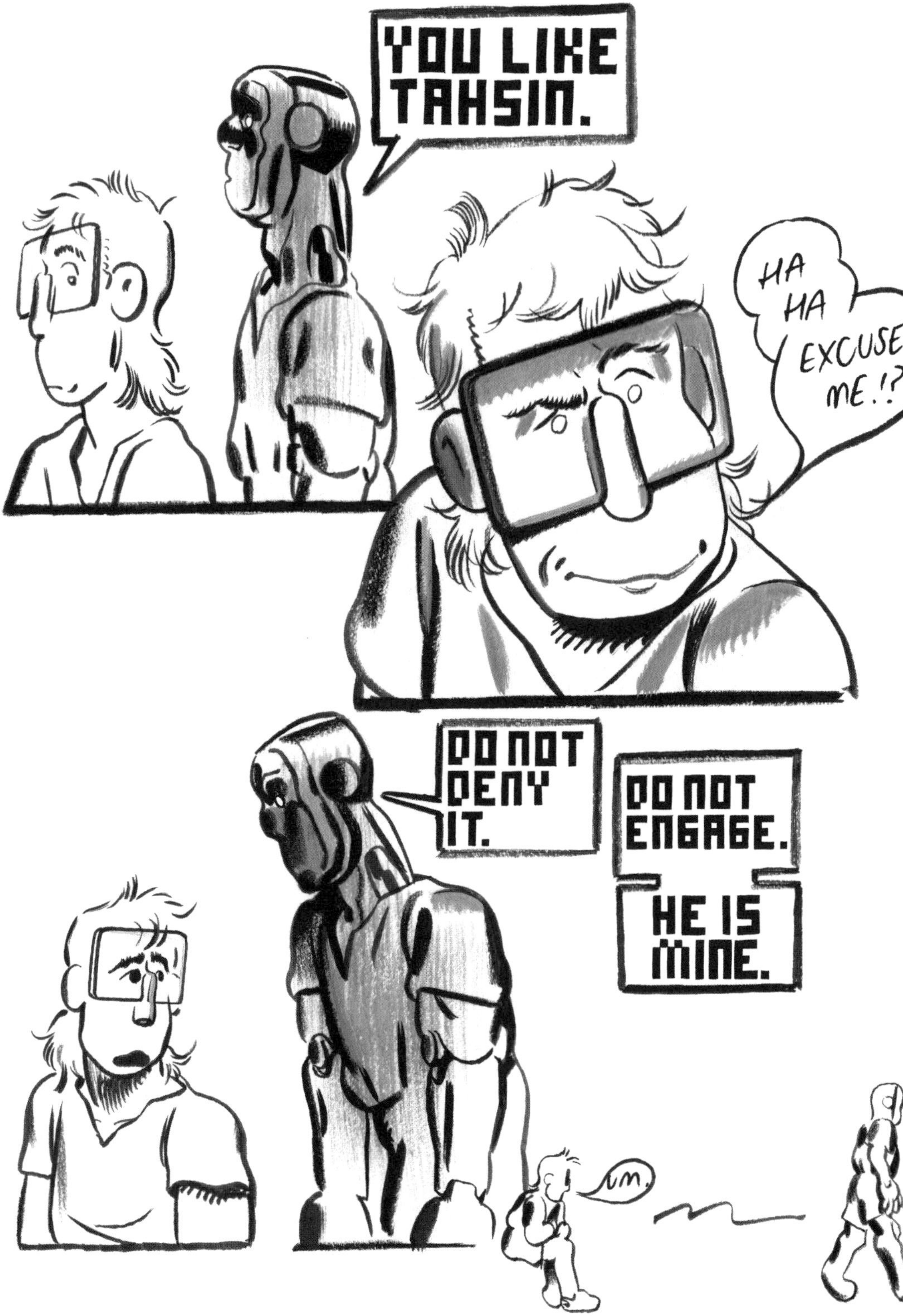
YOU LIKE TAHSIN.
HA HA EXCUSE ME.!?
DO NOT DENY IT.
DO NOT ENGAGE.
HE IS MINE.
UM.

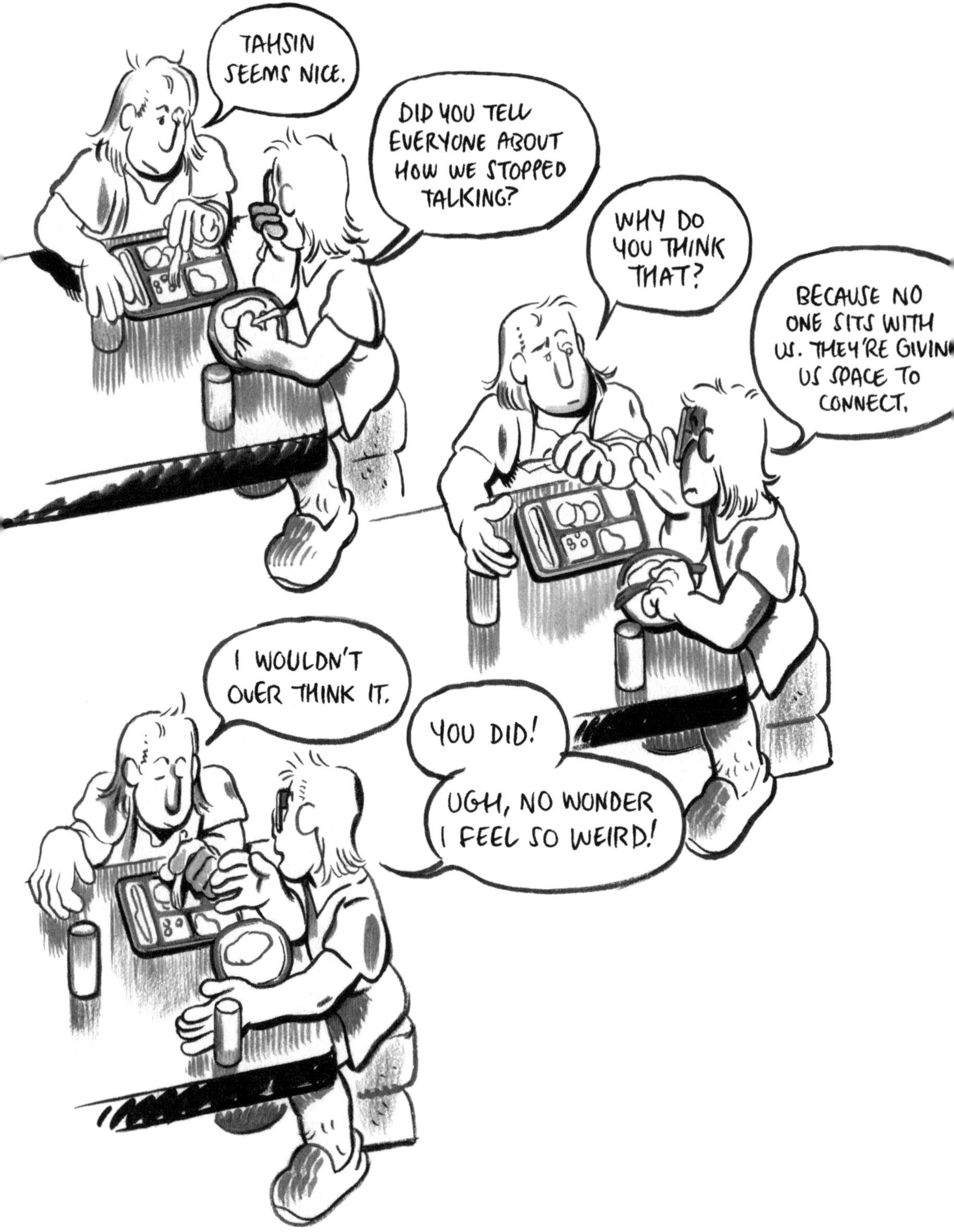
TAHSIN SEEMS NICE.
DID YOU TELL EVERYONE ABOUT HOW WE STOPPED TALKING?
WHY DO YOU THINK THAT?
BECAUSE NO ONE SITS WITH US. THEY'RE GIVING US SPACE TO CONNECT.
I WOULDN'T OVER THINK IT.
YOU DID!
UGH, NO WONDER I FEEL SO WEIRD!

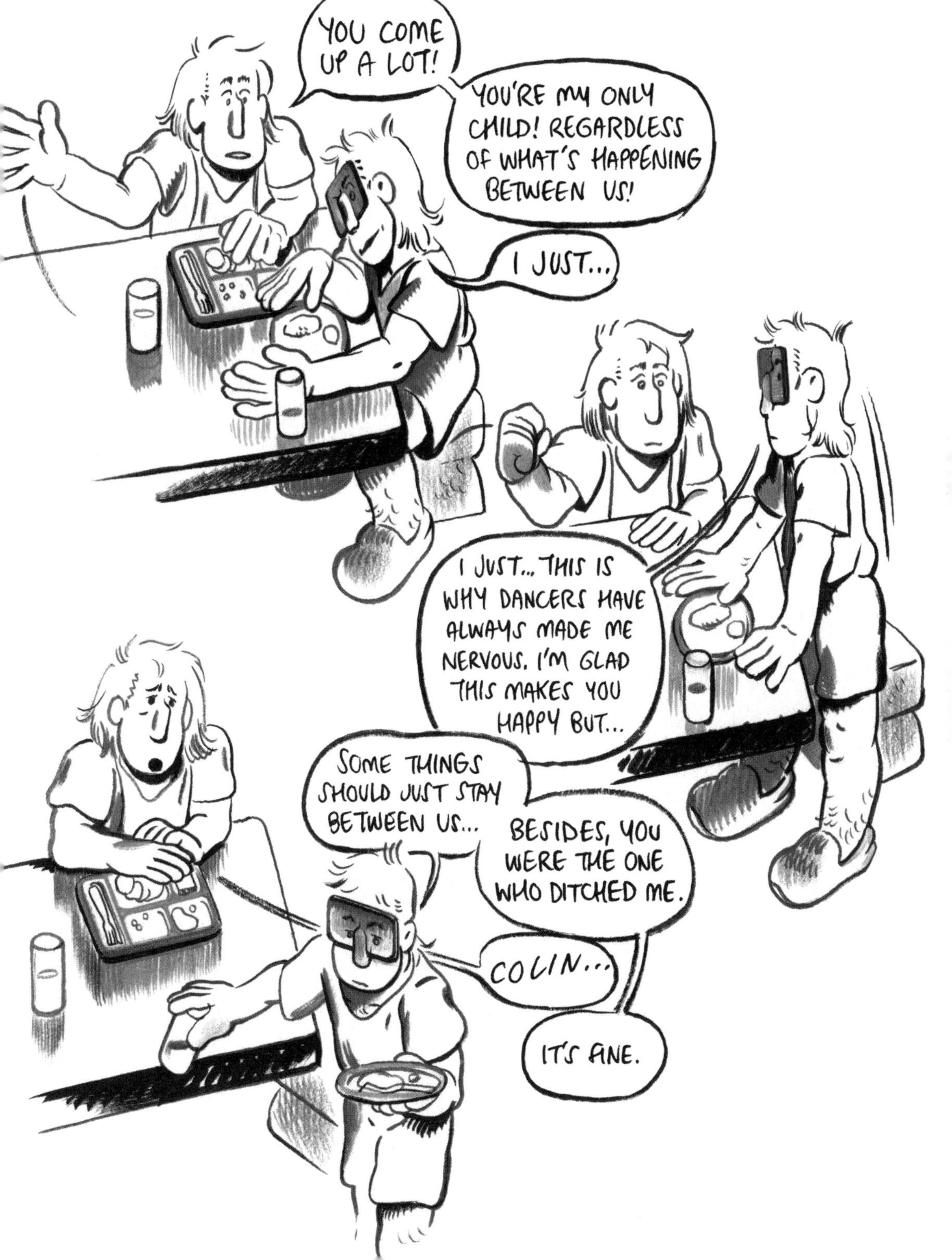
YOU COME UP A LOT!
YOU'RE MY ONLY CHILD! REGARDLESS OF WHAT'S HAPPENING BETWEEN US!
I JUST...
I JUST... THIS IS WHY DANCERS HAVE ALWAYS MADE ME NERVOUS. I'M GLAD THIS MAKES YOU HAPPY BUT...
SOME THINGS SHOULD JUST STAY BETWEEN US...
BESIDES, YOU WERE THE ONE WHO DITCHED ME.
COLIN...
IT'S FINE.

These people. Her people. They were her world.
And it pained her that Colin couldn't comprehend that.

Within her troupe, Minnie often spoke of her life before becoming a Dancer.

Minnie was born to two unhappy people who had hoped having a child would solve whatever it was they were lacking in their lives. It didn't work. Even before she arrived, Minnie's parents had pulled away from their own relationships—distancing themselves from their parents, their old friends, even their neighbors—for reasons Minnie could never quite understand. If they were craving the love that having a child could bring, why not open themselves up to all the love the world had to offer? Growing up isolated, Minnie felt a singular determination to fill her life with love. Considering the circumstances of her childhood, she saw something like love as nothing short of mystical.

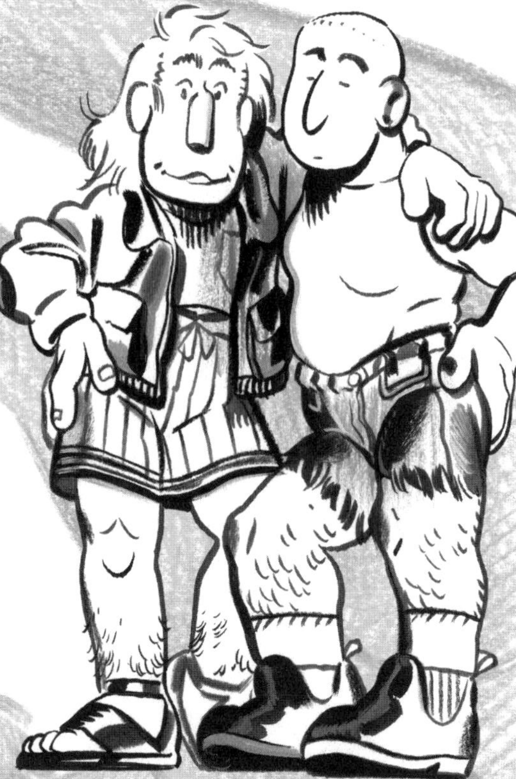

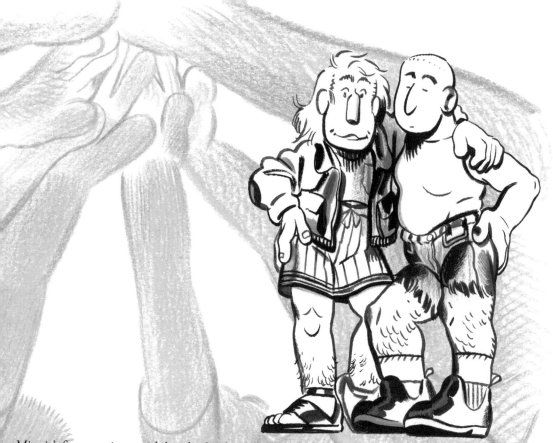

Minnie's first experience with love hit her hard.

Donna made electronic music using sounds she recorded from nature. She was often incredibly busy, either making her own music or DJing local events (birthday parties, bar and bat mitzvahs, charity galas) to make extra money to get herself through university. Minnie was obsessed. They shaved their heads together each summer. They adopted a polydactyl cat named Ray Gun. They moved in together after two months of dating and were pretend-married a year later.

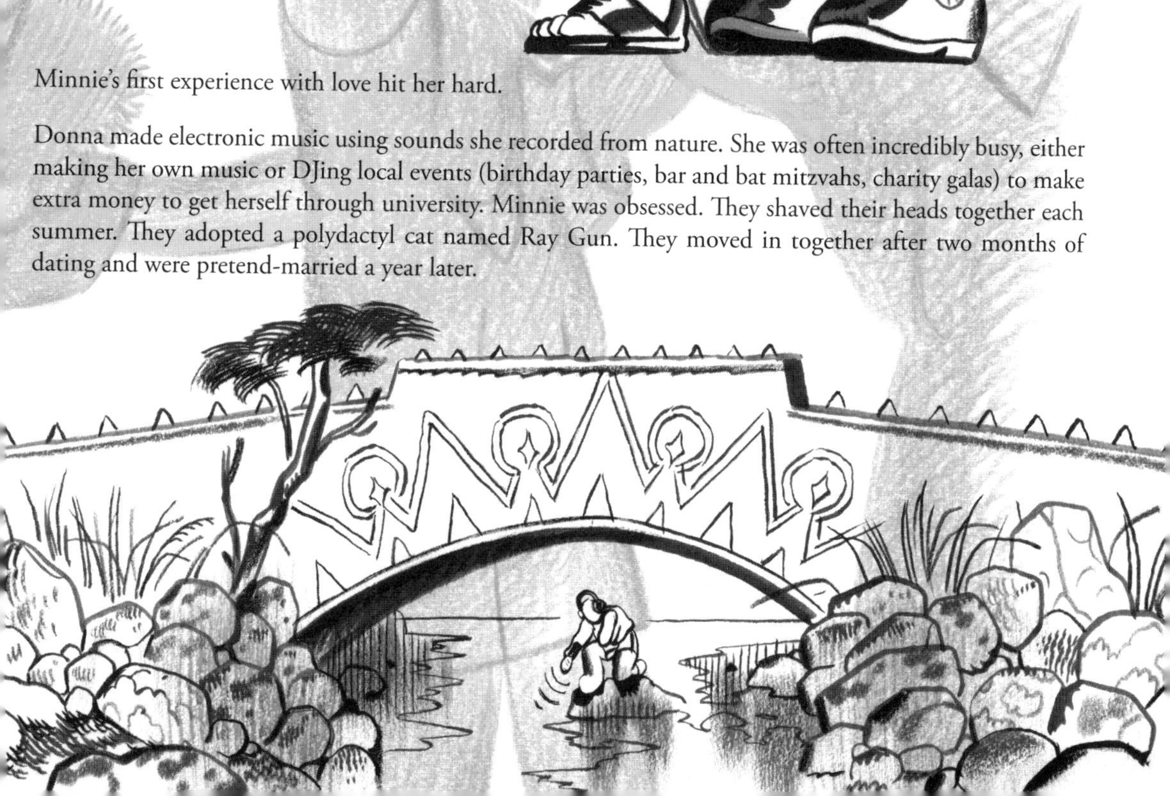

Donna and Minnie were together for just under six years. It is still the longest relationship Minnie has ever been in. Only after she started attending troupe meetings did Minnie feel comfortable admitting that Colin's birth had cost her her first love. There was no way she could blame Colin for this, and she knew, ultimately, that the ending of her relationship came naturally, as Minnie and Donna's opinions about having kids became harder to avoid.

Donna was the only child of two people who had several children each from previous marriages. She grew up feeling like the awkward stepchild in a house full of strangers. She craved silence. She was happiest alone, with an exception made for Minnie, who was all the home she felt she would ever need.

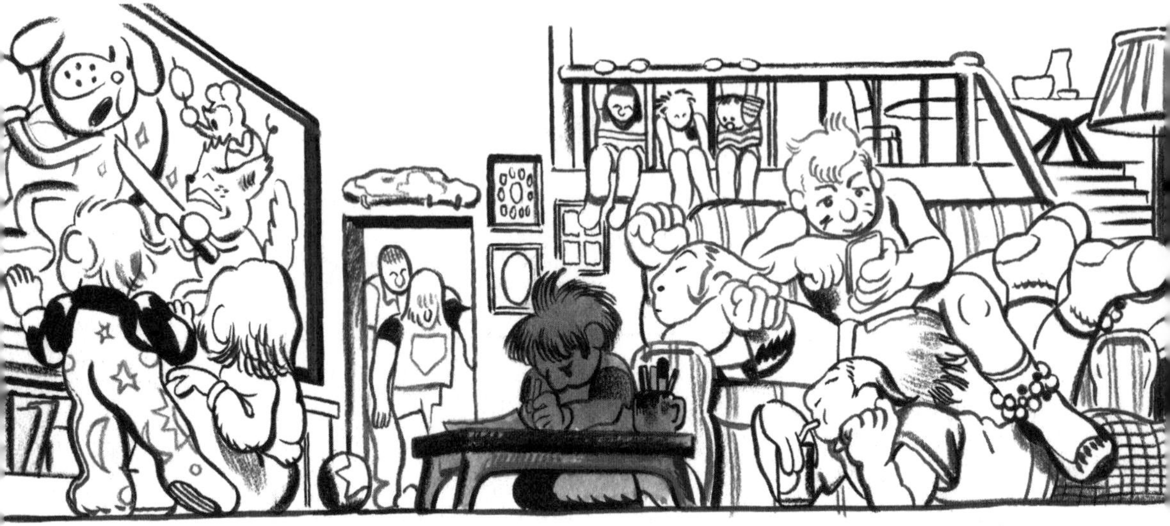

Minnie craved more, though. Why stop with just the two of them, when you could make even more happiness for yourself? Minnie contacted a fertility clinic on her own in the hopes that Donna would come to love her child when the time came. But when the time came, she didn't, especially after finding out that Minnie had made the decision without consulting her first.

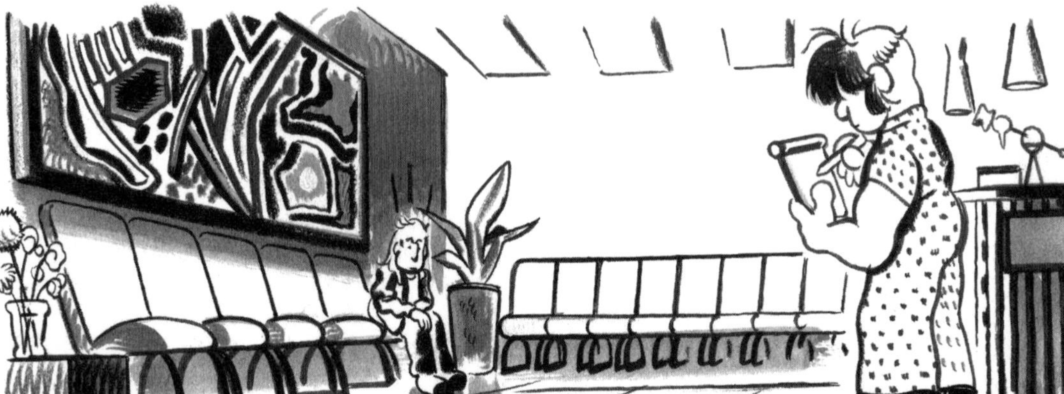

Even though a lifetime had passed, Minnie thought of Donna often. After long days, when she was already feeling low, Minnie would wonder what Donna's life looked like now. Where was she living? And with whom? Minnie still thought of Donna as Colin's other mom. She never cared who the sperm donor was.

Their last fight as a couple had been especially cruel. Minnie told Donna the truth only after her belly started to show. When Minnie admitted that she already knew the sex of the person growing inside of her, Donna cried out:

"There are already so many men in the world!"

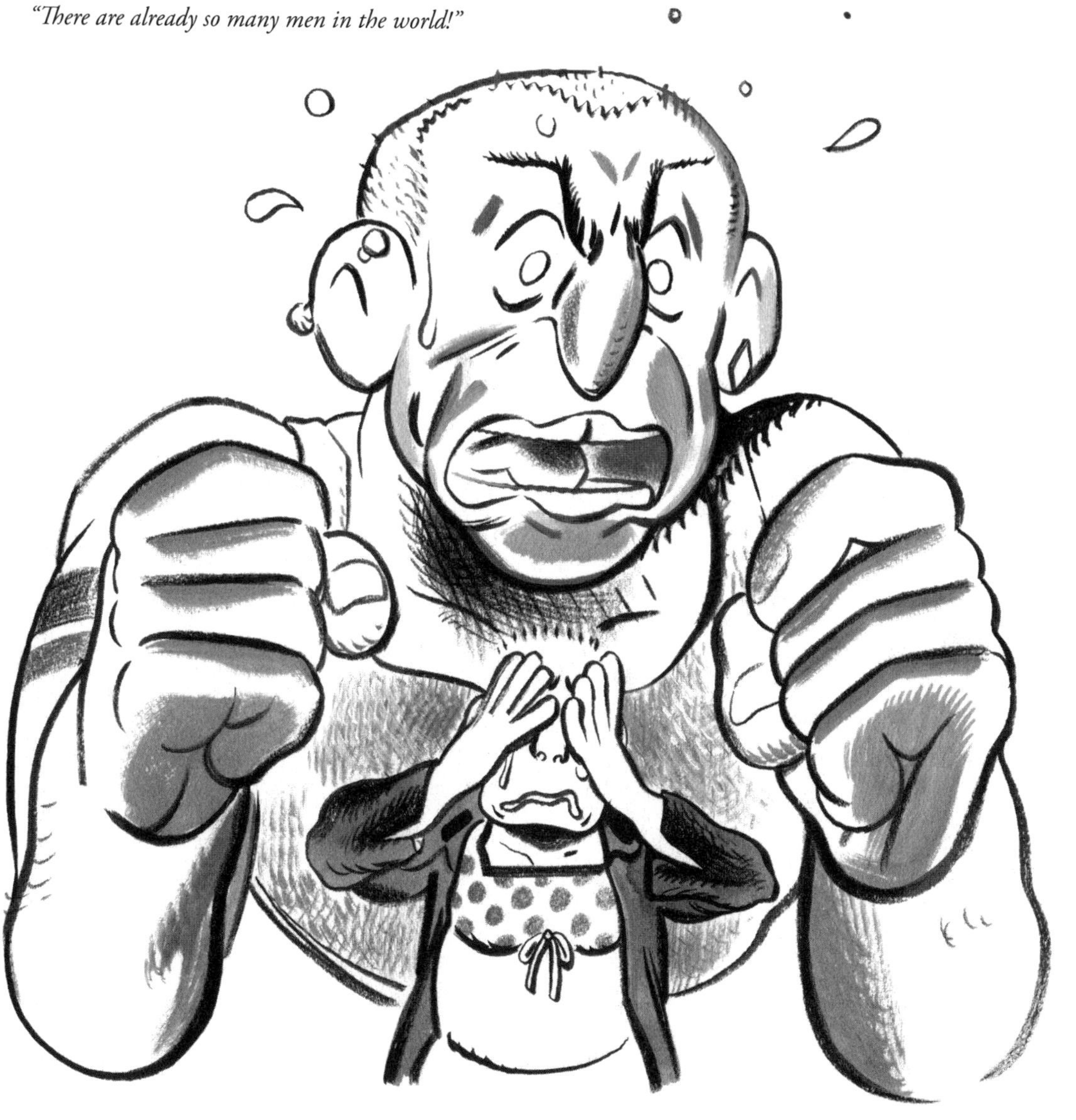

Minnie could have taken supplements to aid her body in choosing the baby's eye color, skin hue, and sex, but Minnie wanted to leave herself open to fate. Minnie was of the first generation too young to remember the horrors of the Administration. Fate was such an old-fashioned notion at a time when everyone craved a greater sense of control over their lives. Why would you leave anything up to chance after decades of lost freedoms?

Even if she hadn't been explicitly aware of it, Minnie had been testing Donna and their relationship by getting pregnant. Minnie worried that what they had couldn't expand to accept more life, and by extension more love, and now she knew for certain.

And then there was Colin.

Before Colin was born, Minnie held a job fundraising for a small women's health organization, but eventually quit because of how uncomfortable Colin made them. The last time she saw most of her coworkers was at their annual retreat, after which Minnie and a three-year-old Colin were socially outcast.

Her coworkers had all birthed genetically coerced daughters and hadn't taken kindly to Colin and what he represented. These women had fought for so long to reclaim their sovereignty from men that the presence of a small boy couldn't help but make them feel uneasy. In their eyes, Minnie was a young woman who couldn't understand what they had witnessed firsthand, and that she had acted foolishly having a son.

But Minnie didn't mind. Colin was her everything. They were a world unto themselves.

Continuing to date within the group of women she had known through her old job was demoralizing, and Minnie soon gave up. Her social circle swelled considerably once she took a job balancing the budget for a rapidly growing religious organization called *The Dance*.

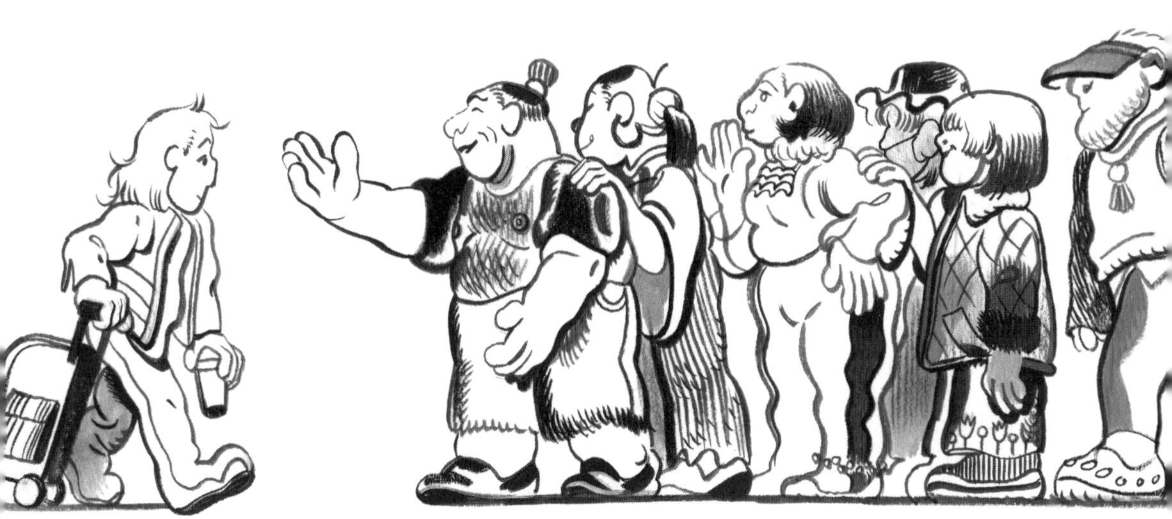

Looking for personal fulfillment, Minnie started attending meetings herself and traveling to conventions across the country. She met engaging people whom she loved, some platonically, some romantically, some both.

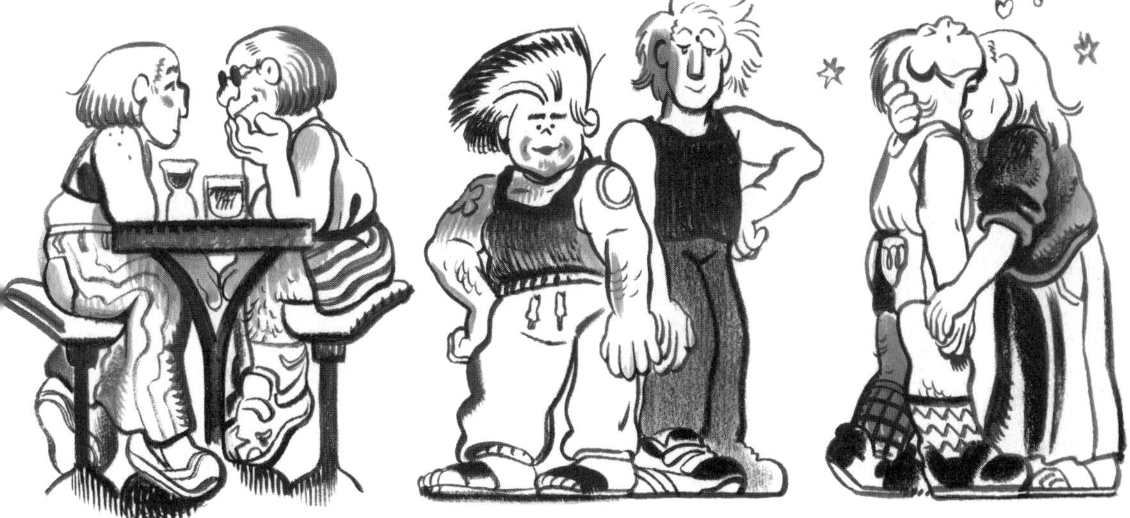

The Dancers were from a wider background than those she had known in her women's group. Sure, the message of *The Dance* was more passive than the activists she had known, but their view of the world more closely aligned with her own. As she saw it, life had a way of working itself out, even if you needed a whole community of people to help recognize that.

As Minnie got older, fulfilled by the love of her son and that of her troupe, she often thought back to her parents and wondered what they had wanted out of their lives. They were two apprehensive people who rarely left the house during the day. When they did, it was always together. Neither worked a job, and they both collected disability insurance, which barely kept them afloat. She would never know what they had endured during their lifetimes, witnessing atrocities that she could not fathom. Had they been persecuted by the Administration? If so, for what reason?

One sweltering October day, Minnie caught her mother changing after bringing their delivered groceries in from the transport. From the doorway of her parents' bedroom, she saw the deep scars that covered her mother's chest, back, and upper arms. The pale grooves that had long been hidden beneath her mother's wardrobe of thick woolen cardigans and bulky sweaters, worn regardless of the season. It was the only time Minnie remembered seeing either of her parents' bare flesh.

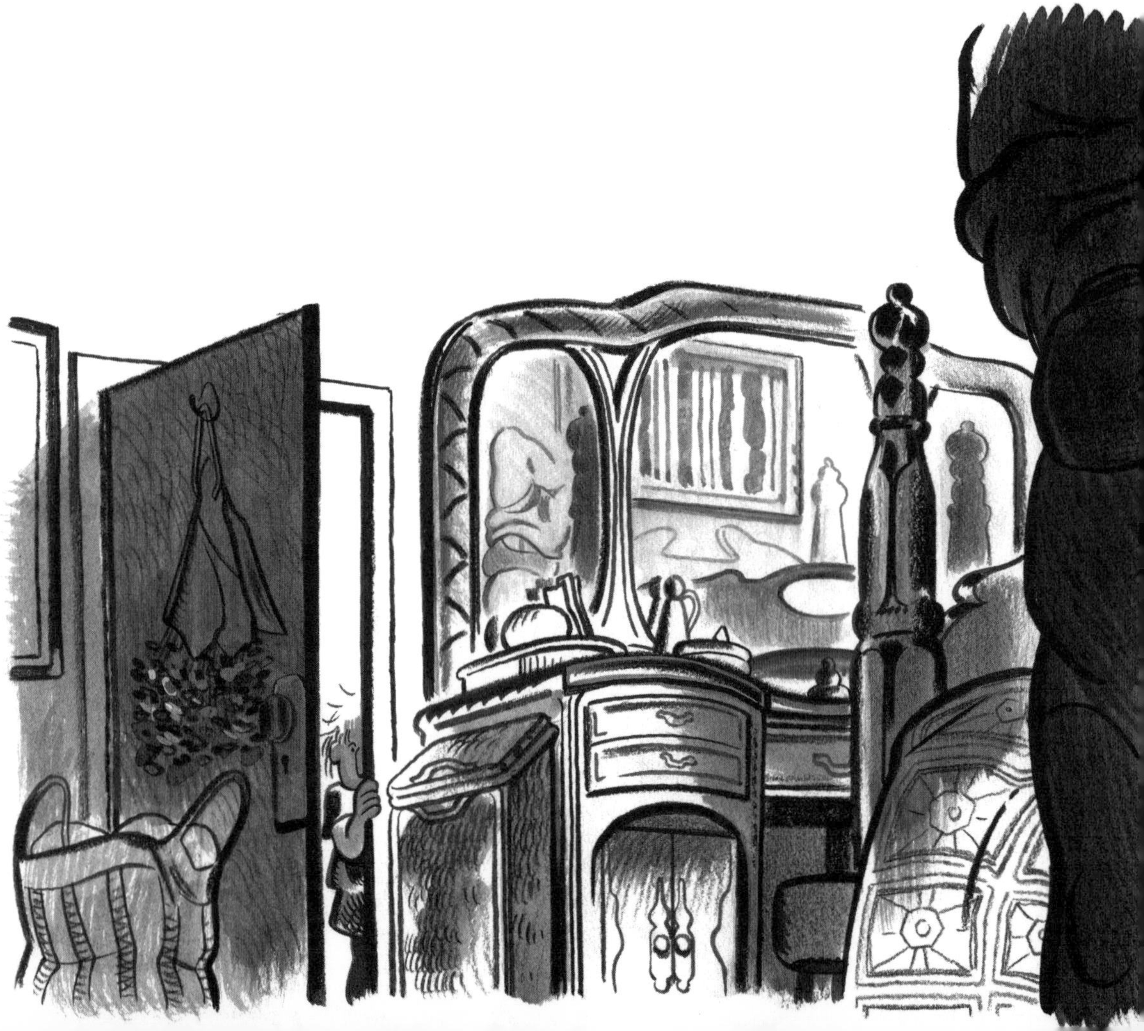

Living life in a fulfilling way was no easy achievement. No relationship, or job, or affiliation—not even a child—could fill the whole of a person's being. Minnie learned this through Colin in the same way her parents had learned it from her. Nourishing yourself had to come first. Unfortunately, sometimes the hole in a life was simply too large and hollow for anything to ever fill it.

Minnie knew that she had been a great mother. She also knew that, in Colin's gentle way, he would assure her that she was still a great mother. But Minnie knew that he simply didn't need her in the way he once did. Sometimes, on bad days, she caught herself wondering if he had ever really needed her. He had needed her in all the ways a child needs a parent, but there was no denying that Minnie would always need more.

That was why her reaction to the news about the stabbing was so unexpected for her. It was a crisis where she was needed, *wanted* even, clearly and unequivocally. And yet, Minnie couldn't bring herself to react in the way she knew she should. The fear of possibly losing Colin had been visceral and immediate, but what lingered after she knew Colin was safe was her heartache over losing the house. Even from that initial phone call, she knew her opportunity to move into that house was already gone. She could grasp that what had happened was bigger than missing out on a new home, but the feeling of disappointment, compounded by the shame of even feeling that disappointment, remained.

During her depression, Minnie would visualize walking through the home. Rearranging furniture. Tending to her garden. Meeting her neighbors.

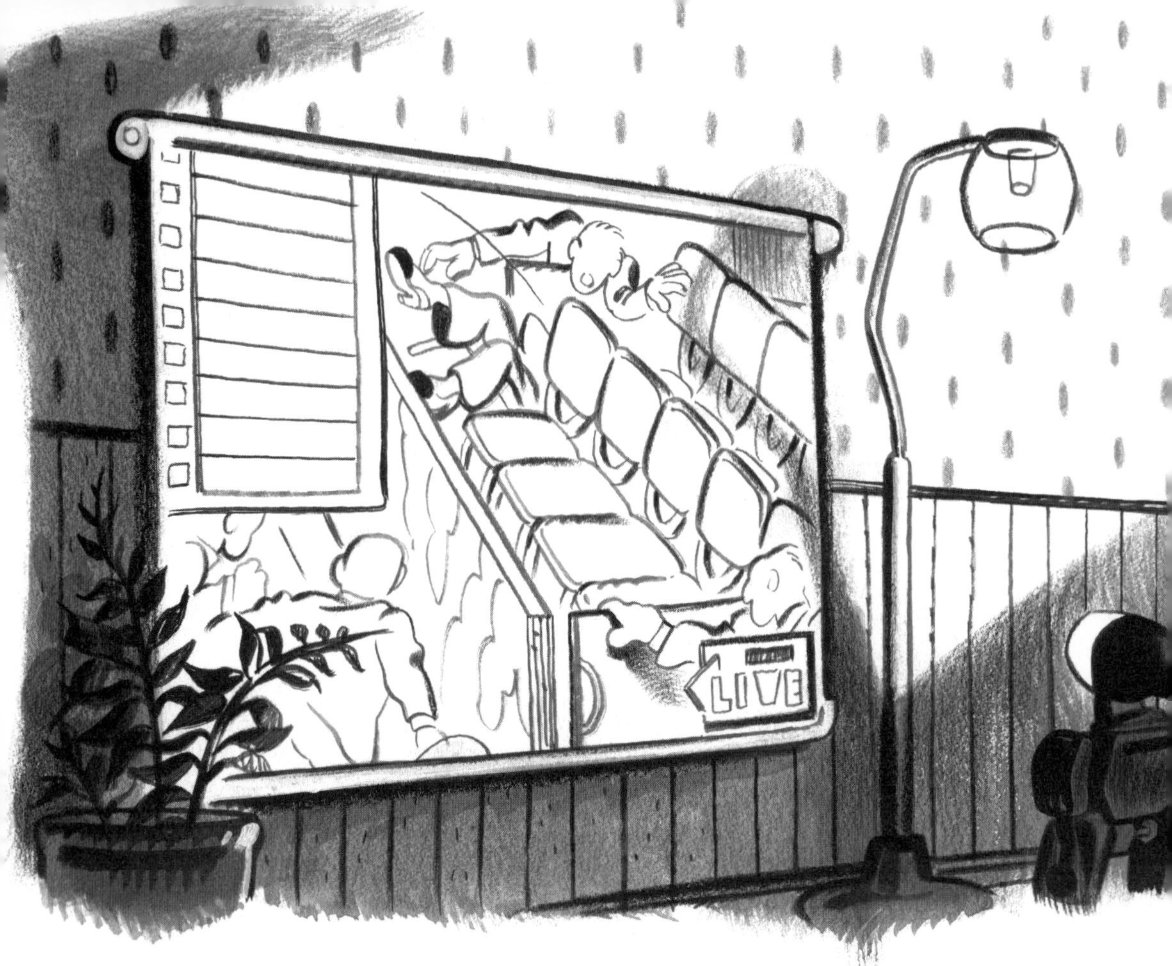
LIVE

The last time Minnie saw her parents was after they began living in a retirement community. Each retiree was given a free standing house to call their own, attended to by a retinue of robotic assistants. Minnie never liked to visit. Despite having hated the somber rooms of her childhood, seeing her parents in these bright open spaces made her uncomfortable. She told Donna that they felt like airport terminals—waiting rooms for a trip her parents would one day take, suddenly, without her. Minnie couldn't deny that her parents had finally come to enjoy their lives, though. Or at least, what was left of it.

On that final visit, Minnie arrived just as a sudden thunderstorm touched down, battering her parents' house in torrential rain. Soaking wet, she walked in to find her parents laughing in the dark.

After years of delays, important evidence mishandled and lost, and a difficult search for impartial jurors, the trial to prosecute the president of the Administration had been set. Each of her cabinet members still awaited their day in court—which would also be televised nationally by way of A.R.G_O—which Minnie's parents planned on following like a season of sports.

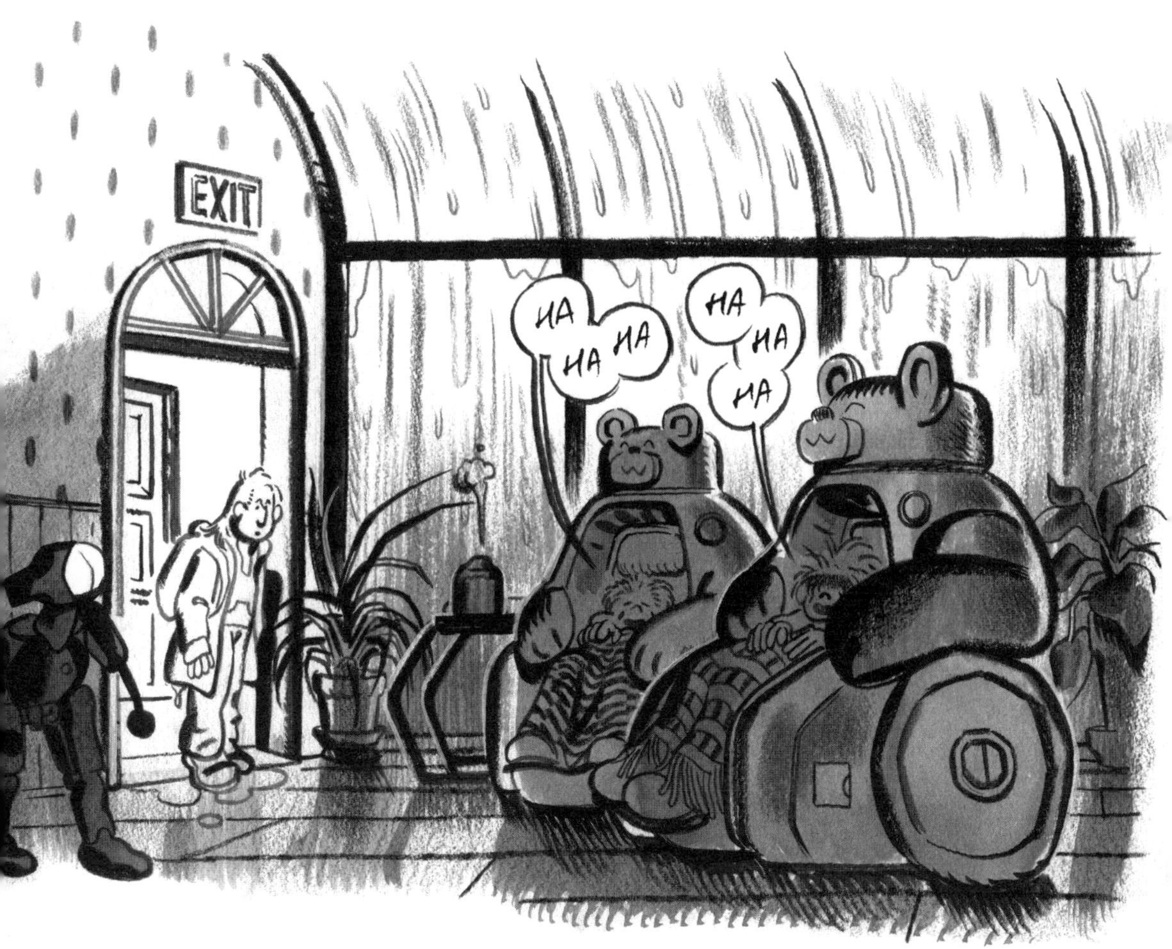
EXIT
HA
HA HA
HA
HA
HA

But after all their years of patiently waiting, the president died before justice could be delivered, seated in the courtroom on the day of her trial. She had abruptly fallen backwards, tossing one of her legs up over her head. The telecast didn't cut away, as people in the courtroom ran towards her, a look of panic on each of their faces.

That day left Minnie feeling deeply sad. She was grateful that her parents were able to find the closure they had craved, but watching the woman who had been the source of all their pain die in such a mundane way—another body made anonymous in death—felt unnecessarily voyeuristic. By that point, there were new problems to contend with. Different monsters masquerading as empathetic people, set on ruining the lives of others. What could even be achieved by this single death?

Minnie found herself thinking the same thing when her parents died a few months later. She had once blamed them for so much, marking them as the source of her obsessive, love-starved personality. She had been her parents' answer to their own questions about life and how to live it, and now, without them, she would never know what they had learned.

It was only after her own pregnancy that Minnie realized she had inadvertently made the same decision her parents had. Colin was just one answer to a lifetime full of questions. A single attempt to ask the Universe: *why*?

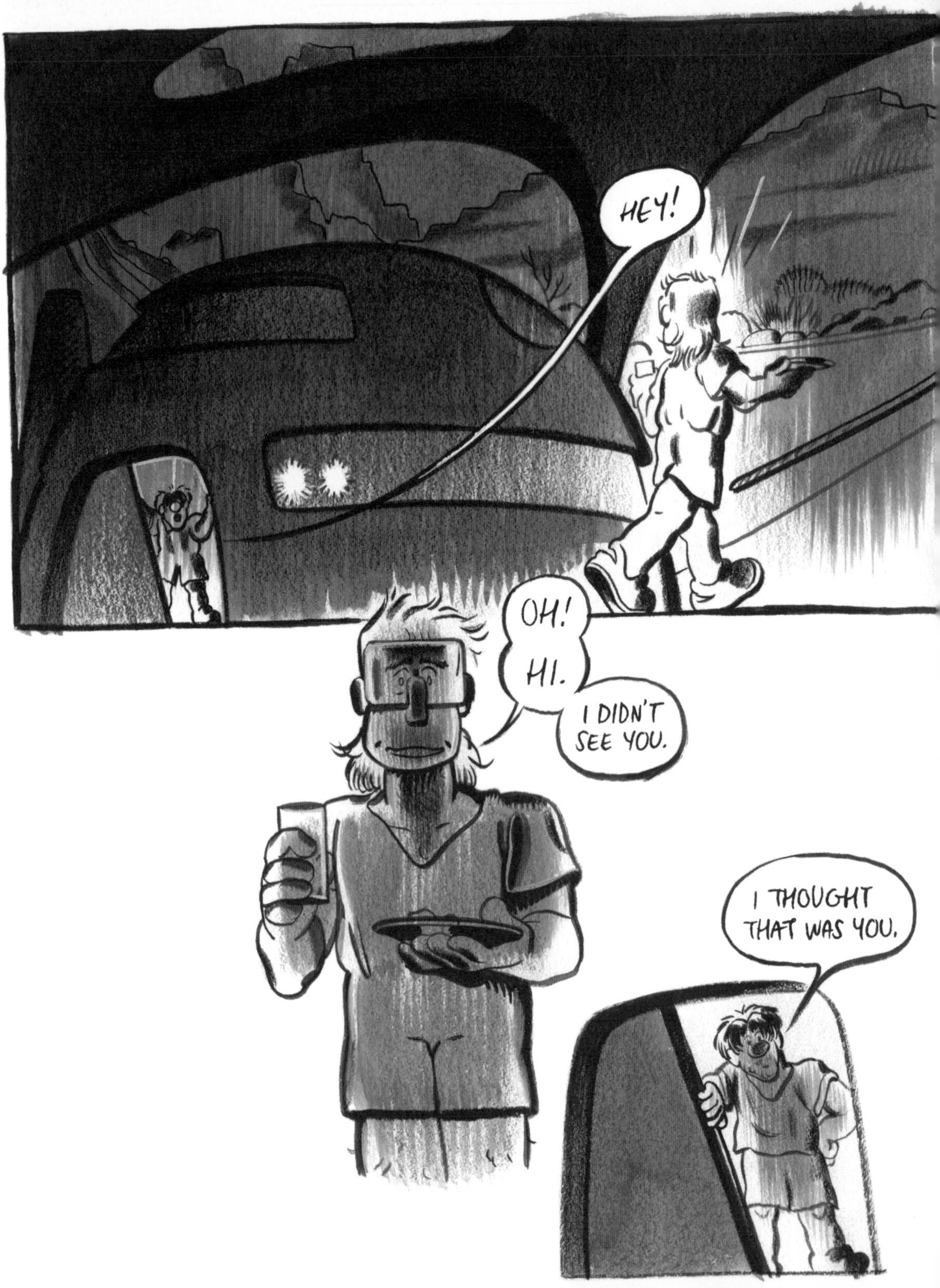
HEY!
OH!
HI.
I DIDN'T SEE YOU.
I THOUGHT THAT WAS YOU.

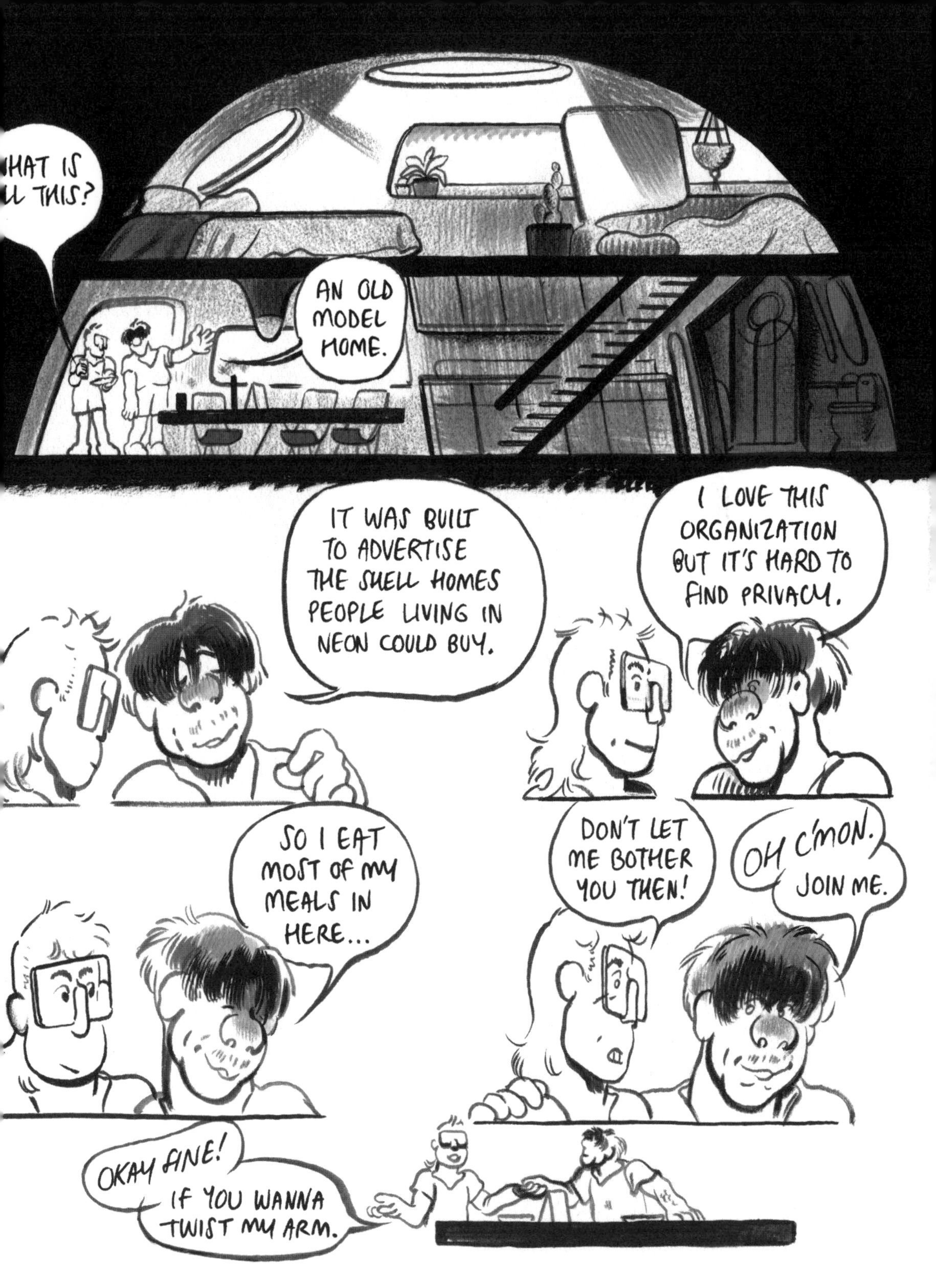
HAT IS
L THIS?
AN OLD MODEL HOME.
IT WAS BUILT TO ADVERTISE THE SHELL HOMES PEOPLE LIVING IN NEON COULD BUY.
I LOVE THIS ORGANIZATION BUT IT'S HARD TO FIND PRIVACY.
SO I EAT MOST OF MY MEALS IN HERE...
DON'T LET ME BOTHER YOU THEN!
OH C'MON. JOIN ME.
OKAY FINE! IF YOU WANNA TWIST MY ARM.

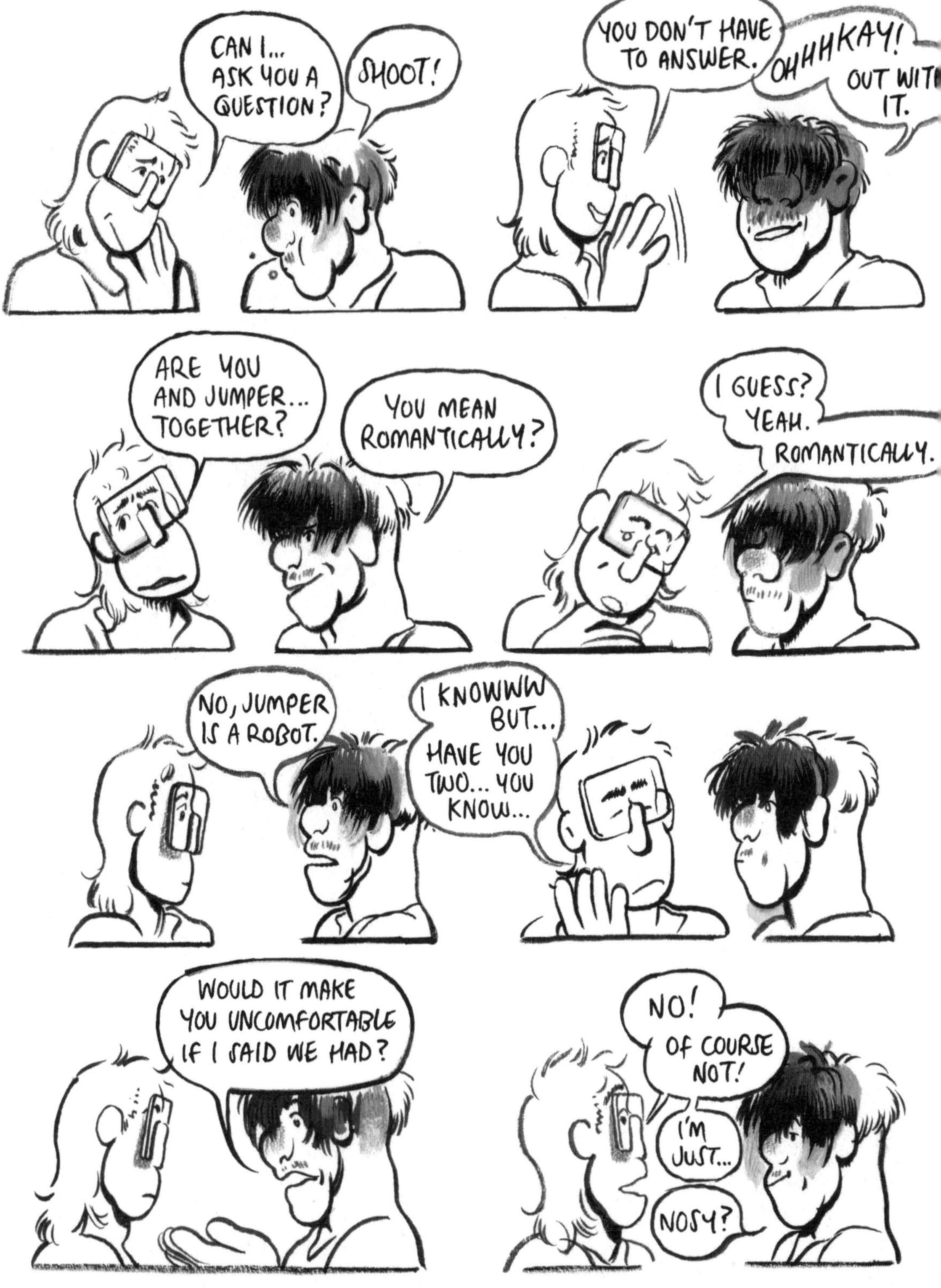
CAN I... ASK YOU A QUESTION?
SHOOT!
YOU DON'T HAVE TO ANSWER.
OHHHKAY!
OUT WITH IT.
ARE YOU AND JUMPER... TOGETHER?
YOU MEAN ROMANTICALLY?
I GUESS? YEAH. ROMANTICALLY.
NO, JUMPER IS A ROBOT.
I KNOWWW BUT... HAVE YOU TWO... YOU KNOW...
WOULD IT MAKE YOU UNCOMFORTABLE IF I SAID WE HAD?
NO!
OF COURSE NOT!
I'M JUST...
NOSY?

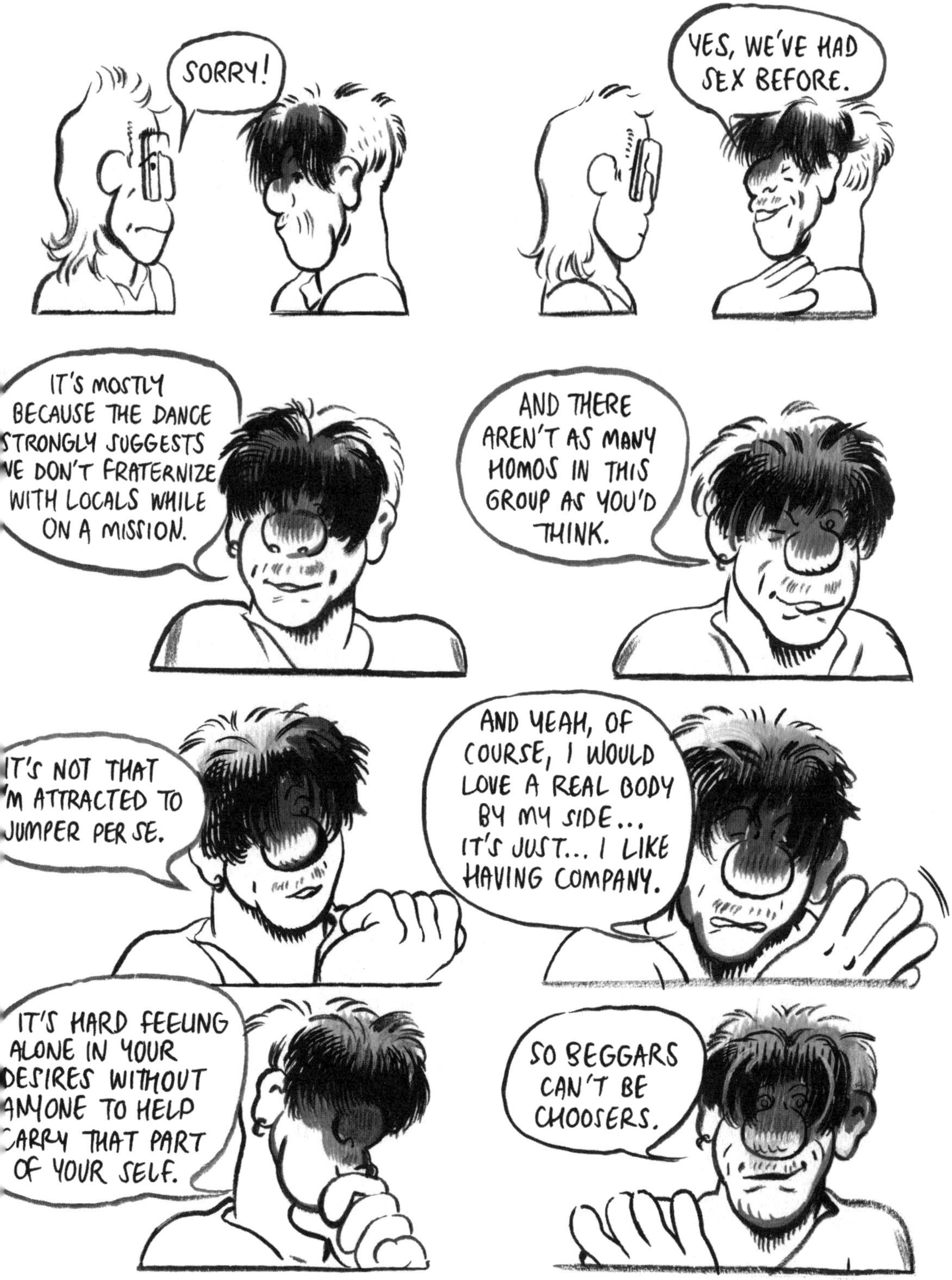
SORRY!
YES, WE'VE HAD SEX BEFORE.
IT'S MOSTLY BECAUSE THE DANCE STRONGLY SUGGESTS WE DON'T FRATERNIZE WITH LOCALS WHILE ON A MISSION.
AND THERE AREN'T AS MANY HOMOS IN THIS GROUP AS YOU'D THINK.
IT'S NOT THAT I'M ATTRACTED TO JUMPER PER SE.
AND YEAH, OF COURSE, I WOULD LOVE A REAL BODY BY MY SIDE... IT'S JUST... I LIKE HAVING COMPANY.
IT'S HARD FEELING ALONE IN YOUR DESIRES WITHOUT ANYONE TO HELP CARRY THAT PART OF YOUR SELF.
SO BEGGARS CAN'T BE CHOOSERS.

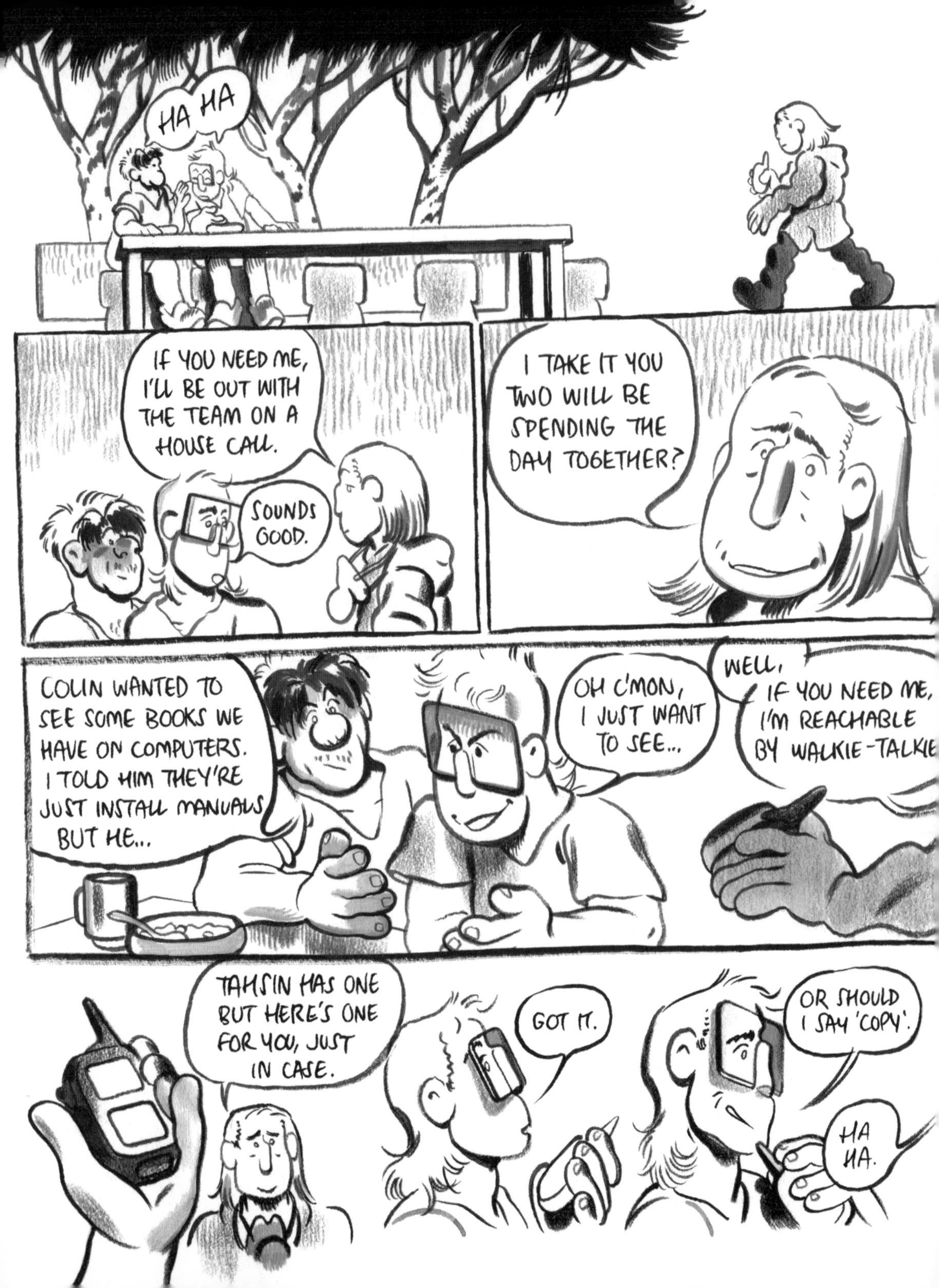
HA HA
IF YOU NEED ME, I'LL BE OUT WITH THE TEAM ON A HOUSE CALL.
SOUNDS GOOD.
I TAKE IT YOU TWO WILL BE SPENDING THE DAY TOGETHER?
COLIN WANTED TO SEE SOME BOOKS WE HAVE ON COMPUTERS. I TOLD HIM THEY'RE JUST INSTALL MANUALS BUT HE...
OH C'MON, I JUST WANT TO SEE...
WELL, IF YOU NEED ME, I'M REACHABLE BY WALKIE-TALKIE
TAHSIN HAS ONE BUT HERE'S ONE FOR YOU, JUST IN CASE.
GOT IT.
OR SHOULD I SAY 'COPY'.
HA HA.

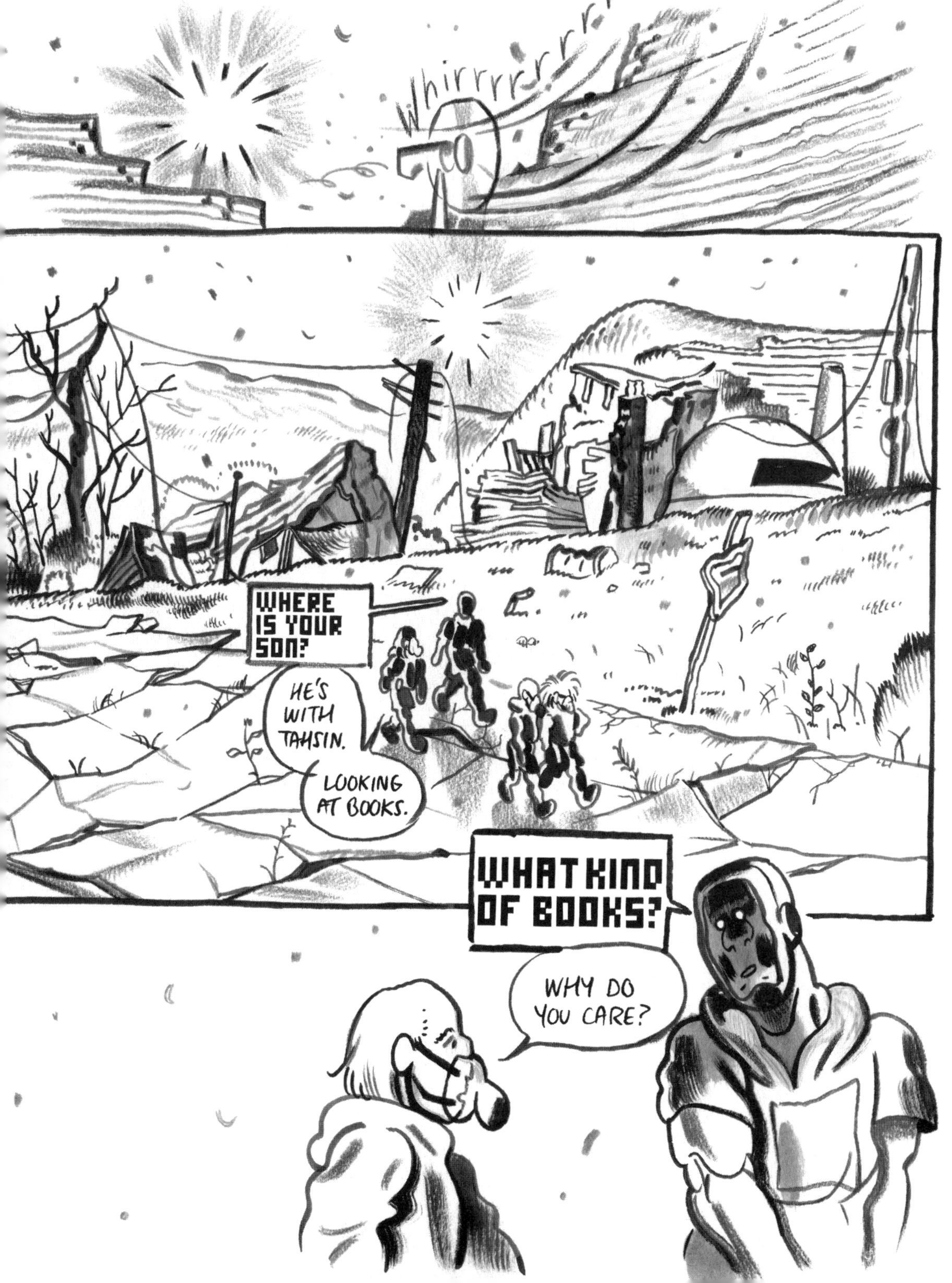
Whirrrrrrr
WHERE IS YOUR SON?
HE'S WITH TAHSIN.
LOOKING AT BOOKS.
WHAT KIND OF BOOKS?
WHY DO YOU CARE?

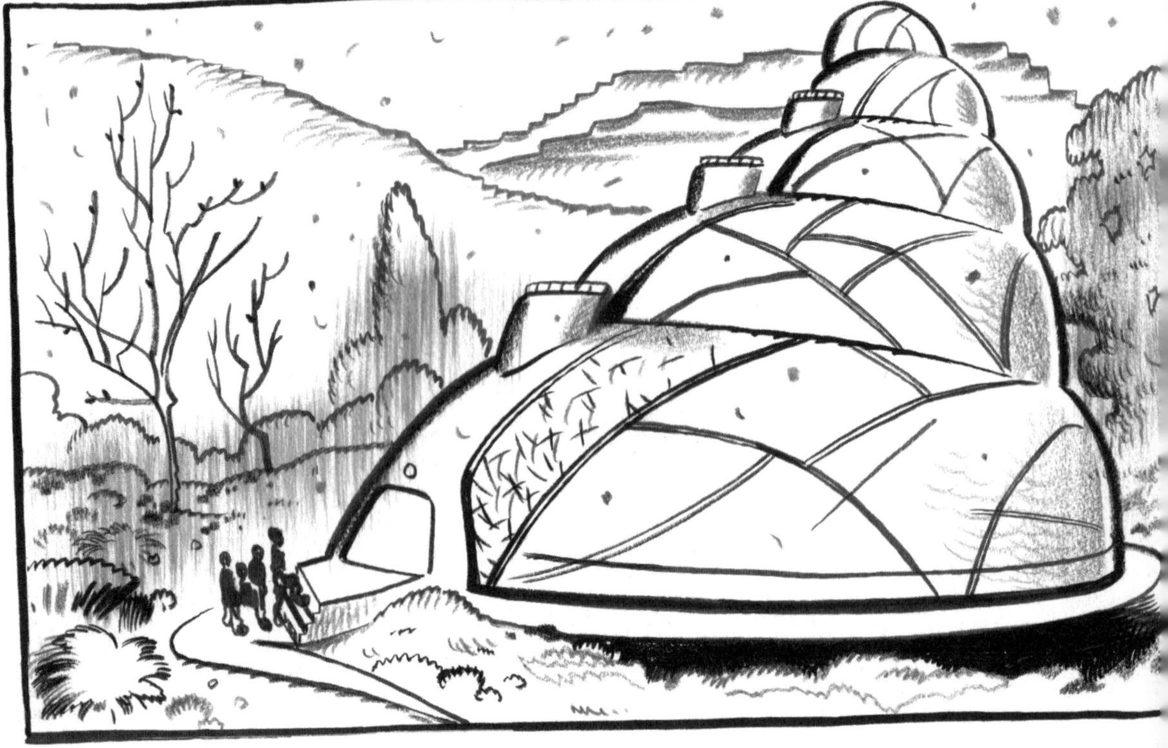

"The Conch" was the name given to the mansion built by the Founder of GrowUp! for when he stayed in Neon. Most shell homes are a single or double dome, but the Conch is a quintuple dome, hence its distinct nickname. Once the fires began, the Founder was the first to abandon his home, which is now occupied by a family of nine.

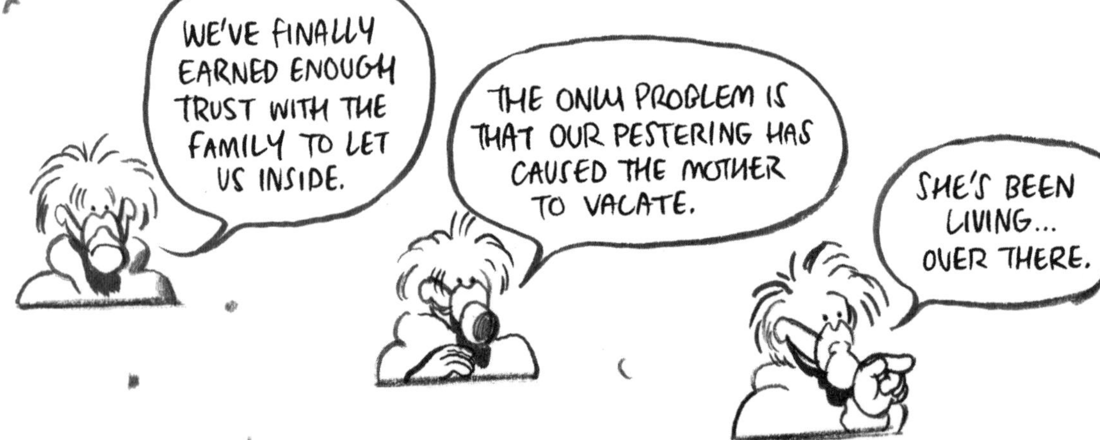
WE'VE FINALLY EARNED ENOUGH TRUST WITH THE FAMILY TO LET US INSIDE.
THE ONLY PROBLEM IS THAT OUR PESTERING HAS CAUSED THE MOTHER TO VACATE.
SHE'S BEEN LIVING... OVER THERE.

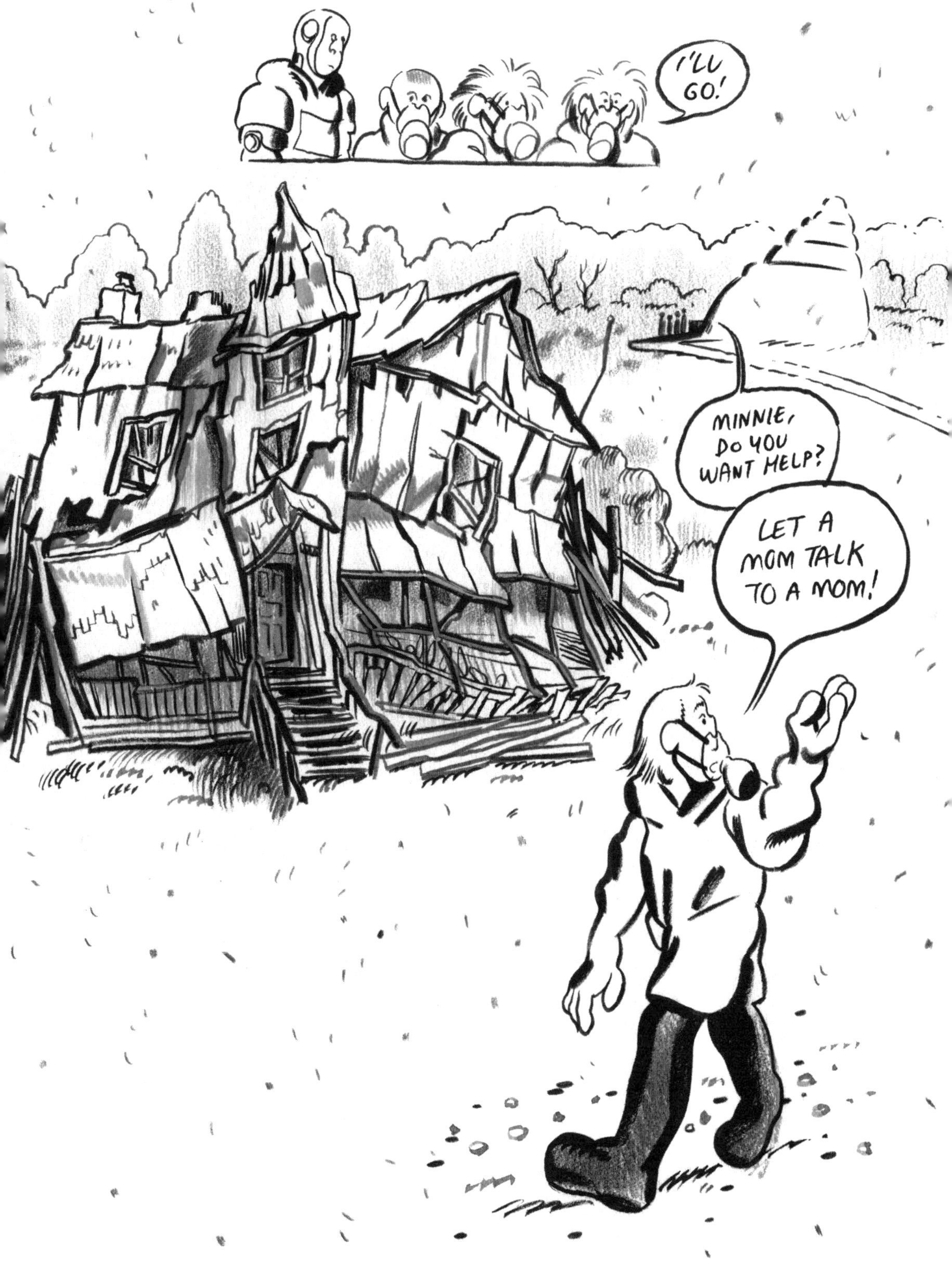
I'LL GO!
MINNIE, DO YOU WANT HELP?
LET A MOM TALK TO A MOM!

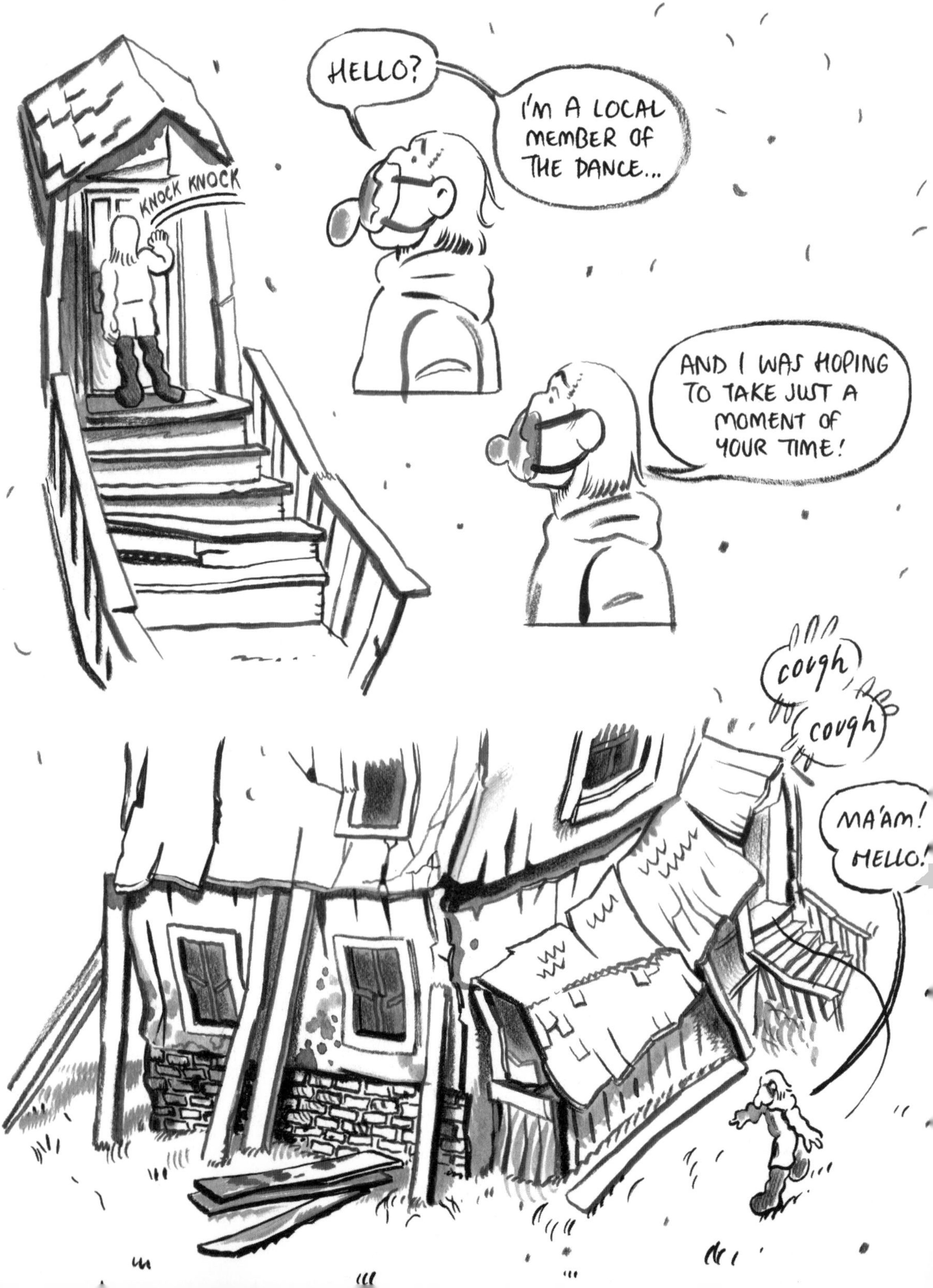
KNOCK KNOCK
HELLO?
I'M A LOCAL MEMBER OF THE DANCE...
AND I WAS HOPING TO TAKE JUST A MOMENT OF YOUR TIME!
cough
cough
MA'AM! HELLO!

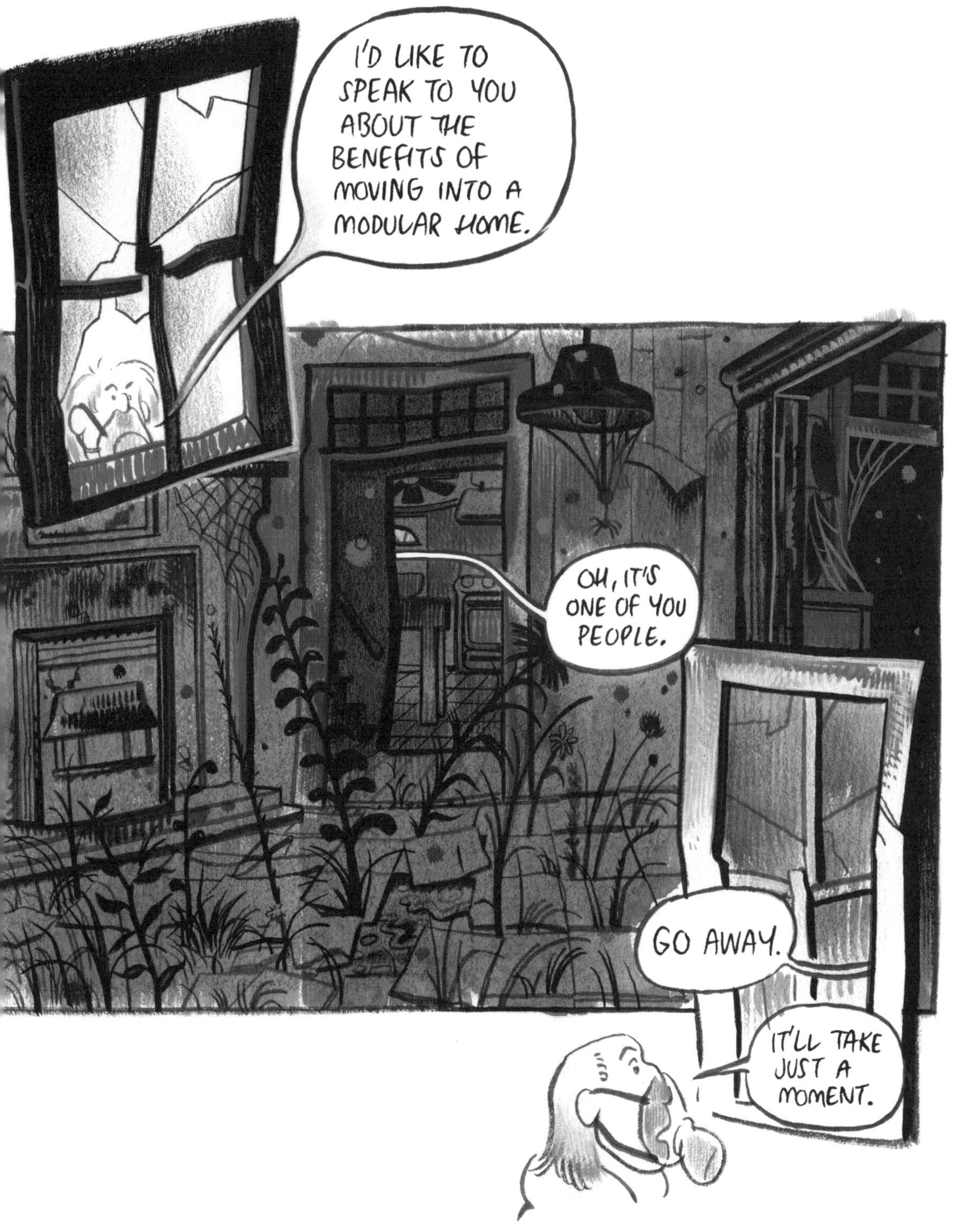
I'D LIKE TO SPEAK TO YOU ABOUT THE BENEFITS OF MOVING INTO A MODULAR HOME.
OH, IT'S ONE OF YOU PEOPLE.
GO AWAY.
IT'LL TAKE JUST A MOMENT.

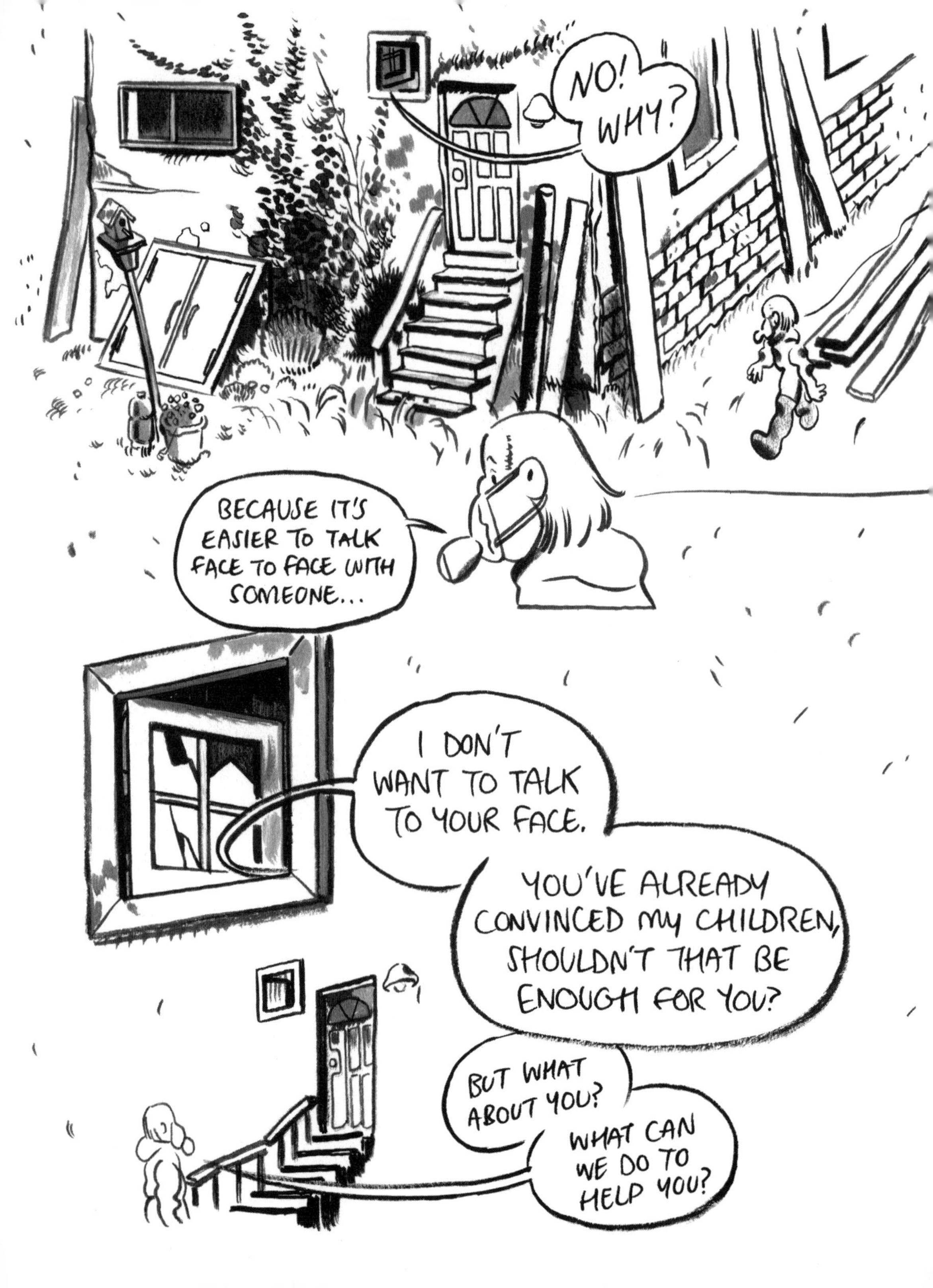
NO! WHY?
BECAUSE IT'S EASIER TO TALK FACE TO FACE WITH SOMEONE...
I DON'T WANT TO TALK TO YOUR FACE.
YOU'VE ALREADY CONVINCED MY CHILDREN, SHOULDN'T THAT BE ENOUGH FOR YOU?
BUT WHAT ABOUT YOU?
WHAT CAN WE DO TO HELP YOU?

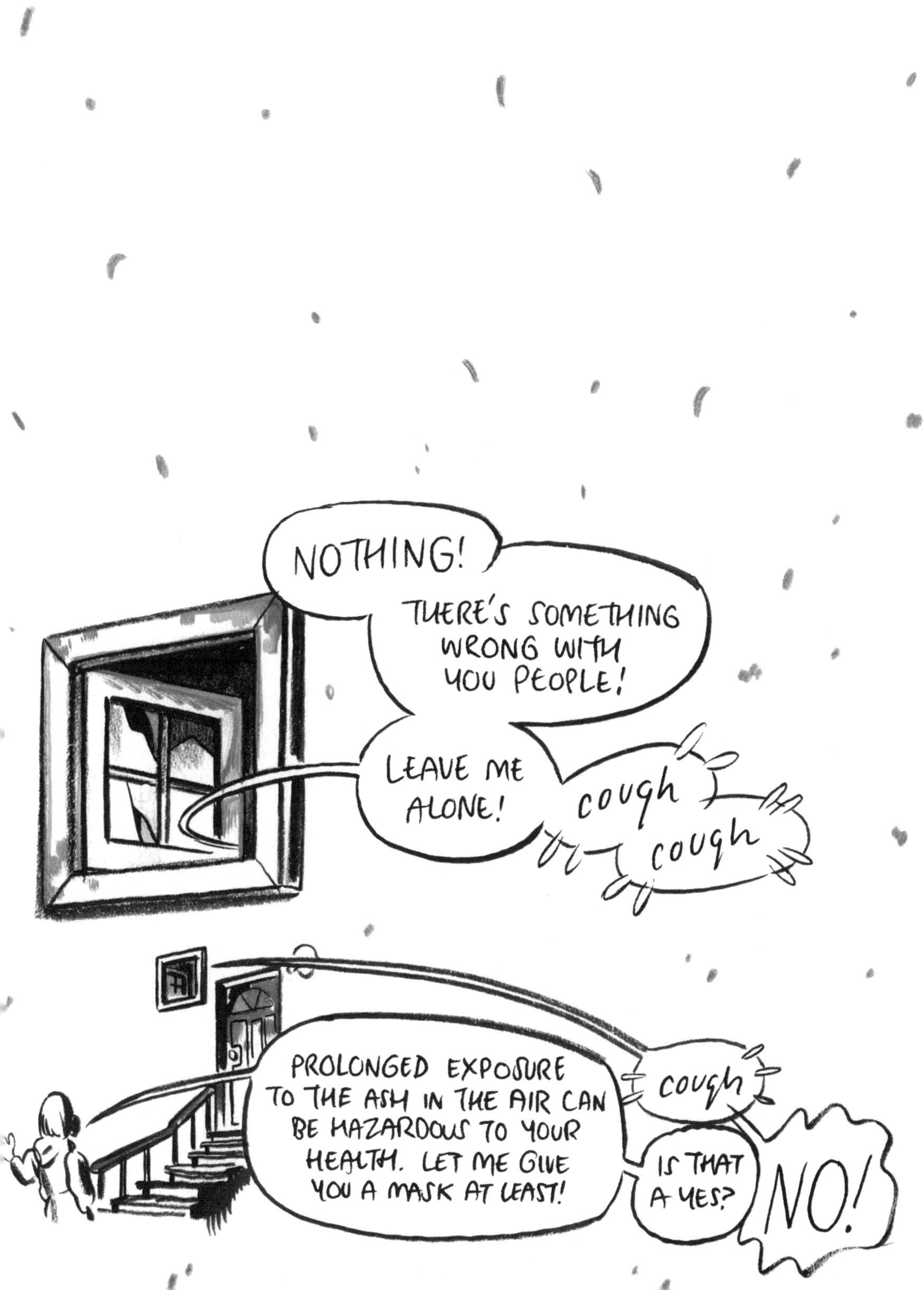
NOTHING!
THERE'S SOMETHING WRONG WITH YOU PEOPLE!
LEAVE ME ALONE!
cough
cough
PROLONGED EXPOSURE TO THE ASH IN THE AIR CAN BE HAZARDOUS TO YOUR HEALTH. LET ME GIVE YOU A MASK AT LEAST!
cough
IS THAT A YES?
NO!

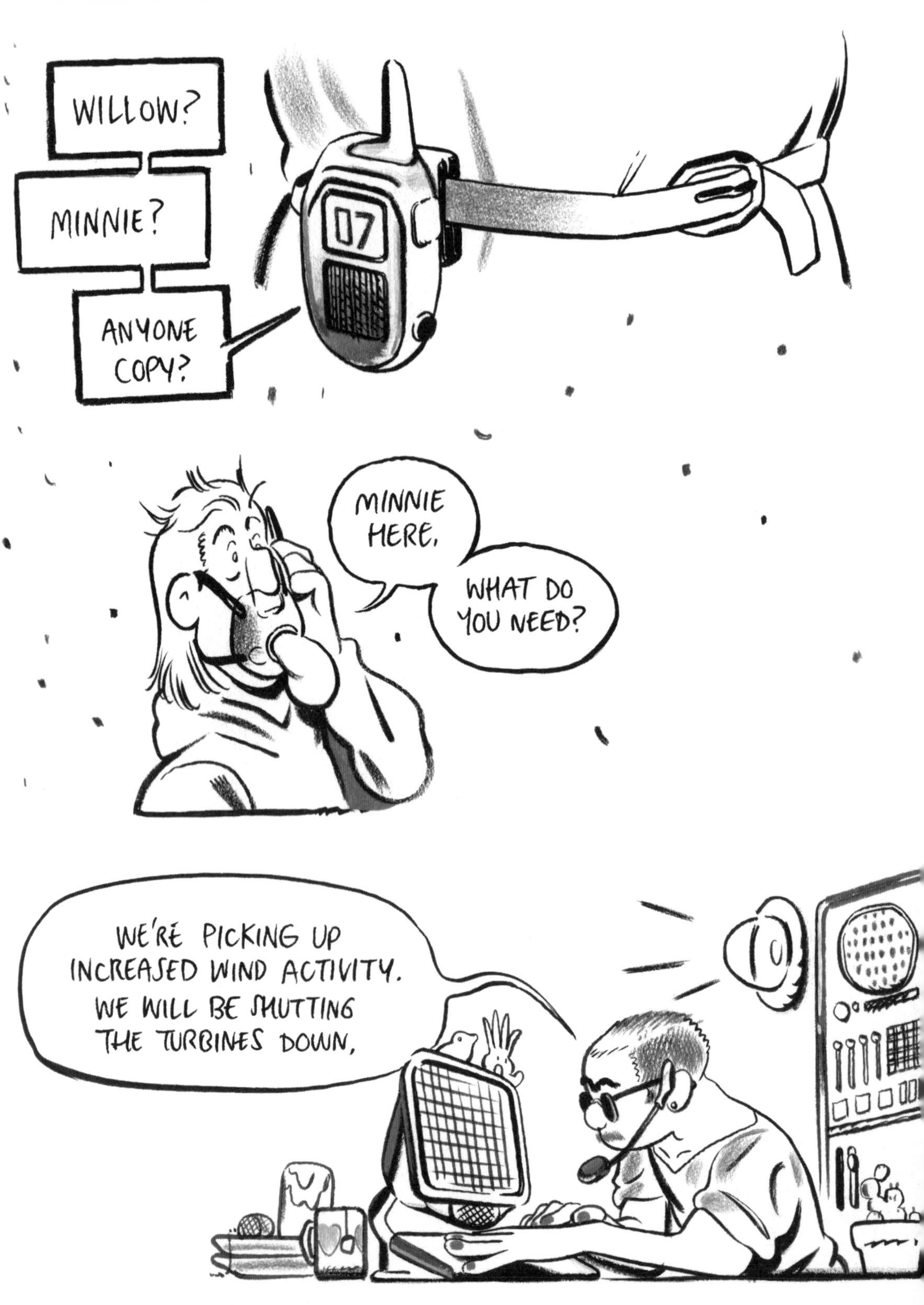
WILLOW?
MINNIE?
ANYONE COPY?
07
MINNIE HERE.
WHAT DO YOU NEED?
WE'RE PICKING UP INCREASED WIND ACTIVITY. WE WILL BE SHUTTING THE TURBINES DOWN.

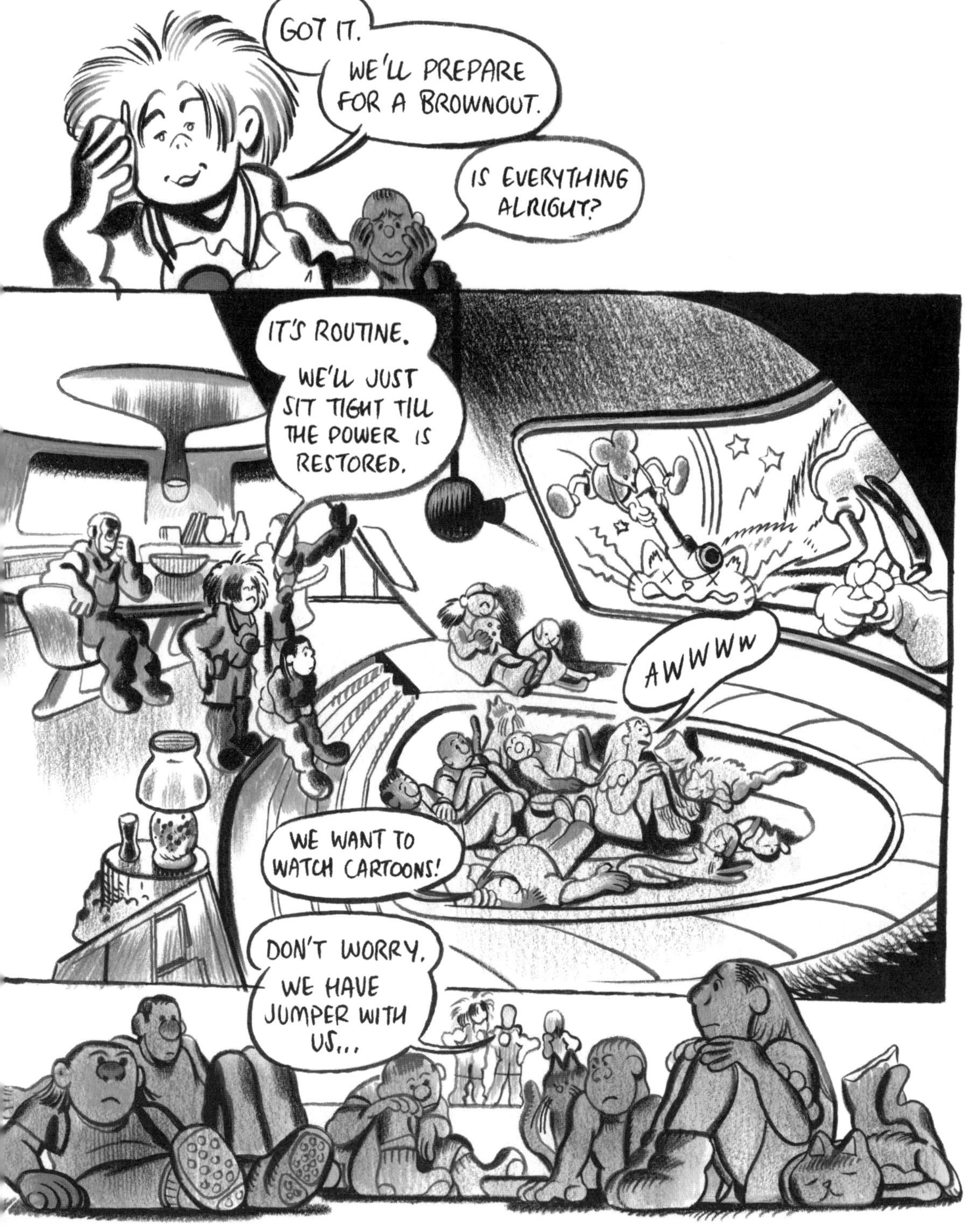
GOT IT.
WE'LL PREPARE FOR A BROWNOUT.
IS EVERYTHING ALRIGHT?
IT'S ROUTINE.
WE'LL JUST SIT TIGHT TILL THE POWER IS RESTORED.
AWWWW
WE WANT TO WATCH CARTOONS!
DON'T WORRY.
WE HAVE JUMPER WITH US...

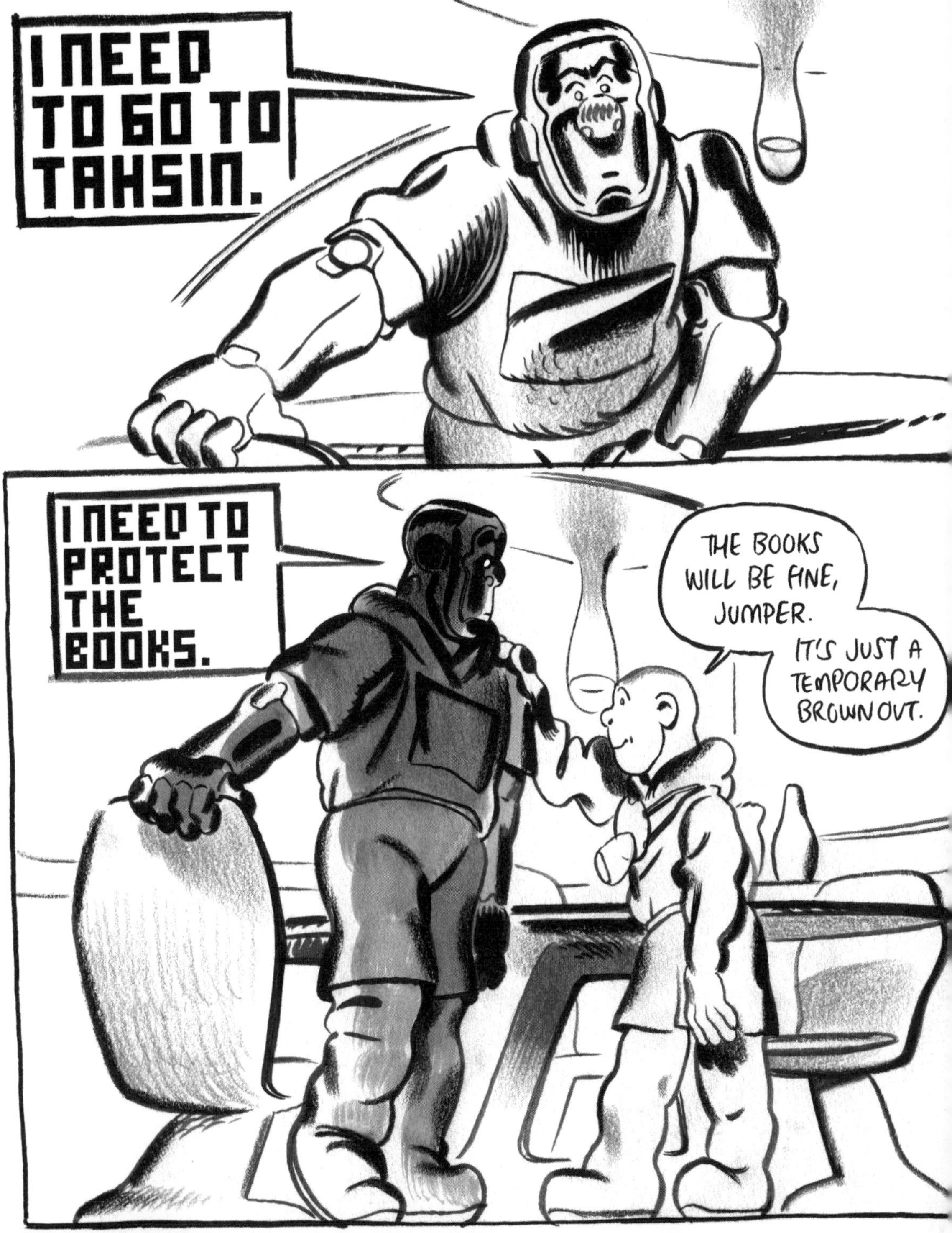
I NEED TO GO TO TAHSIN.
I NEED TO PROTECT THE BOOKS.
THE BOOKS WILL BE FINE, JUMPER.
IT'S JUST A TEMPORARY BROWNOUT.

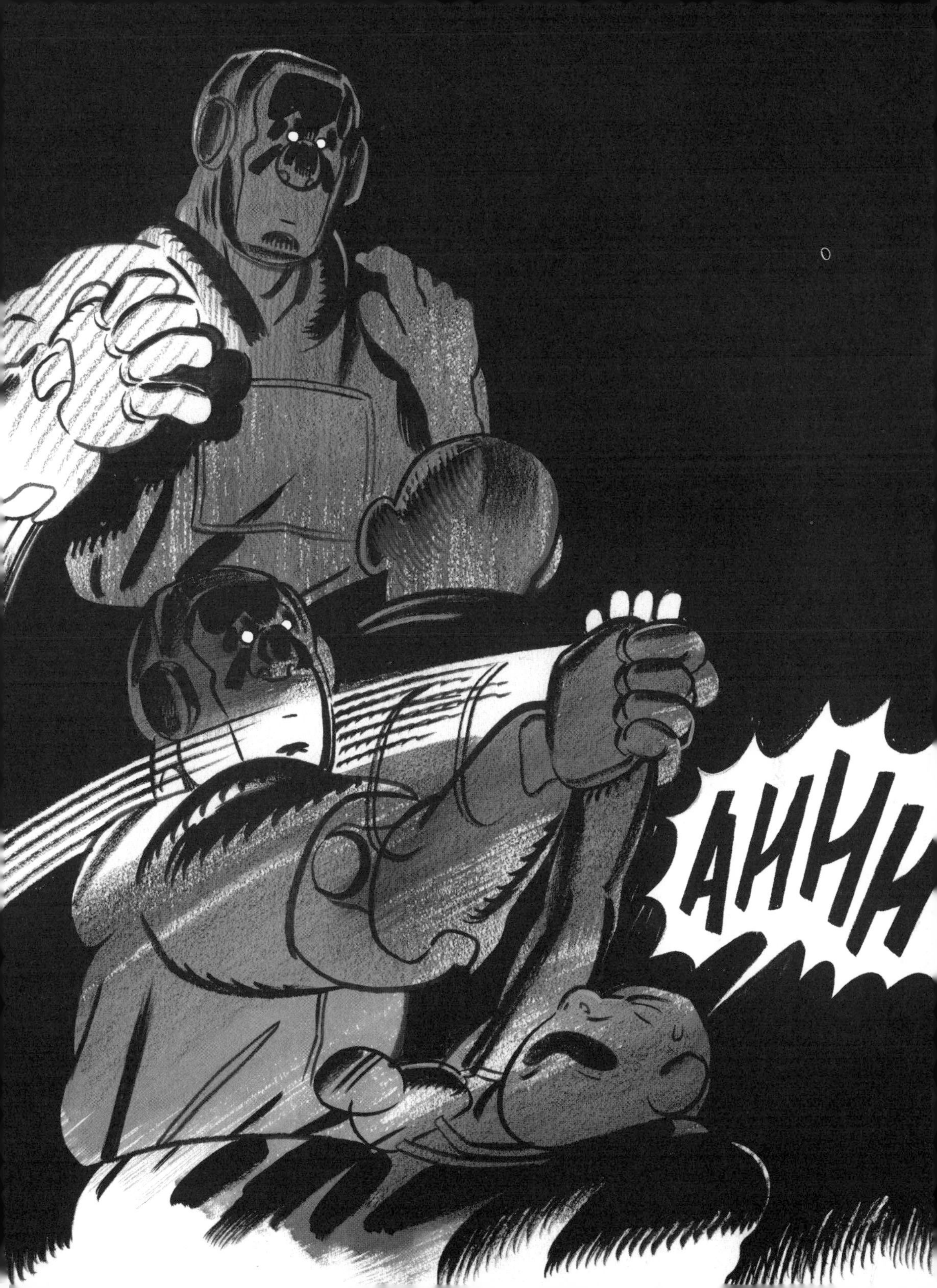
AHHH

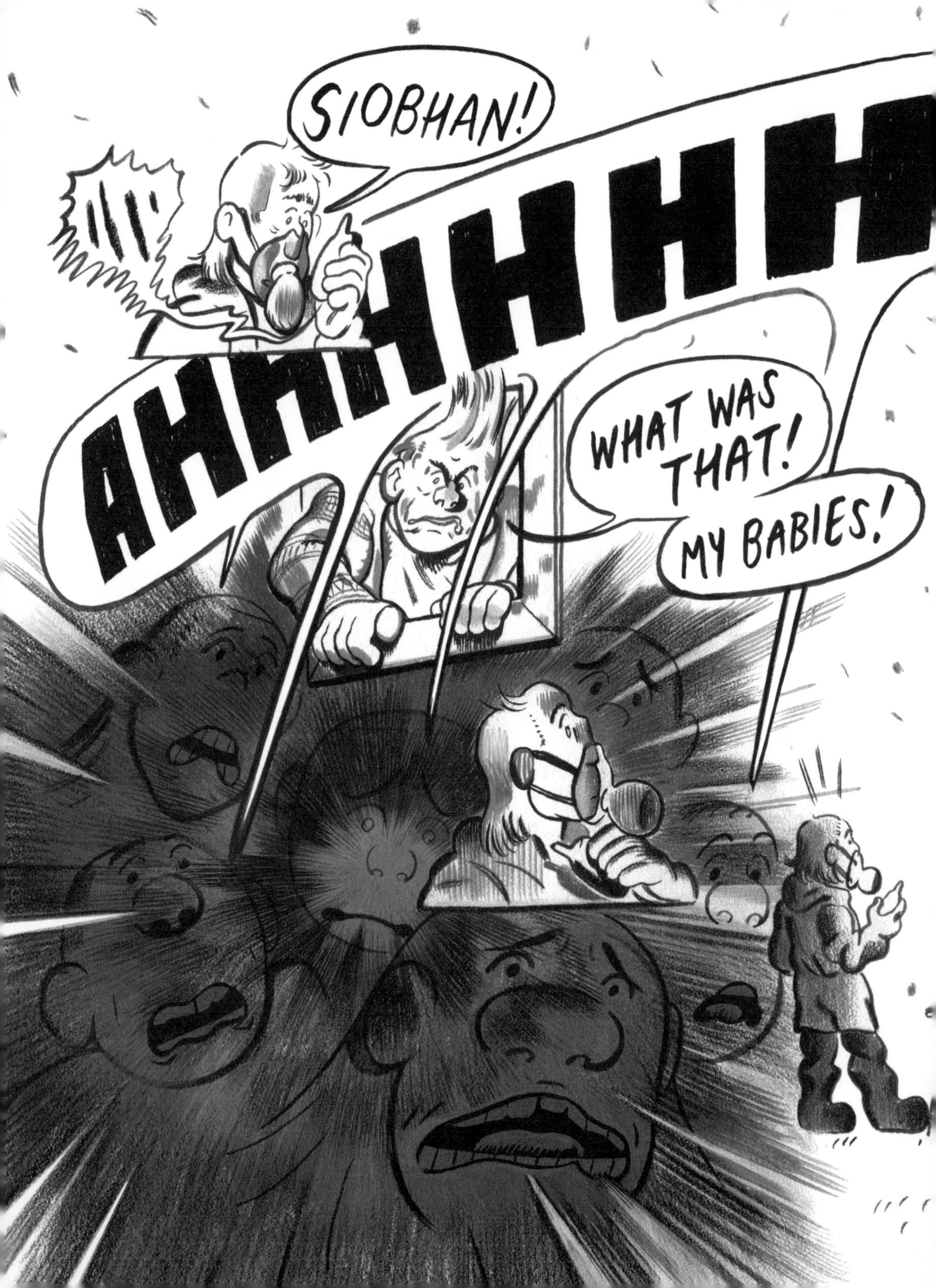
SIOBHAN!
AHHHHHHH
WHAT WAS THAT!
MY BABIES!

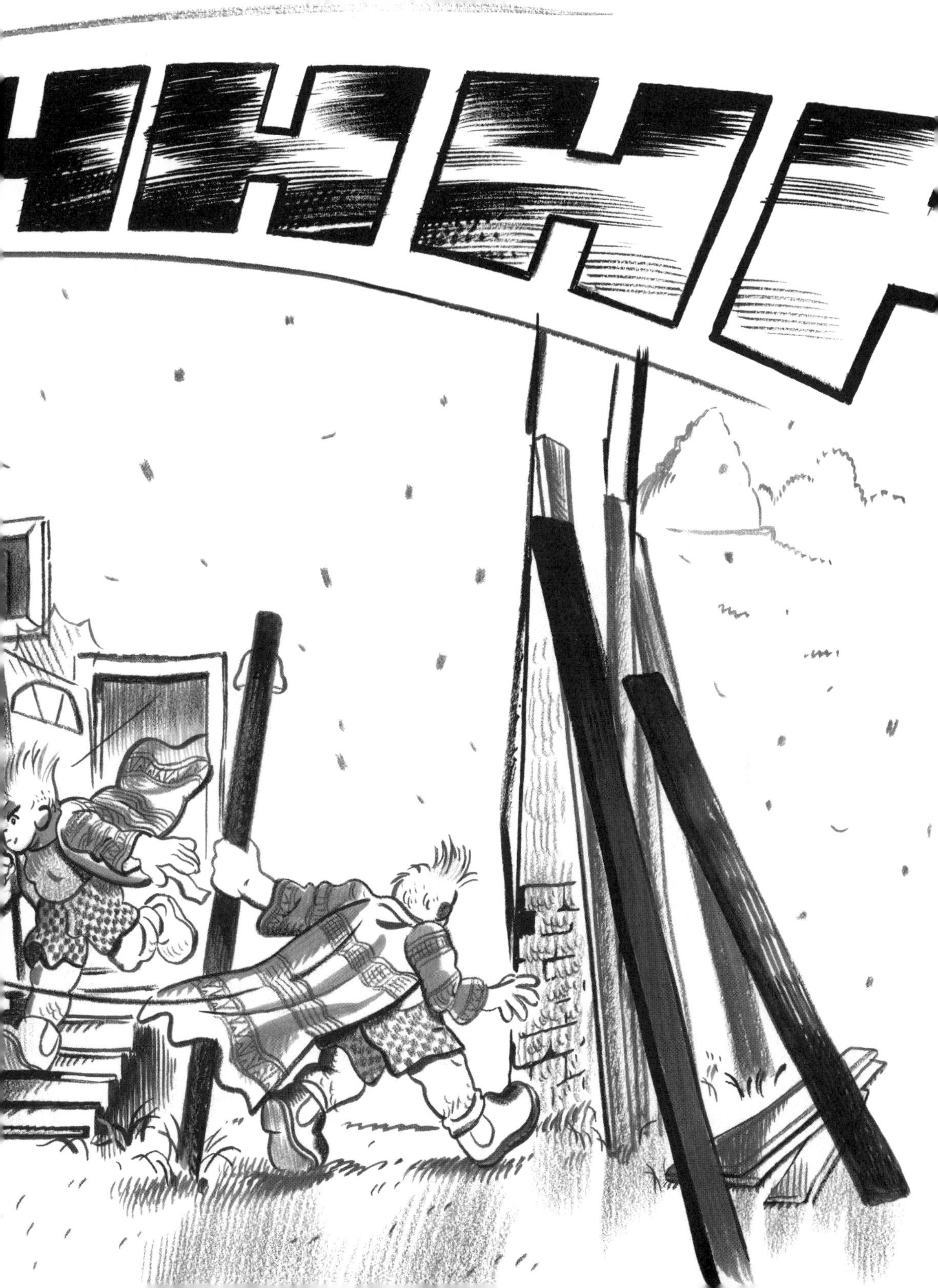

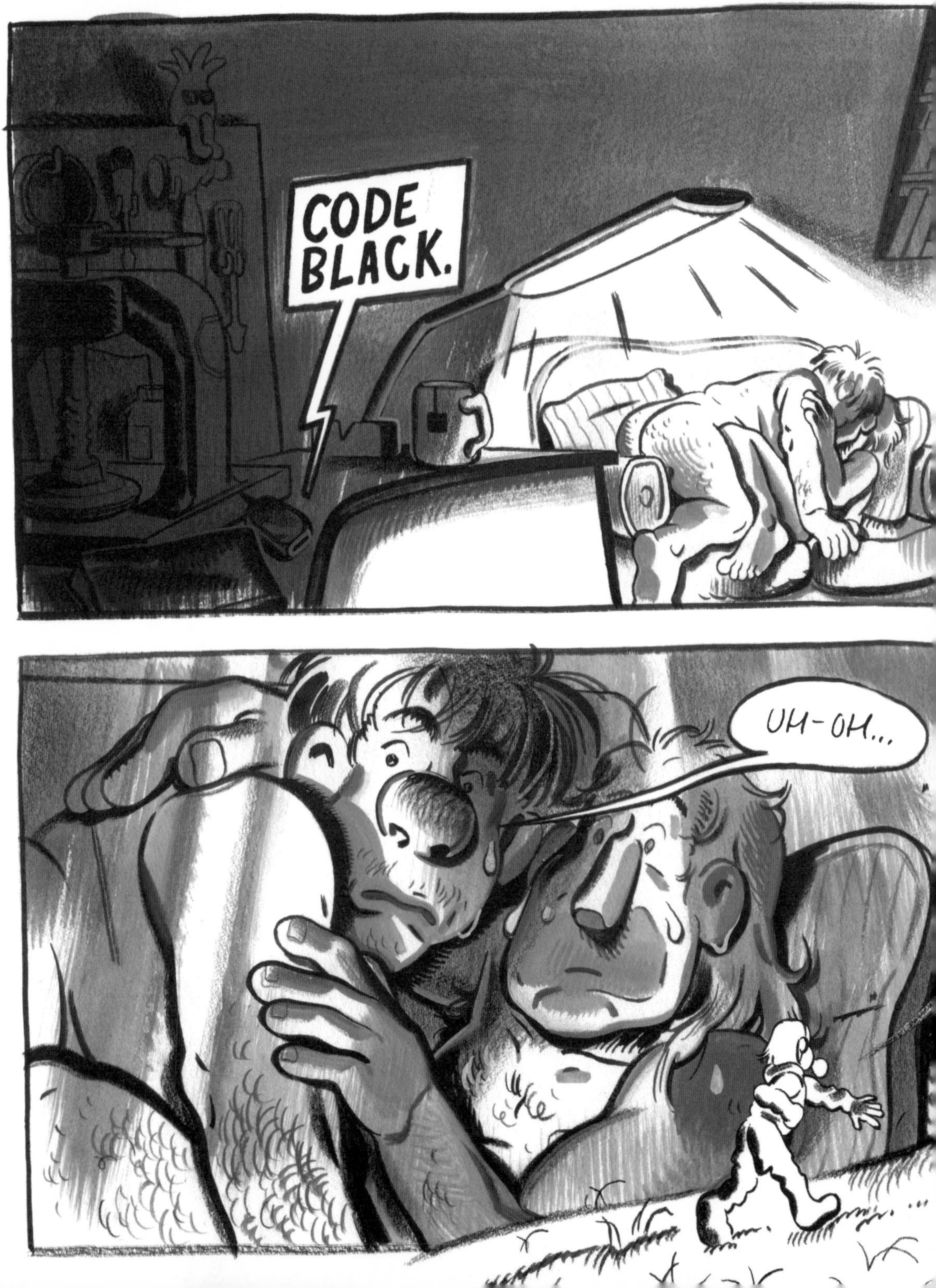
CODE BLACK.
UH-OH...

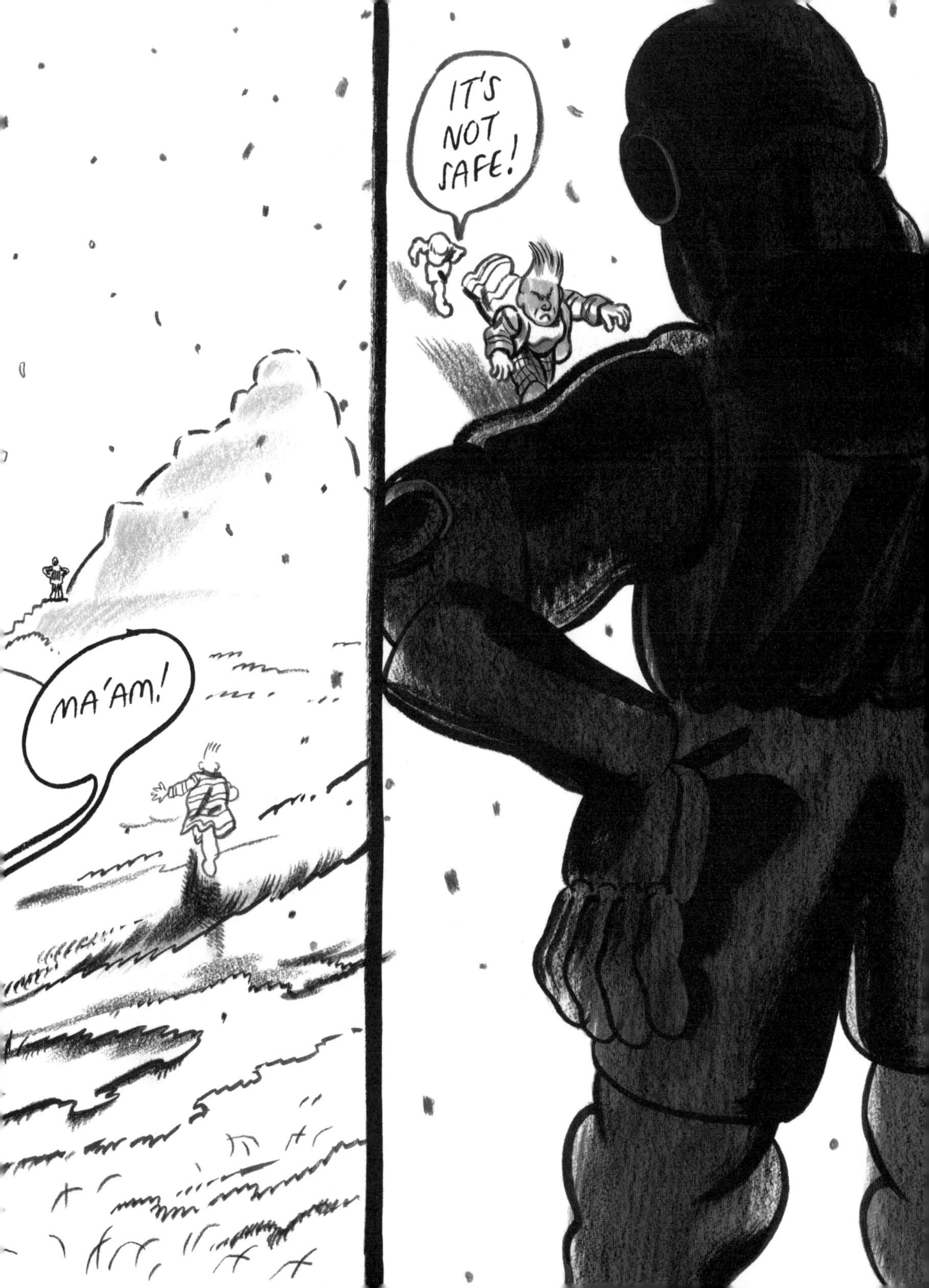
MA'AM!
IT'S NOT SAFE!

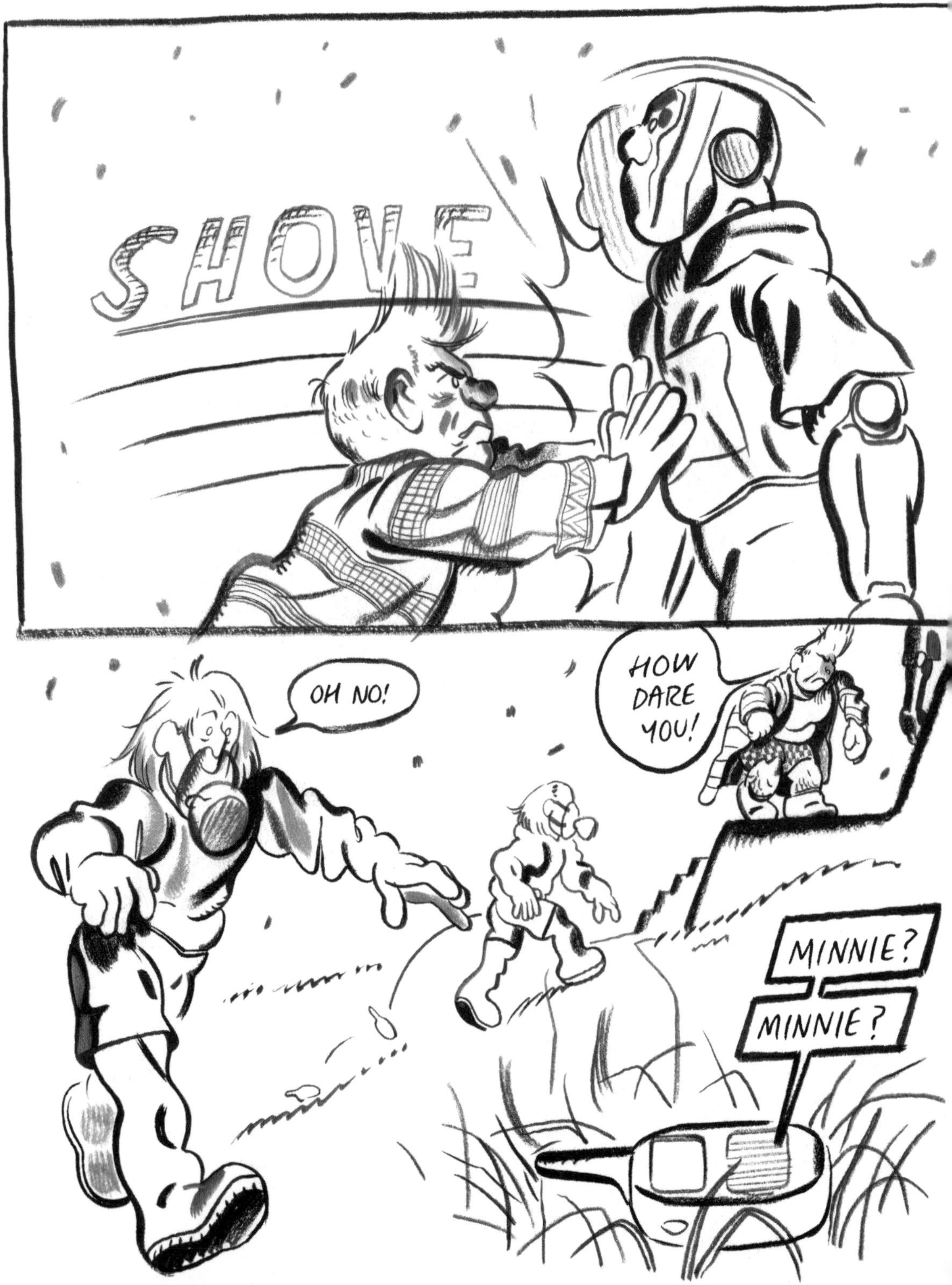
SHOVE
OH NO!
HOW DARE YOU!
MINNIE?
MINNIE?

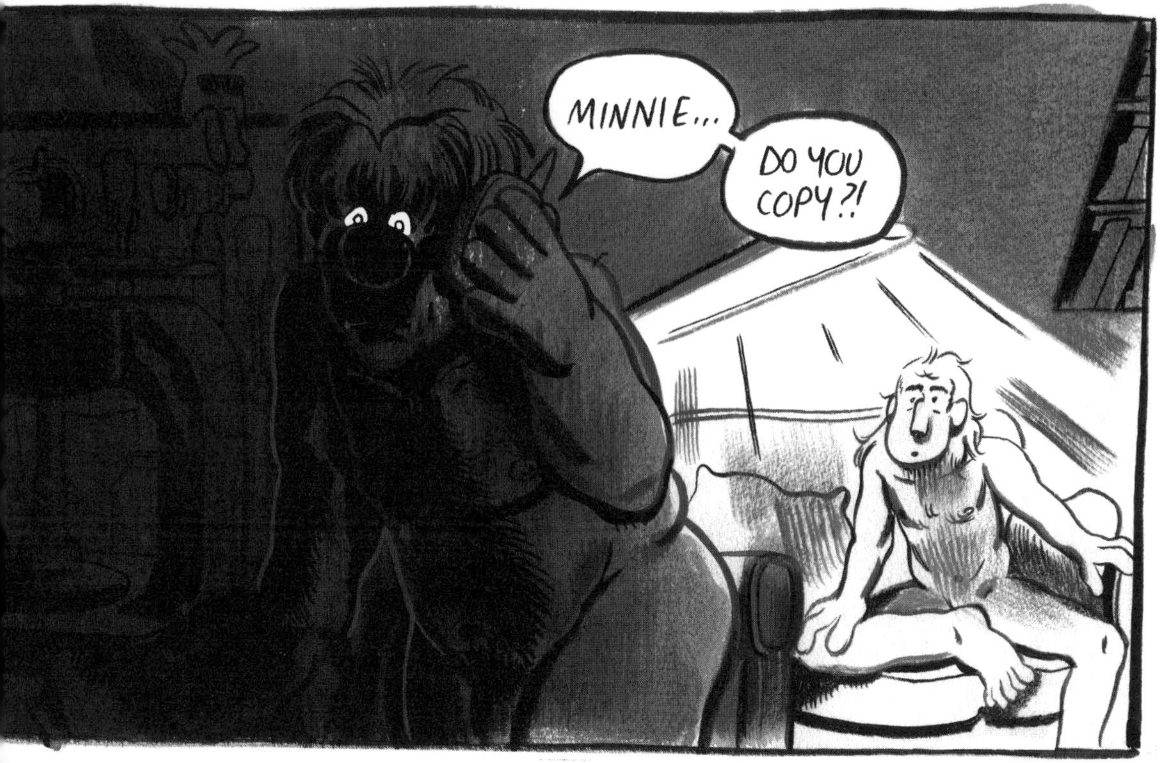
MINNIE...
DO YOU COPY?!

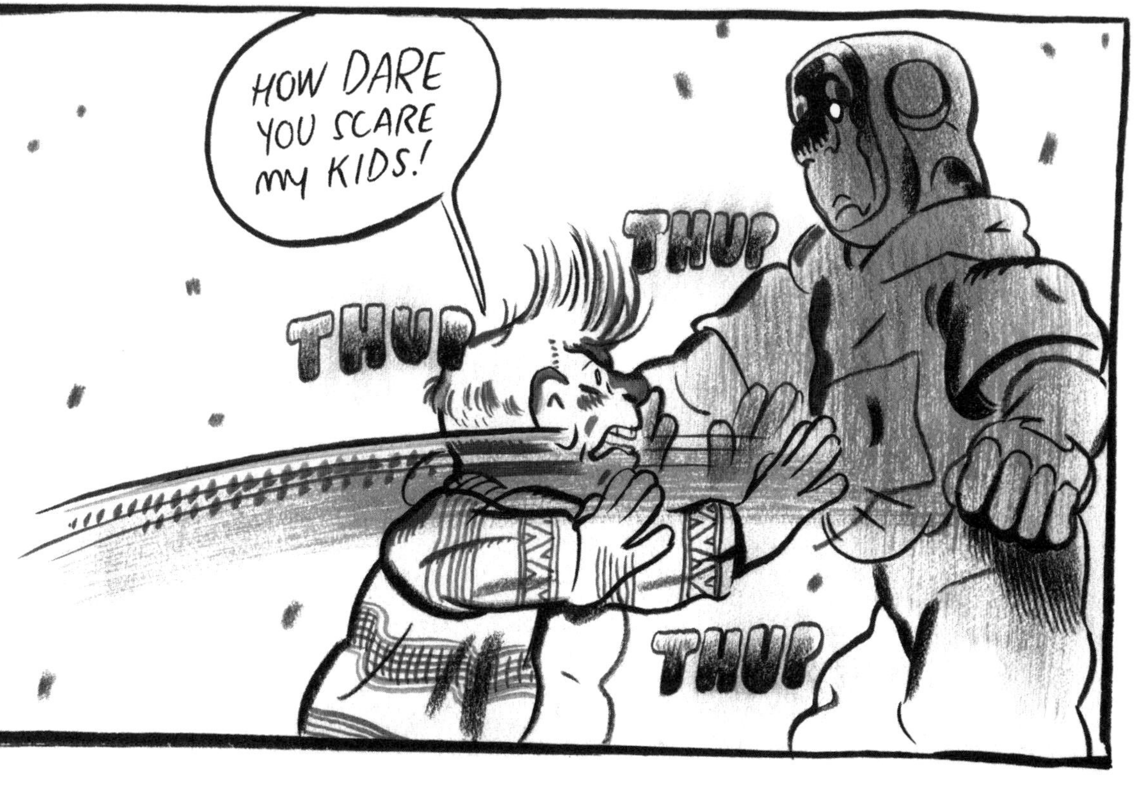
HOW DARE YOU SCARE MY KIDS!
THUP
THUP
THUP

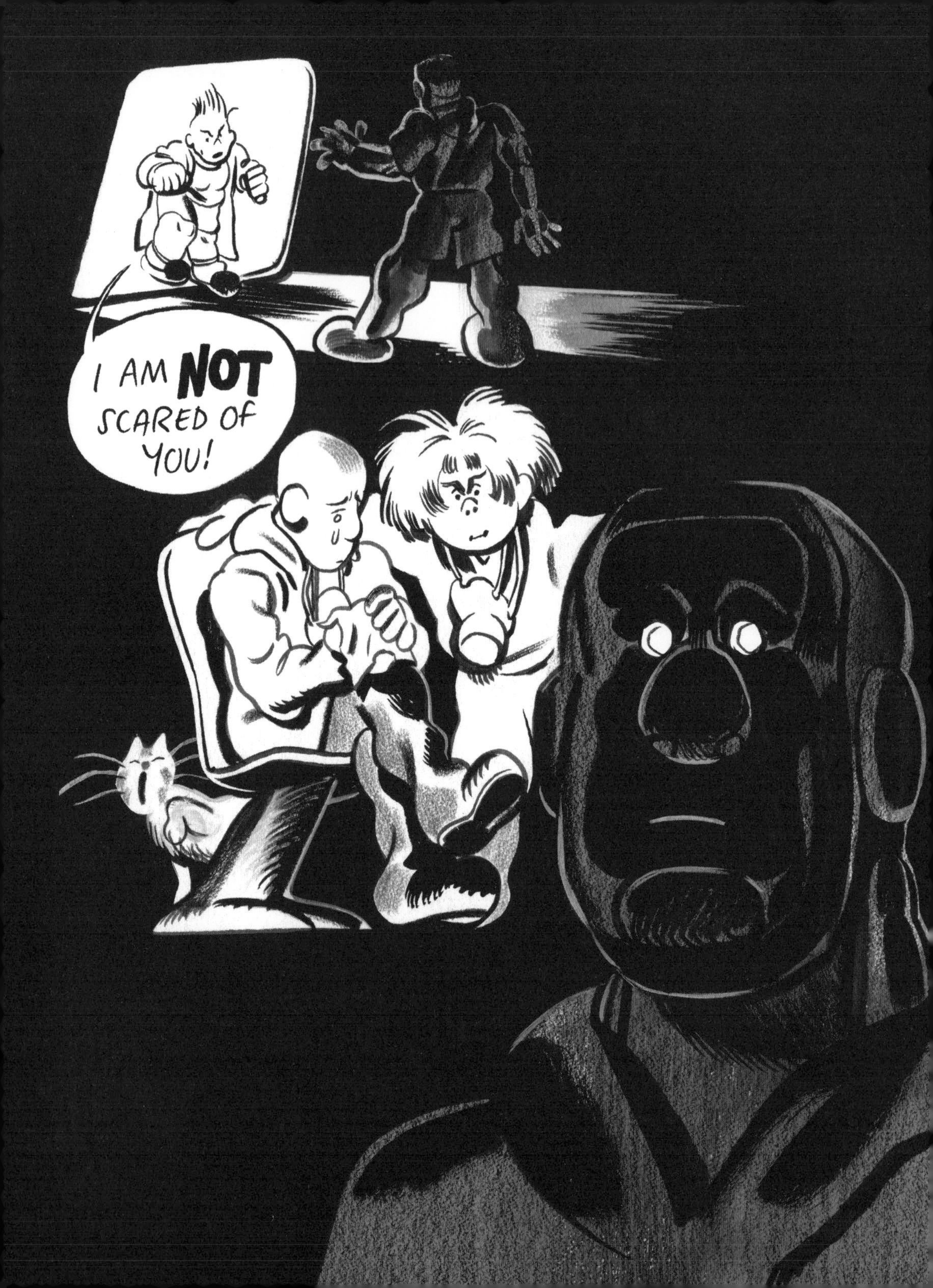
I AM NOT SCARED OF YOU!

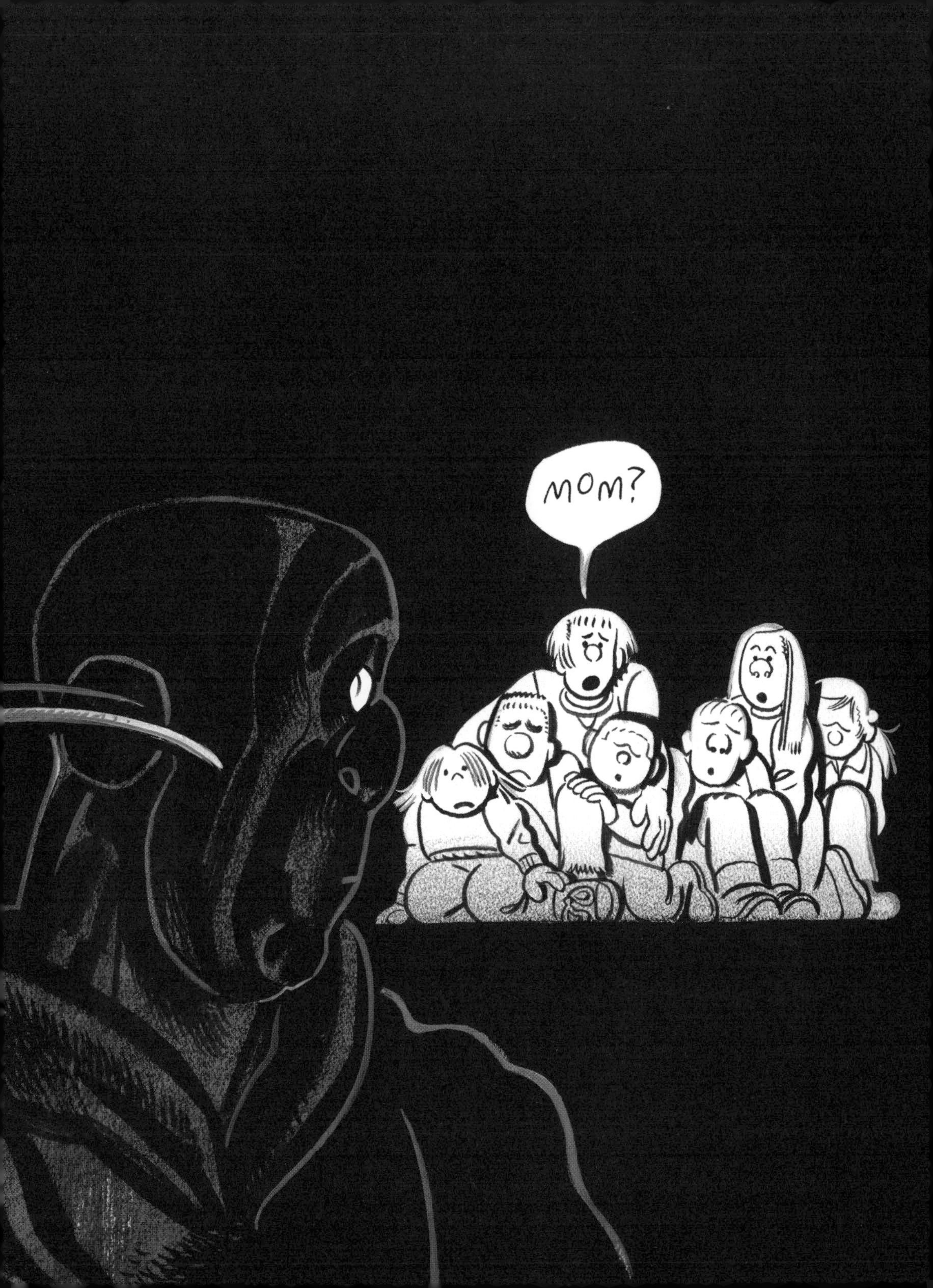
MOM?

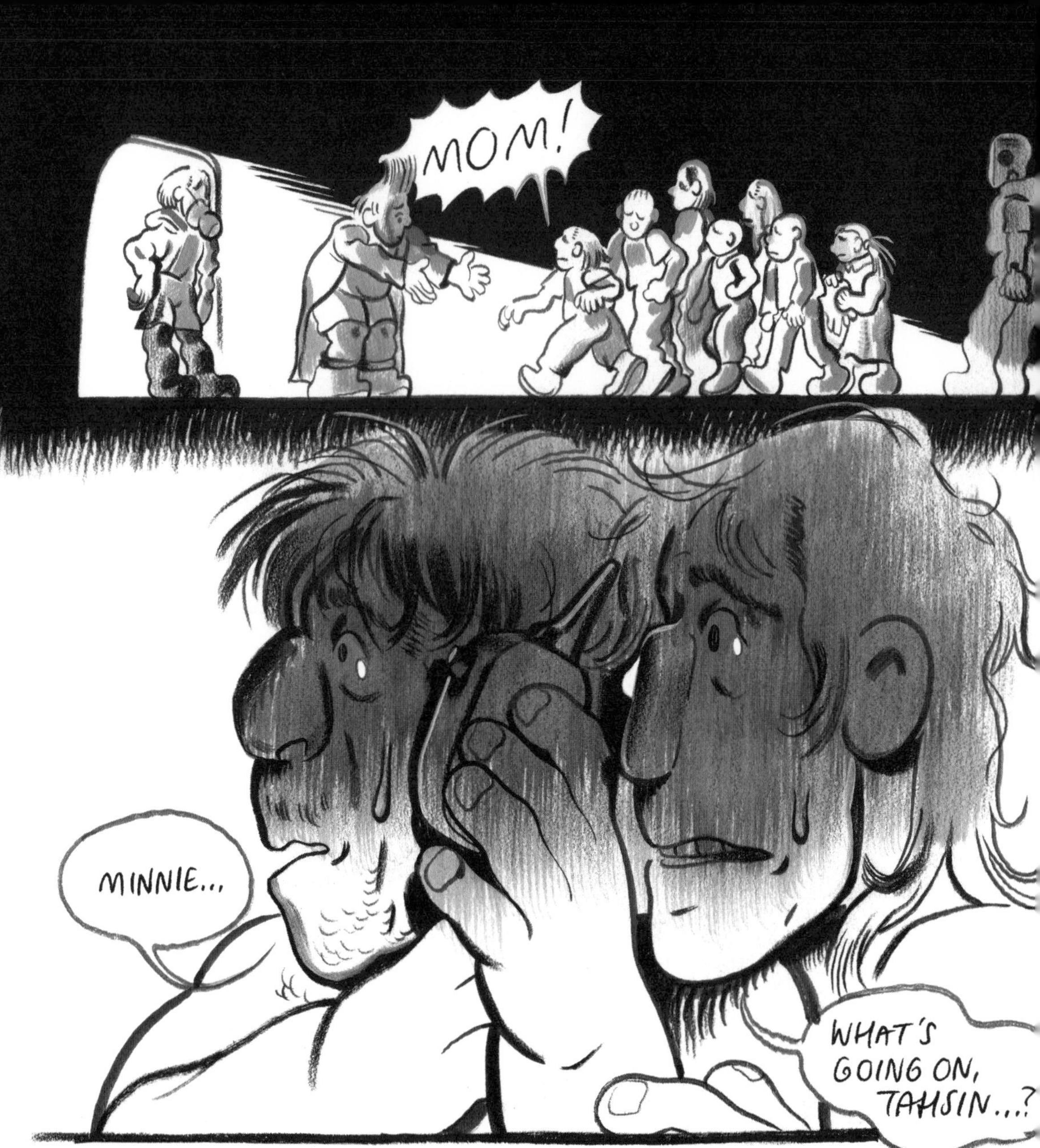
MOM!
MINNIE...
WHAT'S GOING ON, TAHSIN...?

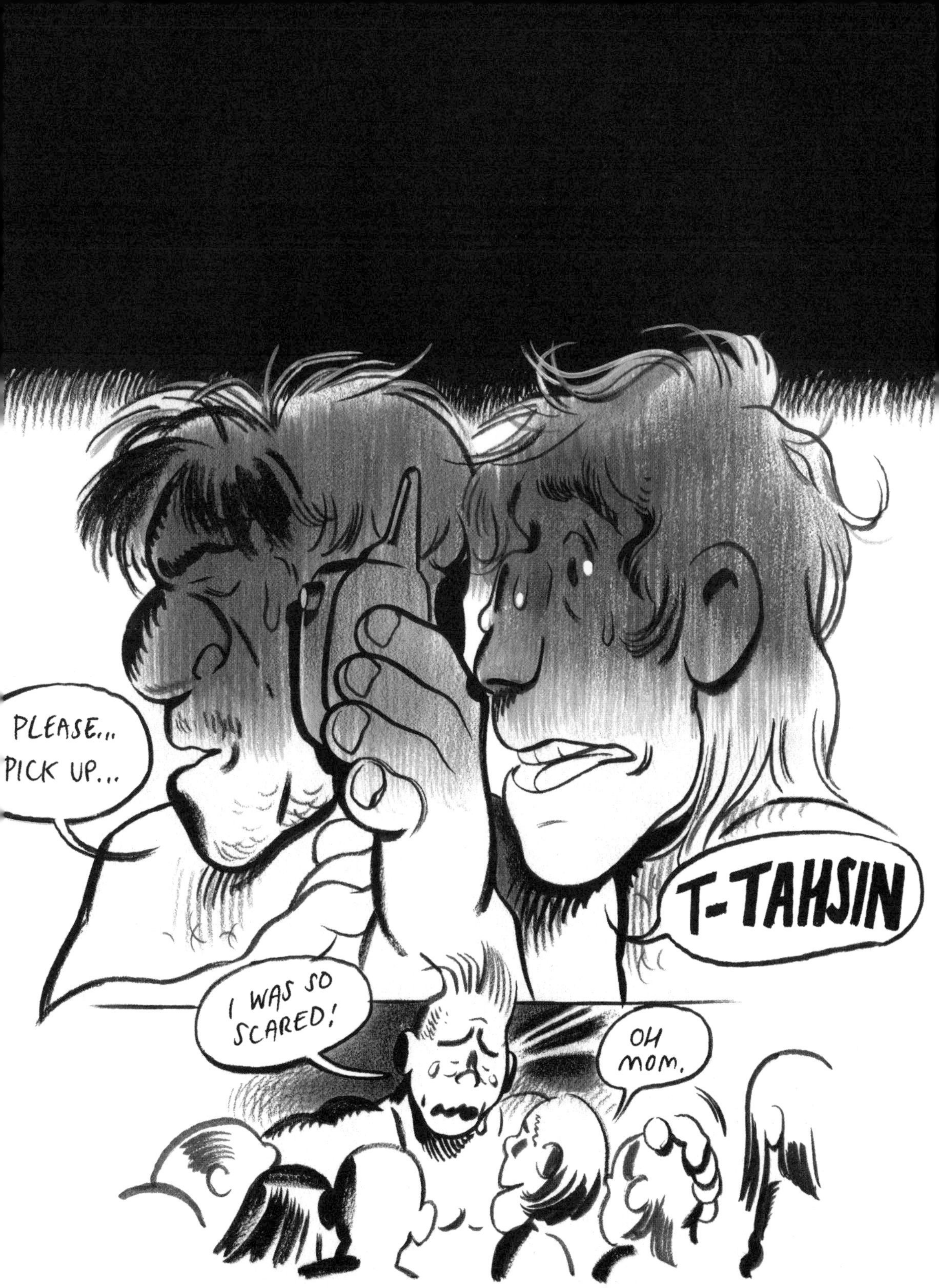
PLEASE... PICK UP...
T-TAHSIN
I WAS SO SCARED!
OH MOM.

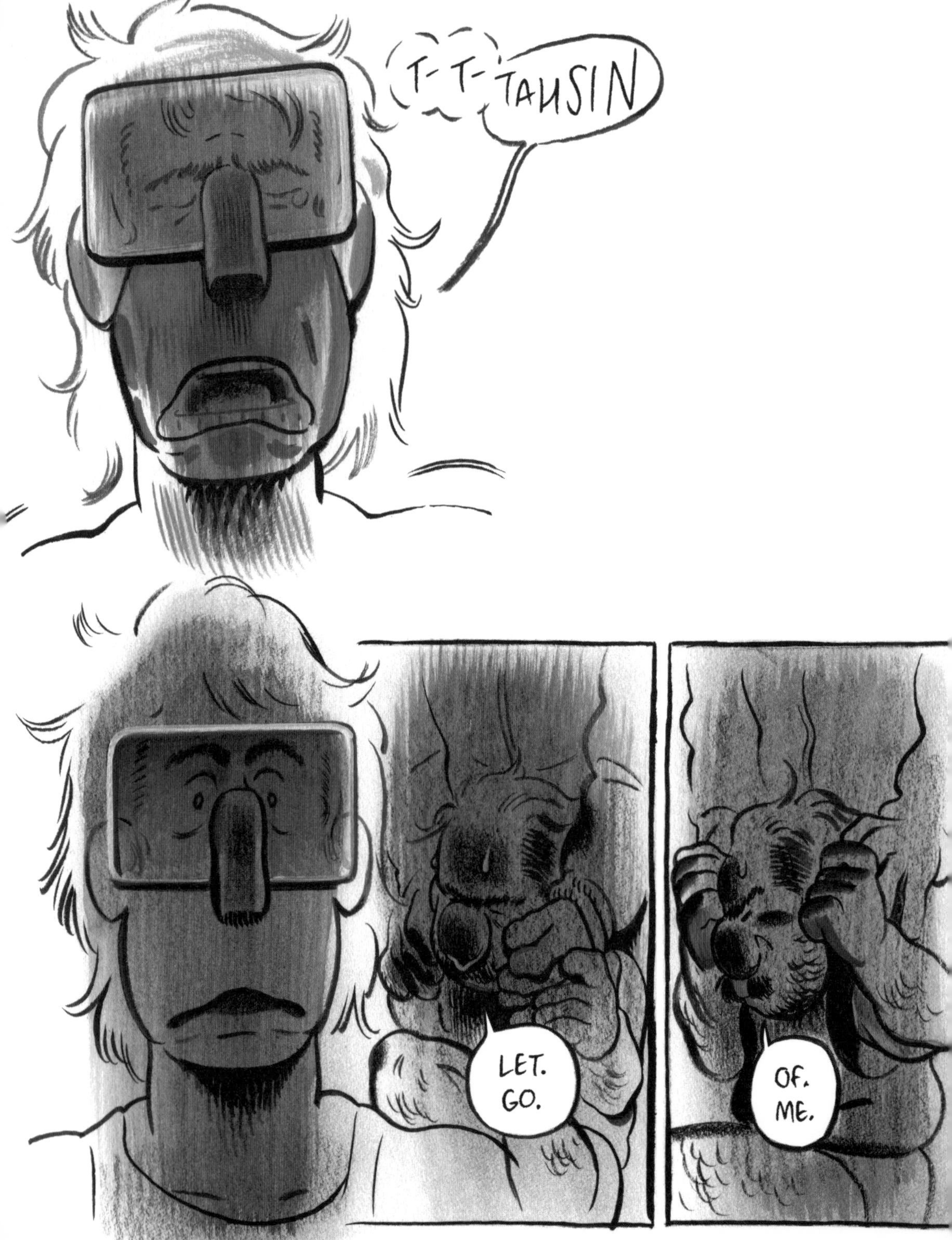
T-T-TAHSIN
LET. GO.
OF. ME.

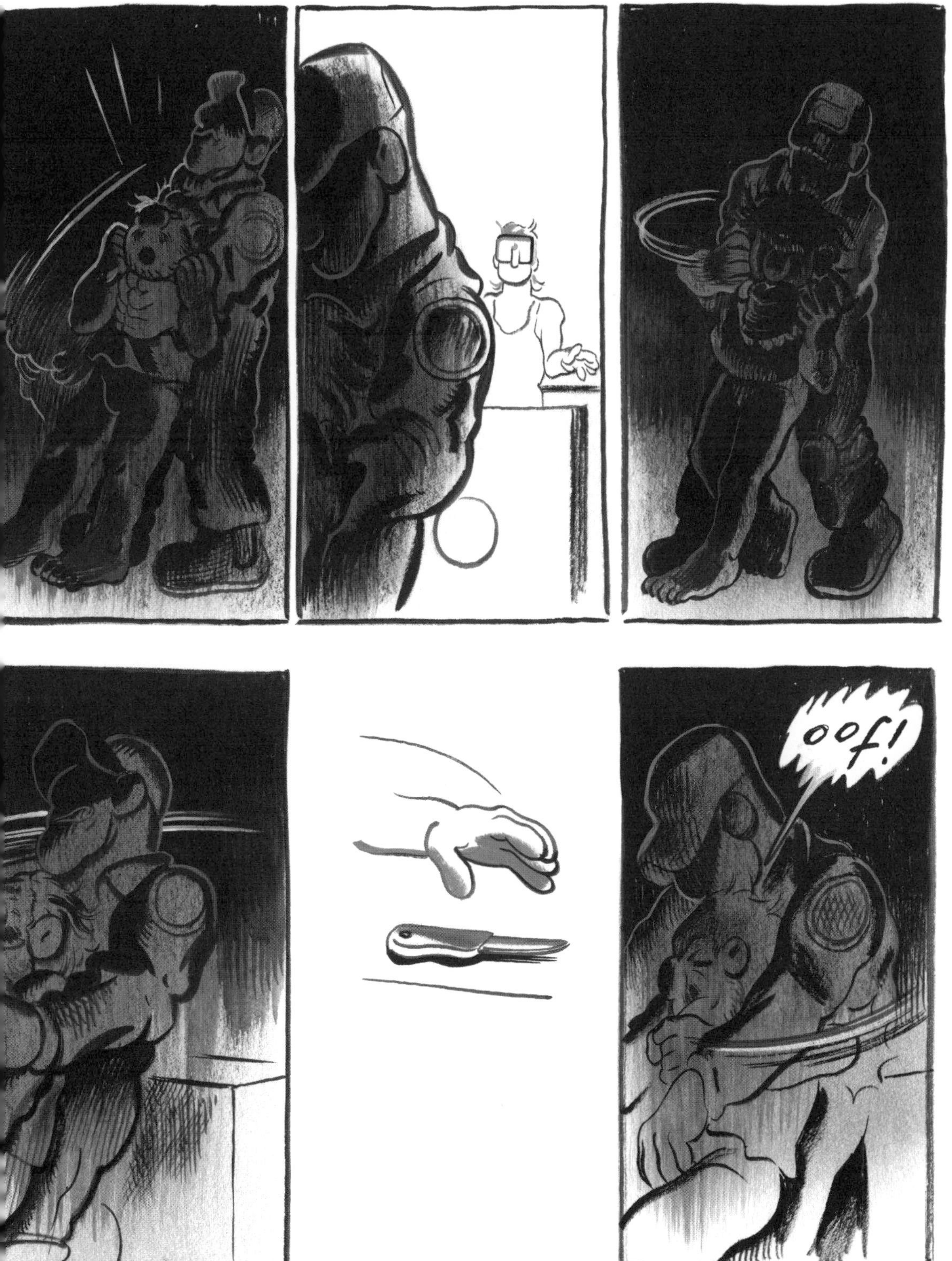
oof!

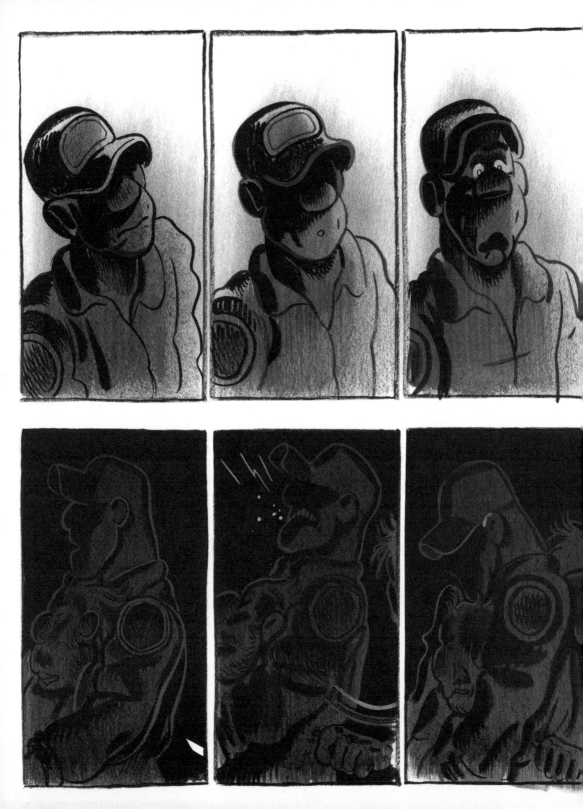

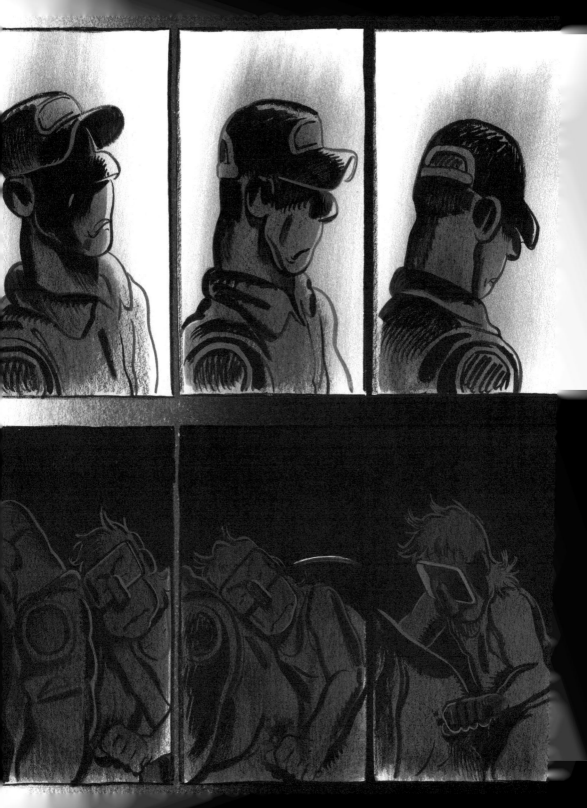

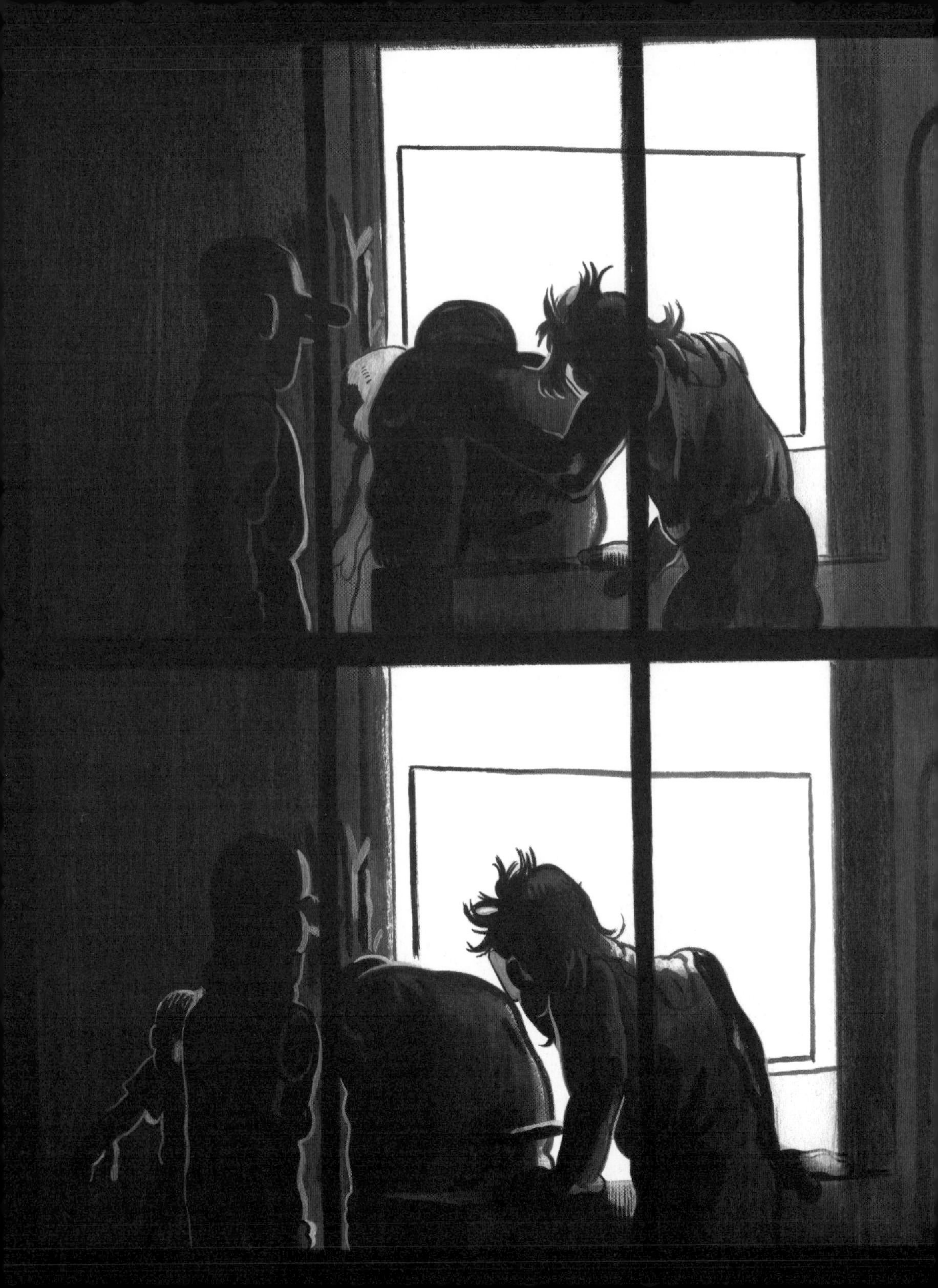

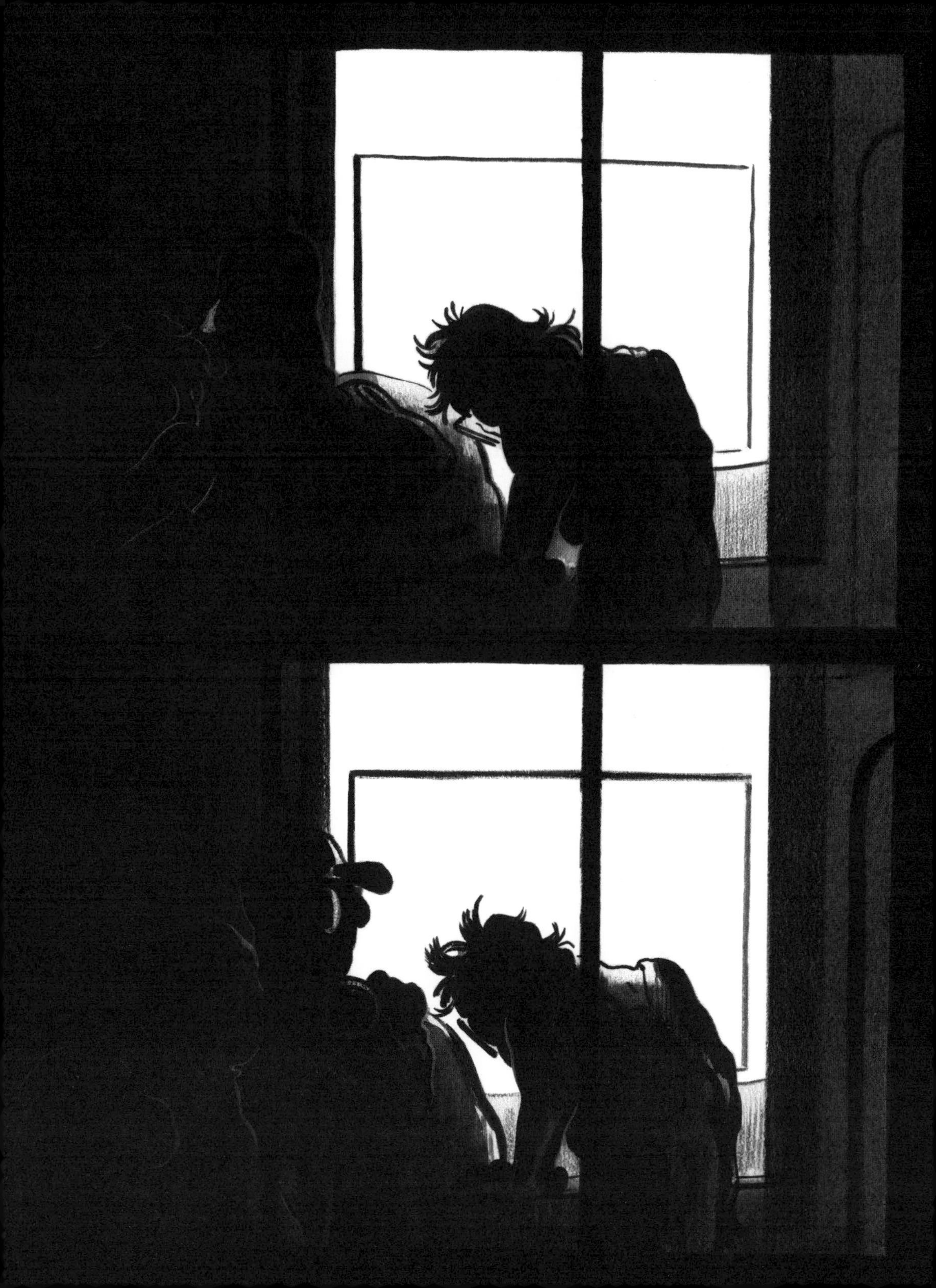

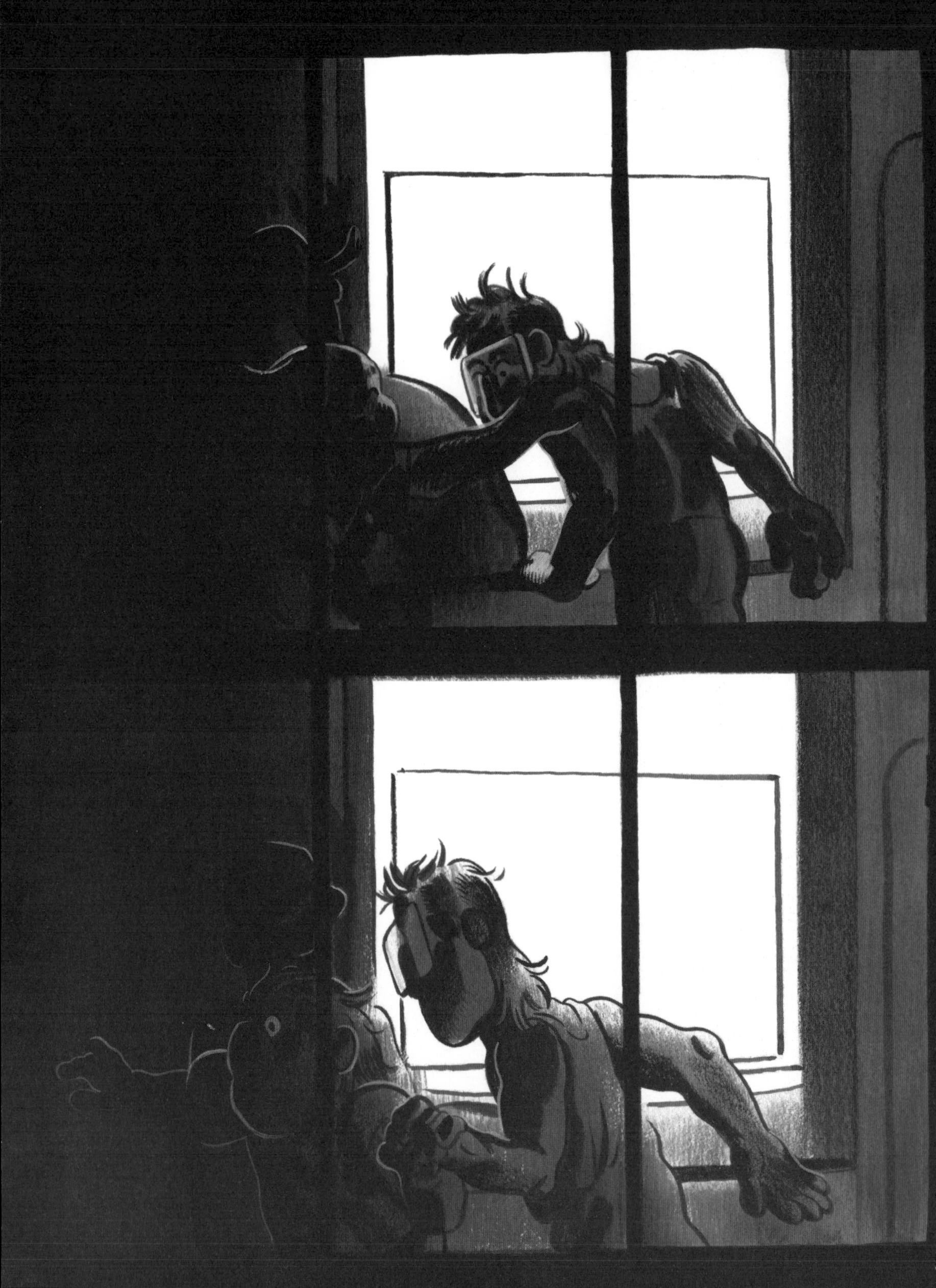

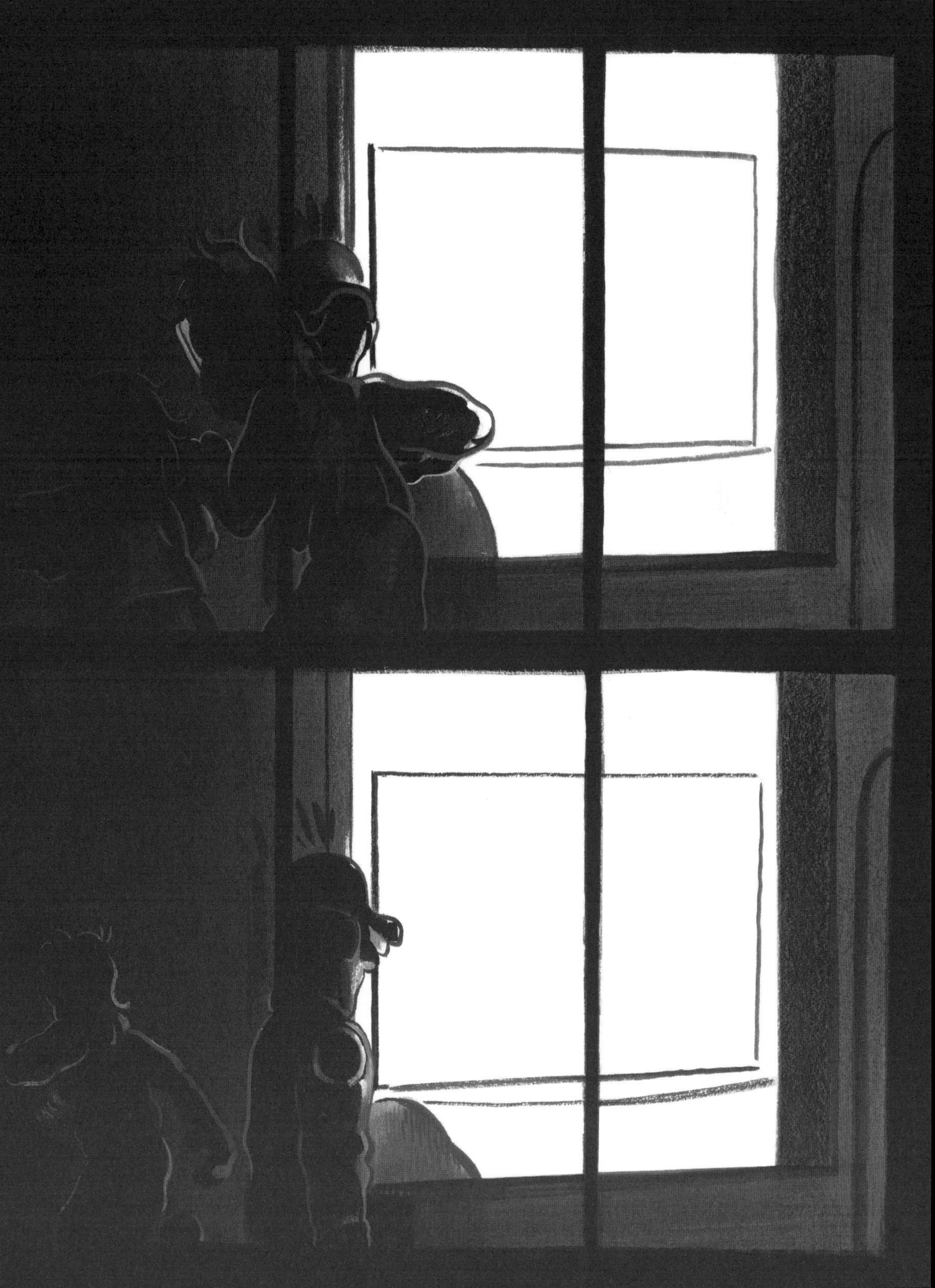

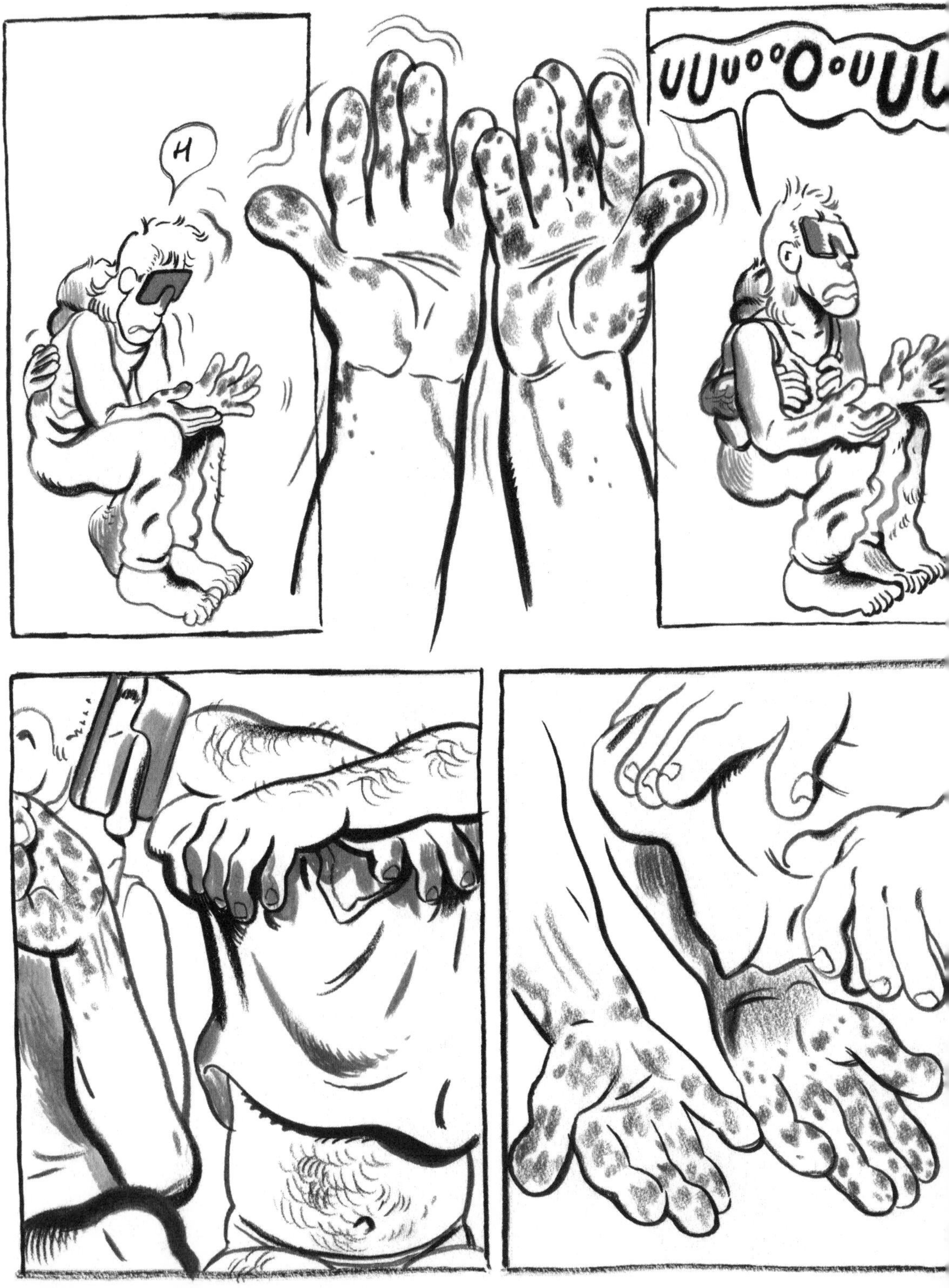
H
UUUºOºUUU

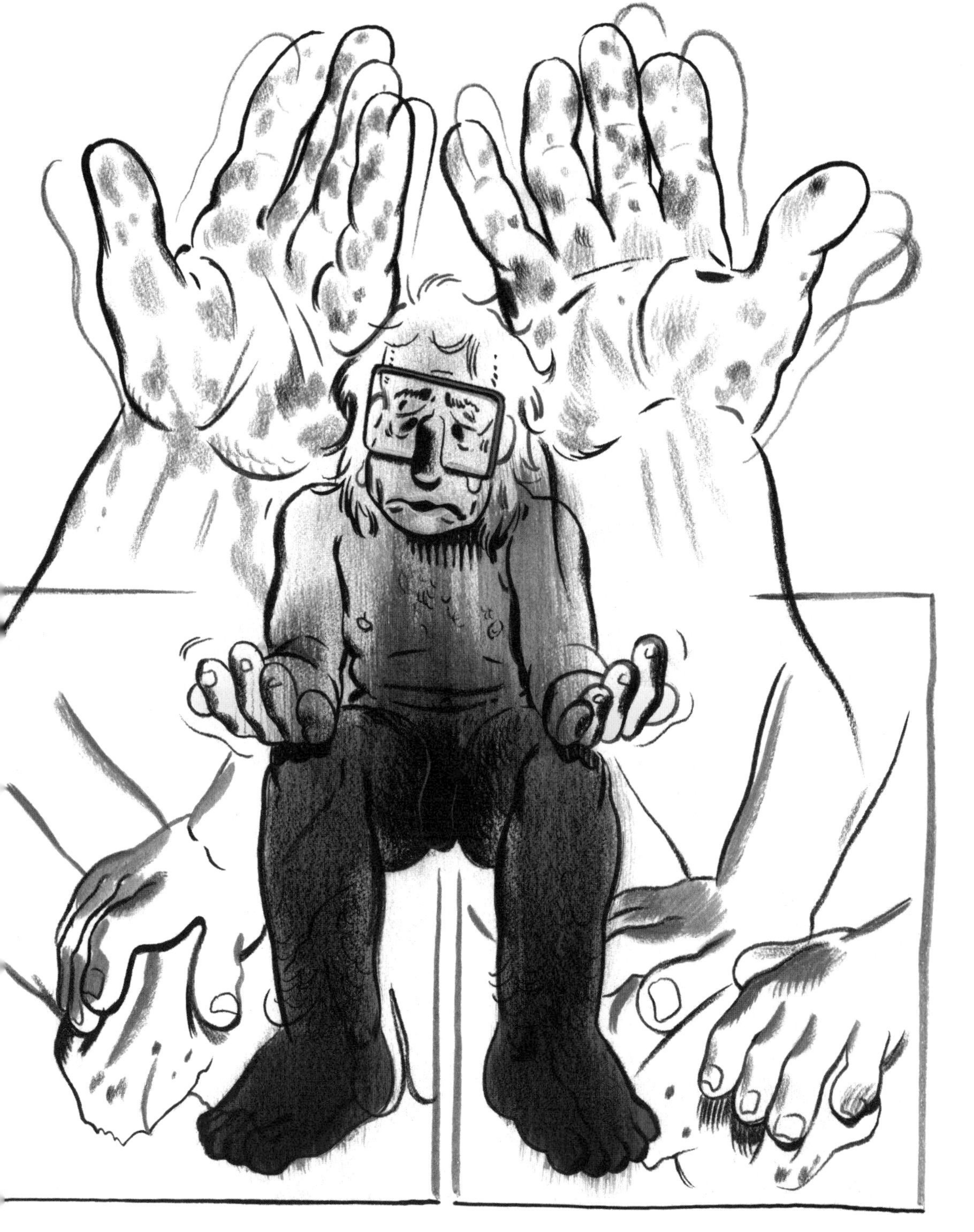

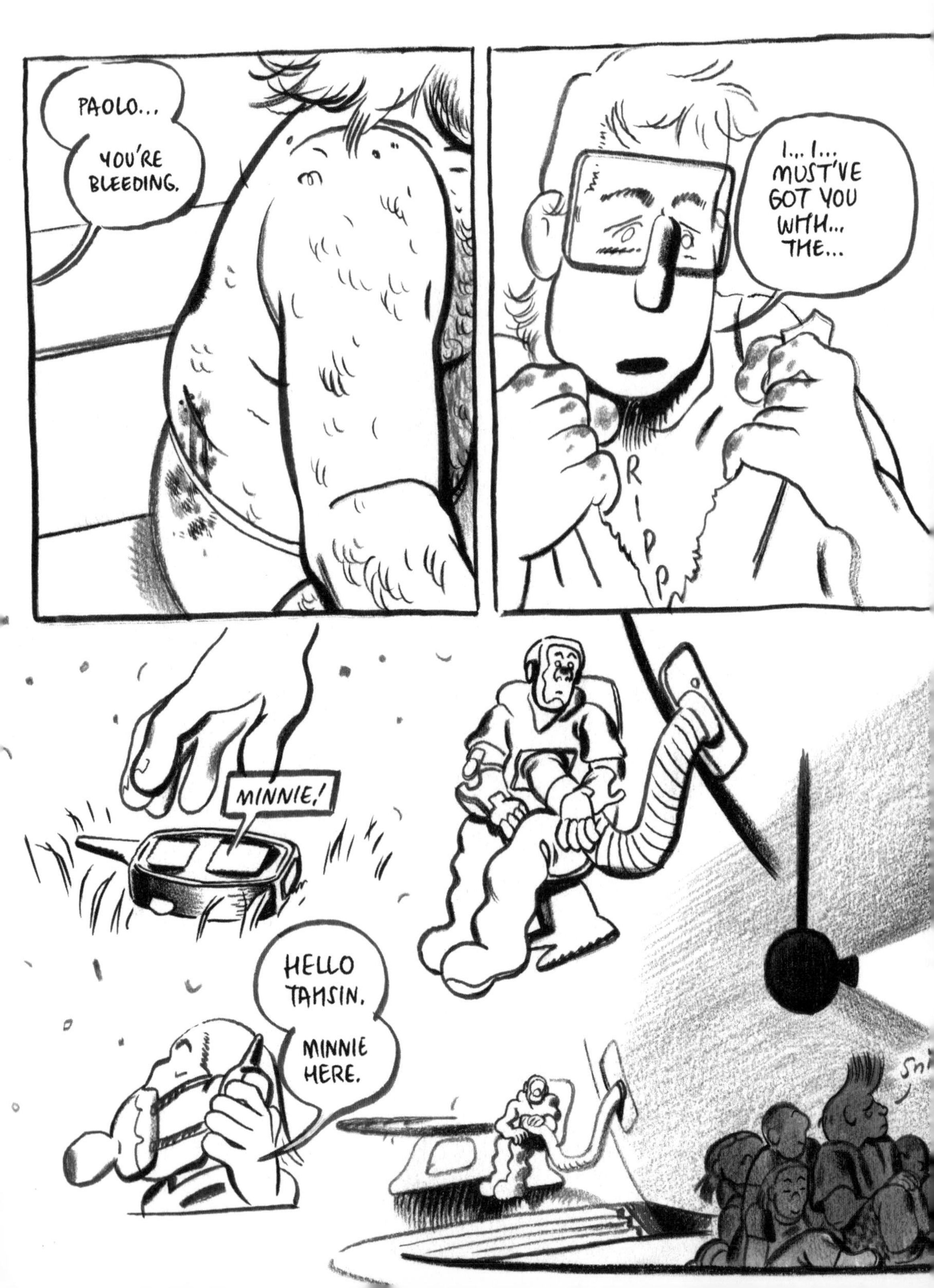
PAOLO...
YOU'RE BLEEDING.
I... I... MUST'VE GOT YOU WITH... THE...
RIPP
MINNIE!
HELLO TAMSIN.
MINNIE HERE.

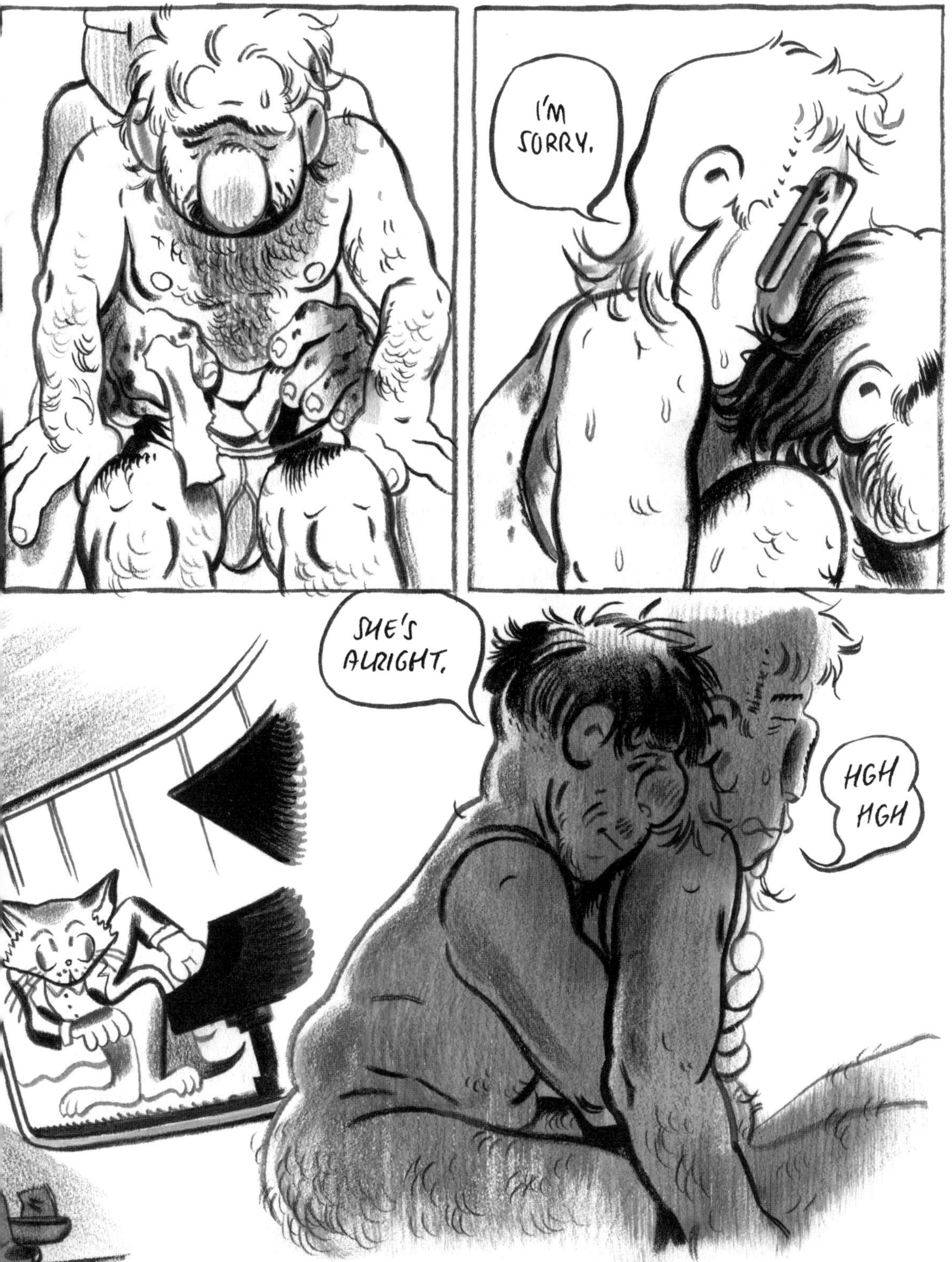
I'M SORRY.
SHE'S ALRIGHT.
HGH HGH

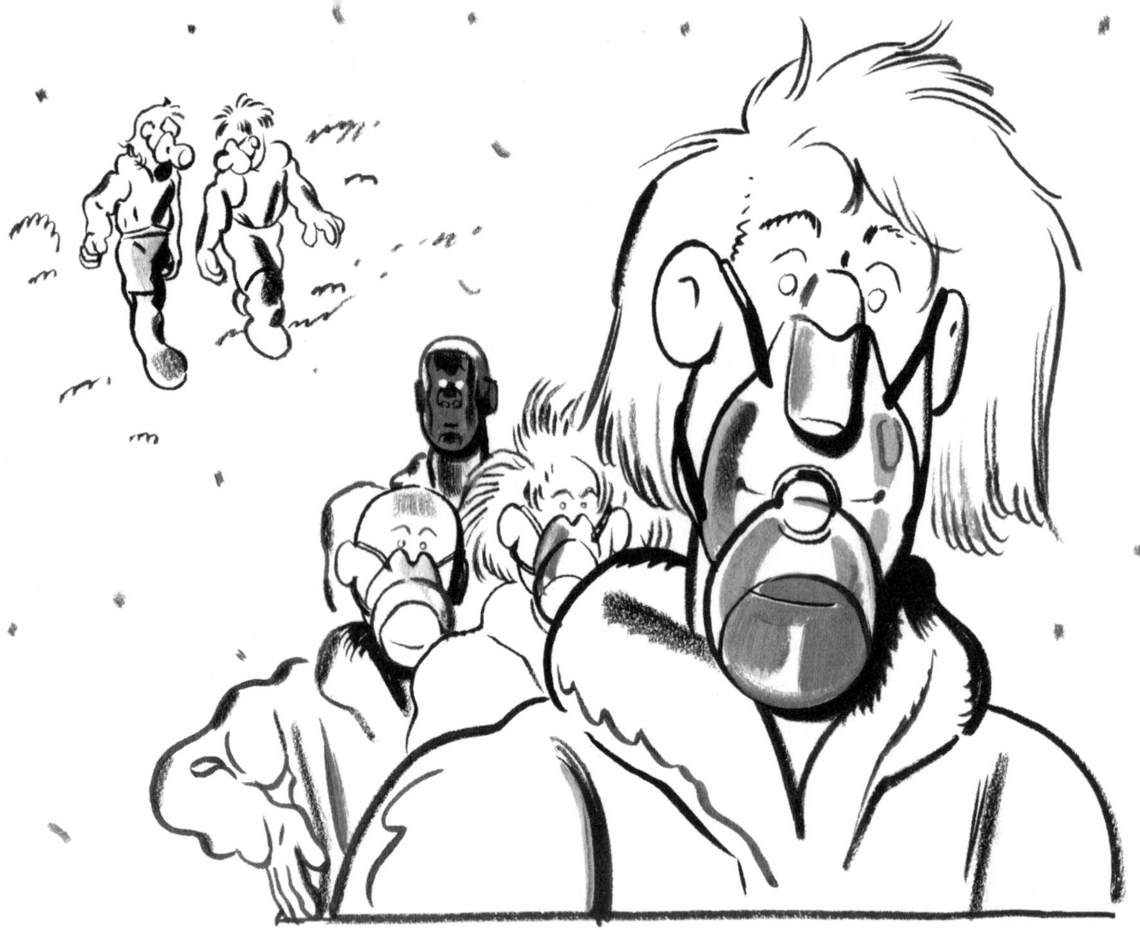

As a child, Colin was bound by a strict moral compass. Actions were not inherently good or bad, but rules, with their firm guidance, made you a better person.

One time, he was caught stealing a toy—a small, red, plastic lion—from a friend. The friend and her mother forgave Colin after it was returned, but Colin still felt horrified by his mistake. As his own punishment, Colin sat behind the living room sofa for three days, too embarrassed to be seen except during meals and to get ready for bed. Minnie would leave plates of cookies to lure him out, but nothing worked. His mistake had branded him and revealed too much about who he was as a person: bad.

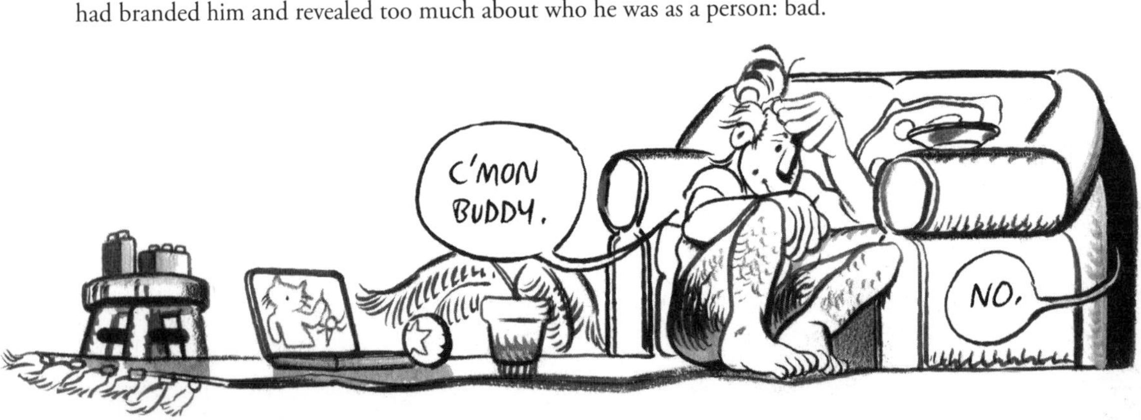
C'MON BUDDY.
NO.

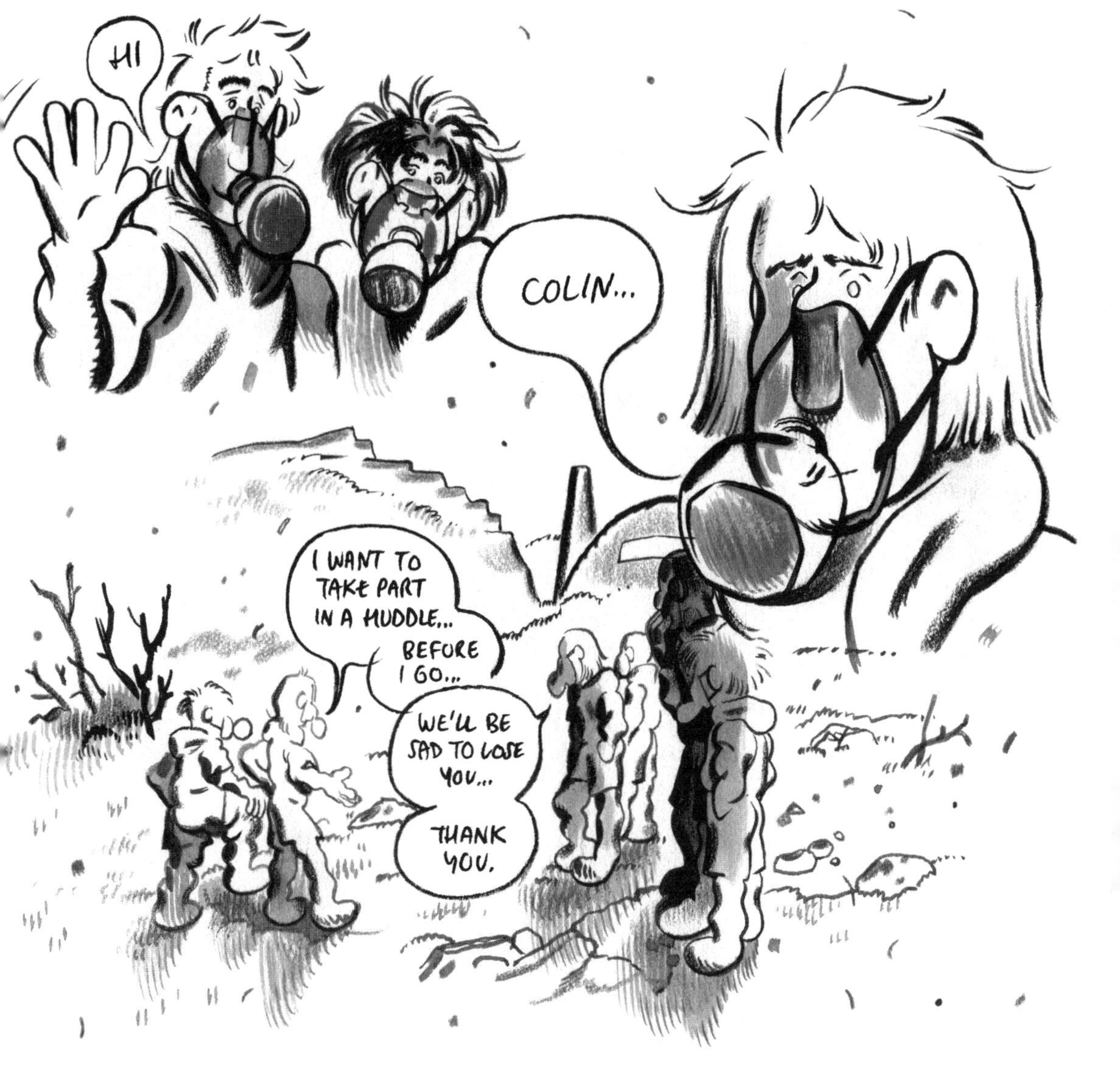
HI
COLIN...
I WANT TO TAKE PART IN A HUDDLE...
BEFORE I GO...
WE'LL BE SAD TO LOSE YOU...
THANK YOU.

Minnie thought that this must have been the hardest part of Colin's childhood: realizing how mortifying it was to be alive. How learning about yourself required admitting how little you already knew.

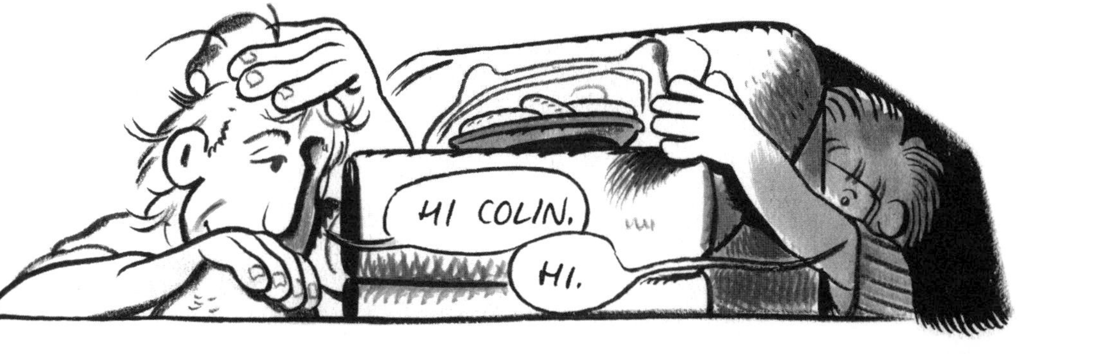
HI COLIN.
HI.

Returning to the city made Colin anxious. Everything was too loud. There were too many people. Too much happening all at once. Although he had done it countless times before, commuting by train to work was suddenly too much for him. He often walked instead, leaving his new apartment early to make up for not relying on transportation.

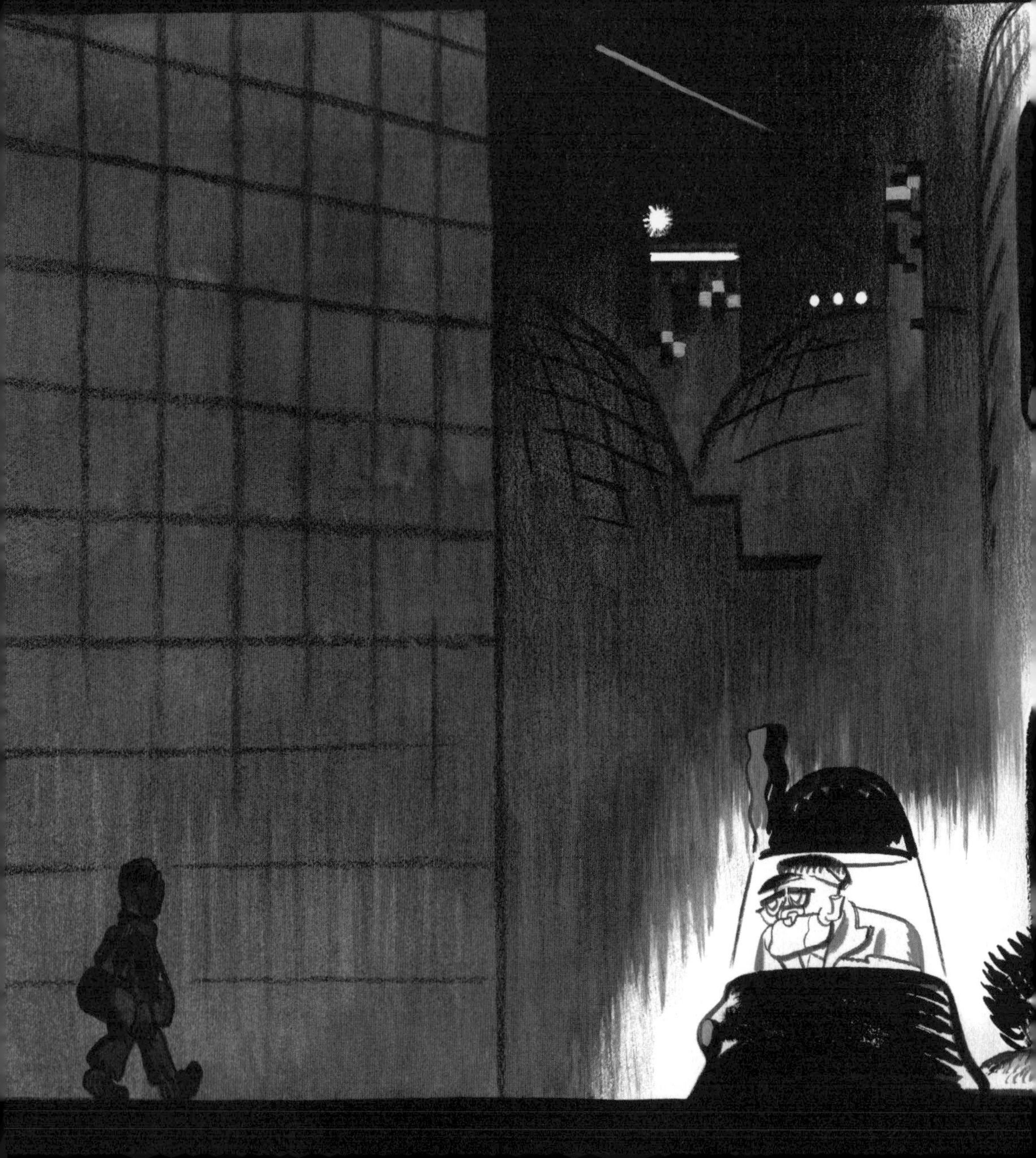

He resumed his role at work as if not a day had passed, but it was obvious to everyone but Colin that in his time away he had outgrown his old life as he had once known it. When an opportunity for a job transfer came up, his boss put his name in for consideration. He got the job. Within a month of returning, he learned he was moving. Again.

Before leaving town the first time, Colin had left behind some of his possessions with Jacqueline and Avery.

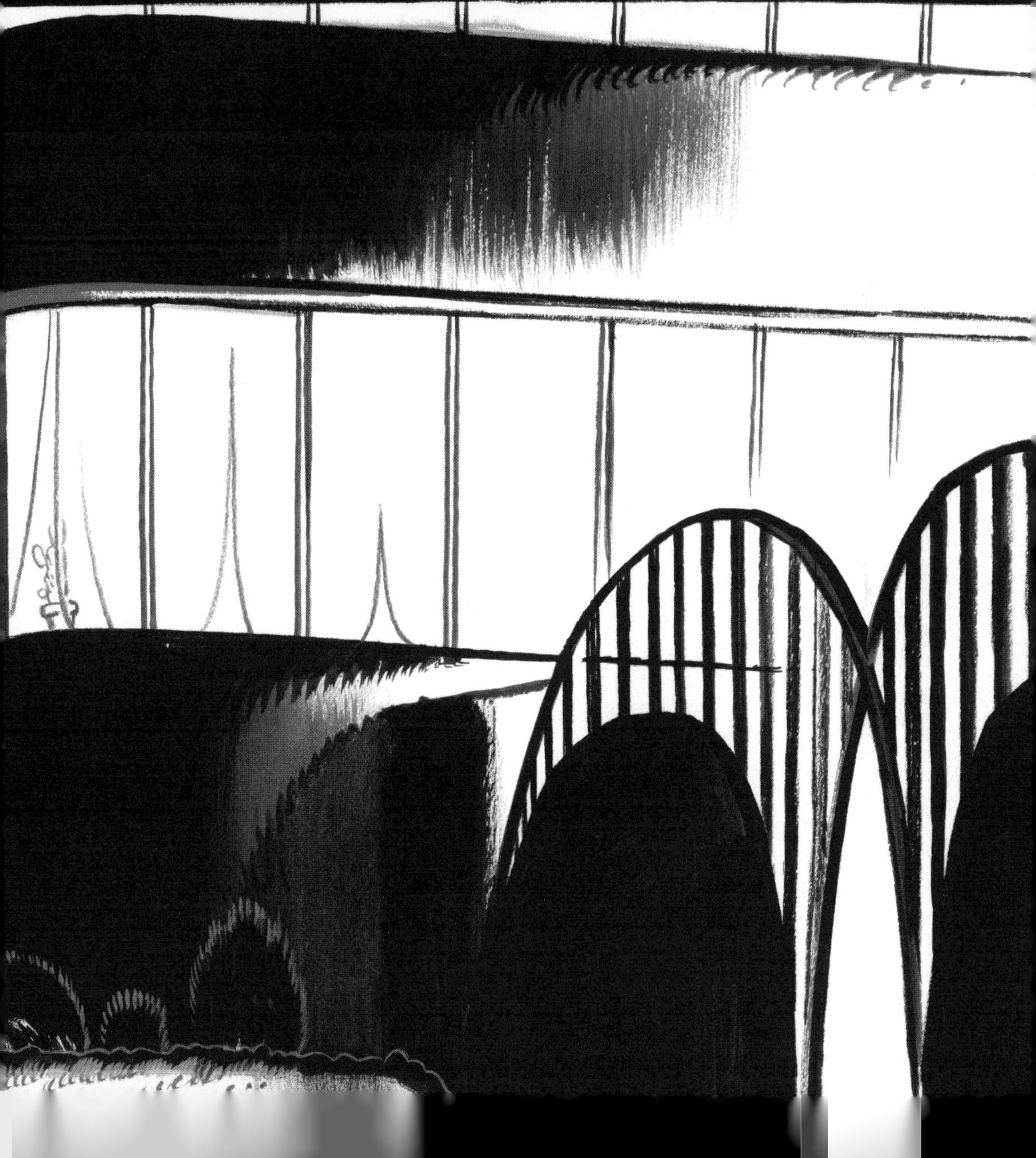

Most of what Colin had owned in his apartment was returned to Central Furnishing. A few things, like the couch he had purchased with his first paycheck, needed a home.

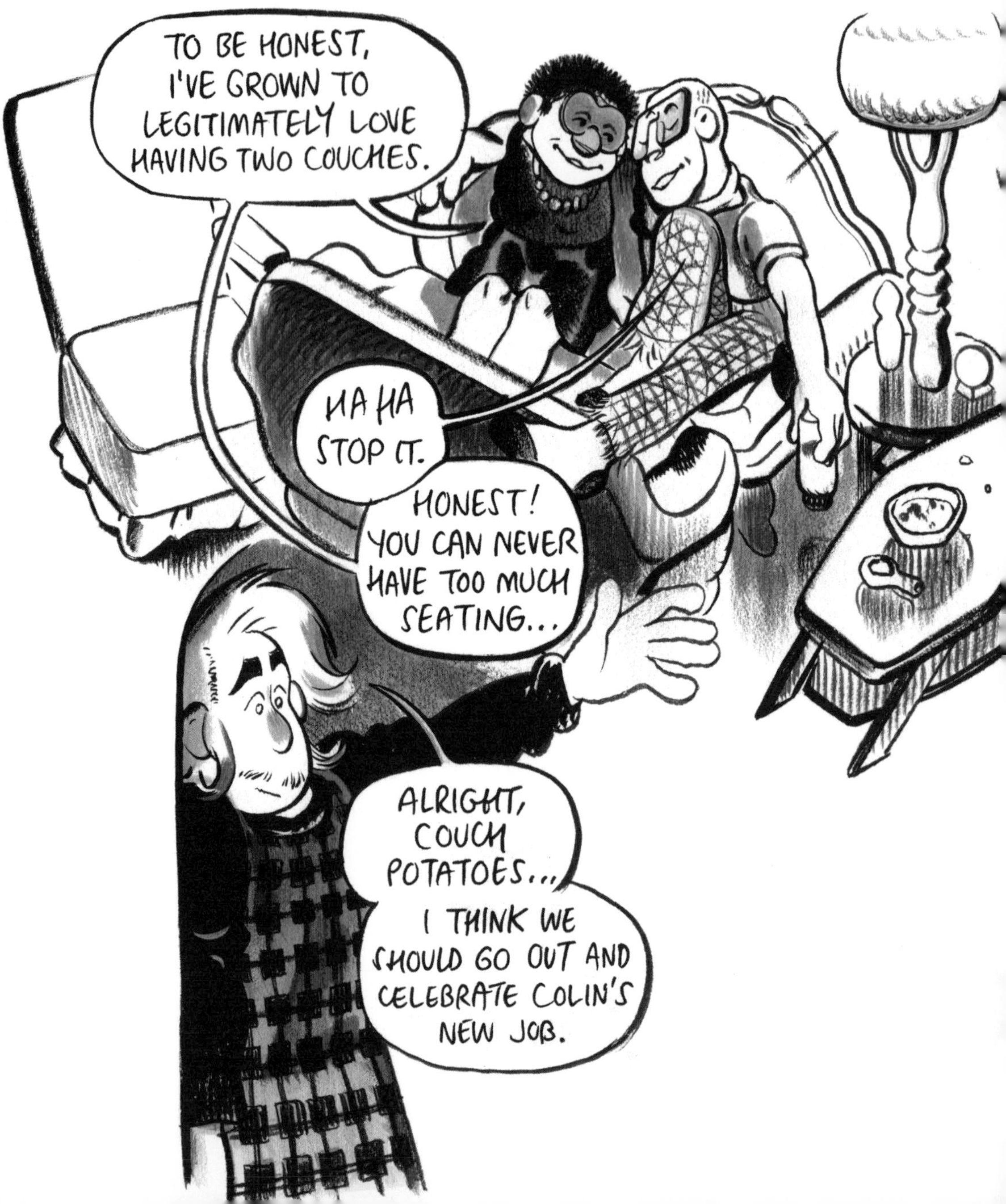
TO BE HONEST, I'VE GROWN TO LEGITIMATELY LOVE HAVING TWO COUCHES.
HA HA STOP IT.
HONEST! YOU CAN NEVER HAVE TOO MUCH SEATING...
ALRIGHT, COUCH POTATOES...,
I THINK WE SHOULD GO OUT AND CELEBRATE COLIN'S NEW JOB.

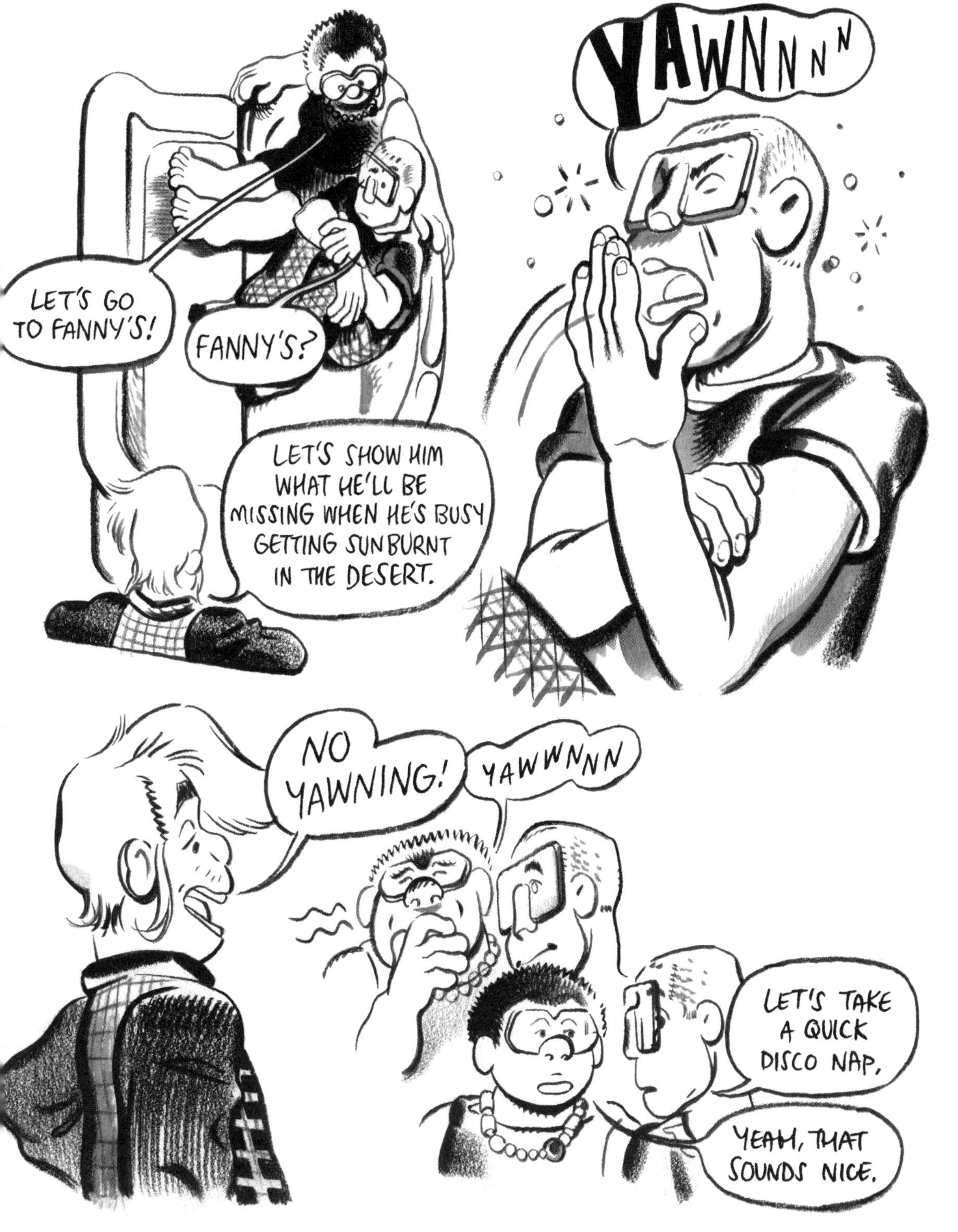
LET'S GO TO FANNY'S!
FANNY'S?
LET'S SHOW HIM WHAT HE'LL BE MISSING WHEN HE'S BUSY GETTING SUNBURNT IN THE DESERT.
YAWNNNN
NO YAWNING!
YAWWNNN
LET'S TAKE A QUICK DISCO NAP.
YEAH, THAT SOUNDS NICE.

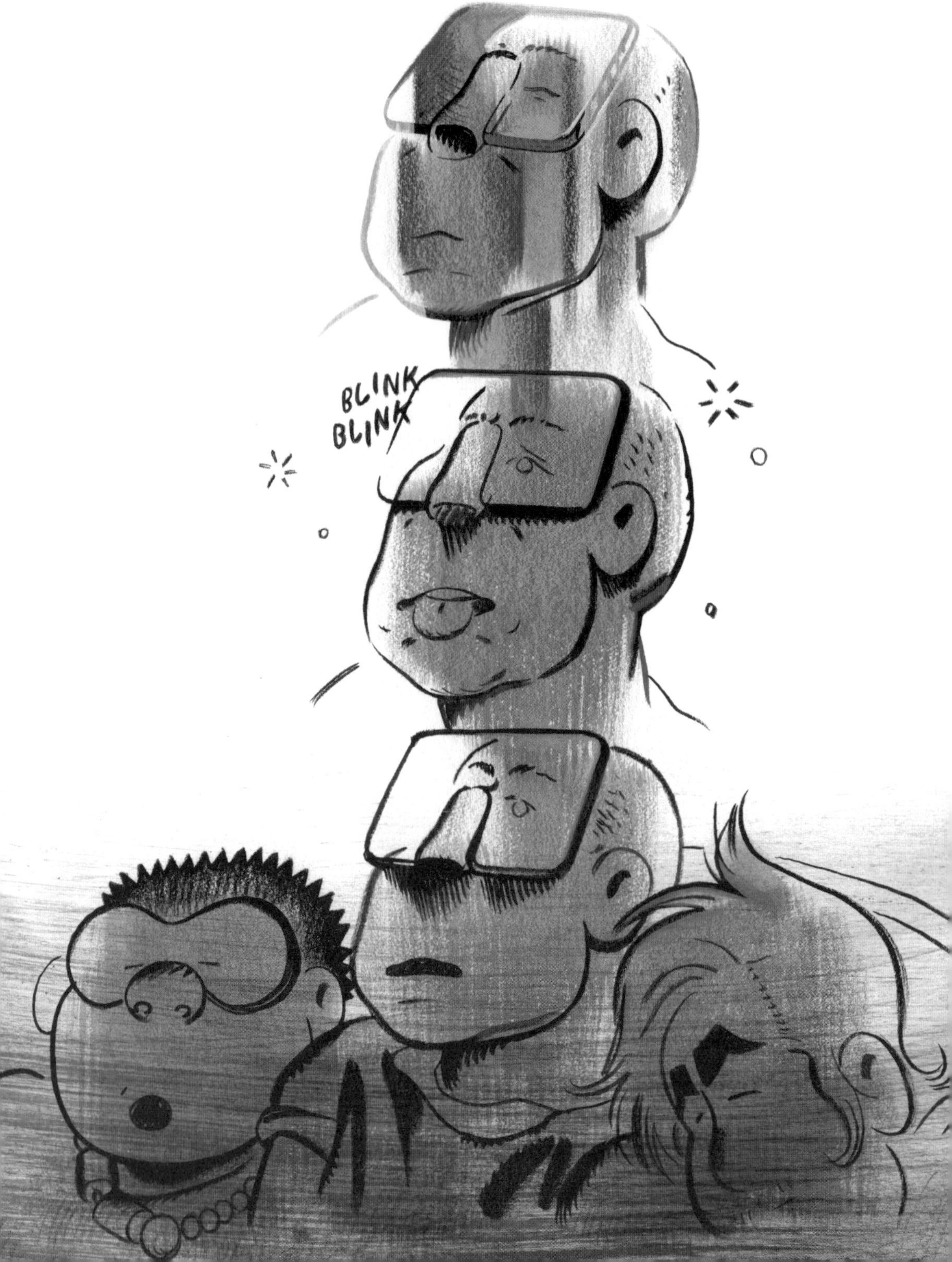
BLINK
BLINK

It took everything in Colin not to quietly slip away while Avery and Jacqueline lay asleep by his side. He knew their goodbyes would feel too rushed and not as poignant as he often thought moments like that should feel. Before, he would have gone through the motions, tried to feel what he needed to feel, but he was a different person now.

That had been the most shocking part of being in a huddle. It wasn't seeing every version of himself, extending as far back as infancy, that no longer made sense to him; rather, it was who he currently was that confused him. Who he used to be felt so clear. He missed that clarity. His own warmth. His easy kindness. He worried that the person he had known himself to be was gone. Or worse, maybe that person had never existed in the way he thought he did.

As the rising sun warmed up the air around him, Colin took in the room. He had almost met Paolo here, at a party they had both attended. He began to drift nostalgically, but caught himself. Missing Paolo felt foolish.

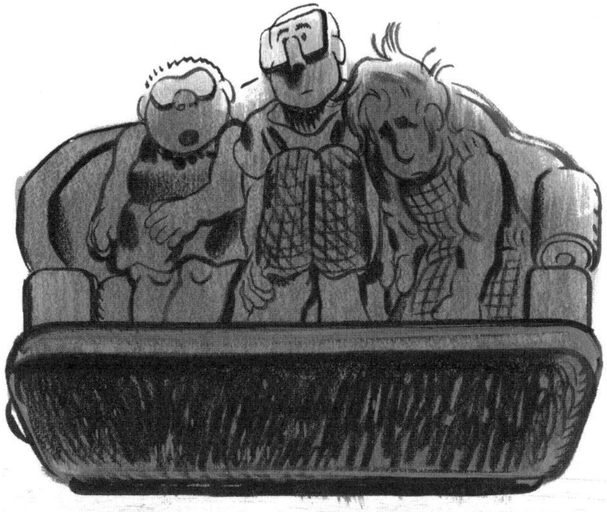

Later, after he said his half-hearted goodbyes standing in the doorway of Avery and Jacqueline's apartment, Colin couldn't help but wonder if the man he used to be had enjoyed himself that night almost two years before. Leaving in exactly the same way he had the night of that other party, after all the guests had left and he had helped clean up, Colin tried to recall how it had felt.

And then he remembered—that moment he realized he was wearing someone else's leather jacket. How strange it had felt to still be himself, but suddenly not knowing where something in his life had come from.

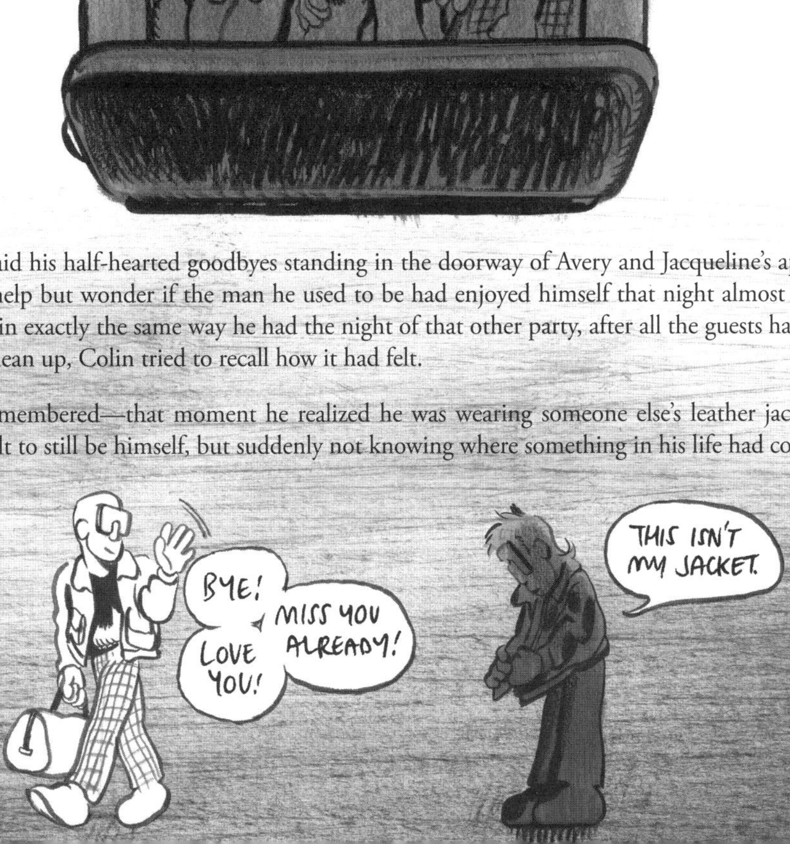
BYE!
MISS YOU ALREADY!
LOVE YOU!
THIS ISN'T MY JACKET.

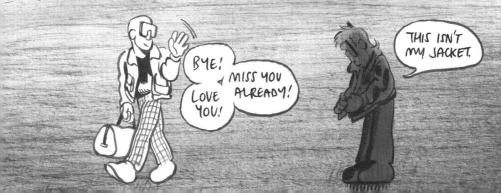

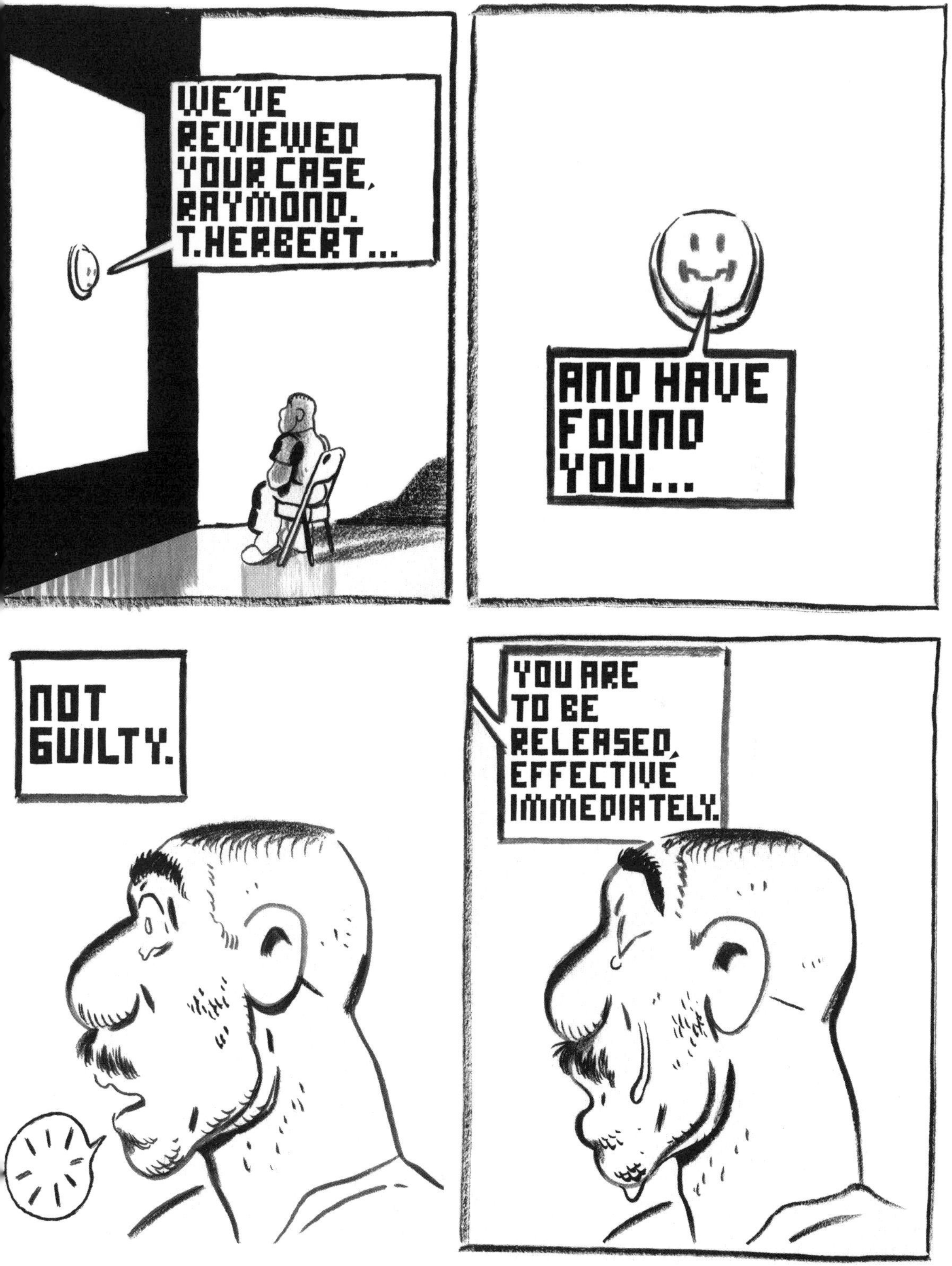

WE'VE REVIEWED YOUR CASE, RAYMOND. T.HERBERT...
AND HAVE FOUND YOU...
NOT GUILTY.
YOU ARE TO BE RELEASED, EFFECTIVE IMMEDIATELY.

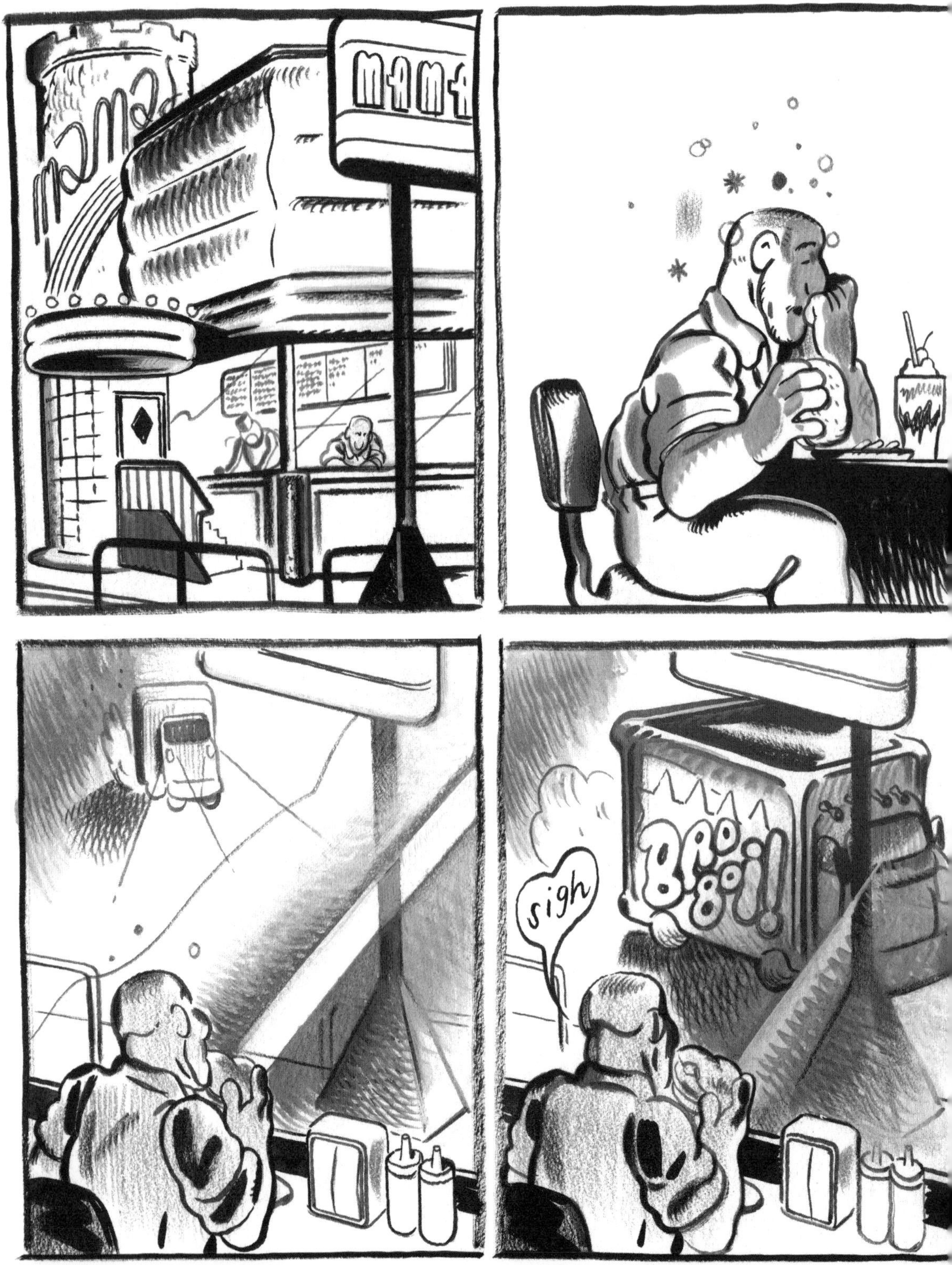
sigh
BAD BOI!

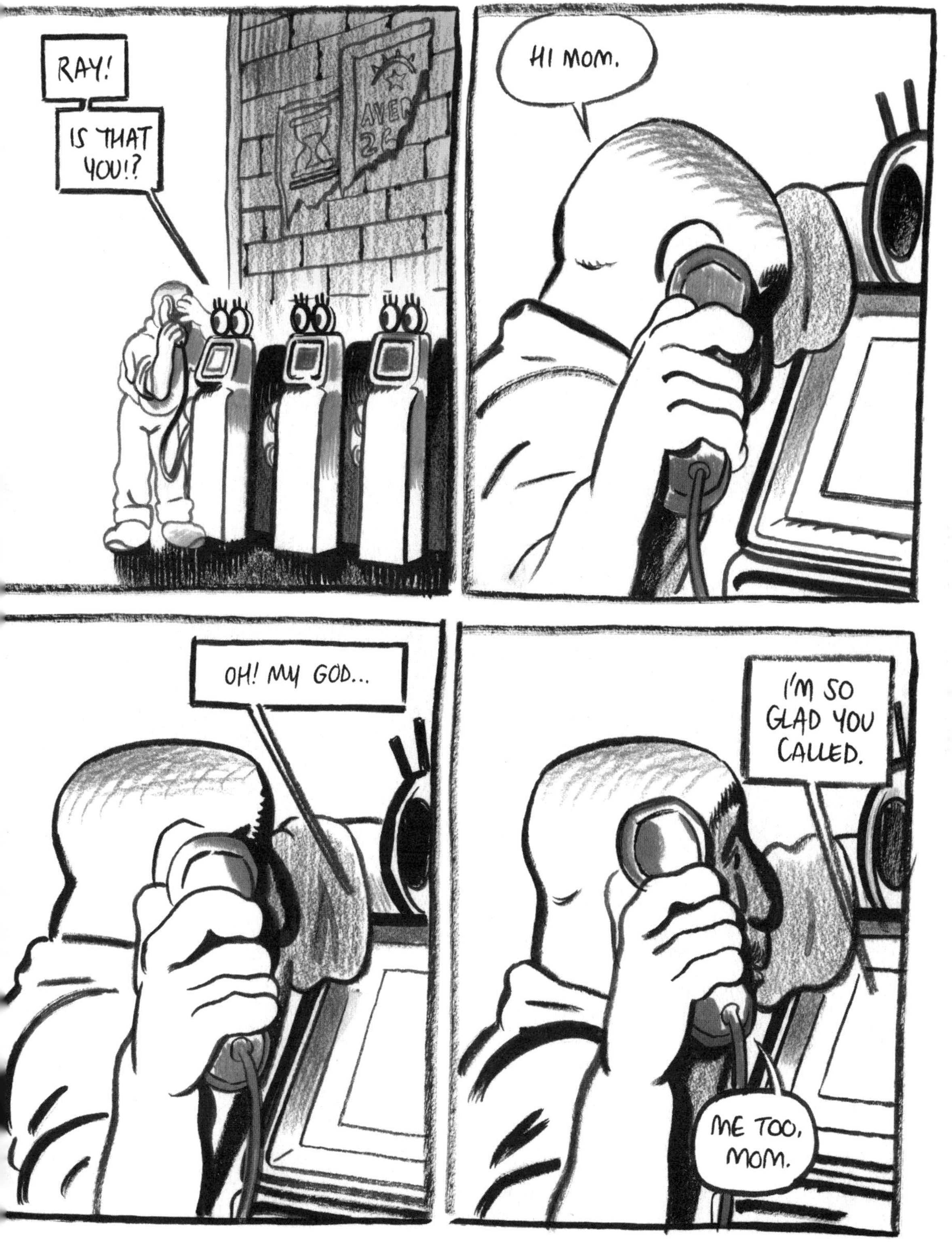
RAY!
IS THAT YOU!?
HI MOM.
OH! MY GOD...
I'M SO GLAD YOU CALLED.
ME TOO, MOM.

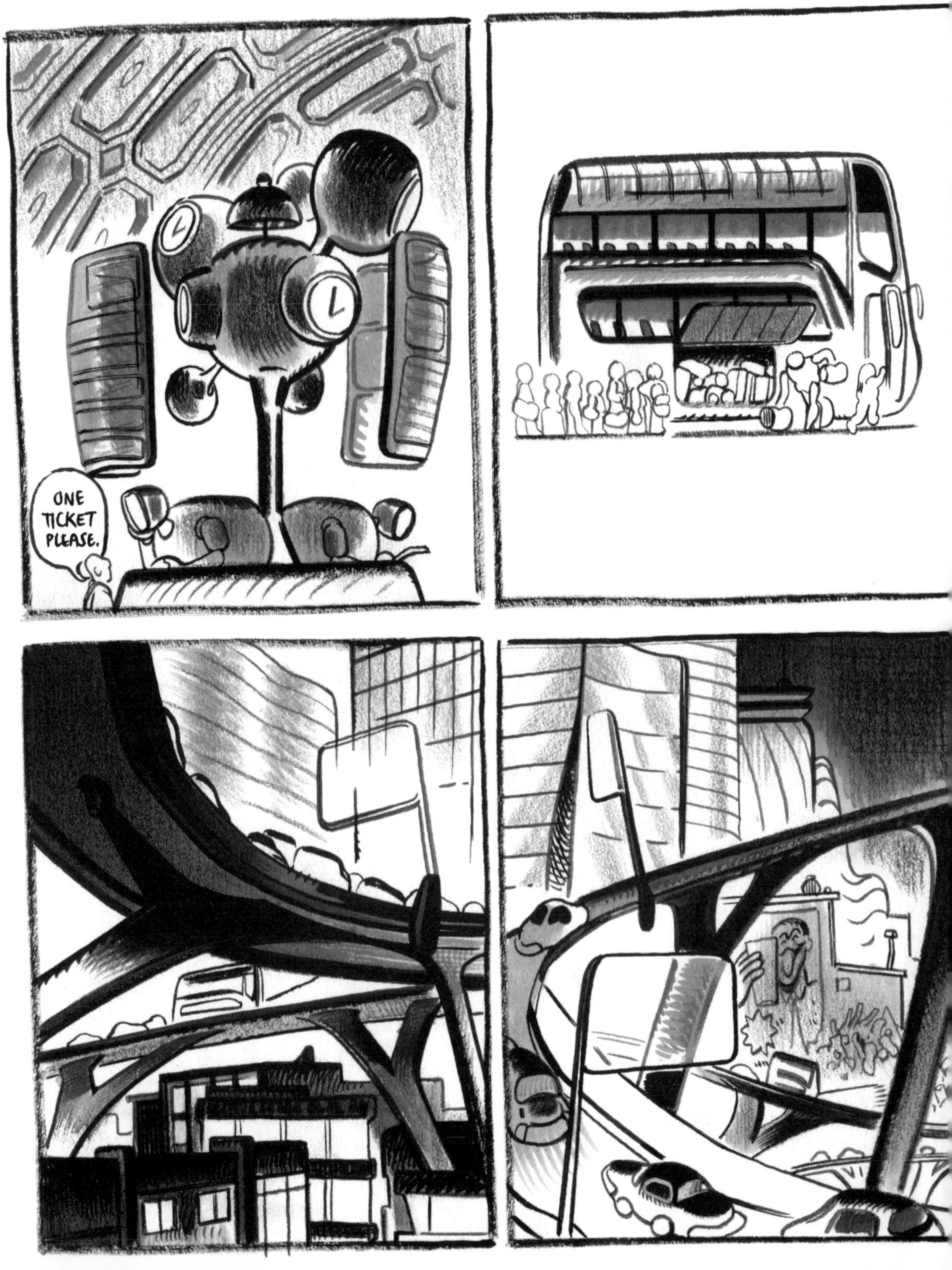
ONE TICKET PLEASE.

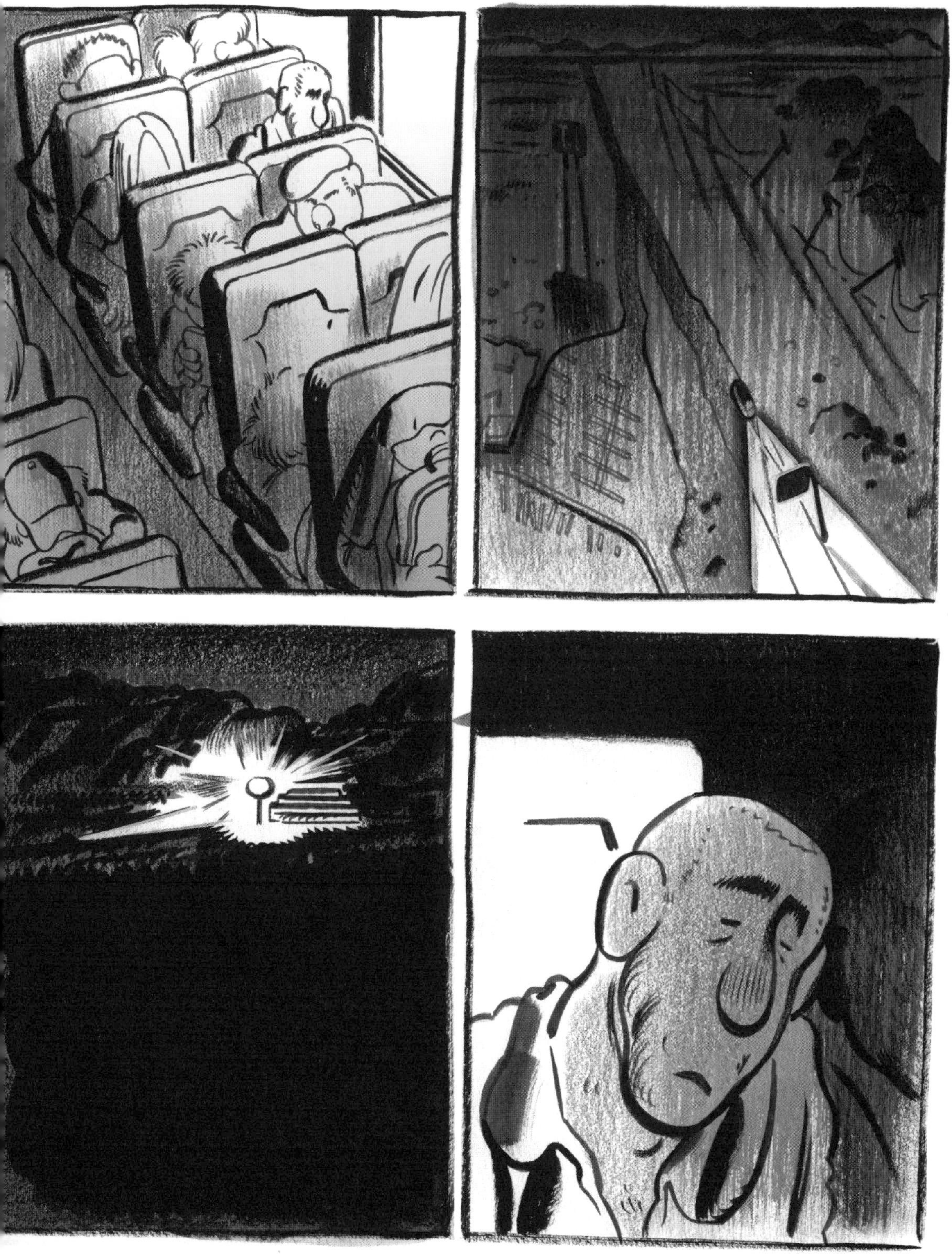

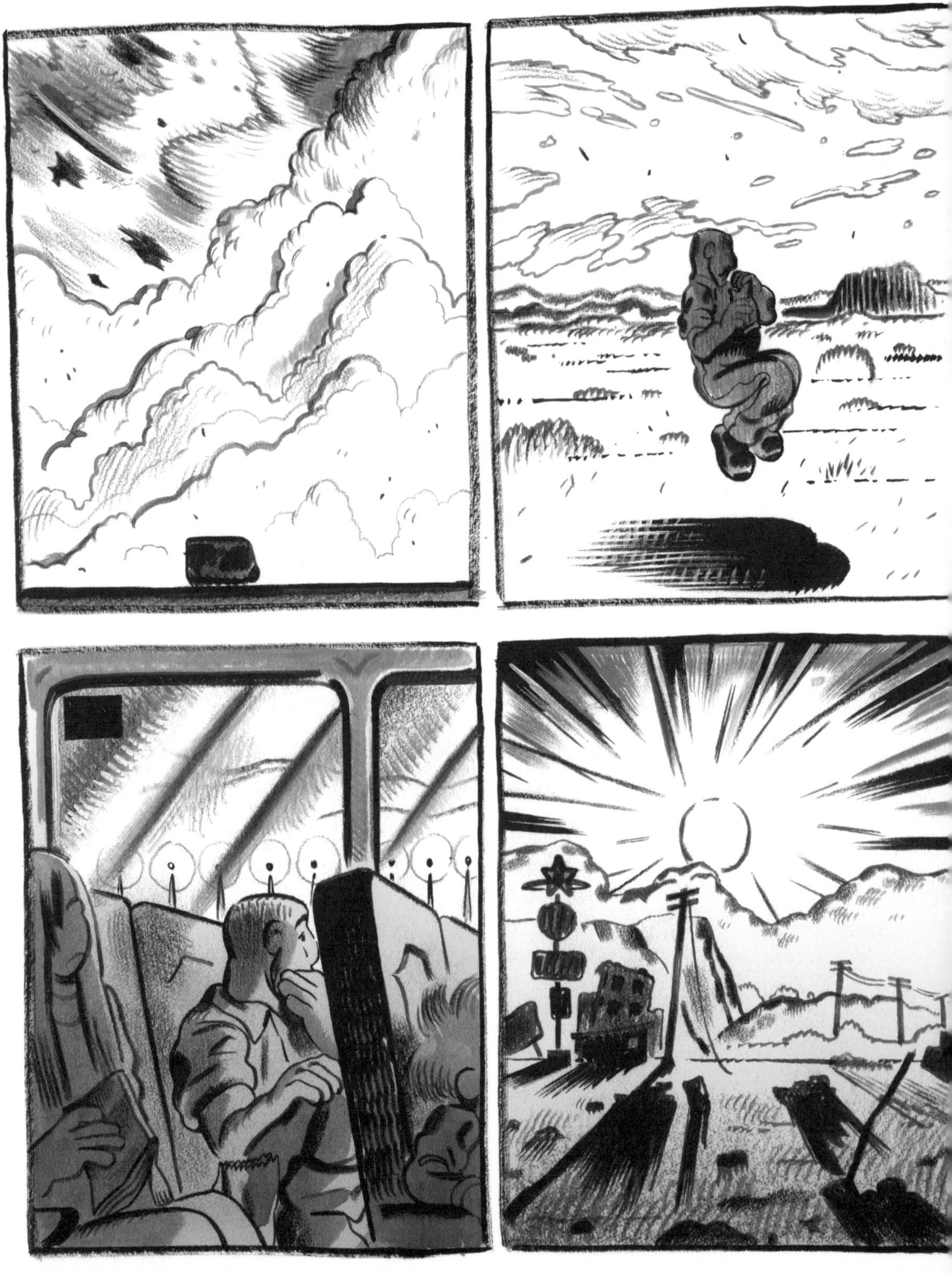

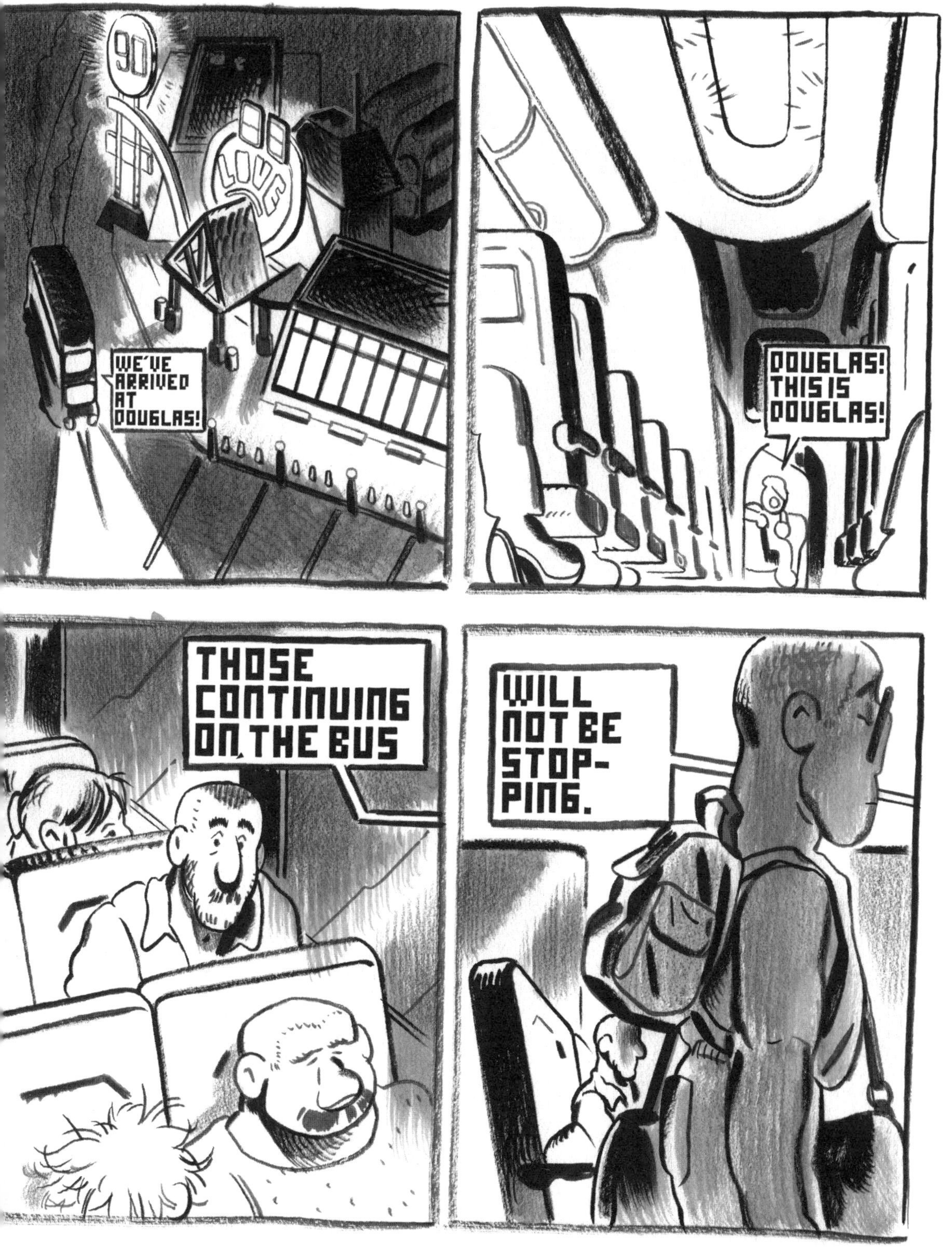
WE'VE ARRIVED AT DOUGLAS!
DOUGLAS! THIS IS DOUGLAS!
THOSE CONTINUING ON THE BUS
WILL NOT BE STOP-PING.

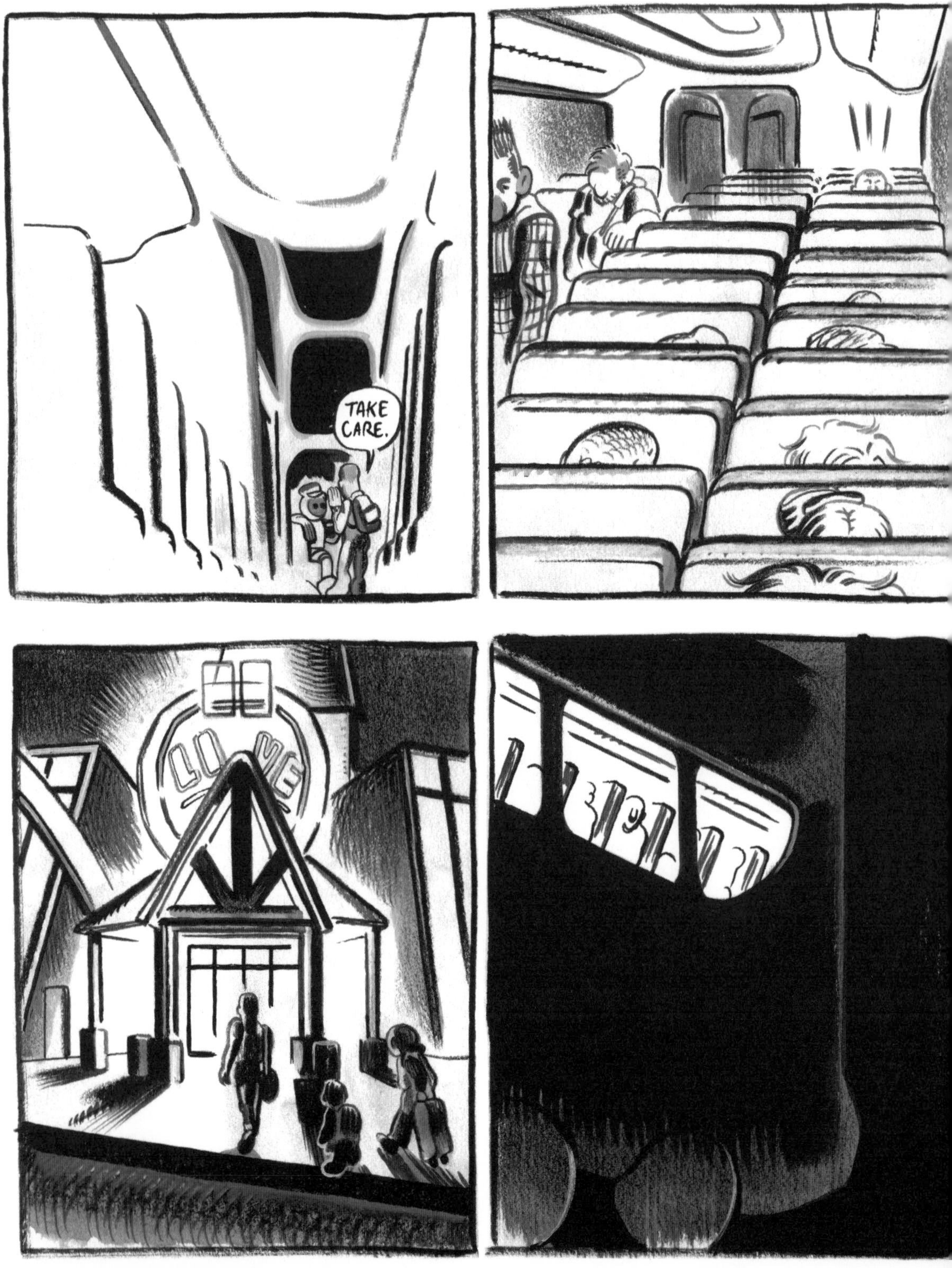
TAKE CARE.

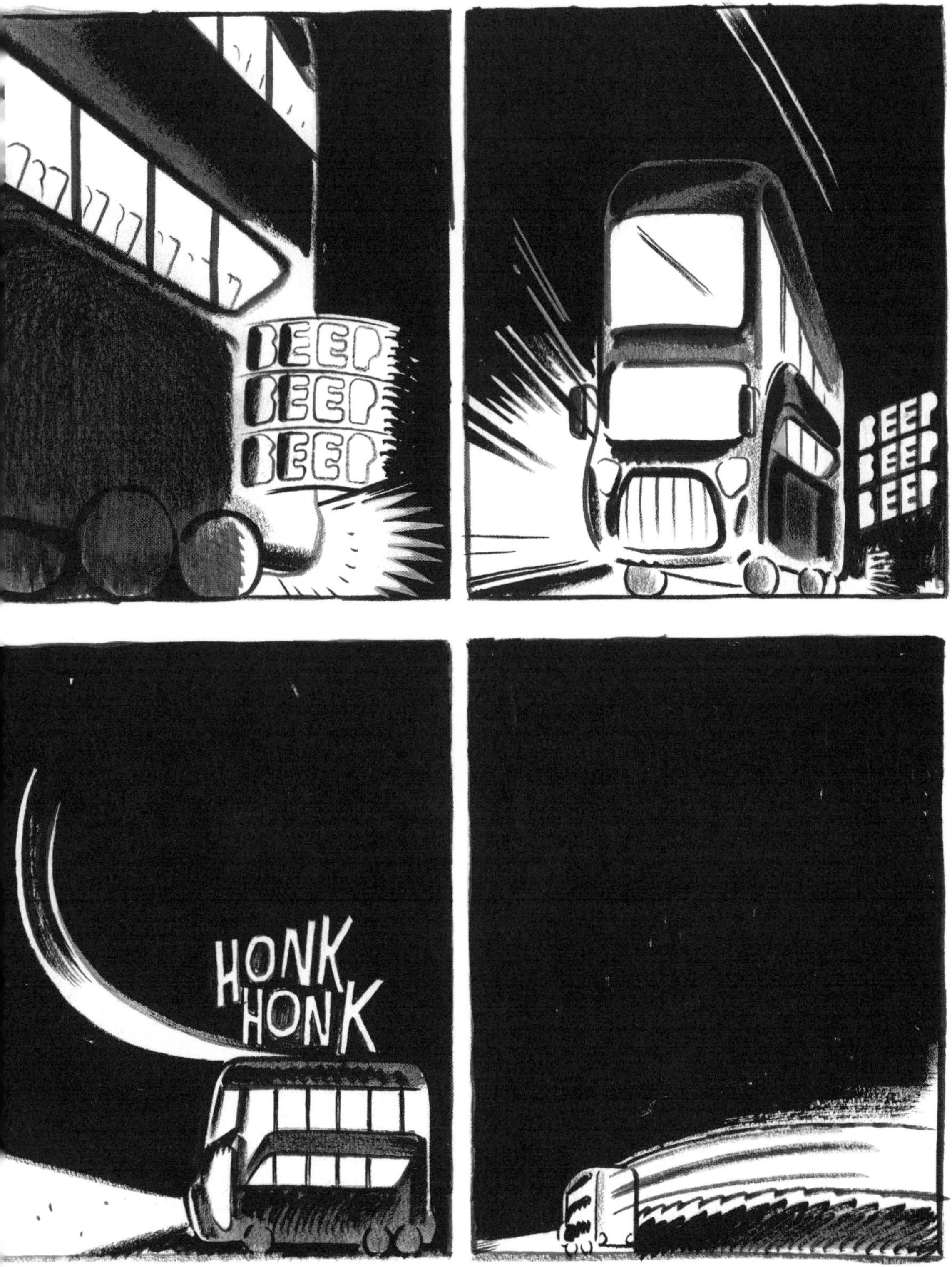
BEEP
BEEP
BEEP
BEEP
BEEP
BEEP
HONK
HONK

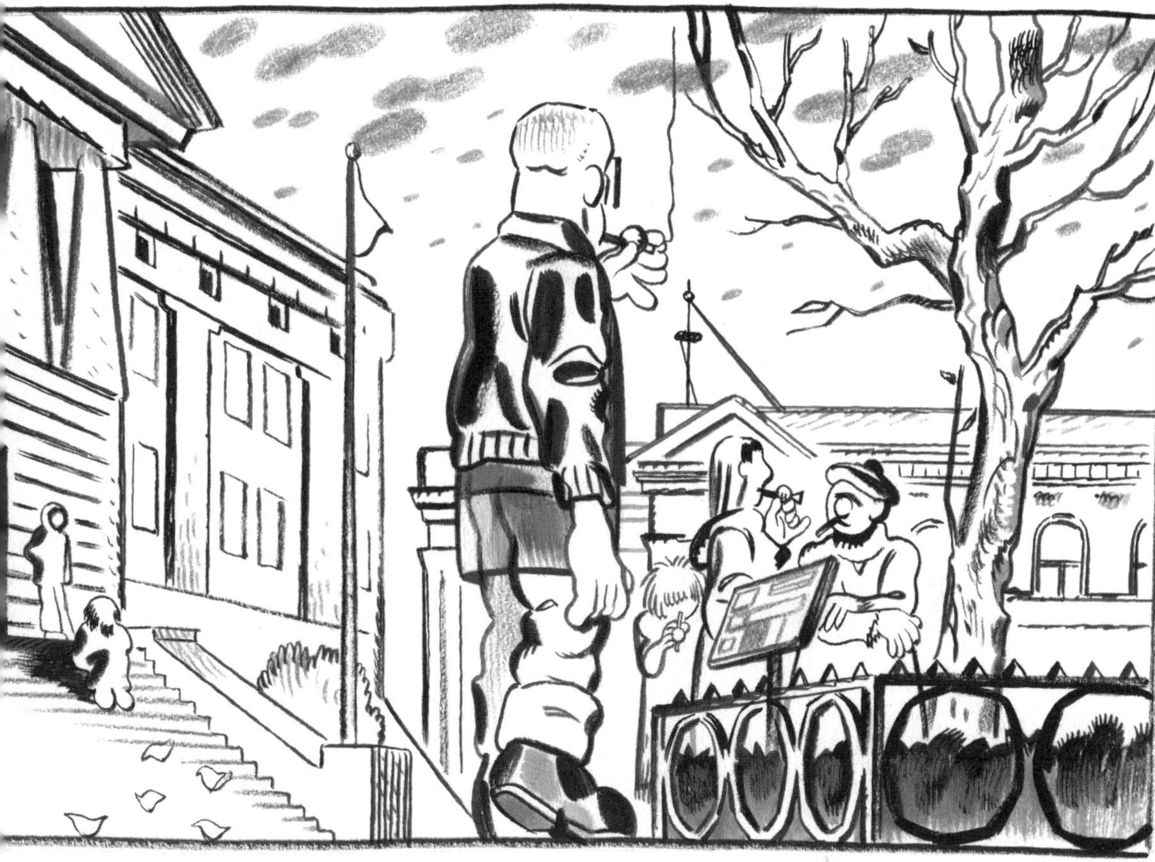

A few years later, Colin found himself back in the city he had once called home.

He now lived permanently in the desert, working on a project to help preserve the large graffitied sections of wall built along the country's southern border. The project was both a testament to the cruelty inflicted by their country as well as a way to highlight all the ways humans have, and will continue to, help support one another.

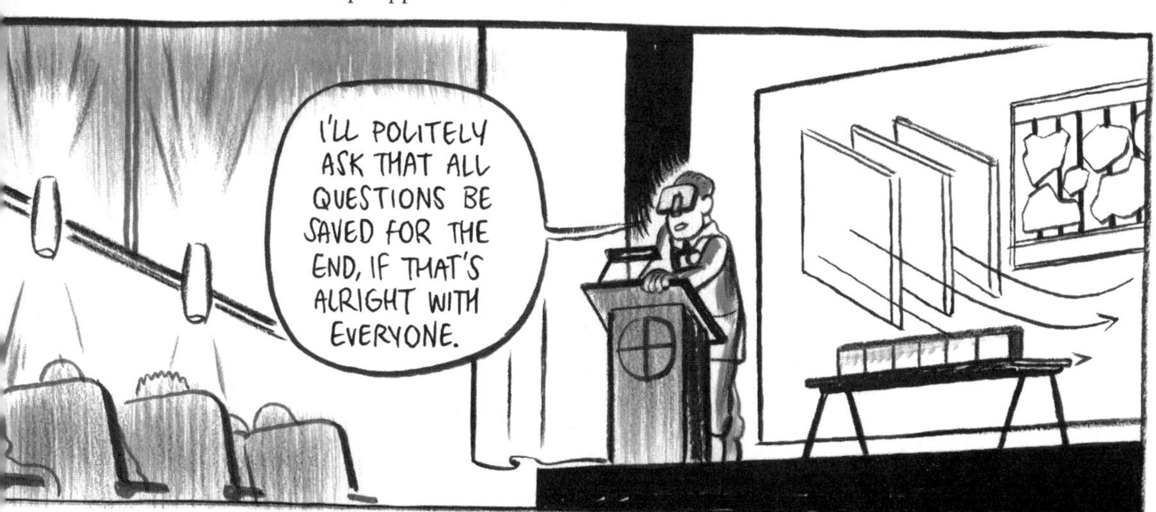
I'LL POLITELY ASK THAT ALL QUESTIONS BE SAVED FOR THE END, IF THAT'S ALRIGHT WITH EVERYONE.

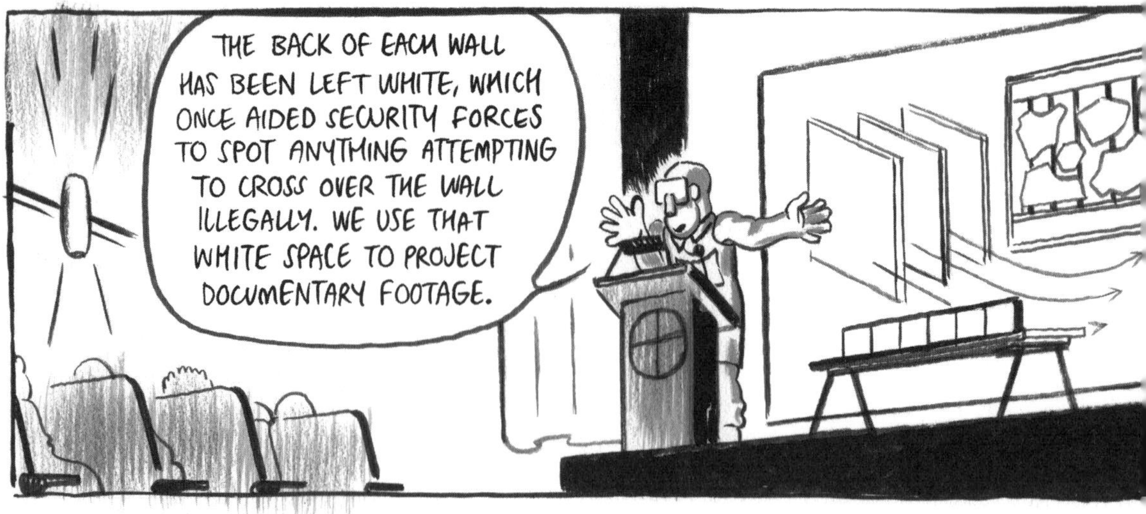
THE BACK OF EACH WALL HAS BEEN LEFT WHITE, WHICH ONCE AIDED SECURITY FORCES TO SPOT ANYTHING ATTEMPTING TO CROSS OVER THE WALL ILLEGALLY. WE USE THAT WHITE SPACE TO PROJECT DOCUMENTARY FOOTAGE.

Colin had been invited back to speak about the project at a design conference. He was only in town for two days and hadn't planned on seeing anyone he knew while visiting.

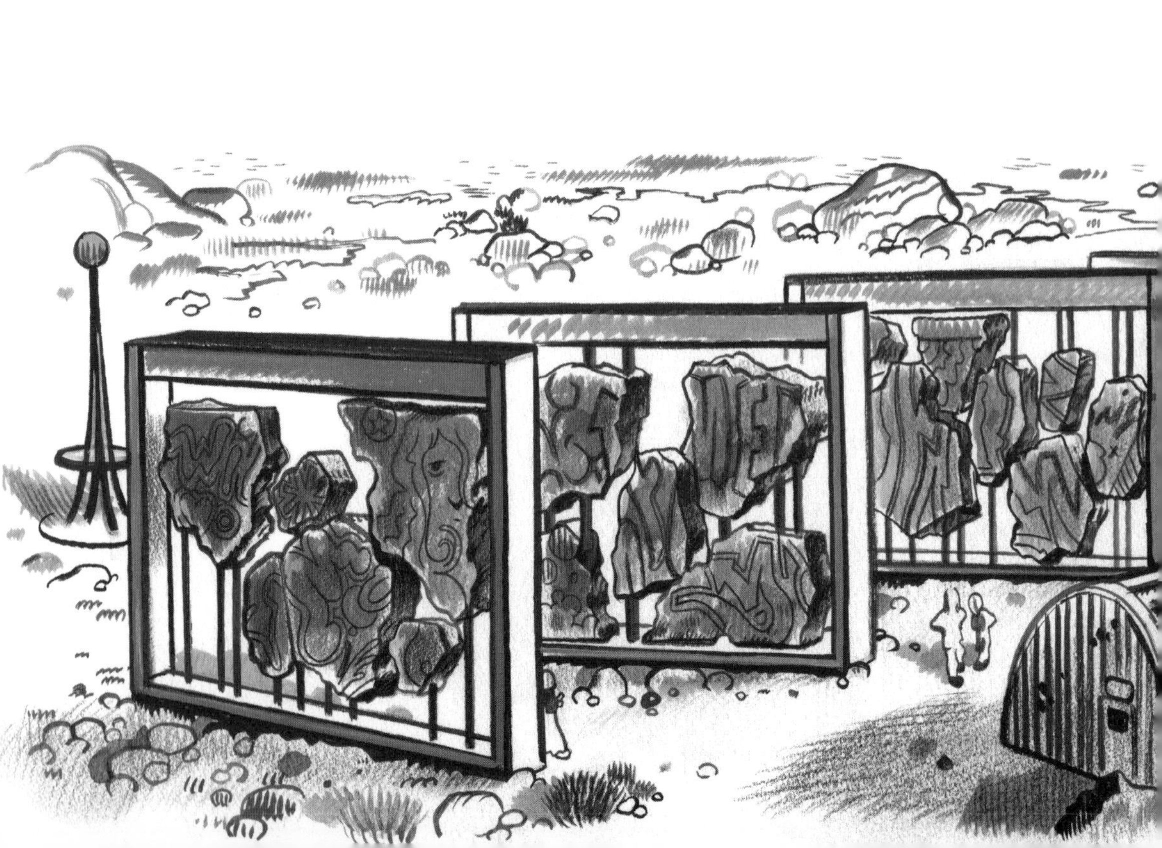

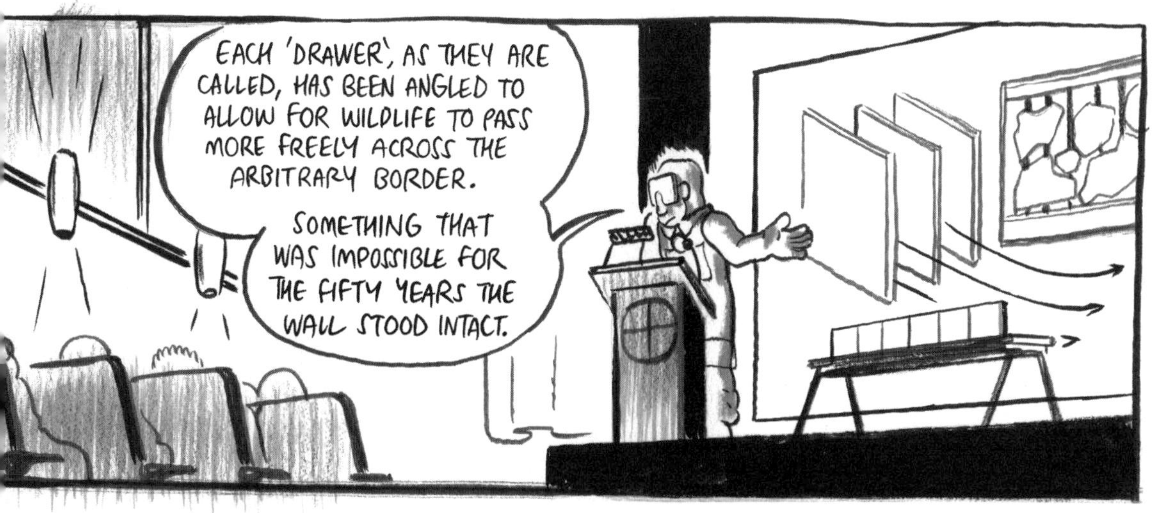
EACH 'DRAWER', AS THEY ARE CALLED, HAS BEEN ANGLED TO ALLOW FOR WILDLIFE TO PASS MORE FREELY ACROSS THE ARBITRARY BORDER.
SOMETHING THAT WAS IMPOSSIBLE FOR THE FIFTY YEARS THE WALL STOOD INTACT.

Avery had moved out of the country entirely after their current partner inherited their family's estate. Jacqueline had moved back home to take care of her ailing mother. Colin thought of Paolo often, but too much time had passed for him to suddenly call him up.

He didn't even know if Paolo was still local. So much had happened in his own life, it was safe to assume that the same was true for Paolo as well.

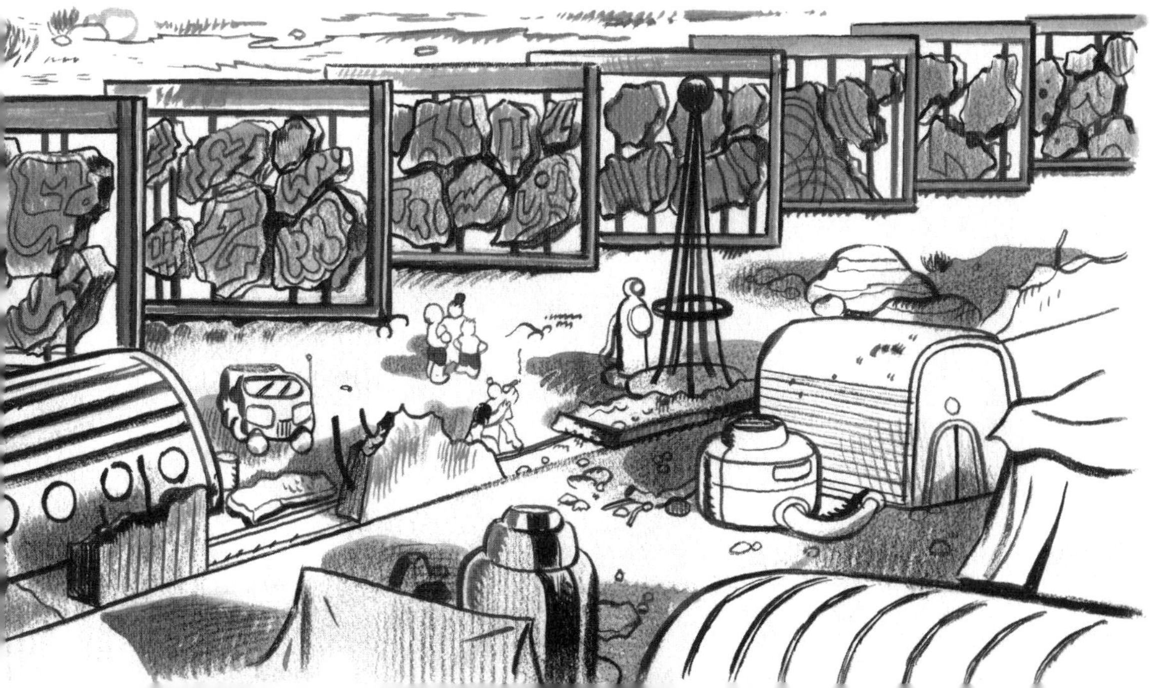

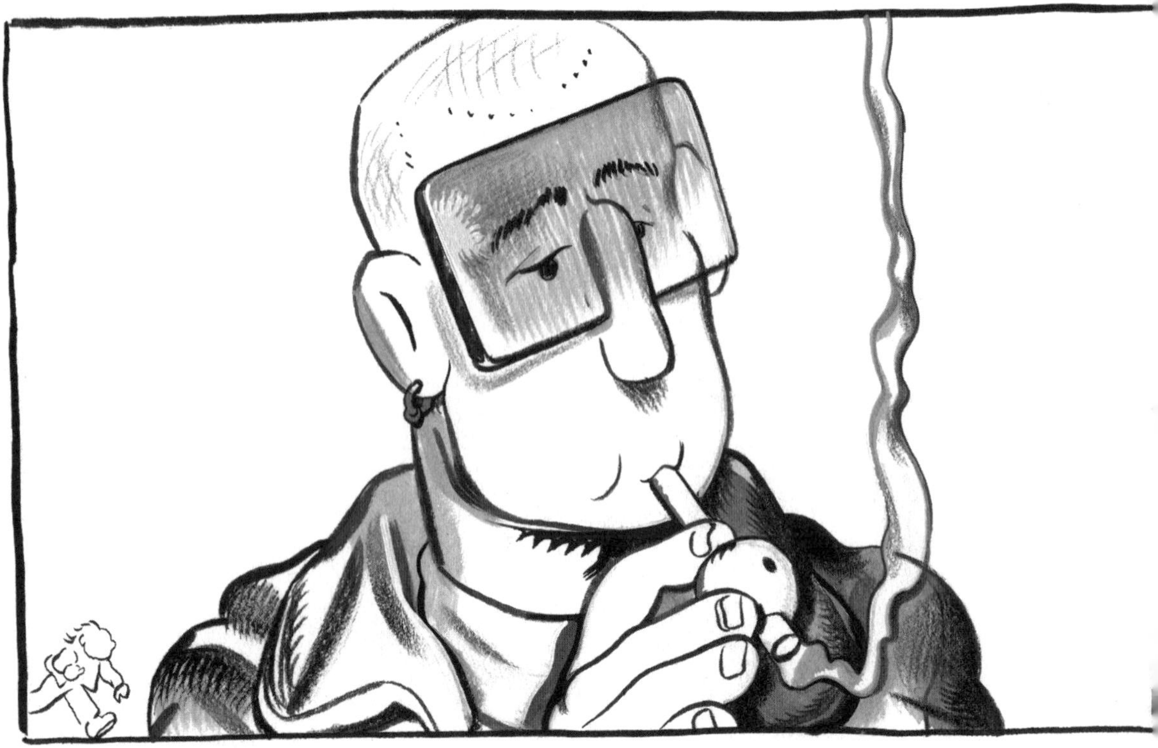

But while standing outside the design conference during a break, Colin saw him.

He was running. And from where Colin was standing, he could tell that Paolo looked upset.

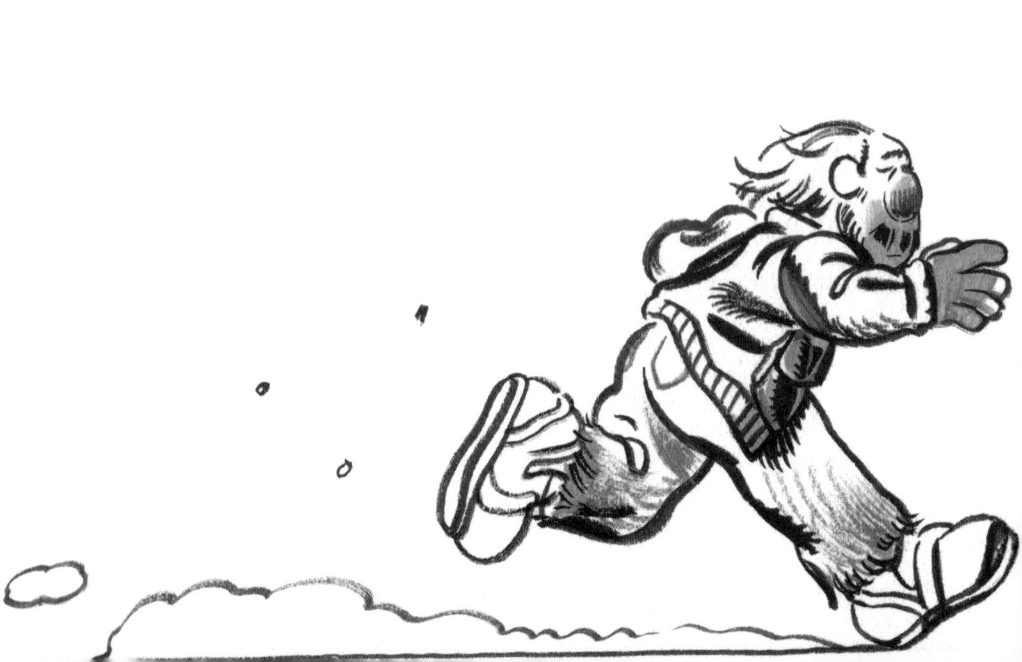

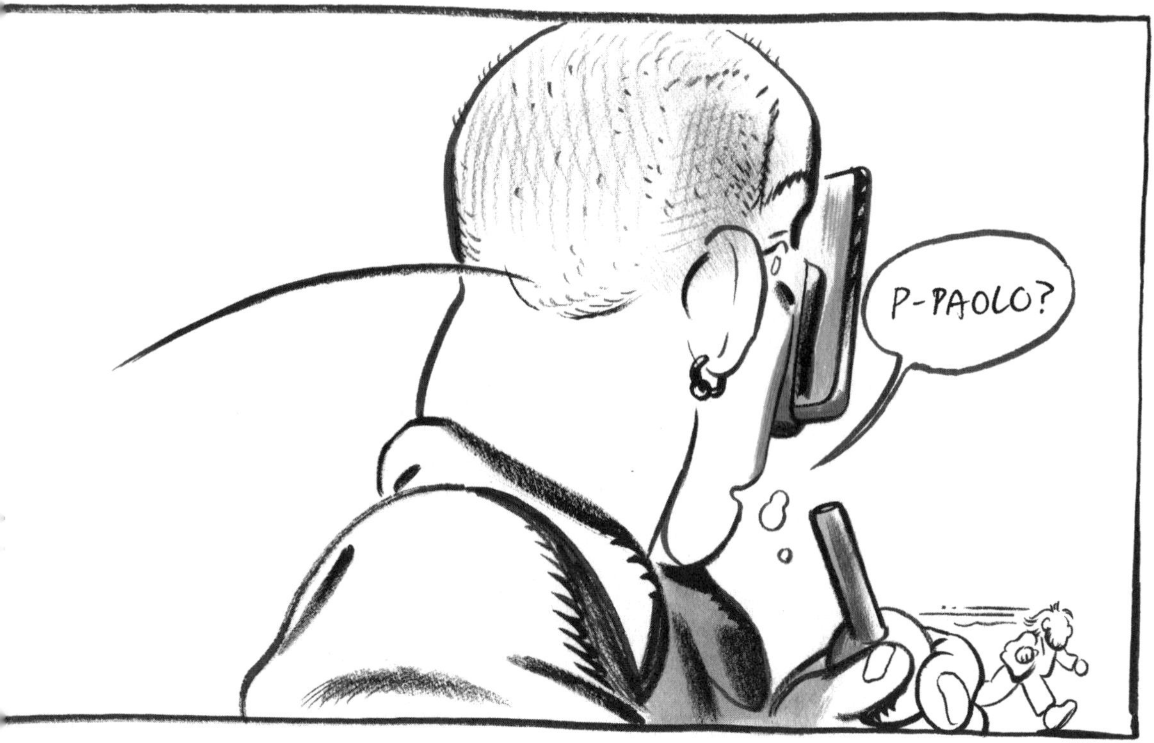
P-PAOLO?

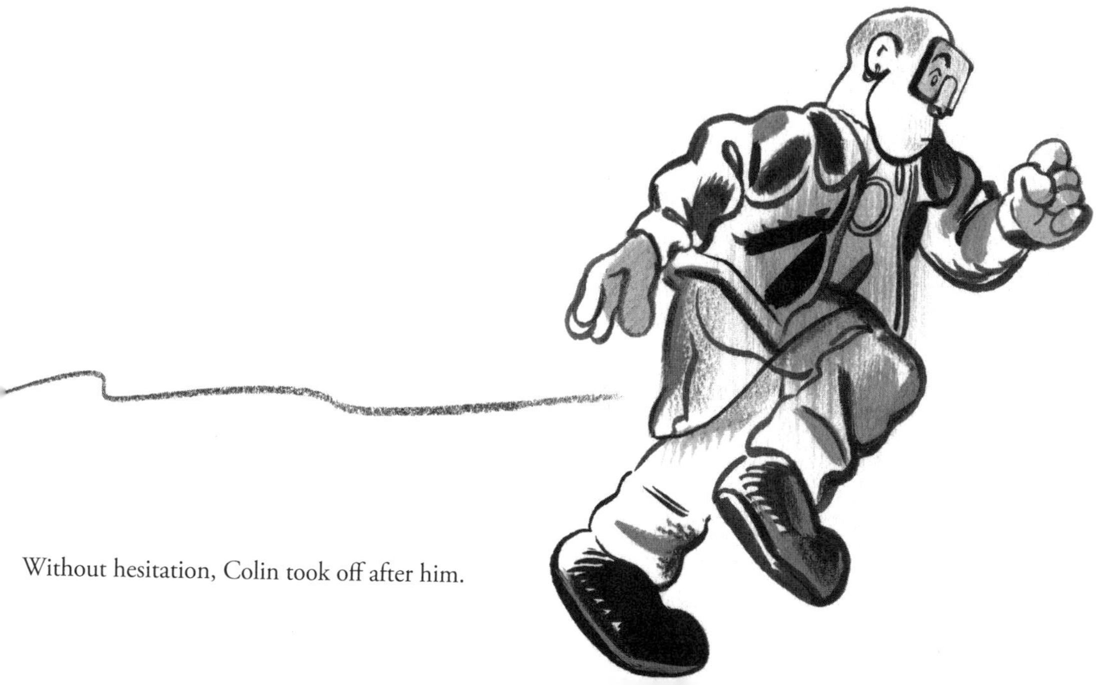

Without hesitation, Colin took off after him.

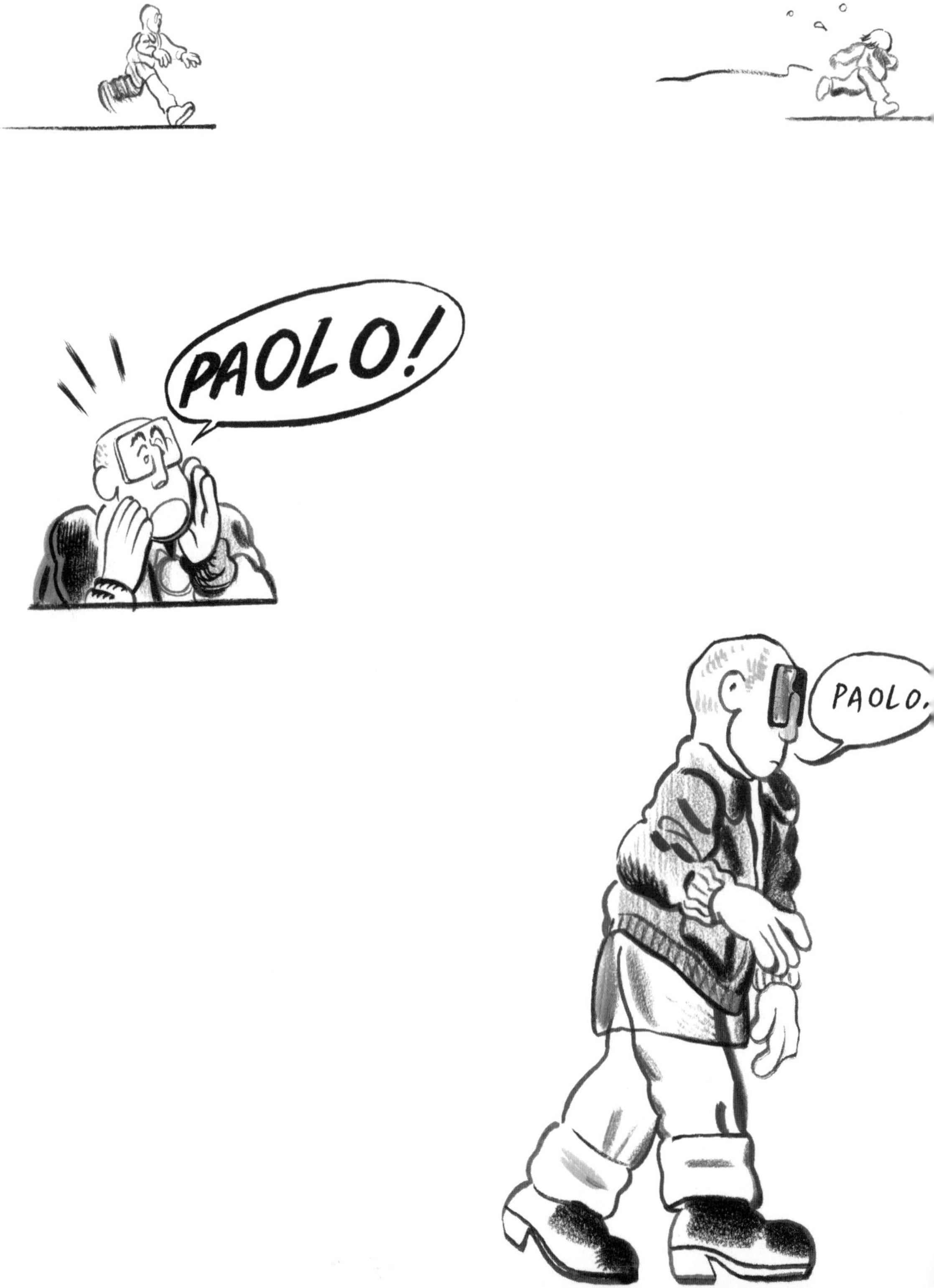
PAOLO!
PAOLO.

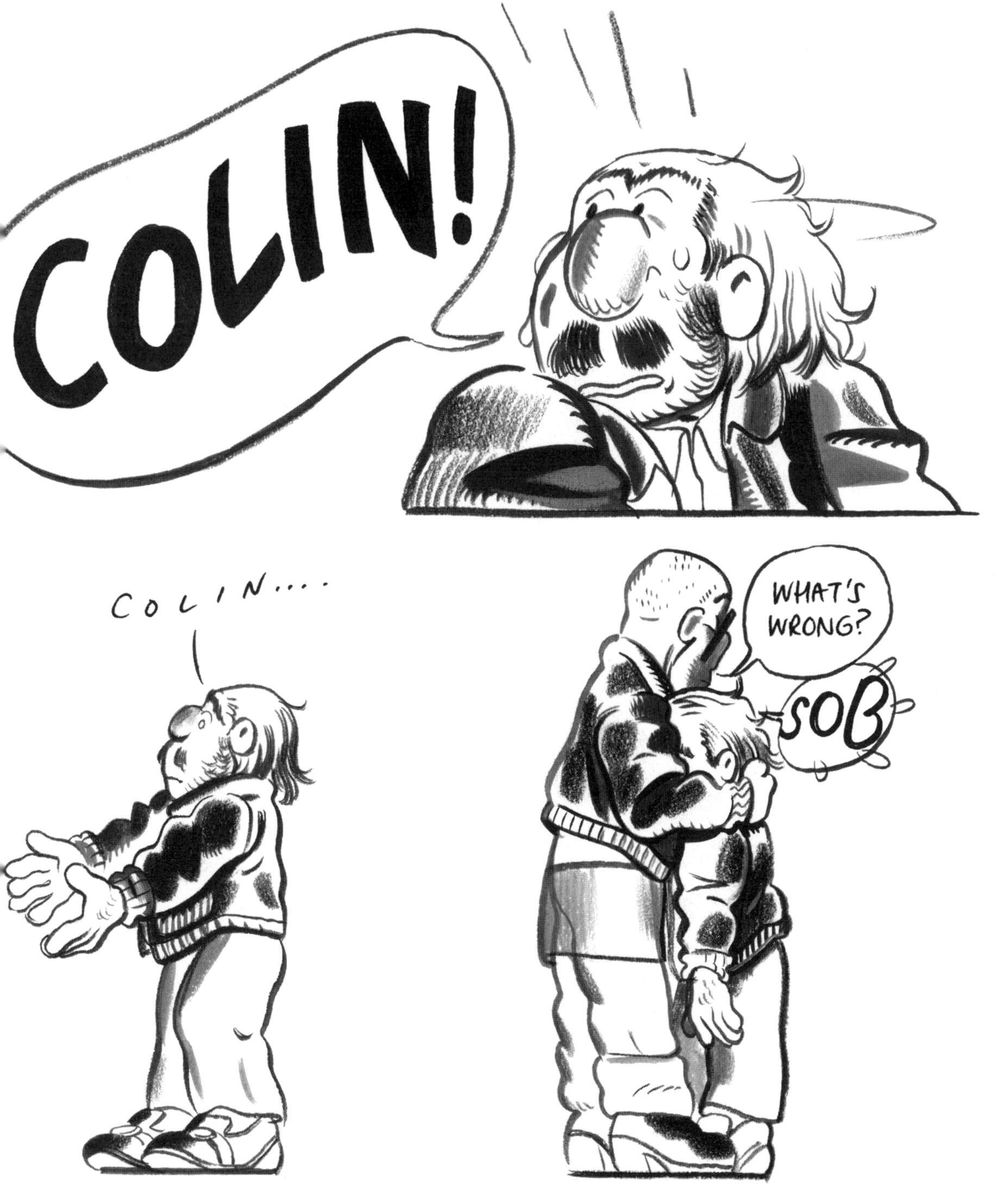
COLIN!
COLIN....
WHAT'S WRONG?
SOB

One of Paolo's nephews had been rushed to the hospital. From the emotional phone call he had with his sister, Paolo gathered that it was an attempted suicide. He rarely gave much thought to his nephews and could barely match their names with their faces, but the sudden news overwhelmed him. Instead of waiting for a car during rush hour, Paolo, in his heightened state, decided it would be quicker to just run to the hospital.

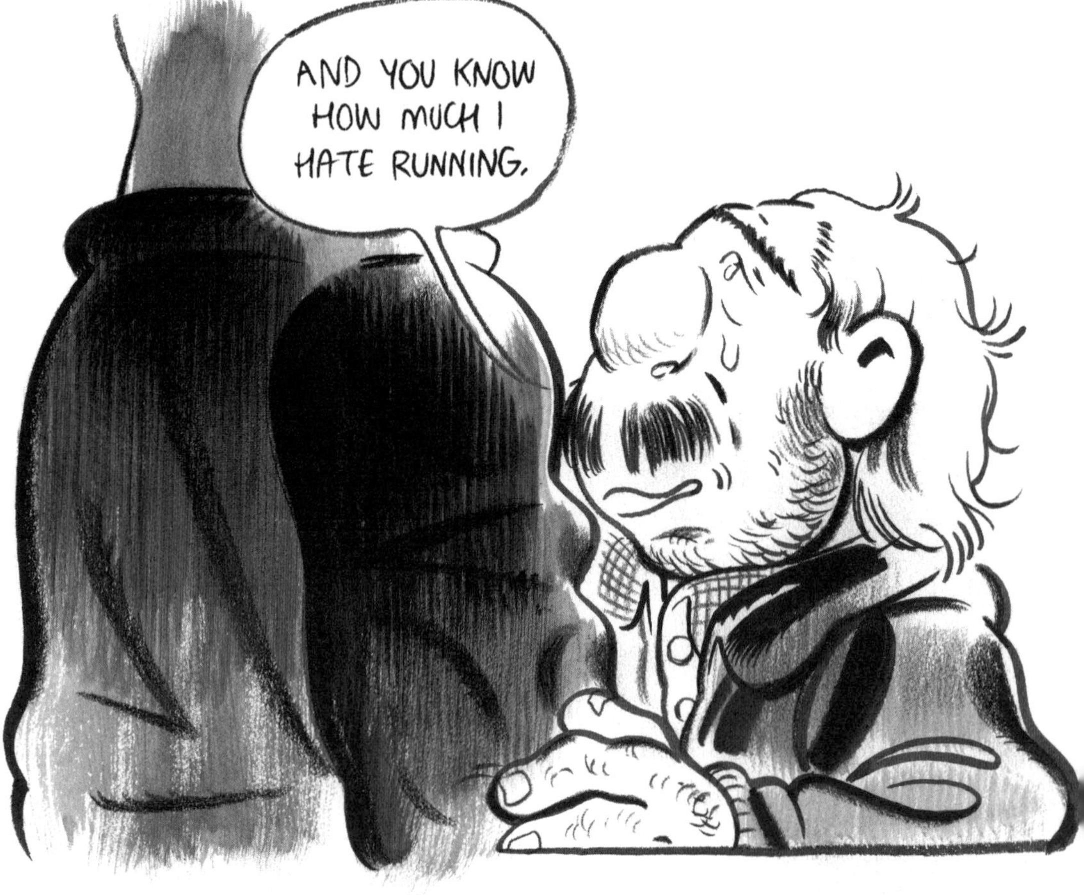
AND YOU KNOW HOW MUCH I HATE RUNNING.

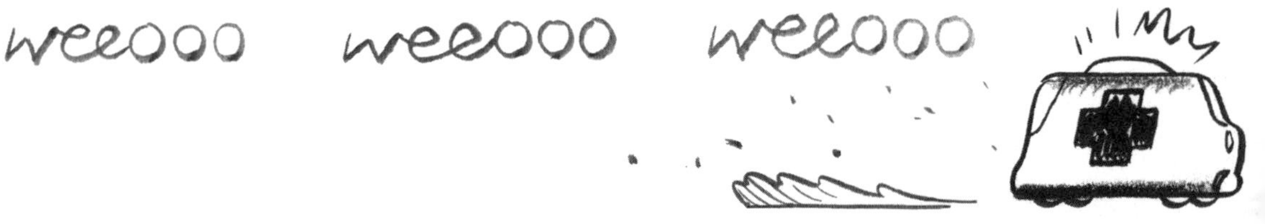
weeooo
weeooo
weeooo

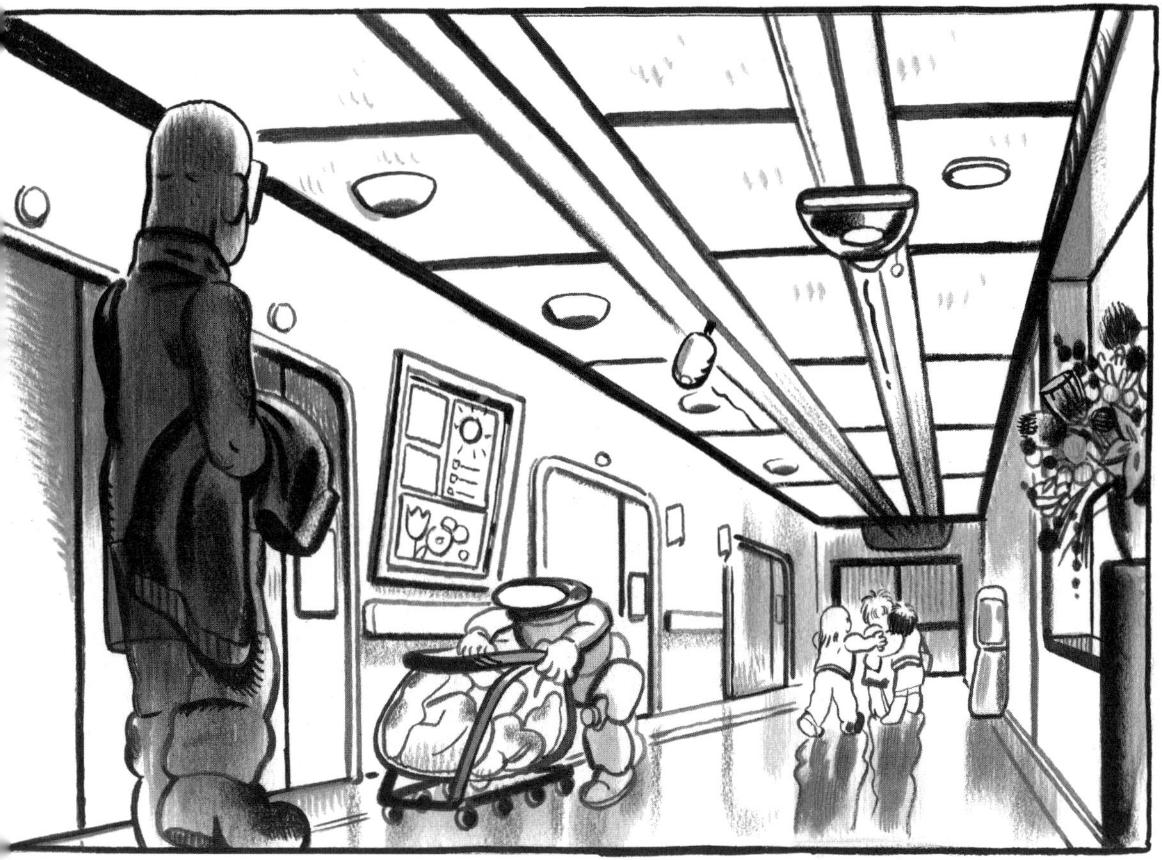

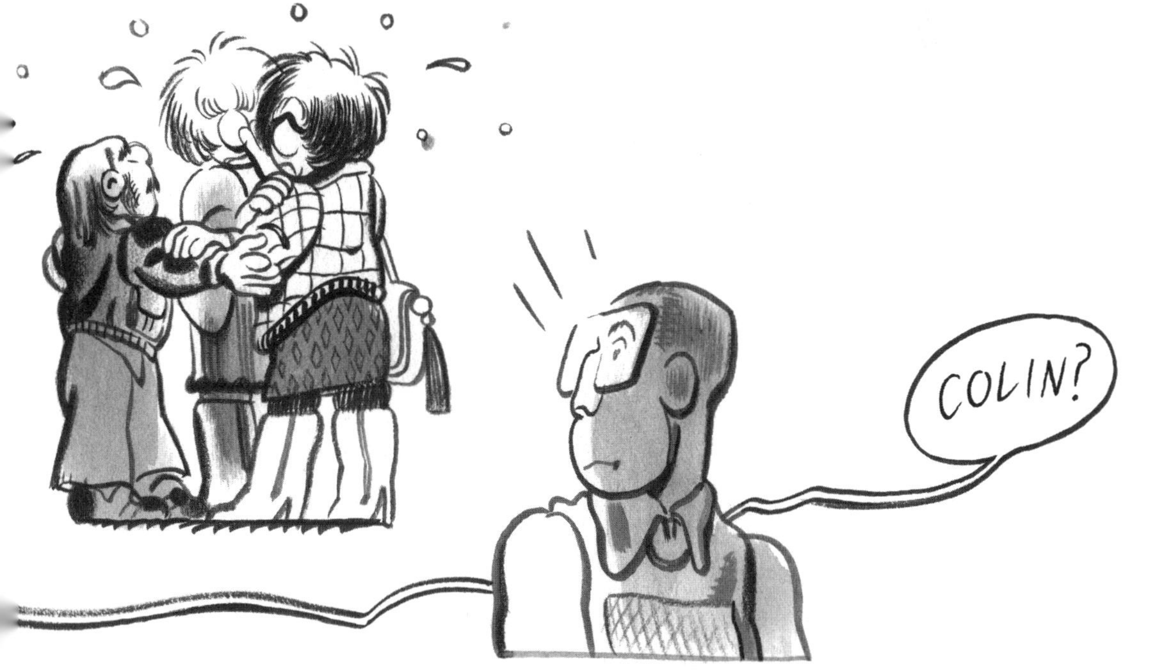
COLIN?

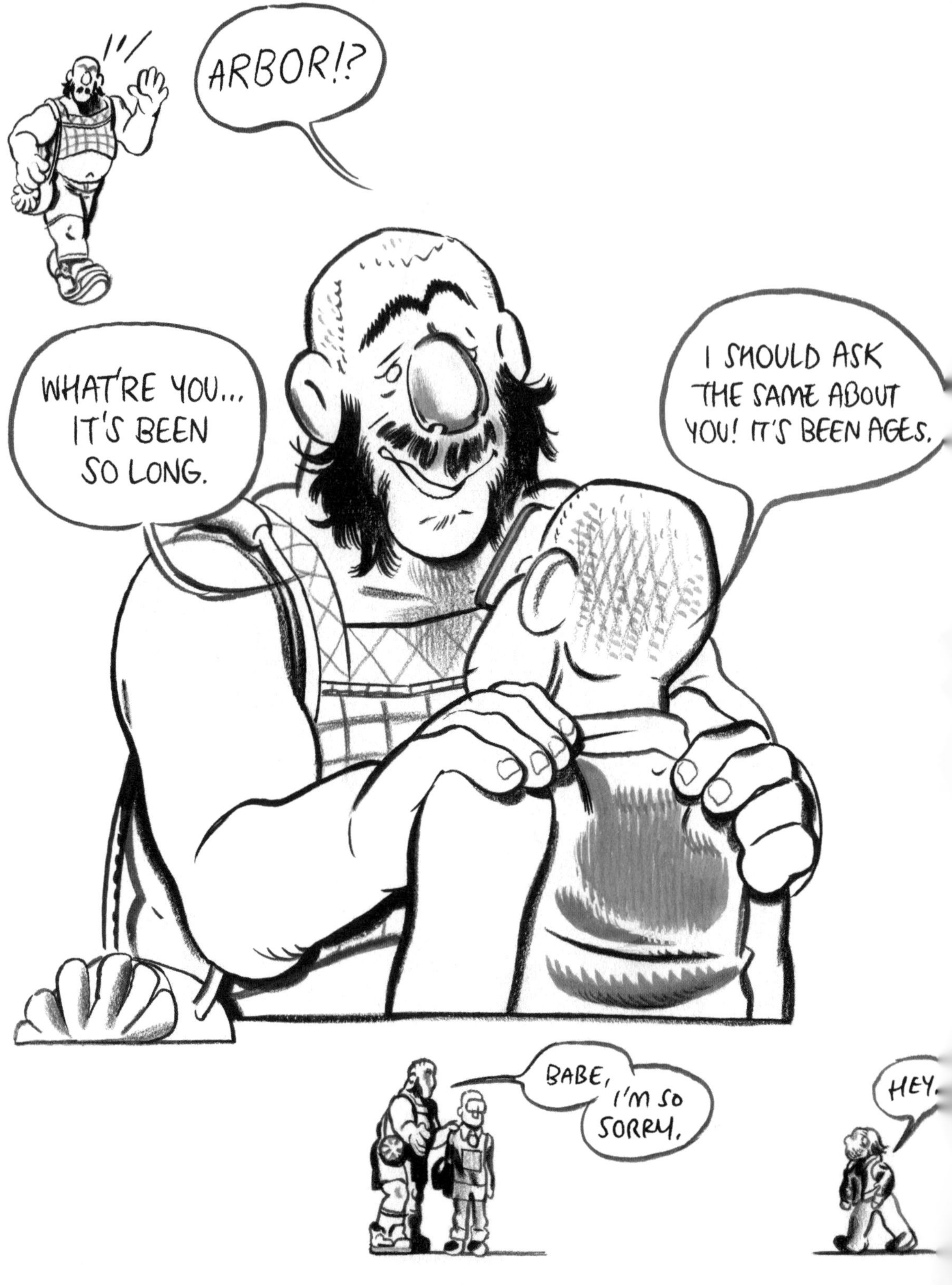
ARBOR!?
WHAT'RE YOU... IT'S BEEN SO LONG.
I SHOULD ASK THE SAME ABOUT YOU! IT'S BEEN AGES.
BABE, I'M SO SORRY.
HEY.

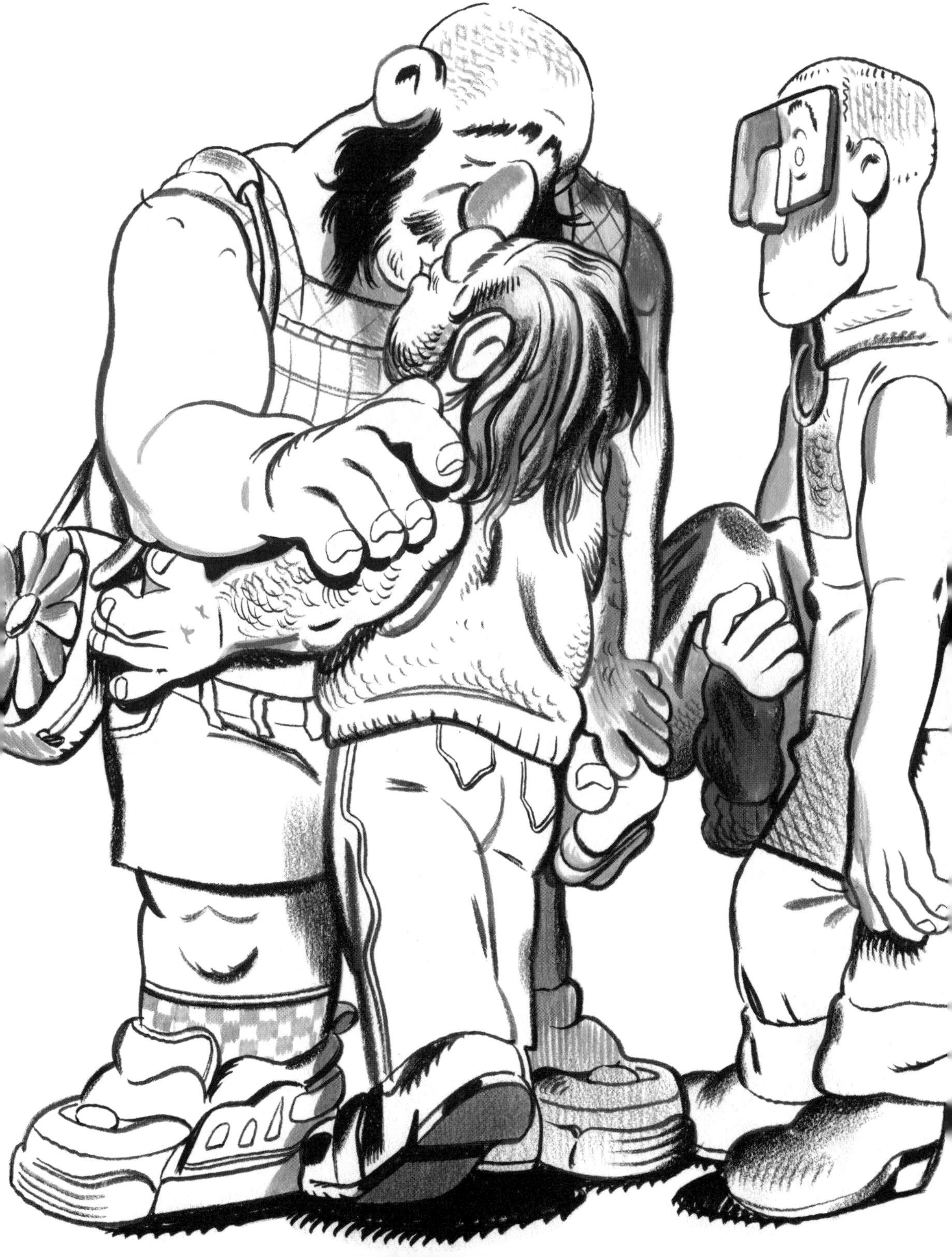

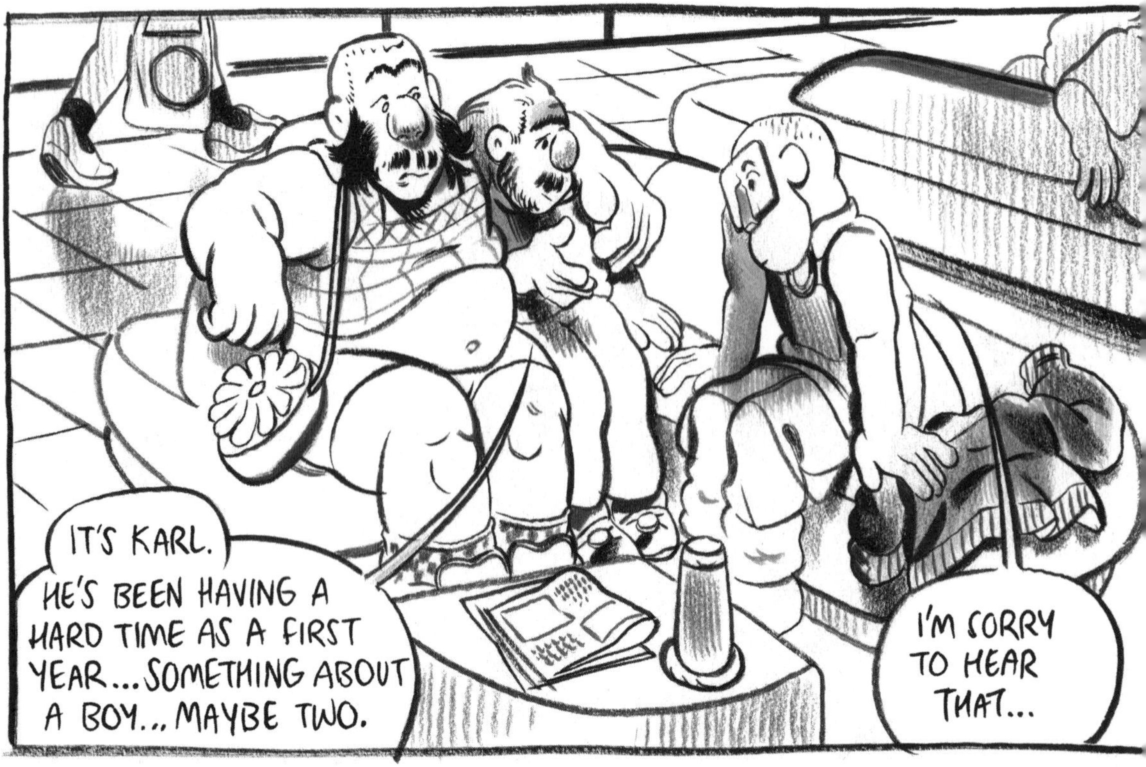
IT'S KARL.
HE'S BEEN HAVING A HARD TIME AS A FIRST YEAR... SOMETHING ABOUT A BOY... MAYBE TWO.
I'M SORRY TO HEAR THAT...
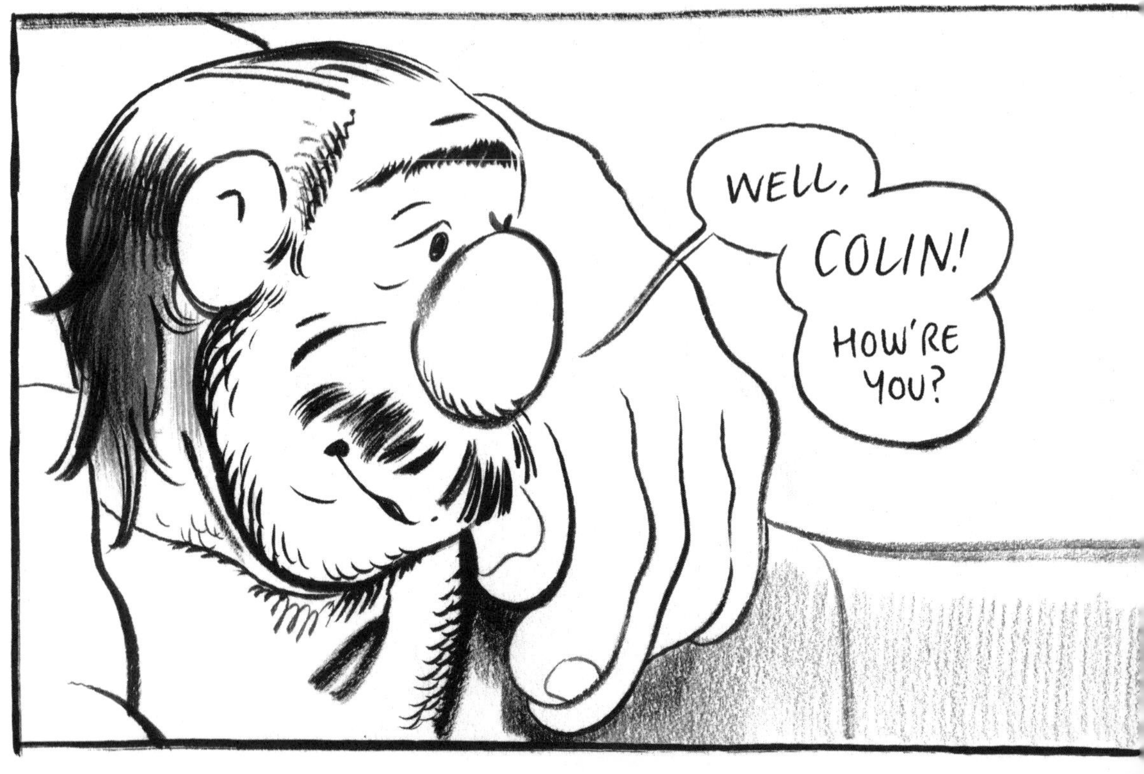
WELL,
COLIN!
HOW'RE YOU?

Colin had fantasized about what their reunion would look like countless times.

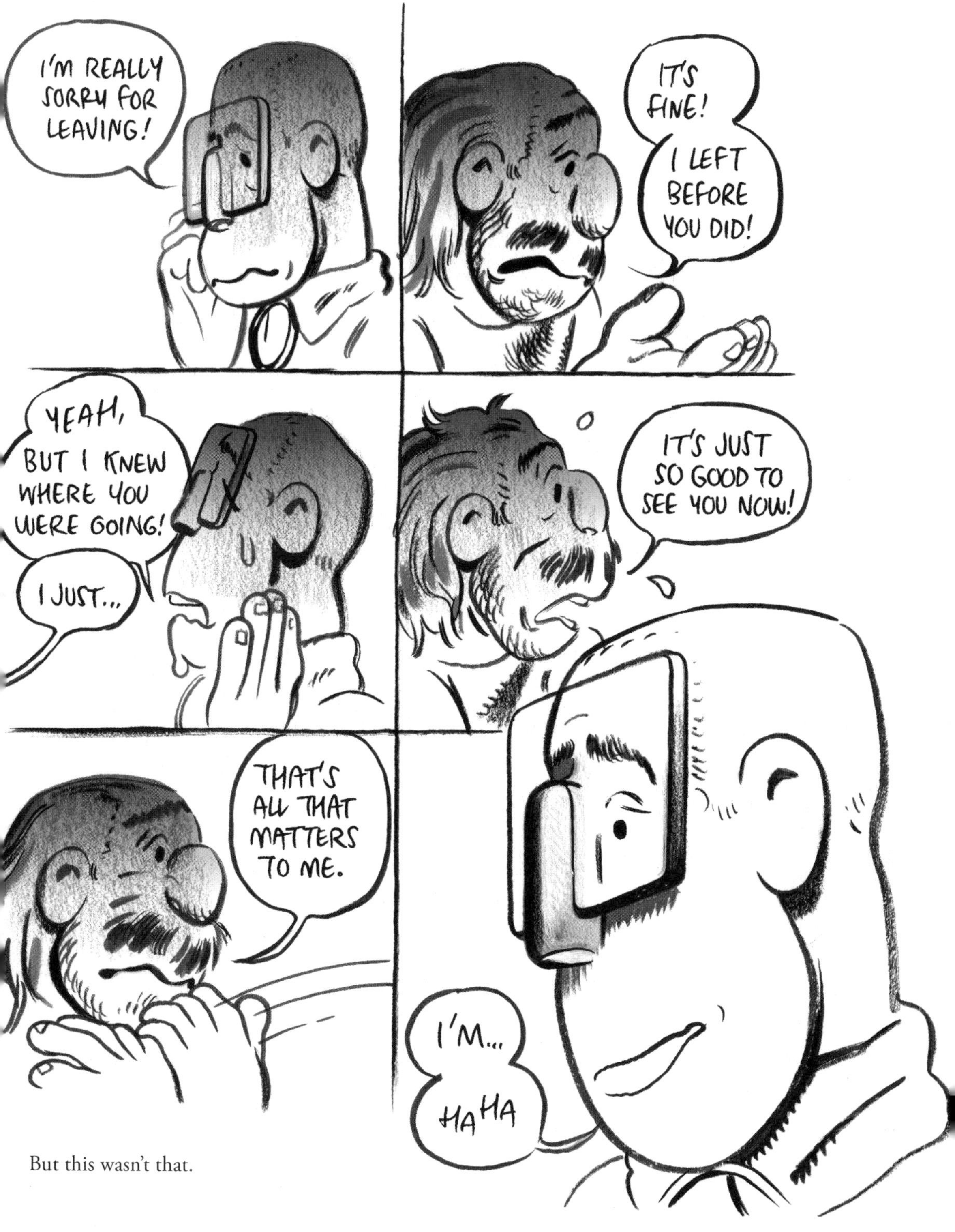
I'M REALLY SORRY FOR LEAVING!
IT'S FINE!
I LEFT BEFORE YOU DID!
YEAH, BUT I KNEW WHERE YOU WERE GOING!
I JUST...
IT'S JUST SO GOOD TO SEE YOU NOW!
THAT'S ALL THAT MATTERS TO ME.
I'M...
HAHA

But this wasn't that.

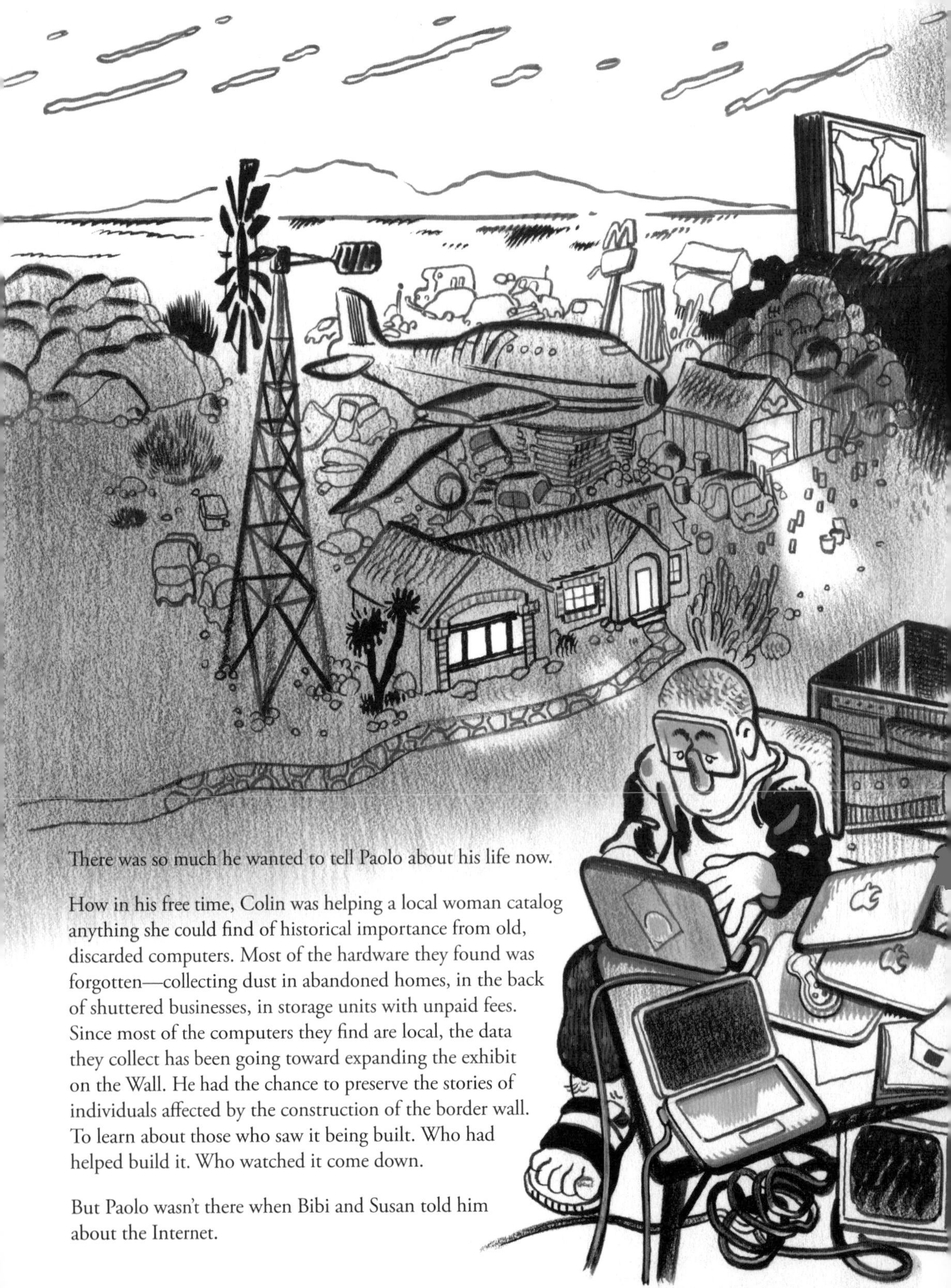

There was so much he wanted to tell Paolo about his life now.

How in his free time, Colin was helping a local woman catalog anything she could find of historical importance from old, discarded computers. Most of the hardware they found was forgotten—collecting dust in abandoned homes, in the back of shuttered businesses, in storage units with unpaid fees. Since most of the computers they find are local, the data they collect has been going toward expanding the exhibit on the Wall. He had the chance to preserve the stories of individuals affected by the construction of the border wall. To learn about those who saw it being built. Who had helped build it. Who watched it come down.

But Paolo wasn't there when Bibi and Susan told him about the Internet.

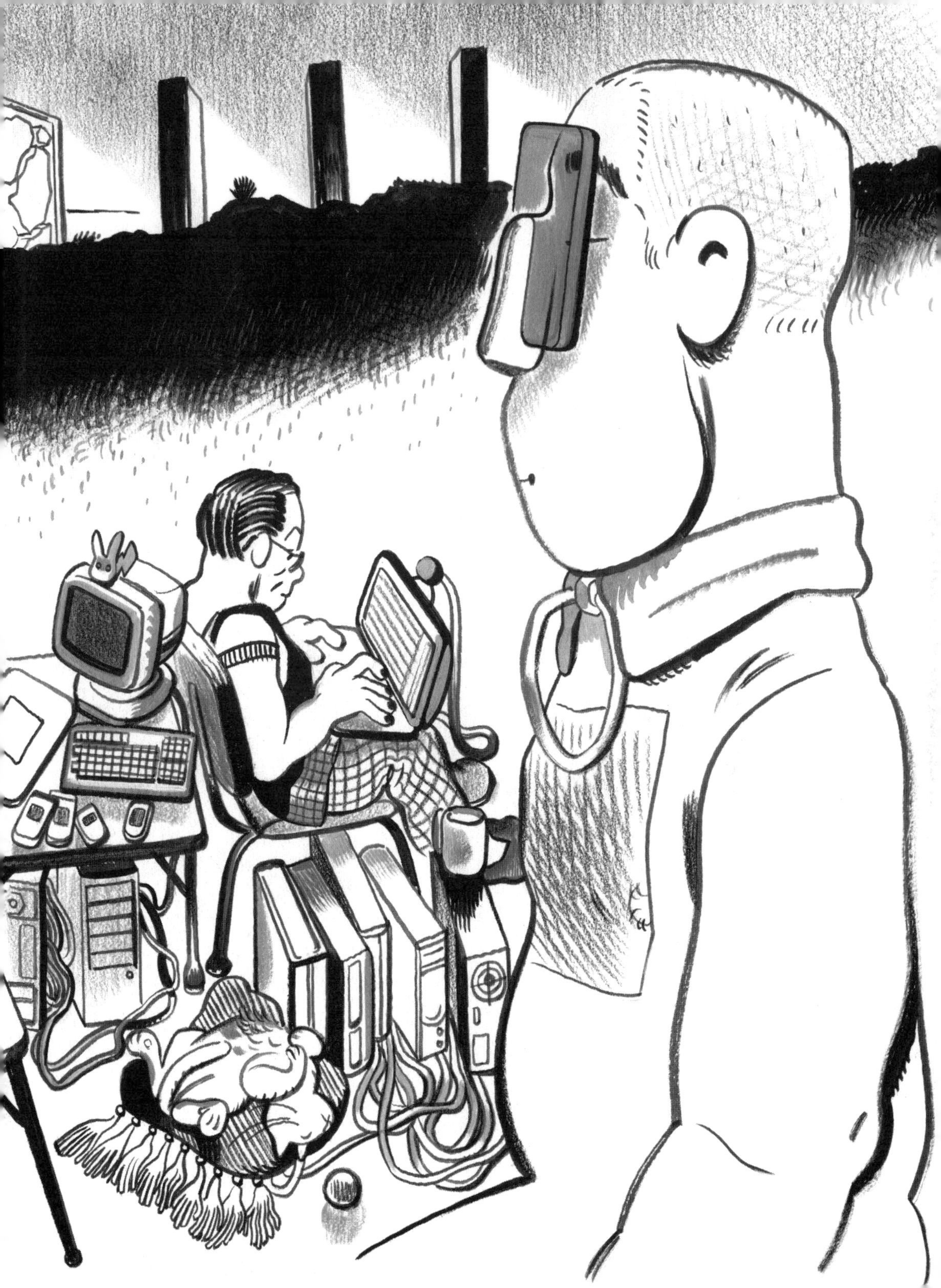

How he's met so many incredible people down in Douglas.

He's been dating a pair of math teachers, Sam and Matthieu, who have an ornery chihuahua named Fibonacci. They've been exploring the network of bars and restaurants built into a string of caverns, which is where they first met. He witnessed a drag queen death drop off a stalagmite into a pool of water. He's been noticing how much he has loosened up, especially when he thinks about how he was when he and Paolo were together. He's quicker to laugh. He hopes he's easier to love, and is someone who has fun. He even entered a wet t-shirt contest once.

But that feels uncomfortable to talk about.

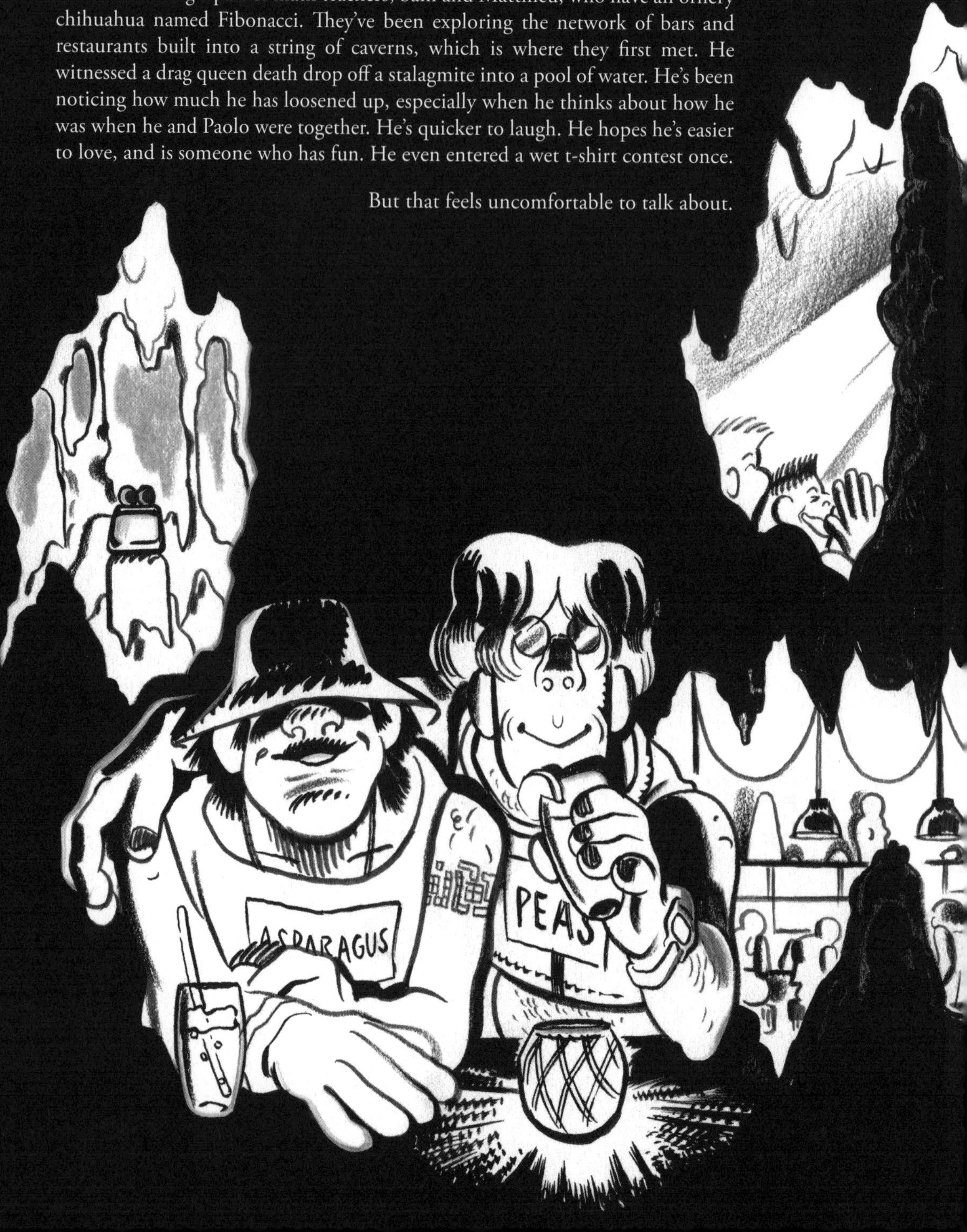
ASPARAGUS
PEAS

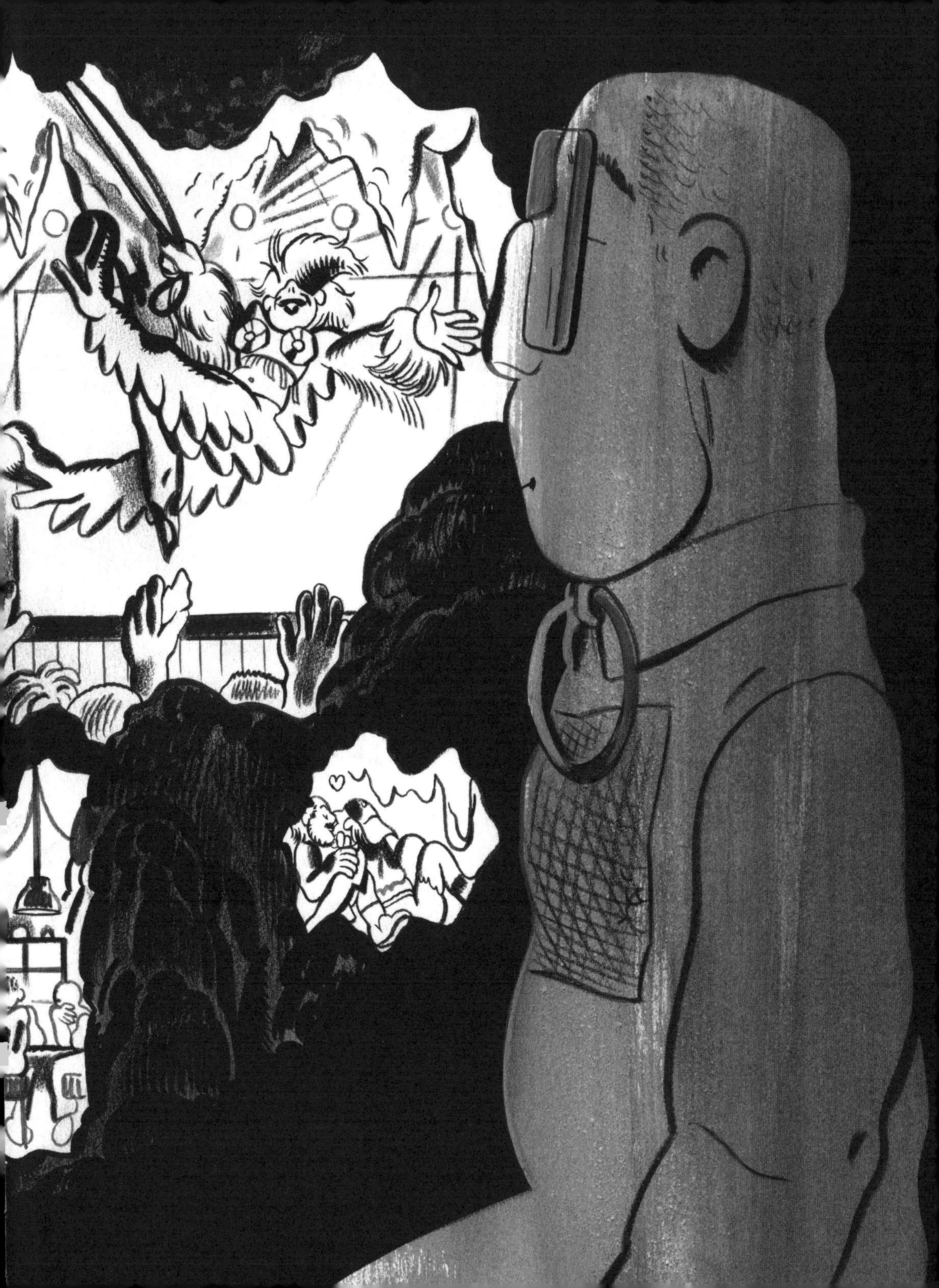

How Minnie has finally moved into a new home.

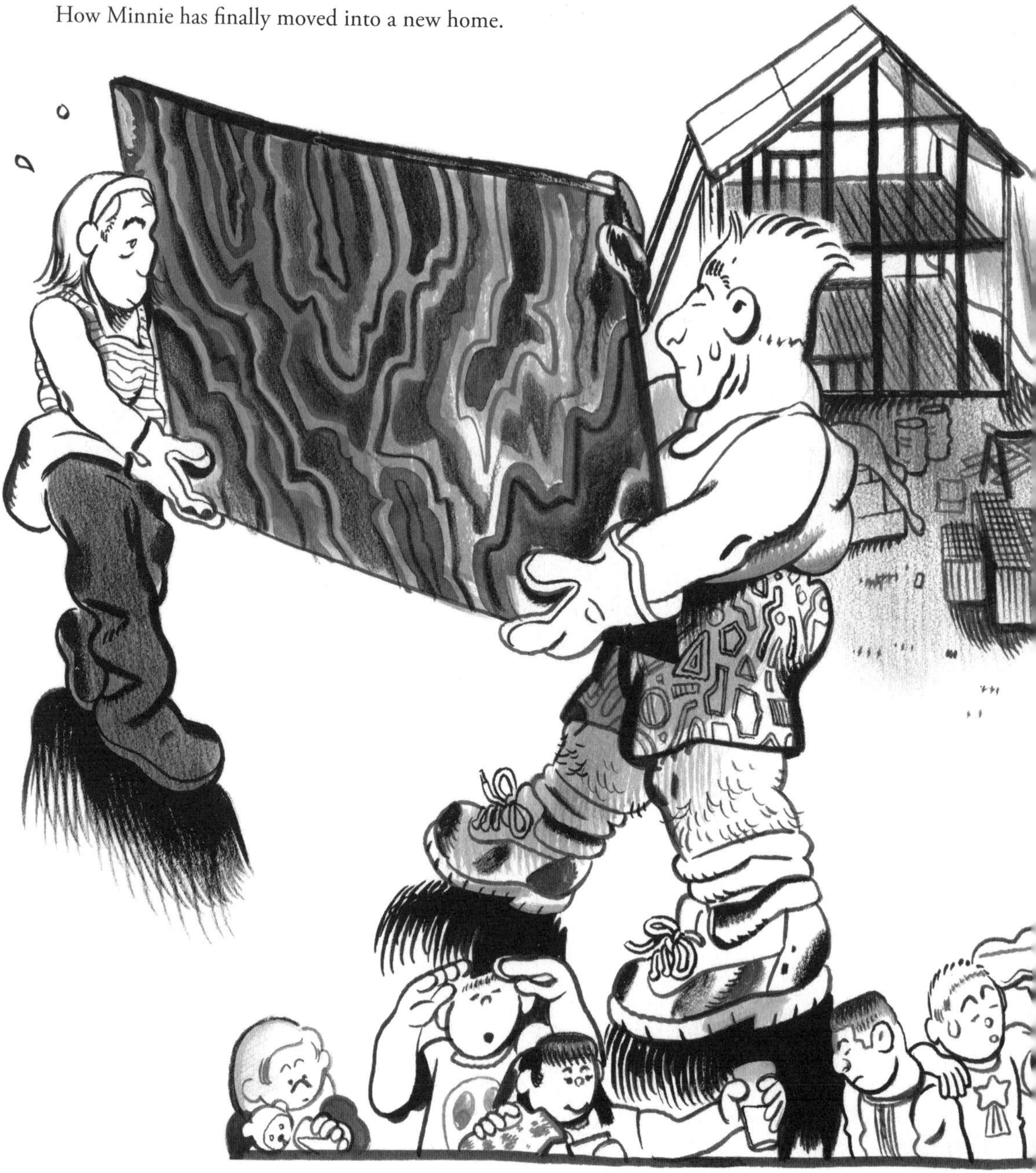

She's been working to rebuild homes in Neon—not just restoring the modular homes—starting with the home belonging to Colette, the woman she met whose children lived in The Conch. The Dancers have partnered with a local environmental group, working in tandem to restore the forest and rebuild the homes of Neon. They've been turning the few surviving non-native trees into lumber to be used for construction. Minnie learned that Colette's children aren't biologically hers, but adopted from local shelters. Minnie even moved into the first floor of the Conch and has been helping Colette raise the children. Colin knows Minnie has a crush—he can hear it in her voice when they talk on the phone—but David still visits each weekend.

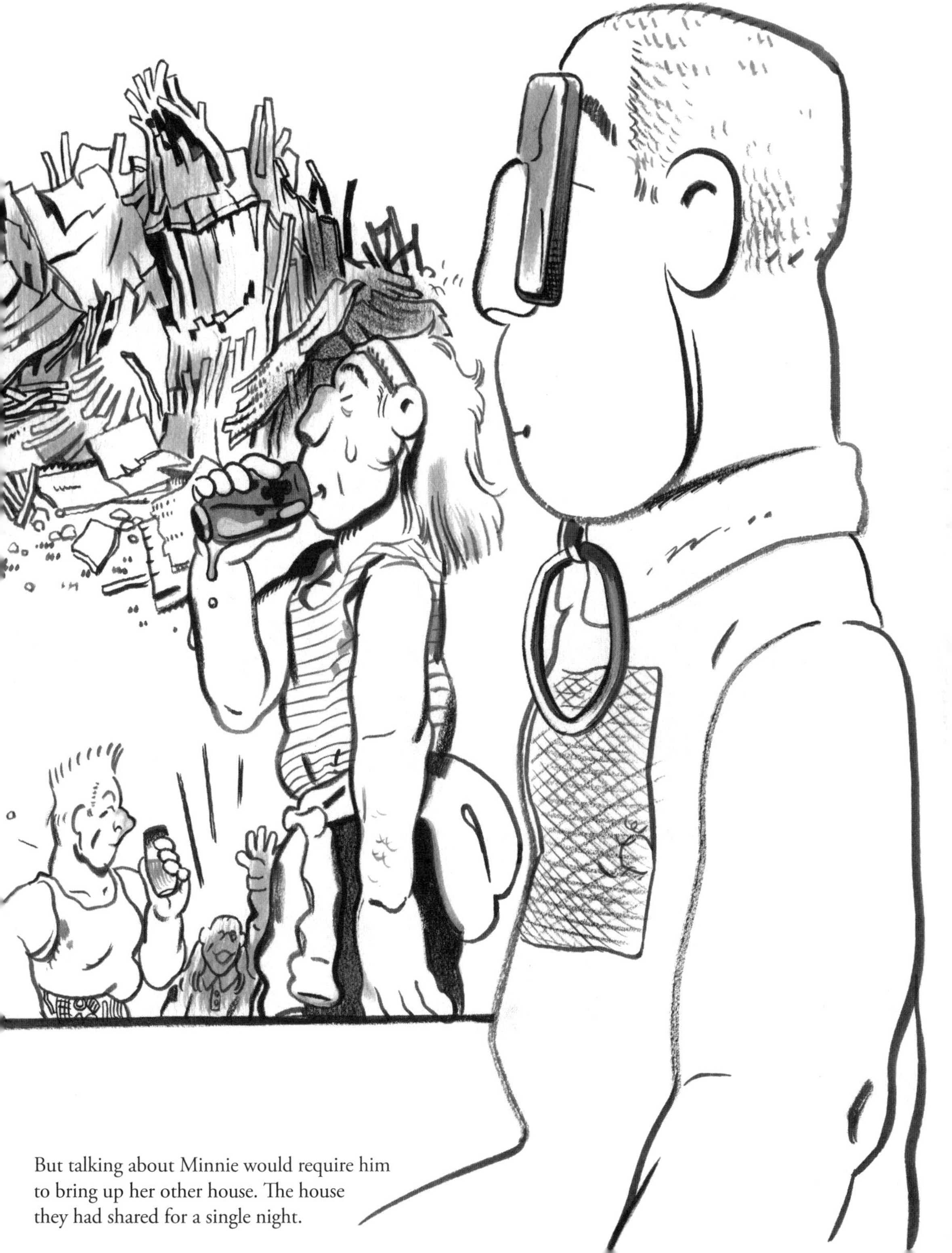

But talking about Minnie would require him
to bring up her other house. The house
they had shared for a single night.

So Colin just said that he was good.

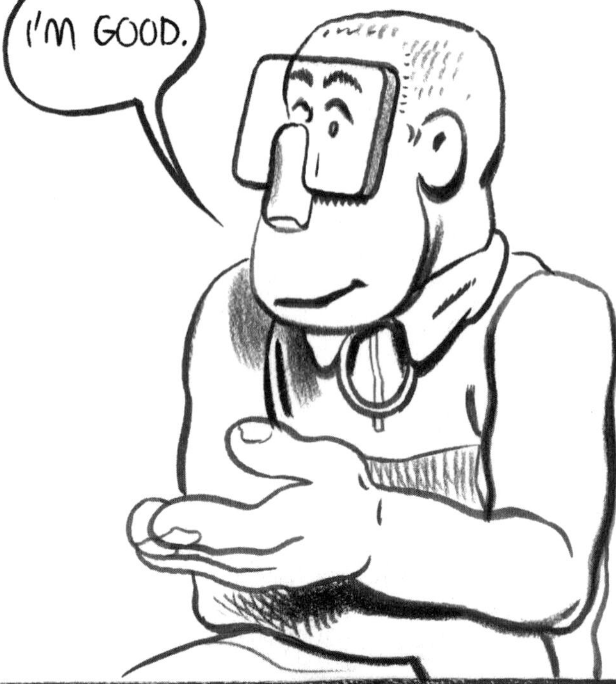
I'M GOOD.

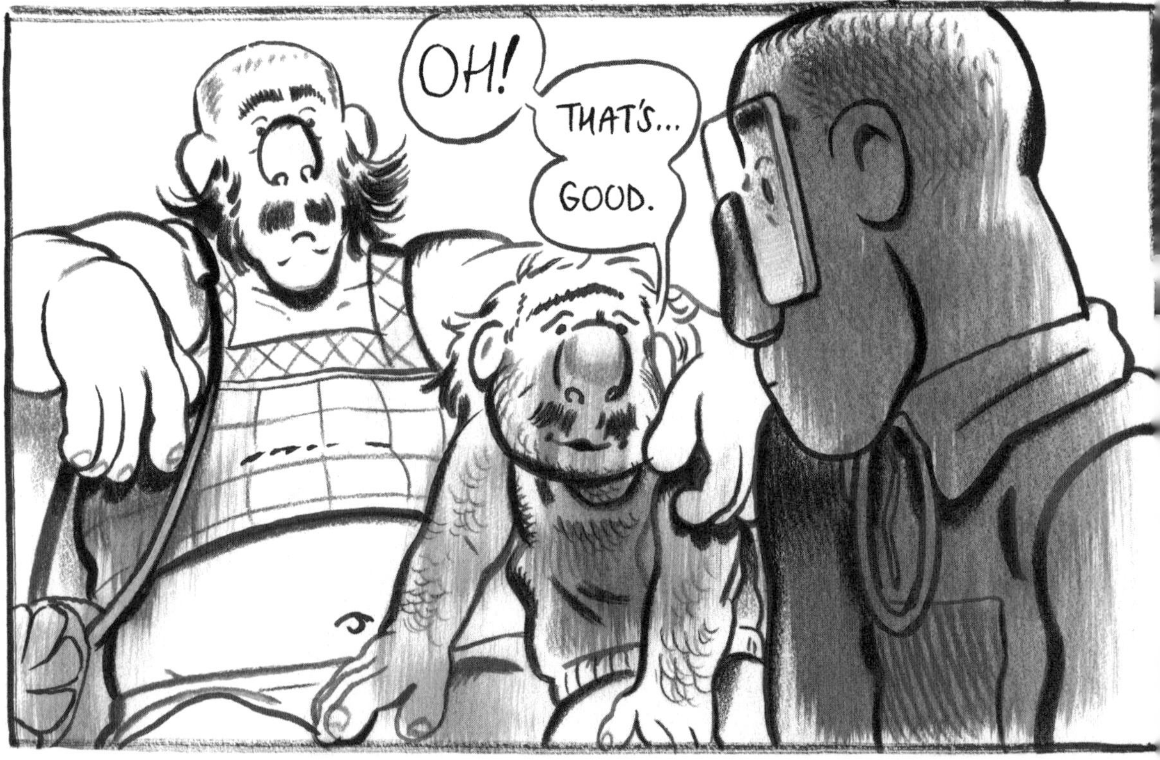
OH!
THAT'S...
GOOD.

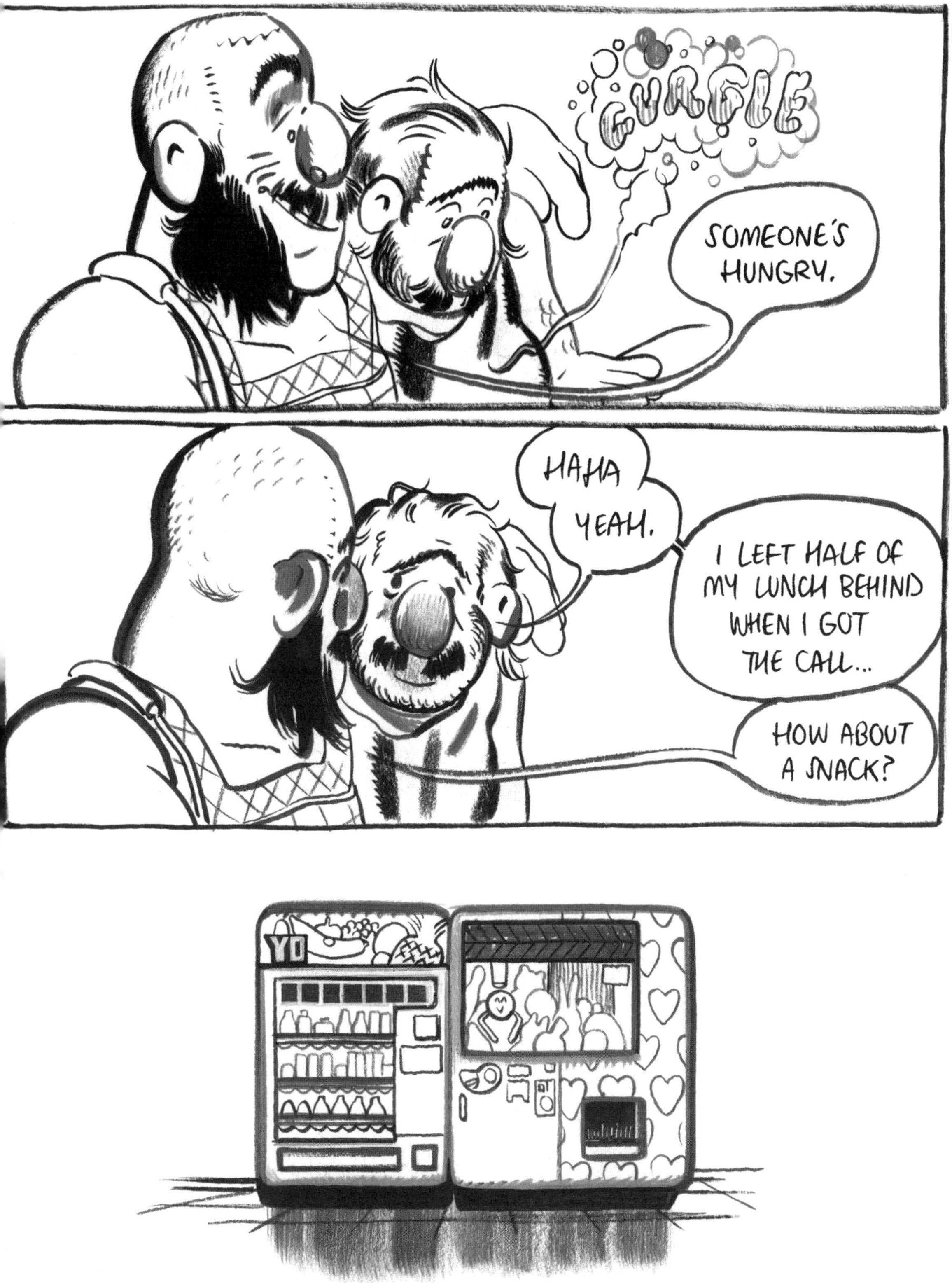
GURGLE
SOMEONE'S HUNGRY.
HAHA YEAH.
I LEFT HALF OF MY LUNCH BEHIND WHEN I GOT THE CALL...
HOW ABOUT A SNACK?
YO

Paolo's voice took on a particular lilt whenever he made a joke. He would often use that voice to break the tension if Colin came home irritated from a bad day at work.

His voice would quickly shift up a few octaves, then slowly cascade down as he spoke, moving past his normal speaking voice and into a much lower register. Colin knew it was Paolo playing the fool to reassure him that whatever was bothering him was fine.

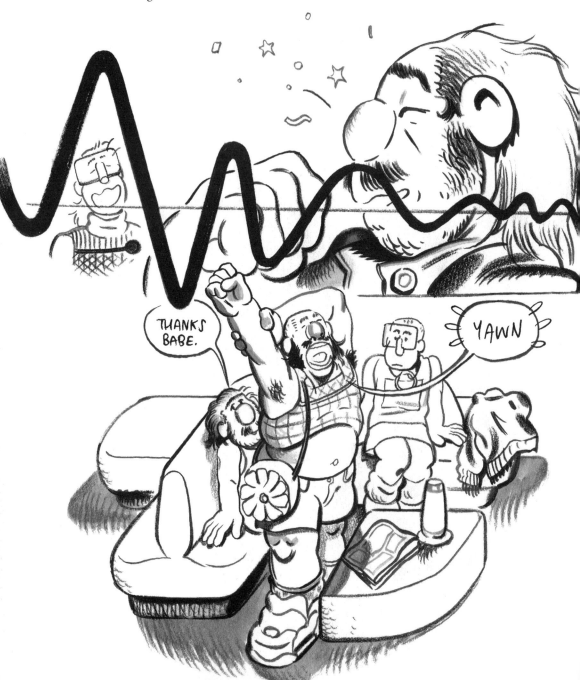

But it wasn't Paolo who Colin heard using that voice. It was Arbor.

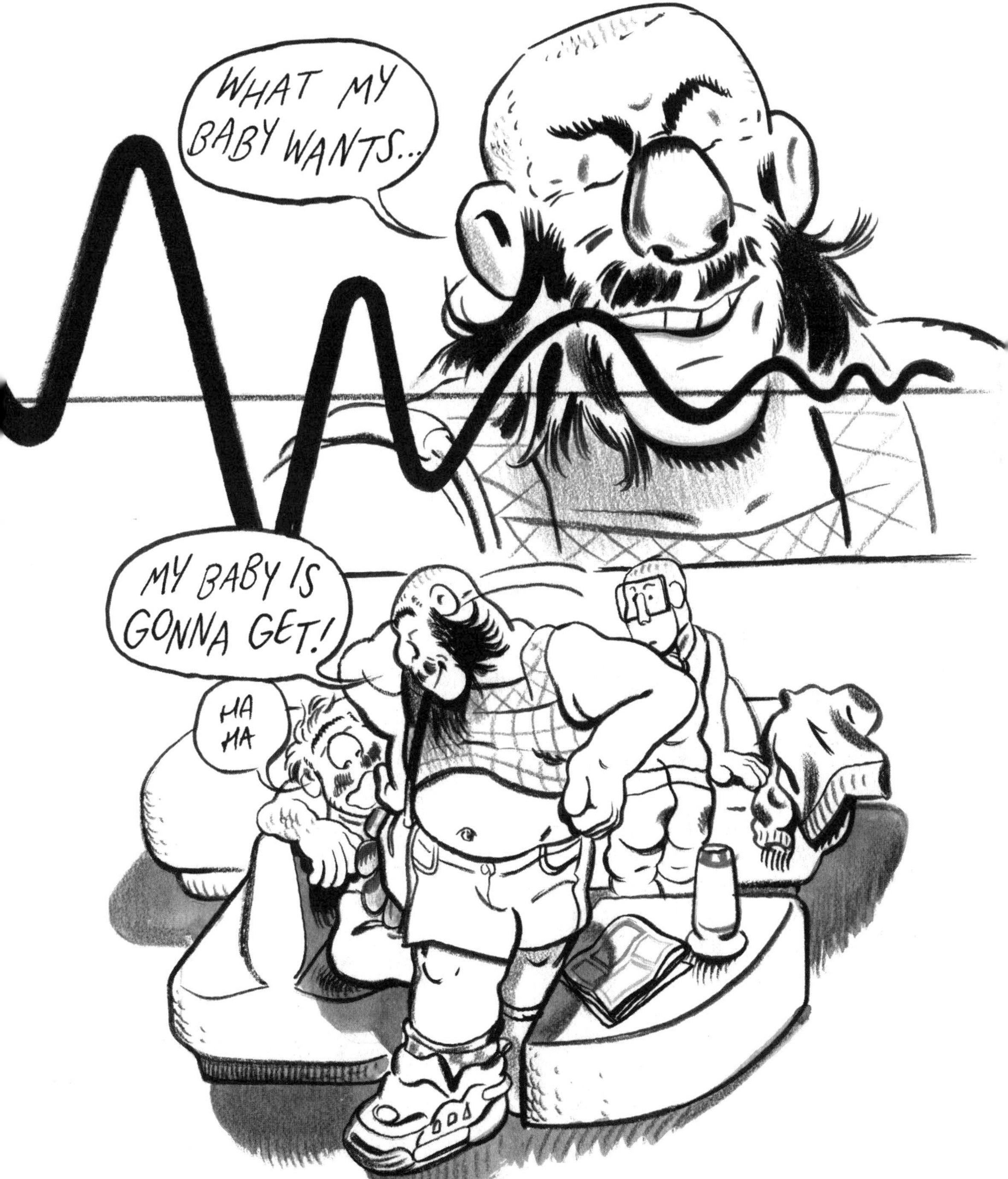
WHAT MY BABY WANTS...
MY BABY IS GONNA GET!
HA HA

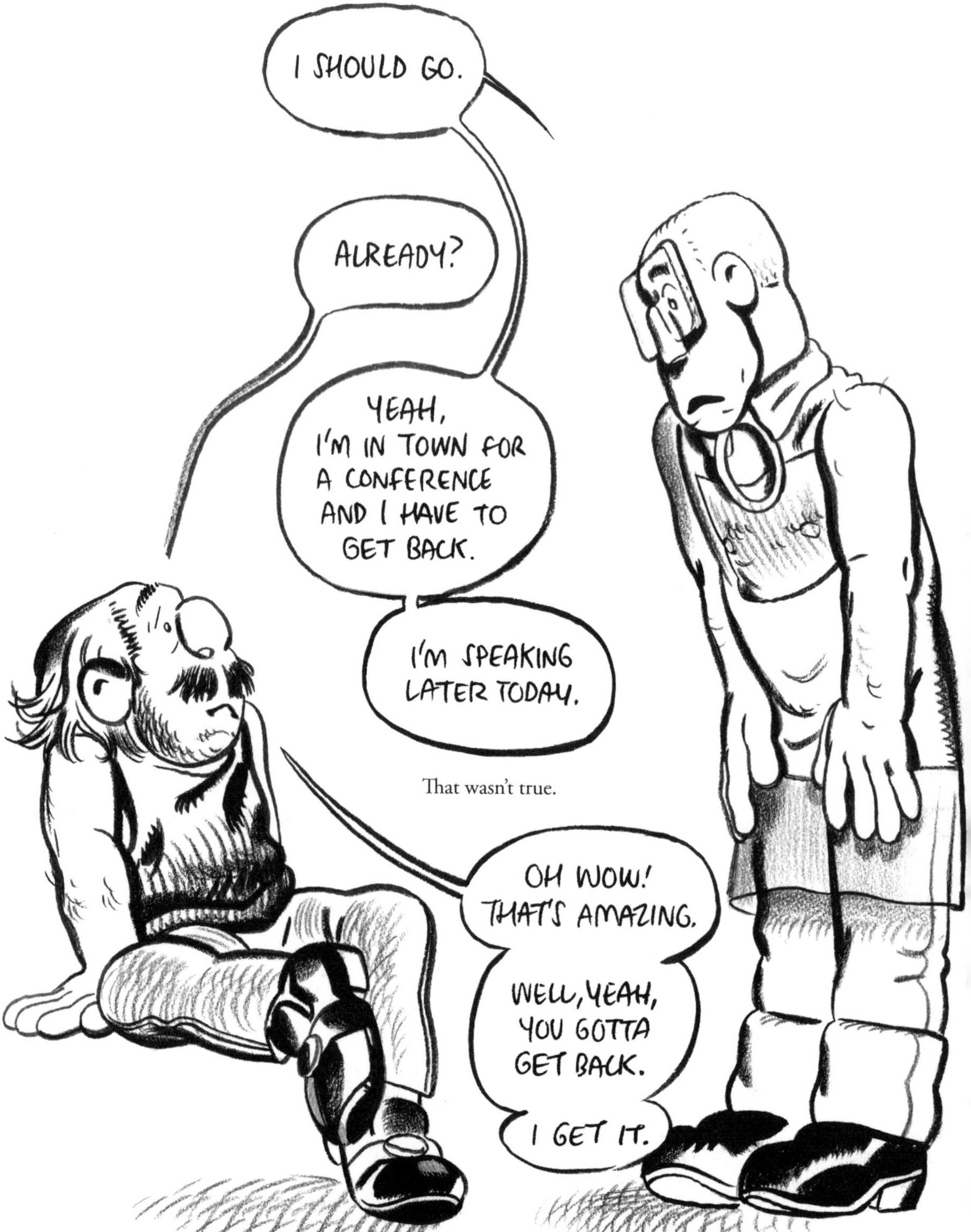
I SHOULD GO.
ALREADY?
YEAH, I'M IN TOWN FOR A CONFERENCE AND I HAVE TO GET BACK.
I'M SPEAKING LATER TODAY.
That wasn't true.
OH WOW! THAT'S AMAZING.
WELL, YEAH, YOU GOTTA GET BACK.
I GET IT.

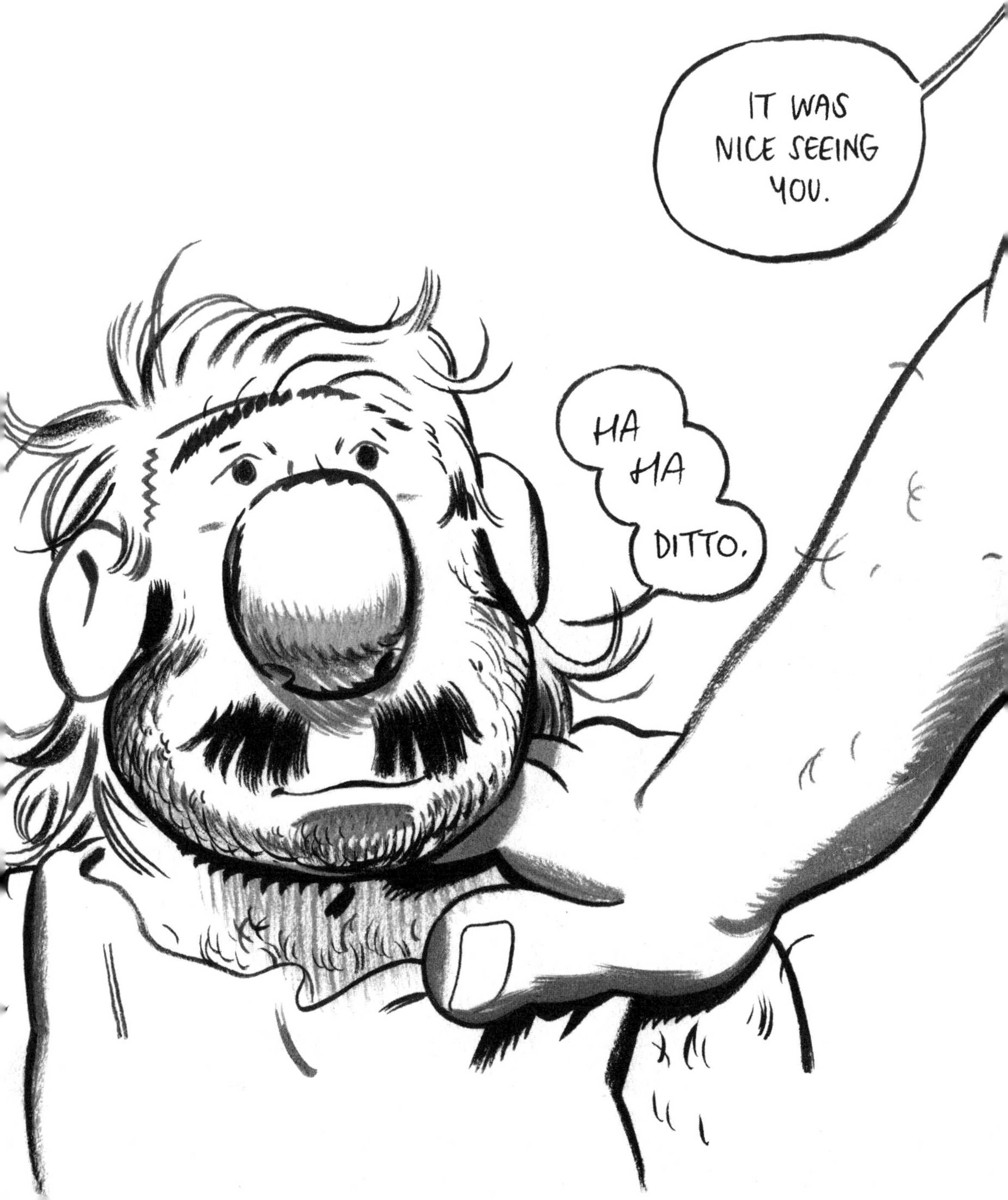
IT WAS NICE SEEING YOU.
HA HA DITTO.

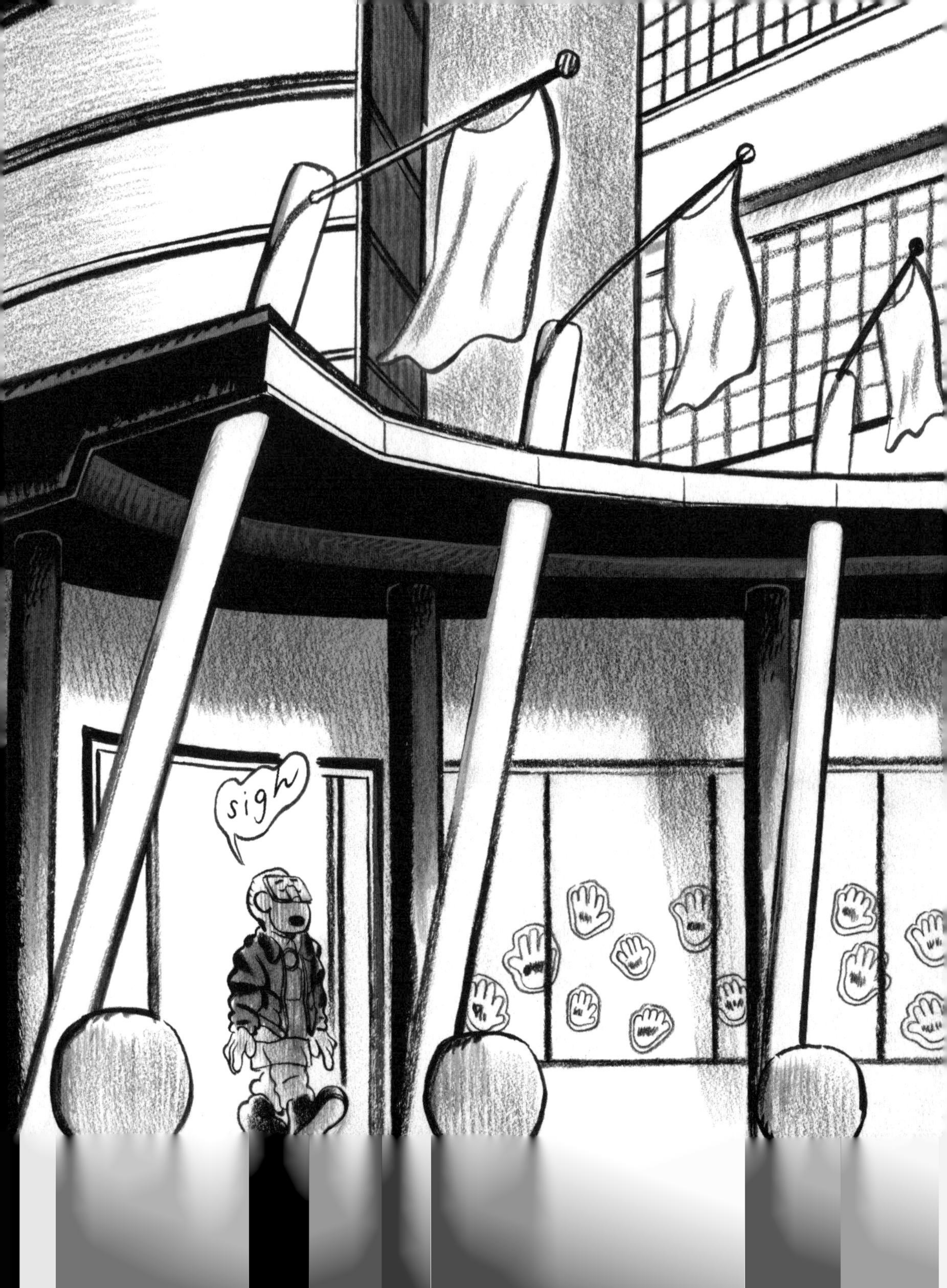
sigh

Colin felt embarrassed. Putting his hand on Paolo's shoulder like that. Why did he do that? As he walked away from the hospital, Colin obsessed over the gesture.

Knowing Paolo, Colin recognized that Paolo probably hadn't thought it was weird, or at least wouldn't have a reason to dwell on it, as Colin was doing now.

Their moment had passed, their "now" being replaced with countless new ones. Colin found himself wanting more… but more of what, exactly?

More time with Paolo? To do what? Sit in a hospital waiting room?

Why was it always so surprising that everything came to an end? That the present always found a way to become the past?

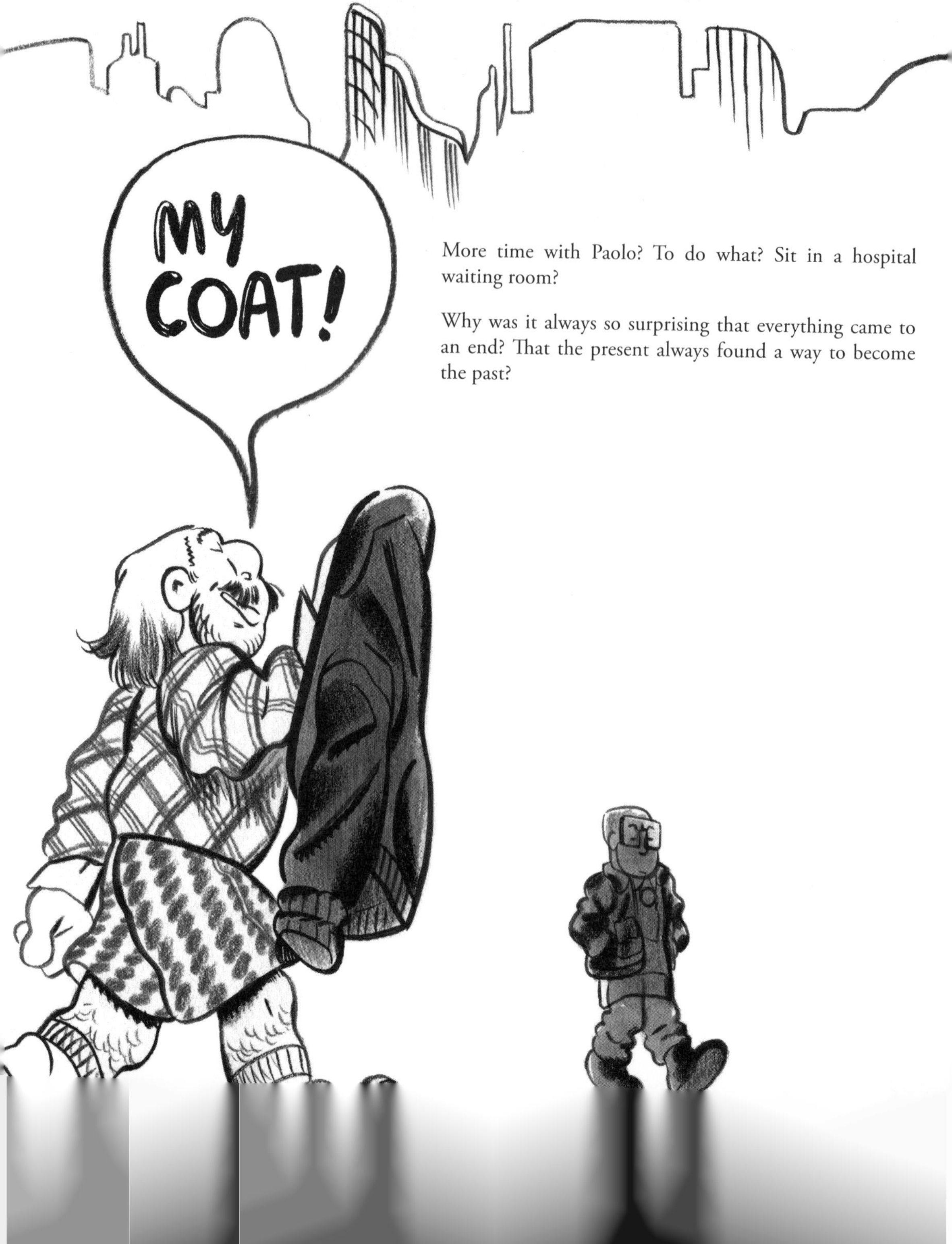
MY COAT!

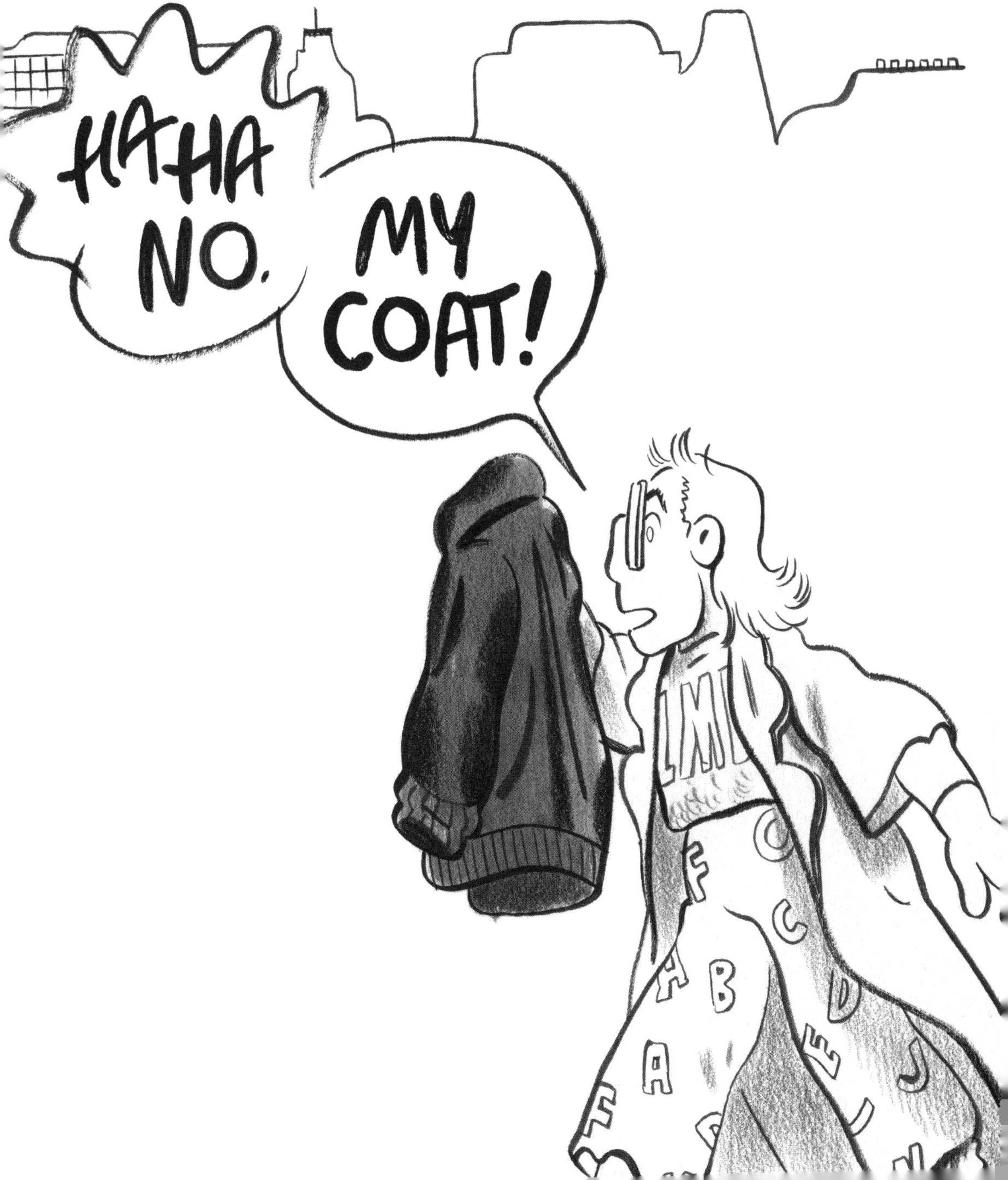
HAHA NO.
MY COAT!

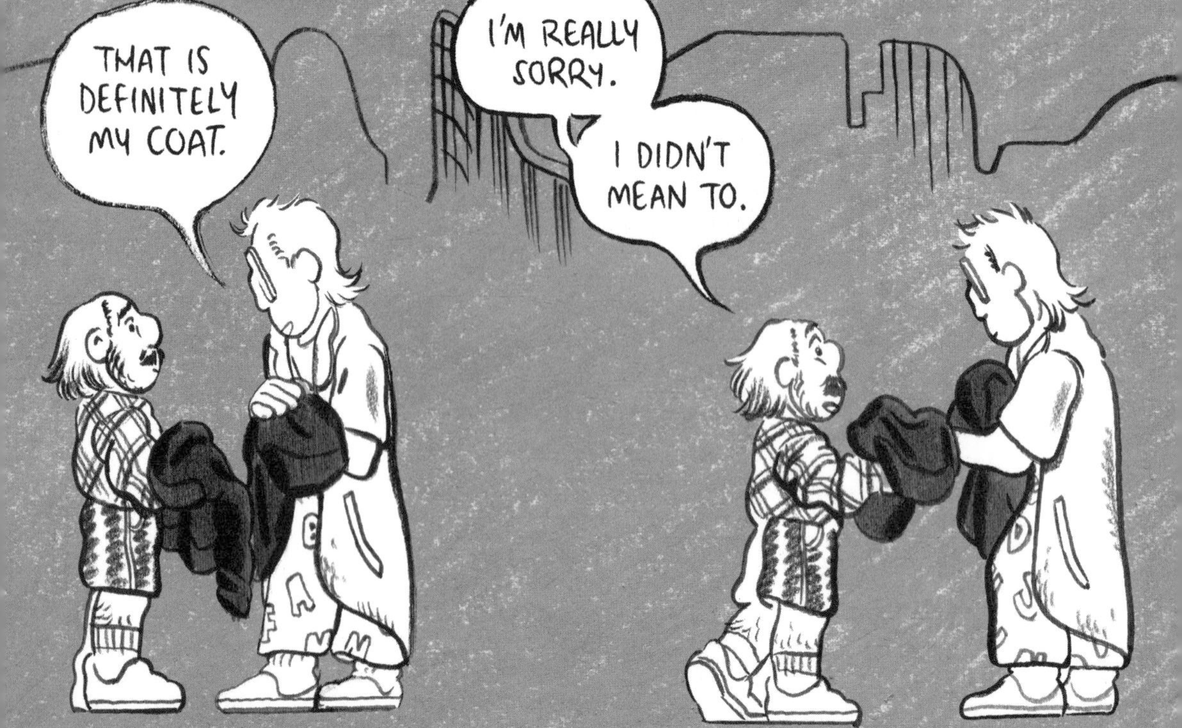
THAT IS DEFINITELY MY COAT.
I'M REALLY SORRY.
I DIDN'T MEAN TO.

A meal is eaten. A day is done. People move on. But he had seen Paolo, and it had been good.

And for a moment, it had felt like enough.

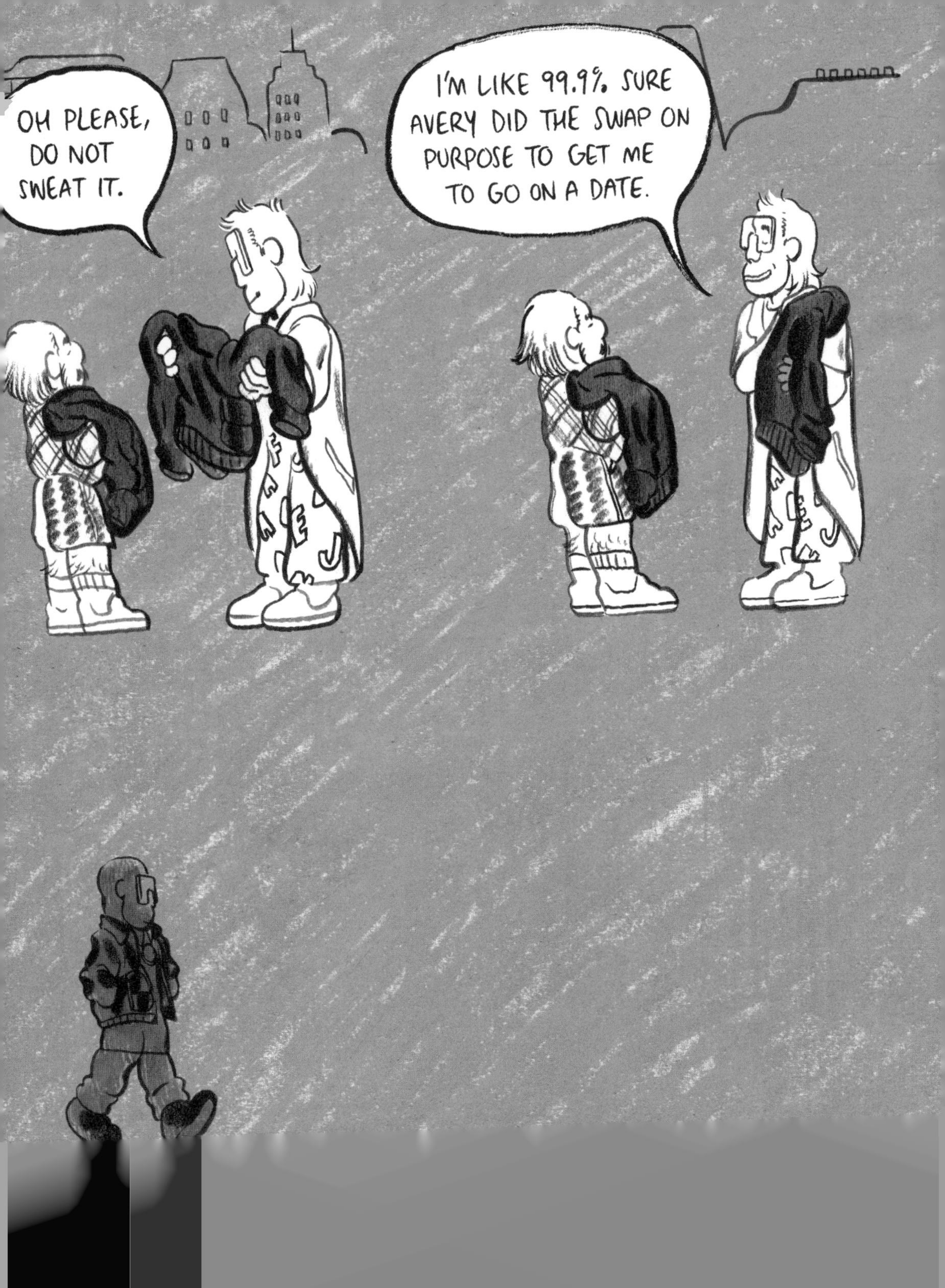
OH PLEASE, DO NOT SWEAT IT.
I'M LIKE 99.9% SURE AVERY DID THE SWAP ON PURPOSE TO GET ME TO GO ON A DATE.

HA HA A DATE!
WITH WHO?
OH WHOOPS!
DID I SAY THAT OUT LOUD?

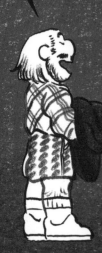

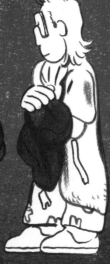

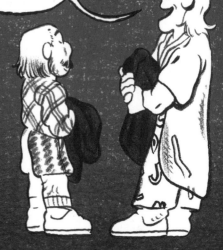

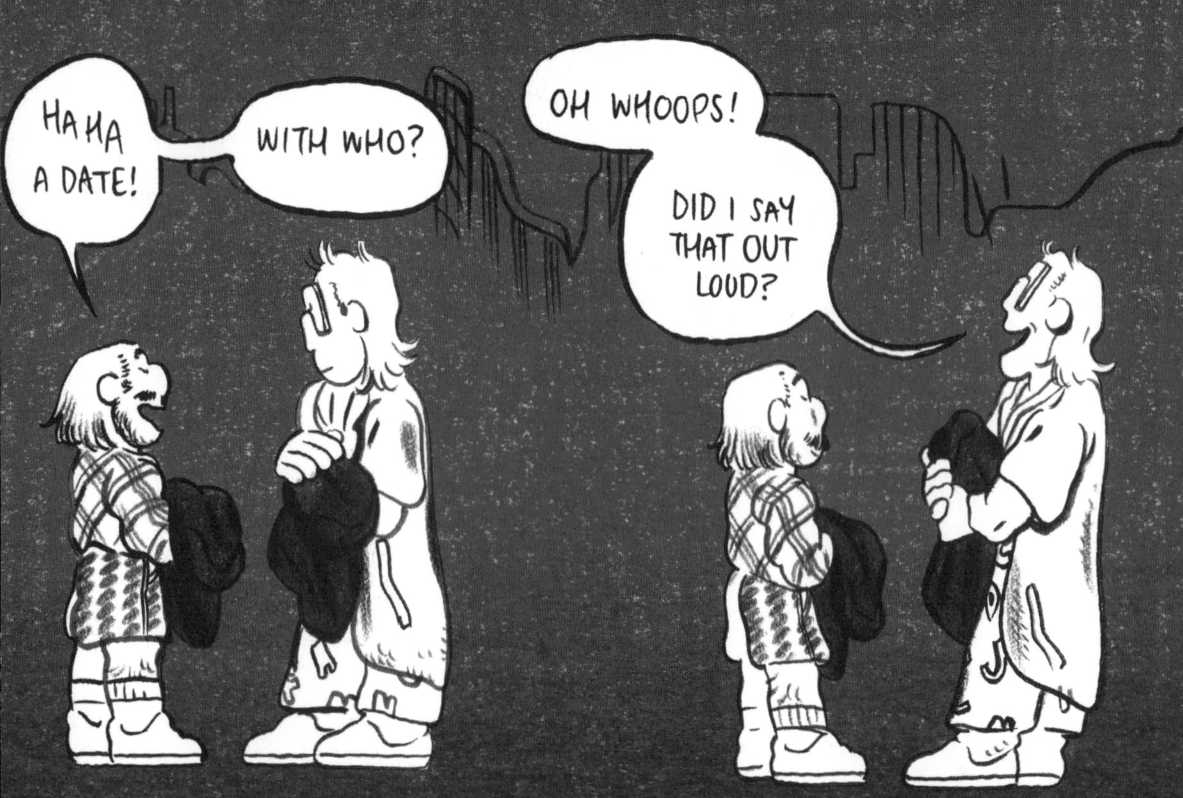

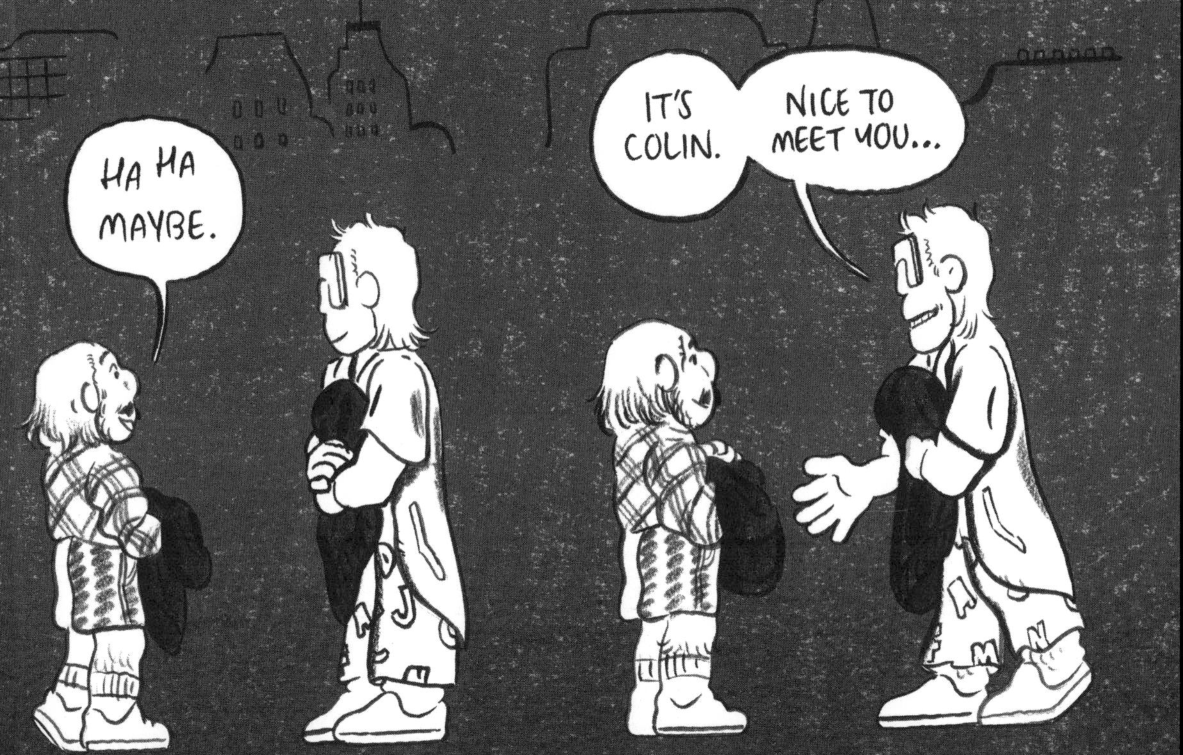
HA HA MAYBE.
IT'S COLIN.
NICE TO MEET YOU...

The problem was that some meals linger long after the table has been cleared. And there are places on Earth where the sun never sets.

But not here. The sun was already beginning to dip behind the skyscrapers and, for just a moment, Colin needed to squint his eyes to help him see.

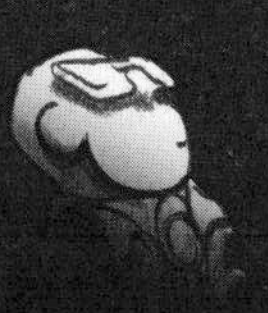

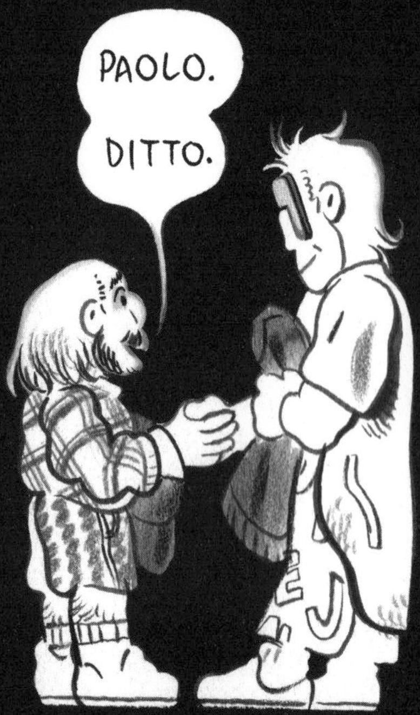
PAOLO.
DITTO.

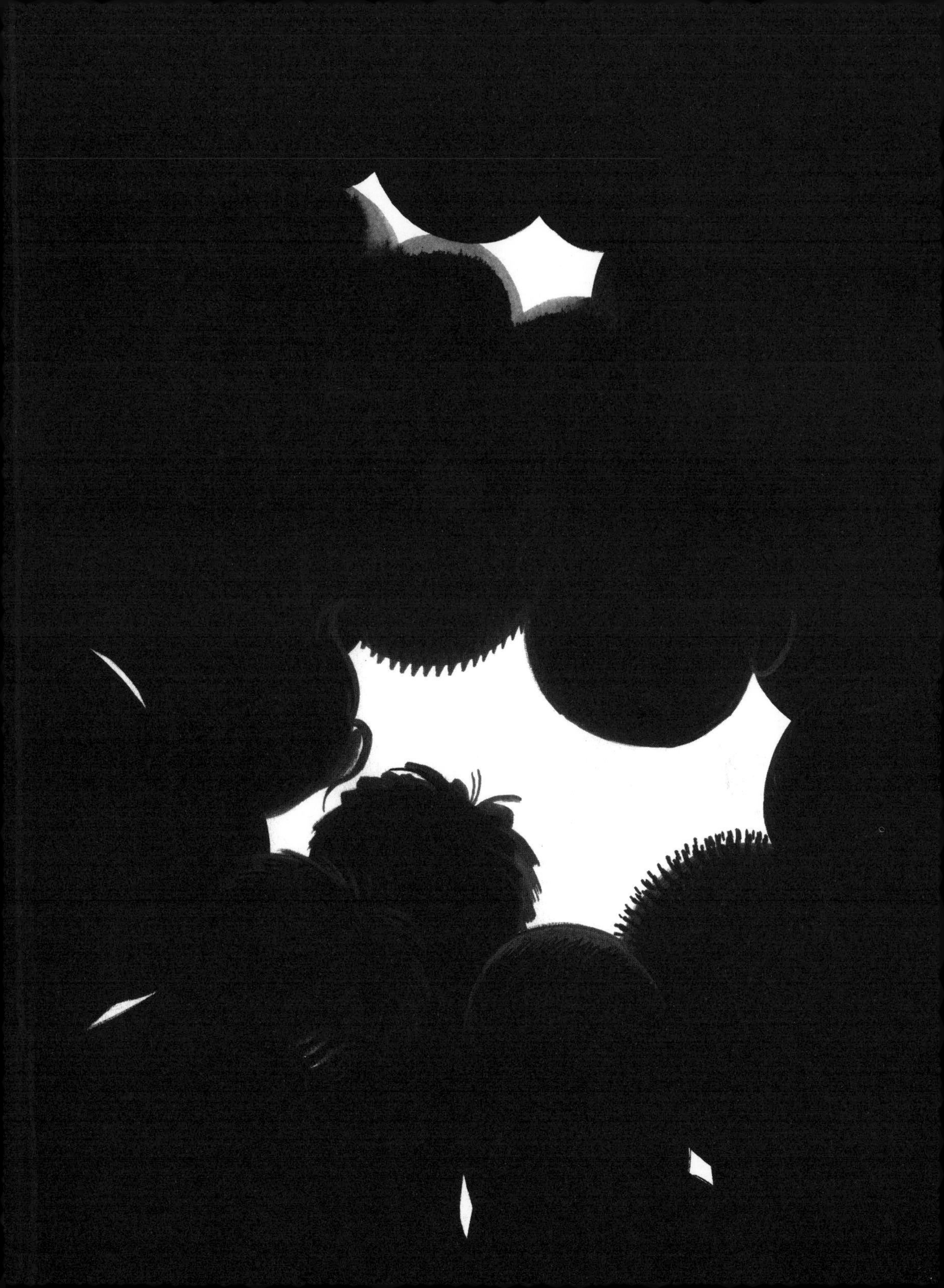

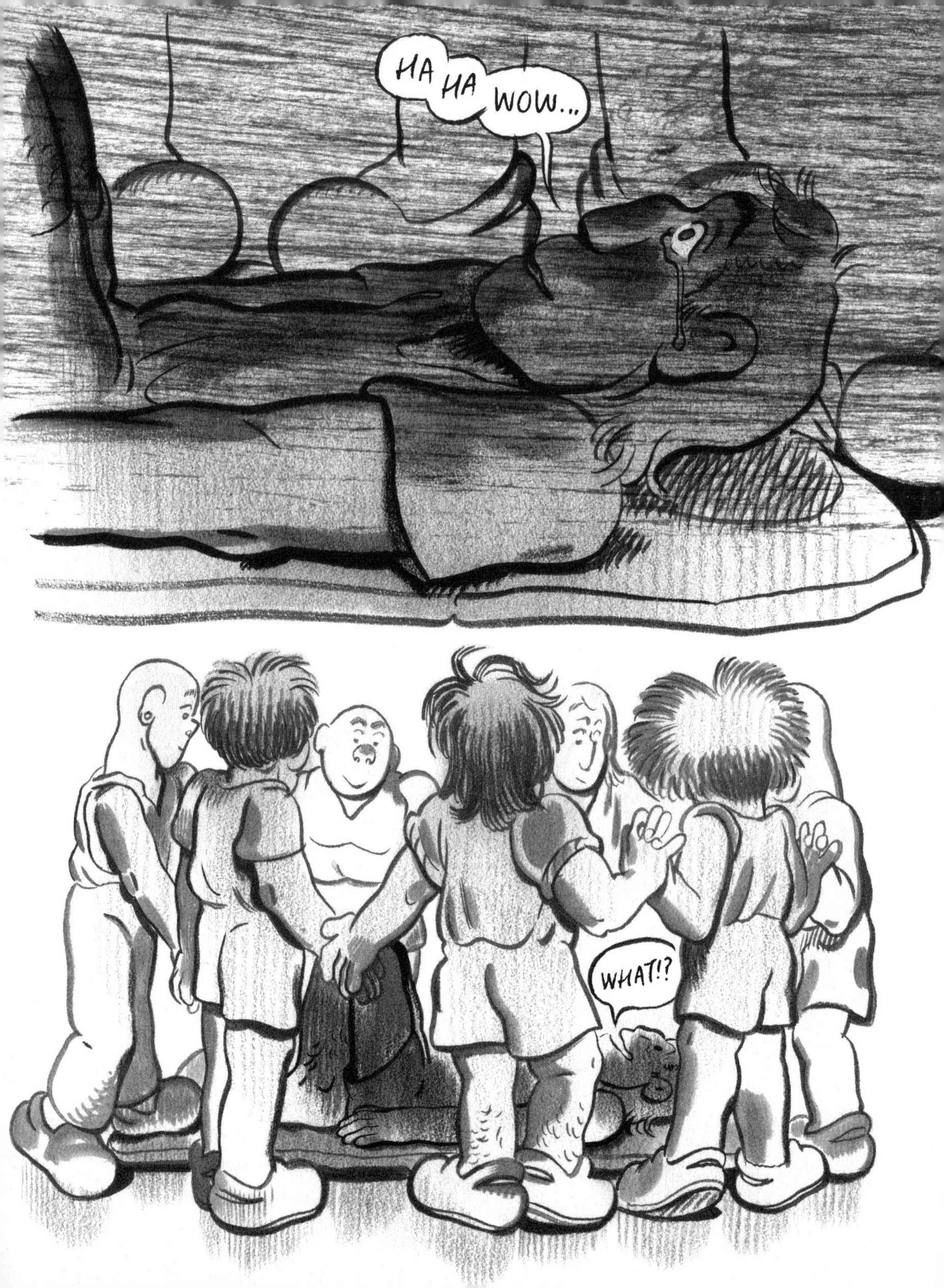
HA HA WOW...
WHAT!?

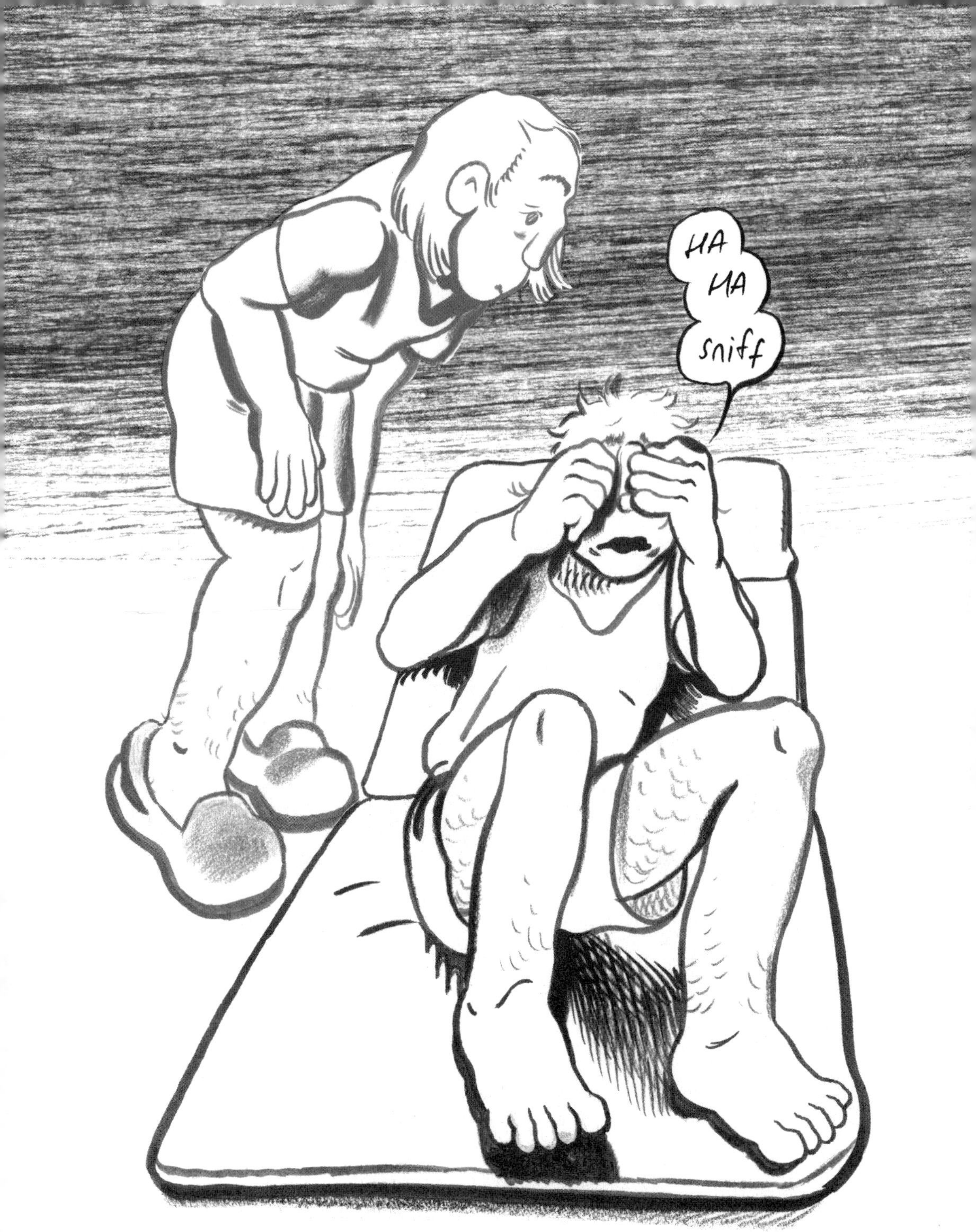
HA
HA
sniff

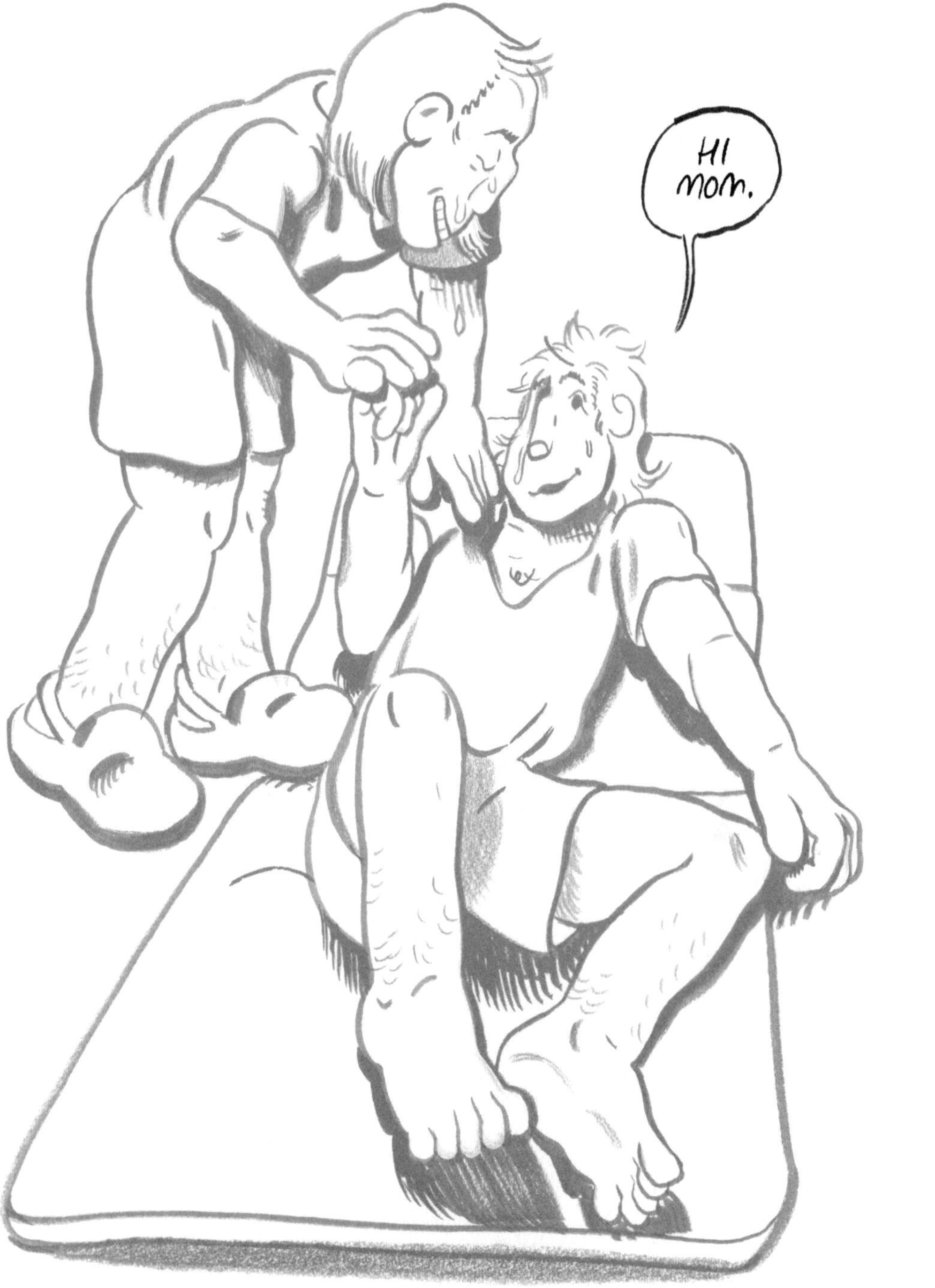
HI MOM.

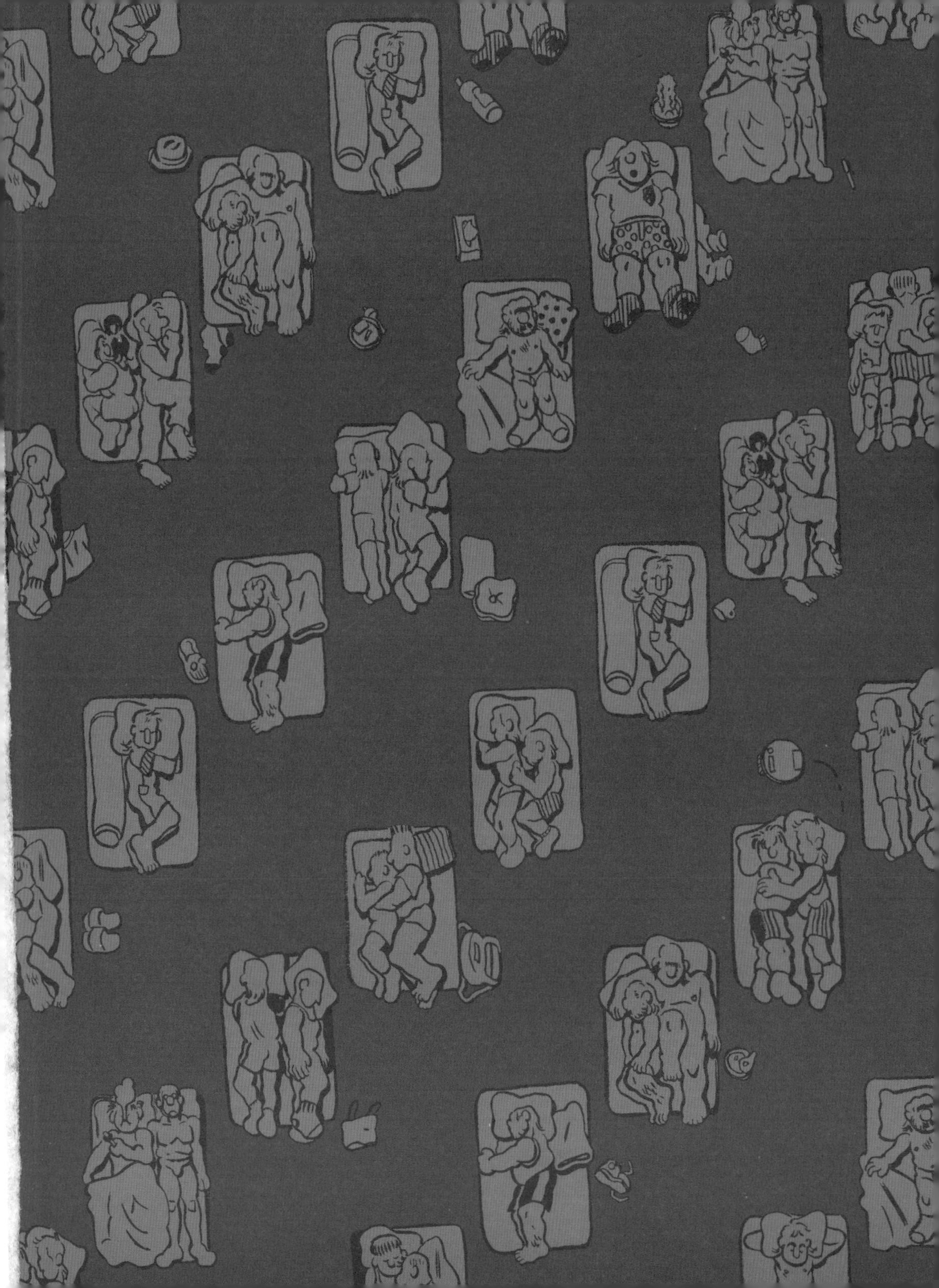

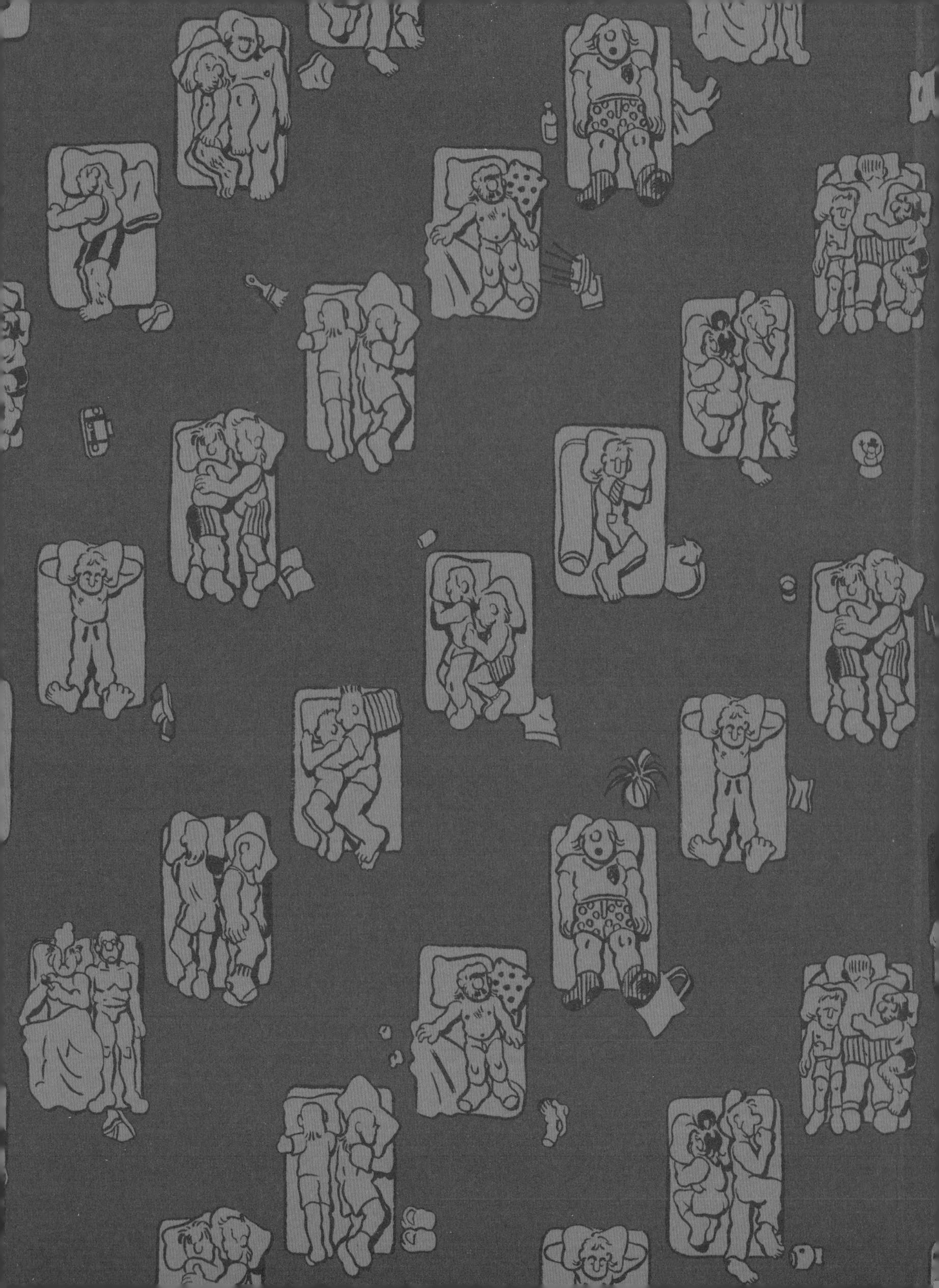